FORTEAN TIMES 63-67
THE PLUMBER FROM LHASA

Rosa Lotti's encounter with the 'men from Mars' in November 1954, as portrayed by Walter Molino for the Italian weekly La Domenica del Corriere. See **FT67:43**. Photo: Mary Evans Picture Library.

FORTEAN TIMES 63-67
THE PLUMBER FROM LHASA

HUNT EMERSON

Fortean Times is now published every month by John Brown Publishing Ltd
It is also available on subscription — inquiries to:
Fortean Times, FREEPOST (SW6096), Bristol, BS12 0BR, UK.
Tel: 01454 202515 Fax: 01454 620080.

Cover illustration: photograph of T. Lobsang Rampa (Topham)

British Library Cataloguing-in-Publication data available.
Fortean Times 63-67: The Plumber from Lhasa

ISBN 1-870870-794

Printed in Great Britain by
Redwood Books, Trowbridge, Wilts.

PREFACE

The five magazines in this book are reproduced facsimile, although not with the original spot colours. Our thanks again go to Steve Moore for compiling the contents lists, which are as detailed as possible to compensate for the lack of a full index. The consolidated index for *Fortean Times* 1–66 is in preparation and we hope to see it in print early in 1997.

Fortean Times 63 was the first issue in the large (A4) format which we have used up to the present. We had long maintained that as *Fortean Times* was a partwork which readers kept in sequence, the smaller formats were more convenient for bookshelves; but an increasing number of copies were being sold through newsagents, where small magazines tended to get lost in wall displays. So we bowed to commercial considerations. The larger format also gave greater scope for our designers.

Contributors to this volume include Peter Bayliss, Janet & Colin Bord, Peter Christie, Eric Crew, Paul Devereux, Bill Ellis, Michael Goss, Richard Holland, Peter Hough, Brian Inglis, John Keel, Ulrich Magin, Kevin McClure, Richard Milton, Jenny Randles, Andy Roberts, Paul Screeton, Karl Shuker, Ian Simmons, Paul Simon, Darren Slade, Dennis Stacy, David Sutton, Nigel Watson, Dwight Whalen, Ion Will – and the regular Gang of Fort (Mike Dash, Steve Moore, Bob Rickard and Paul Sieveking).

Our title comes from the feature on Cyril Henry Hoskins, who wrote under the *nom de plume* of T. Lobsang Rampa. The lama from Lhasa was really the plumber from Plympton (*FT*63:24-26).

Paul Sieveking, August 1996

FORTEAN TIMES 63-67 (1991-1992)
CONTENTS

FORTEAN TIMES 63 - June/July 1992

FORTEAN TIMES 64
August/September 1992

FORTEAN TIMES 65
October/November 1992

FORTEAN TIMES 66
December 1992/January 1993

FORTEAN TIMES 67
February/March 1993

NUMBER 63

UK £2
USA $6 / AUSTRALIA $4.95

FORTEAN TIMES

THE JOURNAL OF STRANGE PHENOMENA

Crop Circles '92

FREE
PULL-OUT GUIDE

Scaly Horrors

ISSN 0308-5899

63

9 770308 589118

T. LOBSANG RAMPA

The Plumber from Plympton who became the Lama from Lhasa

Spontaneous Human Combustion

LSD Scares • Premature Burial • Squirrel Kings
Buddha's Ashes • Stigmata • Dogs Shoot Hunters

The Earth needs all the friends it can get.
And it needs them now.

For thousands upon thousands of years our planet has sustained a rich diversity of life. Now, one single species - humankind - is putting the Earth at risk.

People the world over are suffering the effects of pollution, deforestation and radiation. Species are disappearing at a terrifying rate. The warming of the atmosphere threatens us all with devastating changes in climate and food production.

But it needn't be like this - we know enough to reverse the damage, and to manage the Earth's wealth more fairly and sustainably. But the political will to bring about such a transformation is still lacking.

And that's exactly where Friends of the Earth comes in.

IT'S TIME YOU JOINED US

I'd like to join Friends of the Earth. Please send me your quarterly magazine. I enclose:

£16 ☐ individual   £25 ☐ Family

I'd like to donate £50 ☐   £35 ☐   £15 ☐   Other £☐

I enclose a cheque/PO for total of £ _____

payable to **Friends of the Earth** or debit my Access/Visa No:

Card Expiry date: ☐☐

Signature _____   Date _____

Send to: Membership Dept., Friends of the Earth, FREEPOST, 56-58 Alma Street, Luton, BEDS LU1 2YZ.

Phone 0582 485805 to join/donate anytime

FULL NAME _____
ADDRESS _____

POSTCODE _____

Friends of the Earth   F81 LAHA

Fortean Times
THE JOURNAL OF STRANGE PHENOMENA

FREE
CROP CIRCLE '92 PULL-OUT CENTRE PAGES

LIZARD MEN page 40

UNEARTHED page 28

SHC page 44

SLITHERING FREE page 16

Contents
Issue 63 June/July

THE GANG OF FORT
EDITORS: Bob Rickard,
Paul Sieveking
CONTRIBUTING EDITORS:
Mike Dash, Steve Moore
© FORTEAN TIMES June 1992
ISSN 0308 5899

FORTEAN TIMES

A bimonthly magazine of news, notes, reviews and references on all manner of strange phenomena, experiences, related subjects and philosophies, founded in 1973 to continue the work of the iconoclastic philosopher of anomalies CHARLES FORT (1874-1932). The views of contributors are not necessarily those of the editors, and vice versa.

EDITORIAL ADDRESS
Fortean Times: Box 2409, London NW5 4NP, UK. Tel & Fax: 071 485 5002 or 081 552 5466.

SUBSCRIPTIONS
RATES – One year (6 issues). UK: £12. Overseas inc. USA: US £15 or $30. For two years (12 issues), double these prices.
PAYMENT – US/Canadian cheques acceptable; payments from all other countries should be in sterling drawn upon a London bank. Major credit accepted – just phone details to 0373 451777. Make cheques/money orders payable to JOHN BROWN Ltd, and send to:
Fortean Times: 20 Paul Street, Frome, Somerset BA11 1DX, UK.

ADVERTISING ENQUIRIES
DISPLAY – contact Sean at John Brown Publishing Ltd: The Boathouse, Crabtree Lane, Fulham, London SW6 8NJ, UK. Tel: 071 381 6007 or Fax: 071 381 3930.
BOOKSELLERS' LISTING and **NOTICEBOARD** items – contact the editorial address (above).

SUBMISSIONS
Submissions are invited of suitable articles, news, art, cartoons, reviews, and especially clippings. Preliminary discussion with the editors is advisable. Text can be submitted on floppy disks, but check with the editors first. Submissions may be edited. FT assumes no responsibility for submissions, but all reasonable care will be taken while they are in FT's possession. Requests for return of material should be accompanied by stamped addressed envelope.

CLIPPINGS
All clippings, references, etc, should be identified by source, date and clipster's name. Mail or fax them to the editorial address (above). Ask for our sorting guide.

PUBLISHER
John Brown Publishing Ltd, The Boathouse, Crabtree Lane, Fulham, London SW6 8NJ, UK. ☎ 071 381 6007 or Fax: 071 381 3930.

DISTRIBUTION
UK trade distribution by UMD, 1 Benwell Road, Holloway, London N7 7AX. ☎ 071 700 4600 or Fax: 071 607 3352.
USA newsstand distribution by Eastern News Distributors Inc, 2020 Superrior St, Sandusky, OH 44870, USA. Fax 0101 212 265 6239.

Gene Genies

The leading edge of scientific technology cuts into the future relentlessly, oblivious to our circumstances. Particularly difficult to resolve are the ethical dilemmas created for our creaking legal system. Genetic engineering, in particular, came to our attention this year, because of moves by medical research corporations to patent specially engineered genes. As our columnist Nigel Pennick warned last issue, the Real World is being carved up and copyrighted under our apathetic noses.

In February this year, a small Scottish research company, Pharmaceutical Proteins, successfully patented a genetic alteration to a sheep so that it can produce milk containing a human protein. Already the Scottish company has won a multi-million pound contract from the giant German firm Bayer to develop a flock of these 'supersheep'. London *Evening Standard* 17 Feb 1992.

Worse is to come: a recent application by the Baylor College of Medicine in Texas concerned a gene in the human mammary gland. Baylor also requested a right to patent any human who carried their altered gene. If this were allowed, it might not be just your soul you owed to the company stores, but, quite literally, an arm and a leg. The European Patent Office, thank heavens, has rejected this part of the application. *New Scientist* 1 Feb 1992. However, that will not stop the corporate ownership of altered plants and animals. Will we still own parts of our own bodies if we take on board patented genes? Will we soon have to pay a royalty for living? The mind boggles.

● This issue comes with a souvenir of the crop circle phenomenon. We hope you enjoy it. As we go to press, we hear that the 1992 season has kicked off with three dubious formations near Winchester and Avebury. We await developments with interest.

● We also feature an article by Jenny Randles and Peter Hough on the difficulties they faced during their investigations of mystery fire deaths for their forthcoming book *Spontaneous Human Combustion*. This confirms our own experience, while researching this subject, of the reticence of coroners' offices who seemed convinced we were ghouls.

The localised, rapid and almost total destruction of the body in these strange deaths may well be a rare anomaly, but it is one leaving tangible evidence. Its neglect is a scandal to forensic science.

● We would like to thank all the readers who have sent in clippings. We trust you understand that we cannot write to each one of you, as every minute of the day is spent putting the magazine together. Your reward will come in heaven (and in the credit listings if we use your clippings in a particular issue). All contributions are passed to the Archives for Fortean Research to be preserved for posterity. Please send them to our editorial address (PO Box 2409, London NW3 4NP, *not* the subscription address in Frome. And, please, no more mail to Mansfield Road.

FATE'S FLYING FIST

Secretary Gail Turner of Patterdale Avenue, Blackpool, left the hotel where she works to find that a giant hand, part of Blackpool's illuminations, had fallen onto her Ford Escort. *D.Telegraph* 19 Dec 1990.

BARN-OWL IMPRINTS

New laws aimed at saving the barn owl were demanded in January 1992 by the Royal Society for the Protection of Birds. Farmers have to provide more nesting and feeding sites if the popular species were to recover. The number of breeding pairs in Britain had halved to 5,000 since the 1930s. *Independent* 10 Jan 1992. Meanwhile we present two remarkable photographs illustrating one of the little known hazards of barn owl life …

■ This imprint of a barn owl was left 25 feet from the ground on the blue plate glass wall of Secured Home Loans and Lombard Home Loans, near Solihull, West Midlands. The owl died instantly. "It looked as if someone had etched the owl onto the window", said clerk Jean Roddy, who took the photograph. Every detail, from

eye sockets to individual tail feathers, was visible. "We found the body on the ground, half eaten by a fox which our security officers have spotted roaming around the area," added Jean.

Though the building is sited on a busy road in an urban area, with a railway line at the rear, it has long proved a hazard for low-flying bird life. Pigeons, goldcrests, a jay, a wren, a blackbird and a tree-creeper have all been discovered dead or stunned on the pavement outside.

Professor John Currey at the Department of Biology, University of York, pointed out that the owl's right bastard feather – placed at the small joint in the middle of the wing – was raised to provide extra lift as it attempted to fly out of the way of the obstacle. "It obviously saw the building at the last moment, put down its tail feathers and was forming

a kind of parachute of itself in an effort to slow down. It crammed on the brakes just before the impact, which is why the whole bird is outlined in this marvellous image," he explained. The impression stayed on the glass for nearly two months until it was erased by window cleaners. Portsmouth

News, Sheffield *Star* 9 Jan; *Independent* 10 Jan; and *Bankground Living* (house magazine for National Westminster Group staff) Mar 1992.

■ We recalled a similar incident, and after a quick rummage in the files, found this story from 1986. When Miriam Ehlers, aged four, pulled back the curtains one morning, she thought somebody had been drawing on the window. On the outside of the glass was a perfectly detailed imprint of a barn-owl. She had not heard it crash against the window of her first floor room at Southfield Farm, Backwell, near Bristol.

Her mother Barbara said the imprint was made of dust. "We looked to see whether the bird had fallen injured in the path, but there was no sign of it," she said. Bristol *Evening Post* 1 Sept 1986.

Top: Jean Roddy's photo of the owl imprint on the insurance building.
Left: Miriam Ehlers, menaced by the signature of her night visitor.

OWL SPOOKS PATIENTS

A model of a white barn owl greeted patients in the foyer of the new £400,000 Galn Clwyd Hospital in Bodelwyddan, North Wales, recently opened by Welsh Secretary David Hunt. According to Welsh folklore, the white owl is a sign of impending death. This belief is found all over the world; it is shared, for instance, by the Latoka Sioux Indians (see *FT53*:24). The hospital hurriedly replaced the barn owl with a brown tawny owl. *Evening Leader* (Clwyd & Chester) 3 Dec 1991.

TROJAN HORSE RE-RUNS

◆ The loss of more than half a million pounds in mid-air in July 1991 marked a new category of theft. The money was collected from Corsican banks and post offices by a security company and put in a sack on an Air Inter flight from Bastia to Paris. At Orly airport the guards signed the sack as 'OK' even though the lead seal was broke.

Apparently, this was a common occurrence, usually due to a knock in flight. When the sack reached the company's headquarters in Paris, it was found to contain bundles of old newspapers.

The security firm is used to the attentions of the French underworld, which has held up their vans with machine guns and bazookas. Mid-air robbery is a new departure. One theory is that the thief hid in a trunk in the hold and made the switch at 30,000ft as security guards relaxed in the passenger cabin. (The hold was pressurised.) The trunk weighed more than 150lbs, and the people who collected it had to pay for excess weight, which was probably the 5.7 million francs in cash. As the trunk was barely 5ft 6ins long,

GIVE IT TIME. THEY'RE BOUND TO BE A BIT UNCOMFORTABLE AT FIRST...

BIRD-BRAINS

■ Agnes Lysholm, 81, of Roan, Tröndelag in central Norway, lost her denture as she tried to spit out a fishbone which had got stuck in her throat during dinner. A crow snatched it and flew away. Six days later, the family noticed a magpie perched in a nearby tree. It had something in its beak, and Mrs Lysholm's son Kristian discovered that it was the missing denture. As he ran outside, the magpie dropped the denture and flew off. Said Agnes: "This is almost supernatural ... It seems that it was arranged by 'small invisible men'." *Dagbladet* 10 Feb 1992.

■ Homing pigeons are being used by car thieves in Taiwan to evade police while collecting ransoms from owners for the return of their vehicles. The thieves leave a ransom note and a pigeon, promising to return the car if the bird is dispatched with cash in a container tied to its body. "Once we tried to catch the thieves by using telescopes to follow the pigeon," said a police spokesman. "But it flew too high and too fast and we lost sight of it." *Int. Herald Tribune* 25 Oct 1991.

■ Some homing pigeons are very slow: Percy the pigeon vanished between Rugby and his Sheffield home in 1984, and owner Francis Butler had given him up for lost when he reappeared seven years later. *D.Star* 16 Aug 1991. For earlier seven-year pigeon absences, see *FT45*:21 & *FT51*:13.

■ Pub landlord Raymond Charman had his gold watch, worth £500, eaten by a duck when he took it off to wash his car in Corby, Northamptonshire, last year. The duck flew away. Scottish *Sunday Mail* 11 Aug 1991.

police reckon the thief must have been very small. *D.Telegraph* 25 July 1991.

◆ Two teenage boys entered the Extra Base Baseball Card store in Forest City, Florida, and asked if they could leave a plywood crate in the store overnight. It contained a gift for their father, they said. After the store was locked up, an accomplice in the crate broke out and escaped with $45 from the cash register. [AP] 8 Sept 1991.

◆ A large parcel was wheeled into a bank by a clerk in Siegan, near Bonn, Germany. A gunman burst out of the box and made off with £170,000 after tying up the clerk and five other workers with the help of an accomplice dressed as a postman. *D.Mirror* 11 Dec 1991.

◆ The Commonwealth Bank repossessed a heavy transport and earthmoving site run by the Bryant Group in St Mary's, Sydney, Australia, over a mortgage dispute before the courts in January. Security guards were stationed at the site. On the morning of Monday, 6 January, managing director Joe Bryant arrived at the site with a semi-trailer carrying a 13-foot-long cylindrical metal horse used by farmers during their demonstration against US President Bush in Canberra the previous week. The security guards let him through the gates, thinking he was returning the horse to the factory.

Once inside, about 30 workers leapt from the horse and opened the gates for 20 supporters waiting outside. The outnumbered security guards departed. "It's going to be business as normal this week", said Mr Bryant. "If we are going to have to pay the banks, we are going to need to generate income and we do that by working." [AAP] 6 Jan 1992.

CLAWS THREE

This crab with three perfect pincer claws was caught in the sea close to the outfall pipe of Winfrith atomic power station in Dorset by Ivor Godden, 43, from Weymouth. 'Claws Three', eight inches wide and ten years old, was taken to the Sea Life Park in Weymouth! "It's a true mutant and it must be significant that it was found near the power plant," said Sea Life manager Mike Quarm.

"It is like something from a science fiction film," said local fish merchant John Comben. "I have handled 15 tonnes of crabs a month for the last 25 years and have never seen anything like it." Dr Eric Edwards, director of the Shellfish Association of Great Britain, said that he had seen several three-clawed crabs around the country. *Western Daily Press* 26 Oct; *D.Mirror* 28 Oct; *Fishing News* 8 Nov 1991.

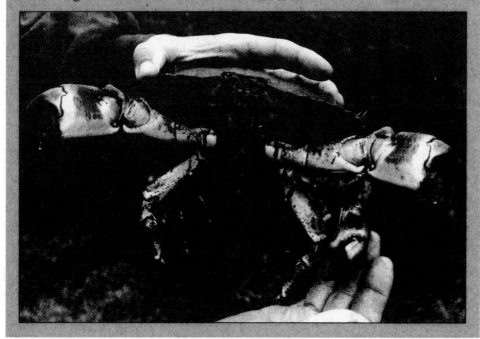

A VIRGINIA STIGMATIC

The Rev. James Bruse, 36, an associate pastor at the Catholic church of St Elizabeth Ann Seton in Lake Ridge, Virginia, developed the stigmata (the wounds of Christ) the day after Christmas: dime-sized pink marks on his wrists, the back of his hands, his feet and his right side. The wounds bleed periodically. Tom Saunders, an engineer and member of the congregation, said a statue "started crying" when he held it in Bruse's presence.

Water came from the eyes of a statue of the Virgin Mary days after Bruse gave it to his mother, said the Rev. Daniel Hamilton,

Bruse's fellow pastor. Other statues in Bruse's mother's home also appeared to weep. "When he gave me the statue, I noticed these marks on his wrists", said Hamilton. "Stigmata …He didn't know what those marks meant. I said 'Didn't they teach you anything at [divinity] school?' …I don't know what is happening. Father Bruse is a normal guy …He is a man of prayer, but he is not a mystic."

The diocese of Arlington cautioned against "any speculation on the causes or possible significance" of Bruse's wounds. In a statement, it called them a "purely physical" phenomenon. A physician and a psychiatrist examined Bruse and were unable to find medical or psychological explanations for the wounds. [AP] 10

Mar 1992. [For a general introduction to the subject of stigmata, see John Michell & Robert Rickard: *Phenomena*, Thames & Hudson 1977, page 42.]

LONG SHOTS

✠ Fisherman Jim Gault, 48, went overboard from the fishing boat *Dayspring* in the Moray Firth 40 miles east of Wick, on Scotland's north-east coast, on 14 January 1992. Despite an air and sea search, he was not found. Three months later, William Gault, 60, who had fished with his brother Jim for 33 years, found Jim's body in his nets as he fished in the same area from the same boat on 7 April. He recognised his brother by his clothes. *Eve. Standard* 8 April; *D.Mail, D.Mirror, Guardian* 9 April 1992.

✠ Pizza chef Richie Barras, 29, had often served take-aways to Stephanie Barras, 17, in Ashington, Northumberland, but only realised she was his long-lost kid sister when she gave her name to join a home-delivery club. They had lost touch when Stephanie went to live with her father in Humberside in 1979. *D.Mirror* 12 April 1991.

✠ Roselyn White of Elizabeth, New Jersey, went to get her eyes examined at the Eye Shop in Newark. Samantha Boyd, the young woman who processed her insurance papers at the shop, turned out to be the daughter White had placed for adoption when she was three days old, 22 years earlier. Newark (NJ) *Star-Ledger* 26 Feb 1992.

✠ Michael Drennen, 34, had been separated from his unmarried mother when he was six, and had been searching for her for years. On 13 March 1992, he was in a video store in York, Nebraska, overheard Mrs Shirley Keener give her maiden name to a clerk, and realised his search was over. Both had lived in York since 1990. Mrs Keener, now 59, had her four children, aged six, five, three and two, taken away from her by county authorities on 24 February 1964 because she was unmarried. Mrs Keener and her son plan to look for the three long-lost daughters. Harrisburg (PA) *Patriot-News* 5 April 1992.

✠ Miner Jimmy Greenfield's past caught up with him when a blast of air blew a 30-year-old newspaper down a ventilator shaft into his face at Westoe Colliery, Tyne and Wear. The paper contained a story about a car crash he had as an 18-year-old in 1962. *Bristol Eve. Post, D.Mirror* 18 Mar 1992.

TO SAVE THE WORLD

Early on 9 September 1991, Marsha Middleton, Frank Flint and Doug Moore dug a six-foot-deep hole outside the Episcopal church of Bruton parish in Williamsburg, Virginia. They were members of the Ministry of the Children, a New Age Christian group from Santa Fe, New Mexico, who believe that a vault in the churchyard contains lost writings by Sir Francis Bacon, including a paper called "The Pattern of Utopia" and proof that he wrote the Shakespeare plays. Also in the vault are the original King James Bible, the Book of St Peter, the Constitution and the Declaration of Independence, plus information about seven (or possibly 144) other vaults including those at St Luke's Historic Church in Smithfield and at Bacon's Castle Museum in Surry County.

Middleton said she saw the Virgin Mary while she was digging, which was a sure sign that she was doing right. In a past life, she was the wife of St Peter. If the documents are not found before the year 2000, world catastrophe will ensue. The Episcopal authorities obtained a restraining order against the group to prevent further digging – anyone would think they didn't give a jot or tittle about world catastrophe.

The quest for the vault was inspired by Mary Bauer Hall, 87, who says she learned about it from codes in an [unnamed] '17th century book', and led an expedition to the churchyard in 1938, with approval from the church. No vault was found and the dig was stopped by church officials because tombs were being undermined. Hall founded something called the Veritat Foundation [sic] about ten years ago. In 1986 and 1987, the Foundation conducted three electronic surveys of the churchyard, and determined that something unidentified was buried there. So maybe the world *can* be saved after all...
Newport News (VA) *Daily Press* 22 Sept + 2 Oct; New Zealand *Dominion* 16 Oct 1991.

SAY IT WITH FLOWERS, BIG!

Andrew Scott, 24, a bedding plant grower, re-created Van Gogh's Sunflowers on a scale that was visible from satellites, the largest reproduction of a painting ever undertaken. His 'canvas' was 46,000 square feet of wheatfield near Duns in the Scottish borders, and his 'paint' was 250,000 flowering plants of six varieties, including nine different colours of French marigolds.

Scott won backing for Operation Sunflowers from 30 other Scottish growers, and sponsorship from major fertiliser, seed and irrigation firms on both sides of the border. Planting took a week, with 20 people working on a grid system, and cost about £25,000. The image was at its best for about a week in August 1991 before being ploughed in.
D. Telegraph 12 July; *Scotsman* 16 Aug 1991

ATTIC GHOST

The recently-opened Café Gallery in Salubrious Passage, off Wind Street in Swansea, is thought to be unique in exhibiting work exclusively by Welsh artists. There are four attic rooms where local artists could work. One artist fled in terror, leaving all his belongings, after spending only two days up there. "He refused to go back up", said gallery owner Ron Banning. "He was working in the room when he heard footsteps walking up the stairs; then everything went extremely cold. He felt there was a really bad atmosphere. I certainly don't think there's anything pleasant about it. I was up there one night doing a bit of repair work to a door and my hair just stood on end."

Banning (pictured here on the attic stairs) has contacted the city archivist to investigate the history of the building. A previous occupant confirmed it had a history of hauntings. "We had a visitor who said there had been a lot of strange goings on when he worked there."

We do wish these reports could be more specific. *Western Mail* 27 Nov 1991.

APPARITION CAUGHT ON VIDEO

Night club boss Cameron Walsh-Balshaw, who runs the Butterfly's night spot, Star Inn, Oldham, Greater Manchester, was telephoned in the small hours by the alarm company and told that sirens at the building had been set off. He hurried to the premises, where police had already checked the outside and found that everything was secure. The display in the reception area told Cameron that the alarm had been triggered from the cash office. He wound back the security video and watched.

At 4:32am – precisely when Cameron was told the alarm had been triggered – a figure was seen to glide down the passageway and enter the secured office. Wearing a white short-sleeved shirt, dark trousers and a hat, the figure appeared for six seconds. According to the security-system company, it is impossible for a tape to be double-exposed, as the cassettes are automatically demagnetised before re-recording. *Psychic News* 30 Nov 1991.

LATEST ROAD GHOST

A lorry driver was heading south at night on the A3 towards Petersfield when he saw a figure in the middle of the road waving its arms near the Pulens Lane junction at Sheet. He was unable to stop and mowed down the figure. He called the police but nothing was found, and the shaken driver continued his journey without leaving his name.

The incident took place on the road just by the Sheet Service Station on the same bend where the driver of a BMW died and his four passengers were seriously injured when the car collided with a 16-ton paper delivery lorry in 1989. Firemen had to cut the five free from the wreckage. *The News* (Portsmouth) 13 Dec 1991.

SPIRITUAL HARASSMENT

A family in Thamara village, Muthithi, in the Kigumo division of Murang'a, Kenya, spent sleepless nights in the cold after their house was allegedly burnt down by ghosts on the morning of Tuesday, 23 July 1991. Mrs Mary Wambui Muchoki said the trouble began at about 9:30pm on Monday night when the roof of their house was pelted with stones as soon as her family had gone to bed. *Nairobi Standard* 27 July 1991.

FATAL ENCOUNTER

Martin Strivens, the only person killed in the Cannon Street rail crash back in January 1991, was also probably the only man among more than 350 passengers known to driver Maurice Graham. *Today*, 10 Jan 1991, which reported this remarkable coincidence, explained that Graham was a close friend of Martin's brother Andrew, a BR guard.

REST IN PEACE

It is reputed that William Stanhope, son and heir of Viscount Petersham, has taken to parking a hearse outside his residence in Stanhope gardens, to the consternation of local residents. He says he bought it as it doesn't offend parking limitations for vans and he can sleep in the back after parties. *Funeral Service Journal* April 1992.

HUMONGOUS FUNGUS

Scientists have discovered what could be the largest and oldest living organism on earth – an individual mightier than the blue whale, the giant sequoia tree or such past pretenders to size and supremacy as the dinosaur.

The organism is a giant fungus, *Armillaria bulbosa*, known to gourmets as the honey mushroom and to gardeners as shoestring root rot. It is an interwoven filigree of mushrooms and root-like tentacles spawned by a single fertilised spore 1,500 to 10,000 years ago and now extending for at least 37 acres (15 hectares), munching away on rotting wood in a hardwood forest near Crystal Falls, Michigan, south of Lake Superior. The same species is found throughout eastern North America and Europe, and there may well be other specimens around that are bigger and older.

Botanists have estimated its size and age by plotting its position since 1988 over an area larger than 20 football pitches. It is genetically uniform from one end to the other, which is why they claim it deserves to be called a single individual. They suggest it has been growing since the end of the last Ice Age. If all its mushrooms and tendrils are considered together, the colossal patch of fuzz weighs about 100 tons, about as much as the blue whale.

The discovery was reported in the April 1992 issue of *Nature* by James B. Anderson and Myron L. Smith of Toronto University and Dr Johann N. Bruhn of Michigan Technological University. Mushrooms are usually identified by their fruiting bodies, the edible portion above ground. The bulk of a mushroom fungus grows below ground as a series of intertwining filamentous strands called the fungal thallus. The humongous fungus might have reached its maximum dimensions: at one, and possibly several, points, it is bumping against competing fungi.

The find will force biologists to rethink their assumptions about what constitutes an individual, a fundamental problem in the study of ecosystems. A single organism is usually thought of as bound by a skin of flesh or cellulose; but fungi, along with organisms like coral, grow as a network of cells and threads (rhizomorphs) with ambiguous boundaries. What is more, the Michigan *Armillaria* has many breaks in its underground webbing, and some of its elements grow independently, thus straining the idea that the entire fungal patch can truly be considered an individual. Nevertheless, the biologists say that its uniform genetic makeup merits its ranking as one giant creature.
Independent, Guardian, D.Telegraph 2 April; *Int. Herald Tribune* 3 April; *New Scientist* 4 April 1992.

TUNING IN

Piano tuner John Hepple, 54, fell 20 feet from a church organ and knocked himself out. Afterwards, he found he was having dreams and visions that came uncannily true. "He writes them down and sooner or later they become fact", said his boss Peter Croucher, of Corbridge, Northumberland. "He predicted a block of flats would collapse. The next day one did in Glasgow. He foretold the San Francisco earthquake, the Iraqi supergun and the Romanian bloodbath".
News of the World 8 July 1990. Psychic powers and other wild talents are frequently associated with a blow on the head.

HUMAN HOOVER

A novel method of jewel theft was uncovered in Bangkok last year. Julio Cesar de Monraes Barros, 28, a Brazilian, was pictured at a press conference in a Bangkok police station on 12 December 1991 holding out his left arm to reveal a scarred wrist and a deformed and scarred little finger. He had had a thin tube implanted under the skin, running from the little finger on his left hand and emerging at the wrist. From there, a thicker tube led to his armpit. A small pump, activated by flexing his muscles, was then used to suck diamonds through a hole in his little finger and up to his armpit.

Barros and another Brazilian, Paulo dos Santos, were arrested for stealing jewellery worth £7,000 from the Anyamee jewellery shop, and police believed they had carried out at least two earlier thefts from Bangkok gem merchants using the same method, and it was possible they had operated in Europe before that. The two men posed as customers. Barros would ask to see a box of gems and, whilst his accomplice distracted the assistant's attention, he would 'hoover' up as many loose diamonds as possible. The hole in his little finger would then close up without trace. [Reuters], 14 Dec 1991.

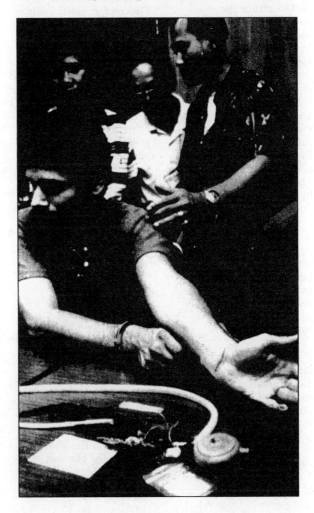

NAME GAMES

✠ In January 1991, samples of the new ten pence pieces, not legal tender until September 1992, slipped into circulation by mistake: they had been issued to the vending industry so that slot machines could be altered to accept them. The first person to find one was Mrs Mabel Shilling, 85, of Whipton, Exeter, who mistook it for an old five pence piece. (The decimalisation of 1971 changed the old shilling into five pence.) *D.Express, D.Telegraph* 3 Jan 1991.

✠ A Dublin scoutmaster complained to a funfair worker that his troop of boys was only given one revolution of the Big Wheel at the RDS Funderland funfair, when they should have got three or four. The worker, Samuel Stephen Ferris from the Crumlin Road, Belfast, struck the scoutmaster on the side of his head, cutting his face. *Irish Independent* 11Jan 1990.

✠ Two Dutchmen put to sea in a yacht called *Chaos* without any charts and got lost near Dorset. They called the coastguard to find out where they were – and their radio broke down. They were eventually found by a lifeboat and towed to Poole. *D.Star* 13 July 1991.

✠ Friends Bill Noy and Bill Fox went out to buy used cars together in Blandford, Dorset, and snapped up two motors with registration plates B111 NOY and B111 FOX. *D.Star* 2 Aug 1991.

✠ Police inspector Steve Bullock was chasing a runaway bull along a busy road near Gainsborough, Lincolnshire, when it did a U-turn and butted his patrol car. He radioed HQ for help, and his SOS was answered by Sergeant Alan Bull. The animal was finally cornered after a 45-minute chase. *Sun* 14 Dec 1991.

Here's Glassi Small, who works as an optical assistant for Wood & Watson opticians in Bridge Street Row, Chester *Evening Leader* (Clwyd & Chester) 3 Feb 1992

✠ Firemen had to free Bill the plumber after he got his head jammed in a lavatory bowl at his home in Puckeridge, Hertfordshire. His full name was W.C. Sticks. *Sun* 17 Dec 1991.

✠ Torrential rain and high wind led to leaking roofs at the newly-opened studio theatre spaces in Glasgow's Citizen's Theatre on 22 February 1992. Theatregoers had to negotiate buckets placed to catch drips. The shows were Craig Raine's *1953* and Alonso Alegria's *Niagara*. *Glasgow Herald* 24 Feb 1992.

✠ Four members of the rock band Violent Storm from Cardiff were killed and a fifth seriously injured when their car smashed into a bridge on the rain-lashed M4 motorway near Bristol on Friday the 13th March 1992. The car was thought to have been lifted six feet by a freak gust of wind and hurled against the bridge, where it landed upside down. *D.Mirror* 14 Mar 1992.

✠ Belgium has a new Minister for the Middle Classes. The Flemish Christian Democrat appointed to the post is André Bourgeois. *D.Telegraph* 16+17 Mar 1992.

PIZZA FRACAS

Bob Briggs, 24, owner of a Domino's Pizza restaurant in Independence, Missouri, dressed as a giant red rabbit and stood in the road to attract business. He was knocked unconscious by Bobo the clown, who was promoting a Pizza Hut across the road. Briggs declined to press charges. Tucson (AZ) *Daily Star* 25 Aug 1991.

DEAD, MORIBUND, NO MORE

✠ A male, green parrot, for 23 years a pet belonging to Maria del Carmen Dotras, died in hospital after incompetent doctors tried to take a blood test from the bird. Ms Dotras claimed one million pesetas (£5,435) in damages, based, in part, on the argument that her parrot could talk. Judge Antonio Nunio de la Rosa ruled that the dead parrot was worth 150,000 pesetas (£815), claiming that it merely "articulated sounds similar to those of people". *Guardian* 1 Oct 1991.

✠ Dave Humphries bought a female orange-crested Moluccan cockatoo from bird breeder David Lloyd for £700, but it died soon after from a respirato-

ry infection. "I thought it was a bit suspicious when the bird fell over in Mr Lloyd's car; but he told me it was a perfect specimen and was just travel sick", said Humphries, in a scene reminiscent of the Monty Python Dead Parrot sketch. He won £1,100 in a breach of contract suit. *South China Morning Post* 28 Nov 1991.

✠ Tony Finn bought a basking shark and placed it in a giant aquarium in his house in Hemel Hempstead. It didn't move an inch, and he took it back to the pet shop to demand a £100 refund. Finn was told the shark was just neurotic. He returned to the shop half a dozen times until the unfortunate creature died from the trauma of all the to-ing and fro-ing.

Finn called in trading standards officers, who told him to keep the corpse in a cool place pending an autopsy. He put it in his freezer, which made a post-mortem impossible. (Ms Dotras had made the same mistake in the Spanish parrot case.) Eventually, Finn made a deal with the pet shop and went home with a fully mobile tarantula spider. *Edinburgh Evening News* etc, 11 Oct 1991.

✠ Dianne Cobb, 23, bought a tortoise for £49 from Timothy Reason, 23, after she saw an advertisement for the Reptile Kingdom in *Exchange and Mart*. Miss Cobb, of Royston, Hertfordshire, named the tortoise Basil. "It appeared not to move at all", she said, "and after about a week I rang the number in *Exchange and Mart* and he said it was probably shy and to give it a bit more time. After another week it was quite obviously dead." Miss Cobb returned Basil to Mr Reason at his bungalow in Luton, but he refused to give her her money back. *D.Telegraph, D.Mirror* 14 Mar 1992.

TANGLED TALES

From time to time we have regaled you with stories of 'Rat Kings' – clusters of rats whose tails have become inextricably knotted together see back to FT40. They do not seem to occur with the frequency they did in earlier times, and they were not common then. Martin Hart, in his loving study Rats (1982), says the phenomenon of tail-knotting has been known to occur in other species of rodents, notably squirrels, but we knew of no case until fairly recently, when we heard of two cases …

The first incident occurred in Easton, Pennsylvania, in 1989. As 16-year-old Crystal Cresseveur set off for church around midday on Sunday 24 September, she noticed a commotion in the hedge outside her house; it was a writhing furry bundle of six young squirrels all squeaking at once. At first she thought they were playing but she soon realised they were in a panic, and as they pulled in all directions at once they had become firmly stuck among the trunks of the bushes. She called her father, Paul, and their neighbour, Charles Kootares, and with help from the growing crowd of onlookers, managed to extract the frantic cluster from the hedge.

In their desperation, some of the squirrels tried to gnaw through their own tails to get free, and one bit through Cresseveur's glove as he swept them into a cardboard box with a broom. Paul Cresseveur pointed up into the branches of the tree in his front yard, saying the mother squirrel watched as her babies were rescued below. "She stood in the crotch of that tree whimpering for them. About half an hour later, she left," he said.

From the photo we have, it seems as if two managed to escape. They must have fallen from a nest up there; but whether they grew up with tangled tails (as rat kings seem to do) or whether the knot developed accidentally as they played in the hedge, we shall never know. Someone called the wildlife conservation department and two officers arrived shortly after two pm and took the boxed tangle to their headquarters in Reading. Reader Scott Deschaine phoned that HQ to enquire after the squirrels. Sadly, he told us, they were put down; an official told him their tails could not be disentangled, and several had legs "crushed together". Easton (PA) *Express*, Allentown (PA) *The Morning Call* 25 Sept 1989.

The most recent, and happier, incident occurred almost two years later exactly – on Wednesday 18 September 1991 – in Baltimore, Maryland.

This time there were five of them, and they fell out of a tree by the Reisterstown Elementary School. "It was really something," said Principal Dena Love. "They were all fighting and squabbling, trying to agree on which way to run." At first the gathering teachers and students were startled, thinking the animals were 'Siamese' squirrels.

By the time Baltimore County Animal Control officers arrived, the frightened cluster of squirrels had managed to get part way up the tree, then, as their consensus failed, the officers managed to brush them into a cage and take them to the county shelter for separation. Officer Tom Strange, who brought them back for release beneath their tree, said the tangle was made up of tree sap, hair and nesting debris it must have oc-curred in the nest – and they were separated quite easily.

Vagn Flyger, a biology professor and squirrel expert at the University of Maryland College, said: "I guess I must have heard of only five or six cases of this happening. It's very rare." Usually the tangled animals are found dead; unless they can disentangle themselves, their survival chances are very slim. The survival odds were even greater for two of the five: they were white. "Albino squirrels are also very rare," Flyger said. We wonder what the odds are for albino members of a rodent king? Baltimore (MD) *Evening Sun* 20 Sept 1991.

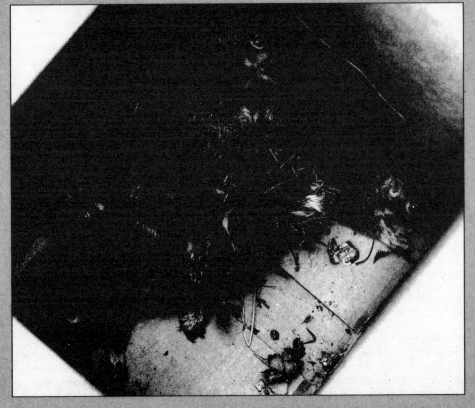

An uncommon tale – four members of the Easton squirrel king, frightened but safe.

STRANGE DAYS

BLAST TO KINGDOM COME

Jay Knudsen, 50, of Des Moines, Iowa, offers a special service to the families of dead hunters, for the cost of a funeral, and sometimes for a lot less. He loads the ashes of the diseased into shotgun shells, performs whatever ritual the family wishes and then blasts away at the sportsman's favourite marsh or bear country. "We can't get you to heaven," he advertises. "But we promise to land you in the happy hunting ground."

Knudsen, a landscape gardener by trade, performs other ceremonies as well. "We just had a lady send us her father's ashes from Missouri to put in golf clubs," he said. "There's no end to this. You could put ashes in bowling balls, in baseball bats, lots of things. We're putting ashes into lures for fishermen, duck decoys for hunters, that sort of thing. One of the things that has been popular is to do this with ashes of the hunter's gun dog. A hunter gets pretty close to his gun dog." There have been about 18 customers since the ad first ran in the Sept/Oct 1991 issue of *Sporting Classics*. [AP] 18 Feb 1992.

AN ANGRY DAY FOR MOTHER EARTH

✠ The strongest earthquake to hit the Netherlands and Germany for more than 200 years caused widespread panic and damage at 3:20am on the morning of 13 April 1992. One person was killed and at least 50 injured. The tremor, 5.6 on the Richter scale, lasted for about 15 seconds, the epicentre being the Dutch border town of Roermond. In the German village of Heinsberg, seven miles away, 150 houses were damaged and 25 people injured.

Shock waves registered as far south as Baden-Würtemberg and east as far as Thuringia. Cracks appeared in dozens of government buildings in Bonn; masonry at the top of the towers of Cologne cathedral crashed to the ground; and seismological devices at Cologne University, intended for measuring much weaker tremors, broke down, spewing ink over the walls.

The quake originated along the Peeil Edge fault, which runs north-west along the Maas river on the Dutch-German border. The last quake of a similar magnitude occurred in the region in 1756.

✠ Meanwhile, Italian experts were detonating powerful explosions high up Mount Etna to attempt to deviate lava which threatened to overrun Zafferana Etnea, a town of 7,000. Some 120 million tons of lava and debris have been spewed out of the 10,948ft volcano in eastern Sicily since a new crack erupted in December.

✠ The 3,000 inhabitants of the volcanic island of Manam, 320 miles south-west of Port Moresby, capital of Papua New Guinea, were preparing to evacuate because of a possible eruption. The volcano in Madang Province is 1,807ft above sea level and has remained dormant for as long as anyone can recall. It is one of 29 in the country.

✠ A teenager was killed after sand gushing from the Cerro Negro volcano in Nicaragua caved in the roof of his home. The volcano was spitting car-sized boulders down its slopes, and worshippers in the town of Leon were praying in an attempt to stop it. And also on the same day, an earthquake measuring 5.3 Richter shook northern Japan. [AP, AFP] 14 April 1992.

BUTANE AND THE BEAST

Transylvanians traditionally eat pork at Christmas and treat the rind as a delicacy. Farmers inflate the dead pigs using the exhaust of a vacuum cleaner or a pump to stretch the skin and burn straw to remove the hair and clean it. Last Christmas, a farmer from Cluj in Transylvania pumped up his pig with butane gas as his vacuum cleaner was broken. Not surprisingly, the pig exploded when he singed its hair with a naked flame. The blast tore the pig to pieces and hurled its owner to the ground. He spent three days in hospital recovering. [Reuters] 20 Dec 1991.

NEPOTISM REIGNS OK?

✠ Margaret Thatcher and John Major, her successor as British Prime Minister, are both descended from a farming family called Crust who lived in East Lincolnshire in the 18th and 19th centuries. Their maternal grandmothers, both called Crust, were born days apart in Boston, Lincs, in 1849. They are listed alongside each other in the birth register. *Sun* 5 Mar 1992.

✠ As it happens, John Major, married Margaret Thatcher 22 years ago. They live at 11 Lilac Walk, Newbury, Berkshire. John, 49, runs a printing firm. As far as they or we know, neither has any connection with their political namesakes. *Sun* 4 Dec 1990.

PEACE OFFERING

Lolita Arellano, 34, from Bacolod on Negros Island in the Philippines, was depressed that Mount Pinatubo had killed 700 people since erupting in June on Luzon Island north of Manila: so she took a scythe and beheaded her three sleeping sons, Manny (7), Everlito (6) and Romulo (4). She also slit her wrist during the 3am episode but a sister rushed her to hospital. She told neighbours that she was offering their heads to pacify the volcano. [AP] 10 Nov 1991.

MARCH HARES

Auberon Waugh in his column (*D.Telegraph* 14 March 1992) mentions that he came across a letter in a local newspaper from two men in Sherbourne, who were walking along a public footpath near Sherbourne Castle on Shrove Tuesday (3 March) when they saw six hares run headlong in single file into a field with sheep in it. In a large open area all six suddenly stopped, simultaneously, and ran in a circle clockwise, then stopped (again simultaneously), ran anti-clockwise for rather longer, and then dashed off, again in single file, into a wood. Waugh comments: "I do not think it presages the end of the world, or even, necessarily, a Labour government."

SEEING DOUBLE

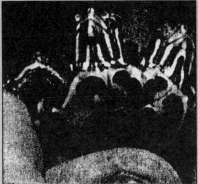

Above left: This two-day-old kitten with two faces is from a litter of seven owned by Linda Lohr in Lancaster, Pennsylvania. [AP] 19 Mar 1991.

Above centre: A two-headed Red Ear Slider turtle. Owner Ken Robertson of Winter Haven, Florida, would not part with it, even when he was offered $10,000. *Saginaw News* 8 Jan 1988.

Below left: Heady Lamarr, pictured a few hours after her birth in Santa Rosa. She had a normal twin brother and was bottle-fed because her mother rejected her. She was authenticated by researchers at the University of California at Davis. (Undated US report.)

Top right: Perry Stowell with the two-headed calf that was born on his dairy farm in Hastings, Michigan, on 4 August 1991. The calf, which had two faces, windpipes and œsophagi, was not strong enough to hold up her head to nurse, so the family was bottle-feeding her. She had only a 50-50 chance of survival. [AP] *San Jose Mercury News* (CA) 8 Aug 1991.

HOW THE ASHES CAME TO HARROW

In 1988, Mr Patel, a mini-cab driver from Harrow, built an extension on his home to house his snooker table. As a devout Hindu, he built a small shrine in the corner of the new room, with the traditional offering of coconuts. Some 50 friends turned up for the opening ceremony, including some devotees of Sai Baba, who sang *bhajans* (devotional songs). During the singing, the coconuts suddenly split open, and a fragrant nectar began to pour from one of them. Then an image of Sai Baba, lightly dusted with *vibhuti* (holy ash) appeared on a second coconut.

Patel wanted to put in the snooker table, but a priest came and told him that devotees would want to come and pray. Devotees brought more pictures of Sai Baba and more *vibhuti* began to appear on those pictures also. Patel added images of Christ, statues of the Buddha, symbols of the Muslim faith; these too produced *vibhuti*, which is collected by Patel to give to those who come.

Sai Baba is believed by his followers to be an avatar, or living god. He is said to have the power to heal, to materialise rings, pendants and, of course, *vibhuti*. Caroline Thomas, a researcher at London University, has analysed the ash which the god-man produces in India. She says it has the same chemical con-

stituents as cow-dung burnt to ash. In March 1992, she visited the shrine in Harrow. "I saw ash appearing on a photograph as I sat in front of it", she said. "I have no doubt that the phenomenon is genuine."

Patel has grown accustomed to the constant procession of visitors coming to his home to pray. "When you look at it, we have been dragged into this, but I don't know why", he said. "I never considered myself holy. I am a mini-cab driver. But I think I have been blessed."

Mick Brown, writing in the *Daily Telegraph* (6 Mar 1992), said: "Looking at the pictures, I could see no sign that the *vibhuti* had been applied by hand, nor any sign that Patel had profited from his miracle. His family

life has been turned upside down; his home is no longer his own. In fact, it seems to have brought Patel only one thing. Happiness. Even if he can't play snooker."

NEW COLLECTING MANIA

A rumour has spread very fast round the country that the 'environment-conscious' Body Shop beauty chain – which bans product-testing on animals – will pay up to £10 for fingernails to be used for testing cosmetics. The company has been inundated with sets of inch-long talons, and boss Anita Roddick has put out a plea for women to stop coming in with them. *Sun, D.Star* 5 Mar 1992.

SLITHERING FREE

■ There must be something about Bristol that is attractive to pythons two of these big snakes made the news there within a few days of each other in August last year.

One, measuring 10 feet, was found in the car park of St Nicholas School, in Lawford's Gate, on the 25th. "I don't think the snake had eaten recently," said RSPCA Inspector Jackie Silk. It was thin and sluggish due to the cold weather, allowing Silk to catch it easily. He took it to Bristol Zoo, where it was fed and warmed up. Bristol *Evening Post* 26 Aug 1991.

Just four days later, another python was alert and hungry (or angry) enough to try to eat four-year-old Terri Paisley knee first. Terri had gone along with her mother, Angela, to visit Angela's boyfriend, Paul Tite, in Bradley Stoke. Paul had left his eight-foot Indian rock python roaming the living room while he and Angela went into the kitchen. "It's our fault," he said. "We shouldn't have left her alone with it."

"I heard a scream," said Angela, "and saw the snake hanging from Terri's knee. Then it wrapped itself round both legs. I went crazy, and I think Terri went into shock. Her eyes were just staring and she said 'I love you, Mum'. I though she was going to die." However, the resourceful mother recovered enough to get a spoon and prised

apart the snake's jaws. "Terri had 30 teeth marks on her left knee and we found three teeth in the wounds." X-ray's at hospital revealed several more teeth embedded in Terri's leg. Despite her ordeal, the girl was treated and allowed home almost straight away. Paul Tite vowed to give his pet to a zoo. Bristol *Evening Post* 29 Aug 1991.

■ A worse experience befell nine-year-old Alex Henry of Long Beach, California, a few weeks earlier. He was alone in the house and after feeding a live rabbit to Damien, their 12-foot Burmese python, took it into his bedroom, where it slithered under his bed. Alex foolishly tried to coax it out with his foot. Damien struck and Alex panicked, his screams attracting neighbours. One of them looked though a window and saw the boy was being eaten alive, his foot down the python's gullet. By the time a rescue squad arrived and smashed their way in, the snake had swallowed a bit more of Alex's leg. Luckily for him, prompt action by a fireman seems to have frightened the python into letting go. *Weekly World News* 20 Aug 1991.

■ Our previous note of a UK python escape was in June 1990, when Sammy, a 12-foot reticulated python belonging to Gary Ansett of St Leonards, West Sussex, vanished from his cage. Gary looked all over, and failing to find Sammy, concluded

that he had been eaten by his other snake, Buster, an Indian rock python who was 15 feet long.

Gary was on holiday in October – four months later – when he heard that police had collared a giant snake gliding across a lawn in a nearby road. "It was a shock," said Gary. "He has really roughed it. He is very thin, his skin is tatty and he is a bit nervous." Gary denies that Sammy would have eaten the neighbourhood cats. "He would never eat anything like that. Pythons can go for a year without feeding. He must have found himself a hiding place." Brighton *Evening Argus* 3 Oct 1990.

■ Most recently, however, we learned that the sewers of Howden, in Tyne and Wear, can boast terrifying creatures the equal of New York's underground alligators. On 4 March 1992, Dave Erickson, a sewerman for Northumbrian Water, opened a hatch and a 10-foot python fell on him. He shrieked and flung the four-stone snake from him as it tried to coil itself around his neck. He said: "It just landed on me all of a sudden. When I realised what it was, I was scared. I thought it was going to kill me."

Northumbrian Water believe it was an unwanted pet, flushed down the loo when it was smaller, continuing to live, hunt and grow in the sewers. It is just as likely that it escaped by sliding down the toilet-pipe bend. However it got there, it was very weak and suffering from the cold, because it died a few moments later. *Sun* 5 March 1992.

Top: Gary Ansett reunites Sammy with Buster. Below: Dave Ericson (left) and workmate Eddie McLoughlan display their surprise visitor from down the sewers.

DEAD MONARCHS

✠ The heart of King Boris III of Bulgaria has been found at last. The discovery was important enough to be announced by Blagovest Sendov, President of the Bulgarian Academy of Sciences. Boris, who died in 1943, was father of exiled Simeon Saxe-Coburg-Gotha, the last king of Bulgaria. Communist authorities had moved Boris' body at least twice, and its current location is unknown.

The discovery was made when the tomb of Boris, in Sofia, was opened in mid-October 1991. "We found two glass jars in the grave: one with the heart of Boris III, and the other containing a document identifying it," said academician Sendov. The relic underwent forensic tests to settle the question whether Boris had been poisoned by the German Nazis or died naturally. [Reuters] 21 Oct 1991. A later report said he had died naturally.

To hide the body and leave the heart – that seems more like the act of devoted nationalists than godless communists; or perhaps it was an act of high magic?

✠ The remains of the Lion of Judah, the former Ethiopian Emperor Haile Selassie, have been found under the office of the deposed President, Mengistu Haile Mariam, in Addis Ababa's former Imperial Grand Palace, according to Ethiopian state radio. The body will be exhumed in the presence of his family and reburied in the Orthodox cathedral.

The body was buried secretly on the night of 27 August 1975. "Mengistu chose this site to see that the body did not rise from the dead", the radio added. There were conflicting reports as to whether the Emperor, who had ruled for 44 years, had been murdered. [Reuters] 10 Jan; [AFP] 17 Feb 1992.

NEVER TO GO AGAIN

✠ Ian Bovis, 18, a cable television engineer from Maidstone in Kent, told his mother that he wanted to sleep in a coffin. Less than two days later, he was injured in a crash and died later in hospital with his mother by his side. When she went home, she found her son's bedside clock had stopped at 10:46am – the exact minute of his death. *D.Star* 14 Jan 1992.

✠ In the same month, Iris Bentley recalled the morning in 1953 when her brother Derek was executed in Wandsworth Prison. She sat with her father William and mother Lillian in their front room. Only the loud ticking of the mantlepiece clock broke the silence. Iris said: "My mum had been sedated. Dad was cuddling my little brother Denis and me. We knew there was nothing else we could do. The clock stopped ticking at 9am. It

has never started up since. We just sat there looking at each other". Derek Bentley was hanged at 9am that morning. *D.Mirror* 29 Jan 1992.

✠ Clocks breaking down at the moment of death is a familiar motif in folklore, reinforced by actual occurrences. As a variation on the theme, we recall that Pope Paul VI's treasured alarm clock went off unexpectedly at the moment of his death (see **FT27**:52).

✠ Here's another appropriate yarn, from the *Sunday Express* of 28 April 1985: Walter Sawchuck ran a fish and chip shop and a grocers in Haddington, Lothian, in Scotland. In 1970, he bought two small electric wall clocks from a stall holder for £1.50 and jokingly asked for a guarantee. The stall holder told him: "I promise these clocks will never break down as long as you are in business". Five years

later, he sold the chip shop, and the day he handed it over the clock in the shop burned itself out. Five years after that, he sold the other shop and the second clock broke down.

GRAVE-Y TRAINS

✠ Three Romanians sat their uncle's corpse upright in a railway seat for the 300-mile journey from Bucharest to their family graveyard in Caransebes, in western Romania, because they could not afford to rent a hearse. To avoid suspicion, they had sloshed alcohol over their uncle's body and told the inquisitive, inclucluding the conductor, that he was in a drunken stupor. The Romanian daily *Adevarul* said the trick only worked because the train had no heat or lights. [Reuters] 6 Dec 1991.

✠ Similarly, a dead woman made an eight-day journey across China to be married to a man who died a bachelor. Dying unmarried is traditionally believed to be unlucky for the deceased, so the man's family employed a professional 'matchmaker for the dead'. The matchmaker, Zhang Jiahua, 44, dug up the body of a woman in Sichuan province and was taking it to be buried with the bachelor in Shanxi when railway officials searched his baggage. The corpse they found had been dead two years. London *Eve.Standard* 18 Feb 1992.

GETTING THE HOTS

Mohammed Jabber, 33, has been jailed for three years for kidnapping a former Bangladeshi politician in Poplar, east London, and forcing a chilli pepper up his rectum in a row over a debt. Jabber, a community worker, photographed the man as he suffered "considerable pain" *D.Telegraph, Sun* 21 Nov 1991.

TOMATOES FROM OUTER SPACE

The first of America's space tomatoes - grown in schoolyards from seeds which had spent six years in space - were being picked and eaten in August 1990, in spite of stern warnings from Washington. The seeds had been sent aboard a satellite to face deep-space radiation exposure for 10 months; but the 1986 Challenger shuttle disaster and other problems left them aloft for five years longer than planned.

Astronauts retrieved the 11-ton Long Duration Exposure Facility in January 1990 and the seeds were distributed to four million schoolchildren across America (see *FT56*:29). The space tomatoes are darker than the earthbound variety. Some of the plants have green, yellow and white leaves instead of the familiar dark green ones. Many mutations did not become evident until a second generation. Since tomatoes belong to the nightshade family, there was a fear that mutations could make the fruit poisonous.

Shortly after their retrieval, BBC space correspondent Reginald Turnill got some of the seeds from NASA. Some were ripened in the BBC's *Blue Peter* studios and some went to schools. Pupils at Holly Hill Primary School, Selston, Notts, volunteered to grow some, and the Ministry of Agriculture granted them a three-month licence to do so. In April 1991, in line with EEC 'phyto-sanitary' regulations controlling seed importation, the Ministry told them to burn the plants, soil and even the pots because of fears that they might carry a virus which could threaten the British potato crop. One British planting escaped the Ministry's notice: Reginald Turnhill himself was growing some in his garden in Sandgate, Kent. In June, some second generation plants were doing very nicely in pots. Men from the Ministry were not amused.

Further reports of American tomato mutations were made public in June, although the vast majority of the plants seemed perfectly normal. Some plants had long central stalks and no fruit, or leaves growing where flowers were supposed to blossom, or stunted leaves and no fruit. The fruit itself tasted normal and was of good size and colour, according to Jim Alston of the South Carolina gardening firm that packed the seeds.

Shrimp eggs were also aboard the satellite, and 10% of them developed into adult specimens with mutations, including shortened extremities and the growth of a second abdomen. The space-flown shrimps also had shorter lives.

The US space shuttle Columbia soared into orbit on 5 June 1991, carrying seven astronauts, 29 rats and thousands of jellyfish, for nine days of medical reasearch in space. The rats and many of the jellyfish were dissected upon their return in the quest for knowledge of how animals function in the weightlessness of space. *D.Telegraph* 14 Aug 1990 + 25 April 1991; *Eve. Standard, Independent*, Atlanta (GA) *Constitution* 6 June; *Observer* 9 June 1991.

SOMETHING AFOOT

A tourist found a human foot on the beach at Coles Bay, Tasmania, on 26 February 1992. Two days later, a second foot was washed up on Swansea Beach nine miles away. Tasmanian police did not believe that the feet belonged to the same person, as one was wearing a sneaker and the other a walking boot. They were sent to the Royal Hobart Hospital for forensic tests. Brisbane (Australia) *Courier Mail* 6 Mar 1992.

MYSTERY BOOMS

@ A huge bang was heard in Radstock, near Bath, on 4 July 1991, and felt as far away as Stratton-on-the-Fosse. Police were inundated with calls and checked with firms, factories, Bristol Airport and the Gas Board. "It is a complete mystery" said a police spokesman. *Bristol Eve. Post* 5 July 1991.
@ At 11:30am the following day, a loud bang shook the Blyth and Ashington area of Northumberland. Again, local police were besieged with calls and couldn't pinpoint the cause. The British Geological Society in Edinburgh assured them it was not an earth tremor. A police spokeswoman suggested, without proof, that it was a sonic boom caused by an aircraft. *Newcastle Journal* 6 July 1991.

PARIS BUZZED AGAIN

Paris, on the morning of 15 September 1991, was disturbed by a low-flying light plane. A female journalist, on her way to work at about 7:20 am, saw the plane make two unsuccessful attempts at flying under the Arc de Triomphe. For the third attempt, the single-engined plane headed eastwards over the Champs Elysées, turned over the Place de la Concorde, and headed for the arch. The arch is 95ft high and 48ft wide, which meant the pilot had to bank his aircraft to gets its 26ft wingspan through the gap. He did so successfully, and headed northeastwards.

The plane was later found in a field to the east of Paris. It was a two-seater Mudry Cap-10 stunt flier, stolen from an unnamed aero club the previous night. Before its audacious dip under the Arc de Triomphe, it had flown under the Eiffel Tower, and waggled its wings victoriously as it banked over the Seine.

The incident could not fail to remind Parisians of the infamous 'Black Baron', who repeatedly buzzed the city in 1988 – see *FT51*:13 and *FT52*:17. At the time, the identity of the flier was unknown and many did not accept the reality of his exploits. Hundreds of policemen and soldiers were used to look-out for the 'Phantom Flier' (as he was also known), and a Mirage fighter was even kept on standby to effect an ærial arrest. Late in 1988, Albert Maltret was charged with the reckless flying; he was fined £8,000 and banned from flying for three years.

Maltret still mixes flying stunts with right-wing politics. In July 1991, he was said to have offered his services to the Iraqi air force. Although he abandoned Baghdad for the more attractive idea of bombarding the Elysée Palace with roses, he was not blamed for the latest excitement.

The stunt of flying under the Arc de Triomphe was annexed to the repertoire of political protest in 1919, when a disgruntled pilot drew attention to the lack of representation of the French air force in a celebratory parade.

Sources: *D.Mirror, D.Mail, Independent* 16 Sept 1991.

Nigel Watson

ALIEN PLANT TERRORIZES CORNWALL

The Hottentot fig – *Carpo-brotus edulis*) related to the genus *Mesembryanthemum* – originated in South Africa, where it is eaten and commonly known as the Kaffir fig. It was imported in 1849 to Tresco, in the Isles of Scilly, in the form of cuttings taken by Augustus Smith; and there are records of the Victorian watercolour artist Tom Hart bringing pieces back from the island to grow in his garden next to the Lizard lighthouse some 30 years later. It is believed gulls may have spread sprigs around the mainland, as it

has been reported since the 1920s in many parts of England, Wales and Scotland. It has also been spotted in Ireland and the Channel Islands.

The fig grows up to six feet a year and hangs more than 40 feet over cliffs. It is overwhelming native plant life on Lizard Point, Cornwall, a grade one Site of Special Scientific Interest. It is immune to herbicides, so methods of control under consideration include hand-pulling, using a herd of Shetland ponies to graze it and, as a last resort, employing a climbing team to remove it from the cliffs.

Fig growth has been especially fast during recent warm summers. "In its own way it is quite attractive," said Nigel Davies, National Trust head warden at Lizard Point, "and many people like it when it is in flower as it has a variety of red, pink, purple and yellow flowers." Its spread is threatening such Cornish favourites as kidney vetch, sea pink and spring quill, as well as rarer species. When the fig is destroyed by winter frosts, it smothers the clifftop in an inert matting that prevents the growth of other species. *D. Telegraph* 3 Oct

Alastair Cameron, of the National Trust, wrestles with the alien plant at Lizard Point.

BAT NEWS

● What is believed to be Britain's last remaining mouse-eared bat – our largest bat species with an 18in wingspan – has died. For the past five years, Mr Flitter Mouse, as he was known, fought off loneliness and rotting teeth to return each winter to a belfry on the Sussex coast. But now

expert Dr Robert Stebbings, who has kept a close watch on the secret sanctuary, believes the 17-year-old specimen is dead. "He hasn't turned up for the last two winters", he said. "I've looked around the area, but I'm sure he is now dead." It was hoped he would live for at least another ten years. This is the first mammal

extinction in Britain since the wolf more than 250 years ago. The number of mouse-eared bats in Britain has declined dramatically since the mid 1970s. The last colony of 50 was decimated by a string of mystery accidents. The species is still found on the Continent, but numbers are falling. *Mail on Sunday* 2 Feb; *Mid Sussex*

Times 7 Feb 1992.

● Fife group of the Bat Conservation Trust filed a report of a pipistrelle bat apparently being mauled by a prawn on a fishing boat 13km south-east of the Isle of May. It survived this ordeal, but died later due to its poor condition. *Bat News* (quarterly) Jan 1992.

MYSTERY CATS AGAIN

RETURN OF THE PEAK PANTHER?

When Mrs Kathleen Topliff, 68, returned to her house in Hayfield, in Derbyshire's Peak District, on the evening of 26 March 1992, she was confronted by a large, jet-black cat. It was described by the police as "about the size of an Alsatian dog with yellow-amber eyes and a pungent smell" (*Daily Telegraph* 3 April); or "having a smooth black coat, muscular appearance, approximately four feet long, with a long tail and pointed ears, green-yellow eyes, and fang-like canine teeth" (*Guardian*, same day). This differed from the earlier description in the local paper (*High Peak Reporter* 2 April): "Two to three foot long with a thick tail, green eyes, pointed ears and fang-like teeth."

Anyway, this two-three-four-foot-long black cat with green-yellow-amber eyes and a long, thick tail was growling and spitting in the dining room. It ran upstairs and hid under a bed, then leapt on top of a wardrobe as Mrs Topliff confronted it with a broom handle. The cat bit her, leaving two wounds in her hand, one of which needed two stitches, and then shot downstairs, disappearing through an open window. This is the local press version of events. According to the *Telegraph*, Mrs Topliff found the cat on the wardrobe, managed to entice it downstairs, and was bitten while trying to open her kitchen door. It had probably entered by the large cat-flap.

The cat had visited Mrs Topliff before. She had chased it out of the house in February when one of her grandchildren was visiting; and it is possible that it spent the night in the house during the week of the March sighting, as there was a very strong smell in the dining room the following morning. Mrs Topliff has a cat of her own, which was shut in one of the bedrooms when the wild animal went in.

Superintendent Mike Whittingham said there was no evidence to link this cat to the 1991 sighting of what was thought to be a black panther on a farm at Laneside Road, New Mills. The 'Peak Panther' has been puzzling inhabitants for over ten years, with several reports of sightings of a big black cat in and around New Mills. A farmer said that some of his lambs had been horribly mauled at Weathercotes in the Spring of 1988; there were huge bite marks on the lambs and paw prints nearby.

Another farmer saw a large black cat the following Spring. In November 1989, a large cat was seen basking in a hollow at Shed Yard Farm, Laneside Road, New Mills, and police marksmen hunted the animal for several days. [See reports *FT53*:9 and *FT59*:20.] Although it was sighted during two of the many sweeps of a steep, tree-lined gully, the search was called off. The police believed it could have been a very large feral cat, or a puma or panther released after legislation on dangerous animals.

Mrs Topliff said of her visitor: "If it was a wild cat, it was a very big one." The probable reason for a wild cat entering a house is to look for food; but this was the lambing season with plentiful big cat food in all directions. Furthermore, local farmers had not reported any stock losses since the 1989 sightings. A further problem is the location of the Topliff house in Swallowhouse Crescent. Though it is adjacent to Ollersett Moor, where the big cat(s) were sighted in previous years, it is in the centre of the village, and wild cats tend to avoid human settlements.

Our man-on-the-spot, Jake Kirkwood of New Mills, knows of one witness to the February 1992 sighting in Mrs Topliff's house, and this person stated that it was merely a large domestic cat. Mr Kirkwood suggests a cross between a Maine Coon and feral or semi-feral stock. "The other cat which would fit the description is the Kellas cat", he writes, "and it is possible that their range extends to the Peak District, although unlikely." [See *FT49*:38 for a description of this cat, shot at Kellas in Moray, Scotland, in 1983.] "We certainly have Pine Martens here, a predator species which require undisturbed habitats, and which are otherwise found mainly in Scotland. However, I remain to be convinced that the Hayfield cat is anything other than an unusually large domestic cat."

THE HAMPSTEAD PUMA

On the morning of Britain's General Election, 9 April 1992, at 9:00am, two businessmen in their forties saw a Labrador-sized golden brown cat. It was climbing along the branch of a tree next to the church in West End Lane, West Hampstead, London.

The animal, "definitely not a fox", climbed onto a flat roof nearby, where they lost sight of it. Neither witness wished to be identified for fear of ridicule, but the West Hampstead police described them as 'unshakeable' (presumably they tried to shake them). A search was made of the area, but no cat was found. Inspector Mike Terry said no registered exotic animal in the borough had gone missing, but didn't rule out the possibility that a cat belonging to a private owner had escaped. One source said there were no registered big cat owners in Camden.

"I have spoken with both witnesses and they are very credible", said Doug Richardson, cat expert at London Zoo. "From the size I would say it could be anything from a jungle cat to a puma. The area has been thoroughly searched. I went down there again on Saturday [11 April]. But a cat like that could stay hidden for months. There are three railway lines nearby with plenty of rabbit warrens – so it would not go hungry. In cities like Nairobi, in Kenya, big cats like leopards live in many suburban areas, raiding dustbins and eating small rodents. They are rarely seen by humans, just like foxes in towns here."

Mr Richardson said the cat posed little danger to humans, although it should not be approached. Domestic pets and very small children could be at risk: "It would view them as meals on legs". The Hampstead ABC (alien big cat) didn't seem to be hungry: two rabbits in a hutch ten yards away were not touched. *Camden & St Pancras Chronicle, Camden New Journal* 16 April 1992.

FORTEAN TIMES MUGS

Take tea in style with our set of four Fortean Times mugs. Illustrated by Hunt Emerson the designs comprise of The Cats Of War, Drunken Bull, Falling Cow and Forest Fire Death. Black designs on high-quality white ceramic mugs. **CODE FTM - £15.00 per set.**

FORTEAN TIMES T-SHIRTS.

CODE FTC

100% white cotton t-shirts, one size XL. £7.99 each

CODE FTT All your favourite strange phenomena illustrated by Hunt Emerson.

CODE FTC Charles Fort's portrait and the slogan "One Measures A Circle Beginning Anywhere"

CODE FTT

TUDOR GATE©

The Green Man is a symbol of great power
and our unity with the natural world.

Tudor Gate's fine antique lead and composite
stone example of this historic ornament can be
purely decorative or used as a functional shelf

Dimensions: 12" x 9"   Price £110 inc. P & P

Please write or ring for catalogue of unusual ornament.

TUDOR GATE, HIGHER GEORGIA, NANCLEDRA
PENZANCE, CORNWALL TR20 8LW. *TEL: (0736) 798411*

MYSTERY HEAD HEAT • PHENOMENOMIX • HUNT EMERSON ∿ ©92

T. Lobsang Rampa

THE PLUMBER FROM PLYMPTON WHO
BECAME THE LAMA FROM LHASA

THE WORLD WAS SHOCKED TO DISCOVER THAT T LOBSANG RAMPA, WHOSE BOOKS ON MYSTICAL ENLIGHTENMENT BECAME BEST-SELLERS IN THE 1950S, WAS ACTUALLY A PLUMBER FROM PLYMPTON. *BOB RICKARD* **INVESTIGATES THIS FAMOUS LITERARY SCANDAL**

The autobiographical writings of T. Lobsang Rampa were the publishing sensation of their day. They began, in *The Third Eye* (1956), as pleasantly told recollections of a Tibetan monk, raised and taught in the Chakpori monastery in Lhasa. In the sequels, Rampa told how he was a pilot in the Chinese airforce, survived internment by the Japanese, and died en route to England having made his way across Siberia, Russia and Europe. Yes, died! He now inhabited the body of an Englishman. Thereafter, the books became progressively more bizarre, incorporating topics which would have been classed as fantasy were it not for the claim they really happened.

The Third Eye saw nine hardback printings in two years in the UK alone, and in its first year was a best-seller in 12 countries. With brilliant timing, the paperback edition of 1959 was reprinted in 1962 to captivate the hippies and disaffected intellectuals who yearned for Eastern wisdom. Rampa's mix of down-home simplicity, exotic occultism and 'Boy's Own' adventure made him a perfect guru for the gullible West. Eventually, he wrote over 14 titles, and lent his name to marketing New Age bric-a-brac (such as incense, personalised prayers and crystal balls).

ANCIENT ASTRONAUTS

The books published after 1962 seemed like rehashes of Theosophical, contactee and 'Ancient Astronaut' literature, deliberately pitched to appeal to the growing New Age readership. They featured astral travel to other worlds, and a Himalayan cave full of machines made by an ancient civilisation, including one which projected images from the past and the future. Rampa also lectured on Adam and Eve, the fictitious 'Philadelphia experiment', relativity theory, telepathy, levitation, psychic healing, lost Atlantis and Lemuria etc etc. One book – *Living with the Lama* (1964) – was the autobiography of his cat, dictated to him telepathically, while another – *My Visits to Venus* (1966) – attempted to forge a link with the growing genre of stories of abductions by our 'Space Brothers' in their UFOs.

Most critics thought Rampa's genial narrative was 'plausible', 'highly imaginative' and a 'good story'. Yet the more the academics and philosophers agonised over the identity of the pseudomymous Rampa and the validity of his claims, the less his public seemed to care. The English editions of *Third Eye*, published by Secker & Warburg, warned the reader to make up his own mind because the publisher's panel of experts could not agree on the authenticity of Rampa's story. Frederick Warburg, who met Rampa several times after 1955, never seemed to question the English appearance of this supposed Tibetan, and accepted as authentic Rampa's medical doctorate from the University of Chungking (strangely printed in English). The editor-in-chief of Doubleday, who published the American edition of *Third Eye*, dispensed with the warning completely, while identifying the reason for the commercial success of the book; it was, he said, "a romantic story [..] from a world that many of us feel may indeed exist."

The most damning exposé occurred in 1958, just over a year after Rampa came on the scene, but it was tucked away in the relatively unknown American review of psychic research, *Tomorrow*. Editor Eileen Garrett had asked Chen Chi Chang, a fellow of the Bollingen Foundation, to do a critique of *The*

Portrait of T Lobsang Rampa, apparently taken in a high-street photographers

Third Eye for their Spring 1958 issue. Chang was eminently suitable; he had lectured on Tibetan tantra at the University of Nanking, and qualified as a medical doctor at Kong Ka in Eastern Tibet. His verdict was unequivocal: "It would be dangerous to regard it as a serious work offering genuine information concerning Tibetan Buddhism."

A FANCIFUL FABRICATION?

For Chang, Rampa's statements about the discipline and education in a monastery did not ring true; to a scholar of Tibetan, they contained obvious doctrinal and ceremonial errors and bogus Tibetan prayers taken from Chinese texts. The book's main talking-point – the one on which the book was marketed – concerned a secret initiation in which the eight-year-old Rampa's 'third eye' (a putative organ of clairvoyance said to be between and just above the eyes) was 'opened' by surgery; this, said Chang, was "a fanciful fabrication". Such a procedure, if it existed, undermined the whole basis of the personal struggle to understand the scriptures and to obtain realisation through one's own efforts and merits (not through surgery or drugs).

> Rampa's mix of down-home simplicity, exotic occultism and 'boys own' adventure made him a perfect guru for the gullible West.

Most inventive of all was Rampa's claim that his final lamaic initiation was in a secret chamber, deep below the Potala monastery, where he meditated alone for three days. He lay beside the stone coffins of three giants; they were gold-plated and not quite human, seeming to be asleep rather than dead. In the darkness he left his body and seemed to experience the time, in a distant millennium, when the land that became Tibet was by the shore of a warm ocean, inhabited by those dormant giants.

Chang, a US citizen, checked with no less than the elder brother of the present Dalai Lama, then resident in the USA, and other leading scholars of Tibetan Buddhism, and "all expressed similar reservations". These doubts included Rampa's exposition of astral travel, and a doctrine of subtle bodies linked to the physical by a 'silver cord', which Chang said were largely "alien to Buddhist thought".

DETECTED IN DUBLIN

While the *Tomorrow* critique was being prepared, Rampa's true identity was discovered by a Liverpool detective, Clifford Burgess, who had been hired by a group of Tibetan scholars, including Marco Pallis. Burgess claimed to have followed a trail of 3,000 miles to the door of Cyril Henry Hoskins, then (in 1958) 47 years old and living with his wife Sanya in Howth, Dublin, "in a dimly-lit house overlooking Dublin Bay". Hoskins had never been to Tibet, and never had a 'third eye' operation on his forehead. He was born in Plympton, Devon, in 1911, and after leaving school helped his father in the plumbing trade. After his father died in

1937, Hoskins lived with his mother in Nottinghamshire, working first for a surgical instrument company and then as a clerk for a firm in Weybridge (a suburb of London) that taught engineering by correspondence.

There is an hilarious account – in Christopher Evans' *The Cults of Unreason* (1974) – of the recollections of several people who knew Hoskins in the mid-1940s, traced by John Pitt, a reporter for *Psychic News*. One recalled Hoskins limping on crutches claiming he had been badly injured in a plane crash while working as an instructor in the Chinese airforce. Another remembered him "full of strange stories about China where he claimed he had been taken as a child". He was known for his interest in occultism, and in 1948 he began, for reasons unknown, to shave his head, grow a beard and call himself 'Dr Carl Kuan-suo', which, as Evans puts it, surprised people because "'The Doctor' both talked and looked remarkably like an Englishman".

When the detective found him in Dublin, Hoskins seemed to be suffering from a heart condition and other ailments; when he realised the press would not go away, he allowed himself to be photographed in his sick-bed attended by his wife and a secretary. The press had much sport with this *menage*, suggesting a Svengali-like Hoskins had enticed this "pretty society woman" away from her "old Etonian" husband.

At first, Hoskins boldly maintained that his story was true, and that the identity of the author could not be revealed for fear of jeopardising relatives in Chinese-occupied Tibet. When faced with the discrepancies between his humdrum life in Thames Ditton (near Weybridge) and the exploits of his lama-pilot alter ego, Hoskins began to claim that at the time of writing, his "body was actually taken over by the spirit of an Easterner". This inspired explanation offered Hoskins a remarkable way out, one he developed in his next book – *The Rampa Story* (1960) – the first to be published after his exposure.

With breath-taking audacity, the book explained that those who claimed to have known Hoskins, with his occult leanings and strange habits, were not wrong – and neither was his on-going tale of 'Lobsang Rampa'. Hoskins, he said, was a deeply unhappy man who wanted to move on and agreed to a plan to reduce his 'Karmic debt'. Hoskins' spirit was to be relocated (like an occult version of one of those new identity jobs for witnesses of serious crime) and the essence of Rampa was to take over his body. The swap took place on 13 June 1949, when Hoskins fell out of a tree photographing an owl, and disembodied Tibetan super-surgeons effected the psychic transplant. Immediately, Rampa continued his autobiographical mission (without the impedi-

ment of his unhappy medium) and presumably with no objection from Hoskins' wife.

Later, Hoskins and his entourage emigrated to Canada, hounded out of Ireland, he claimed, by the Press. He died in 1981. He left behind the mystery of where he obtained his `plausible' knowledge of life in Tibet. Hoskins was an avid reader of anything to do with the Orient, and constructed for himself a fantasy world from the writings of anthropologists, travellers, philosophers and mystics; in this there is a strong analogy with Carlos Castaneda's equally inspired and influential creation of the world of Don Juan, 'a Yaqui shaman'. Hoskins' pseudo-Tibetan mysticism and religion undoubtedly came from an immersion in Theosophical literature and the writings of the remarkable female-lama Alexandra David-Neel, laced with lashings of *Lost Horizon*.

Hoskins must have marvelled at the controversy over the authenticity of his invention, and wrote the subsequent books to keep a 'good thing' going. There can be few researchers and writers on the paranormal who were not influenced in some way by Lobsang Rampa, because, as Kevin McClure noted, in the first issue of *Common Ground*, "there was a time not twenty years ago when his were almost the only books on the subject that were generally available." Hoskins' legacy is a generation of New Agers who have swallowed his bogus-Buddhist ancient magic and mysticism hook, line and sinker; while a new generation of believers will see in it confirmation of the 'Indiana Jones' school of mystical anthropology.

We are left with a disturbing thought; what if soul transplanting is possible, and Rampa was telling the truth? Could you tell whether a lama was driving a plumber's body (or vice versa) – and would it have made any difference to the outcome of this classic hoax if you could?

FT

Acid Tattoo Scare

Why do people persist in believing that children are under threat from psychedelic transfers?

TRANSFER
TATTOOS LACED
WITH LSD ARE AN
IMAGINARY PANIC
THAT WILL NOT
DIE.
*PAUL SIEVEKING
INVESTIGATES.*

Last year, a pamphlet called *Metropolitan Police Neighbourhood Watch* (Issue No. 10, February 1991) dropped through my door in Hampstead. The lead story began: "Information has been received from HQ EAOR of a worrying new drug danger to school children which has emerged on the continent. To date it is confined to Holland and Switzerland [..]

"Gifts, in the form of self-adhesive stickers, designed to be stuck to the skin for decoration, are being offered to children of all ages. The stickers are soaked with LSD and strychnine which causes a quick and unpredictable reaction. The aim is ultimate dependency and therefore new customers. The drug is absorbed through the skin, even if only held in the hand.

"The stickers discovered to date are: Blue star on white background; small card with ROTE PYRAMIDE (Red Pyramid) printed on it; small tokens named `Window Pane' with motifs to cut out and tiny coloured grains/seeds to swallow.

"If either you or your children see or are offered any of the above, DO NOT TOUCH, prevent contact to the skin and inform local police. If contact has been made and the following occurs the individual must be taken to hospital immediately: hallucinations, vomiting, headaches and/or fluctuating temperature."

As any informed student of contemporary folklore, chemist or drug squad policeman will tell you, there is not, and never has been, a distribution of LSD 'tattoos', but two decades or more of official denials seem to have no effect. (The reference to 'dependency' shows that the instigators of this hoax know nothing about LSD anyway: the drug is not addictive.) The story is a bit like a vampire; no matter how many times it is cut down it rises again to scare the pants off another generation of ill-informed parents.

This was not the first police bulletin to help spread the story; a Baltimore police precinct bulletin did it in August 1986. One version of the story had a brain-damaged child dying in a Baltimore hospital after handling the blue stars. In Tacoma around the same time, a police query, apparently a response to the rumour, was worded: "Have you seen any drug-laced tattoos?" This was repeated as: "We have seen many drug-laced tattoos!" That's one way these stories build up steam. (See *Curses! Broiled Again!* by Jan Harold Brunvand, W.W.Norton & Co. 1989.)

In March 1991, a similar letter was pinned on a noticeboard at BICC Cables in Wrexham, North Wales. This one was said to have first circulated in Merseyside. One sentence read: "A young child could happen upon these [tattoos] and have a fatal trip." Wrexham drug

CHEMISTRY

Lysergic Acid Diethylamide is an amine alkaloid resembling ergonovine and has an oxytoxic action comparable to the latter drug. Unlike the amino acids of ergot (i.g. ergotamine), it produces only slight vasoconstriction. It has the following structural formula:

LSD and many of its congeners have been extensively studied. Although a number of other drugs capable of producing psychotic reactions have been found, LSD still remains the most potent psychotogen

Lysergic Acid Diethylamide, as the chemists see it. From *IT* 19, 5 October 1967.

squad officer DS John Atkinson said: "These are just stupid chain letters that cause nothing but alarm". *Evening Leader*, (Clwyd and Chester) 1 Mar 1991.

In July 1991, Detective Inspector Neil Kingman, head of Hampshire drug squad, was busy rubbishing similar leaflets circulating in Portsmouth. *The News* (Portsmouth) 4 July 1991. A week later, the Yeovil (Somerset) *Star* (12 July) said a similar letter was being distributed in schools and workplaces in Somerset, with the added detail that the 'tattoos' depicted "brightly coloured cartoon characters such as Bart Simpson and the Turtles characters." The dire symptoms included "uncontrolled laughter and changes in mood". Yeovil police spokesman Paul Hardiman said that the letter was panic material, an "elaborate hoax started in Canada some years ago." (Have you noticed that hoaxes are nearly always 'elaborate'?)

POLICE WARNING LETTER

Obviously, the West Midlands police had never heard of the 'elaborate hoax' because they were busy frightening parents in September 1991 with a tattoo warning letter. Additional tattoo images were mentioned: Superman, clowns, butterflies and Mickey Mouse. "Each one is box wrapped in foil" the parents were told. A facsimile of the letter to Grestone Junior School in Birmingham, dated 10 September 1991, is reproduced in *FLS News* (The newsletter of the Folklore Society) No.14, Jan 1992.

Despite the earlier denials in March, LSD transfer scare letters were again circulating in Wrexham in November. This time they purported to come from the Welsh Office, and the chief environmental officer of Wrexham Maelor Borough Council did the rumour-trashing. *Evening Leader* 13 Nov 1991.

The fear spread to France in December. A much-photocopied leaflet, apparently bearing a French police stamp, turned up in offices and schools. The drugs, it stated, were "probably already circulating in Switzerland and will rapidly invade the rest of Europe." A spokesman for the narcotics department of the French Interior Ministry asserted that the hoax surfaced in Western Europe a few years ago. *Int. Herald Tribune* 19 Dec 1991.

MICKEY MOUSE ACID

A poster warning parents about LSD transfers was given to a sub post office in Gunard, Isle of Wight, in March 1992. A spokesman for South West Surrey Health Authority, whose name was printed at the foot of the poster, said the posters were bogus. "We have been receiving calls from all over the country where these posters are appearing", he said. *Isle of Wight County Press* 3 April 1992.

The Blue Star acid transfer story was long discredited when it reappeared in a big way across America in 1986. In *Newsweek* (24 November 1986), reporters investigated rumours of LSD microdots, resembling blue stars, in New York, New Jersey, Texas, Georgia, Kansas and Nebraska, and concluded that some ``may have existed'' around 1971. By the end of 1987, the scare letters had been circulated coast to coast in the USA and Canada.

The folklorist Jan Harold Brunvand studied the acid transfer legend in 1981, calling it "Mickey Mouse acid" because this character was most often named in the warnings. I remember seeing tiny squares of LSD-impregnated cellulose with a picture of Mickey Mouse back in 1969, but they weren't skin transfers.

A 1980 New Jersey police bulletin did warn: "Children may be susceptible to this type of cartoon stamp believing it a cartoon transfer"; but there is no evidence that actual cartoon 'tattoos' have ever circulated.

LSD can, of course, be ingested through the skin if the amounts are large enough. The police dismantling the Hampton Wick 'acid factory' in the London suburbs a week after the massive 'Operation Julie' bust in March 1977 had been warned by the chemist that a carpet was saturated with LSD after a mishap where enough acid for 150,000 trips had been spilt. Three policemen took insufficient precautions and soon afterwards headed for outer (inner?) space after handling the carpet and other items. After some hilarity down the pub, they became confused and had themselves arrested and carted off to Kingston Hospital. Leaf Fielding gives a colourful account of the policemen's trip in *City Limits* (1-7 Nov 1985).

A string of debunking newspaper articles in the American press a few years ago seemingly had little effect: "Tattoo Tripped Up" (Chicago *Sun-Times* 20 May 1987); "Only a Folk Tale" (Dubuque *Telegraph-Herald* 6 October 1987); ``No Cause for Alarm'' (*Washington Post* 2 June 1988). No drug enforcement agency has ever seen an LSD transfer; but the "stupid chain letters" carry on to eternity.

THE ARK OF THE COVENANT (1)

Author Graham Hancock has traced the lost Ark of the Covenant (reputed to contain the tablets upon which the 10 Commandments were written) to Axum in Ethiopia. There's nothing new here so far: the Ethiopians have long claimed to have the Ark, saying that it was carried off by Menelik, the son of Solomon and the Queen of Sheba. What is new is that Hancock seems to have traced the history of how it got there. His research is set out at length in a book, *The Sign and the Seal*

UNEARTHED
Steve Moore

Lost and found time: we seem to have aquired a clump of stories recently about lost cities and artefacts suddenly reappearing (or at least, so say their 'discoverers'), so here's a quick round-up ...

(Heinemann), but we must summarise briefly here. Hancock dismisses the Menelik story, as the Ark seems to have remained in the Temple at Jerusalem until about 650 BC. At this point he believes the Ark was removed by Jewish priests when the apostate King Manasseh installed a pagan idol in the Temple. At about the same time, a Jewish colony built a temple at Elephantine in Egypt. This is the only known Jewish temple apart from the one at Jerusalem, and there is evidence of animal sacrifice, which

should not have been possible without the presence of the Ark. After a conflict with the local Egyptian community in 410 BC, the temple was destroyed and the Jews appear to have fled to Lake Tana in Ethiopia. There the Ark seems to have remained until 340 AD, when the country was Christianised, and it was removed to Axum, where the church of St Mary of Zion was built to house it.

Various wars and destructions caused by the intervention of Jewish and Muslim rulers led to the Ark's removal (to Lake Zwai in 950, to Lake Tana in 1535) but since about 1640 it has remained in Axum. An Ethiopian Christian monk remains in constant attendance on the Ark (the current incumbent being one Abba Fameray) chanting and burning incense before it. So far so good. Hancock's evidence sounds

reasonably convincing, but the only problem is that the Ethiopian church will not allow anyone, except its guardian, to actually see the Ark. This is unfortunate, and under the circumstances we really have to leave the verdict as `not proven'. *Independent* 21 March, *Observer* 22 March 1992.

THE ARK OF THE COVENANT (2)

And while the case is not proven, the field remains open for different interpretations. Yehuda Getz, Chief Rabbi of the Wailing Wall, also claims to know where the Ark is: in Jerusalem. According to Getz, the Ark was removed from the Temple about 100 years before its destruction by the Romans in 70 AD, by King Josiah. It seems that the prophetess Huldah predicted the destruction of Jerusalem, so Josiah had the Ark moved to a maze of tunnels carved deep in the Temple Mount. The Temple was originally on the west side of the Mount; Getz believes he knows its present location, "within 2 or 3 metres", on the east side... under the Dome of the Rock and the al-Aqsa Mosque. But, "in the actual political climate, we cannot go and look for it. It would cause trouble with the Arabs". Again, one is forced to say that this is unfortunate, or perhaps in this case, convenient. Unless someone can actually 'produce the body', this one could run and run. *Courier Mail* (Brisbane) 29 Jan 1992.

ATLANTIS ON THE SHORE

German geologist Dr Eberhard Zangger has found lost Atlantis, and (surprise!) he's written a book about it: *The Flood from Heaven* (Sidgwick & Jackson). According to Zangger, Atlantis wasn't in the Atlantic Ocean, or even an island; it was the ancient city of Troy. He argues that the 'Pillars of Hercules' refers not to the Straits of Gibraltar, but to the Dardanelles, near Troy. That hot and cold

Egypt in California: part of Cecil B DeMille's gigantic set for *The Ten Commandments*

Another view of *The Ten Commandments* set of 1923 (see Ancient & Modern)

springs, mentioned as being present in Atlantis, were also present at Troy. That both places were buffetted by strong northerly winds. That Atlantis means 'Daughter of Atlas', and that the Trojans were supposed to be descended from Electra, daughter of Atlas. He suggests that the city was destroyed in the Trojan War, and that part of Troy, located on the plain below the city, was then submerged by river silt and buried, rather than the city sinking below the sea. *Independent* 14 March 1992. And so the Atlantis story runs on and on. Where next?

A ROMAN CITY IN CHINA

David Harris, a 49 year old writer and teacher from Adelaide, believes he has found a Roman settlement in what is now the Gobi desert, in western China. Inspired by the work of the wonderfully named Oxford professor, Homer Hasenpflug Dubs, Harris has made three trips to China, exchanging western historical information with Chinese academics at Lanzhou University. Now, unsurprisingly, he's written a book: *Black Horse Odyssey*.

It seems that in 35 BC, about 145 Roman mercenaries were captured by the Chinese in a battle near what is now the town of Vzhambul, in Kazakhstan.

They were carried off eastwards and settled in what was then a fertile region known as Li-jien, which is now at the edge of the Gobi. The exact location of the city at Li-jien was lost, but in 1989 Harris and his Chinese associates found what *seems* to be the place, along with three other possible settlements. There are remains of walls 5.5 metres high, pottery, and uninvestigated tombs which are said to contain the remains of "yellow haired" people. A joint Chinese-Australian archaeological expedition was due to investigate the site this May, and we await developments with interest. *Sunday Mail* (Aust) 8 Dec, *Evening Post* (Wellington, NZ) 14 Dec 1991.

ANCIENT AND MODERN

In 1991, California was in the grip of a drought which had some interesting side-effects. At the end of World War II the federal government built 30 large dams to provide reservoirs. Now the water levels have dropped so dramatically that flooded towns, bridges, abandoned railway tunnels, cemeteries and flights of steps that lead nowhere are resurfacing. In Lake Isabella, which has dropped 50 feet, the entire town of Kernville has reappeared, allowing old-time residents to wander nostalgi-

cally through the streets. Other reservoirs have revealed 1850s gold-mining equipment, old mule trails, and a number of skeletons.

While all this is going on, something else is reappearing in the sands near Guadalupe, 150 miles north of Los Angeles. A city with a 120 foot high, 800 foot long stone gateway bearing bas-reliefs of Egyptian archers in their chariots; four 35 foot high statues of Ramses the Magnificent; and an avenue of 21 sphinxes, each weighing 5 tons. Yes, it's the city from which Moses led out the Israelites... and it isn't. In 1923, Cecil B. De Mille built an enormous set for his silent movie, *The Ten Commandments*, and being the man he was, he built it all out of concrete and plaster, rather than plastic and papier-mache. When filming was over, it was cheaper to bury the set than dismantle it, and after that the site of the set was lost. Now it's been relocated with ground-penetration radar, and plans are afoot for a full excavation. *Guardian* 3 Jan, *D.Telegraph* 14 Jan 1991.

We're struck by the strange coincidence here: in the same time and place, real recent towns and fake ancient ones are reappearing together. But before you start to wonder whether it's really worthwhile excavating a modern fake of an

ancient Egyptian city, you might care to consider the following tale.

Archæologists from London University believe they've located the Persian Portico at the foot of the acropolis in Sparta. This was originally built in 479 BC as a war memorial to celebrate the Spartan part in the Greek defeat of the Persian invasion. It was famous for the stone columns which held up the roof, which were sculpted in the form of Persian prisoners of war. The columns themselves have not been located, but a large Doric capital has been found; yet this is Roman work of the 2nd century AD, done in a deliberately archaic Greek style. It appears that the Portico was rebuilt and embellished at this period when the Greek cities had lost their power under the Roman Empire, and in order to make money they had to turn themselves into showcases of local history for the rich Roman tourists.

The Athenians were just as bad, putting up reproduction buildings and even importing a disused temple of the 5th century BC and rebuilding it block by block in the city centre. In other words, they faked it. It may not be quite the same as a film set, but let no one tell you that a historical theme-park is a new idea! *D.Telegraph* 17 Dec 1990.

MEDICAL BAG

Dr Faustroll

FACULTIES REGAINED

◆ Simon Davis of Colebourne Road, King's Heath, Birmingham, lost his hearing when he caught meningitis at the age of seven months. When he was nine years old, his mother Jackie heard him singing along to the theme tune of Home and Away, and realised he could hear again. "This is unprecedented", said consultant David Proops. "We have no idea why it should have happened." *D.Mirror, D.Telegraph, Sun* 17 Mar 1992.

◆ Margaret Gresser of Godfrey, Missouri, lost her voice from polio at the age of four. Fifty-two years later, she regained her voice. Gresser, who was also left profoundly mentally retarded by polio, now has a vocabulary of 14 words that can be understood easily. She is being taught to make the sounds of words slowly, to avoid straining her vocal chords and the muscles in her mouth and tongue. Harrisburg (PA) *Sunday Patriot-News* 5 April 1992.

◆ For a round-up of anomalous returns of faculties, see 'Headbangers' *FT53*:28.

GETTING STUCK IN

◆ Sara Fletcher of Crowthorne, Berkshire, swallowed a one-and-a-half-inch screw unobserved when she was two and immediately started choking. Her mother, Sheila, was convinced she had swallowed something, and Dr Lord, the family doctor, sent Sara to Heatherwood Hospital, Ascot, for an X-ray. The doctor who saw her didn't do an X-ray; he diagnosed her as asthmatic. Dr Lord accepted the diagnosis and refused Mrs Fletcher's repeated requests for an X-ray, even though he witnessed the little girl coughing up blood.

Sara suffered from infections and was miserable for two years. Then Dr Lord retired and an X-ray located the screw in the girl's windpipe. After an operation, she made a dramatic recovery. Sara, now eight, was awarded £10,000 damages against doctor and hospital, both of whom admitted liability. *Scotsman, Independent* 8 May 1991.

◆ Another supposed asthma sufferer was Gavin Marshall, who swallowed a plastic sweet box lid during a cross-country run when he was 16. He thought nothing of it at the time, but for the next 13 years, his constant coughing baffled all the doctors and specialists he visited. Diagnoses included a weak lung causing chest infections, asthma, allergies, and malignant growth. Finally he began coughing blood, and the lid was removed from his lung using bronchoscopy, an operation in which a small tube fitted with forceps is inserted into the lungs via the mouth or nose. Mr Marshall, an insurance agent aged 29 from Worthing in Sussex, was cough-free for the first time since childhood. *D.Telegraph* 17 Oct 1991.

◆ A man in his 30s had complained for some years of an odd sensation in one ear, but doctors found nothing wrong. Last September, he was cleaning his ear when he felt something. After groping around with a hairpin, he removed an inch-long pencil lead, which he believed could have been in his ear for over 20 years. *Independent* 8 Oct 1991.

◆ Brian Wheeler was eight when a playmate shot him in the ear with a toy pistol loaded with cigarette filters. He forgot about the incident, but after 16 years of earache and deafness, he went to hospital where his ear was syringed and a filter tip dropped out. Nat. Enquirer 31 May 1991. For two tales of bus tickets stuck in ears for many years, see *FT53*:12.

◆ Frank Curry, 50, of Hillsborough, Sheffield, suffered from an itchy scalp for 40 years. Then a barber removed a piece of plastic comb embedded in his scalp. It had snapped off in a childhood fight in 1951. *D.Star* 8 May 1991.

◆ A woman fell on a needle she was carrying when she tripped over her cat. Some time later she went to the emergency room of the Frisco Medical Center in Denver, suffering from chest pain, nausea, vomiting and sweating, symptoms of her immune system trying to expel an object. The sewing needle was found in her heart, and was removed with open heart surgery. The case was written up by Dr James J. Bachman in the March 1992 *New England Journal of Medicine*. [AP] 13 Mar 1992.

STICKY PROBLEM

A 62-year-old man from Fort Lauderdale recently found that everything he touched stuck to his fingers. He visited his dermatologist, Neal S. Penneys, who found that the man was suffering from a weird reaction to the drug etretinate which he was taking in high dosages for psoriasis. The drug increased a sugar protein molecule in the man's skin that made his palms and the soles of his feet sticky. The condition was overcome by reducing the dosage of the drug. *Nat. Enquirer* 9 Oct 1991.

CYCLOPS NEWS

◆ Luzinete Josepa Silva, 27, gave birth in a hospital near Recife in Brazil on 19 April 1991. The baby had one large adult eye in the place where the nose should have been and a penis in the middle of its forehead. It died two hours later. Large crowds attended the funeral. *O Globo* (Brazil) 22 April 1991.

◆ Students from a military academy in Soviet Azerbaijan spotted a 'cyclops' near Baku. Ali Ahverdiyev, chairman of the Baku Anomalous Phenomena Club, said the students "ran into an enormous one-eyed creature covered in black hair". The eye – a red orb in the centre of the creature's face – was the size of a pomegranate. *Independent* 9 Aug 1991.

◆ The Bulgarian news agency BTA reported the discovery of a 'cyclops' skeleton near the town of Razlog in southwest Bulgaria back in 1973. It was 5ft 8in tall and had one eye socket in the coronal bone above the nasal cavity. The discovery was made in a burial ground near the ruins of a building of unknown age. UPI 4 Aug 1973.

DEXTER GORDON

Dexter Gordon, the tenor and soprano saxophonist, died in Philadelphia aged 67 in April 1990. He achieved his apotheosis in Bertrand Tavernier's film *Around Midnight*, where he played Dale Turner, a black jazz genius struggling against drink and drugs, for which he was nominated an Oscar.

Gordon had a history that made him an enigma to medical science. During the making of the film, studio doctors found that he was a diabetic, had virtually no liver and a percentage of alcohol in his bloodstream that defied belief. The

MIRROR-IMAGE PEOPLE: Ryan Perkins, the mirror-image baby at ten weeks, with his parents. Sisters with mirror-image organs: Jo Stark, left, and Jane Toon.

average is measured at 33; at over 150, a driver's licence is automatically forfeited. If it is over 250, one is considered clinically insane. Gordon's alcohol content registered at 1,200. *D.Telegraph* 26 April 1990.

MIRROR IMAGE PEOPLE

◆ Ryan Perkins was born to Martina and Brian Perkins of Desford, Leicestershire, in November 1991. An ultrasound scan when he was two weeks old revealed that his heart, liver, appendix and all his major organs were on the opposite side to the normal position. "I occasionally see children whose hearts are on the right side, but in 95% of cases they have abnormalities to the heart", said Dr Chen Chan of Leicester's Groby Road Hospital. "What makes Ryan so unusual is that he is perfectly healthy." *Leicester Mercury* 11 Jan 1992.

After the report on Ryan Perkins, other 'mirror image' people in

Leicestershire came forward, including Mrs Jane Toon, 32, from Glen Parva and her sister Jo Stark, 31, from Narborough Road South – *pictured above*. Also, Mrs Jacqueline Gee of Narborough said her soldier son, Scott, 21, had the same unusual characteristic.

Delving back into the archives, I discover a clipping from the *News of the World* for 17 April 1927, which reports on a miner called Joseph Johnson, of Oaks Green, Sheffield, "who has his heart on the wrong side, and all his other organs are vice versa to those of normal people… He declares that he is as strong and healthy as any man."

BUBONIC PLAGUE WATCH

Bubonic plague, the Black Death, is still with us. About five years back we recall reading about some cases in Texas. In 1990 there were more than a hundred cases in China, while there was an outbreak in Kenya

at the end of August that year. It came from a rat-infested grain store near Jomo Kenyatta Airport, and was passed to humans by rat fleas. Three people died and 23 were in hospital. *D.Mail* 3 Sept 1990; *Middlesbrough Eve. Gazette* 17 April 1991.

TWO HIT BY POLIO NAPPIES

An unnamed 48-year-old man developed polio in November 1991 after touching the soiled nappy of his niece days after the baby was vaccinated against the virus. He was taken to Southampton General Hospital, where he developed paralysis of the lungs and was placed on a ventilator.

Only one case of polio was recorded in Britain in 1989, none in 1990, and only the case mentioned here in 1991. Seven million doses of the polio vaccine are given in sugar every year in Britain and it is regarded as one of the safest of all vaccinations. The victim was unlucky not to be

vaccinated himself. "There is no specific treatment available", said consultant Martin Whale, adding, in a virtuoso display of probability calculation: "It is literally a one in three million chance that he contracted polio."

Nevertheless, four days later, reports of a second victim appeared in the papers. The 30-year-old father from Bournemouth, Dorset, caught the disease in an identical way from his baby daughter. He was paralysed but stable in the Royal Bournemouth Hospital, where he was admitted in January 1992. "The two cases are in no way connected, and two different strains are involved", said Dr Keir Kimmance, Consultant in Public Health Medicine for Wessex Regional Health Authority. "For it to happen twice within a few months to two people living 30 miles apart is truly remarkable." *Guardian* 24+28 Jan; *D.Telegraph*, *D.Mirror* 28 Jan 1992.

FT

OVER REACTIONS

⬤ Naomi Parker, 32, threw liquid drain cleaner in the face of Demetrius Moore, 27, during a church service in Lexington, Michigan, causing serious burns. He was singing off-key. *South China Morning Post* 27 Nov 1991.

⬤ When Kevin and Denise Childerley sold their home in Mansfield Woodhouse, Nottinghamshire, they agreed to leave the cooker for the new owner, Alan Bryce. Bryce, however, thought the cooker left behind was not the one agreed. Correspondence and solicitors failed to get satisfaction, so Bryce and his friend Bryan Clark killed Kevin Childerley with an axe and disfigured his wife. *Independent* 21 Feb 1991.

⬤ Max Hoffmann, 39, went berserk 11 hours after his wedding, when his camera failed to work, and gave his father a black eye. His mother Astrid then stabbed her son to death with a kitchen knife in front of the bride and 40 wedding guests in Traunreut, Bavaria. Scottish *D.Record* 21 Oct 1991.

⬤ A bus passenger in the Philippines chased a man into a restaurant and shot him dead after the man had drenched him with a pail of water while celebrating the feast of St John the Baptist. Some Filipinos honour the feast day by throwing water on people in the street. *Dundee Eve. Telegraph* 25 June 1991.

⬤ Paul Franklin Carter, 62, of Santa Ana, California, suffers from cancer, is paralysed on one side and confined to a wheelchair. When he ate the chocolate Easter bunny which had been given to his wife June, 71, she doused him with rubbing alcohol and set him on fire. She then went shopping, and only called paramedics six hours later

NOWT SO QUEER

Paul Sieveking

on her return. Mr Carter was rushed to hospital with third degree burns over 27% of his body. [Reuters] 18 April 1992.

⬤ A snake appeared under a peepul tree in Hapur near Delhi, and was perceived by Hindus as a divine sanction for plans to construct a temple at the site. A group of Muslims objected and the ensuing street battle left eight dead and several injured. According to *The Pioneer* newspaper: "The

snake itself left as soon as the clash erupted, but its devotees plunged headlong into violent battle." *Independent* 15 Feb 1992.

FANCY FOOTWORK

⬤ Back in the summer of 1990, Michael Wyatt, the Toe Sucker of Little Rock, Arkansas, was sent down for 90 days [see *FT60*:22]. Now, the authorities have nicked Edgar Jones, 29, whom they believe to be the St Louis Serial Toe Sucker. He faces two charges of sex-

PHANTOM STRIPPER

All the wallpaper was meticulously stripped from a ladies' lavatory during a rock concert at the famous Floral Hall in Southport, Merseyside. The paper was taken off in complete rolls and neatly stacked in a corner. Furious tourism chief Phil King stepped up security after a similar incident three years ago (!) "It's the work of an expert", he said. *D.Mirror* 4 Jan 1992.

ual abuse and five other related offences against seven schoolgirls.
Jones, posing as a jogger, knocked the girls to the ground, tore off their shoes and sucked their toes. Some of the girls, aged 13 to 19, were also fondled in the fiend's three-month reign of torment. *Today* 20 Mar 1992.

⬤ Jonathan Thomas was walking home through Oxford after a night out with friends on 10 April 1992. Shortly before 1pm, on a secluded footpath in the Headington Hill area, he was seized by a man in his late 20s who tied his hands behind his back and blindfolded him with sticky tape. His assailant forced him to the ground, stripped him of his shoes and socks and, showing no mercy, tickled his feet for several minutes. He then engaged Mr Thomas in a brief conversation before untying him and vanishing into the night, leaving him shaken but unhurt, his wallet and other possessions intact. *Independent* 11 April 1992.

BIRDMEN

⬤ Michael Balama, a 45-year-old farmer and father of nine from the village of Mhweli in Nigeria, had a row with one of his two wives in 1987 and spent the following five years up a locust-bean tree. He only fell out once. His wives fed him by leaving meals on low branches. In February 1992 he came down, rowed with the other wife and ran away. After a search by neighbours, he was found up an olive tree on top of a mountain a kilometre from his house, where he said he was 'fine', but couldn't come down because of spirits.

A healer, Doctor Kaya, hoped to appease the tree spirits with blood sacrifices. "There are evil spirits holding him from coming down from the tree, and until these spirits are appeased, there is no hope of his coming down", he said. ☛ P34

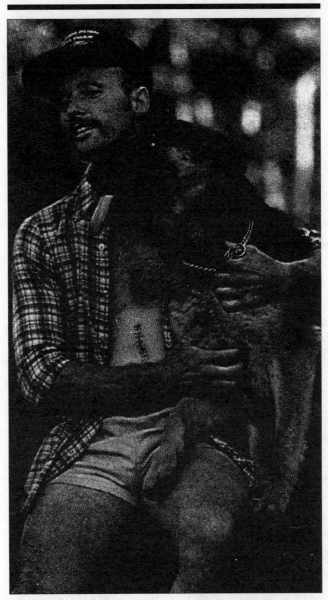

ASSORTED REVENGES

▼ Mitchell Lee Franklin, 31, was fishing with three friends when he hauled in a 5-pound catfish, which he tossed to a friend, who tossed it back. A 5-inch bony fin went through Franklin's lung. He underwent surgery on 7 March 1992 to stabilise his collapsed right lung and was taking antibiotics to reduce swelling caused by toxic slime on the catfish. The fish was filleted. [AP] 12 Mar 1992.

▼ Poacher Marino Malerba, 35, shot a stag dead as it stood on an overhanging rock in Trento, Italy. The stag fell on top of him and broke his neck. *European* 23 Aug 1991. This story was also reported in the *Sun* and *Daily Star*. Curiously, 11 months earlier, exactly the same thing happened in Trento to a poacher called Giacomo Montara, aged 40. [*Daily Star* 29 Sept; *Weekly News* 13 Oct 1990.] A good story is always worth repeating (changing the odd detail, of course).

▼ Rabbit-hunting farmer Vincent Caroggio of Chartres, France, paused for a rest and laid his gun down. He was immediately shot dead by a rabbit, which rushed from its burrow and bumped against the trigger. Scottish *Sunday Mail* 14 April 1991.

▼ Ali-Ashgar Ahani, 27, an Iranian hunter, tried to catch a snake alive near Teheran by pressing the butt of his shotgun behind its head. The snake coiled around the butt and pulled the trigger with its thrashing tail, firing one of the barrels and shooting Ahani fatally in the head. His colleague tried to grab the shotgun, but the writhing reptile triggered the other barrel, according to the *Islamic Republic News Agency*. [AP, Reuters] 24 April 1990.

TABLES TURNED ON HUNTERS

Patrick Herne

VEGAS STILL A WINNER: Joe Petrowski of St Laurent, Manitoba, with his dog Vegas, who accidentally shot him in the back when her fur got caught in the trigger of a .22 rifle. Notice the long scar on Mr Petrowski's stomach.

▼ We have notes on two hunter's wives severely injured by plummeting pheasants. One was a 50-year-old woman sitting on a shooting stick who had her spleen ruptured when the bird hit her in the back in late 1987; the other was Emmanuelle Argand, 31, the pregnant wife of Swiss businessman Luc Argand, who was sitting on a wall at the Duke of Roxburghe's 60,000 acre Floors Castle estate near Kelso in the Scottish Borders. The couple were in a party of European businessmen on a day's shooting. Mme Argand was sitting on a wall beside her husband when the bird struck her, forcing her backwards nine feet into a ditch. She was paralysed from the waist down, while the baby was aborted.

"One is frequently hit by birds", mused Douglas Sutherland, author of *The Good Shooting Guide*, who himself once had three ribs broken by a falling grouse. *D.Express, Today, Sun, D.Telegraph* 19 Nov 1991.

DOGS GET THEIR MAN

▼ Dog-Shoots-Master is the most common type of incident in this genre. German shepherd dog Vegas gave new meaning to the term 'hair trigger' when her coat got caught in the trigger of Joe Petrowski's .22 calibre rifle in St Laurent, Manitoba, on 19 June 1991. Petrowski, who was home alone at the time, was adjusting the scope on his gun, aiming at a target 36 metres away. The gun was clamped into a vice in front of a bench where he'd placed Vegas's ball before walking across the yard to check the target.

Unfortunately, Vegas went for the ball at the same time, catching the trigger and shooting her master in the back. The bullet went to the right of his spine, slicing through his stomach and liver. When he passed out moments later, Vegas ran to his aid, licking and scratching at his shirt and neck to revive him. The one-year-old dog dragged her master toward the house, until he could get on his feet and call for help.

Six weeks later, Petrowski had almost completely recovered, but Vegas couldn't seem to get over the accident. If Petrowski was home alone, she wouldn't let him lie down – she scratched and pawed at him until he got up. Victoria (BC) *Times-Colonist* 28 June + 30 July 1991; *Eve. Standard* 28 June 1991.

▼ Lars Ingvar Karlsson, 48, went hunting for elk and deer with a group near Ryda in central Sweden on the weekend of 21/22 October 1989. Putting his rifle on the ground, he went to separate two fighting dogs. His own dog stepped on the gun and shot Karlsson in the chest, killing him instantly. *Aerzte Zeitung* 24 Oct 1989.

▼ Barry Woodcock, 15, was shot in his right leg at point-blank range after his grandfather's Jack Russell terrier knocked over a shotgun, which was leaning against a haystack at Willoughby Farm, Norwell, near Newark, Notts. The boy was hospitalised with a severe leg wound. *D.Telegraph, Sun* 4 Dec 1989.

▼ A 50-year-old hunter

and his companions laid down their shotguns when they stopped to rest during a rabbit hunting trip near Lyhndal, Norway, on 2 December 1989. Terna, his Finnish hound, jumped on the guns and the hunter suffered minor injuries when he was hit by pellets. [AP] 6 Dec 1989.

▼ Belgian hunter Jean Guillaume, 66, was driving down an unpaved country road in the Ardennes Forest with a friend when he was shot dead by his spaniel, Ben. The dog jumped onto the back seat of a jeep and pulled the trigger of a loaded shotgun with his teeth. [AP] 23 June 1991. The British press (*Today, Sun, D.Mirror, D.Star* 24

June) changed the shotgun into a rifle.

▼ Gennady Danilov, 33, was found dead in snowy woods near Novgorod with his hunting rifle in his left hand. The Soviet police concluded that he had been shot in the stomach by his

dog as he tried to free it from a trap. Scratches on the rifle butt proved that the struggling animal, near the body, pulled the trigger as Danilov tried to free it. [Reuters] 6 Mar 1992.

For the last round up of hunted hunters see *FT52:22.*

NOWT SO QUEER
Continued from page 32

Brisbane (Australia) *Courier Mail* 27 Feb + 11 Mar; *D.Mirror, Sun* 6 Mar 1992.

● Bungkas, the birdman of Madura Island, Indonesia, is still up his palm tree after 22 years. We last heard of him in 1987 [see FT53:24.] He climbed the tree in 1970 after the death of his wife. By weaving leaves and branches together, he built himself a makeshift nest 45 feet above the ground. Since then, the tree has grown another six feet. His only clothing is a sarong tied around the waist. Now 58, the 5ft 4in man weighs no more than 90 pounds, but seems in good health. His family sends up food in a bucket three times a day, plus one pack of cigarettes daily. Bungkas sends down his waste and any other rubbish. The 'birdman' is famous throughout Indonesia, and there are many visitors to his tree. *Nat. Enquirer* 23 July 1991.

HOME SNUFF MOVIE
Rose Langton, 51, was quick off the mark when her husband Robert, 51, had a heart attack: she grabbed her camera and panned and zoomed as he writhed in agony on the living room floor. She recorded his groans as he lapsed into unconsciousness and it took the stricken man's 14-year-old son to call the ambulance when he got back from school.
Rose was planning to send

the videotape to a game show which offered £20,000 for the best home video. She continued to shoot as paramedics arrived and struggled to save her husband's life. She even tried to carry on filming in the hospital coronary unit. A hospital security guard said: "She told us, 'My husband's dying. I've got to get it on tape'. We literally had to drag her away."
Doctors in New York said the man would have died if help had been delayed another few minutes. Rose said later that she had thought her husband was having stomach pains. The husband was considering divorce. *Shropshire Star* 11 Dec 1992.

ROSENBAUM'S MOMENT OF TRUTH
Searcy County, Arkansas, Sheriff Kent Griggs was called to a rural home to investigate complaints that its owner, Howard Rosenbaum, had threatened relatives over the telephone. When he got there, Griggs found the house burnt to the ground and Rosenbaum standing there with two other men. All three were stark naked and had shaved all the hair from their bodies. Rosenbaum admitted setting his house on fire, but referred all other questions to a nearby chicken, which he said housed the spirit of his dead grandmother. [Russell Ash's *Midweek* column, 23 Jan 1992.]

SIMULACRA CORNER

This railway sleeper (you can tell he's asleep as his eyes are closed) was photographed at Victoria Falls by Alex Bratall. We are always glad to receive pictures of spontaneous forms and figures, or any curious images.
Send your snaps to the editorial address – with SAE – and we'll pay a fiver for any we use.

BACKGROUND & THEORIES

Crop circles, the mysterious geometric patterns appearing in fields of ripening cereals and other crops, first came to general attention in 1980. Typically, they are neatly flattened circles, with well-defined edges, in which the plants are swirled in spiral patterns; sometimes several layers are interwoven with the tautness of thatch. Significantly, the bent stems are almost never damaged and the crop continues to ripen till harvest. In the early 1980s, the sporadic appearance of circles caught the interest of a few meteorologists and chroniclers of anomalies, and formed an occasional news filler during the silly season, but each successive summer brought greater numbers of circles. To date, many hundreds of circles have been surveyed, photographed, analysed, or simply admired for their undeniable beauty. Circles-enthusiasts - cerealogists - believe that the patterns are evolving in complexity from single circles to multi-ringed geometric clusters. Since 1990, the world has marvelled at rectangular and triangular shapes, 'French curves' and formations that look like archaic picture-writing (dubbed agriglyphs).

Now, the circles have firmly entered human consciousness and theorising about their origins has become a planet-wide sport; here are a few notions...

HOAXES & ARTISTS

Numerous attempts by pranksters, young farmers, squaddies and students, crusading skeptics and newspapermen, using a variety of ingenious methods, have failed abysmally to mimic the precision and complexity of the 'true' circles. Their hasty or clumsy efforts are betrayed by crushed or broken crop stems, footprints or other evidence of their arrival and movements, and pale imitations of the complex swirling patterns and interwoven layering which are characteristic of the originals. The precedent was set in 1983, when journalists from the Daily Mirror confessed to commissioning a circle at Westbury to fool their rivals on the Daily Express. There have been many other hoaxes since then. In 1986, the perpetrator of a message "WEARENOTALONE" gave away his terrestrial origin by using 'we' instead of 'you'. In July 1990, under the massed cameras and survey equipment of 'Operation Blackbird' at Westbury, hoaxers made a crude circle and left a ouija board in the centre to the embarrassment of the watching investigators.

In 1991, hoaxers were to the fore. The Today newspaper promoted the claim by Doug Bower and Dave Chorley, two retired artists from Southampton, to have made most of the Wessex circles since 1979. Some doubts have been cast on this claim by the sheer scale of the manifestations, but it does highlight the possibility that some

of the better circles and probably most of the elaborate pictograms could be the work of conceptual artists using the landscape as their canvas. We also saw, in 1991, several disconcerting episodes in which an anti-paranormal group, calling themselves the Wessex Skeptics, constructed circles with the deliberate aim of catching out the more serious circles researchers.

THE WEATHER

One of the first people to take an interest in the circles back in 1980 was Dr Terence Meaden, founder of the Tornado and Storm Research Organization (TORRO) and the Circles Effect Research Unit (CERES). At first, he speculated about some kind of fair-weather stationary whirlwind. It became increasingly obvious that this could not account for the precision and developing patterns, such as the five-circle 'dice' or 'Celtic cross' formations.

Over the last decade, Meaden expanded his theory to include something he calls a 'plasma vortex', which begins as a spinning column ball of air highly-charged with electricity, caused by winds passing over high ground and perhaps related to the odd phenomenon of ball lightning. A bulge of electrified air, formed on the central column, plunges downwards to create the formations below.

This was the most scientific of the available theories, but it was by no means accepted by meteorological orthodoxy. However, Meaden has also drawn attention to a number of anomalies that should be considered seriously, these include: witnesses to the moment of creation; the sounds, lights and other characteristics of such

vortexes; and the possibility that similar phenomena in the ancient past may have provided the location and inspiration for the megalithic stone circles.

Despite supposing a variety of ingenious scenarios for his collapsing vortices, Meaden's theory failed to account for the bizarre patterns being reported in 1991, and after the disclosures by 'Doug and Dave' and the Wessex Skeptics, Meaden now restricts his theory to the simpler formations of circles, because, in his view, they are more likely to be genuine.

LITTLE GREEN MEN

The original investigators of the Wessex crop phenomena were the UFO buffs. At first it was thought the circles might be the landing traces of flying saucers, similar to the swirled depressions in crops and grass reported from Australia, USA and South Africa in the 1960s and nicknamed 'UFO nests'. It is to the credit of these early investigators that they quickly realised the UFO explanation was quite inadequate; nevertheless, much of the world's sloppier media coverage continues to plug the UFO association.

Some ufologists teamed up with the independent meteorologist Dr G.T. Meaden and began a careful research programme. Others

retreated from the scientific approach, finding supernatural explanations more appealing.

TECHNOLOGY

The down-draught from a helicopter was an early explanation for the circles, but the complexity of the formations has rather overtaken it; in any case, the down-draught would flatten crops in a tapering effect, not a spiral. Some daft soul suggested helicopters flying upside-down over the same spot; but they would, of course, crash.

The proximity of many of the circles sites to large Ministry of Defence establishments prompted speculation about the testing of secret weapons. A retired soldier wrote to a British newspaper to say that his squad formed crop circles in the 1960's with an electromagnetic transmitter.

There are several rumours that the telephones of crop circle researchers are being tapped, reinforcing the belief that the Government is somehow involved. The Government denies this.

ANIMALS

One of the sillier theories blamed rutting deer or demented hedgehogs running in circles, and, like the UFO theory, was only taken seriously by journalists and cartoonists. Someone calculated that it would take 40,000 hedgehogs running in unison to create a smallish circle. More complicated geometry would require master tacticians, veritable hedgehog Napoleons.

SUBTERRANEAN THEORIES

It is well known that the underground remains of ancient roads and buildings can affect the growth of the crops above them, and archaeologists frequently locate prehistoric ruins by studying aerial photographs. Although many crop circles occur in proximity to megalithic sites, there is no evidence to support the idea that the crop circles are caused by underground artifacts.

An analogy has also been drawn between crop circles and the phenomenon known to folklore as 'fairy rings'. These rings are in fact cause by successive radial growths of fungus threads (hyphae). Above ground, the mushroom or toadstool (a fruiting body) is the only visible part of the fungus itself which remains underground. The suggestion is that the spreading of these hyphae, like a slow outward ripple, somehow weakens the crop stems which then fall over in circular fashion in the next strong wind. There is no evidence from soil samples to support this.

A similar weakening of stalks has been blamed on the use of old-fashioned circular irrigation machines, which leach the soil of their nutrients; and on the effects of ozone depletion above the circle causing an increase in ultraviolet ►

◀ radiation. None of these theories can account for specific details such as the sharply-defined edges and the complex symmetry.

SUPERNATURAL FORCES

British folklore contains many beliefs and traditions relating to corn and the seasonal cycle of planting, ripening and harvesting of cereals. It is most odd, therefore, that scholars can find only a single mention of a crop-circle-like event in the entire literature of folklore. This exception is a pamphlet called <u>The Mowing-Devil</u> published in 1678, and tells of the fate of a farmer in Hertfordshire who refused to pay the reasonable rates for mowing his oats. In the night the field appeared to be on fire, and when the farmer came to his field at dawn "he found the crop was cut down ready to his hands, and as if the Devil had a mind to shew his dexterity in the art of husbandry, and scorned to mow them after the usual manner, he cut them in round circles, and plac'd every straw with that exactness that it would have taken up above an age for any man to perform what he did in that one night." The stems in today's crop circles are bent, not cut; but this could be an historical record of crop circle if you accept that in his reference to 'cutting' the narrator was simply trying to describe the astonishing edge-precision noted in many circles today.

Mention of 'fairy rings' reminds us of the old fertility cults and the belief that daemons or fairies preside over growing crops and have power over the wind, and dance in circles. The humming noises heard by witnesses during circle formation may have given rise to the old belief that humming or buzzing sounds reveal the passage of invisible fairies.

The crop circles have provided a focus for modern supernatural beliefs, uniting the mystical ideas of the New Age, Theosophical and Green movements. In this view, the circles are venerated as places where divine beings have attempted to communicate with mankind. The pictograms are interpreted as mandala-like messages warning us to change our harmful ways, sent by a wounded Mother Earth (Gaia), nature spirits, the UFO-piloting Cosmic Brothers, perhaps even mankind's collective unconscious, according to your beliefs.

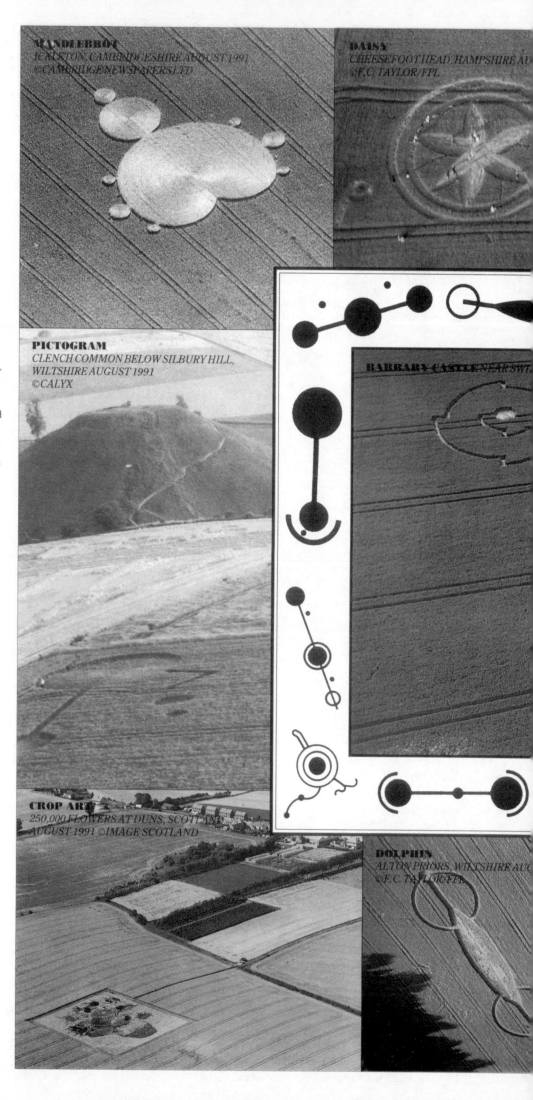

MANDLEBROT
ICKLETON, CAMBRIDGESHIRE AUGUST 1991
©CAMBRIDGE NEWSPAPERS LTD

DAISY
CHEESEFOOT HEAD, HAMPSHIRE AU
©F.C. TAYLOR/FPL

PICTOGRAM
CLENCH COMMON BELOW SILBURY HILL,
WILTSHIRE AUGUST 1991
©CALYX

BARBARY CASTLE NEAR SWI

CROP ART
250,000 FLOWERS AT DUNS, SCOTLAND
AUGUST 1991 ©IMAGE SCOTLAND

DOLPHIN
ALTON PRIORS, WILTSHIRE AU
©F.C. TAYLOR/FPL

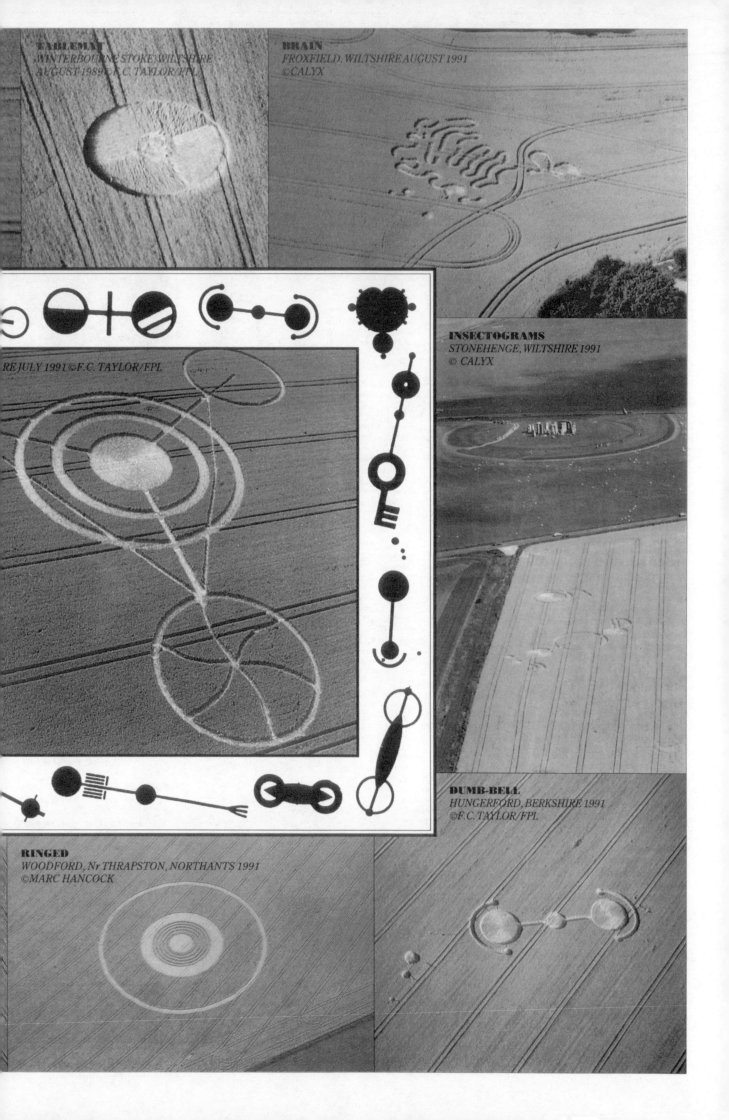

TABLEMAT
WINTERBOURNE STOKE, WILTSHIRE
AUGUST 1989 ©F. C. TAYLOR/FPL

BRAIN
FROXFIELD, WILTSHIRE AUGUST 1991
©CALYX

INSECTOGRAMS
STONEHENGE, WILTSHIRE 1991
© CALYX

RE JULY 1991 ©F.C. TAYLOR/FPL

DUMB-BELL
HUNGERFORD, BERKSHIRE 1991
©F.C. TAYLOR/FPL

RINGED
WOODFORD, Nr THRAPSTON, NORTHANTS 1991
©MARC HANCOCK

CROP CIRCLE WITNESSES

People have seen crop circles forming naturally, and their stories are important evidence for the 'plasma vortex' theory. Nearly all the witnessed formations were simple circles, confirming the view that the likelihood of a hoax increases with the complexity of the design.

The formation of the circles is often accompanied by remarkable sounds, possibly made by the electrostatic charges inside the vortex. Other effects - like eerie lights and electrical interference with vehicles - recall similar details reported in some UFO cases. Here are some examples...

The earliest eye-witness case occurred in 1934, when Kathleen Skin observed a whirlwind in a field at Eversden, near Cambridge. She heard "a crackling like fire" as the whirlwind spun out two small circles. Inside the circles the stalks were "plaited" and, curiously, "hot to the touch".

As farmer Tom Gwinnet drove past his wheatfield at Woolaston in Gloucestershire, in July 1988, his car stalled and its headlights failed. He saw myriads of small flashes of light running through the heads of his crop, and heard a "whirling, humming" sound coming from a spinning mass of the orange-yellow lights. Returning to the site the following morning, he found a clockwise circle where he had seen the lights.

Gary & Vivienne Tomlinson were walking near the hamlet of Hambledon (Surrey) in May 1990 when they were engulfed by a whirlwind. They felt a change in air pressure, and static electricity made their hair stand on end. From inside the vortex they saw numerous miniature whirlwinds laying the crop down clockwise.

WHAT TO DO...

WHEN VISITING A CIRCLE... OR IF YOU SPOT A NEW ONE

Crop circles almost always appear on private land and you are probably comitting criminal trespass for which you can be successfully prosecuted - if you visit crop circles without obtaining the landowner's permission.

Remember...

1 Do not enter private property without the permission of the landowner, or unless the farmer is charging for people to enter his land.

2 Having gained permission from the landowner to visit the circle walk along the tramlines rather than through standing crop.

3 Do not smoke in the field. Crops are easily set on fire and high winds can fan sparks into major fires.

4 Always close gates behind you. Do not take dogs onto private land.

5 Crop circles often appear during harvesting, when farmers are already very busy. Please consider the farmer's property and livelihood at all times.

A WHIRLWIND HISTORY OF CROP CIRCLES & RELATED PHENOMENA

Because of the difficulty in accurately dating events for which there is only fallible memory, some dates given span a likely period. Historical research into many of these cases continues.

YEAR	LOCATION
1678	The 'Mowing Devil' incident in Hertfordshire.
1880	Circle scoured out of cropless field in Ontario, Canada.
1914-56	Maiden Bradley, SW of Warminster.
1918	Large single in green oats at Bilsington, Kent.
1935-37	Single and a triplet at Helions Bumpstead, SE of Cambridge.
1936	Several circles in corn at Aberystwyth, Wales.
1936-40	Two singles at Whiteparish, Wiltshire.
1939	Circle at Kilmacanogue, Co Wicklow.
1940/41	Triplet at Earl Shilton, Leicestershire.
1940s	Multiple single circles at Cilycwm, Dyfed and at Elton, Cheshire.
1946	Single in barley at Ivinghoe, Bucks.
1947	Single among turnips at Pilling, Lancashire.
1950s	Circles at Heytesbury near Warminster.
1951-91	Headbourne Worthy.
1954	St Souplet, Nord, France; and in grass at Redlynch, Somerset.
1958-91	Singles and quintuplets at Whiteparish.
1960	Double rings at Evenlode, Gloucestershire.
1963	Charlton, Wiltshire (adjacent to the famous crater); also circle in grass at Epping, Essex.
1966	Single seen forming among reeds at Tully, Australia (followed by hoaxes); single at Sharnbrook, Bedfordshire (in Brussels-sprouts); single at Colloway Clump, Warminster.
1967	Ringed circle at Bowden, Alberta, Canada.
1968	Circle in broad beans at Bolnhurst, Bedfordshire.
1969	Two ringed circles at Chapeau, Canada; circle in capim grass at Ibiuna, Brazil; circle in soya beans nr Garrison, Iowa.
1970s	Single at Starr Hill, Warminster.
1971	Ring in grass near Draguignan, France.
1972	Double rings in grass at Orebro, Sweden; ringed circle at Cradle Hill, Warminster.
1973	Bordertown, Tooligie Hills, Wokurna [Australia]
1974	Triplet at High Point, North Carolina; circle in Stockton/Darlington area, North Yorkshire; 5 circles at Langenburg, Saskatchewan, Canada.
1975	Single at Headbourne Worthy; and in snow at Anatolia, Turkey.
1976	Singles at Litchfield, and Headbourne Worthy.
1977	Single at Aix-en-Provence, France; in grass at Crook, Cumbria; and at Cheesefoot, Corsley (Wilts), Woburn Green (Bucks), Twywell (Northants).
1978	Double rings at Twywell, Northamptonshire, and quintuplet at Headbourne Worthy; singles at Beacon Hill, Newbury, and Corhampton (Hants). Ring in rice paddy at Nakano, Japan.
1979	Singles at Bratton, Cheesefoot, Blackdown (Hants)
1980	The 'first' modern circles at Westbury, Wiltshire, investigated by Dr Terence Meaden (TORRO/CERES). The British UFO Research Association begin their 12 year investigation by rejecting UFOs which the media rapidly blamed. Local farmers blame "whirlwinds".
1981	Pat Delgado sees his first circles at Cheesefoot Head. Circles reported at Trans-en-Provence (France), Litchfield, Headbourne Worthy, Worthy Down, Goodworth Clatford, Mere Down (Wilts), Ross-on-Wye (Herefordshire).
1982	An oddly quiet summer with very few reported events. Ray Barnes sees circle forming at Westbury, Wiltshire. Singles reported at Cheesefoot Head, Headbourne Worthy, Litchfield (a triplet), South Wonston, Cley Hill (Warminster) and Bratton (Wilts).
1983	The first media hoax at Westbury and the arrival of quintuplets.
1984	Again a quiet year. Singles reported from Long Hill (Oxon), Marlborough, Bratton, Corhampton, Cheriton.
1985	A year of quintuplet patterns appearing on Friday nights. Busty Taylor begins his investigations.
1986	Colin Andrews begins investigating the phenomenon. BUFORA publishes Mystery of the Circles in an attempt to explain the mystery. Stages first ever circles debate in London bringing together Andrews, Delgado, Meaden, Fuller and Randles on the same stage for the first - and last! - time. Famous hoax at Cheesefoot Head.
1987	BUFORA carries out the first survey of crop circles.
1988	The formations become more complex but still essentially circular.
1989	Circular Evidence is published, becoming an instant best seller. Dr Meaden publishes The Circles Effect and Its Mysteries. The patterns become more complex. 'Operation Whitecrow' fails to film a crop circle happening. BBC produce its first documentary. BUFORA publish Controversy of the Circles to update Mystery, claiming that affected crops are "contaminated" by a "molecular change" cause concern in the farming community.
1990	The world's media descends on Hampshire and Wiltshire. 'Operation Blackbird' farce at Westbury. Crop Circles A Mystery Solved published. CCCS formed. First pictograms appear. First scientific conference at Oxford brings scientists from three continents to present papers.
1991	Dr Meaden and Busty Taylor caught out by Wessex Skeptics' hoax at Clench Common. Doug Bower and Dave Chorley claim of mass hoaxing. CCCS responds with claims of government disinformation. Mass crop circle hoaxing. Fantastic formations appear. Sceptics dismiss entire subject as a manmade hoax. American researchers claim to have discovered significant evidence of radiation emissions. Meaden claims link with ancient stone circles.
1992	What next ???

---

6 Keep a watch out for Hoaxers. Report any suspicious behaviour to the police.

7 If you see a crop circle that you think is new and unvisited please contact CERES - the Circles Effect Research Unit - on 02216-2482 or on 0794-522862.

8 Make any measurements or observational notes you can; and if you have a camera of any kind, use it.

ORGANISATIONS & MAGAZINES

that deal directly or indirectly with crop circles, covering a range of approaches. Contact them for recommended reading and other details.

BUFORA
The British UFO Research Association, Suite 1, The Leys, 2c Leyton Road, Harpendon, Hertfordshire AL5 2TL. UFOCALL: 0898-121886.

The Cerealogist
20 Paul Street, Frome, Somerset BA11 1DX. Editor: John Michell.

CCCS
The Centre for Crop Circle Studies, 20 Paul Street, Frome, Somerset BA11 1DX.

CERES
The Circles Effect Research Unit, 54 Frome Road, Bradford-on-Avon, Wiltshire BA15 1LD.

The Circular
at CCCS address above. Edited: George Wingfield.

CPRG
The Circles Phenomenon Research Group. 96 Salisbury Road Andover Hants SP10.

The Crop Watcher
3 Selborne Court, Tavistock Close, Romsey, Hampshire SO51 7TY. Editor: Paul Fuller.

Fortean Times
Box 2409, London NW5 4NP. Editors: Bob Rickard & Paul Sieveking.

The Journal of Meteorology
at CERES address above. Editor: Dr G.T. Meaden.

Northern UFO News
37 Heathbank Road, Cheadle Heath, Stockport, Cheshire SK3 0UP. Editor: Jenny Randles.

CREDITS
Many thanks to Dr Meaden and especially to Paul Fuller who provided considerable research at short notice.

CROP CIRCLES '92
The Fortean Times Guide to Cornography

FAR OUT EAST

K. Tendzin Dorje

There seems to be a strange affinity between Tibetans and native Americans. For instance, 1,200 years ago, Padmasambhava left this prediction in Tibet: "When the iron bird flies and horses run on wheels, then the Dharma [ie., Buddhism] will come to the land of the red man."

During 1991, the year of Tibet, the man westerners call the Dalai Lama (he is more properly the Gyalwa Rinpoche) travelled the world championing the cause of Tibetan independence. One of his less publicised visits was to Santa Fe Indian School, New Mexico. About 500 native Americans crowded into the school to present gifts and receive blessings.

Thomas Pela is a Hopi priest from the village of Shungopavi, northern Arizona. He is the leader of the ancient Wuchim Society, which initiates Hopi youths into manhood. He stood on line with the others, in his hands a box

which he was hoping to get rid of. According to a story in the *Arizona Republic* (7 April 1991), the simple wooden crate had not been opened in the ten years since it was entrusted to Earl Pela, Thomas's father, by a mysterious Japanese priest, at 1:15 in the afternoon of 27 November 1980.

Earl was told that it should be handed over to the Dalai Lama, if the opportunity arose. Thomas knew the box contained someone's ashes, someone of such importance that monks "dressed like the Dalai Lama" came from India every two years to check on it and "say prayers" over it. When asked about the contents of the crate, all the monks would say was that "they are not just for the Hopi but for the whole universe." Of

course, rumours soon multiplied among the Hopi community. Many supposed that the box held the ashes of the Buddha himself.

"I don't know if this box contains the ashes of the Buddha", said Pela. "I hope it does not." Human remains are taboo to the Hopi and Thomas was eager to complete his mission. He had adorned the wooden crate with an ear of multi-coloured corn, a Hopi gesture of welcome. As the line shuffled past His Holiness the Dalai Lama, Thomas was only able to mutter a few words. H.H. the D.L. reached out and took the corn and a dazed Thomas was ushered away, carrying his box back into the crowd.

For the first time, Thomas was persuaded to open the box. But before we examine its contents, a little historical perspective:

At the age of 80, having

outlived his two most prominent disciples, the perfectly awakened one passed into the great extinction which liberates from suffering. He'd been travelling near Kushinagara and had eaten a dish of *sukaramaddava* provided by Chunda, a smith. Opinions differ as to the exact nature of this delicacy. Some say it was pork, or maybe bamboo shoots, or perhaps a trufflelike fungus. Whatever, if you see it on the menu of an Indian restaurant, maybe you could ask the waiter. So, in the year 483 BCE, the Buddha passed away. Nobody blamed Chunda, but, curiously, some blamed his monks: not one of them thought to ask him to stay alive.

The cremation was taken care of by Anuruddha, the Buddha's cousin. At the request of many devoted followers, the remains were divided into eight and taken away for veneration. Even the gods are said to have taken a tooth (but as all Buddhas have 40 teeth, no-one missed out). The messenger from Pipphalivana arrived too late and had to be content with the ashes of the fire.

Currently, we know the whereabouts of only two of the portions. One is in Thailand, property of the king, and the other is in Patna, India, property of the state of Bihar.

As for the other portions, we may assume that some have been destroyed or discarded. For instance, during the period of Hindu ascendancy, a Maharaja ordered the demolition of the original brick monument at Bodhgaya, site of the Buddha's enlightenment. When an urn containing human bones and ashes was found, an orthodox Brahmin funeral was conducted and the remains were scattered in the Ganges. Even so, it is just barely possible that the other urns could be around

Thomas Pela holds the box given to his father. The Hopi holy man hopes that it doesn't contain the ashes of Buddha.

... somewhere. After all, the Patna remains were not discovered until 1958.

Opening the box, Thomas Pela found an empty brocade pouch, a bronze Buddha-statue and a pouch of 'sacred herbs'. There was also a brass container with a screw-top lid, believed to hold 'the ashes' and a four-page letter written in 'Japanese' and its translation into English. The letter explained that war would ravage parts of Asia in 1991 and that these sacred relics were being

moved to the Hopi reservation for safety. It was signed S. Kendo.

But was Mr Kendo really Japanese? Why would a Japanese monk leave instructions concerning the Dalai Lama? While he may be a Nobel prize-winner and international celebrity, His Holiness holds no special status among the international community of Buddhists. Perhaps Earl Pela was just a little shaky in his geography. Is Kendo actually a Japanese name? It

could easily be a Tibetan abbreviation. And these monks from India ... there are several Tibetan monasteries in India and as they were dressed like the Dalai Lama we must presume that they were Tibetan.

Has anyone shown the letter to somebody who actually reads Japanese? I doubt it. I would confidently wager a small amount of someone else's money that the letter is in Tibetan.

So the mysteries clear a little to reveal yet more

mysteries. The prediction of an Asian war in 1991 seems to predict the Gulf War and also echoes the Tibetan prophecies of the great war between Shambhala and the Muslim world. And if the ashes aren't the Buddha's, whose are they? And why wasn't the Dalai lama expecting them?

Meanwhile, back in Shungopavi village, the elders are considering sending Thomas to the Dalai Lama in India to get rid of the box once and for all.

FT

As I said in my last round-up of resurrections, *Cheating the Grim Reaper* [**FT49**:55], "...death itself is not always final. Recognising it can be a tricky business; various states of coma, epilepsy, hypothermia, or trance can mimic death pretty accurately." I remember, years ago when I was a paste-up artist on the British Library updated catalogue, being amused by the mention of the Association for the Prevention of Premature Burial; but the statistics show that the fear of such a fate is not entirely irrational or just the morbid imagination of Edgar Allen Poe!

SUSPENDED ANIMATION
The power of suspended animation has long been claimed by yogis. As I wrote last time, Haridas supposedly survived 40 days' burial in 1837. In November 1977, Swami Satya Moorthi, who claimed to be 102, had sensors attached to various parts of his body before assuming the classic contemplative position. He was then lowered into an eight-foot by eight-foot box, six feet under the Delhi suburb known as Friends Colony. The hole was bricked up, and technicians under the direction of Dr Y.G. Mathur

RESURRECTIONS
Paul Sieveking

settled down in a recording van to monitor the Swami.

After 15 minutes, the yogi's pulse began to plummet, and within two hours it was down from the normal 128 beats per minute to a mere 68. His temperature fell to 80.6 degrees Fahrenheit. On the second day, his pulse began to increase until the 40th hour when his heart was racing away at 178 beats a minute. Then, suddenly, the heartbeats stopped, and the cardiograms displayed a steady line. The Swami showed no sign of life for the next seven days. There was no heartbeat and, since no air could get into the box, no respiration.

Then the police arrived to arrest the medics, dig up the yogi, and prefer charges of murder, suicide or GBH. They were persuaded to leave and the experiment continued. After 192 hours without heartbeat or respiration, the yogi was dug up and climbed to the surface in good condition.

Mathur said it was "man's answer to hibernation: it could prove very effective in forcing the body to rest. It is man's way of extending his life here on earth. The Swami has done

it 278 times already for as long as 48 days. No wonder he is so old." *Manchester Guardian*, via *San Francisco Chronicle* 17 Nov 1977.

■ Kasmani, a 40-year-old man from the village of Tosari in central Java, insisted on being buried to receive divine revelations. Police warned against it, but he said: "Only God can tell us how humans die!" He was buried without food or oxygen. Seven days later, watched by a large crowd, he stepped calmly out of the grave and went home. Relatives said he was in good condition. *Arzte Zeitung* 11 Sept 1989.

LIGHTNING RESURRECTION
On 17 August 1901, storm clouds gathered over Hanston, Kansas, as a horse-drawn hearse led a solemn procession to the cemetery. Inside the hearse, in a metallic coffin, lay the body of a five-year-old daughter of Samuel McPreaz, a local farmer.

As the sky darkened, mourners noticed "a peculiar, soft mellow light" in the sky. There was a clap of thunder and the hearse was struck by lightning. The

bolt knocked down both horses, stunned the driver and burst open the coffin. Mourners found the 'dead' girl sitting up, crying for her mother.

"Her parents believe the bolt was sent as a miracle and the people of the vicinity speak of it in whispers", reported the Cincinnati *Enquirer*. "Physicians declare the little girl was in a cataleptic condition and the shock revived her, but many residents believe she was dead and came back to life." Belief in the miraculous was bolstered by the fact that nobody was killed or even seriously injured by the lifesaving bolt of lightning.

RUDE AWAKENING
It was no great shock to her family when Kalenben Balabhai died on 2 January 1989 at the age of 100, in Malanka village near Rajkot in Gujarat, India. They took her to the cremation ground and placed her on the funeral pyre. As the relatives prepared to light the pyre, the 'dead' woman sat up and demanded to be taken home. Her flat had been let to Amuan and Selim Kahaan by her son Luxan. When she returned, Mrs Balabhai flew into a rage and threw some of the Kahaans' furniture out of the windows before calling the police. [*Press Trust of India*] 4 Jan; *Times of India* 5 Jan 1989.

THE MYSTERY OF THE SWEDISH MORGUE

A 40-year-old woman was brought to Danderyd Hospital north of Stockholm at the beginning of January 1989 after a heart attack, and was declared dead the same evening. She was shrouded in a sheet and wheeled into the mortuary. The door was locked. About 24 hours later, a nurse walking by saw that blood had been pouring under the mortuary door into the passage-way. She was convinced that the woman had regained consciousness, sat up on the stretcher and fell, hitting her head on the floor which had killed her for good. A dead person does not bleed.

The nurse reported the incident to the chief doctor, Sven Dahlgren. He believed that the woman was already dead when she fell from the stretcher, according to Gunilla von Hall who interviewed him for *Expressen* (2 Feb 1989). Though her head was gashed, the blood had come from the stomach and was mixed with stomach fluids. The corpse had fallen off the narrow stretcher, according to the doctor, because the woman was probably placed on her stomach. Furthermore, the mortuary was very cramped (what this has to do with anything we are not told). The doctor did not report the incident to the relatives or the 'medical committee of responsibility' for an impartial investigation. "What happened is rather gruesome", said the doctor. "But apart from the ethical aspect it's really a mere trifle".

Bengt Robertsson, chief of the clinic at St Gren's hospital with 30 years' experience of pathology, told *Expressen*: "I have never heard of a corpse falling off a stretcher. I don't understand how it could happen."

DON'T BURY ME YET

Allison Burchell, 57, suffers from cataplexy, a bizarre disease which leaves her apparently dead when her pulse becomes almost impossible to detect. Her condition was diagnosed in 1951 when she was 16, and she was monitored in hospital for a year. Since then, she has been declared dead at least six times in hospitals. Once, she woke up freezing on a stone slab in a hospital morgue.

"An attendant came in", she recalled. "I called out 'Please may I go back to my room?' He took one look at me, screamed and bolted." Two nurses rescued her. Her attacks can be brought on by any sudden fright, shock or even laughter. By February 1989, she was taking a 'life drug' and had not had an attack for nearly six months. As a young woman, she might have two or three attacks a week which could last up to eight hours. She had moved from Surrey to Melbourne, Australia, in 1971, where she worked as a computer operator. After she described her condition to a newspaper, her employers gave her the sack. *Sunday Mirror* 22 Jan; *Computer Talk* Feb 1989.

ARABIAN GRAND GUIGNOL

Muattak Zafer Al-Shaani, 49, from Aseer in southern Saudi Arabia, was fixing a windmill when one of the vanes knocked him unconscious. When his family failed to revive him, they thought he was dead and buried him. About 27 hours later, he awoke to the sound of hooves from grazing sheep walking above his grave. Shepherds heard his screams and dug him up. He walked home in his burial shroud. The newspaper *al-Riyadh* quotes him as saying that when his mother and sister saw him, "they went mad and dropped dead." The story could not be officially corroborated. [Reuters] 17 Aug 1989. The French paper *Quotidien* in Réunion added that he went mad as well and was sent to an asylum. The whole family must have been teetering on the edge of sanity.

ON THE THIRD DAY, HE ROSE AGAIN

A Romanian woman fainted when she opened her front door in Bucharest to see her husband, Neagu, 71, back from the grave, according to the Romanian weekly, *Tinerama*. Neagu had collapsed coughing after swallowing a fishbone, and had apparently stopped breathing. The family doctor, who knew Neagu had a bad heart, confirmed that he had died of a heart attack. Three days after he was buried, gravediggers at the cemetery heard him knocking and found him lying in the coffin among wilted flowers. On his return home, he found his wife and children would have nothing to do with him. His wife, fearing he was a ghost, barred him from spending nights at home. His two sons told him to stay well away from his grandsons. It took Neagu three weeks to convince the police, town hall officials, doctors and priests to erase his death from their registers. [Reuters] 20 July 1991.

HIS BEST TRICK

George Barr, 82, complained of severe chest pains on 30 March 1990, before a massive heart attack. When he arrived at the Valley Hospital, Ridgewood, New Jersey, he had no pulse. He failed to respond to half an hour of emergency treatment with drugs, cardiopulmonary resuscitation, electric shock therapy and a respirator.

Thirteen minutes after being pronounced dead, Barr began breathing. Dr Sheldon H. Gottlieb, a cardiologist and professor of medicine at Johns Hopkins University in Baltimore, explained that a primitive reflex sometimes allows the brain to use oxygen saved by virtually shutting down other body systems.

Mr Barr was comatose until the next day, when he awoke with a craving for chow mein. He was released from hospital on 19 April 1990, and finally died in his sleep of an apparent heart attack on 20 February 1992. He was a science teacher in New York City schools and wrote over 40 books, as well as being New York's first city-wide science coordinator. He was also a longtime amateur magician. *The Record* (NJ) 3 April 1990 + 21 Feb 1992; [AP] 29 April 1990.

INTERRUPTED FUNERALS

■ An Omani woman from Liwa province, northwest of Muscat, who had apparently died after a long coma, was being prepared for burial. As she was splashed with water by her son as part of traditional Muslim rites, she sat up and shouted "I'm still alive!" according to the Omani news agency. [Reuters] 19 Feb 1990.

■ During a burial service in Longano, northern Italy, the 'deceased', Ernest Quirino, 60, opened his eyes, looked round in horror, leapt out of the coffin

and ran. He collapsed after 100 yards, but a doctor said later he was well. *D.Express, Sun* 6 April 1989.

The same scenario played out in Guastalla, central Italy, in September 1990. Mourners praying at the open coffin of Rubens Incerti, 78, screamed in terror as he sat up, clambered out and fled. He was found having a stiff drink at a table laid for his own wake. Or so the *Daily Star* (17 Sept 1990) would have us believe. Sounds a bit like a recycling job.

■ Julie Carson, 42, dropped dead in a New York funeral parlour when her mother Julia "came back to life". Julia, 65, thought to have died from heart disease, sat up in her coffin and asked what was going on. *D.Mirror, D.Star* 30 Mar 1992.

■ When a hearse carrying Theodore Zaete's body crashed into a tree at Toluca, Mexico, mourners were surprised to hear a voice from the coffin shout "I'm not dead. Please don't bury me!" *The People* 19 Aug 1990. ['Saved by the crash' is a recurrent motif. See, for instance, the tale of Gerry Allison in *FT49:58*.]

RECENT RESURRECTIONS

■ Nine-year-old Rachel Nation was pulled from the Ohio River after more than half an hour under water on 2 August 1990. She had no heartbeat, but was revived by paramedics. The following December, three-year-old Brittany Eichelberger

wandered out into the snow dressed only in a nightgown and froze to the point of clinical death, her body temperature 13 degrees Celsius below normal. She was revived by doctors and was in critical but stable condition in a Pittsburgh hospital, suffering from frostbitten fingers and toes. [AP] 4 Aug, 28 Dec 1990. [For other hypothermia revivals, see *FT45:28*.]

■ Curt Coleman Clark, 22, was pronounced brain dead after a car crash in North Carolina. After his family agreed to donate his organs, he was put on a respirator and driven 150 miles from Hickory to Winston-Salem. Doctors were about to remove his organs when they noticed his foot move. He was then rushed to intensive care and upgraded from 'brain-dead' to 'critical'. [AP] 29 Sept 1990.

■ Ernest Wilmhurst, 83, certainly appeared dead. Doctor Mohammad Hasan found the old man ice cold, stiff with rigor mortis and with no pulse. Then he opened his eyes and groaned. Dr Hasan was struck off by the General Medical Council. *Daily Express* 5 July 1991. This seems rather harsh in view of the frequency with which death is prematurely diagnosed. Besides the cases summarised here, I have on file 26 others from the newspapers since my last round-up in 1987.

■ Steve Castledene, 39, from Newcastle, was knocked off his motorbike in Bangkok, Thailand, where he was teaching English. His body was picked up by a pirate ambulance crew who eavesdrop on emergency radios, arrive first at crash sites and make fast money charging accident victims for their services. Steve was unconscious and covered in mud and blood from head wounds, but the untrained ambulancemen thought he was dead and dumped him at the city morgue. He woke up an hour later, crammed between corpses. *The People* 3 Nov 1991.

■ An 18-year-old Romanian girl, declared clinically dead, regained consciousness while being raped on a slab by a Bucharest mortuary attendant. Police arrested the shocked rapist, but the parents refused to press charges because their daughter "owed her life to him". [AFP] 29 Jan 1992.

■ Emma Brady, 75, was declared dead after a cardiac arrest and wrapped in a plastic sheet at Palms of Pasadena Hospital, St Petersburg, Florida. Her children arrived an hour later and found her gasping for air. A doctor said that "every known indication" suggested that Mrs Brady was clinically dead. She was listed as 'critical, but stable' five days after the incident. [AP] 30 Jan 1992. **FT**

THE ULTIMATE LEGAL HIGH

Ever wished for a Legal Smoke that gave a Euphoric High. A nicotine-free, non-addictive antidote to the Blues? Whole Earth Herbs Laboratory have researched and developed an exclusive range of Cigarettes and smoking mixtures.

Cloud Swept, our first and Mildest High is soothing to the Mind and Nerves. The combination of Stimulant and Sedative herb is similar to home-grown but costs only £6.85 per Oz.

A rare psycho-active extract from Fiji gives Rococan a long lasting high, instant buzz and creates a smooth yellow smoke. Improves art, music and meditation without loss of identity. Rococan Cigarettes cost £11.45 for 50 or £8.95 per Oz Pouch.

The Ultimate legal high is Yuba Gold. Our latest combination of Stimulant, Sedative, Narcotic, Tranquilliser and Euphoriant herbs are flavoured with mint. The result when smoked in the finest Marijuana-like high ever (especially in a waterpipe). The high is so close to the original smoke. Why be illegal?

At last the six rare herbs used in Yuba Gold are available as Eclipse cigarettes. In exotic yellow with purple marbled filters, they look as potent as they smoke. We are confident you will be delighted with the high or your money refunded. Introductory offer £19.90 per 100. Yuba Gold is £10.45 per Oz.

READ WHAT THE OTHERS SAY:
a selection of unsolicited testimonials which are regularly received and held on file.

"Dear All at W.E.H.L., I tried Rococan and experienced very warm, smooth feelings. Thank you very much – as for Yuba? – you bet. A truly choice blend."

"Dear Sirs, I doubt you no more! How can this be legal ... it smoked like ... wow, the real McCoy. Genuine 100% Wacky Baccy!"

"A few days ago I received your sample of 'Yuba Gold' and I must say I was impressed. The effects are quite authentic and the taste and aroma are superb. I must compliment u on an excellent herbal mix."

"Many thanks for sending me your Rococan cigarettes, which have brought something like serenity into a lie not heretofore renowned for it."

"The Yuba Gold is very good and fulfils the promise of your literature."

"Dear Sir, I did have my doubts about the 'effect" of your 'Rococan', thinking any feelings would be merely psychosomatic. How wrong I was!"

"Me and my companion found that we achieved a relaxed, mellow high. We found that Cloudswept is a different high from illegal herbs, and just as enjoyable!"

"Dear W.E.H.L., Having just had a few joints of your Yuba gold, we feel compelled to congratulate you on this remarkable smoke."

"Congratulations on what I and a few friends consider a major breakthrough."

"Unbelievable! The best tasting legal cigarettes by far. I have ordered another 2 boxes and could you please send another order for future orders."

Prices include VAT and P&P ● Make Cheques/POs payable to W.E.H.L. ● (allow 28 days delivery)

WHOLE EARTH HERBS LABORATORY (FT),
103 HIGH STREET, SAWSTON,
CAMBRIDGE, CB2 4HJ.
(Sorry, no callers, strictly mail order) Enquiries 0223 833343

SCALY HORRORS

Amphibious aliens, frogmen and UFOs

by **ULRICH MAGIN**
leading German
Fortean, UFO
researcher and editor
of **Bilk**, a cryptozoology newsletter.

WATER SPIRITS

After a heroic struggle, the Baltic states have finally achieved their political and cultural independence from the defunct Soviet bloc. Westerners have tended to see the old Soviet Union as an amorphous mass of Slavs; we can redress this ignorance by taking an interest in the lore of their regional and national cultures.

In keeping with the traditions of most European peoples, the water spirits of the Balts, which date back to the earliest times, include beautiful maidens with fish-like tails. They could not vocalise human speech, and when encountered would try to hide their fishy parts and flowing long hair. In Latvia, the *Juras mãte*, the sea-mother, was a ubiquitous water goddess. The Lithuanians had a sea-goddess called *Bangpûtys*, a river-goddess called *Upinis*, and a lake goddess called *Ezerinis*. White-skinned pigs were sacrificed to *Upinis* to keep the water fresh and clean.

The ancient Prussians – A Slavic people, not the inhabitants of the later German state – revered *Autrimpas*, a sea spirit who looked after fishermen and mariners. [1]

Similar beings are known in Norse legends as *Selkie* (Orkneys), *Nogle* (Shetlands), *Nykur* (Iceland), and *Nakk* or *Nakki* in the Ugro-Finnish culture. This Germanic word gave rise to the generic word for mermaids in German *Nixe*. These northern legends of water-gods and goddesses are based, in my opinion, mainly upon the importance of seals to these peoples; they have a parallel in the Amazon, where the mermaids – *chichas preciosas* – are based on dolphins. Their male counterparts, the mermen, are said to be dolphins transformed into beautiful young men who come to dance and seduce

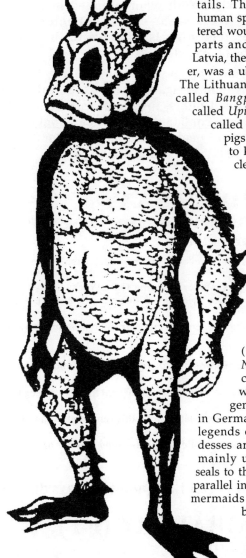

The monster of Thetis Lake, British Columbia, seen on at least three occasions during August 1972.

Indian women. Their proof is that when they become pregnant, the fœtus resembles a fish or a dolphin. [2]

These water spirits have survived in the popular imagination into the modern era, and traces of them can be found, unexpectedly, in UFO-related stories of close encounters. For example, in the autumn of 1938 or 1939, two Estonians saw a "frog-man" at Juminda on the Baltic coast. The three-foot tall creature had a mouth and eyes that were slit-like, a browny-green skin and a general resemblance to a frog. It appeared to have difficulty walking on dry land, but when pursued it fled from sight very quickly. Although Jacques Vallée lists this elemental in his catalogue of UFO encounters [3], he does not mention any associated lights. Can we establish a link, then, between the water spirits of old and today's UFOs?

I recently found a tale from Laibach – once in southern Austria, but now, under its Slav name Ljubljana, capital of the independent republic of Slovenia – in which the water-man plays the role of abductor, a role assumed today by ETs. At a dance-festival held in Laibach in July 1547, the girls noticed a beautiful young man with soft, cold skin. These characteristics are a typical disguise for water-spirits in folktales, and he soon displayed his true nature; before long he made off with one of the girls and dragged her into the river.

Grimm tells another story, from 1630, which hints at the fate of those abducted by the water-man. At Breulieb, near Saalbach in Austria, a priest taking the death-bed confession of a midwife, was told that her mother, also a midwife, had been summoned one dark night. The stranger took the woman's mother, blindfolded, to a lake; there, he beat the surface with a stick and the waters opened to reveal a stairway. They descended to a room where a woman was in labour. She had, she said, been abducted by the water-man years before. The midwife delivered the baby, but the elemental creature ate it three days later. [4]

These stories – fairly typical of a widespread body of tales – show clearly that today's ETs are replicating or continuing the sinister seductions and abductions of their elemental forerunners. For example, one of the most prominent abductees, Betty Andreasson Luca, tells that she was taken – like the midwife of Breulied – to comfort another abducted woman; only Betty Luca's ETs stole the woman's fœtus for their genetic experiments. [5]

Left: *The Creature From The Black Lagoon* from Jack Arnold's classic SF film of 1954. Arnold, who died as this issue was going to press, was born on 14 Oct 1916 in Connecticut,. After an early acting career he became a documentary director, before making the chillers for which he is best known. These include *Tarantula* (1955), *It Came From Outer Space* (1953), adapted from Ray Bradbury's *The Meteor,* and *The Incredible Shrinking Man* (1957). Arnold's trademark was brooding menace, as Spielberg noted of *Creature*: "It plays upon a basic fear people have about what might be lurking beneath the surface of any body of water."

ALIEN GILL-MEN AND THE BLACK LAGOON

For his innovative 1954 science fiction film *The Creature from the Black Lagoon*, director Jack Arnold created a humanoid lizard or fish. This monstrous gill-man, with its shell-like skin, bone plates and webbed fingers, preceded by many years seemingly genuine reports of similar creatures.

In an instructive article in *FT40*, Loren Coleman reprints a sketch of a monster reported from British Columbia, where several witnesses told of seeing it in Lake Thetis on three occasions in August 1972. [6] It is remarkably like Arnold's gill-man [see illustration]. We recognise here the phenomenon in which modern incidents echo not only the concepts of traditional folklore but also of fiction.

Arnold's gill-man and the Thetis Lake humanoid resurface a few years later as the crew of an extraterrestrial vehicle in Italy. On the night of 6-7 December 1978 – during one of the country's biggest UFO flaps – a young man, Fortunato Zanfretta, was abducted by scaly aliens near Marzano in Liguria. An artist's impression [reproduced overleaf] should suffice to show that the beings reported by Zanfretta are our aquatic humanoid friends. [7]

It is sometimes said that UFO abduction stories *must* be true because the aliens described in report after report are so similar. Unfortunately, this is the argument of those who believe the aliens to be malevolent, big-headed, grey and gnome-like. In fact there is a variety in the morphology of reported aliens, which makes nonsense of any argument based on body type. In Britain, for example, there were bearded abductors with black dogs; in South America, hairy aggressive dwarfs do the job. Uniformity is only possible if you choose a uniform sample in the first place. I hesitate to believe that a gill-man from Zeta Reticuli, like Bud Hopkins' sinister 'Greys', will delight in raping Earth-women with needles. The Zanfretta case, with its echoes of ancient water spirits and popular SF, indicates the need for a more folklore-oriented approach to these mysteries.

Contrary to the impression given by the 'grey alien' school of abduction ufology, the gill-man type is not just an exception. From my own survey of the literature, I judge that ETs with the characteristics of frogs, fishes or lizards are reported just as often as the more 'acceptable' form of the grey humanoid.

Frogman eats human, an ad from *Fate* Dec 1991

NOTES

1. Marija Gimbutas, *Die Balten* (Herbig; Munich, 1983), p221.
2. Jacques and Jean-Michel Cousteau, 'Abenteuer Amazonas', *Hessische Fernsehen* 26 July 1985. Michel Meurger has traced 16th century records of belief in encounters with the Amerzonian merfolk – see his *Lake Monster Traditions* (Fortean Tomes, London, 1988) p199ff.
3. Jacques Vallée, *Passport to Magonia* (Regnery; Chicago, 1969), p189.
4. Grimm, *Deutsche Sagen* (Winkler; Munich, 1956), pp711 & 74. For a tale of a merman abducting six women in Swaziland see FT60: 8.
5. Whatever the reason, there are a great number of folk stories in which humans have been taken by chthonic fairies to act as their midwives – see, for example, Katherine Briggs, *A Dictionary of Fairies* (Allen Lane; London, 1976), 'Midwife'. Betty Luca's story spans a number of books by Raymond E. Fowler, the latest being *The Watchers: The Secret Design behind UFO Abductions* (Bantam, NY, 1990). I used the German edition: *Die Wächter,* (Bastei Lübbe, Bergisch Gladbach, 1991, p56 & p92).
6 - Loren Coleman, 'Creatures from the Black Lagoon', *Fortean Times* 40:43-47 (1983).
7 - Antonio Ribera, *Secuestrados por extraterrestres* (Planeta; Barcelona, 1981), pp155-67.

8. M. Spingler, 'Fifty little green Frog-men', *Flying Saucer Review* 22: 6. In the Menuge case, only the `frogs' were seen; no UFO. However, because it was nighttime, and the creatures were clearly seen by the witness, Gordon Creighton, in a commentary to Spingler's account, supposes there must have been a source of light nearby (which the witness did not notice!) Somehow the light becomes a UFO, ergo the frogmen must have been ufonauts!

9. Ulrich Magin, *Kontakte mit `Außerirdischen im deutschen Sprachraum* (GEP; Lüdenscheid, 1991), p10.

10. Hans Van Kampen, *CENAP Report* (July-August 1991).

11. Robert Temple, *The Sirius Mystery* (Sidgwick & Jackson, London, 1978).

One night in May 1976, Dominique Menuge was driving through north-eastern France when he saw "fifty little green frog-men" crossing the road in front of his car [see illustration]. Because a bright source of light was believed to be nearby, ufologists – who are unable to resist the association between 'strange experience' and 'bright light' – annexed this incident to their interminable catalogues [8], just as Vallée did with the Estonian merman.

A witness, close to Lake Constance in Germany, observed a large meteorite on 24 February 1977, and believed it was a UFO. He was shocked, shortly after, to encounter several frog-like creatures, between 1.1 and 1.3 metres tall. They were significantly different from the Juminda creature: they had long ape-like arms, large round heads, and, most curious of all, a frill around their necks. The witness's drawing [see illustration] shows something very like Jim Henson's muppet Kermit. [9] Once again the association with UFOs is assumed, compounded by the witness's misidentification of the meteoric light.

A spherical UFO hovered a field of grain at Nördling, Germany, in July 1984. An iris-like opening appeared in the side of the object, permitting one of the female witnesses to see a couple of figures inside. According to the investigator's report, the "two strange creatures looked like fish. They walked erect, but their motion was jerky. Their heads and hands moved abruptly and they exchanged a kind of `nose kiss' like the Eskimos do." [10]

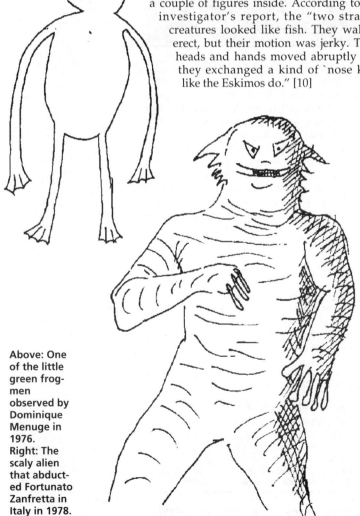

**Above: One of the little green frog-men observed by Dominique Menuge in 1976.
Right: The scaly alien that abducted Fortunato Zanfretta in Italy in 1978.**

THE LIZARDS ARE COMING

Were Vallée and Gordon Creighton right to include stories of frog-men in their collections of UFO reports? Are some space-beings amphibians, as Robert Temple [11] and other 'ancient astronaut' advocates have suggested? We find the same pattern recurring when we study false UFO reports; hoaxes and psychologically conditioned observations.

In 1990, a rather clumsy hoax managed to fool some of the more gullible UFO researchers. According to Tony Dodd, a 'flying saucer' crashed into the Kalahari desert in southern Africa on 7 May 1989. The story asserts that the bodily remains of the dead alien pilots were traded for a brace of nuclear bombs from the US government. The hoax was so crudely executed that the full name of NASA was misspelled, and an illustration from the famous Socorro, New Mexico, 'saucer landing' case of 1964 was used to depict the hoax UFO. More interesting to our inquiry is the detail that the fictitious pilots were fish-like humanoids with webbed fingers. [12]

An Austrian called Hartwig Rüdiger Bayerl fled to Australia believing that atomic disaster would destroy the rest of the world, the ruins of which would be ruled by lizard-like aliens aided by the Freemasons. In Adelaide, in 1984, Bayerl built and kitted-out a survival shelter. In 1989 he claimed to be Jesus Christ reborn. Moving to Cairns later that year, he met fellow-Austrian Johann Manfred Weissensteiner and the woman he later married. All three worked on converting Bayerl's yacht, and when it was deemed WW3-proof, they sailed into the Pacific. In September 1990, Weissensteiner was found on the vessel alone, and has since been charged with the murder of

The cover of *Fantastic Adventures* (1939) eight years before the 'official' flying saucer period began

Bayerl and his pregnant wife. He refused to explain what happened, saying only that Bayerl was a prophet and the Gulf War heralded the 'great destruction'. [13]

Disguised as humans, the aliens in the successful SF serial *V*, televised in the late 1980s, were Nazi-like lizards, bent upon dominating earthlings by terror and deceit. In the 1985 SF movie *Enemy Mine*, the foe was again a reptilian warrior; and the aliens in Germany's own 1960s SF serial, *Raumpatrouillie*, were called "frogs". In 1988 there was worldwide interest in sightings of a lizard-man in South Carolina [14]; perhaps he was checking on the progress of those fiendish Freemasons?

The water spirits of the Balts threatened to drown anyone who swam in their sacred places, or who neglected the annual sacrifices. Driven from their rivers and lakes by pollution and environmental engineering, these dangerous entities, or their relatives, have returned in spaceships. [15]

Water spirits have always had an aura of eroticism; so many of their encounters with humans are characterised by abduction or seduction. This is acknowledged as much in the tales in Grimm's great anthology of folktales as in Arnold's *Creature from the Black Lagoon*. The gill-man combines eroticism with menace; he lurks below the heroine as she swims unawares, attracted by her near-nakedness, waiting for the right moment... Abduction here means drowning, and death an end to innocence. Now, according to Hopkins et al., the ETs are abducting and inseminating innocent American housewives; they are obviously as dangerous and as powerful as their archaic fellows, made solid and technological by the scientific materialism of our age.

There is little difference between the conspiracies imagined by the insane, popular rumours of conspiracies, and the beliefs of some 'scientific ufologists' that governments retrieve crashed UFOs and that ETs violate earthlings in genetic laboratories. Somewhere between the fantasies of an abducted Zanfretta and the reptilian nightmares of the tormented Bayerl, the real meaning of these encounters is lost; lost in the pseudo-scientific terminology of the Hopkins school of alien abductions, and lost in the pseudo-rationalisations of lawyers and psychiatrists.

FT

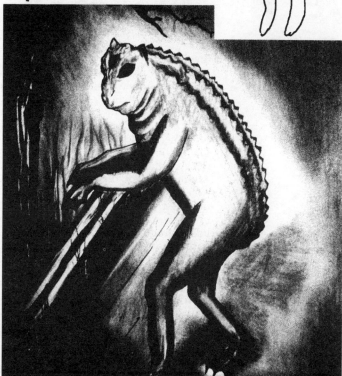

Below: The Lizard Man of South Carolina, as imagined by the Houston (TX) Chronicle 1988. Below right: witness drawing of a frogman seen near Lake Constance in 1977.

12. CENAP Report #170 (April 1990). Details of the Socorro case can be found in most UFO casebooks, including *Project Bluebook*; a good summary appears in Hilary Evans, ed., *UFOs 1947-1987*, (Fortean Tomes, London, 1987) pp66-69.
13. *Darmstädter Echo*, and *Süddeutsche Zeitung* 12 Sept 1991.
14. FT51: 34-37, FT53: 10.
15. Transitional forms of the water-man, from floating log, to mystery submarine, to UFO, are discussed in some detail by Michel Meurger, in *Lake Monster Traditions* (op.cit). See his indexes.

THE FAR SIDE By GARY LARSON

Larson
© Chronicle Features
Distributed by Universal Press Syndicate

The frog-like creatiure of Loveland, Ohio, according to a 1972 witness, police officer Mike Matthews (see FT46:*19*)

SMOKESCREEN:

Spontaneous Human Combustion (SHC) is an intense localised combustion, burning from within, which has no obvious cause. It rapidly reduces the bodies of its victims to heaps of calcinated ashes. SHC does not officially exist, and most investigating authorities will not even consider its possibility. **JENNY RANDLES** and **PETER HOUGH** describe here the difficulties they encountered while investigating possible SHC cases for their forthcoming book, *Spontaneous Human Combustion*.

In the spring of 1985, the police invited Peter Hough to attend an inquest on Merseyside the following June. It was an invitation too tempting to be ignored by any researcher into strange phenomena. The inquest was on the death of a teenage student who had burst into flames as she walked downstairs at her Cheshire college. The event had occurred in January, and at the rapidly adjourned initial inquiry, some unguarded official comments were made to reporters that implied spontaneous human combustion (SHC) would be considered.

The fire had seemingly sprung from nowhere to cause the girl's back to erupt in flames. A mature student only yards away later told us how one second the girl had been happily chatting to her friends, and the next she looked like 'a stunt man on television'. If the fire service was baffled and normal explanations proved unworkable, then, of course, paranormal options deserved careful and cautious attention.

SHC is a phenomenon generally familiar to the public, but seemingly based more on legend than scientific fact. It forms a part of our popular culture and briefly featured recently in the Australian TV soap *Neighbours*. In 1853, Charles Dickens, the great soap writer of the day, used SHC to kill off a character in his novel *Bleak House*. Whilst SHC often features in general 'pop' books about the supernatural, these recycle a few old tales from a magic roundabout used by one potboiler after another as an example of 'just one of those things' that defy explanation.

The belief is that in rare circumstances, people can suddenly burst into flames and be consumed by a fire apparently from nowhere. The victim is often reduced to a pile of ash with just fragments of limbs remaining. Although it would seem that temperatures in excess of those used in crematoria are involved, surrounding furnishings are often untouched. Theories have ranged from alcoholics struck down by the wrath of God, to the sudden explosion of intestinal gases and Martian death rays.

Whilst magazines such as *Fortean Times* have done a sterling job in recording accounts from the mass media, we saw the invitation to an inquest as an exciting opportunity. We were able to follow a case through its physical, evidential and sociological manifestations toward its eventual 'conclusion'.

In fact, this case became more important for what it told us about the psychology of SHC participants than the nature of the phenomenon itself. Our previous paper in this magazine (*The Creation of a Myth? FT47:60*) summarised our research on that 1985 fire death, and showed why the SHC option could never be proven or disproven because of the flawed official investigation. It highlighted the problems arising for officialdom when the mere possibility of SHC is contemplated.

The coroner instructed the jury to ignore all media speculation about SHC. In other words – true or false, real or imaginary – it was officially a non-option. On the face of it, this may seem a reasonable request; coroners and judges make similar remarks all the time about cases which have been the subject of intense media speculation. What seemed suspicious here was that the coroner singled out SHC without mentioning any of the less exotic rumours which had also appeared in the papers.

Worse – the coroner also refused to admit as evidence a vital 30-page report by the Cheshire Fire Brigade and the Shirley Institute in Manchester, which conflicted with the Home Office's conclusions. Although this report did not endorse the SHC option, it apparently demonstrated that the girl could not have caught fire through leaning against a lighted cooker.

While preparing our investigation of the Cheshire case, we needed a reliable source of SHC data. It did not exist. Michael Harrison's *Fire From Heaven* (1976) was a brave attempt to tackle the subject, but had many problems, not least that it relied on ancient cases and showed no sign of an investigative journalist attempting to wheedle out the facts from police, coroners, fire officers and forensic scientists. In addition, the book rambled around the issues and was hard to follow.

We therefore decided to write a SHC book ourselves. While we had no pretensions that we could 'solve' the mystery, we could at least demonstrate whether there was a mystery at all, and if there was, what the various official parties were doing about it.

This sounded a simple task, but in reality it was far from that. We struggled to persuade any British publisher to take an interest. Bloomsbury, for example, who published the first book about crop circles in July 1989, called us into their offices the week that book was released and spoke at length on the shock value of horrific photographs. They kept us hanging on for months and we gave up when they seemed strangely unable to communicate a simple 'yes' or 'no'. Indeed, we started work without a publisher and only found one by fluke two years later.

We faced enormous problems, which fell

Investigating SHC

into three main groups. Firstly, we didn't know whether SHC was real or illusory; if real, we had no idea if the solution lay in biology, physics, psychology or any number of fields, even without considering paranormal possibilities. This was too much to explore in one book, so we concentrated on sketching in the facts and establishing the basic pros and cons of the main options. Others can probe deeper at their leisure.

Secondly, we had great difficulty assessing material about SHC that was not many years old. Nobody was recording the cause of death of contemporary cases as due to 'spontaneous combustion'. One of the first fire officers we talked to told us plainly: "These cases are filed as unexplained fire deaths. They could be anything. A very few might be SHC. Most are not."

As we could not gain access to the cases in an official capacity to make any such judgement for ourselves, we were reduced to finding leads wherever we could, such as press clippings, tip-offs from people we were working with or paranormal magazines. From these we went back to first base and – not infrequently – found that the stories had no relevance to SHC. When they did, we found ourselves confronting our third problem – official stone-walling.

The records about cases that look as if they might be about SHC are not available to civilian investigators. Whilst inquests are invariably held in public and any local hack can attend and write what they like, when we came along later the chances were that we would be denied access to inquest records. The situation was sometimes even worse: more than once we were given the bureaucratic runaround. At least once we were apparently given false information to put us off the trail.

A newspaper cutting from February 1989, headlined "Rescuers Found Man Was Human Fireball", told of three men who saw smoke from a pensioner's window. They broke in and found an elderly man standing in the hallway, with his upper body ablaze. The flames were put out, but he died ten hours later. There was some doubt about the cause of the fire. The journalist who wrote the story put us onto the local coroner's office. They said they would look up the file, but never actually did so.

An officer at the local fire brigade headquarters looked up the file and rang us back. "I have our report in front of me", he said, "but I've been told that I cannot reveal any of its contents." We explained that we needed to know whether it was worth pursuing the case or not. After all, the information he was with-

holding had been, or would be, presented at the inquest, where anyone could hear it and take notes. He would tell us nothing at all. Back at the coroner's office, they advised us to inquire at the District Coroner's Office, where there were files on every death in the area. This we did, and eventually received a call from the District Coroner.

He said he had received our request for 'inquest evidence', but unfortunately the inquest had not yet been held. When we pointed out that it was two and a half years since the incident, he replied that there was a backlog of cases still waiting to be heard. He would

A fiery fate envisaged by Max Ernst. (Is that Hecate throwing up her hands in the distance?)

A QUICK TOUR OF SHC

"Call the death by any name [..] it is the same death eternally; inborn, inbred, engendered in the corrupt humours of the vicious body itself – Spontaneous Combustion, and none other of all the deaths that can be died."
Charles Dickens.

With these words Dickens writes off the drunkard Krook from his novel *Bleak House* (1853); all that remained of the villain were calcined ashes, a film of greasy soot and a horrid smell. When some critics protested that Dickens' imagination had gone too far, he responded with a detailed discussion of Spontaneous Human Combustion (SHC), citing many cases and the opinions of those who had investigated this arcane death of fiery disintegration. Charles Fort studied the collections of cases by previous academics, novelists, historians and scientists and added to them his own cases, gleaned from periodicals and scientific literature from around 1800 onward.

The idea that living people can suddenly burst into flames and be rapidly reduced to calcined bone and greasy ashes is an uncomfortable one. Despite many studies of SHC by scientific minds – going back to the pioneering anatomist Thomas Bartholin in 1673 – the subject is still tainted by the kind of supernaturalism in which it is seen as a punishment from the gods. It was often touted (in Dickens' day) as the inevitable fate of all boozers who consume too much inflammable spirit and are then consumed in turn by the fires of Hell – see SHC THEORIES panel.

It is not surprising that SHC is rejected by medical science today as a preposterous superstition. Nevertheless, baffling and suggestive cases continue to accumulate, and the phenomenon nags at the minds of investigating police and fire officers. In 1988, for example, John Heymer, a retired Scene of Crime Officer of 25 years experience, 'went public' by describing, in *New Scientist* and on TV, the mysterious fiery death of a man in Gwent in 1980, which he had investigated personally. Heymer's Case (as it is now known) had all the classic characteristics of SHC – see CHARACTERISTICS panel. Only the feet (in unscorched socks) and a blackened skull remained on a charred area of carpet; less than three feet from the victim a sofa with loose covers, and plastic tiles below the burnt carpet were undamaged. The hearth was tidy and the dead ashes of an old fire in the grate. An intense heat had melted the plastic lampshade and TV knobs, but the light and TV remained on. A sticky, orange substance coated the bulb and window. The room dripped with condensation.

Regular readers of *FT* will know that incidences of SHC continue to be reported although at a very low rate; and because of risk of upsetting relatives, contemporary cases are notoriously difficult to investigate. Our records hint that the phenomenon is met with, more frequently than generally supposed, by policemen, firemen and doctors, but confidentiality and a fear of ridicule prevent cases becoming better known. The facts are often very hard for an unaccredited inquirer to obtain (as Randles and Hough demonstrate in their article). Coroner's courts have a problem with 'unexplained' deaths, and prefer to return an open verdict or rely on speculation by experts about 'likely' causes.

Apart from the aura of gothic horror about SHC, the main obstacle to official interest is the word 'spontaneous'. Unfortunately, it is used very loosely in the literature, and the scientific mind is repelled by any suggestion of physical processes 'springing out of nowhere', or worse, having supernatural origins. By 'spontaneous' in this case we mean 'no immediately obvious or discernible cause', for cause and process there must be to produce such physical destruction.

Conservative explanationists have difficulty with SHC because they insist in thinking in terms of conventional combustion. An analysis of cases accumulated over several hundred years reveals a variable pattern of strong characteristics – see CHARACTERISTICS panel – each one of which presents a challenge to our understanding. Some of these characteristics will be more real than others, and they will be substantiated by sound investigation; the false or illusory ones will soon drop away.

Fort was fascinated by the paradoxical selectability of SHC, particularly those stories of people who burned while the bedclothes or cushions around them, or even the clothes they were wearing, remained untouched by fire. Fort also drew attention to other curious – non-physical – aspects of SHC, such as the way its victims rarely seemed to object or resist, the similarities with the kind of fires associated with poltergeist outbreaks, and those unfortunate people who are fire-prone (ie. fires regularly break out in their presence).

Just as fascinating, for the folklorists among us, are the references to SHC-like phenomena in the myths and lore of other cultures, suggesting the puzzling aspects of the phenomenon are widely known. A good example was quoted by Michael Harrison from Wu Ch'eng-en, author of the 16th century Chinese classic *Monkey*: "Heaven will send down a peculiar fire [..] It is neither common fire nor celestial fire, but springs up from within and consumes the vitals, reducing the whole frame to ashes…"

inform us when a date was fixed so that we could attend.

We traced one of the men who had rescued the deceased. "If the inquest hasn't taken place," he said, "then what was it that I attended over two years ago, where I had to stand up and give evidence?" Could this have been a preliminary hearing, an adjourned inquest while the incident was investigated more fully? He was sure it was not, so we got back to the District Coroner. This time, he sounded annoyed.

"Look, I've told you, the inquest has not taken place! I have the file in front of me. It contains the result of our official investigation. This evidence will be heard at the inquest, *once it is arranged*." He repeated that he would duly inform us of the date. Perplexed, we let the matter drop. A week later, we received a call from the District Coroner's Office. This time it was a woman; she sounded embarrassed and was very apologetic.

"I'm sorry to tell you that you've been given some wrong information about the inquest. It did in fact take place on 23 May 1989." When we asked how we had been misinformed by the District Coroner when he had all the information to hand, she muttered something about `holidays' and continued.

"Look, we can't let you have the inquest evidence, but if you would like to arrange an appointment at the office, you can read the file and take notes." We thanked her and agreed that it was a good compromise. Once again, she apologised. At the office, we were given the file to examine under guard of an employ-

THE ARMCHAIR OF OBLIVION

"No! No! Not the comfy chair!"
                    M. Python.

In the annals of SHC, probably the best known case is that of Mrs Mary Reeser [inset], who was almost totally consumed by a fire of unknown origin as she reclined in an overstuffed armchair in her apartment in St Petersburg, Florida, in the night of 1 July 1951. In the morning, her landlady took her a telegram and found the door-knob too hot to handle. She called for help, and the party were met by a blast of hot air as they opened the door. In a charred circle lay the few remains of Mrs Reeser and her chair: burnt springs, fragments of backbone, a cooked liver, and a skull shrunk to the size of fist.

The photo shows the damage in the region of the chair; above a four-foot line, heat had buckled, cracked and melted fragile items and coated walls with greasy soot. The inquest deter-mined that heat in excess of 2500F was needed to reduce a living body to this state, yet a pile of papers less than a foot away had not caught fire.

An FBI statement suggested that Mrs Reeser had fallen asleep while smoking, having taken her usual sleeping pills, but this was refuted by experts at the inquest who testified that even if her clothes had ignited this way it would have caused only superficial burns, and even if the armchair stuffing smouldered it could not have generated enough intensity to ignite or char a living body so completely.

ee. The coroner who presided at the inquest was the same one who had twice denied that it had taken place...

In another case from north-west England, two people had emerged from a high-rise flat as human fireballs and died as a result of their injuries. The story had made the front page of one regional newspaper, but it never carried details of the post mortem or the inquest (which we discovered was held remarkably fast and established an 'open verdict'.

We visited the scene of the tragedy and found the area rife with rumours. Staff on the local paper were puzzled that they had never carried the story at all. "We covered every little chip pan fire", noted a senior reporter incredulously. But this double fire mystery on their door step which was common knowledge locally, with all sorts of connotations (love triangle, suicide pact, even murder allegations) got not one word. We never found out why.

As for official help on the matter, we were sent from one department to the next, faced with replies such as: "I don't think I can tell you that". At one stage the person we spoke to had to go and check if they could give us a department phone number we could have got from the phone book!

After weeks of on-the-beat investigation, we were able to tell the police more than their press officer could tell us when they finally agreed to say anything at all. Ultimately, the coroner agreed to provide a few quotes that, frankly, made the case more contentious.

The point is that, while we were asking for nothing that could not be obtained by reason-

CHARACTERISTICS OF SHC

SHC does not ignite or burn like a 'normal' fire. Typical cases share a number of consistent characteristics (though not always all of them at once).

● The victims often seem to feel no pain, or at least make no cry. Fort likened this effect to the lulling of a vampire's wings. During a series of unexplained fires on a farm at Binbrook, Lincolnshire, in 1905, a maid was observed to carry on her sweeping unconscious of the flames that engulfed her shoulders. If she had not been rescued in time, she could have become another unexplained fire death.

● The heat must be intense. Several experts have confirmed that crematoria require a temperature of about 900 degrees C, intensified by a forced draught and sustained for several hours to reduce a dead body to ashes. Then a pulveriser is used to crunch up the lumpy bits. Somehow SHC accomplishes this without the hi-tech equipment.

● SHC not only reaches the required temperatures rapidly, but pursues its course quickly and quietly.

● SHC seems to burn from the inside outwards, beginning in the chest, abdomen, or in the deep muscles.

● SHC can be weirdly selective. The author of *Proverbs* (6:27) asked: "Can a man take fire in his bosom and his clothes not be burned?" The answer must be in the affirmative. In 1908, Wilhelmina Dewar burned to death in her unscorched bed in Blyth. Likewise, in 1943 in Sussex, Madge Knight lay in bed unaware she was burning; later she awoke screaming, her back burned so badly she died later, but there was no trace of fire on her sheets. Fort mentions many other cases.

● The intense heat of SHC can be focussed or localised. Often, easily combustible materials nearby are untouched or merely scorched. When Dr Irving Bentley died in Pennsylvania in 1966, he seemed to have been taken by a pillar of fire intense enough to burn through the floor where he was standing, yet the bath nearby was barely scorched. Bentley's left leg, burned off below the knee, lay by the hole. See also the cases of Mrs Reeser and the old man of Aberdeen [in panels] for similar effects.

● In many SHC cases, the body is consumed leaving a hand or foot (the latter sometimes still wearing an unscorched slipper). To confound matters, there are also cases where the extremities are the first to be consumed.

● A frequently reported detail is an unpleasant greasy brownish tar that coats most of the smooth surfaces at the SHC scene. It seems to be a byproduct of burning human flesh.

---

able research, we encountered bureaucratic barriers that made the straightforward look mysterious. Conversely, we found that various suspect cases which might potentially relate to SHC were being hastily concluded with any mundane explanation to hand. Was this to avoid facing the possibility of SHC?

At other times, we were officially assured that there was no evidence for SHC in a case. When asked how such a conclusion was reached – to help us look for this non-evidence ourselves in other incidents – we learned, as expected, that nobody knew. This was, of course, just a way to be rid of the problem.

It was as if, for some people, the very thought of anyone seriously investigating SHC was not to be contemplated. It upset the status quo or exposed dilemmas they would rather not have to confront. We respect this view and know we are dealing with a widespread attitude – from fire officers to coroners. It caused us many difficulties, but has a lot to do with an unavoidable fact: we were investigating people who have died in harrowing circumstances. Their families obviously don't want to face further pressures. How would you feel if someone probed the recent death of a loved one to find out whether they died as a result of a bizarre phenomenon, unknown to science and used as light entertainment by the media?

For example, we treated the family of the girl from Cheshire with what we hope was respect. Although it was the subject of national media attention and some ludicrous coverage abroad in supermarket tabloids (in most cases before the second inquest), we decided not to cause more grief by publishing our work. We refused to help BBC TV on a serious item because of this. Only later, when inaccurate versions of the case appeared in some general supernatural books, did we write our article for *Fortean Times* and a chapter in *Death by Supernatural Causes?* (Grafton 1988).

We never stated that this girl died as a result of SHC. We merely presented our interviews with witnesses and a review of facts known only to us. However, the media were not so considerate. We saw features based on our work with provocative titles, imaginative scenarios and garish presentations. We learned (from the front page of the *Liverpool Daily Post*) that one of these greatly offended the girl's relatives. We felt very badly about this and made several entreaties to them about this difficult matter.

It is not serious enquiry into alleged SHC which creates the problem, but the media's treatment of the paranormal as High Farce. We were even asked to help a TV comedian write a humorous script for a children's show based on SHC! We have visions of a TV games show one day screening video clips of SHC, perhaps entitled *You've Been Flamed!*

We have said little in this article about SHC itself or our conclusions. Readers will have to read our book. We will say, however, that there is a phenomenon worthy of investigation. Whilst a number of 'SHC' events crumbled upon investigation, others do not have easy explanations. We uncovered several new cases and photographs, and produced a chronological database of SHC cases that we came across, with sufficient information to produce some rudimentary statistics.

We also assessed some of the classic SHC cases, which usually receive a very one-dimensional approach, glossing over the real issues. For instance, we obtained the FBI report on the famous Mary Reeser case. Mrs Reeser, of St Petersburg, Florida, was reduced almost com-

DEATH IN A HAYLOFT

On 19 Feb 1888, Dr J. Mackenzie Booth, a lecturer at Aberdeen University, was called to a loft of a stable in the town. There, he found the charred body of a 65-year-old man; most of the abdominal flesh was burned away leaving the calcined ends of bones. The body had burned through the floorboards and was resting on a charred beam; and directly above the body the roofing slats had burned away causing slates to fall onto the corpse's chest.

The man was known to be a drunkard, and was last seen the previous night, climbing into the loft with a lamp and a bottle. The obvious conclusion – that he knocked over the lamp and was incapable of putting the fire out – is confounded by the facts of the case. Firstly, a witness saw the light extinguished and observed no further glimmer of light or fire during the night. Secondly, we have the peculiar death scene preserved for us by this engraving – from the *British Medical Journal* 21 April 1888, and based upon a police photograph - which shows the body surrounded by untouched wood and bales of hay. Dr Booth noted that the features of the man's face were preserved, and concluded "from the comfortably recumbent attitude of the body, it was evident that there had been no death struggle."

pletely to ashes, along with her armchair, on the morning of 2 July 1950. The rest of the apartment was relatively untouched. The police report included witnesses' statements and presented new information. We also contacted the victim's son, Dr Richard Reeser, who may have been the last person to see her alive.

One of the most surprising things for us was our review of the BBC TV feature on SHC which appeared as part of the *Q.E.D.* series in April 1989. We felt its cautious approach – whilst a little overbearing – was at least a sober presentation of a subject often treated with undue mystical reverence. It concluded that there was no such thing as SHC and the mystery was explained away as the result of a natural process of burning.

Without revealing too much – indeed you have to see the data unfold damningly as it does in our chapter – we can say that when we interviewed most of the people who appeared in the programme, we established a consensus that differed markedly from what we expected or had felt at the time. While the programme was undoubtedly an attempt to tackle the problem and was well received by many, we now have very serious reservations about its primary contention. We only wish that SHC was as readily explicable as *Q.E.D.* suggested!

[*Spontaneous Human Combustion* by Jenny Randles and Peter Hough is published in hardback by Robert Hale, London, in July 1992, price £14.95]

SHC THEORIES

There are many more theories of SHC than we can present here, from the outright superstitious to the ultra-rational, and all shades of plausibility. Most of them fail to account for all the observed facts, nor the variety of victims or their circumstances. There is no discernible profile of an SHC victim, so that theories based upon age, sex, sociability, health, culture, indoors or out, drunkenness, sin, obesity, or smoking can all be contradicted by established data. Here are a few of them...

● **SUPERNATURAL** – By far the oldest explanation of SHC is that it is some kind of divine weapon for punishing sinners, iconoclasts, blasphemers and inebriates. The thunderbolts of the gods were feared in most archaic cultures. (The biblical 'pillar of fire' has been revived and incorporated into the popular computer 'god simulator' game *Populous 2*; players can invoke it to consume an opponent's men.) SHC has even been blamed upon demons and witches, as in the case of Grace Pett of Ipswich, who burned to a crisp in 1744. She had a reputation for drunkenness and her combustion was used widely as an example of divine retribution; only it was not the whole story. Patient research by Peter Christie – *FT35*:6 – showed that she was also believed by her contemporaries to be a witch, and to have cast one spell too many when it rebounded with fiery consequences.

● **MURDER** – Most of the discussion of SHC in textbooks on forensic toxicology concerns its use as a cover for murder, based on a famous French case from 1725 in which an accused man successfully persuaded a court in Rheims that his wife had spontaneously combusted in her armchair. Some medical textbooks acknowledge a few cases where the almost complete destruction of the body and the localisation of the fire are baffling, and grudgingly suppose that the human body can, under circumstances unknown, develop an unusually combustible constitution.

● **THE 'WICK' THEORY** – This makes an analogy with the candle. Prof David Gee, of Leeds University, has argued that burning clothes boil off the body water, then absorb the melted fat, becoming in effect a wick around the body which continues to burn until the fire has consumed all its fuel (fatty tissue, clothes, or alcohol-saturated flesh). Serious experiments, however – including those performed by Baron Justus von Liebig, a father of modern chemistry, in the mid-1800s – only demonstrate the limitations of this theory. Ignition of *living* tissue by sparks or smouldering cloth is extremely difficult due to being 72% water with an active blood supply to redistribute the heat. If clothing smouldered long enough to 'boil off' the nine or ten gallons of water in the average-sized body before it could dessicate the flesh, there would be none left to act as a wick. The old notion of boozing yourself into a human firelighter is also untenable; a drinker would die of alcohol poisoning long before his tissues were saturated enough to make them combustible.

● **FORCED DRAUGHT** – Really a corollary of the 'wick' theory. Under normal circumstances, any smouldering fire (eg. in clothes or an armchair) would not be intense enough to inflict more than serious surface burns. The theory speculates that the body *must* have been in a draught between a door or window and the chimney. The draught provides extra oxygen, allowing the fire to reach greater temperatures than it would unaided, just as fan-forced oxygen is required by incinerating machines in crematoria. Even so, it is doubtful that draught-fed fires could reach the temperatures required to fuse bone or reduce it to ash, and the theory as applied to SHC has been rubbished by actual investigators – see panel on Mrs Reeser. Heymer's case actually occurred in a room sealed with draught-excluders.

● **THE HUMAN FUEL CELL** – Heymer's experience with the Gwent SHC and its subsequent investigation made him scathing about the way his forensic advisors relied on the wick and draught theories. "Let them try to incinerate to ashes a clothed corpse in an airless room without damaging the furnishings," he wrote in *New Scientist* (15 May 1986).

Instead, he bravely proposed an ingenious theory of his own, based upon the same electrochemical processes that power the US space-flights. Electricity passed through water can split it into hydrogen and oxygen. Heymer wondered if an unknown biochemical action in the human cells, powered by a build-up of electrostatic charge, caused the water in those cells to split into its constituent gasses. "The burning hydrogen would use up all the oxygen, leaving none to support the combustion of other materials." A biochemical fire of this nature could accelerate rapidly from cell to cell, like a bushfire, from the deep tissues outward and be extinguished just as quickly when it loses its momentum. No scientist has yet commented on its feasibility.

● **BODY CHEMISTRY** – The Fortean writer Ivan Sanderson supposed that loneliness might affect the metabolism causing an accumulation of inflammable nitroglycerine-like phosphagens in muscle tissue. From the annals of medical curiosities, we also know of cases of inflammable perspiration, electric people who emit sparks and glows, and of accumulations of methane and 'phosphoretted hydrogen' gasses. What if the heat-generating processes in the liver and brown fat layers went out of control; could that be a factor in SHC?

● **PSYCHIC HEAT** – According to yogic teachings some kind of biofeedback control over the body's heat generation is possible. In the Tibetan rite of Tumo, for example, the adept has to sit naked in the cold air and by meditating upon fire increase his body heat so that he can survive. There are stories of monks being able to dry out dozens of sheets soaked in freezing water this way. Normally, the body's autonomic nervous control system is beyond conscious intervention, but perhaps in SHC a kind of negative interference is operating.

Again, in Eastern and esoteric traditions, the use of psychic powers can also generate heat as a byproduct, either in the body or in a magical object. In some poltergeist cases, for example, objects flung through the air, or on materialising, are found to be hot. If this notion has any substance it may provide a link between SHC and undisciplined psychic activity.

● **ELECTROMAGNETISM** – In a few modern cases of unexplained fires, tests to detect possible microwave radiation have proved negative; nevertheless as a method of generating heat at a distance, which can also cook from the inside out, it should not be ruled out definitively in cases of SHC. Similarly, some have wondered about the effects of ELF radiation from power-lines. These ideas, however, do not account for SHC cases that occurred before the availability of power broadcasting and distribution. Lightning is a natural source of microwaves, and can create weird balls of plasma energy which play poltergeist-like tricks; this was writer Maxwell Cade's candidate for triggering SHC.

The biochemical mass of the human body still has sensitivities both unexplored and undiscovered. One researcher, Livingston Gearhart, in 1975, found a correlation between SHC events and changes in the peaks of the Earth's geomagnetic field, as though the fluctuations of the field had triggered the combustions.

● **NUCLEAR DISINTEGRATION** – This notion bridges the mystical and the physical; it supposes that there is a life-force which holds together the constituents of the body. If this malfunctions, the body structure begins to disintegrate, giving off heat in an uncontrolled equivalent of the way nuclear fission is used in a power station. As far as we know, no one has yet taken a Geiger counter to the scene of an SHC to check for residual radiation.

FORTEAN EXTRACTS
FROM THE
GENTLEMAN'S MAGAZINE

Charles Fort did not study pre-1800 records in any depth, and many useful records remain to be discovered.

The Gentleman's Magazine was first issued in January 1731, and appeared monthly for nearly 200 years. Sprinkled across its closely printed pages are the record of odd events of interest to Forteans.

Since 1982, Fortean Times has been publishing PETER CHRISTIE'S chronological selections with his comments. Continued from FT61.

1752

● To round off the year, the December issue carried two reports of fireballs. At Bristol on 16 December "A great ball of fire was seen to issue from the clouds, which shot with great swiftness to the northward". Nine days later at 4 pm, Glasgow was treated to the sight of "a large ball of fire with a long tail" which travelled NE-SW "and after having exhibited, for some time, the various colours of the rainbow, it burst into a thousand sparks of fire, and was immediately follow'd by a great shower of hail." (p.582)

1753

● The New Year opened with the death of Mrs. Mary Jenkins at London aged 110, about whom it was noted that she "never used spectacles". (p.52)

● February saw an involved numerological exercise which conclusively proved that the Great Beast of Revelations (i.e.666) was China. Has anyone ever sat down and tabulated how many people/places or whatever have qualified as the Great Beast? – it would be a fascinating list if only to show the amount of time wasted on such fruitless activities. (p.90)

● Also in this month there is an account of a paper read to the Royal Society concerning a fatal lightning strike in Cornwall in December 1752. The lightning bolt

"bored several holes thro' banks, cut several channels like plough furrows, and shattered a rock, as if blown up with gunpowder. Another flash beat down a chimney of 4 foot square, and mov'd it to some distance from the house; made fractures in the partitions, rent the roof, broke into the kitchen, where the farmer and the family were most of them struck down. The farmer's son was kill'd, his clothes rent to shivers, his shoes much scorched, and one of his toes cut off so as only to hang by a bit of skin, and a dog between his legs struck dead also; Neither man or dog stirr'd at the shock, nor was the countenance of the former at all alter'd, and a person in another room was thrown 12 feet from her place." (p.98)

Could death be so instantaneous that a man's face wasn't at all changed? It seems unlikely.

● March saw a long article about John Tallis of Bromsgrove in Worcestershire. In 1724, when he was 48, he retired to a virtually sealed room, went to bed, swathed his head in 100 yards of flannel and finally had "stoppers fitted to each nostril". All apparently because he feared infection via air-borne germs – clearly the late Howard Hughes had nothing on Mr. Tallis! (p.123) [See *FT53*:31.]

● As post was slow in those days, it wasn't until March that a letter from the American colonists reached the editor. This was sent from Boston on January 1st. A shower of rain had fallen "which turn'd into ice, or congeal'd, as it fell; and many flocks of wild geese that were flying, had their wings suddenly frozen, and fell down as if shot." (p.147) This must have been an odd storm as the atmosphere generally warms the closer one gets to the earth – thus water tends to warm as it falls – not cool down.

● April 1753 saw a woman burnt at the stake in Gloucester for poisoning her husband (p.198) and May saw the use of ginseng advocated.

● The following month the Royal Society published the reports that had been sent to them regarding the earthquakes experienced in Britain in February and March 1750 (see my coverage of that year). This prompted *Gentleman's Magazine* correspondents to send in some of their own and these make interesting reading – especially as they deal with other 'quakes in August and September of that year. At Norwich in June 1750 there was a 'hollow' sounding explosion in the air which puzzled many as there was no earth movement associated with it (pp.220,262,263). The August earthquake in Lincoln occurred at the same time as an Aurora Borealis display "which turn'd to a very deep red."

● The magazine continued its interest in meteorological conditions in June with a report from Rome. On the second day of that month there was a fall of hail there in which "some of the stones were as big as a hen's egg." (p.290)

2 June was also memorable in Bridgwater, Somerset, as a storm began and after an hour turned very nasty. Hail stones of "6,7,8 and 9 inches about [..] made holes in the ground like cannon balls." Intriguingly, these large hailstones fell "for half an hour with this rapidity" – far longer than is usual with hail and certainly a very unusual event. People were injured by these stones though no details are given. (p.294)

● In the July issue appeared the illustration **[opposite]** showing the contemporary view of the earth's structure – note the air and water layers (pp.312-4). One assumes that Verne and Wells picked up ideas like these for their later stories.

● This issue also answered one long-standing question – why are Red Indians red? The answer comes in an article entitled *"Some Account of the NATIVES of Louisiana"*. Apparently,

> *"As soon as a child is born, both the mother and child are washed in river or spring water: a few days after, the child is rubbed with bears oil; this unction, together with their continual exposure to the heat of the sun (for both sexes go quite naked till they are 12 years old) gives a red colour to their skin, which is as white as ours when they are born, that no time can efface."* (p.326)

So now you know! Though how do the Chinese become yellow? Sunflower oil? The mind boggles.

● This highly-coloured tale was followed by another in the same month. We read that "Don Andrew Bueno lately died at Badajoz (Portugal), aged 124." (p.340) This old soldier "was only a lieutenant of foot, tho' he had been in the service above 100 years." As the obituarist noted, "A sure sign of want either of merit or friends."

● August saw an article and illustration on an aura around the sun (p.370), whilst September had a discussion about tarantula bites and the beneficial effects of playing jig music to sufferers in order to "dance the frenzy out". (p.433)

● Also in the September issue was an account of a journey undertaken by a 'civilized' or Europeanized Red Indian to the North West coast of North America around 1700. At one point he joined an attack on some white 'slavers' who had long black beards, stocky bodies and were heavily clothed. The traveller "thinks it probable that the bearded men are the inhabitants of some isles in the neighbourhood of Japan." They sound more like Russians to me but could any reader add anything to this strange story? (p.407-10)

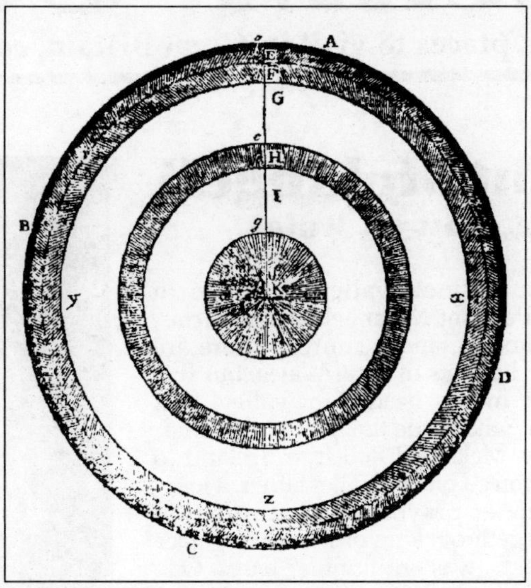

A CROSS-SECTION OF THE EARTH

"The thickness of the upper crust a b is impossible to be known, but as the semi-diameter of the earth is nearly 4000 miles, so vast an arch must be very strong and therefore we cannot suppose its thickness to be less than 11 miles. E represents the zone of water; its depth b c we will suppose 200 miles. F is the zone of solid matter supporting the abyss or zone of water, its thickness d e we will estimate at 1000 miles. H is the superior Terella, the thickness of its crust or surface e f we will suppose 400 miles. I is the second or lower interior atmosphere, its breadth or thickness f g may be supposed equal to the former, viz. 1000 miles. K is the central Terella, its semi-diameter g h therefore will be 1000 miles. All which dimensions added together are equal to A, K, the semi-diameter of the globe, viz. 4000 miles." Gentleman's Magazine July 1753, page 313.

● Late news in the September issue came from Munich where, at the end of August,

> *"the workmen employ'd in enlarging and repairing the vault of the church of our lady, found in an hollow pillar a lamp, which, they say, was burning when they opened the vault. It was in the form of a chalice, closed at the top with wax; at the bottom there was a tube of 4 or 5 inches long, in the shape of the glasses fix'd to a cage, out of which birds drink their water, and through the tube a match was introduc'd. Little of the oil was wasted."* (p.439)

The unfortunate thing about this report is that one is not told when the vault was sealed and how long the lamp had been burning. The story could almost be taken as a pre-electric forerunner of the 'whale tumour' story about the everlasting lightbulb.

● Another, possibly original, story of this sort surfaced in October, when a young man called Holmes was arrested in London. He was an apprentice baker who had run away from his master in Lincolnshire. When he left, "some of the neighbours reported that he had been killed, and baked in the oven; which occasioned the poor man (i.e. the baker) to lose his custom, and to be threatened to be prosecuted as a murderer." (p.490)

One can here perhaps distinguish certain features of the Sweeney Todd legend. This 'demon barber' had the charming habit of dispatching his victims/customers and then using them as raw materials for his pies. Is this the first appearance in print of this sort of story?

● On 18 October, Evan Price of Dolgelly, North Wales, died, having claimed to be 120 years old. The report notes that "within a month of his death he used to walk 4 miles twice a week, in that hilly country." (p.492)

SECRET COUNTRY

Mysterious places to visit in Great Britain, compiled by Janet & Colin Bord

3: Pennant Melangell
Llangynog, Powys, Wales.

Tucked away in a remote valley in the north Powys hills is Pennant Melangell: a few farms, some holiday homes, and a church. There are many forgotten hamlets in rural Wales, but this one is special. 'Pennant' means 'head of the valley', and Melangell was the saint who made this place her home.

In the sixth century, Melangell fled from Ireland to avoid a marriage being forced on her by her father, a king. One day, her quiet life of prayer was disturbed by huntsmen. Brochwel Ysgythrog, king of Powys, together with his men and hounds, was out hunting hares. One ran to Melangell and hid beneath her skirts. She pleaded with the prince to leave the animal alone, but he urged on his hounds. They seemed afraid and refused to approach the girl. One of the huntsmen lifted his horn but it stuck to his lips and no sound came from it. Brochwel realised that Melangell was no ordinary country girl and he asked her who she was. She impressed him so much that he gave her land for a sanctuary, and she stayed in the valley for the rest of her life. A religious community developed, and eventually the site became a focus for pilgrimages. An annual fair was held to celebrate her feast day. Melangell also became known as the patron saint of hares, and locally they were called 'wyn bach Melangell' (Melangell's little lambs).

Melangell's influence is still very strong in the valley 1,400 years later. A rock platform in woods just south of the church is known as Gwely Melangell, or Melangell's Bed. On the hillside above the church is a holy well named after her: today it is little more than a hole in the ground, but its situation high above the valley, with fine views into the surrounding mountains, is magnificent.

The heart of Pennant Melangell is the old church. The present building dates back to the 12th century, but stands on the site of the original church in a large 'llan' enclosure, a sure sign of antiquity. The present church is a small, simple building. The most important feature is the reconstructed shrine, built around 1160 to hold the saint's remains. This was rebuilt in the late 1950s, and until recently stood in the 'Cell-y-Bedd', a small room on the east end of the church, and entered from outside. In the

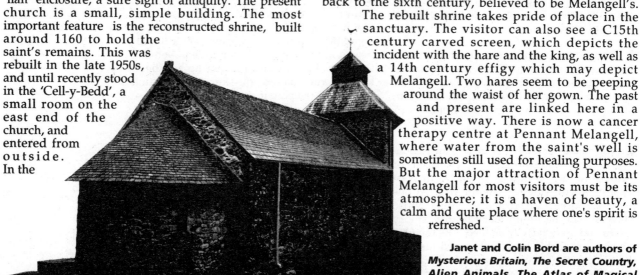

last few years a major project of excavation and reconstruction has been carried out. Important discoveries have been made, including a grave dating back to the sixth century, believed to be Melangell's.

The rebuilt shrine takes pride of place in the sanctuary. The visitor can also see a C15th century carved screen, which depicts the incident with the hare and the king, as well as a 14th century effigy which may depict Melangell. Two hares seem to be peeping around the waist of her gown. The past and present are linked here in a positive way. There is now a cancer therapy centre at Pennant Melangell, where water from the saint's well is sometimes still used for healing purposes. But the major attraction of Pennant Melangell for most visitors must be its atmosphere; it is a haven of beauty, a calm and quite place where one's spirit is refreshed.

Janet and Colin Bord are authors of *Mysterious Britain, The Secret Country, Alien Animals, The Atlas of Magical Britain*, and *Modern Mysteries of Britain* among many others.

A Local Legend

The subtle codename Operation Napoleon was well chosen. Keeping the location secret was essential. A red alert test of emergency services to see how they would cope with a simulated rail-borne nuclear consignment being damaged had to be kept under wraps. When it took place recently, the cryptic historical connection became clear. It had to be at Hartlepool.

According to legend, the fishermen of Hartlepool hanged a monkey which had been washed ashore. It was during the Napoleonic Wars and the monkey was mistaken for a French spy. Chattering away and dressed in a military-style uniform, it was decided that as a precaution it should be hanged.

This is the basic and simplistic version of the legend. Hartlepudlians, wherever in Britain or abroad they go, are remembered for this deed and dubbed 'monkey-hangers'. The majority take no offence; indeed, they regard it more as a compliment. However, on occasions when a questioner might have sarcastically inquired: "Is this where they hung the monkey?" the reply would be: "Why, have you lost your father?"

Delving into the archives, I was able to find an account several times removed from an original witness, giving details of the shipwreck on the Longscar Rocks of a French privateer named *Chasse Maree*. The spoils from the warship included a piece of wreckage to which hung a bedraggled, shivering monkey. A 'lobster-pot court martial' was held and the verdict was that it was a spy. A coble's mast with halliard rove was erected on the Fish Sands and the monkey hanged.

Problems immediately arise, as inquiries have failed to establish the historicity of *Chasse Maree*, despite the account's keen observation and technical detail. In any case, commonsense suggests that any monkey found floating on a spar would be of a small breed and common as a ship's pet, whose size and innocence wouldn't qualify it as a French spy. More reason for doubt is that none of the prominent regional folklore collectors of the period found the story worthy of mention, had they heard it. Unless, of course, they considered it as history.

If documentation of the monkey-hanging legend from the Napoleonic

Folklore

Paul Screeton is a feature writer and sub-editor on a newspaper in North-East England. Formerly editor of *The Ley Hunter*, he currently produces the controversial magazine on urban folk tales, *Folklore Frontiers*. He has had published several books on earth mysteries, the paranormal and folklore. The latest is *Who Hung the Monkey?* In this column, Paul sets out the main elements of this monkey-hanging legend. Copies of the book are available from Atkinson the printer, 11 Lower Church Street, Hartlepool, Cleveland, TS24 7DJ. (Make cheques out to Printability Publishing. Price, inc p+p, £4.50).

era speaks volumes by its absence, then there is a tantalising reference made in a political pamphlet of the 1840s to 'aquatic monkies'. Accounts of the historical development of railways throughout the North-East rarely touch upon the intense rivalries which were stirred. It was the battle to export coal more cheaply which led to rival railways converging upon Hartlepool, creating the larger and more prosperous West Hartlepool (the two boroughs amalgamating in the 1960s). Initials on the small bill announcing 'aquatic monkies' likely stand for those who favoured the West Dock scheme.

If these people were to be regarded as charlatans, then we can suggest that the 'aquatic monkies' jibe turned on association with 'jenny hanivers'. These mermaid-type creations, half-

fish, half-monkey, were popular in the last century. The bill was dated 1844, and we know that showman Phineas Barnum was exhibiting an example in 1842. Indeed, in Hartlepool, a small skate is folded, smoked and can then take on the appearance of a small monkey, demonstrating a possibly unbroken tradition of 'aquatic monkies' in the town spanning 150 years.

What most firmly established the legend, however, was a song composed by Ned Corvan (1829-65). Corvan's policy was to discover some local disturbance and extend it into an epic. This he would declaim with suitable gestures and those dramatic asides so essential to music-hall gatherings when everyone was in their cups.

Corvan's song includes:
"Still you may hear to this day, / Boys crying, Who hung the Monkey, O?"

Perhaps Corvan heard this catcall on Hartlepool's ancient Headland. There was a popular play at the time called "Jack Robinson and his Monkey". One rival railway had a Stephen Robinson as engineer; was his opposite number a 'monkey'? Robinson's monkey was called Mushapug; Corvan called the monkey Pug, as shortened in the play. The song made its stage debut at the Dock Hotel Music Hall, Southgate, Hartlepool, on an unspecified date. The ballad sheet contends it was greeted with immense applause, but it has also been suggested Corvan was run out of town for performing it. Whether Hartlepudlians liked it or not, they had to be resigned to the fact that Corvan had put them on the map.

However, it is only fair to record the fact that Hartlepool is not alone in having a monkey-hanging legend. Another features Boddam, Aberdeenshire, where the delightful inhabitants lit beacons deliberately to lure cargo boats to be wrecked on the rocks. When a monkey was washed ashore, it was hanged, as there were fears that as the sole survivor it would claim the remaining merchandise.

Boddam fishergirls followed the herring fleets and would have gutted fish ashore in Hartlepool. Perhaps this could be the genesis of the tale. There again, the tale surfaces on Clydeside at Greenock, in distant Cornwall at Mevagissey and even inland in a Derbyshire village.

Just as legend relocation is common, so are examples of 'blason populaire' – a simple expression for a distinct form of local tradition, a jeering slogan or jibe, a taunt levelled in semi-malicious fun by the inhabitants of one town or region against those of another. In fact, both Hartlepool and Boddam also share the catcall: "I hear they're painting the end of the new pier red to save lighting the beacon at night".

More than 100 years ago, Robert Chambers observed: "There is a nationality in districts as well as in countries: nay, the people living on different sides of the same stream, or of the same hill, sometimes entertain prejudices against each other, not less virulent than those of the inhabitants of different sides of the English Channel or the Pyrenees."

West Hartlepool born and bred, I must record that there is still a rivalry between the people of the former boroughs of Hartlepool and West Hartlepool; equally, a shared insularity, shunning connection with either Teeside or South-East Durham. More positively, Hartlepudlians can laugh at themselves and have capitalised upon the monkey legend rather than decried it. The monkey today is mascot in sporting and military contexts; regaled in modern traditional songs; used in advertising promotions and even for sugarcraft modelling; and has appeared as a high-gravity beer.

A century ago, the tale gained national prominence when Hartlepool Rovers Rugby Football Club was having a glorious period during the 1890s. A stuffed monkey was hanged from the crossbar before a match and national newspapers reported this novel behaviour.

The club still associates itself strongly with the legend. When recently a Rovers' team went to a match at Twickenham, they had a live monkey as mascot. On the way back to Hartlepool, the bus crashed and the only survivor was the monkey. A police officer tried to communicate with the monkey to ascertain what had happened. Eventually, he had some success and when asked what was happening at the rear of the coach, the monkey made a gesture indicating people playing cards.

In response to the question of what was happening in the centre portion, the monkey gesticulated as if singing and waving a scarf. As for those at the front, the monkey demonstrated the drinking of cans of beer. When asked about the driver, it held its hands as if reading a newspaper. Lastly, the police officer asked what the monkey was doing itself. Its hands moved as if controlling the steering wheel...

Colossal Misunderstanding

Five years have gone by since I picked up the telephone one morning to hear a literary agent ask whether I would like to earn – I forget the precise sum, but it was more than I had earned from all my books put together. And it would not be difficult: all that would be required was an account of the discovery, thanks to a psychic, of the remains of the Colossus of Rhodes.

To refresh your memories: on a visit to Rhodes the previous year, the psychic Ann Dankbaar had 'seen' the remains on the seabed, a few hundred yards from Rhodes harbour. Divers, descending at the point she indicated, found what looked as if they might indeed be the remains. It was too late in the season for further exploration, but plans were laid to carry on the investigation the following summer.

Curtis Brown – Ann's agents – scented the story of a lifetime; if she turned out to have been right. The *Sunday Times* agreed to sponsor her return visit to Rhodes, and to have me there to report progress. The Greek Shipping Minister put his department's resources at the searchers' disposal. And they found ... a giant fist.

It looked very impressive, in the film taken of it on the seabed. Alas! It clearly was not a fist, or any other part, of the Colossus; when brought to the surface, it turned out to be some kind of sandstone. For various reasons, my hopes that the resting place of the Colossus would be found had never been high. I had an enjoyable holiday, and provided the *Sunday Times* with a front page story about the involvement of the Greek government; but as Amit Roy, on the *Sunday Times* staff, had come out to Rhodes, I came home.

As a result I missed the denouément, in which charges of fraud were thrown around. Roy's account was full, and in general fair; but the headline – 'Clairvoyant says Colossus is a Fake' – left the misleading impression that the whole enterprise, and her part in it, had been a hoax, or sting. What she had in fact said was that the *fist* – which at first she had thought confirmed her clairvoyance – was a fake.

If it was a fake, what was it, and how did it get to its place on the sea bed? Certainly there were individuals in Rhodes who stood to make their fortunes if the remains of the Colossus were found; but as I pointed out at the time, those fortunes would depend on

Psychic Research

Brian Inglis is a London-based veteran of over twenty books in the fields of parapsychology and fringe medicine, including a history of psychic research, *Natural and Supernatural* (1977).

genuine, or at least cleverly-faked, remains.

So far as I know, the 'fist' remains a mystery. It weighed a ton; why should anybody have gone to the trouble and expense of planting it where it was found? It was suggested that it had been picked up during dredging, a process which could also have accounted for the gaps between the 'knuckles' which had made it fist-like; but this was quickly ruled out.

My guess was that Ann Dankbaar's clairvoyance was genuine, but 'dyslexic'. The divers found some indications that there had been a settlement – as if the level of the land had fallen, or that of the Mediterranean had risen. If there was, she may have 'seen' something but put the wrong interpretation on it. If so, the discovery of the 'fist' could have been an unfortunate accident, distracting attention from what might have been a profitable investigation, even if it had not disclosed the Colossus.

Or the whole affair may have arisen simply because Ann's psychic powers – which I witnessed at first hand, in trivial ways, in Rhodes – let her down. I felt sorry for her that the impression left – echoed, I fear, even in FT [see **FT49**:22] – was that she had been involved in a calculated deception. One or two of the Rhodesians I met were certainly chancers, but they were not so stupid as to plant that 'fist'.

So that leaves the questions: what was it? and how did it come to be where it was found? Perhaps some psychic can enlighten us!

Black Shuck

Cryptozoology

Michael Goss is a freelance writer living in Essex. He has written *Evidence for Phantom Hitch-Hikers* (1984) and contributed articles on folklore and the paranormal to many periodicals.

Black Shuck the demon dog is back again; or he was as recently as Summer 1989 around Buckhurst Hill, Essex, where he alarmed a trio of 17-year-old boys walking to a party through a local graveyard, and soon thereafter a motorist, on the bonnet of whose car he landed. These incidents are fondly recalled among Epping students to whom I teach English literature. Black Shuck greatly enlarged their comprehension of the 40th chapter in Thomas Hardy's *Far From The Madding Crowd*, in which the pitiable Fanny is befriended by a preternaturally large black dog who materializes in the vicinity of Grey's Bridge on the outskirts of Casterbridge (a.k.a. Dorchester):

> *a huge, heavy, quiet creature... of too strange and mysterious a nature to belong to any variety among those of popular nomenclature... the ideal embodiment of canine greatness... Night, in its sad, solemn and benevolent aspect... personified.*

Now as then, Grey's Bridge spans the river Frome. It is mildly interesting that Hardy (who almost certainly knew of the Black Dog – Wessex being one of its most heavily-trodden stamping grounds) should choose *that* venue for Fanny's encounter. The Black Dog's association with water has long been noticed by researchers, starting with Ethel Rudkin's seminal review of current Lincolnshire stories in *Folklore*

(Summer 1938) and continuing through Steve Moore (*FT16*, June 1976) and Ivan Bunn (*FT17* August 1976 and *Lantern 18*, Summer 1977).

Conventionally, the Black Dog is described as being as big as a calf and with eyes (usually flaming ones) as large as saucers. Eyes in the plural: the Buckhurst Hill version had but one, planted Cyclops-style in the centre of its forehead.

This is unusual, but not unprecedented. The Norfolk writer W.A. Dutt (quoted in the better-known James Wentworth Day's *Ghosts & Witches*, 1954) specifies that Black Shuck has but a solitary Cyclops eye – he even uses that phrase. Several years ago, I came upon an illustration in a children's ghostie book which portrayed Shuck in the same way. It is tempting to guess that the Buckhurst Hill creature was derived from some such source. But that would suggest that the four witnesses had come across the same books I had; that they based their fabricated stories upon them, if they *were* fabricated; or that the Cyclopsian detail had permeated their consciousness deeply enough to make them perceive (hallucinatorily?) their own Black Dog as one-eyed. If the stories were *not* fabricated, that is.

I used to be rather fond of speculating that popular iconography, oral or printed, influences how witnesses perceive and/or describe apparitional events. I'm less fond of

this 'model' now, if only because there seems so little experimental evidence to confirm it. But let all that pass; whether the Buckhurst Hill phenomenon was a folk-legend, hallucinatory fact or anything else, it intrigues me to think that the Black Dog is still around. We seem to be losing, or to have lost, so many of our traditional revenants. Does anyone still tell phantom coach stories – as facts, I mean, and preferably as first-, second-, or even third-person, within-living-memory experiences? Do screaming skulls still scream? And what the hell became of the Cauld Lad of Hylton? [*Editors' note: for an Italian 1968 phantom coach story, first-hand, see FT53:78.*]

Jeremy Harte's *Cuckoo Pounds and Singing Barrows* (1986) makes the fascinating point that the Black Dog formerly occupied the place in the popular imagination since usurped by the Alien Big Cat – or rather:

"It is as if the great cat apparitions formed a secondary class of ghosts which only began to thrive after the eclipse of black dog traditions; one thinks of the parallel conflict of red and grey squirrels."

In the past, Black Dogs were significant: omens of dire misfortune, guardians of treasure, or (as per Hardy) of unprotected females. Now, when they appear at all, we're at a loss to decipher their purpose – unless startling teenage partygoers in churchyards or dancing on car bonnets be purposes in themselves. Given the endangered status of the species, though, perhaps we shouldn't complain too loudly. Nor care how many eyes it has.

Illustration from the title page of *A Straunge Wunder in Bongay*, which describes the black dog seen in Bungay, Suffolk, in 1577

UFOs: Really Fantastic?

Many books about UFOs confidently assert that flying saucers are real vehicles visiting our planet. The craft are made of solid nuts and bolts and their pilots are the alien equivalent of flesh and blood. They can have a tangible impact on people or animals if they try to abduct them, and their craft can leave traces on the ground.

A basic problem for such ideas is that UFOs and alien beings have a ghost-like manner. Alien beings walk through solid walls; huge UFOs hovering over highly populated areas are seen by a few 'selected' witnesses; and the messages from the aliens are esoteric and confusing if not downright deceitful.

Very few UFOs are seen in broad daylight by several independent witnesses. More often they are encountered by a lone witness at night, in a remote location.

Fair enough; there are cases that involve traces of landing marks, photographs, movie film, video or radar recordings. These indicate that physical objects have been present, but the majority of this data is very controversial and ambiguous. For example, photographs of an out-of-focus blob of light could be anything on, or out of, this world. On the other hand, photographs that show a detailed, structured craft in bright sunlight look too faked!

In the past, instances of 'good' photographic evidence have been undermined when they were submitted for rigorous analysis. Photographs that have been accepted by ufologists can cause embarrassment when, perhaps years later, the photographer reveals that they are fakes (and often simply done). We have only to consider the classic photographs of the Cottingley fairies to realise how fakes can fool the great and the famous for long periods. (No doubt there are still people who believe them to be true.)

To get around this problem, researchers, such as Jacques Vallée, have proposed that UFOs are indeed technological, and that "during the observation, the UFO is a real, physical material object" and "The (UFO) technology triggers psychic effects, either purposely or as a side effect of the presence of a UFO." (*UFOs 1947-1987*, Fortean Tomes, 1987, p318.)

In addition, Valée believes that 'their' technology is being used to manipulate our social and cultural conditions, but does not say why they are doing this. Certainly, they are not exploiting it definitively to convince us of their presence in our everyday reality.

I respect Vallée's work, but I feel that he wants to have his cake and eat it. If UFOs are a combination of ghost and machine, we do not have to play by the rules of normal scientific inquiry. It would be impossible for us, given our own level of technological development, to capture or even adequately record them. Worse: such a viewpoint would allow us to explain lots of other baffling things, because if UFOs are ghost-machines, anything we cannot explain might be caused by them or have similar attributes.

Vallée's logic leads us to this conclusion, which implies that we now have to research UFOs in a special manner. We have to be aware that they are intelligent and cunning; that they can elude the fastest fighter jet; and, if they wish, they can turn your mind to jelly – a fate that has befallen several notable ufologists over the years. Indeed, we are entering a psychic twilight zone where the magical of the UFO operators might entrance you at any moment.

Ufology becomes a type of fantasy game that confirms the worst fears of sceptics and non-believers. This apparently explains why some UFO investigators can be sane in most areas of their lives, yet incredibly naive and gullible in their chosen subject. They want to believe in exotic

Ufology

Nigel Watson works as a copywriter in North London. He has had a long interest in the sociological aspects of the UFO phenomenon. He recently self-published a book about UFO witnesses *Portraits of Alien Encounters* (1991). He has just published, with Darren Slade, an analysis of Steven Spielberg's use of supernatural motifs, to be featured in *FT* next issue.

visitors from beyond – but deep down, even they might not really believe that the aliens are solid, physical beings.

A case that indicates this view is the report of a 'grey alien' by Terry Jones. In the early hours of the morning, he saw from his bed that "the visitor was outlined in a dark cherry red colour". What did he do next… strike up a conversation about the intergalactic fellowship? Welcome the visitor to planet Earth? Ask for the secret of immortality, or three wishes? What did you do, Terry? "I just looked at it, thought they would not do anything now, so turned over and went to sleep."

Surely, if he had seen a real alien, he could at least have made the effort to keep awake! No wonder conclusive proof has not been placed before an expectant world; we are just too blasé.

SPECIAL CORRESPONDENTS

AFRICA: Cynthia Hind (Zimbabwe), Ion Alexis Will (Here & There). **AUSTRALIA:** Greg Axford (Vic.), Paul Cropper (NSW), Rex Gilroy (NSW), Tony Healy (ACT). **BELGIUM:** Henri Prémont. **CANADA:** Brian Chapman (BC), Dwight Whalen (Ont.). **DENMARK:** Lars Thomas. **ENGLAND:** Clare Blamey, Bruce Chatterton, Peter Christie, Mat Coward, Hilary Evans, Peter Hope Evans, Alan Gardiner, Mick Goss, Chris Hall, Jeremy Harte, Brian Inglis, Jake Kirkwood, Joseph Lang, Alexis Lykiard, Nick Maloret, Valerie Martin, Kevin McClure, John Michell, Ralph Noyes, Nigel Pennick, Andy Roberts, Paul Screeton, Doc Shiels, Karl Shuker, Bob Skinner, Anthony Smith, Paul R. Thomas, Nigel Watson, Owen Whiteoak, Steve Wrathall. **FRANCE:** Jean-Louis Brodu, Bernard Heuvelmans, Michel Meurger. **GERMANY:** Walter J. Langbein, Ulrich Magin. **GREECE:** S.C. Tavuchis. **HONGKONG:** Phillip Bruce. **ICELAND:** V. Kip Hansen. **IRELAND:** Peter Costello. **JAPAN:** Masaru Mori, Shigeo Yokoyama. **NEW ZEALAND:** Peter Hassall. **NORTHERN IRELAND:** Caryl Sibbett. **POLAND:** Leszek Matela. **RUSSIA:** Vladimir Rubtsov. **SCOTLAND:** David Burns, Stuart Herkes, Roger Musson, Roland Watson, Jake Williams. **SWEDEN:** Anders Liljegren, Sven Rosén. **USA:** Larry E. Arnold (PA), Mark Chorvinsky (MD), Loren Coleman (ME), David Fideler (MI), Mark A. Hall (MN), Michael Hoffman (CA), John Keel (NYC), Phil Ledger (CA), Kurt Lothmann (TX), Gary S. Mangiacopra (CN), Ray Nelke (MO), Scott Parker (TX), Jim Reicken (NY), Ron Schaffner (OH), Margo Schwadron (NY), Chuck Shephard (DC), Dennis Stacy (TX), Joseph Swatek (NB), Joseph Trainor (MA), Jeffrey Vallance (CA), Robert Anton Wilson (CA), Joseph W. Zarzynski (NY). **WALES:** Janet & Colin Bord, Richard Holland, Joe Kelly.

THE SUPERNATURAL

Due out in the spring, so probably already published when you read this, are: Alan Robson's *Grisly Trails and Ghostly Tales* (Virgin Books, £4.99 pb, March), which is a 'magical mystery tour of hauntings and happenings' in the north of England; and *The Supernatural Murders* (edited by Jonathan Goodman), thirteen true crime stories by well-known writers, all with some supernatural connection (Piatkus Books, £13.95, April). *Places of Witchcraft* by Kevin and Ingrid Carlyon (Robert Hale, £13.95, June) investigates British sites with witchcraft connections from the past to the present.

Hecate's Fountain by Kenneth Grant (Skoob Books, £24.99) describes magical contact with alien intelligences. Not having seen this text, I do not know whether these aliens include any claiming to originate from other planets, a subject tackled by Peter Hough and Jenny Randles in their book *Looking for the Aliens* (Blandford, £14.99 hb, £8.95 pb, March, and in the USA from Sterling in late April). *Life Beyond Planet Earth?* by Janet and Colin Bord (Grafton, £7.99 pb, June) also explores the possibility of alien intelligence having visited Earth. A very different approach to ufology is taken by David Morris who relates it to 19th-century occultism and theosophy, and examines them as modern cultural phenomena in his book *The Masks of Lucifer: Technology and the Occult in 20th Century Popular Literature* (Batsford, £17.99, March).

UFOs AND COSMOLOGY

Several potentially interesting UFO books are due from American publishers this spring, notably Jacques Vallée's *Revelations: Alien Contact and Human Deception* (Ballantine, $20), a hard-hitting criticism of some aspects of ufology in the 1990s to be released in the UK by Souvenir Press in April (£14.99 hb). Vallée is also publishing *UFO Chronicles of the Soviet Union* (Ballantine, $18); and a third title, *Forbidden Science*, is due in May from North Atlantic, being his journal of his work with Professor Hynek in the aftermath of the famous Condon Report on UFOs. David M. Jacobs is another respected American ufologist; his *Secret Life* (Simon & Schuster, $21) contains extracts from hypnotic regression sessions with 39 people who believe they have been abducted by UFO entities. The second volume of Jerome Clark's impressive UFO encyclopædia publishes this spring: *The Emergence of a Phenomenon: UFOs from the Beginning through 1959* (Omnigraphics, $$85 hb). The first volume was *UFOs in the 1980s; volume three*, due in late 1993, will be titled *Abductions and Other Events of 1960-79*.

From ufology to cosmology, and three titles for those who like to stretch their minds... *The Mind's Sky: Human Intelligence in a Cosmic Context*, by Timothy Ferris (Bantam, £16.99 hb, March), explores the relationship between the perceived universe and the mind that perceives it, also touching on dreams, precognition and life after death; while John Gribbin deals with time travel and black holes in his new book *In Search of the Edge of Time* (Bantam, £14.99 hb, April). Robert Matthews tackles basic questions about the origins of life on Earth in his attempt at *Unravelling the Mind of God: Mysteries at the Frontier of Science* (Virgin, £15.99 hb, March).

PARAPSYCHOLOGY

Parapsychology also encompasses basic questions whose answers have eluded us thus far, and two encyclopædias demonstrate the breadth of the subject: *The Encyclopedia of the Paranormal* by Lynn Picknett (Papermac, £12.99 pb, April), and *The Paranormal: An Illustrated Encyclopedia* by Stuart Gordon (Headline, £18.99 hb, May). Richard Broughton's *Parapsychology: The Controversial Science* (Rider, £19.99 hb, £10.99 pb, March) is a serious study of recent research by an active parapsychologist; while at the other end of the spectrum is Robert Wood's biography of Maryanne Foyster, the wife of the one-time vicar of Borley who was heavily involved in the 'haunting' of the rectory there, *The Widow of Borley* (Duckworth, £14.99 hb).

A thorough study of the spontaneous combustion of the human body is badly needed, and Jenny Randles and Peter Hough are offering one this year – *Spontaneous Human Combustion* (Robert Hale, £14.95 hb, July).

EARTH MYSTERIES

Some books on prehistoric sites and antiquities which are likely to interest readers are Dr G.T. Meaden's *The Stonehenge Solution: Sacred Marriage and the Goddess* (Souvenir, £18.99 hb, April), which presents a new view of Neolithic peoples and their monuments; Michael Poynder's *Pi In the Sky* (Rider/Shambhala, £25 hb, April), which explores the skills and beliefs of Stone Age man via mathematics, cosmology, physics and archaeology; Paul Devereux's *Symbolic Landscapes: The Dreamtime Earth and Avebury's Open Secrets* (Gothic Image, £12.95 pb, July), which discusses mythologized landscapes (Celtic, Australian, Greek, etc) and the interaction of mind and land in ancient times; and also by Paul Devereux, *Secrets of Ancient and Sacred Sites* (Blandford, £18.99 hb, July), which is a big, full-colour book describing over twenty World Heritage sites.

Later in the year, look out for a third title from Paul Devereux, *Shamanism and the Mystery Lines* (Quantum, September), a major new study of Leys and landscape lines. Jenny Randles' autumn book is *UFOs: An Observer's Illustrated Guide* (Anaya, October), a heavily illustrated book described as 'a complete guide to UFOs and how to see them'.

This instalment of Book Alert contains no cryptozoology titles, but a major work is due out this autumn from Dr Karl Shuker, *The Encyclopedia of New and Rediscovered Animals* (HarperCollins, October).

Finally, a research request from Jenny Randles in connection with a new book project. She would like to hear from "any reader who during 1992 has, or comes across, a paranormal experience which they believe is probative of the supernatural as opposed to being potentially explicable. All cases will be credited to their investigators and any used in any significant way will receive a free copy of the book, when published in 1993." Write to her at 37 Heathbank Road, Cheadle Heath, Stockport, Cheshire.

BOOK ALERT

Janet Bord

From magic to murder, from SHC to shamanism: quite a mixed bag of books of likely interest to Forteans is on offer this year.

REVIEWS
New and recent publications of interest

THE NOX ANTHOLOGY:
DARK DOCTRINES
Ed. by Stephen Sennitt & Gareth Hewitson-May.

New World Publishing, Fairpiece, Mill Rd, Gringley on the Hill, Doncaster, DN10 4QT; 1991, pb £7.99 inc p&p, pp160, illus.

It's curious, perhaps, that Forteans generally make little use or reference to the work of occultists and magicians ... they, after all, seem to know our work well enough. Surely there are parallels worth investigating between the conscious evocation of entities and, say, the unconscious evocation of a poltergeist; or between the deliberate exploration of other realities and the unsought intervention of another reality in a UFO abduction case.

Perhaps because so much of Fortean research interfaces with a scientific and academic establishment we tend to use the same methods, with references, `facts' and `proofs', while a great deal of magical material is subjective or anecdotal; even so, the theory and methodology of magical practice must be of interest. Perhaps we fear that if we admit the possibility that reality can be changed by something so tenuous as the magician's will, then at best our rationalist opponents will laugh at us, or at worst, our *own* reality structure will come under threat. After all, whether you're a Fortean or a Chaos mathematician, who *really* wants to believe that the flapping of a butterfly's wing across the ocean can result in a hurricane that blows your house down? Worse still if a magician has done it deliberately!

It has to be said that even a convinced magician would find a considerable amount of the magical books on the market, especially those from `New Age' publishers, pretty half-baked (and some may say, deserving of total incineration!), but then that's also true of many commercial `Fortean' books. Nonetheless, there are a number of serious magical writers, especially in this country, whose work tends to appear in small press magazines and limited edition books. Some of those writers are represented here.

Like all anthologies, the contents of *Dark Doctrines* are of varying interest, and one or two assume the reader to be

already conversant with occult theory and terminology. But we have here a broad range of material on the `darker' side, including Jivaro head-hunting; the magical aspects of H.P. Lovecraft's Cthulhu mythos; conspiracy theory and the magical side of serial-killing; and alleged Satanic ritual abuse. Two items might be picked out as of particular interest to Forteans. Phil Hines' `The Physics of Evocation – A Mythos Perspective', roams through Chaos maths and Chaos magic to the Earth Lights phenomenon and the possibility of evoking entities in fault areas. And there's a splendid analysis of the psychology of the Satanic ritual abuse panic, `In Praise of Devil Worship', by the everentertaining Ramsey Dukes. Highly recommended, and well worth exploring, if only to get another viewpoint on things.

Steve Moore

THE SEARCH FOR THE MANCHURIAN CANDIDATE
by John Marks.

W.W. Norton (London & New York), 1991; pb £7.95, pp264, notes, bib, index.

In the aftermath of World War II, the United States was startled to confront the rapid establishment of Communism in Eastern Europe and Asia. Military muscle, including nuclear capability, was developed with alarming dispatch by the Russians and Chinese, and their Marxist ideologies seemed to

preach global domination. Into this world, where a shooting conflict could lead to atomic destruction, the Cold War was born. Its front-line army was the CIA.

In recent years, much has been written about the CIA's clandestine ventures into foreign policy, but little has been documented about their pioneering research into the field of human behaviour. In this book, John Marks tells an alarming story about the CIA's quest for the ultimate psychological weapon – a sure-fire process of mind control. He has based his research on numerous interviews and volumes of once classified documents, and his narrative style is clear and objective.

The goal of CIA research in this field was to determine whether technologies could be found utterly to transform and control normal or usual patterns of behaviour. Practically, could an enemy spy be unwittingly manipulated to divulge sensitive information, or could a CIA operative be triggered, becoming an automaton capable of committing any desired act? Successful attainment of these goals would give the United States incalculable advantage over its communist enemies and little expense was spared in funding research and field studies. Top-rank academics and private-sector researchers were funded by the CIA to engage in behavioural studies (often without a subject's knowledge or consent), and two areas came to dominate their activities: chemical substances and psychological manipulation.

In the early 1950s, the CIA first heard of a chemical compound, developed in Switzerland, which induced hallucinations and psychosis. The substance – LSD – was odourless, colourless and could easily be slipped to an unwitting victim. During the early days of LSD research by the CIA, the drug was widely and frequently tested by some of America's most eminent physicians and academics (eg. Norbert Weiner, Buckminster Fuller, etc), as well as by their own top-level operatives. The profound effect on mental perception caused by the drug gave the CIA hope that it could be used to disorient entire populations as well as single targets, thus causing havoc and disorder among the enemy.

The extent to which the CIA believed in the potential of LSD is a subject central to Marks' work, and he uncovers a shocking catalogue of abuses meted out by the CIA in its tests. Numerous people – usually from minorities, mental patients, prisoners or low-life urban dwellers – were unwitting day-trippers whose reactions were carefully recorded by the CIA experimenters. In one extreme case, a black mental patient from Kentucky was kept on LSD for 77 successive days.

In the field of psychology, the CIA funded research into a wide variety of phenomena and practices. Everything from hypnosis and parapsychology to extremes of sensory deprivation and electro-shock therapies were explored. Marks highlights some gruesome cases in great detail, where CIA experiments into personality repatterning were attempted by Canadian doctors. Their methods included a variation of long-term sedation and heavy-handed electro-shock treatments. Similarly, ethics were abandoned in the exploration of hypnosis; using many of its own employees, the CIA pushed unwitting individuals to wild extremes of behaviour in their quest for mind control.

In a decade of this kind of research and millions of dollars in expenditure, the CIA learned absolutely nothing new. Its utter disregard for scientific method and ethics and its destruction of numerous lives (including a few documented deaths) was pursued with a genuine belief in the national interest. Finally, they discovered their best methods of manipulation were those already in their arsenal: blackmail, threats or outright violence. John Marks' readable and compelling book documents a unique American tragedy which portends the dangers of blindly combining patriotic enthusiasm and unharnessed 'scientific' research.

John O'Brien

THE SUPERNATURAL MURDERS
edited by Jonathan Goodman.
Piatkus, London; 1992; hb £13.99, pp198, photos.

Subtitled 'Classic True-Crime Stories', this book would seem to be ideal for the reader intrigued by the psychology of crime and welcoming an added supernatural dimension. In reality, however, the collection is disappointing. It consists of tired old cases (eg. Amityville, Charles Walton), with some of the chapters written over 50 years ago; and many have only the barest mention of supernatural factors. Certainly no attempt is made to discuss or analyse inexplicable features when they do arise, such as a mother's recurring dream of her murdered son lying at the bottom of a well, which led to the discovery of his body in 1922.

The book is fine for an afternoon's entertaining reading, but makes no pretence to be a serious study of the supernatural in murder cases. That's a subject still waiting to be researched by someone with a detailed knowledge of both the supernatural and violent crime.

Janet Bord.

A DICTIONARY OF CELTIC MYTH AND LEGEND
by Miranda J Green
Thames & Hudson, London; 1992, hb, £16.95, pp240, subject index, bib, 243 illos.

A welcome reference work that covers the length and breadth of Celtic Europe, from Ireland to the Black Sea, although limited in time to the decline of Celtic paganism, about 400 AD; Arthurian, later legendary, and fairy-lore material is not included. Even so, with its double-column pages, the book contains an immense amount of material. A concise introduction covers the Celts and their society, and the nature of the evidence, which is largely drawn from archæology, references in Classical writers, and surviving Welsh and Irish literature. The entries themselves cover divinities and legendary persons, sites, symbols, animals, natural phenomena and concepts.

The dictionary is particularly strong on deities from the Romano-Celtic period, and those known only from inscriptions and archæological finds, which makes it a valuable companion to the usual run of books concentrating only on the literary sources. Like most mythological dictionaries, the entries are necessarily brief; but unlike many similar books, each entry carries its own references to the extensive bibliography, which is a valuable resource in itself. A necessary work for anyone interested in Celtic mysteries.

Steve Moore

CROP CIRCLES:
HARBINGERS OF WORLD CHANGE
Edited by Alick Bartholomew.
Gateway Books, Bath; 1991; hb £14.95, pp192, colour plates, photos and other illus, refs, index.

The cerealogical 'anomaly cluster' continues apace. Having banished the plasma vortex, the contributors set out to approach the circles phenomenon through meaning rather than mechanics. While there are some excellent articles, too often a pattern develops where the writer takes refuge in his/her particular brand of esotericism, using crop circles as no more than a closing argument. Too often a failure of imagination leads to anthropocentrism, taking us back to benign Space Brothers bombarding benighted Earth with good vibes, Atlantis, Native Indians, and the general state of the world/cosmos. This leads to over-credulity, especially with the 'channelled' material (banal as ever) and some of the more obvious hoaxes. We do need this kind of 'brainstorming' to approach the phenomenon, but such wishful thinking and pseudo-religiosity are a dead end.

There is much stimulating thought and image elsewhere in the book, with impressive contributions by John Michell, George Wingfield and Peter Cedrowen Taylor. The best comes at the end, in Stanley Messenger's 'Creating the Phenomenon'. He develops a surprisingly under-developed area: the medium of the crop and the field, and the nature of the affected part of the crop itself, raising rather different questions from those of the rescue-fantasists.

Of course, the book is replete with superb photographs (though some incorrect captions are irritating): forget the sun-lamp, and spend an evening contemplating the Barbary Castle and Ickleton manifestations. It's a pity that John Michell's *Cerealogist* article on the 3:1 symbolism of Barbary isn't here to extend the force of the image. However, the inclusion of several of John Langrish's plans is most welcome.

While recognising that this book is not intended to be a 'Crop Circle Yearbook 1991', the lack of factual data is disappointing. Thus one is told that many circles are of the same dimensions as Stonehenge, but it is impossible to check this factoid. Given the past decade of cerealogical activity, the tabulation of data concerning places/time of year/formation is essential.

I can't recommend this book wholeheartedly, because of the patchiness of the material. It's a pity the photos aren't available in a cheaper format (see last year's *Crop Circles – The Latest Evidence*). However, any cerealogist impatiently awaiting the summer should find some stimulation here.

Denis Browne

BEYOND THE BLUE HORIZON:
by Edwin C. Krupp.
HarperCollins, NY; 1991; hb $35, pp387, illus, bib, index

Beyond the Blue Horizon is big in size and ambition. Dr Krupp aims high; he wants to do for astronomy what Joseph Campbell's *Masks of God* did for mythology. A better comparison would be with de Santillana and von Dechend's *Hamlet's Mill*, a pioneering study of the origins of human knowledge which forged a mighty bridge between the magic of mythology and the practicality of the earliest sciences, or with the great encyclopædic works of the French astronomer Flammarion.

Chapters are devoted to broad subjects, for example: the sun, the planets, the zodiac, thunder and lightning, the morning star, the seven sisters, the Milky Way, the pole star, the great bear, calendars, the sky as the location of heaven and the abode of the gods, the seasons and agriculture, creation myths and so on in no discernible order. The book is saturated with paintings and photos as well as explanatory drawings, making this an exciting visual reference work as well.

In reaffirming the view that the origin of astronomical ideas, terms and names was concurrent with the origins of human culture itself, Dr Krupp has in effect brought *Hamlet's Mill* up to date. He confines his discussions to the anthropological origins of astronomy, and popularises the many detailed scholarly arguments about dating, language, customs, history and archæology there is an extensive bibliography if you want it.

Dr Krupp writes very well, and is always mindful of his audience; not surprising as he is director of the Griffith Observatory in Los Angeles and has been instrumental in raising the public appeal of its services. In case younger readers miss the point, Dr Krupp demonstrates the universality of mythologising about the heavens with significant discussions about

UFOs, aliens, abductions, science-fiction films, the 'ancient astronaut' school of cosmology, and New Age cults based on these and related subjects. For me, this was the most fascinating aspect of the book; reading the considered views of a widely-read and articulate astronomer about our favourite subject-matter. Dr Krupp can take his place alongside his eminent heroes because he shares their open-minded and inspirational values.

Bob Rickard

CROPCIRCLE COMMUNIQUÉ
Circlevision, Box 36, Ludlow, Shropshire SY8 3ZZ, UK; 1992; video (PAL for UK) £14.99, or (NTSC for USA) $35, 75 mins.

Sceptics and avid fans of crop circles, despite their many differences about the origins and meaning of these artifacts, have been unanimous in declaring their peculiar beauty. The main reason for the success of books on crop circles – like those reviewed above – has been the power and attractiveness of the large glossy full-colour photographs; seeing these agriglyphs or pictograms (as the main researchers are fond of calling them) on living film has an even greater subliminal impact.

This professionally made 75-minute documentary, produced and directed by John McNish, uses the best footage from a variety of sources – from pilot-cerealogist Busty Taylor, to media-commissioned news-gathering teams – intercut with specially-shot studio interviews with some of the leading players representing a spread of views: Colin Andrews, Pat Delgado, Terence Meaden, Busty Taylor, Michael Green and George Wingfield, together with Leonie Starr (an astrologer and co-founder of the Centre for Crop Circle Studies),

Richard Andrews (a dowser), and Jürgen Krönig (a journalist). The absence of many other leading, able and qualified commentators is a puzzle; nevertheless this is a video everyone, even the know-it-alls, should have.

The presentation standards are of high, network quality and it usefully documents the evolution of circle design complexity. It was actually quite enjoyable, unless you take notice of the number of sweeping and unsubstantiated statements, and the closing appeal to New Age adoration of the weeping Earth Mother. Other doubtful points were: the disappointingly vague animation of Meaden's vortex theory; the visually stunning yet quite incidental voyage into fractal geometry (inspired by the Cambridge design); film of the 'UFO' which seemed to buzz a test flight of Concorde, then explained as "perhaps an object in the gate of the camera"); and Ms Starr's out of place arrogance ("Only astrologers can understand these symbols").

Some of the choicest bits include: film (by German tourists) of a ball of light crossing a corn field near a circle; Doug'n'Dave chortling over several they might have made earlier; the point that normally brittle stems of the oilseed rape plant had been bent intact in formations on the Isle of Wight and elsewhere; and an instance during an ærial view in which the corn moves mysteriously and parts as a hare (a witch-animal to mediæval Britons) penetrates the ovate circle, bounds across the flattened corn and is gone.

The many stunning ærial sequences in which the camera lovingly caresses the fertile curves of the feminine circles suggest a new field of subliminal eroticism – soft corn, anyone?

Bob Rickard

PARAPSYCHOLOGY:
THE CONTROVERSIAL SCIENCE
by Richard Broughton.
Rider, London; 1992; hb £19.99, pp408, sources, notes, index.

Dr Broughton is an experienced parapsych-ologist with an open-minded yet scientific approach to his subject, and so his overview is relatively free of bias. He explain the nature of psychic experiences, describes the current research, and assesses its future, all in a readable style uncluttered by jargon.

Well worth reading for an honest appraisal of parapsychology; and it is to be hoped that a cheaper paperback edition will follow, to bring the book within reach of more pockets.

Janet Bord

All illustrations are taken from *Beyond The Blue Horizon: Myths and Legends of the Sun, Moon, Stars and Planetss* by Dr E C Krupp

LETTERS
Readers write

CHRISTIAN ABUSE

■ Michael Shoemaker [*FT61*:61] is quite right that there is a germ of truth to the ritual child abuse rumours, though unfortunately (as I pointed out in *Magonia* 40) the amply documented cases involve Christian parents who abused their children under the guise of exorcising the devil from them. It is ironic indeed that one of the rumours circulating in the UK involves a child roasted in an oven. This is partly derived from the worldwide urban legend, 'The Hippie Babysitter'; but it also owes something to the horrific 1984 Auburn, Maine, case in which Cynthia Palmer, assisted by her fundamentalist boyfriend John Lane, pushed her four-year-old daughter Angela into a red hot oven and propped the door closed until she was dead, drowning out her screams with religious music. (Cuttings are available for those of steely stomachs).

Still, directing readers to Terry's *The Ultimate Evil*, Kahaner's *Cults That Kill* and Wedge's *The Satan Killer* for "hard evidence" is like recommending *Mein Kampf* and *The Protocols of the Elders of Zion* as good sources for Jewish history. These three books have been lambasted by every authority on the phenomenon as illogical and unprofessional. Shoemaker might better look at Robert Hicks's *In Pursuit of Satan*, Phillips Stevens Jr's essay "Satanism: Where Are The Folklorists?" in *New York Folklore* 15(1989):1-22, Jeffrey S. Victor's and my own essays in *Western Folklore* 49(1990):27-81, and the soundly skeptical collection *The Satanism Scare* ed. James T. Richardson, Joel Best and David G. Bromley.

Yes, kids in the US (and probably in the UK as well) do go out into the woods and perform weird rites (usually around a keg of beer). They do vandalise graveyards and paint 'satanic' graffiti on buildings. But how does this support in any way the claim that there are hundreds of thousands of multi-generational families of Satanists who hurt children just for the hell of it? To make another analogy, one might just as easily say that the presence of unexplained glowing lights in the sky somehow proves that aliens are stealing hundreds of gallons of cattle blood for reasons not easily explained in human terms. Maybe so – but let's see the evidence that *directly* supports the claim.

Professor Bill Ellis
Hazleton, Pennsylvania

DUTCH FUNNY BUSINESS

■ In your round-up of 'satanic abuse' cases [FT61:34], you made mention of the happenings at Oude Pekela in the Netherlands. It might interest you to know, especially as you did a round-up of sinister clowns in the same issue [p38], that the children in Oude Pekela were allegedly lured away by several clowns.

The authorities have never successfully got to the bottom of what happened there. Up to 300 children were lured away according to some press reports – which would mean practically every child in the place. The emphasis was on pædophilia, not satanic abuse, but the conclusion seemed to be that it was a case of mass hysteria.

Robin Pascoe
Amsterdam

HALF-BAKED NEW AGE

■ I hope that FT is not going to degenerate into an anti-rationalist science bashing rag, because judging from the last issue (FT61) that's the way it seems to be heading.

We have Dennis Stacy concerning himself with attempted murder amongst biologists; so what? His column is called Science Watch, not Scientists Watch. We have Bob Rickard sneering at astronomers because they admit to making a mistake. Good for them, I say. It's interesting to compare the reaction of the astronomical establishment with that of certain elements within the crop circle establishment who are never going to admit that crop circles could be man-made artifacts and that their hypotheses could be wrong. We have Brian Inglis criticising people who realise they may have been fooled by the likes of Uri Geller. Finally we have Anthony Shiels's piece degenerating into abuse towards James Randi.

There are enough publications around peddling half-baked New Age mysticism to the gullible; there are few which aim to present curious, entertaining and possibly unexplained reports to the public without ramming a point of view down their throat.

John Rowe
London

■ *The editors reply: We can assure our readers that our non-partisan editorial position remains unchanged and we disagree with Mr Rowe's interpretations. We don't see why Science Watch cannot occasionally include observing the behaviour of scientists. We don't think that Bob Rickard was "sneering at astronomers": after all, he says "chortling at the mistakes of scientists holds no real appeal for us"; And what is the "crop circle establishment", for heaven's sake?*

Brian Inglis wasn't so much criticising those who realise they may have been fooled by the likes of Geller, as those who succumb to retrocognitive dissonance against their better judgement, which is not the same thing at all. While we hold no brief for Geller, we think Doc Shiels was quite restrained about Randi, whose humbug and bullying 'fundamentalist materialism' give scepticism a bad name (see, for instance, his behaviour in the CSICOP sTarbaby scandal of the 1970s exposed in Fate October 1981, or during the Benveniste inquisition, detailed in FT52:40). Randi is about as 'skeptical' (as they spell it across the pond) as the Democratic People's Republic of Korea is 'democratic'.

We would be delighted to run original and/or entertaining columns from genuine sceptics; come on, send us your contributions!

LETTERS

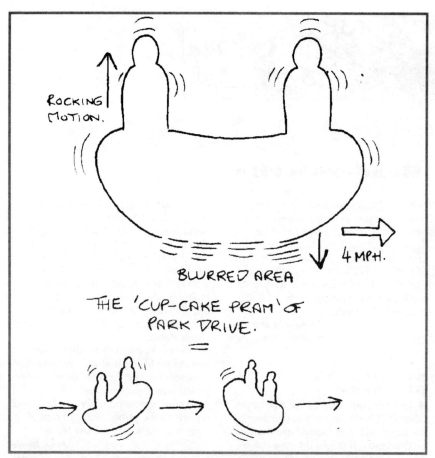

Art Wetherell's drawing of the 'cup-like pram' he saw in Park Drive, Grimsby, in June 1975. Was Art's youthful imagination running riot, or did aliens really appear in this phalic object?

WHAT WAS IT?

■ I must tell you of a mysterious object which I encountered in June 1975.

I recall sitting on the grass of our local park, in Grimsby, one night with a schoolfriend. We were planning a shopping trip to Hull the following day, and were eagerly discussing the records we wanted to buy. From where we were sitting, at the very edge of a large expanse of lawn used for bowling, we had a clear view of Park Drive to our right; it's stretch broken here and there by clumps of trees.

It was definitely fully dark – thought I forget what time – when an object came into view, travelling left to right along Park Drive and in full illumination of the street lights. I estimate our distance from the road to be no more than 30 yards – I frequently re-visit this spot so I am pretty sure of the distance – yet for some strange reason, we could not make optical sense of the object we both turned to look at.

Firstly, it was luminous white and its edges were blurred, while it travelled about walking speed along the centre of the road. The main body of the object resembled a large pram without wheels. At each end of the 'pram' was seated a figure, featureless and white; in fact they were hardly figures at all, but more like skittles or milk bottles with rounded 'heads' [*see accompanying sketch*].

The most alarming aspect of the object and 'occupants' was the way 'they' rocked up and down in see-saw fashion, in unison with the carriage. There was no-one pushing this object, and it was devoid of superstructure (handle, hood, wheels, etc). It did not hover above the ground, but seemed to blur into the ground where the wheels should be.

We watched it for around two minutes before it disappeared behind trees – it may have turned into a driveway at that point – and never re-appeared.

Strangely, and I still can't understand why, we never gave chase for a closer look – we just gazed at the object in bemused acceptance.

Art Wetherell
Stallingborough, South Humerside.

COME IN NUMBER 27

■ Recently, I spent the night with a woman I had just met. In the morning we exchanged telephone numbers. The second half of her number began with a 27, the same as her house number. How appropriate, I thought, since it was the 27th (of March 1992).

Shortly after arriving home, I thought I'd do some writing. I found concentration difficult with a hangover creeping up on me, and pulled out a box of half-finished stories. I saw I had given one of them the working title "27 Angels from the Great Beyond". I couldn't understand why I had called it that, and I replaced it with something else. With a fine headache now, I looked through my tapes for something to listen to and selected *I'm Your Man* by Leonard Cohen. Haven't heard this for ages, I thought. When it arrived at *Tower of Song*, the line "27 Angels from the Great Beyond" leapt out at me. So that's where I got that title from! No doubt the unconscious was at work when choosing to play this tape for I had no conscious knowledge of where the line came from.

In the evening, I met up with a friend I hadn't seen since a party a while ago. "Last time I saw you", he recalled, "you were 27 sheets to the wind". I asked him why he chose to say this number. "I don't know", he said. "It just popped into my head".

Neil Wilsher
Hampstead, London

IT'S NOT FOR YOO-HOO #1

■ Back around 1982/83, I was working in a 12-storey office block, with our department situated on the fourth floor. Eileen Campbell, a work colleague of mine, had taken the main lift from the ground to the fourth floor. In the lift was an emergency telephone with a direct line to the main reception. The phone rang, something which happened very rarely and not once in my presence during my five years working there. Eileen picked it up cautiously, and the caller asked if she could speak to Eileen Campbell! When she had recovered from surprise, she said that she was Eileen Campbell and was in a lift travelling between floors. The caller then realised that she had dialled the wrong number and wanted another Eileen Campbell, working in another building in the town and for another company.

Steven Shipp
Devon

IT'S NOT FOR YOO-HOO #2

■ In the Summer of 1990, I was living in a bedsit in Swansea, and reading a famous Victorian novel by 'Mrs Craik', *John Halifax, Gentleman*. One night, I answered the telephone and a woman asked to speak to 'John Halifax'. When I mumbled in astonishment that I didn't know who this was, the caller said that "Mr Halifax is a *gentleman* who lives upstairs". I subsequently fetched him to answer the telephone on numerous occasions.

Simon Cooke
Liskeard, Cornwall

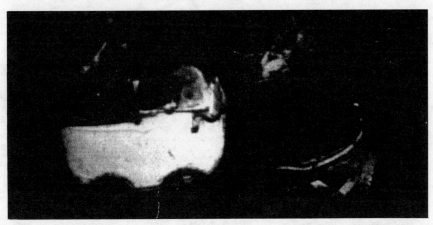

PUSSY POWER: Mother cat pushes her young around in an Irish pram. Photo by Barry McLean's mum (see letter)

FINDING THE MILITARY ORCHID

■ Your item about the chance discovery of a New Zealand orchid [FT62:19] reminded me of a story often told, allegedly dating from the 1950s, when the whole country was surveyed for *The Atlas of the British Flora* (1962). Two botanists were working in a rather boring area of forestry plantations in Cambridge-shire, out of obligation to cover as much ground as possible more than hope of finding anything interesting.

Noticing what seemed to be a glade among the dark tiers of conifers, they pushed through some tangled undergrowth. The ground gave way, and the leading botanist fell, rolling down a slope into what turned out to be an old chalk quarry. At the end of his fall, somewhat dazed, he opened his eyes, bracing himself for the sight of his own blood, but what he saw, the story goes, made him wonder if he were dead and had woken up in heaven. The grass at the bottom of the quarry was studded with military orchids, a species not seen in Britain for 15 years, and feared extinct.

This yarn was originally told me by a friend who had a friend who knew one of the botanists involved. John Fisher, in his *Wild Flowers in Danger* (Gollancz 1987), states that the military orchid was last seen in Britain in the 1920s, and believed to be extinct, until in 1947 the botanist J.E. Lousley chose a picnic spot in Buckinghamshire and decided to check the vicinity for any interesting plants. He didn't actually sit on them, but they were close by.

Lousley gives his own account in his *Wild Flowers of Chalk and Limestone* (Collins 1950), which tallies with Fisher's, except that he says the military orchid was last seen in England 'about 1914'. Fisher adds that a second colony was found in 1955, "during a routine survey made for *The Atlas of the British Flora*", which ties in with my foaftale, except that there is no mention of the discoverer literally falling on them. The site was indeed a chalk pit on Forestry Commission land, but in Suffolk, not Cambridgeshire.

Chris Hall
Fleet, Hampshire

AUNTS OF ONE MIND

■ I was interested to read, in *The Best of Fortean Times* [p19], the letter from a woman who received two identical greetings cards from her two sons, in different countries. Last November, on my birthday, I received identical cards from two of my aunts (who are sisters). One lives in Belfast, the other with her family in the Transvaal, South Africa. They had also written "Barry!" after the "Happy 18th Birthday" message printed inside the card, both put two x's below their names, and one wrote "Have a great day however you choose to spend it", while the other wrote "Enjoy your day however you spend it".

I enclose an old photograph of a cat my mother owned as a child. She trained it to wear a dress and to push its kittens around in a pram.

Barry McLean
Balimena, Co. Antrim, Northern Ireland

DALLYING WITH DOLPHINS

■ I would have thought that love affairs with dolphins would have been, in the UK at least, hampered by the weather and British reserve. [See 'Animal Lovers' *FT59*:8 and 'Dances with Dolphins' *FT61*:20 for our reports on the dolphin molestation trial.] In 1974 in Hong Kong, I met a young woman employed as a dolphin handler at the Hong Kong Sea World aquarium where a pod of dolphins was obliged to perform various acrobatics. Dolphins, being reasonably intelligent, are fairly amenable to training, but, the young woman confided, the males seem to be in a perpetual state of rut and only really became tractable if they were regularly masturbated. This was, apparently, so effective that it had become a standard reward when training the beasts to perform their more publicly acceptable acts. I wondered about the female dolphins, and was referred to the male handlers, who confirmed that they had their own way of calming their female charges. This gave me an idea.

Asia has a surprising number of discrete, luxury, holiday-hideaways that don't appear in the ABC hotel guide, and are always on the lookout for fresh entertainments. The rest, as they say, is history. There is now a number of 'dolphinariums' where adventurous men and women can establish a relationship with a difference. As an enterprise, it has been quite successful. The human participants seem to be generally satisfied.

As with all water sports, there has been the occasional drowning and a few appalling injuries, but, by and large, everyone is happy. Recalcitrant dolphins are cycled through the resort restaurants (which proved very popular with the Japanese) and, prior to the depredations of the long line fishermen, were easy to replace. I no longer have any connection with the enterprise. The resorts don't advertise, but discrete enquiries at any of the better diving shops should get you connected.

R J Henry
Pearce, Australia

CREDITS FOR THIS ISSUE

CLIPPINGS & TRANSLATION

Larry E. Arnold, Sherry Baker, Greg Bale, Lisa Ann Barnes, K. A. Beer, Lionel Beer, Ron Bishop, Claire Blamey, Janet & Colin Bord, Cuyler Warnell Brooks Jr, Linda Brown, Des Burkinshaw, David J. Burns, Brian Chapman, Arthur Chrenkoff, Peter Christie, David Coe, Terry W.Colvin, Mark Conti, J. B. Coombs, R. Coombs, N.P.R.Cooper, Richard Cotton, COUD-I, Mat Coward, Miss J. Critchley, Scott Deschaine, Tim Donaghy, Jill Doubleday, T. Elias, Peter Hope Evans, Ian Faichnie, George Featherston, Eric Fitch, FLS News, Jon Fry, Rob Gandy, Alan Gardiner, Wojciech T. Gaworzewski, J. Geal, Mark Gillings, Joan Good, Matthew Goulding, Chris Hall, Lucy Hall, Jim Haslam, Peter Hassall, Tuuri Heporauta, Stuart A. Herkes, Richard Holland, Mike Howard, R. Hudspith, Ros Jay, Dionne Jones, Joe Kelly, Jake T. Kirkwood, Denise Kleine, Roger Laidlow, Walter J. Langbein, Jim Lippard, Cynthia Newby Luce, John Macmillan, Jen Magson, Celia Maier, Nick Maloret, G. Markie, Valerie Martin, Otto Martinussen, Will Maudling, Barbara Millspaw, Pat Missin, Ian S. Murray, Roger Musson, Jackie Neervoort, Ray Nelke, Cecilia Örning, Tony Parkes, Gary Parslow, Nigel Pennick, Ian Peters, G. Pottle, T.Powers, Les Prince, John Reid, Barry Reynolds, Sam Rickard, Jim Riecken, Jean Roddy, John Rowe, Mike Roycroft, Tom Ruffles, Gregory Sams, John Sappington, Ronnie Scott, Paul Screeton, Caryl Sibbett, Ian Simmons, Anthony Smith, Iain S. Smith, Raymond T. Spears, Peter Stallard, Joe Swatek, Paul R. Thomas, B. E. Tolley, Joe Trainor, Mike Travers, Michael Truelove, UFONS, John Viney, Nicholas P. Warren, James Webster, John Whiskin, Owen Whiteoak, Terry Wilkin, Ion Will, Jan Williams, Jace Winter, Steve Wrathall.

PROOFREADING:
Val Stevenson.

ILLUSTRATION COPYRIGHTS

5 Unknown. 6 Merrily Harpur. 7 (TR) Jean Roddy; (B) Bristol United Press. 8 Bournemouth News & Pictures. 9 Image Scotland. 10 Western Mail. 11 Reuter / Popperfoto. 12 Mark Hibbin / Wrexham Leader. 13 Ross Cameron / (Easton; PA) Express. 15 (TL) Associated Press (AP); (TC) Saginaw News; (TR) Unknown; (BL) AP. 16 (T) Alan Jones; (B) North News & Pictures. 17 Merrily Harpur. 19 John Redman. 22 (All) Janet & Colin Bord. 23 Hunt Emerson. 24 Topham Picture source. 26 International Times. 27 Hunt Emerson. 28+29 Unknown. 31 Leicester Mercury. 32 Merrily Harpur. 33 Unknown. 34 Alex Bratall. 35 Michael Ging/Phoenix Newspapers. 37 Felix Bennett. 38 Pierre Hollins. 40 Unknown. 41 United Artists. 42 Witness Drawings from FT Archive; pulp cove from Mary Evans P.L. 43 Farside – Intercontinental Features; Witness Drawings; Loveland Frog from FPL. 45 Max Ernst. 47 (both) FPL. 49 FPL. 54 (both) Janet & Colin Bord.64 Art Wetherell 65 Barry McLeans Mum.

EXCHANGE & MART

● **UFO NEWSCLIPPING SERVICE** – keeps you up with the real 'close encounters'. Many fascinating UFO reports from the world's press are reproduced facsimile, along with news-wire items from the major agencies. UFONS is 20 foolscap pages monthly, with a Fortean section strong on cryptozoology. Foreign language reports are provided in translation. For information and sample pages, write today to: UFONS (Dept FT) – Lucius Farrish, Route 1 – Box 220, Plumerville, AR 72127, USA.

● **THESE DAYS EVERYONE TAKES VITAMINS,** even if it's only because they are in the morning cornflakes. But is the next step legal drugs that stimulate the mind and enhance the memory? For further information, please send SAE to: HDC, 2 Lavender Mews, Bishops Cleeve, Cheltenham, Glos GL52 4LN – or tel (0242) 677347 (24hrs).

● **CELLULAR AUTOMATA T-SHIRTS** – Striking full-colour artificial designs generated by computer. SAE for brochure to: Ray Girvan (FT), 160 Stonor Road, Birmingham B28 0QJ.

● **BOOKSEARCH SERVICE** – Out-of-print books a speciality. Dedicated, personal attention. No obligation to buy – no find no fee. For details send SAE to: Ian Murray (Dept FT), 6 Nevis Close, Loundsley Green, Chesterfield, Derbyshire S40 4NS.

● **UFO AFRINEWS** – edited by Cynthia Hind. The only UFO magazine in Africa. #1-4 available at £2; #5 at £2.50. Write: Gemini, Box MP 49, Mt Pleasant, Harare, Zimbabwe.

● **NORTHERH EARTH MYSTERIES** – celebrates its 50th issue with a change of editor and name. NORTHERN EARTH will take a slightly broader approach to the subject. Send £3.95 for four issues to: John Billingley, 10 Jubilee St, Mytholmroyd, Hebden Bridge, W.Yorks HX7 5NP.

● **FED UP BEING A MUSHROOM?** – Tired of being kept in the dark and fed shit? Get NEXUS magazine for suppressed news, UFOs, prophecies. Send equivalent of A$5.00 for airmail sample to: Nexus Magazine, PO, Mapleton, Queensland 4560, Australia.

RESEARCH

● **FORTEAN CURIOS** – Fortean Times is collecting information on private and museum collections of bizarre and mysterious objects such as unicorn horns, vegetable lambs, bits of alien craft, fafrotskies, rat-kings, fairy artifacts, mummified cats etc. If you know of any, please write to FT at the editorial address.

● **OLD PULP SF MAGS WANTED** for FT Library. Also FATE MAGAZINE vol 1, no 4 (1948); nos 50 (1954) & 90 (1957). Write to Bob Rickard, c/o FT editorial address.

● **FORTEAN PICTURES** – The Fortean Picture Library is a self-funding project for the rescue and preservation of valuable documentary material, photographs and drawings etc. If you have anything of this nature please let FPL look after it. 50% of any revenue from the commercial use of the material (in books etc) could come back to you. FPL covers all expenses from its half. Contact Janet Bord, FPL, Melysfan, Llangwm, Corwen, Clwyd, Wales LL21 0RD. Tel: 049 082 472. (FAX 321)

EVENTS

● **PERSPECTIVES ON CONTEMPORARY LEGEND** – 10th international seminar, 15-18 July 1992, at the Halifax Hall, University of Sheffield. £31/day full board – For further information contact Paul Smith, Dept of Folklore, Memorial University of Newfoundland, St Johns, Newfoundland, Canada A1C 5S7 – or via E-mail: ifsbac#at#kean.ucs.mun.ca

● **TEMS** – (Travel & Earth Mysteries Society) is a new non-sectarian group for SW London, Surrey and Middlesex, for those interested in ancient sites, leys, hauntings, crop circles, UFOs, unexplained animals, etc. For the programme of speakers, social events, trips and further info, contact Lionel Beer (081 979 3148), Barbara (081 942 3447), or Ann (081 542 3110).

● **SOCIETY FOR PSYCHICAL RESEARCH** – Lectures. 18 June: Beyond the Paranormal; (Colin Wilson). Venue: the lecture hall of Kensington Central Library, London W8, at 6:30pm. Entrance £1. Further information from the SPR at 49 Marloes Rd, Kensington, London W8 6LA. Tel: 071 937 8984.

● **LONDON EARTH MYSTERIES CIRCLE** – Evening meetings in St Andrew's Seminar Room, Maria Assumpta Centre, 23 Kensington Square, London W8, at 7pm on the 2nd and 4th Tuesdays in each month. Members £1.00, non-members £2.00, unwaged £1.50. Lectures: Contact: Rob Stephenson, 18 Christchurch Ave, London NW6 7QN, or tel: 081 459 0652.

● **BUFORA LECTURES** – 6 June, `Psychic questing and the UFO phenomenon' (Andy Collins). 6:30 pm. Venue: London Business School, Sussex Place, Outer Circle, Regents Park, London NW1.

● **FOLKLORE SOCIETY CONFERENCE** – `First international on Celtic folk studies', 19-23 July 1992, possibly in Cardiff. Contact Juliette Wood, The Folklore Society, University College London, Gower St, London WC1E 6BT, or tel: 071 387 5894.

MISCELLANEOUS

● **WELSH HOLIDAY COTTAGE** – Self-catering accomodation in historic North Wales town of Denbigh. For further details, contact Janet Bord, Melysfan, Ll Llangwm, Corwen, Clwyd LL21 0RD. Tel: 049 082 472. Fax: 049 082 321.

● **JOSS (INCENSE) STICKS** – cones etc. Exotic perfumes, Tarot Cards etc. Send SAE for list to: Cabarri (JOSS) 45, Terminus Road, Eastbourne, East Sussex BN21 3QL.

● **HAVING AN EVENT?** – Publicize it in Fortean Times. Fax us details on 081 552 5466.

WHERE TO BUY FORTEAN BOOKS

Most of these book shops ◆, mail-order services (including second-hand book dealers) ✗ will send you further information on request. Please mention FT when you respond.

✗ **AARDVARK BOOKS** – secondhand books on UFOs, ghost and folklore. Free list – 8 Braddon Ave, Urmston, Gtr Manchester M31 1UE.

✗ ◆ **DEJA VU BOOKS** – Rare Forteana, psychic research & esoteric books & artefacts from the 17th century to now, including signed etc. Catalogue & search service – 31 Trafalgar St, Brighton, Sussex BN1 4ED – ☎ 0273 600400.

✗ **EXCALIBUR BOOKS** – New, secondhand and imported titles on folklore, paranormal and UFOs. Free List. – 1 Hillside Gardens, Bangor, Co. Down, N. Ireland BT19 2SJ – ☎ 0247 458579.

✗ ◆ **THE INNER BOOKSHOP** – Parascience, mysteries, mind-body-spirit-planet. Big catalogue (send 6 first class stamps) – 34 Cowley Rd, Oxford OX4 1HZ. – ☎ 0865 245301.

✗ **MIDNIGHT BOOKS** – New & secondhand books on the unexplained. SAE for catalogue. Free searches. – The Haven, 21 Windsor Mead, Sidford, Sidmouth, Devon EX10 9SJ – ☎ 0395 516806

◆ **MUSHROOM BOOKSHOP** – 10 Heathcote St, Nottingham NG1 3AA. – ☎ 0602 582506

◆ **MYSTERIES BOOKSHOP** – 9 Monmouth St, London WC2. – ☎ 071 240 3688

✗ **MYTHOLOGICAL BOOKSHOP** – Specialists in myth, legend & folklore. Send for free catalogue – 174a High St, Townhead, Biggar, Lanarks ML12 6DH, Scotland. ☎ 031 447 6750.

✗ **NANTMAWR BOOK SERVICES** – New books on all aspects of the paranormal & unexplained. Send for list. – Stone House, Quarry Lane, Nantmawr, Oswestry, Shropshire SY10 9HL.

✗ **SPACELINK BOOKS** – Since 1967 Britain's leading stockist of UFO and Crop Circle books and magazines, plus wide range of Fortean titles. Free lists. – Lionel Beer, 115 Hollybush Lane, Hampton, Middx TW12 2QY.

✗ ◆ **SPECIALIST KNOWLEDGE SERVICES (SKS)** – Internationally renowned specialists in new books on the paranormal, Forteana, mysteries, philosophical & unusual. Send for free lists. – 20 Paul St, Frome, Somerset BA11 1DX. – ☎ 0373 451777.

FORTEAN TIMES

THE JOURNAL OF STRANGE PHENOMENA

SOME PEOPLE WILL GO THROUGH ANYTHING TO GET A FORTEAN TIMES SUBSCRIPTION ...

FORTUNATELY YOU DON'T HAVE TO. JUST COMPLETE THE COUPON BELOW, RETURN WITH PAYMENT AND WE WILL SEND YOU A YEAR'S SUPPLY OF FORTEAN TIMES PLUS A FREE T-SHIRT (WORTH £7.99)!!!

Postage and Packing FREE   Special offer on subscriptions for 12 issues

FREE T-shirt with every new subscription

If you have enjoyed this issue, why wait two months for more? Order some back issues today. £2 each (see coupon).

I would like to subscribe to Fortean Times:

For one year (6 issues)   ☐ UK £12   ☐ overseas inc USA £15 US$30

For two years (12 issues)   ☐ UK £20   ☐ overseas inc USA £26 US$50

Back Issues No(s) – £2 each _____

Name: Mrs/Miss/Ms/Mr _____

Address _____

_____ Postcode _____

I enclose a total payment of £   made payable to: John Brown Publishing Ltd, or debit the above amount from my Access/Visa/Mastercard/Eurocard (delete where applicable) account.

Account no ☐☐☐☐   Expiry date ☐☐

Signature _____ Date _____

Please return order form to: Fortean Times, 20 Paul Street, Frome, Somerset BA11 1DX
or phone credit card details on 0373 451777   **FT63**

A *Gordon's & Tonic* DURING HAPPY HOUR

NUMBER 64

UK £2
USA $4.95 / AUSTRALIA $4.95

FORTEAN TIMES

THE JOURNAL OF STRANGE PHENOMENA

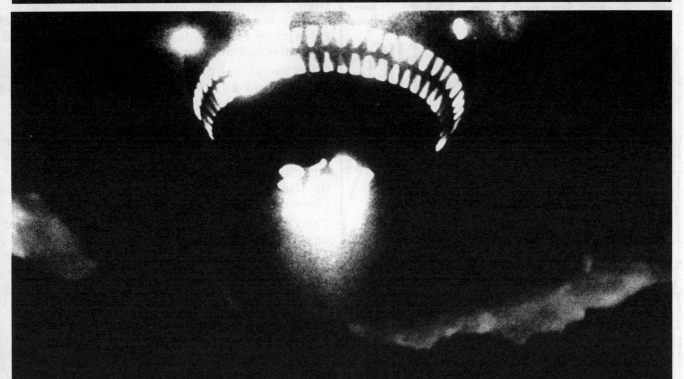

SUPERNATURAL SPIELBERG:
Close Encounters of the Fortean Kind

Alternative 3: Slave Labour on Mars?

Michael Bentine Interview ● Escape From A Killer Wave
● Pregnant Man ● Satanic Video Fiasco ● Crop Art '92
● Computer Demons ● Swedish Horse Ripping

0308 589118

64

Contents

Issue 64 August/September 1992

CORN CIRCLES P6

SPIELBERG P25

BENTINE P32

CHARLES FORT
(1874-1932)

Fortean Times is a bi-monthly magazine of news, reviews and research on all manner of strange phenomena and experiences, curiosities, prodigies and portents, founded in 1973 to continue the work of the iconoclastic philosopher CHARLES FORT. Fort was sceptical about scientific explanations, observing how scientists argued for and against various theories and phenomena according to their own beliefs, rather than the rules of evidence. He was appalled that data not fitting the collective paradigm was ignored, suppressed, discredited or explained away (with is quite different from explaining a thing).

Fort was born in Albany, New York, in 1874 into a family of Dutch immigrants. Beatings by a tyrannical father helped set him against authority and dogma, and on leaving home at the age of 18 he hitch-hiked around the world to put some "capital into the bank of experience." At 22 he contracted malaria, married his nurse and settled down to 20 years of impoverished journalism in the Bronx. During this time he read extensively in the literature of science, taking notes on small squares of paper in a cramped shorthand of his own invention, which he filed in shoe boxes.

In 1916, when he was 42, Fort came into a modest inheritance, just enough to relieve him of the necessity of having to earn a living. He started writing *The Book of the Damned*, which his friend, the novelist Theodore Dreiser, bullied his own publisher into printing in 1919. Fort fell into a depression, burnt all his notes (which numbered some 40,000) as he had done a few years earlier, and in 1921 set sail for London, where he spent eight years living near the British Museum (39 Marchmont Street) and wrote *New Lands* (1923). Returning to New York, he published *Lo!* in 1931 and *Wild Talents* in 1932, shortly before he died. He left 60,000 notes, now in the New York Public Library.

Fort was perhaps the first to speculate that mysterious lights seen in the sky might be craft from outer space. He coined the term 'teleportation', which has passed into general usage through science fiction. His dictum "One measures a circle beginning anywhere" expresses his philosophy of Continuity and the 'doctrine of the hyphen', in which everything is in an intermediate state between extremes. He had notions of the universe-as-organism and the transient nature of all apparent phenomena. Far from being an over-credulous man, Fort cut at the very roots of credulity: "I cannot accept that the products of minds are subject matter for beliefs ... I conceive of nothing, in religion, science, or philosophy, that is more than the proper thing to wear, for a while."

THE GANG OF FORT:

Editors:
Bob Rickard
& Paul Sieveking

Contributing Editors:
Steve Moore
& Mike Dash

© Fortean Times August 1992
ISSN 0308 5899

Bob Rickard

EDITORIAL:
X Marks the Spot

Paul Sieveking

EDITORIAL ADDRESS
Fortean Times: Box 2409, London NW5 4NP, UK. Tel & Fax: 071 485 5002 or 081 552 5466.

SUBMISSIONS
Submissions are invited of suitable articles, news, art, cartoons, reviews, and especially clippings. Preliminary discussion with the editors is advisable. Text can be submitted on floppy disks, but check with the editors first. Submissions may be edited. FT assumes no responsibility for submissions, but all reasonable care will be taken while they are in FT's possession. Requests for return of material should be accompanied by stamped addressed envelope.

CLIPPINGS
All clippings, references, etc, should be identified by source, date and clipster's name. Mail or fax them to the editorial address (above).

SUBSCRIPTIONS
RATES – One year (6 issues). UK: £12. Overseas inc. USA: US £15 or $30. For two years (12 issues) UK: £20, overseas inc USA £26 or US$50.
PAYMENT – US/Canadian cheques acceptable; payments from all other countries should be in sterling drawn upon a London bank. Major credit cards accepted – just phone details to 0373 451777. Make cheque/money orders payable to: JOHN BROWN PUBLISHING Ltd, 20 Paul Street, Frome, Somerset BA11 1DX, UK.

ADVERTISING ENQUIRIES
DISPLAY or CLASSIFIED: contact Ronnie Hackston or Dan Squirrel at John Brown Publishing Ltd: The Boathouse, Crabtree Lane, Fulham, London SW6 8NJ, UK. ☎ 071 381 6007 or Fax: 071 381 3930.
BOOKSELLERS' LISTING items – contact the editorial address (above).

PUBLISHER
John Brown Publishing Ltd, The Boathouse, Crabtree Lane, Fulham, London SW6 8NJ, UK. ☎ 071 381 6007 or Fax: 071 381 3930.
Managing Editor: Fiona Jerome.
Publisher: Vic Lime.

DISTRIBUTION
UK trade distribution by UMD, 1 Benwell Road, Holloway, London N7 7AX. ☎ 071 700 4600 or Fax: 071 607 3352.
USA newsstand distribution by Eastern News Distributors Inc, 250 West 55th Street, New York, N.Y. 10019, USA. ☎ (0101) 212 649 4484.

● We noticed a couple of giant sigils recently. The Hubble Telescope has recorded a huge cross-shape in the heavens, supposedly marking the location of a black hole, silhouetted against the centre of the M51 spiral galaxy. Astronomer Holland Ford of Johns Hopkins said that this was "due to absorption by dust" (*Standard* 9 June). Also, a giant swastika formed by a forest of larch trees and measuring approximately 100 yards from tip to tip was spotted near the German town of Zernikow. It was probably planted by Hitler Youth members in the 1930s, and can only be seen for what it is from the air (*Reuters 5 May*).

● The world's first crop-circle-making competition was held over the weekend of 11-12 July (- see page 7). The location of the barley field was kept secret until the last minute and each of 12 teams paid a £50 registration fee. There was enough sponsorship to compensate the farmer, and offer a £3,000 prize for the best emulation of a 'perfect' formation. What an ingenious and genial way for circles experts to study at close quarters the techniques used by the flesh and blood hoaxers! Whether this will become an annual event remains to be seen, but we congratulate *The Cerealogist* magazine for its hard work in organising the event.

● Speaking of sponsorship, we note the recent announcements in the press that Project Urquhart is under way. In fact the project was launched a year ago – see *FT59:10* – and it has taken all this time to secure the £2 million backing. The project, fronted by BBC newsreader Nicholas Witchell, is a scientific expedition to Loch Ness to make a detailed study of its wildlife (worms and fishes are mentioned). We should be thankful, because this is the nearest the establishment zoologists will get to an official monster hunt, and it should determine, once and for all, whether creatures larger than salmon or the occasional seal live in the depths of the loch's peat-stained waters.

● Our breath was quite taken away by the simple announcement in the personal column of the *Daily Telegraph* for 23 March 1992, signed 'B.P.'. It said, simply: "St Jude. Grateful thanks for the Election results." This followed the publication, in the same column, of a prayer to St Jude, which, its author claimed, if said nine times a day for nine consecutive days, "never fails".

We infer that 'B.P.' either prayed for a Conservative win or Labour failure. Either way, a divine fix of the election demolishes, in one stroke, the whole concept of democracy. If someone else had used the prayer to secure the reverse outcome, how would the equation balance out? Do numbers count? If we believed in such things, anyone can now perform miracles, thanks to the *Telegraph*.

We'll let the bishops argue whether God can veto the infallible St Jude, and suggest the ideal experiment is coming up with the US presidential election. Whoever more people pray for will take high office. Good heavens! that's almost like democracy.

THE EDITORS

STRANGE DAYS

18 pages of worldwide weirdness

A SATANIC THREAT TO LIBERTY?

This ominous cloud was photographed over New York's Statue of Liberty in early December 1990 by two tourists from Ballymena in Northern Ireland, Clifford Scullion and Denise McNinch. The cloud image was only noticed after the film was developed. Since they were both using the same camera, they are not sure which of them took the picture.

CORNUCOPIA

It is a sure sign of arrival when a new phenomenon makes its way into the collective image-bank, not to mention kiddies' comics. It was a pleasant surprise, therefore, to find that Dr Meaden's 'plasma vortices' have spiralled down to imprint themselves on the tranquil vales of Nutwood.

In episode five of 'Rupert and the Spaceship' – *D.Express* 30 April 1992 [**below left**] – Rupert and Gregory discover a huge circle of crushed grass in a meadow. "Do you think it's where a spaceship landed?" marvels Gregory. "I don't know," says Rupert fairly. "My father thought it might have been caused by a gust of wind, but I've never seen grass that's been flattened like this..."

We wonder what the sage little bear would make of 'The Cornfield' [**below**], painted by John Nash at Chalfont St Giles in 1928, and on display in the Tate Gallery? It provides a four-square antidote to circle-mania – but is it actually evidence of a pre-1980 manifestation?

HIGH SEAS DRIFTERS

Two emaciated fishermen who drifted around the South Pacific in their 13ft dinghy for 175 days – more than six months – were washed onto a beach in Western Samoa in May. The relatives of Arenta Tebeitabu, 40, and Tabwai Mikaie, 24, in the tiny island state of Kiribati had held funeral services for them months earlier.

A third man, Nweiti Tekamangu, 47, died within sight of land (or a few days earlier). The boat was somehow steered through a dangerous reef, off the island of Upolu. The survivors believed the spirit of their dead comrade, whose body was put overboard, pushed them to shore. "We prayed every day, four times a day, asking for God's help", said Mr Mikaie. Samoan villagers found them, lying motionless, in what they thought was an empty dinghy. They were just bones and skin, too weak to walk. Daniel Galuvao, Western Samoa's police chief, said they would be in hospital for quite some time.

Their ordeal began 900 miles north west on 17 November 1991, when a cyclone swept them out to sea from Nikunau, one of the Kiribati coral atolls. They lost their outboard motor as the dinghy capsized, but righted their craft, salvaging a spear, a fishing line and a small basin, and began to drift further away from land. They used the spear and line to catch fish, including 10 sharks, and the basin to catch rainwater. There was also the occasional floating coconut. *D.Telegraph 14 May; Independent 15 May; The Australian 16 May 1992.* If verified, this journey of 175 days would be the longest recorded marine drift, surpassing the 119 days spent by three New Zealanders and an American in an upturned trimaran off New Zealand in 1989 (see **FT53:18**. For another ordeal and miraculous deliverance for Kiribati fishermen, see **FT48:16**.)

Josephine Sanders, 57, from Nottingham, and an American, William Heil, 70, were adrift in a dinghy off Brazil for 23 days after their trimaran struck a whale and sank on 2 February 1992, about 550 miles north-east of the island of Fernando de Noronha. Three days later, the dinghy capsized in a storm and they lost their emergency supplies. They survived on rainwater caught in a piece of cloth, four seagulls they caught and two flying fish that jumped into the dinghy. They were picked up by a fishing boat, and seemed in remarkably good shape, although they had lost a lot of weight. *D.Express, D.Telegraph 3 Mar 1992.*

Over the weekend of 11-12 July 1992, the world's first crop circle competition was held – with the farmer's permission – in fields at West Wycombe in Buckinghamshire. A three-man team from Yeovil, called 'Masters of the Cereal Universe', beat 11 others to win the £3,000 prize. The event was sponsored by *The Cereologist* magazine, the *Guardian*, the German Magazine *PM* and the Koestler Foundation, in order to learn more about the techniques used by hoaxers.

CROP ART '92

NEARY'S EAR GETS LEG-UP

Patrick Neary, 32, a Channel Tunnel worker from Aberdare in Wales, had his right ear bitten off in a brawl on 4 October 1991. Plastic surgeons at the Queen Victoria Hospital in East Grinstead didn't think sewing the ear back in place straight away would succeed, so they stitched the cartilage of the ear inside his thigh to maintain its blood supply.

By February 1992, the surgeons thought the ear would be ready for sewing back into position, but there was no response to a letter sent to Mr Neary's last address in Kent. The hospital feared he could be working 'anywhere'.

According to Gus McGrowther, Professor of Reconstructive Plastic Surgery at Middlesex Hospital, London, ear-biting is quite common. "In Scotland and the Northeast we still see women who have been bitten by other women. This is a traditional thing. The wronged woman bites the woman who has been with her husband or partner." A month before Neary's mutilation, steeplejack Vic Harfield, 39, had his ear bitten off in the Black Cat pub in

Southampton; while twins Alan and Barry Marshall from the Rotherham area of South Yorkshire both had their ears bitten off, Barry in 1986 and Alan in 1989. Said Alan: "Biting off ears is a bit of a sport round here."

The temporary graft is an established surgical procedure. Five years ago, a Yugoslav's severed hand was sewn onto his chest before eventual transfer to his damaged arm, a year later. In 1990, a French surgeon reattached a man's foot to his leg, after it had spent seven months sewn to his arm. The foot was severed when the man fell under a Metro train. *Sun 2 Aug 1989; Guardian 19 Oct 1990; Sunday Mirror 1 Sept; Wolverhampton Express & Star 9 Oct 1991; Independent 20 Feb 1992.*

THE PHANTOM HUNGARIAN SHAMPOO SALESMAN

The hair of eight people in the Hungarian village of Heves turned bright lilac overnight. Shortly afterwards, there were six more cases in the village of Ecsed, less than four miles away. The local doctor suggested that the phenomenon could have been caused by an unknown shampoo, sold by a travelling salesman passing through the area. Did he only have 14 bottles, we wonder? *[Deutsche Press Agentur] 13 Mar 1992.*

PREGNANT MALES?

Time, it is said, is the greatest diagnostician. This was certainly upheld in the dubious saga of the Filipino fellow who caught the world's attention, in May, by claiming he was pregnant. Edwin Bayron (whom reports variously called 'Carlo', 'Blaka' and even 'Duenne-Mae') is described as a male-nurse (some said midwife), which in this case makes a poor joke of these terms.

Edwin, 32, claimed he was born a hermaphrodite, and undertook surgery, in 1985, to remove his penis and create a vaginal passage. After hormone treatment, he says, he began menstruating.

Urine Samples

According to the reports, Edwin went to see Dr Clarita Paggao, a gynæcologist in the town of Malaybalay, after he missed a period and thought he might be pregnant. He took with him a "full medical history" and urine samples. Dr Paggao said that the urine tested positive, and that the six-month-old fœtus showed up on her ultrasound scanner. Some reports said she had even felt the baby's kicks while palpating Edwin's stomach. Edwin and his homosexual lover – a junior army officer called Roel Enriquez – announced to the world that they were so happy they had cried. "Now I can prove to the world I am a real woman," blubbed Edwin. "I'm really feeling fulfilled."

Obstetrics

The *Sun* (25 May 1992) asked the opinion of Sir John Dewhurst, the obstetrics expert; he said: "I have known five or six cases of people with both sex organs giving birth, but they were all women." According to our trusty reference, *Gould and Pyle*, there have been instances in which the full set of female sexual and reproductive organs, including uterus, have been found in a male; but generally, hermaphrodites are considered to be sterile. Even breast-feeding would not necessarily have been a problem; there being ample cases in the records of male lactation. Such was the worldwide interest that Antonio Periquet, Minister of Health, could not bear to be left out; he was proud his country had such a rarity and offered to pay all the medical expenses involved.

Effeminate

The photos which accompanied the reports were hardly convincing. They showed a rather self-conscious Dr Paggao pos-ing with an effeminate General Noriega lookalike who sported a Little Richard hairdo and what looked suspiciously like a beer gut.

At some point, Edwin had applied to the courts to have his sex officially changed to female so that he could marry Enriquez. The court, reasonably, asked for proof of his adopted femininity and ordered a new examination. When the medics found no evidence of pregnancy, nor any sign that Edwin had ever been a hermaphrodite, he and Enriquez promptly went on the lam.

It transpires that Edwin and the doctor worked at the same hospital. Dr Paggao admitted she had been fooled: "Being a co-worker I took all his words on trust," she added, acknowledging that she "had made a mistake in not having insisted earlier on a physical examination of his genitals." We are astonished to hear this because any doctor would make his or her own examination of a new patient. Wasn't she curious? She said: "I had all sympathies for him before and was supportive of his claim of pregnancy." Edwin had used urine samples from a real pregnant female, and his medical history, it need hardly be said, was faked using the experience and opportunities from his hospital work; but Dr Paggao had totally misread her ultrasound scans. We have to wonder if she was a dupe or an accomplice.

Hormones

An even later source said that the actual moment of truth came when a team of doctors from the World Health Organisation approached Edwin, who was strutting about the hospital wearing a maternity gown. He refused their request for an examination, so they rushed him; his pants were forced down to reveal an underdeveloped penis "the size of a thumb" and no sign of surgery or vagina. The distended stomach was variously blamed on hormones, muscle control and gallons of Coca-cola.

Sources: the original story came from Reuters but appeared in papers world wide between 24-28 May 1992.

Almost exactly two months before the Edwin story, a tiny item in the *Daily Mirror* (24 March 1992) said that Rosalinda de Hernandez was stunned to hear that an autopsy on her murdered husband revealed that he was in fact a woman *and* pregnant. Rosalinda, of Tegucigalpa, in Honduras, who had been married to Gustavo for nine years, said: "Our love life was a bit strange but I never suspected he was a woman."

BEES STUNG BY MITE PLAGUE

Millions of British bees are threatened by a virulent plague of mites sweeping across southern England.

The outbreak of Varroa disease, discovered in Devon on 4 April, is already reckoned to be the most severe bee plague to hit the country since the native black bee population was wiped out by the so-called Isle of Wight disease before and during the First World War.

Isle of Wight disease entered bees through their breathing holes and left them unable to fly. Varroa is carried by parasitic mites, *Varroa jacobsoni*, which weaken adult bees and suck the blood of larvæ, causing exhaustion and birth deformities. And in an echo of the killer bee plague threatening humans as it sweeps from South America to the United States, the new disease is moving rapidly from the south of Britain to the north of the country.

By the end of April, the plague had been identified in 57 apiaries from Devon to Surrey and the Ministry of Agriculture had slapped an exclusion zone around the town of Okehampton as well as banning the movement of hives from Devon without a special licence. By 8 June, 109 infested apiaries had been identified. Among the bees affected by the exclusion zone are those of Brother Adam, the 93-year-old monk from Buckfast Abbey famed for his 70-year breeding programme to produce a disease-resistant bee.

Varroa originated in the Far East and remained localised until an unexplained explosion in the late 1970s saw it move across Russia and Western Europe. Britain remained immune for several years thanks to an import ban, but the mites reached the Americas and now only Australasia, Sweden and the Canaries remain uncontaminated. Apiarists predict that the disease, nicknamed "bee rabies", will sweep the country in less than two years. There is no known cure for the mite, which can decimate bee populations and cut honey production by 20%. *Independent 8+27 Apr + 8 June; Western Daily Press 18 Apr; Observer 19 Apr; Bristol Evening Post 23+26 Apr; D.Telegraph 4 May; (AP) Newark (NJ) Star-Ledger 15 May 1992.*

With Varroa sweeping the country, the last news bee-lovers wanted to hear was the tragi-comic tale of amateur entomologist Ray Gabriel.

Gabriel was out recording the numbers of bees in the Coate Water park near Swindon when he spotted an unusual specimen, which he chased and killed. Taking the dead bee home, Ray stuck it under his microscope – and realised it was a cuckoo bee (*Nomada xanthostica*), the first one seen in Britain since 1949.

The cuckoo bee is on the endangered species list and is feared to be nearing extinction. "When I found out what it was, it crossed my mind that this might be the last one in existence – and I've just killed it," he confessed. *Western Daily Press+D.Mirror 26 Feb 1992.*

THE LIVINGSTON UFO PLAQUE

THIS IS THE SITE REFERRED TO IN ARTHUR C. CLARKE'S "MYSTERIOUS WORLD" WHICH DESCRIBES AN ENCOUNTER BETWEEN A FORESTRY WORKER OUT WALKING AND WHAT APPEARED TO HIM AS AN UNIDENTIFIED FLYING OBJECT

LDC 1991

Livingston Development Corporation have at last erected a metal plaque, set in a rock at Detchmont Low, West Lothian, near Edinburgh, to commemorate Scotland's most famous close encounter with a UFO. It is probably the first time anywhere in the world that a public body has officially recognised such a claim.

On the morning of 9 November 1979, forestry worker Bob Taylor (now 73) came upon a circular 'craft', about 30ft across, in a clearing. Two 'creatures', balls with spikes looking like World War II mines, approached him. There was a terrible smell and he passed out. When he came to, his body was bruised and his trousers torn. Odd indentations were found at the site by police later that day. [See *FT31:30, FT56:46 & FT60:63*.]

NOWT SO QUEER ...

CAR PARK MYSTERY

● A man with a camera took pictures of 40 motorists as they arrived at the Trenchard Street NCP car park in Bristol on Tuesday, 11 February 1992. Later, they found the photographs under their windscreen wipers, accompanied by a printed card.

The card read: "You and your car are invited to take part in a performance entitled Environmental Forces this Friday. You and your car must leave your place of residence and travel into the centre of Bristol in search of resources without which you would not even get home. You will be in direct competition with other car driver teams and subject to unknown factors."

Four drivers complained to the police, whose spokeswoman said: "I wouldn't blame anybody who took a look at this and thought it was suspicious." The police had no clue concerning the identity of the conceptual artist (or whatever he was), except a car park attendant who questioned the man and was told he was "part of the university". Among those who had nothing useful to add were a spokeswoman for Bristol University, the students' rag week treasurer and Tony Ambrose of the Bristol Cycling Campaign. We wonder whether any of the drivers took part in 'Environmental Forces'... perhaps they couldn't help it. *Western Daily Press 13 Feb 1992.*

OUT OF THIS WORLD

● Richard Price from New York claimed he had been carrying a extraterrestrial homing device in his groin for the last 35 years. The space creatures who abducted him were about four feet tall and wore red and blue skintight uniforms and helmets. They sounded more like machines than people and showed him a film before they implanted the device.

Price said he had sent the contraption to the Massachusetts Institute of Technology who have told him the material is not of this Earth. The two-millimetre-long device isn't metal and feels like a brown, stale piece of licorice. *Lancaster (PA) New Era 5 Nov 1991.*

● A man walked into Orca Bay Seafoods in Seattle on 10 September 1991 and asked for three days' back wages. He was carrying an AR-15 assault rifle and wore a bandoleer of cartridges across his chest. He told employees not to be frightened, that he was armed only because he was going to a firing range with some friends. Although he was calm, he spoke of having a legal right to kill all communists and said that "President Bush would be next." Police searching his home found a large arsenal of weapons. When asked about the tattoos on his arms, the man explained that they had been stencilled by the CIA and that he received messages from outer space through them. *Seattle Post-Intelligencer 12 September 1992.*

FILTHY PEOPLE

● A Kenyan man in Othaya, 60 miles north of Nairobi, who had not washed for three years, was pursued through the streets by an exasperated mob of fellow workers who seized him, peeled off his clothes and scrubbed him with soap and a piece of gunny sack. His clothes were burnt and he was given a new set after friends held a collection for him. Frog-marched to a barber shop, he had his hair cut and beard trimmed. "After the dramatic exercise", said the *Kenya Times*, "the artisan was escorted to a nearby bar, where his colleagues bought him several beers." *San Francisco Chronicle 23 August 1990.*

● Sri Kuncoro [above], 83, lives in the village of Desa Sumokaton, near Jogjakarta on the island of Java. He has not washed for over 43 years. "I wanted to let God know that I am prepared to make a sacrifice to help convince Him to wipe out war, other violence and poverty ... If I gave up showering, God would realise I was serious." At the same time he gave up meat and rice, and has subsisted on vegetables, fruit and tea. He is widely known as a mystic and healer, and spends several hours each day receiving visitors from all over Indonesia who come to him for psychic guidance. *People (South Africa) 27 Mar 1991.*

OVER REACTIONS

● Jacob Mandel, 18, went into a barber shop in Los Angeles and asked for a short back and sides. He was not satisfied with the result, so he burned down a four-million-dollar shopping mall and three barbers' shops. *D. Mirror 15 June 1992*

● A man with a machine gun wounded 20 people at a brothel in Tripoli, Lebanon, after learning that his sister worked there. *Sun 29 Feb 1992.*

● A woman motorist in Seattle, angered by blocked traffic, drove her car onto the sidewalk and ran over Janice M. Gaston three times, killing her. Ms Gaston and three other women were standing at a corner talking to a male friend whose van was blocking traffic. The incident happened after a violent argument with the van driver. *St Louis Post-Dispatch 29 Nov 1991.*

● An Australian man was jailed for five years for stabbing his wife to death after she refused to change the TV channel so that he could watch a football match. *Edinburgh Evening News 30 April 1992.*

● Milkman Dave Walters grabbed customer David Blackley by the throat when he cancelled an order and threatened to kill him, Nottingham Crown Court was told. Walters, 42, sacked from his milk round, was given a conditional discharge. *D.Mirror 3 June 1992.*

● Lillian Ramsay, 36, got fed up with the barking dog of the Wrights next door; so she dressed up as a man in black and at 3am poured petrol through their letter box, followed by lighted rolled-up newspaper. Mrs Doreen Wright, 43, died in the fire. Her husband and two teenage daughters were rescued by a neighbour with a ladder. *D.Express 16 Jan 1992.*

COMPUTER DEMONS

SEE? THIS IS WHAT HAPPENS WHEN I TRY TO GET DOUBLE SPACING

O ne of the most sent-in clippings in recent months comes from 'Backbytes' in *Computing* magazine (5 Dec 1991), and concerns a possessed computer terminal. The new system was installed in a bank in Valparaiso, Chile, in the spring of 1991 and soon afterwards a bank custodian saw a hideous horned demon on the screen. The machine was said to have killed two bank employees, by decapitation and heart attack, and put another in a coma. A computer expert babbled like a madman after going within ten feet of the machine "and a dozen more were thrown to the floor like rag dolls by some unseen force." Anyone trying to turn the machine off blacked out. The firm that installed it said that the demon was almost certainly created by a computer virus. The yarn comes complete with an exorcist, Father Hector Diaz, and a police detective Raul Lopez.

New Scientist (1 Feb 1992) quotes the same yarn from *Computer Fraud and Security Bulletin*, who got it from an unnamed supermarket tabloid. The story omits useful details like the name of the bank, the type of computer involved, and even whether the 'demon' was possessing a single terminal or the whole system. Computer programmer Roy Stilling pointed out that the obvious solution of disconnecting the external power supply to the bank goes unmentioned; perhaps the Chilean Electricity Board is chaired by Beelzebub.

S imilar items do pop up in the press now and then: according to *Le Parisien Liberé* (27 May 1988), a new computer was terrifying staff at a

Stockport architect's office. No one wanted to touch the 12 megabyte PC, which emitted strange groans even when unplugged. Its screen would emit an incandescent light and letters appeared and disappeared. Experts verified that the machine wasn't picking up static electricity and wasn't affected by the radar of a neighbouring airport.

THE MANILA VAMPIRE

In the run up to the Philippine presidential election on 11 May, politics took second place to supernatural rumours in the slums of Manila's Tondo district. It was said that a 'mananang-gal', a creature similar to a vampire, was terrorising the area.

According to Filipino folklore, the manananggal appears as a woman who can cut her body in two. The top half flies around at night searching for babies to devour, but must return before daybreak to rejoin the rest of the body. The demon's latest exploits were reported in most of the tabloids.

"It's scary", one housewife told a vendor in the crowded Divisoria market as she paid for fresh fish. "That's why I don't sleep alone at night." The largest circulation tabloid, *People's Journal Tonight*, published an interview with Martina Santa Rosa, who purportedly battled with the demon a few days earlier.

"She attacked me", Santa Rosa said. "I was just lucky I was able to get free. I saw half of her body. it was naked. She had long, scraggly hair, long arms, nails and sharp fangs." The account was 'corroborated' by her neighbours. One, Alfonso Bernardo, said: "We saw it fly away from her house."

On 6 May, about a dozen young men, accompanied by a TV crew, barged into the home of Teresita Beronqui to investigate rumours that she was the manananggal. ABS-CBN television showed a terrified elderly woman denying the rumour. Actually, she said, she herself had been attacked by the demon, and as proof showed that her foot was missing several toes.

"Vampire experts in the neighbourhood said the woman was lying" the TV reporter, Cesar Soriano, told a nationwide audience. That was followed by an 'explanation' from an unidentified expert that the woman was indeed the manananggal and had already changed back into human form, albeit without some of her toes.

To resolve the mystery, Soriano produced a dried tail of a stingray and asked the woman to touch it on camera. (Manananggals are repulsed by stingray's tails.) The woman touched it to the satisfaction of all concerned. [AP] 8 May 1992.

LOVESICK ALBATROSS

Mollymawk, the lovesick black-browed albatross with an eight-foot wingspan, was back in Scotland this April. He joined the gannet colony at Saito outcrop at Hermaness nature reserve in the Shetland Islands, gazing out to sea searching for a mate, just as he has done every spring for over 20 years. He goes through the ritual of putting on a display to attract a female albatross. The chances of success are astronomically remote. The gannets are impressed, but quite unmoved emotionally.

Back in 1967, an albatross (probably the same one) turned up on the Bass Rock in the Firth of Forth, returning in 1968 and 1969. The next spring (or pos-

sibly spring 1972), he came to Hermaness. Mollymawk, Dutch for 'foolish gull', has been stranded on the wrong side of the world, about 8,000 miles from the nearest breeding colonies, since adulthood. He must now be 25, although albatrosses can live to a considerable age, possibly more than 30 years.

It is not known where Mollymawk (or Albert, as he is called in one report) spends the winter. Michael Everett of the RSPB said that he probably travels thousands of miles roaming the North Atlantic, resting on the water and feeding on fish. *Scotsman 26 Mar 1991; D.Telegraph 21 April; Int. Herald Tribune 23 April 1992.*

Scotland. Its only known competitor in the antiquity stakes is an ancient shrub in Tenerife. The yew's vast trunk, split into two, has a circumference of 56 1/2 feet. The split is thought to go back to pre-Christian times and to have been caused by fire. According to legend, Pontius Pilate was born under the tree when his father was the regional Roman commander. *Scotsman 4 April 1992.*

■ The world's largest bacterium has been discovered in the intestines of a surgeonfish. *Epulopiscium*, with a width of 0.5mm, is 1,000 wider than its smaller cousins with a volume a million times larger – a behemoth in the bacterial world – and has also been identified in mice and guinea pigs, though not in humans. Visible to the naked eye, it was discovered in 1985 and identified as an unusual protozoan because it was thought that bacteria could not become that large. However, genetic testing showed that it was most closely related to the Clostridium bacteria family.

"Bacteria have always been considered to be structurally simple – basically bags of enzymes", said Norman R. Pace, professor of biology at Indiana University, who directed the research. But the huge bacterium is too large to survive with such a simple structure. "That means to us that bacterial cell organisation is much more complex. It's not just a bunch of stuff floating round in a bag." It does not seem to harm or help its host. "It has the same function that we do", said Professor Pace, "to grow and reproduce and die – to be part of the turning wheel." *[AP] 30 May 1992.*

■ An alligator skull almost five feet long was found on the banks of the Amazon

NEW WORLD RECORDS

Just a month after the announcement of the world's largest (and oldest) organism - a 15 hectare honey fungus, comes news of a much bigger one in Washington state, near Mount Adams. This *Armillaria ostoyae*, a close relative of the Michigan *Armillaria bulbosa* (see *FT63:11*), covers 600 hectares (ie 1,480 acres or about two-and-a-half square miles).

Terry Shaw of the US Forest Service Rocky Mountain Experimental Station in Fort Collins, Colorado, measured its extent several years ago. From its size, he estimates that it is between 500 and 1,000 years old (in other words, much younger than its Michigan cousin: the discrepancy is not explained.)

It spreads from root to root, passing between trees where they make contact below the ground, and can double in size every 20 years if left unchecked. The *ostoyae* has a greater ability to kill trees than the *bulbosa*. Both types produce small edible mushrooms. Shaw suggested that the record might well be broken again. He said there was another *ostoyae* west of La Pine, Oregon.
[AP] 18 May; New Scientist 30 May 1992.

■ We must add to these fungal superlatives what is reckoned to be the world's largest truffle, found near Rimini, Italy, by Fernando Gianessi, head waiter at the Green Dragon Hotel, Hereford, who was on holiday in his homeland. The 5lb truffle was promptly sold to a

local restauranteur for £6,000, which Fernando donated to leukæmia research. "I normally can't afford truffle", he said. "Now I think I've eaten enough for a lifetime." *D.Telegraph 20 May 1992.*

■ Various clonal organisms compete for the record of oldest living 'thing' on the planet. A clone of box huckleberry has been found with a diameter of 2,000 metres and an age of 13,000 years, while an aspen (*Populus fremaloides*) covers 81 hectares and is over 10,000 years old. [Letter from James Bullock in *New Scientist 30 May 1992.*]

■ Europe's oldest piece of vegetation is believed to be a 3,000-year-old yew tree in the churchyard of Fortingall in Perthshire,

last year. The beast to which it belonged lived about eight million years ago. It is estimated to have been about 8ft tall, 40ft long with a weight of about 12 tons: about a ton heavier than *Tyrannosaurus rex*, the mightiest of dinosaur predators, which lived 60 million years earlier.

"This giant animal with its 4in teeth preyed on birds, turtles and on giant rodents that were themselves the size of cattle", said Professor Carl Frailey from Kansas. "We found the shell of one giant turtle with 20% of it bitten off." The alligator was probably heavier than an extinct ancestor of the great white shark, which reached 45ft, making it the largest carnivore the world has ever seen. *D.Telegraph 16 Nov 1991.*

THE De CLINTON CURSE

Something seems to be preventing developers building houses in the mediæval town of Kenilworth in Warwickshire. The first planning application, to build 80 houses on land near Finham Brook, was submitted to Warwick District Council in 1984. Since then, the original applicant has died in a hunting accident, the land has changed hands three times as successive owners have gone bust, council officers have been struck down by illness, and both the chairman of the planning committee and the leader of the council have lost their seats after agreeing to the application, now reduced to 20 houses.

The Manor of Kenilworth was given to Geoffrey de Clinton by Henry I in about 1130. He built the famous castle on the site and founded a Benedictine priory, later upgraded to an abbey. He granted the people of Kenilworth the right to graze their livestock around the abbey and the church of

RAINMAKER FAILS

In an attempt to relieve Indonesia's long-lasting drought, inventor Sunaryo Wirodirjo demonstrated his 'Sinkar XP-SE' rain-making device at the Ancol marine resort in Jakarta on 23 October 1991. After three days firing 'electromagnetic beams' into the sky, which, Wirodirjo claimed, would "provoke the formation of large clouds" he had to admit defeat.

Commenting on the story in *New Scientist (9 Nov 1991)*, a spokesman for the UK's Meteorological Office said: "Most clouds form through convection currents which would not be affected by an electromagnetic beam.

Electromagnetic fields only appear when thunderclouds form." He added: "The beam from his device must be many orders of magnitude less than the fields already existing up there in the formation of a thunderstorm."

We were unable to find out what was in Wirodirjo's rain-gun, or how it was intended to work; but the Met Office man did add an aside which relates to the topic of Jean-Louis Brodu's article [*FT60:50-53*]. Cloud-seeding has been out of fashion for two decades, he said, ever since "an American farmer took legal action to prevent a neighbour from stealing his rain."

St Mary; but he warned that if anyone "should attempt to take away or diminish anything which I have granted to the aforesaid church, he shall incur the curse of his father and the anger of God."

The proposed building site once formed the basin of the abbey's fishing lake. The latest mishap has been waterlogging from a mysterious regeneration of the springs that fed the lake, holding up work for months. Locals opposed to the housing scheme now believe it will never be built. Avril Redman, whose family have lived

at Kenilworth since Cromwell's time, said: "The curse...has passed into local folklore. The land has remained undeveloped for centuries. It's madness to build here." She believes the waterlogging – in an area hit by drought – is a dire warning to keep off. Balfour Beatty, the latest developers to own the land, refused to comment. *Observer 29 Mar 1992.*

FROZEN IN TIME

An 84-year-old woman sat for over two months on her balcony in the Stockholm suburb of Traneberg last

winter. She may have died while watching fireworks on New Year's Eve: police found newspapers from the beginning of January on her door mat. She was finally noticed on 16 March, sitting on a chair on her balcony, dressed in a coat and hat. Her forehead was leaning against the railing.

Neighbour Margaretha Marsellas realised something was wrong when she saw the woman on the balcony around the clock despite freezing temperatures. "I blame myself for not having seen her earlier", she said. [*AP*] *18 Mar 1992.*

COATIMUNDI CAPERS

In moments of weakness, sometimes, we find ourselves echoing the famous cry of Louis XIV: "Oh God! Send us a new animal!" However, where the Sun King was merely bored with beef for dinner, we find that unidentified big cats make for the largest proportion of clippings in our 'Mystery Animals' tray – see report on p44. Perhaps our half-hearted prayers were answered …

It began on the evening of 24 February, when Will Tuxworth, of Monksthorpe, near Spilsby in Lincolnshire, was walking home and spotted a strange animal close to a building in which his neighbour, farmer Robin Woolford, kept 400 pigs. Although it was the size of an average fox, he couldn't recognise

> *"'I was very concerned about it getting in among the pigs, especially the breeding sows, and causing them to panic or stampede, which could result in abortions and very serious injuries.'"*

it, and called in to the farm to ask Woolford if he was keeping any exotic pets.

Woolford and his wife joined Tuxworth in trying to trap the beast in an empty pig shed, but it escaped and was eventually cornered elsewhere. Woolford went to phone the Ministry of Agriculture for advice, and later decided to shoot it. "Although we didn't think it likely to be dangerous," he said, "I was very concerned about it getting in among the pigs, especially the breeding sows, and causing them to panic or stampede, which could result in abortions and very serious injuries." Another farmer, Peter Bark, who had a rifle, was asked to do the deed.

The browny grey animal weighed about 14lbs, and had a pointed head with small sharp tusks on either side of its snout, long claws, and a long brown-ringed tail. The dead creature was taken away by a Ministry official, who was unable to make a positive on-the-spot identification, but thought it likely to be a coatimundi, a kind of badger from South America.

Sightings

The *Spilsby Standard* (28 February 1992) said that police had no reports of such an animal escaping, or any other sightings. The intriguing question of its origin was left hanging, until about two months later when another coatimundi turned up in Wrawby, South

Above: The Wrawby coatimundi.
Bottom Left: Farmer Robin Woolford with dead beast.

Humberside, as reported in the Grimsby *Evening Telegraph* (6 May 1992). Luckier than the Spilsby Beast, this one was taken alive in a garden in Kettleby Lane in a joint police, RSPCA and Ministry of Agriculture operation.

RSPCA Inspector Alan Horan said he believed it had been in the area for about a week "upsetting the neighbourhood dogs"; but apart from a suspicion that the coatimundi was an illegal pet that escaped, there were no clues as to how it got there or where it came from. Wrawby is about 37 miles from the Spilsby area as the crow flies; could both animals have escaped from somewhere between the two towns? If the two appearances are independent events, just how many coatimundis might there be wandering around out there?

Capture

Just two weeks after the capture at Wrawby, we read in the *Times* (20 May 1992) that farmers in Lincolnshire have been warned to look out for a South American tapir "believed" to have escaped from an unnamed wildlife park. We have seen too many of these stories to accept, without qualification, that there is a tapir on the loose in an area which has yielded two coatimundis. The long snout of these latter creatures has already been noticed, so our tentative guess is that this warning is based upon a misperception of a third coatimundi. To date we have no note of its, or the tapir's, capture. It's still out there.

SEEING IS BELIEVING

● An elderly woman woke up during the nuns' chorus of *The Sound of Music* at a Birmingham theatre and caused chaos. She thought she had died and was being welcomed to heaven. *D.Record 4 May 1992.*

● A man walking on the North Wales shoreline at Pwllheli saw part of a man's body in an advanced state of decomposition and alerted the police. They rushed the jeans-clad remains 30 miles to Home Office pathologist Donald Wayte in Bangor. When he cut into it, he discovered it was a latex mannequin. *D.Post 18 Nov 1991.*

● Isle of Wight police ordered a post-mortem after a woman stumbled on what was thought to be a severed hand on a Seaview beach. A pathologist identified the 'hand' as a cuttle fish, a member of the squid family, which breeds in the Solent. "It did look like a badly decomposed hand", said Inspector Malcolm Turner, "especially with the tentacles." *Independent 18 June 1992.*

● Last November, two policemen in Newport, Gwent, reported seeing a woman in a window brandishing a weapon. Armed police surrounded the flat for three hours, using nine police vans to seal off roads. Eventually, two terrified teenagers emerged, shouting "Hold your fire!" What the policemen had seen was a 13-year-old girl with a television hand-control. *D.Telegraph 11 November 1991.*

FRUITY BULGE

● A banana caused a French passenger aircraft to go on hijack alert and turn back in mid-flight on 18 June. A passenger on board an Air Inter Airbus from Paris to Malaga, Spain, mistook a bulge in another traveller's trousers for a gun and alerted the crew. After the return to Orly Airport, paramilitary gendarmes discovered the fruity nature of the bulge. Two hours behind schedule, the plane took off again. *[Reuters] 19 June 1992.*

BANANA CRIME

● Last January, Nigel Hayward was released from a two-year sentence for robbery using a banana. The next day he walked into a bank with a banana under his shirt and a cashier gave him £295. The same trick worked in a building society where he got £1,500. Later, he was arrested for arguing in a nightclub called Joe Bananas in Bristol. He was jailed for another six years.

The following month, Ian Gaffney was jailed for robbing a Leominster bank with a banana. The defence said that, at the time of the raid, Gaffney was "suffering from a brain problem". *D.Mirror 21 Jan; Western Daily Press 12 Feb 1992.* For further crimes using fruit, vegetables and eggs see **FT53:14, FT57:31 & FT61:6.**

THE DANGERS OF TOURISM

...AND ACCORDING TO LEGEND IT HAS ONE HUGE EYE, HAIRY LEGS, AND CLAIMS IT'S DOING A FEATURE FOR A MAGAZINE...

● Pini Mauro, a Swiss tourist visiting the Indonesian island of Sumba, was severely beaten by villagers who took him for a demon or ogre of local legend who kidnapped and ate children. [AFP] *Daily Telegraph 2 June 1992.*

● The recent extensive riots in Conakry, the capital of Guinea, West Africa, seem to have grown from a rumour that a Spanish business-man was offering young women to have sex with dogs. Alseny Gomez narrowly escaped from a lynch mob which then ran amok for three days, stoning foreign cars and raping Guinean women dressed in Western-style clothes. Later, investigations by the interior minister said that Gomez's nightwatchman had made up the story to scare off an unwanted girlfriend. *Sunday Times 26 April 1992.*

NOT THE TIME OR PLACE

A 30-year-old man tried twice to hurl himself to death from the same window in Kenmore, New York, on Saturday morning, the 4th of April. In the first attempt, he had to take a running leap at the fourth-storey windows, because they didn't open. He smashed through the double-glazing, fell 40 feet and landed on a car, buckling the roof and doors and smashing the rear windows. Although dazed and bleeding from facial cuts, he got up and walked to the building's elevator, leaving a trail of blood.

Kenmore Police lieutenant Ronald Sardina arrived at the six-storey building in time to see the man make a second jump onto the crumpled car. This time he suffered more serious injuries, as the car no longer absorbed the impact and "kind of flattened out like a dumpster", said police captain Emil Palombo.

The man was in a Buffalo hospital with a broken wrist and ankle. He had lived in the building in 1991, moved out, then moved back in a week before the jumps, according to neighbours. "God bless him, he's alive" said Palombo. "Whatever help he needs, he's going to get it." [AP] *6 April 1992.*

STRANGE DEATHS

THE DEMON DRINK

✝ A 20-year-old woman with a severe allergy to milk died merely from smelling it, when she delivered census forms to a dairy near Treviso, Italy. *Observer 10 Nov 1991.*

✝ A Treviso wine enthusiast drowned in 500 gallons of home-made wine. Orfeo Agostinetto drank too much of last year's wine and fell into the new vat he had just made. *Scottish D.Record 11 Nov 1991.*

TOUPEE TOPPING

✝ Eager to try on a £750 toupee, shop manager Claude Jules, 53, of Abbeville, France, stopped his car, dabbed on special glue and applied the wig. Then he lit a cigarette. The glue fumes ignited and the car exploded, killing him instantly. *Scottish D.Record 2 Jan 1992.*

KILLER DENTURES

✝ A 56-year-old man tricked his way into a house in Alicante in Spain by saying he was a sewing machine technician, and then stole £80 worth of pesetas from a woman. As she chased him, he tripped, swallow-ed his false teeth and choked to death. *Johannesburg Citizen 16 May; European 17 May 1991.*

JEALOUSY KILLS

✝ Priscilla Brayboy and a friend drove down a street in Houston, Texas, looking for her husband, Joe, whom she suspected of visiting his lover. On spotting a grey Volvo parked in a driveway, she knocked on the door and began to force her way inside. A resident heard the commotion, armed himself with a shotgun and shot her dead. When Mrs Brayboy's friend saw what had happened, she ran down the street screaming and then noticed the light grey Volvo parked in a different driveway a few houses away. *Independent 7 Dec 1990.*

MINCEMEAT

✝ Only the legs of a 27-year-old meat worker could be seen when he was discovered by a colleague in a giant mincing machine at a meat packing plant in Pico Rivera, California. The victim was alone cleaning the machine when it was somehow switched on. Police questioned workers to discover if it was a freak accident or murder. *Standard 28 Feb 1992.*

WHEELY DANGEROUS

✝ Michael Bennet, 22, from Driffield, Humberside, burst into tears after overturning his 'pride and joy', an E-reg Citroen AX, on a bend after he hit some boulders. Hours later his body was found hanging from a tree – by the same rope he had used to tow his car home. *D.Mirror 26 Sept 1991.*

✝ Widow Pany Jagger, 81, from Wakefield, killed herself with paracetamol after being told her old car was beyond repair. *D.Express 1 Jan 1992.*

SPACE EMBASSY

The Raelian sect, founded by a French contactee, has commissioned Swiss architects to design a flying-saucer-shaped embassy to welcome space aliens with hot baths, fresh food and comfortable beds. They hope to build it near Jerusalem before the expected arrival of the aliens in the year 2000.

The Raelians, who say they have won 31,500 supporters across the world since the sect was founded in 1973, claim they are already in contact with the extraterrestrials, dubbed 'Heloims'. They are discussing the embassy project with the Israeli government. *[Reuters] 22 Feb 1992.*

PECKED BY PENGUINS

A 76-year-old South African gentleman, rejoicing in the name of Nimrod Nbini, was recently charged with the somewhat unusual crime of stabbing and beating a penguin to death. He told a Cape Town magistrate that he acted in self defence after being pecked. *Brisbane (Australia) Courier-Mail 31 Mar 1992.*

NEW FISH FOUND IN PUDDLE

A new species of brilliantly coloured fish - the tiny red-finned blue-eye named *Scaturiginichthys vermellipinnis* - was discovered in December 1990 in a shallow Queensland puddle no more than three inches deep. The fish has made its home in just five shallow pools on Edgbaston Station, a grazing property near Longreach. Not only is it an unknown species, but also a new genus and a new subfamily. It has a bright blue belly and eyes, a yellow body and red-tipped fins, and a maximum length of about an inch. The discovery was made by a member of the amateur Australia-Papua New Guinea Fishes Association, Peter Unmac. *Brisbane (Australia) Courier Mail 11 Jan 1992.*

WEB OF LOVE

Mrs Elizabeth Wells, 58, a wealthy American divorcee living in Axford, Wiltshire, lifted the lid on a heart-shaped pink satin gift box on 7 November 1991 and found a poisonous four-inch red-kneed tarantula inside, capable of paralysing humans with its bite. Mrs Wells, an acute arachnophobic, screamed and dropped both box and spider, but her housekeeper trapped the spider until police arrived. The surprise gift had arrived in a Jiffy bag mailed from London. The following day, the police web was said to be closing in on a love rival of Mrs Wells. *D.Telegraph 8 Nov; Today 9 Nov 1991.*

THE EFFECTS OF PROZAC

Bite-sized pieces of flesh were found at the San Francisco home of Mildred Mortenson, 87, on 6 November 1991. Police said she was being 'cannibalized' by her daughter Barbara, 61, who had dried blood covering her face and was wearing a nightgown completely soaked in blood at the front. The daughter claimed she had been taking the anti-depressant Prozac, a drug believed by the Church of Scientology to inspire suicides and other violence (charges rejected by the American Food and Drug Administration).

The daughter was treated in hospital for a cut before being booked on charges of attempted homicide, assault with a deadly weapon (her teeth), aggravated assault, mayhem and infliction of physical pain to a senior. The mother was in stable but critical condition in hospital, with at least 20 bites on her face and arms. Several of the bites were bone-deep. *[AP] D.Star 8 Nov 1991.*

● Jason Wayne Laberge, 20, high on Prozac, opened a cage in a downtown zoo in Toronto to set free some flamingoes. When they refused to leave their cage, he beat six of them to death with a broom handle. Laberge was jailed for eight months and ordered to pay £4,500. *Rocky Mountain News 29 April 1992.*

PERPER'S PEEPERS

Passengers on bus 61A (East Pittsburgh to Wilkinsburg) noticed two eyeballs, slightly larger than human eyes, on a back seat shortly after 2am on 2 February 1992. The bus driver placed the eyes in a cup

and took them to the garage, where a dispatcher gave them to the police, who passed them to Allegheny County Coroner Joshua Perper, who held on to them (in a manner of speaking). He said that the eyes were "not in any bottle or bag or box". *Pittsburgh Post Gazette 4 Feb; NY Post 5 Feb 1992.*

LAST ORDERS

A bottle thrown into the sea off the Scilly Islands with the message: "Send more gin please. Desperate" has been washed up in France ten years late. *The People 22 Sept 1991.*

BARKING MAD

The latest craze in California is apparently sex changes for pets. A doctor who charged £3,000 for the surgery said: "Like humans, pets can find themselves trapped in the bodies of the opposite sex." *Edinburgh Evening News 20 Aug 1991.*

THE FAR SIDE By GARY LARSON

Earthquake's a-comin'.

yup.

The mysterious, innate intuition of some animals

STRANGE DEATHS

HEADJAMMERS

✝ Francis McCorry, a civil servant aged 38, of Ruddington, Nottinghamshire, suffocated when his head jammed in a wash basin in his bathroom on 12 November 1991. A policeman broke into the house and found Mr McCorry slumped forward in the basin with his head under the tap, which had not been turned on. The inquest recorded an open verdict. *Nottingham Evening Post 18 Nov 1991.*

✝ Paul Ferguson, 25, from Eccles, was found dead, stuck headfirst down a fox hole in waste ground by Davyhulme sewage works, off Rivers Lane, Stretford, near Manchester. He was out hunting rabbits with his six terriers and a ferret, and police believe he was trying to free one of the terriers, which was later found alive. He either suffocated or froze to death. *Bradford Telegraph and Argus 27 Jan; Eccles Journal 30 Jan 1992.*

✝ Two months later, Philip Edwards, 26, from Edmondstown, Mid Glamorgan, also died trapped head first down a hole while trying to rescue his pet terrier. *Bristol Eve. News 7 April 1992.*

FATAL PHONE CALL

✝ Hester Fourie, 19, was talking barefoot on the telephone when lightning struck overhead telephone wires near East London in South Africa on 11 February. She died later in hospital. *Johannesburg Star 13 Feb 1991.* For other telephones struck by lightning, see *FT45*:8.

REST IN PEACE

✝ Marshall Gambrell, 25, from Alexandria, Virginia, lost control of his car, crossed a grassy area, went through a hedgerow into Beaverdale Memorial Park, Hamden, Connecticut, and was fatally hurled head-first into a marble headstone. *[AP] 18 Jan 1992.*

DEAD RIGHT

✝ Armando Cassa, 24, got so depressed when he was reported to have died in a fire that he jumped to his death from a high-rise in Puerto Rico. *Sun 15 Oct 1991.*

ICED

✝ Piera Rutelli, 40, was killed by a falling piece of ice that pierced the roof of her car as she drove through a tunnel outside Genoa in Italy. *Daily Record (Scotland) 28 Feb 1991.*

HIGHWAY HORROR

✝ Snake-like steel cables from a blown-out tyre tore through a bus floor, snatched sleeping four-year-old Ramon Prado from his mother's arms and dragged him to his death beneath the bus's wheels. The boy and his family were returning to Santa Ana from Michoacan, Mexico, when the rear tyre blew out near Oceanside, California. *[AP] 12 May 1992.*

SWEDISH HORSE RIPPING

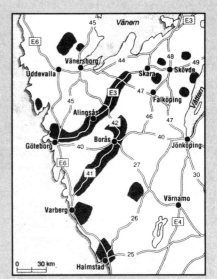

The grey areas show where horses have been assaulted. The perpetrator is likely to have a car; note the proximity of the attacks to roads. However, since most big farms, riding schools and studs are situated near roads rather than in the middle of nowhere, this may not be significant.

For two or three years, someone – or something – has been attacking and mutilating horses and cows in western Sweden. About 200 horse attacks had been reported to the police when the mystery was brought to national attention by journalist Siewert Öholm's TV programme *Svar direkt* on 25 February 1992.

In the summer of 1989, the number of reports increased. In 90% of the incidents, the victims were horses, almost always assaulted in the same way. They were cut with a sharp, scalpel-like instrument, in or beside their sexual organs. The wounds were often 30cm long, and five or six cm deep. About 50% of the animals were so severely maimed that they had to be put down.

Fanatic

Most of the attacks were near main roads, and the original police hypothesis was that a single madman or religious fanatic was motoring from one enclosed pasture to another; then several horses seemed to have been assaulted in different places at the same time, although this is not certain. According to Marie Rådén, police investigator in the Vänersborg district, it requires an astonishing knowledge of animals to be able to approach the horses, and hurt them so badly, without causing them to offer resistance. There were cases where watchdogs didn't react, even when they were only a couple of yards away, nor was there any indication that the animals had

been drugged.

In August 1991, several horses were assaulted in the neighbourhood of Färgelanda in Dalsland. It began when a mare, belonging to Marianne Göthberg, was cut round the vagina. Another of Mrs Göthberg's horses was cut the following day, and the day after that a foal was found bleeding on a neighbouring farm. More horses in the area succumbed, and some 40 farmers formed a sort of equine `home guard'. Pairs of farmers policed the roads at night, armed with whatever weapons their farms could provide. They caught a suspicious individual one evening, and turned him over to the police; but he turned out to be a frightened bilberry-picker who had lost his way.

Assaults

Tord Haraldsson from Alingsås, who belongs to the investigating task force, said that similar assaults in Denmark and the USA have turned out to be sectarian rituals, where fanatics have been drinking horses' blood to gain strength. This is news to us; the widespread cattle mutilations across the American Midwest in the last two decades are variously blamed on cultists, aliens or government experimentation, but, as far as we are aware, no actual *proof* has ever been found to back up any one of these hypotheses.

Several farmers and horse breeders appeared on the TV programme. They stressed that several attacks had taken

place almost in their presence, and couldn't understand why their horses had submitted without offering resistance. The perpetrator was like a phantom or a supernatural being. A vet said that the attacker had a good knowledge, not only of animal behaviour, but also of animal anatomy. Some of the wounds had been very professionally cut.

Prostitute

The reviewer of the programme in *Sydsvenska Dagbladet* the next day drew a parallel with "the horrible murder and cutting up of a prostitute, Catrin da Costa, in Stockholm a couple of years ago." It was not possible to determine how the woman had died, since she was dismembered and her head was never found.

When the horses were turned out to pasture again after the winter, the Färgelanda `home guard' was again mobilised, and others were organised all over western Sweden. The first mutilation of the year was reported in *Expressen* on 14 April. A mare was found at a place called Vitehall near Kyrkekvarn, bleeding from wounds in her vagina and hind legs. A `mysterious' red car driven by a young man sped away from the spot as the mare was found; but it was not clear at the time of the report how the wounds had been inflicted. The mare might have been kicked by another horse.

EQUINE HOME GUARD. Left to right: Marianne Göthburg, Tina Lindblom, Karin Svedberg, Vera Svedberg, Anita Andersson

CROCODILE BOY

Archæologists in Istanbul have been thrown into confusion by the discovery of a bizarre mummy in the museum at the Topkapi Palace. *Sunday Times* 8 March 1992. Once the seraglio of the Turkish sultan, Topkapi now houses one of the world's most dazzling collections of manuscripts, jewellry and other articles from the ancient Middle East. Visitors are still shown the room where they strangled unfortunate wives, bundled them into bags and tossed them into the Bosphorus – the origin of the phrase 'getting the sack'.

During an attempt to unwrap and study one of their many mummies, the archæologists were astonished to find the preserved upper half of a young boy joined to the lower half of a crocodile. Their first thoughts were that this was an elaborate practical joke; if so, it was a grim and unprecedented one. The only facts established so far are that the mummification techniques were undoubtedly Egyptian, as is the wooden sarcophagus in which the unusual mummy lay.

A discussion in the Australian journal *Digging* (May 1992) referred to the frequency of hybrid human-animal gods in old Egypt – eg. Anubis, Thoth and Horus – but these usually had the heads of animals on human bodies. It was even proposed that "the child was half-eaten by a crocodile and his parents, either in revenge or simply so that the child should not arrive in the other world incomplete, arranged for this macabre mummification."

If anyone learns more of this enigma, do let us know.

PETS' CORNER

■ Above: Sophie Nowell, six-year-old daughter of a trawler skipper, spotted a goldfish in the gutter near her home in Goldsithney, near Penzance, Cornwall. She wanted to give it a proper burial, but her mother Nell refused. Twenty minutes later, they passed the lifeless fish again and Nell relented. As Sophie was rinsing the grit off the 'corpse' in the kitchen, it flipped its tail and started gasping for breath. Sophie named her new pet 'Lucky'. *D.Mirror* 4 April 1992. [For another goldfish resurrection, see *FT60*:6.]

■ Glen Maloney, 30, thought his Jack Russell terrier, Mugsy, had died when he was hit by a car in Maryland USA; so he buried the pet three feet under as his two young children sobbed indoors. Mugsy turned up on the doorstep 14 hours later, presumably having dug himself out of his grave. Apparently, shock can cause dogs to go into a lifeless 'coma'. *Sun* 22 Nov 1990.

■ Arnold, a young pig, was frozen and clinically dead when he arrived at the office of vet Campbell Mercer in London, Kentucky. His skin was purple, he had stopped breathing and he had no pupil response. Arnold belonged to Elizabeth Strunk, eight, who had only had him a couple of days when he froze to death in the family garage. Elizabeth and her mother took Arnold home for burial. Her father Frank returned from work and suggested soaking the animal in hot water as a last resort. Elizabeth soaked Arnold and massaged him, and a few hours later he was squealing up a storm. *Country Vol 4 (7) Feb/Mar 1991.*

■ Louise Duguid, 15, and her brother Graeme, 12, found their two-year-old pet hamster Hector cold and lifeless at their Gifford home in East Lothian. They packed him in a small cardboard box and buried him a foot down in the garden. Two hours later, a neighbour called to say that Hector was running about her garden. He had come to in the warmth of the box and dug himself out. The children, whose father is a pet insurance salesman, renamed him Lazarus. *Edinburgh Eve. News 17 Jan; D.Star 18 Jan 1992.*

■ A second hamster dug itself out from the grave in Sutton Benger, Wiltshire. Carly Gough, 11, and her brother Lee, six, buried two-year-old Hammy the hamster six inches underground in a shoebox lined with cotton wool after they had found him apparently dead in his cage. Seven hours later, they watched as he burrowed his way out. *Bristol Evening Post, D.Mirror 3 Feb 1992.*

MY GOD!

In Concord, California, two modern witches have asked the Mount Diablo District School Board to ban the story of Hansel and Gretel from local school libraries. Karlyn Straganana, high priestess, of the Oak Haven Coven, complained: "This story teaches that it is all right to burn witches and steal their property." We find this a bit one-sided; surely, the same story could be said to endorse the kidnap and baking of children? But Ms Straganana protests: "Witches don't eat children and we don't have long noses with warts and we don't wear concial hats." *Rockland (NY) Journal News 28 May 1992.*

The issue raised here is far greater than a petty squabble between the system and an offended minority. Already many councils in the UK have forbidden from schools anything that hints at witchcraft, however lightly treated. Under pressure from extremist Christian organisations, even Hallowe'en festivities are outlawed, forgetting, it seems, that this festival traditionally ends with the triumphant banishment of evil for another year.

These same organisations published, a couple of years ago, an extensive list of things which they regarded as being the thin end of the wedge of Satan propaganda, including the Care Bears, yoga, the 'ban the bomb' symbol, computer games and all fairy tales. For other councils – notoriously the barmier Labour ones – have tried to purge themselves of racist, sexist and blasphemous publications, and the telling of 'offensive' jokes. Offence, of course, is a highly variable and

arbitrary concept, difficult to define in any absolute enforcable way.

We learn from the *Pagan News* (May 1992) that the Pagan Federation is trying to restrict common usage of the word 'Pagan'; and from a US Satanist's magazine *The Bladk Flame*, that the Church of Satan has actually applied to copyright the sign of the goat's head in an inverted pentacle. Can one legally annex words and images that have been in the public domain for centuries?

Where does it stop, if indeed it will or ever can? Meanwhile, with Nigel Pennick's warnings about the copyrighters' encorachment on everyday reality, we noted the following curious development. According to the *Daily Telegraph* (29 May 1992) Mrs Chitralekha Bolar, a classical Indian dancer from Tamworth, Staffordshire, has complained to Matchbox Toys, the makers of the popular 'Monster in my Pocket' figurines, about a tiny model of an elephant-headed, pot-bellied humanoid in a box of other monsters bought for her nine-year-old son Ashwin.

We don't know if this figurine is actually named Ganesha in the Matchbox literature, but Mrs Chitralekha chose to interpret it as a representation of this popular Hindu god. "I am not a religious fanatic," she said, "but imagine how I felt when I found a figure of the god whom we worship every day in a box alongside models of the Loch Ness Monster, the Ancient Gorgon and the Ectoplasmic Phantom."

Quite. But who's to say that these – like My Little Pony, Batman, perhaps even Satan – aren't, or cannot be, the objects of a pious devotion themselves?

NIGHT CURSES

A father who attempted to murder his stepson while asleep was cleared on the grounds that he was not responsible for his actions in a unique legal ruling at Newcastle Upon Tyne crown court in June.

The man, who was not named, told police he remembered a strange dream in which he attempted to smother the eight-year-old boy with a pillow and contemplated attacking his other two children. When he awoke he phoned his wife, who was working a night shift, and told her he had done "something stupid".

Under the recently-introduced 1991 Criminal Procedure (Insanity and Unfitness to Plead) Act, Mr Justice Kennedy was able to rule on the case without referring it to a jury – and he decided the man was a victim of 'insane automatism'.
D.Telegraph+D.Express 6 Jun 1992.

● It was not the first time such a case had come before a British court. Back in 1986 Colin Kemp of Caterham, Surrey, was cleared of murdering his wife, whom he had strangled in his sleep, after the jury heard that he had been having a nightmare in which he dreamed he was chased through a jungle by two Japanese soldiers. His defence was also automatism; psychologists said he had experienced a condition known as 'night terror', an arousal from normal sleep accompanied by intense anxiety. Similar cases dating back to the 17th century were detailed in *FT48:25.*

● A sleepwalking policeman who claimed he unwittingly tried to strangle his uncle during a nightmare was cleared of attempted murder on 25 June. PC Robert Short, 24, slipped a cord round Patrick Barrett's neck as he slept and only awoke when he heard him cry out: "You are killing me!" The prosecution maintained that Short set out to murder the 58-year-old draughtsman after quarrelling about the house they shared in Shooter's Hill, south London. Short said he had suffered bouts of sleepwalking since he was five years old and that the condition ran in the family. *D.Telegraph, Sun 26 June 1992.*

● In the only two Canadian murder trials where automatism was put forward as a defence, one man was found not guilty and the other guilty. In May 1987, Kenneth Parks, 28, allegedly drove 15 miles in his sleep to Scarborough, Ontario, where he picked up a tyre iron and a kitchen knife and killed his mother-in-law and wounded her husband in their bedroom. He was found not guilty of first degree murder.

Fifteen months later, William Wade, 58, fell into a deep sleep following an argument with his wife of 19 years. A few hours later, he was rhythmically bashing her head against a curb outside their house in Bolton, Ontario. He was found guilty of second degree murder, but is appealing the sentence.

Both men came from families of sleepwalkers and themselves had a history of serious sleep disorders. Neither had shown any propensity for violence, asleep or awake. Both murders occurred when the men were having marital problems and were facing considerable stress for other reasons as well.

The prevailing view among psychiatrists is that "the sleeping mind cannot form an intent"; but medical opinion is not unanimous and court rulings on sleep crimes are inconsistant. *Victoria (BC) Times-Colonist 15 July 1988 & 6 Mar 1992; Scientific American Jan 1990; Toronto Globe & Mail 25 Apr 1992.*

GUN-HO!

Here are some tales of amazing escapes from guns fired at lethally close range. It would be hard to top the dramatic twist of the Florida shopping mall shoot-out in 1987, when a police agent caught a bullet, aimed at his chest, in the barrel of his own gun [*FT50:4*. For similar tales, see also *FT54:6* & *FT56:31*.]

BANG!

Hiroshi Oyama, a 62-year-old dentist from Osaka, western Japan, was confronted by a gunman outside his house after returning from dinner late on 30 January this year. The gunman was middle-aged with a mustache. "Are you Mr Oyama?" he asked. The moment Oyama replied "Yes", the man fired once into his chest, jumped into a car and drove off. Mr Oyama was not injured: the bullet was found lodged halfway through a bundle of 42 banknotes, amounting to 242,000 yen (£1,084), in his fold-over leather wallet... which just goes to show that it's safer to carry a bankroll than a credit card. The dentist had no idea why he was shot at. [*AP*] 1 Feb 1992.

BANG!!

Charles Kobel, 50, a retired New York City policeman, was confronted by a mugger who demanded his watch and wallet. He was complying when the mugger said, "I might as well kill you anyway", aimed at Kobel's neck and fired. The knot in his tie apparently deflected the .22-calibre bullet. Mr Kobel drew his own gun and the mugger fled. He was treated for powder burns to his neck. *Int. Herald Tribune 9 Dec 1991.*

BANG!!!

The escape of John M. Rainey, a 43-year-old doctor, was even narrower. Rainey and his wife Carol were walking along E 18th Street in Cleveland, Ohio, about 9:00pm on 25 March 1992. They were returning to their car after going to the ballet (it was Mrs Rainey's birthday). Suddenly, they were confronted by a robber, who pulled a gun and demanded money. The doctor tried to push the gun away, but the robber brought it back toward him and fired, before running off.

Rainey didn't realise he was wounded until he was in a police station reporting the incident. Police examining his overcoat noticed blood and a bullet tear, and as a bloody chequebook was removed from his breast pocket, a small calibre bullet fell to the floor. It had gone right through the chequebook and broken his skin, but he was not seriously injured. *Cleveland Plain Dealer 26 March 1992.*

BANG!!!!

Dentures can sometimes save lives. Cab driver Ignatius Nwandilibe, 47, was shot in the mouth by a teenage robber in Denver this June. The bullet cut his lip and tongue, shattered his dentures, which slowed its speed and probably saved his life, before bullet fragments lodged in the roof of his mouth. The attacker fled. Police held the shattered bridgework as evidence. [*AP*] 14 June 1992. The same denture deliverance was provided for Charles A. Hinkle, 38, in Riverview, Florida [*AP 25 August 1990*]; and to Albino Biasilo, 75, in Cavazzale, Italy [*Sun 18 Dec 1991.*]

BANG!!!!!

Ronnie Ware, 15, went to the kitchen sink for a glass of water in Memphis, Tennessee, when a bullet zipped through the window's two panes of glass and a heavy curtain into his open mouth. It struck a back tooth, chipped it and dropped out of his mouth when he fell, knocked unconscious by the impact. He wasn't able to walk for two or three hours. Police had a suspect with a pellet gun. Such weapons can fire bullets up to .22 calibre with compressed air. [*AP*] 17 Sept 1990.

MONKEY BUSINESS

The corridors of power in India have been ruled for over 20 years by a group of monkeys. The monkeys, which number at least 200, are descendants of a group that escaped from laboratories at the All-India Institute of Medical Sciences in New Delhi. They not only roam the institute, but rule the roost in India's 'Whitehall' three miles away. They conceal themselves in cavernous niches high up in the Lutyens-designed building, ready to chase the unwary or embark on "orgies of file shredding" during holidays.

Private wards in the institute are equipped with expensive wire mesh. Dozens of people have been bitten by the monkeys, who often chase nurses and patients. Surgical patients have been known to emerge from anæsthesia to find a monkey either sharing their bed or fiddling with their drips. Shooting and poisoning are not an option as the monkeys are sacred because of their association with Hanuman, the monkey god. Efforts to tranquillise them were abandoned when they hid. *Sunday Telegraph 17 Feb 1991.*

■ Romeo, a rude rhesus monkey, was banished to the jungle last February after 66 days behind bars for

I HATE PAPERWORK BUT IT'S GOT TO BE DONE...

YEAH

OFFICIAL DOCUMENT

being a sex beast. He had molested at least 30 young women, mostly nurses, at the government-run Sir Maharaja Ghulab Singh hospital in Jammu, Kashmir. He groped at their breasts and tried to kiss and cuddle them. Staff threw stones at him, but this failed to deter. The last straw came when he started making obscene gestures, and the nurses threatened to strike. Wildlife officials and police finally lured him into a trap. *Straits Times, D.Telegraph 3 Feb 1992.*

■ Monkeys drove officials out of the Public Works Department office in Tezpur, north-eastern Assam, in December 1991, and spent 25 minutes destroying official documents. Police were summoned, but made no attempt to intervene. The holiness factor saved them again. *D.Post 10 Dec 1991.*

■ Israel's former Chief Rabbi Ovadia Yosef has ruled that trained monkeys may turn off lights or do other chores forbidden on the Sabbath. However, only a borrowed animal can be used by observant Jews between sunset on Fridays and sunset on Saturdays. Their own beasts must rest on the Sabbath. *[Reuters] 15 Nov 1991.*

SPECIAL CORRESPONDENTS

AFRICA: Cynthia Hind (Zimbabwe), Ion Alexis Will (Ivory Coast). **AUSTRALIA:** Greg Axford (Vic.), Paul Cropper (NSW), Rex Gilroy (NSW), Tony Healy (ACT). **BELGIUM:** Henri Prémont. **CANADA:** Brian Chapman (BC), Dwight Whalen (Ont.). **DENMARK:** Lars Thomas. **ENGLAND:** Claire Blamey, Bruce Chatterton, Peter Christie, Mat Coward, Hilary Evans, Peter Hope Evans, Alan Gardiner, Mick Goss, Chris Hall, Jeremy Harte, Brian Inglis, Jake Kirkwood, Joseph Lang, Alexis Lykiard, Nick Maloret, Valerie Martin, Kevin McClure, John Michell, Ralph Noyes, Nigel Pennick, Andy Roberts, Paul Screeton, Doc Shiels, Karl Shuker, Bob Skinner, Anthony Smith, Paul R. Thomas, Nigel Watson, Owen Whiteoak, Steve Wrathall. **FRANCE:** Jean-Louis Brodu, Bernard Heuvelmans, Michel Meurger. **GERMANY:** Walter J. Langbein, Ulrich Magin. **GREECE:** S.C. Tavuchis. **HONGKONG:** Phillip Bruce. **ICELAND:** V. Kip Hansen. **IRELAND:** Peter Costello. **JAPAN:** Masaru Mori, Shigeo Yokoyama. **NEW ZEALAND:** Peter Hassall. **NORTHERN IRELAND:** Caryl Sibbett. POLAND: Leszek Matela. **RUSSIA:** Vladimir Rubtsov. **SCOTLAND:** David Burns, Stuart Herkes, Roger Musson, Roland Watson, Jake Williams. **SWEDEN:** Anders Liljegren, Sven Rosén. **USA:** Larry E. Arnold (PA), Mark Chorvinsky (MD), Loren Coleman (ME), David Fideler (MI), Mark A. Hall (MN), Michael Hoffman (CA), John Keel (NYC), Kurt Lothmann (TX), Ray Nelke (MO), Jim Reicken (NY), Ron Schaffner (OH), Margo Schwadron (NY), Chuck Shephard (DC), Dennis Stacy (TX), Joseph Swatek (NB), Joseph Trainor (MA), Jeffrey Vallance (CA), Robert Anton Wilson (CA), Joseph W. Zarzynski (NY). **WALES:** Janet & Colin Bord, Richard Holland, Joe Kelly.

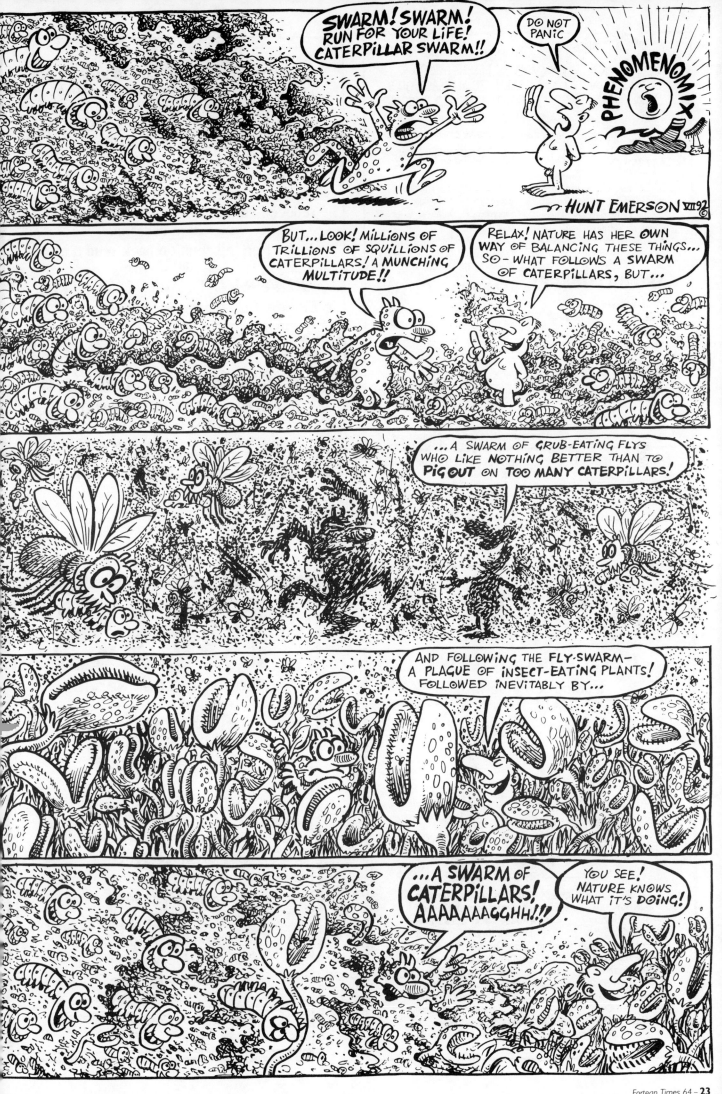

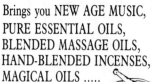
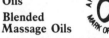

SUPERNATURAL SPIELBERG
Close Encounters of the Fortean Kind

Steven Spielberg can easily be regarded as the premier promoter of Fortean topics in contemporary popular cinema. His films about UFOs and aliens - *Close Encounters of the Third Kind* (1977), and *E.T. The Extraterrestrial* (1982) - broke all box-office records when they were released.

Close Encounters publicized the classification system for UFO experiences, devised by Dr J. Allen Hynek; he can even be seen in the final reel, stroking his beard. The character of Lacombe, played by the respected French film director François Truffaut, was based on a combination of two influential French UFO researchers, Claude Poher (a director of the French equivalent of NASA) and the computer scientist Jacques Vallée. Spielberg hoped the publicity generated by the film would encourage research into UFOs. In Britain, newspaper stories about the film boosted the work of the UFO Investigators' Network (UFOIN) and brought to light many new cases; indeed, those from northern England were the basis for Nigel Watson's study *Portraits of Alien Encounters*.

E.T. was originally intended to be a sequel to *Close Encounters*. Spielberg was intrigued by a version of the filmscript, by John Sayles and Ron Cobb, in which one of the benevolent aliens is left behind by his comrades. This became linked with another of Spielberg's filmic projects concerning the adventures of a group of children. The first encounter with E.T., and the alien itself, was largely inspired by one of the earliest group 'contacts' with mysterious entities in the casebook of modern ufology. In August 1955, a terrified Kentucky family, living in a remote farmhouse near Hopkinsville, became convinced they were under attack by glowing goblin-like creatures hiding in the surrounding woods. Shots fired at these long-armed 'aliens' seemed to knock them down, but they soon got up again, scurrying away apparently unharmed.

What Spielberg regarded as a small-scale movie became one of the most popular films of all time. Jeffrey Drezner - 'E.T.: An Odyssey of Loss' in *The Psychological Review* vol 70, no 2 (Summer 1983) - attributed the success of the film to the way it tackled the problems of "latency age". Elliott, the chief protagonist, is a latency age child who is on the verge of choosing between rational and magical thinking. His older brother takes longer to accept the existence of E.T. because his thinking is already more adult and rational; whilst Gertie, his younger sister, immediately accepts E.T. because her mode of thinking embraces magical things almost without question. Translated into the language of ufology, we might say that younger children are more fantasy-prone than teenagers and adults generally less so.

It has also been argued - in *E.T.: You're More than a Movie Star* by Al Millar - that the film's success lies in the way it echoes central Christian themes. For example: E.T. is discovered in a shed (an approximation to a stable); the name of the alien's earthly 'mother' is Mary; E.T.'s message of love is ignored; and as a climax E.T. has his own death, resurrection and ascension. However, both Spielberg and Melissa Mathison, his script-writer, have denied that these themes were used consciously or deliberately.

It is clear that there are large numbers of people - not all of them ufologists - who want to believe in the existence of living beings elsewhere in the universe, and that they are friendly. The skill with which Spielberg shows how innocence and love can overcome obstacles that inhibit cold, rational science usually affects even the most hard-hearted and cynical viewer.

> "It is clear that there are large numbers of people – not all of them ufologists – who want to believe in the existence of living beings elsewhere in the universe, and that they are friendly."

MAGICAL THINKING

The emotional power of Spielberg's films arises from his recreation of ancient myths for a contemporary audience. Like Jacques Vallée (in his classic *Passport to Magonia*), Spielberg is aware that today's obsession with alien visitors is nothing new. Our aliens both resemble and behave like the fairies of folklore and

DARREN SLADE has followed Spielberg's work since viewing *Duel* in the 1970s. His film studies range from the Hammer horror series to the films of Orson Welles. In 1986 he graduated from Warwick University with a BA in film and Literature. He now works as a journalist.

NIGEL WATSON was so enthralled by *Jaws* that he has followed Spielberg's films ever since. He gained a degree in Psychology, Film and Literature, so that he could explore the role of the news media in forming society's beliefs about UFOs and related subjects. He works as a copywriter in London.

AMAZING STORIES: Steven Spielberg (below) has become the world's most successful film director

folk-tales; the only difference is that today we have a different set of theories to explain them. This aspect of his work has been noticed by some perceptive critics, among them Andrew Gordon, who wrote: "Because of his tendency to magical thinking, Spielberg's films are closer to fairy tale and horror than to SF. They deal not in the rationality of SF but rather in the implausibility of fantasy, the inexplicable intrusion of the extraordinary into the everyday. His alien beings, as one critic points out, 'partake more of folklore and superstition than of alien visitation'. They are not so much extraterrestrials as versions of trolls, dwarves, elves, leprechauns and other enchanted creatures who populate folklore and fairy tales." ('Steven Spielberg's Career' in *Metaphores* #12-13, Faculté des Lettres et Sciences Humaines de Nice, 1988, p180.)

After the success of *Close Encounters* came *1941*, a wild satire on the war-time rumours of an imminent Japanese invasion that raged through Los Angeles, actually, in 1942.

> "Spielberg shows that adult ambitions and desires divorce you from the essential aspects of being human; whereas, if you are a child, or a child at heart, you can believe strongly enough to really feast on an imaginary banquet or fly like Superman."

BELOW: E.T. explores in detail contradictory impulses – towards inspiration and repression, towards wonder and cynicism, towards emotion and rationality. More than any of his other films, E.T. crystallises Spielberg's complex vision of suburbia and elucidates his view of the world.

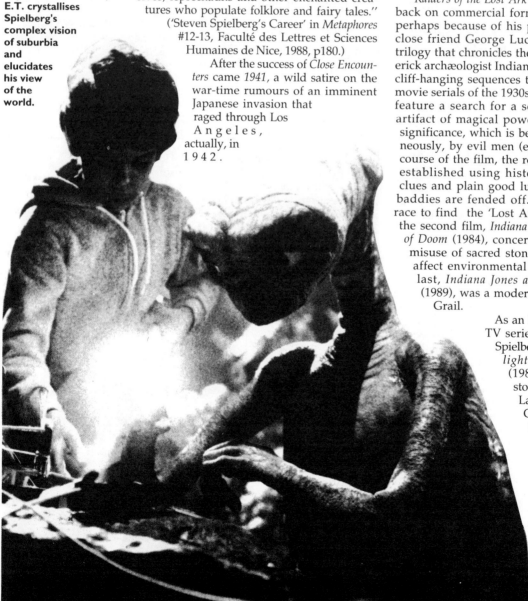

Citizens thought they saw Japanese aircraft attacking, and it is a matter of record that on the night of 26 February 1942 the local defense forces expended 1430 rounds of ammunition. This seems to have been a case of 'war nerves' or collective panic - similar to the 'siege' at Hopkinsville - because there are no corresponding records of enemy planes hit or of bombs dropped. The film's release in 1979 was met with only lukewarm praise from critics and it failed to match up to Spielberg's other successes. Since then, however, it has become a cult classic and is regarded by some critics as his best film.

Raiders of the Lost Ark (1981) saw Spielberg back on commercial form and surer ground, perhaps because of his partnership with his close friend George Lucas. It kicked off the trilogy that chronicles the adventures of maverick archæologist Indiana Jones, and is full of cliff-hanging sequences that hark back to the movie serials of the 1930s and 40s. All of them feature a search for a seemingly legendary artifact of magical power and supernatural significance, which is being sought, simultaneously, by evil men (eg. the Nazis). In the course of the film, the reality of the object is established using historical and folkloric clues and plain good luck, while persistent baddies are fended off. *Raiders* involved a race to find the 'Lost Ark of the Covenant'; the second film, *Indiana Jones and the Temple of Doom* (1984), concerned a sinister cult's misuse of sacred stones with powers that affect environmental prosperity; and the last, *Indiana Jones and the Last Crusade* (1989), was a modern quest for the Holy Grail.

As an homage to the classic TV series *The Twilight Zone*, Spielberg put together *Twilight Zone The Movie* (1983), which included stories directed by John Landis, Joe Dante and George Miller. Spielberg's own contribution concerns a group of depressed old folk who are given the chance to become children again. It is too sentimental for the general taste, but it does reveal Spielberg's continued interest in Peter Pan-type motifs.

RETURN FROM THE DEAD

In 1990-91 Hollywood produced a glut of films that feature spirits of the recently dead interacting with the lives of their loved ones. The most popular – Jerry Zucker's *Ghost* (1990) – was credited with initiating this trend, but the accolade for finding this profitable theme should have gone to Spielberg's *Always* (1989). The ever-popular theme of a return from the dead has a venerable history in the cinema, and a number of excellent examples of this genre were made in the wake of World War Two; noticeably *A Matter of Life and Death* (1946) by Powell and Pressberger, Frank Capra's celebrated *It's a Wonderful Life* (1946), and Victor Fleming's *A Guy Named Joe* (1943) of which *Always* was a devotional remake.

These films were undoubtedly popular in the post-war period because they addressed (and perhaps even helped to alleviate) the grief, shock and hopelessness that are the consequence of war by dramatising positive and optimistic values which would help society rebuild itself. The current cycle of similar films is attributed by some critics to the loss and adjustment needed to cope with the Aids epidemic. Joel Schumacher, the director of *Flatliners* (1990), suggested they were a response to wider issues... "Think about it! There's terrrorism, wars, drugs, homelessness, a growing suicide rate, and what's happening to the planet itself. Young people aren't protected from that insecurity. It's on the news every night. It raises profound questions."

Spielberg's latest work, *Hook* (1991), brings to fruition his ambition to film the Peter Pan story. It centres on a man of today, very much rooted in this 'real' world, who has to travel to the elusive, magical, parallel world of Never Never Land to rescue his children from the clutches of Captain Hook, an incarnation of the supernatural abductor. At the same time, Peter Pan has to regain his youthful joy and innocence. Spielberg shows that adult ambitions and desires divorce you from the essential aspects of being human; whereas, if you are a child, or a child at heart, you can believe strongly enough to really feast on an imaginary banquet or fly like Superman. The message of *Hook*, according to Spielberg, is that Peter Pan "rescued his past. He rescued the memory of himself as a child and carried that best friend with him the rest of his life. It will never leave him again."

Spielberg's love of old TV anthology series, like *The Twilight Zone*, inspired him to produce a similar series in 1985, called *Amazing Stories*. A mixture of famous film directors and newcomers were hired for the shows, making it a proving ground for new ideas and techniques. This, combined with high production values and stories in the SF, comedy and adventure genres, seemed like a formula for success - but it did not meet the expectations. (It was recently shown on British TV). A theatrical release in 1987 featured the pilot episode of Spielberg's series *The Mission*, portraying the claustrophobic conditions onboard a WW2 bomber return-

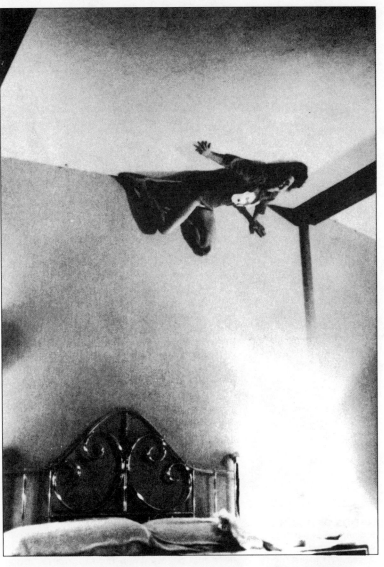

LIVING ON THE CEILING: One of the incredible special effects from Spielberg's 1982 movie *Poltergeist*, in which an unscrupulous property developer pays dearly for building a housing estate on the site of an ancient Indian burial ground

ing from a mission, and stars Kevin Costner and Keifer Sutherland. The main premise is that one of the crew - a budding cartoonist who wants to work for Disney after the war - is able to visualise a new set of wheels for the battered aircraft. This happy ending is the most disappointing part of this 50-minute story, but it does show that Spielberg's fascination with the power of belief long before *Hook*.

A rescue mission into another dimension, home of another supernatural abductor, also featured in Spielberg's *Poltergeist* (1982). Spielberg wrote the story to explore the dark side of supernatural experiences as a counterbalance to the Christ-like benevolence of the alien in *E.T.*, and chose Tobe Hooper (best known for *The Texas Chainsaw Massacre*, 1974) to direct it.

In *Poltergeist*, an unscrupulous property developer builds a new estate over an ancient burial ground, hiding the fact from his customers and staff. His best salesman is rewarded with a magnificent new house in which poltergeist events begin to occur; an invisible force stacks chairs after sliding them across the room; an animated tree nearly makes off in a whirlwind with the son; and a freshly-dug

HANDS OF DOOM:
Indiana Jones battles
with a sinister
Aztec-style priest for
possession of the
all-powerful mystic
stones

swimming pool becomes a swamp in which
corpses dislodged from their subterranean
graveyard bob up alongside startled swimmers.
This 'siege' begins when the salesman's young
daughter is enticed into the other dimension,
through the TV set, by voices emanating from it.
A spiritualist medium senses the girl is alive in
another world surrounded by demonic entities.
The girl's mother ventures into this other realm
via a 'gateway' that opens in the children's bedroom; it is a terrifying sucking vortex, the psychic equivalent of a black hole. Eventually,
through love, courage and determination, the
girl is brought back to the 'everyday' world.

In 1984, Spielberg produced *Gremlins*, written by Chris Columbus and directed by Joe
Dante. It features cute but zoologically
unknown and indeterminate animals called
Mogwai, who breed on contact with water,
become vicious if fed after midnight and die
when exposed to light. The film shows how a
small town community corrupts these sinless
creatures: there is the bigot who hates Japanese
imports; the money-obsessed old spinster; the
ambitious yuppie; the science teacher who
regards living creatures as things to dissect.

BACK TO THE FUTURE

After *Gremlins*, Spielberg produced the first of
the *Back to the Future* trilogy (1985-1989), scripted by Bob Gale and Robert Zemeckis, who also
directed them. The plot develops around the
adventures of the hero, Marty McFly, and his
inventor pal, Emmett Brown, who travel backwards and forwards through time in a suitably
equipped DeLorean sportscar. The complica-
tions arise from their interactions with their
ancestors and their future children; for example, in the first film, Marty has to put his future
mother and father on course for their eventual
marriage, but inadvertently makes his mother-
to-be fall in love with himself, while in the second film, Marty has to save the world from his
own awful progeny. Each time Marty and
Emmett return to the present, they find it
changed by their intervention in their own
past.

If we examine Spielberg's filmic past, we
can see that his films have always concerned
other worlds, supernatural, mythic or pseudo-
scientific. As a boy, he created many 8mm
films. At the age of 16, he made a 16mm film
called *Firelight*, a two-and-a-half-hour epic in
which the Earth was invaded by aliens. The
$500 production cost was recovered by show-
ing it at a local cinema for one night. This pre-
cocious movie director then made a short
35mm film called *Amblin'* which impressed
Universal so much they gave him a seven-year
contract as a TV-director. At the age of 21 his
first assignment was a segment of *The Night
Gallery* series, with Joan Crawford as his star.

Spielberg still had ambitions to shoot feature films, and his chance came with *Duel*
(1971); although shot and first released as a TV
movie, it won such acclaim that it was length-
ened for theatrical release in Europe. The relatively simple story begins with a near-accident
between a car driver and an oil-tanker. An
escalating series of revenges develops into a
murderous pursuit of the car by the tanker. By
skilful filmwork, the tanker (whose driver we
never see) gains the menace of a mechanical
demon; it is a gigantic and malevolent version
of the toy vehicles activated by poltergeists or
UFOs in so many of his films.

Something Evil (1972) is an equally modest
TV movie, which tried out many of the themes
developed in *Poltergeist* ten years later. Here,
the family of an advertising executive move
into a farmhouse haunted by a spirit which
had already hounded the previous owner to
death. This supernatural force causes the death
of a film director and actress using the farm as
a location for shooting a TV commercial, and
nearly succeeds in driving the mother of one of
the boy-heroes to kill herself. Once again love
triumphs, as the mother fights back to save her
children from the supernatural abductor.

The first film to be made by Spielberg pur-
posefully for the cinema was *The Sugarland
Express* (1974), starring Goldie Hawn. Although
there are no supernatural elements in it, it does
develop another of Spielberg's favourite
themes: that people can be motivated to
behave in crazy and incredible ways by their
inner lives and visions. In the film, a young
couple kidnap a policeman so that they can

retrieve their son from his foster parents. They flee in a stolen police car pursued by police, TV crews and others. At first the chase is comic, but as the serious implications of their actions dawn on them, it ruins their dream of family life.

Spielberg hit the box-office jackpot with *Jaws* (1975), which draws on the influence of Jack Arnold's *Creature from the Black Lagoon* (1954) and John Houston's *Moby Dick* (1956). Considerable tension is generated by keeping the monster (a great white shark) from view as it terrorises the bathers and boats of the coastal town of Amity. In the opening sequence, for example, the beast lurks in the depths below a lone swimmer, and after it strikes the mournful toll of a sea buoy adds to the poignancy.

The three men who hunt for the shark are typical Spielberg characters. The law enforcement officer is a newcomer to the small community who wants to save his family from the deadly threat. The other two are a technological whizzkid who represents the scientific view of the menace; and a loner, a throwback macho-man who sees the shark as a personal challenge leading to the inevitable duel. Just as the truck in *Duel* became, in the end, an almost supernatural menace, the unstoppable shark in *Jaws* metamorphoses from a big fish into a terrifying monster.

These three human roles are revisited in *Close Encounters*, where we have a family man who triumphs over formidable adversity, a scientist who interprets the phenomenal events, and, in place of the macho-man, the equally pugnacious and obstructive military.

A partial explanation for the huge success of Spielberg's films is that they validate the viewer's notions of supernatural or anomalous phenomena (in Spielberg films these ontological terms are usually interchangeable). *Close Encounters* began with the excited discovery of the long-missing planes of 'Flight 19', suggesting that some sort of UFO-related time-warp was involved in their disappearance. In the end, the missing pilots, together with many other 'disappeareds' from the Fortean annals, come down the ramps of the great mother ship. In the *Indiana Jones* films, the folkloric

belief in magical objects is validated; the lost Ark of the Hebrews, the 'Sankara stones', and the Holy Grail all turn out to be real objects as powerful and dangerous as their reputations foretold. In many of the films, the enemy is a relentless supernatural evil that animates everyday objects and possesses ordinary people. This is counterbalanced by the triumph of positive virtues and the unseen guidance and protection of angels and friendly spirits. In both *E.T.* and *Close Encounters*, for example, there is reassurance that UFOs represent a benign and magical force watching over us and helping us towards our destiny.

> "Spielberg challenges us to break free from the straitjacket of conventional, rational thought and regain the imaginative world of our childhood."

STRANGE PHENOMENA

Many critics have condemned Spielberg's films as juvenile; something aficionados of strange phenomena often hear about their own pursuits. Certainly *Close Encounters* - hotly debated as it was among ufologists - gave inspiration to many UFO believers who were tired of being dismissed as cranks. Nigel Watson's *Portraits of Alien Encounters* shows how the film appealed, also, to some UFO percipients, because it both validated and shaped their understanding of their experiences. Evidence that *Close Encounters* has influenced reports of UFO experiences can be seen in Budd Hopkins' book *Intruders,* which powerfully argues the case for the reality of UFO abductions. Sketches made by the abductees depict aliens very like those appearing at the end of Spielberg's film. It is interesting to note that aliens of this description were rarely reported before the film's release.

There is a hint of conspiracy latent in the lack of 'official' corroboration of supernatural

GREMLINS: not to be fed after midnight!

MOUNTAINS OF MADNESS: A deranged Richard Dreyfus creates a scaled down replica of Devil's Tower, Wyoming, in the privacy of his own living room

RAIDERS OF THE LOST ARK: Nazi underlings attempt to make off with the Ark of the Covenant

phenomena. Spielberg ignores the more obvious explanations (eg. the difficulty in proving something which might not exist outside the imagination or will to believe), and opts every time for the suggestion that there is 'something' behind the myths after all and that scholars and authorities have known all along. Spielberg's authority characters - usually scientists or government officials - conspire to conceal what the rest of us want and ought to know. The conspiratorial activities of scientists are usually mitigated by the fact that they have to work for secretive government or military agencies; Spielberg's view is that if science were only freed from such control, it would acknowledge and validate supernatural phenomena. An example of this kind of authentification is the short discussion of paranormal phenomena by the late D. Scott Rogo, a respected researcher, with which Spielberg prefaced the early release of *Poltergeist*.

In *Close Encounters*, the government disseminates, via mass media, a story of deadly gas leaks to keep people away from the mountain where the ETs will land. In *E.T.*,

there are mobile squads of scientists out to track down alien visitors and cruelly study them. At the close of *Raiders of the Lost Ark*, the government confiscates the Ark itself and has it boxed and stored with thousands of other identical crates; the implication is that there could be many more of these magical artifacts or weapons of supernatural power, but their existence and numbers are 'Above Top Secret'.

The release of *Hook* sees Spielberg returning to the more magical/supernatural themes which made him Hollywood's most successful director. His films show us, in an entertaining way, that there are more things in heaven and earth than our governments want us to know; that we're not crazy for believing there's more to life than work and TV; and that almost anything is possible. Spielberg challenges us to break free from the straightjacket of conventional, rational thought and regain the imaginative world of our childhood. To do so is to see the world as it really is - made up of our wildest dreams and worst nightmares, yes; but always full of magic.

This article is based upon *Supernatural Spielberg*, a privately published book by Darren Slade and Nigel Watson, available at the following bookshops: The Cinema Bookshop, 13 Gt Russell St; Forbidden Planet, 71 New Oxford St; MOMI Bookshop, South Bank; Offstage, 37 Chalk Farm Rd; Vintage Books, 39/43 Brewer St; all in London. Or by mail order from SKS 20 Paul St, Frome, Somerset BA11 1DX, or Valis Books 52a Lascotts Rd, Wood Green, London N22 4JN.

FT

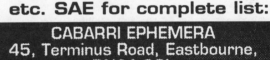

TALES OF THE PARANORMAL

The editors remember how their Fortean attitude was influenced early on by programmes like *The Bumblies,* *It's A Square World* and *Potty Time,* which pioneered the use of surrealist comedy on British TV. We therefore thought it appropriate to speak to their creator, Michael Bentine. Bentine was a founder-member of the much-loved **Goon Show,** which was first broadcast by the BBC in 1951. By the time he left the Goons in 1953, he had performed in about 50 shows, leaving Harry Seacombe, Peter Sellers and Spike Milligan to go on to even greater fame.

Besides his career as a radio and TV comedian, Bentine has maintained an eclectic interest in the paranormal, especially psychical phenomena and healing; an interest inspired by his father's own investigations into spiritualism and poltergeists.

Bentine was conceived in Peru, but born in Watford, outside London, in 1922. He grew up in Folkestone, saw active service in WW2 as an intelligence officer in the RAF, and has gained acclaim for his novels and memoirs.

Bentine's autobiography – **The Reluctant Jester: My Head-on Collision with the 20th Century** – has just been published by Bantam Books; and he is currently on tour with a one-man show (see NOTICEBOARD on page 66 for details).

SWEET SMELL OF SUCCESS: Michael Bentine with Diana Dors, his co-star, in a publicity shot for *The Sandwich Man* (1965).

FT: You have frequently mentioned your father's interest in paranormal phenomena and how he involved the whole family in his investigations. How did it all begin?

MB: My father's first experience of the paranormal was of a phantom that vanished while surrounded by a crowd of boys.

My father came over to England at about thirteen years of age. He stayed in London with a Mrs Southery, who used to eke out her widow's pension by lodging foreign students in her large house in Holland Park Avenue.

During summer holidays, Mrs Southery hired a rambling house at Hayling Island. This was before the First World War, and everyone had a marvellous time in a simple, naive sort of way. Late one summer, about 30 girls and boys had a weekend party under the eagle eye of Mrs Southery, on a beautiful moonlit night. Suddenly there was a yell of absolute terror let out by one of the girls who said she saw a rather peculiar face at the window. From their brief glimpse, father said the figure was unnaturally thin.

Of course the young lads wanted to show their manhood; they rushed out, chasing the intruder through the garden, and eventually cornered him on the tennis court. In the bright moonlight this tall, skeletal entity seemed to repel them. For a while, none of them actually wanted to touch him. Then suddenly they all shot forward to grab him, but he just vanished.

Later, in 1929, father had unexpected confirmation, by a medium, of an incident he had quite forgotten, occurring when he was about 18 and studying at the London School of Electromagnetism. From then on, he, and some of his closest friends - all fellow scientists, like my tutor Bill Hope Jones - formed a team to investigate the paranormal.

FT: You became one of your father's mediums at the age of 13. How did this happen?

MB: Quite simply, from the start, my father never did anything without the whole family being involved in some way. My mother had a fantastic sense of humour as well as a very bright mind. I wouldn't say my father had a great curiosity, but he had the curiosity of a scientist. He was a very fine mathematician, with a balanced, logical brain. He would play chess blindfolded, or against several people at the same time. He was a leading ærodynamisist and pioneered many of the developments of flying boats and sea planes.

Father turned one of the rooms in our home into a type of laboratory. He helped my elder brother and me to develop clairvoyance. We are both visual thinkers, and we started with simple experiments using Zener cards - the wavy line, the circle and the square and what have you. Transmitting the visualised card from one part of the room to the other or from one room to another, we developed an enormously high hit rate. We felt quite safe, and it was the most exciting time of my life.

FT: You have talked of witnessing astonishing feats of materialisation and telekinesis. What was most convincing about them?

MB: Let's take telekinesis first. We had a table we used for table turning; a very primitive form of communication, but by golly it worked. With the whole family sitting round this rather heavy, single-pillared, massive Victorian occasional table, we would get various types of phenomena. My mother and I yawned like it was the end of world, as though power was being drawn from us, and our fine curly hair went straight up on end. Static electricity was also indicated by a strong smell of ozone. There were rapid temperature drops of about 15 to 20 degrees. These phenomena would precede the levitation of the table. We only had our fingers resting lightly on the table to maintain contact, but the thing would whizz round the room with us chasing it, trying to keep our hands in contact.

I loathed materialisation, I only went to one, and I didn't like the sight of very thick mucous coming from the medium's nostrils and the base of her throat. This, apparently, was ectoplasm. Before we could analyze it, we had to have the permission of whatever entity was controlling the medium; if you start touching the stuff you can harm the medium. In this case, in lowered light, part of it was taken off and analysed in our kitchen by the chemical member of our team who came back and said it was mucous. But the damned thing was alive! It moved around, forming into a mass at the base of the throat, and inside the mass something like a face would appear. My father took a number of pictures; sadly most of them didn't come out.

A transfiguration medium, called Mrs Enid Barmer, came down one summer and performed in the presence of 20 people and three cameras, including my father's, in the light of a summer afternoon. She sat in a big Chippendale style chair and said a short prayer to herself. After about three minutes what seemed like a mist started to form around her throat. It was drawn upwards to cover her face and suddenly another face appeared, superimposed on Mrs Barmer's face, almost as though she'd put on a mask.

These were living faces - an elderly judge in a full wig, a young girl with red hair, a young lad, a middle aged woman - one after the other. Each would take about a minute to form and then a few seconds to dissolve back into the mist again. The mist seemed slightly out of focus and contrasted with the clarity of the faces. This went on for something like an hour, during the course of which people were saying my god look it's aunt so and so... My brother saw the second demonstration under much the same circumstances the following day.

The series of pictures taken by all three photographers begin and end with Mrs Barmer sitting in the chair, but those in between are totally fogged as though by intense radiation. In fact, Dr Roussack, who was a great friend of my father's, examined one film and said that exposure to radiation of that intensity should have pro-

> "Why was Rudolf Hess, at the age of 90, the only prisoner in Spandau prison, guarded by four different nationalities 24 hours of the day?"

duced some harmful effects, but it didn't; so it couldn't have been gamma or x-ray radiation. What the hell was it? All I know is that I saw those faces one after the other - all alive. There was no way she could have faked it, or hypnotised us.

FT: You have claimed that your own talent for clairvoyance has helped your career. How?

MB: It helped me with the death of my son in a flying accident, and in my investigations for the three years following that. It certainly helped me make a living because I've been able to think up original ideas. To give you an example, in a dressing room in Cardiff, in 1964, just waiting to go on, I looked up at the wall and saw the entire process of my invisible flea circus, from the fleas jumping along the sand to

climbing up the ladder to the bendable platform at the top, diving into the teacup with a splash, and rolling the ball up the slope. I thought good Lord! what have I just seen? It was, of course, a preview of something I developed later, which was not only seen throughout the entire world, but was also nicked by other, not quite so inventive, comedians.

FT: Your novels warn of the consequences of misusing psychic powers or tampering with other realms to satisfy corrupt ambitions. Your baddies develop their paranormal powers in the context of evil cults.

MB: I put warnings in my books because anyone of an extremely neurotic or nervous disposition could find themselves in dead trouble if they played around with tarot, or table levitating, for example, and became totally obsessed by it or too reliant on it. It can affect your mind. To do it alone is a very foolish thing; likewise, to do it without proper instruction.

FT: The last few years have seen an increase in reports of the sort of phenomena you associate with institutionalised worship of evil: suicides, drug abuse, the breakdown of law and order, and even child sacrifice. How do you interpret these developments now?

MB: Every religion has chanting and ritual. It is used to get the totality of the will of the congregation into one force; in other words, to guide the belief of the people, as in the climax of the Eucharist, or in Islam, or among the North American Indians (with whom I've stayed), or in the beautiful Jewish ceremonies, etc.

Similar types of mental manipulation, ritual exercises if you like, release pressure from the unconscious mind through the conscious mind. If the ritual is based on positive ways of thinking, such as love or healing, then obviously you are in no danger whatsoever; but if it uses profound hatred, such as the Nazis felt towards the Jews and the gypsies, you are dealing with an extremely negative force - evil. You can see this, today, in any fanatical form of fundamentalism.

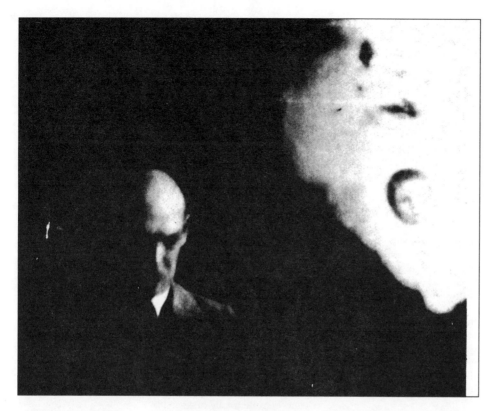

Photograph of Michael Bentine's father with two ghostly forms on the right. It was taken by psychic photographer John Myers during a visit to Myers' South London home. Bentine's father took his own camera and film, which was developed in his presence. Subsequently, relatives from Peru confirmed that the faces resembled those of deceased members of the family. The photograph is one of the few mementos of Bentine's father's psychic exploits; shortly before his death he destroyed all his papers because he thought they might be dangerous in the wrong hands.

FT: Like Dennis Wheatley, you have written about the use of occultism in wartime, particularly by the Nazis. It has been claimed that a recent release of war-time documents from the Public Records Office confirmed Aleister Crowley had been hired by British military intelligence to drive an occult wedge between Hess and Hitler.

MB: It is a fact that most of the Nazi hierarchy were involved with black ritual. What we are talking about is the summation of will to bring about a change in future circumstances, and that is the definition of magic: black, grey or white.

My authority is my friend and war-time mentor Airy Neave, who started MI9 in which I was trained as an Intelligence officer. At that time I talked to many Poles, Czechs, Norwegians, Danes, French, Belgians and even Germans (because there was a German Resistance as well) and they all said the same thing; that the Nazis were using ritual methods to whip up the normal down-to-earth German mentality into a completely bamboozled form of manipulated entity.

At the Nuremberg trials only the minimal part of their involvement in such extraordinary concepts as Shamballah,

Agarti and Valhalla, was mentioned and played down. Airy Neave explained to me that if we exposed the enormous amount of evidence that they were involved in black ritual practices, the Nazis' defence lawyers - they had a brilliant team - would have pleaded insanity or diminished responsibility and the whole lot would have been consigned to a lunatic asylum. Even the pathetic 150, or whatever it was, who did pay the supreme penalty, would have got off.

If you doubt that, ask yourself one question: why was Rudolf Hess, at the age of 90, the only prisoner in Spandau Prison, and guarded by four different nationalities 24 hours of the day? Or why, when he died, or committed suicide, his body was spirited away to an unknown burial? Or why the bulldozers came in, within 10 days, and raised Spandau Castle to the ground. Very ordinary types of political action, I'm sure you'll agree!

FT: These subjects are very grim and often frightening; yet we are constantly amused and delighted by a dark surreal humour behind the events we chronicle. You once described one of your father's devices for recording mediumistic phenomena sitting silently –

struck dumb, perhaps - on a table, while the table itself rose into the air. Is the Cosmic Joker a deity in your pantheon?

MB: The apparatus was a spelling machine father invented, involving spring balances and an incredibly sensitive Morse key. We would sit solemnly around it for weeks on end, during which nothing happened... but the table went up in the air! On its own! All my father said was "I think they're trying to tell us something."

Well, surely we're talking about an archetype of the human unconsciousness. So vivid are these archetypal forces that I can say to you 'Sherlock Holmes' or 'Robin Hood' and you instantly see roughly the same sort of thing I do, even though they never actually existed in that form. These are examples of archetypal entities being created in the universal, global mind. Representations of evil have been created in much the same way - for example, Satan, Kali, or Lilith, demonic forces or even Angelic Hosts. We are talking about archetypes of the human unconscious, and it is odd that you do get the existence of the universal joker, the fool figure. It is man's way of rationalising the fact that terrible things happen to him, and that a sense of humour can get you through your own vicissitudes. That is why that archetype of the universal jester is acceptable to me.

FT: You have denied that you are a Spiritualist, yet you seem to have accepted the likelihood of some sort of personal survival of bodily death. Do you believe that there is a natural process involved which has nothing to do with theology?

MB: Not being the Almighty I couldn't possibly answer that question. Death is an enormous business on this earth. Fear of death is built into our survival mechanism. The question is: does the individual entity, the persona – whatever you want to call it – retain its individuality after the death change, or does it go back into some general fund of energy? Knowing that it is universally accepted in scientific circles that you cannot destroy energy - you can only change its form - has helped me accept the physical death of my three children.

I have had the out-of-body experience a number of times. During the war, when I was given an injection (paratyphoid, tetanus and ATTAB) which went sadly wrong; one cadet died and another was paralysed. My family was sent for, and I was gone. During that time I had an experience of the enormous light, light which would have blinded my physical eyes. I felt I was waiting for something, and felt myself drawn back. It makes you think that there must be something beyond all this; or is it that, in the last final nanosecond in which you are still conscious, your own beliefs come to the fore? I don't know, and neither does anyone else on this earth.

FT: Do you have an interest in the riddle of UFOs?

MB: When I was an intelligence officer in a bomber command in the winter of 1943-44, I debriefed several crews about some lights that had attacked them when they were over the Baltic. They fired at the lights, which didn't shoot back. These lights didn't seem to do anything, just pulse and go round.

We put it down to fatigue, but later, after I had sent the reports in, an American G2 Intelligence officer told us that their day bombers saw lights in the sky – "foo fighters" he called them. The next time I heard about UFOs was when Kenneth Arnold reported his "flying saucers" in 1947; and when Captain Mantell crashed his F-51 after reportedly attacking a great metallic disk at extreme altitude in 1948.

My family once owned an airline in Peru, and two of our respected and experienced pilots reported lights flying around their DC6Bs over the plains of Nazca, and knocking out their radios. In both cases the lights were seen by the passengers as well.

FT: How did you first became aware of the work of Charles Fort?

MB: I read about Charles Fort before the war, and how he found his info in the newspaper morgues. I thought now here's a tough old journalist. At that time Arthur Clarke, Patrick Moore and I, used to go down to our various Woolworths and buy these marvellous Street & Smith pulp fiction magazines at thruppence at time - they were used as ballast for cargo ships - and Fort was often mentioned in them. His books *Lo!* and *The Book of the Damned* I thought were marvellous, absolutely wonderful. Incidentally I believe the character of Kolchak, *The Night Stalker* (played by Darren McGavin), is supposed to be Charles Fort.

FT: Do you have any closing advice?

MB: I can pass on my father's advice: "Keep your mind and your bowels open". The Romans had the right idea - a healthy mind in a healthy body. **FT**

BELOW: Michael Bentine today.

KILLER WAVE

GAVIN CRAIG'S compelling account of the night he escaped a monster seiche wave.

The late Gavin Craig (d. 1989) was helmsman on the **Cape Horn** the night it escaped the killer wave. The size of the wave, its colour and motion, its crest of geysers and other details are unlike anything we know of in the records of anomalous wave phenomena. If anyone has seen anything similar at such close quarters before, they are almost certainly now in Davey Jones' locker, so we are pleased to present this eyewitness account with the author's own drawings. Craig had previously published an account of his life as a seaman — **Boy Aloft** (1973).

When I saw the killer wave from the bridge of the Cape Horn, I took it for a natural peril; it was only much later that I realized that I might be one of the very few people to have observed a rare marine phenomenon – a monster seiche wave – at close quarters ... and survived.

The *Cape Horn* was the standard 'three island' ship of the period. When I joined her in 1930 she was almost a new ship. The man in charge, Captain E.S. Wilkie, had commanded the last active square-rigged ship on the British register. He and I were the only sailing ship men aboard, and for this reason he would talk to me occasionally.

The incident happened during a Force 9 or 10 gale in the Pacific, sometime between April and June 1935. We were about 10 or 12 days out of a Canadian or US west coast port taking sawn lumber to Shanghai. It was blowing hard with 25-foot seas running and the distance from crest to crest exceeded the ship's length (425ft). The phosphorescence given off by the breaking seas provided plenty of light to see by as I made my way over the deck-load towards the bridge.

Gavin Craig, pictured at about the time of the incident

"I knew beyond question that I was a dead man, but the idea didn't seem to worry me unduly."

It was 4am and my wheel. Ahead and to port one could see for a couple of miles, but the horizon was not clearly defined. The starboard window of the wheelhouse was constantly drenched by heavy spray and useless for observation. The temperature was around zero. I had the helm hard-a-starboard continually, but from time to time eased the wheel a few spokes, then slammed it down again. (It was a common seaman's belief that if [modern] steering gear were held hard-over too long, a bubble of air would form within the cylinder or tubes and prevent movement of the rudder.) In a full gale I was taking no chances.

About 4:30am, I noticed a change in the regular run of the seas ahead. A larger wave was forming, to judge from the gaps of blue water between the crests. The Chief Mate, Mr McKenzie, had the watch and I drew his attention to it. "Here's a 'ninth wave' bearing down, Mister." He examined it with the glasses, took a bearing from the ship's compass, checked the ship's head, then moved back to the corner window.

THE NINTH WAVE

A 'ninth wave' is a common expression, meaning a single wave larger than the others. As I kept my eyes on it, it slowly increased in size. Hoping the Mate would increase the engine revolutions to face up to this new threat, I said: "She's nearly five points off and won't answer." He remained silent. Later, I added: "It's not just one big wave, there are others behind it just as big. I can see their crests breaking here and there." His left hand moved towards the engine telegraph, hesitated and drew back.

By this time the wave had become so huge that I knew it would capsize the ship. No increase in speed would save us now. I was puzzled by the slowness of the advance of the sea; we seemed to be drifting together. Then I noticed that what I had initially taken for wave crests were actually widely-spaced geysers, dancing on the upper surface. These geysers – or whatever

The Cape Horn – built by Lithgow's of Port Glasgow in 1929, and owned by Lyle Shipping of Glasgow.

they were – were rising to a height of about 20 feet and dropping to half that before rising again, sometimes curving against the wind. The upper surface of the sea appeared flat and endless, stretching towards the unseen horizon. By 'flat' I mean there was no defined wave motion; the surface boiled gently in whorls, exactly like the water filling a lock of the Panama Canal.

I knew beyond question that I was a dead man, but the idea didn't seem to worry me unduly. Rather, there was an absence of feeling. Suddenly I was shocked back to the present. I could plainly hear the thumping and rattling of the rocker arms of the main engine and the noise of the big exhaust in the funnel. Then, like the slamming of a watertight door, the wind dropped from a full gale to a calm. I knew what was happening; the height of the sea had cut off the wind making a temporary lee for the ship. Glancing at the compass, I saw with surprise

"I've seen some big uns off the Horn, but nothing like this."

and delight that the ship's head was coming up to windward. In fits and starts it moved in the right direction. I talked to her: "C'mon my sweet beauty, get up there. Hurry 'fore the bastard wind comes back. Do it for me lover..." stuff like that, but meaning every whispered word.

The bows were only about 30 feet off the far end of the 'sea' when she rammed it. Then all hell broke loose. I felt the shock as the fo'c's'le head went in and the deck-load forrard tore loose. There was another crunching thud beneath my feet as the sea demolished the lower bridge rail. I thought: "There's the [life]boats gone for a burton."

Just then, and with incredible speed, the whole face of the wave altered. A curtain of water rose from the sea and enclosed it. Where the existing face was deep and flat, this curtain appeared to be made of joined vertical columns about three feet in diameter, uniform and crested, and sloping at the same angle as the great wave behind it. They looked exactly like huge steel pistons coated with oil. The crest passed the wheelhouse windows downwards in about three seconds.

SPLAYED RUNNELS
I gripped the wheel harder (for all the good it might do). The forrard windows were struck by a sea that I fully expected to demolish the whole front of the structure. This was strange; it acted like water but didn't have the character of water with force behind it... no shattering explosion of glass, no rendering of woodwork... just a heavy thump. In that instant - as if a switch had been pressed - the three front windows turned pure white. This, again, was strange; there were none of the movements you'd expect from water on glass... no splayed runnels... no small bubbles... just the purest white I have ever seen, as if they had turned into three blocks of ice. In the blink of an eye it

was gone, and you could see out of them again.

Then the big wave was gone. I looked for the Mate, but he was outside on the bridge wing, trying to pull down the bone-hard canvas dodger so that he could see over it. As the vessel listed heavily to port, I saw a normally big sea pass by us as the water drained from the bridge. The Old Man arrived, much to my relief, and immediately rang the telegraph. He was barefooted in soaked pyjamas and his uniform cap, shivering, for the wind had returned. He had words with the Mate (beyond my hearing), who departed at great speed. Captain Wilkie glanced briefly at the compass and said: "All right Craig. What really happened?"

His question relieved me. It meant the Mate had not seen me alter course to windward

(Top) The wheelhouse of the Cape Horn showing the position of the Mate and author Gavin Craig at the helm. Drawn by the author. (Below) against a background of heavy seas, the anomalous wave stood like a pillar with waterspouts or 'geysers' dancing around its top surface. The area delineated at the pillar's base represents the view from the weelhouse as it passed the Cape Horn. The drawing also shows the relative sizes of ship and wave.

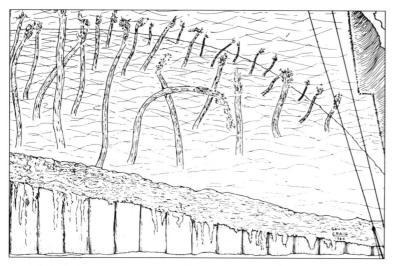

A view of the top of the great wave seconds before its dissolution (drawn by Gavin Craig). The 'geysers' break into crests at their upper ends as they weave about, rising and falling. The sides of the base of the great wave (or the 'curtain' around its base) are shown as a wall of smaller columns.

without orders. If anything had happened to anyone down below, the sea would get the blame, not me. I answered: "She wouldn't answer her helm, sir; not enough anyway. It was the biggest sea I've ever seen. I've seen some big uns off the Horn, but nothing like this." He nodded towards the binnacle: "Keep her at that while I dry off. If you want me, stamp on the deck." After I struck the four bells at the end of the watch, I wanted a good look at the lower bridge. The stanchions on the fore part remained, but all the woodwork except the capping rail had gone. The boats were in perfect order, canvas covers intact. The afterdeck was untouched. I could hardly believe it, after taking onboard such a heavy sea.

Part of the deck-load was floating alongside still attached by a few wires; elsewhere the stacks of timber were intact but in disarray. The fo'c's'le had been flooded to the level of the upper tier of bunks, but this was quite normal in this run in any sort of weather. Nobody made any more comments about it

than usual; it seemed as if nobody but the Mate and myself had seen what we went through. He never spoke about it afterwards – we never hit it off well, anyway – and neither did I.

I am left with my memory of those critical minutes, like a stretch of film with neither beginning nor end. Contrary to usual storm conditions, visibility was excellent. Wherever one looked, the air was charged with phosphorescence, and the water was alive with it. The prevailing colour of the solid water was a dark blue, with the breaking crests and 'geysers' showing a normal white. When the great wave had passed, the colour of the seas changed back to grey. The sky was gradually becoming lighter in colour, except directly over the ship, where it had assumed an arrowhead formation (the point facing the wind and the two sides clearly defined).

The course of the enormous wave was directly towards the ship's bow, yet the wind was on our quarter throughout. It made no leeway until the wind stopped and the ship reached to wind'ard and hit it. The wave appeared independent of the rest of the sea, while the 'geysers' seemed like a great pumping system, raising and lowering the water level within it. If there was any gas involved, it was imperceptible; there was no smell, and the oil lamp lighting the compass card burned steadily through the whole incident.

So what was it? Where did it come from – and where did it go after it left us? Are there 'holes' in the sea as there are said to be 'black holes' in space? I've often wondered. My own conclusion is that it was hollow – a gigantic bubble. **FT**

This article is abridged from Gavin Craig's original account in *Coast and Country* vol 9 no 3 (June 1980) pp22-25. The chief omissions were extraneous detail of the life afloat, cargo, and descriptions of the ship. Our grateful thanks go to *C&C*'s editor Pat O'Driscoll, and the magazine's publisher at that time, Parrett and Neves of Sittingbourne, Kent, for their kind permission to reproduce Craig's narrative.

Waterspouts can vary considerably in their shape, size, colour and even numbers. (Right): A waterspout near Gerona, on Spain's Costa Bravo, dwarfing the jetty in the foreground. Its opacity is due to water vapour condensing out as the air pressure drops inside the column. Notice the wider curtain of spray about the base. (Far right): A beautiful waterspout on Lake Geneva in Switzerland in 1956. Its hollow tube-like structure can be clearly seen in its upper parts, while its base is almost invisible except for the darkened patch of agitated surface water.

SEICHE WAVES, BUBBLES & WATERSPOUTS

Gavin Craig was, without doubt, an experienced seaman. Throughout his original account - in *Coast and Country* – he refers to the anomalous wave as a gigantic form of seiche wave, an opinion apparently shared by the then editor of the magazine, Pat O'Driscoll, herself an old salt. Turning to William Corliss' *Earthquakes, Tides, Unidentified Sounds and Related Phenomena* (Sourcebook Project, 1983; section GHS2) we learn that seiche waves occur when a secondary wave system, generally with a smaller amplitude created by seismic or barometric disturbance, is superimposed on the usual wave periodicity so that every-so-often there is a wave bigger or stronger than the rest. It seems to correspond to the sailors' belief in 'ninth waves', to which Craig refers.

Seiche waves are seldom encountered on the open sea, however; they are more usual in inland seas or lakes and rarely higher than two or three feet. Even supposing Craig saw the mother of all seiche waves, it is hard to believe it could have reached the monstrous proportions reported here.

BIZARRE

As the narrative develops, another difficulty arises - not, we hasten to add, because of yarn-spinning, but most likely arising from the attempt to describe an extraordinary phenomenon. We refer here to the bizarre representation of the wave as a pillar-like formation.

Unless Craig is trying, impossibly, to depict a new kind of quantum event - ie. the ocean attempting to be a wave and a pillar simultaneously - we ought to consider another possibility. Pillars of water, encountered during storm conditions, are usually a type of waterspout. Waterspouts can vary in shape and colour, and in size – Frank Lane's *The Violent Earth* (1986) reports one estimated at 500ft across. The whirling column of air can draw up a column of water in tube-like structures as well as solid ones. These can rise up and fall back into the sea within a short time, and many waterspouts have a curtain of spray around the base.

If, indeed, the *Cape Horn* encountered a waterspout, it was a truly anomalous one - gigantic, as well as possessing a crest of smaller waterspouts, and sides composed of a solid mass of adjacent columns of water. Craig's references to "pistons" and "a pumping system" raising and lowering water levels, seems to imply a dynamic complex of vortexes all transporting water in different sub-systems. At the centre of the great outer vortex of the whirling winds there was a kind of calm. Craig attributes this to being shielded from the gale by the giant waves, but it might well have been the phenomenon known as the 'eye of the storm'.

WATERSPOUT

Could it be, then, that the ship sailed through a giant waterspout? A significant detail prevents too ready acceptance of this idea. Inside the perimeter of the waterspout - in the 'calm' region - the atmospheric pressure would be considerably lower; if this could affect the oil-lamp flame illuminating the compass, the effect was not noticed or reported.

In conclusion, Craig states his feeling that the mass of water was hollow, like a "gigantic bubble". Certainly, if the wave mass had been solid when it struck the ship, we might reasonably expect to find the *Cape Horn* among the 'Posted Missing' on Lloyd's Register. On the other hand, Craig's impression that the impact of the wave-water both lacked force behind it and behaved unexpectedly could be interpreted in favour of passing through a relatively thin wall of water in a giant tubular waterspout.

ODDITY

Another oddity, given the huge and violent nature of the wave and storm, is that the surface of the column "boiled gently". Perhaps, vast and complex though it was, this particular waterspout had reached some kind of equilibrium about the time it encountered the *Cape Horn*, and that saved the ship from destruction. Alas, we cannot ask for further clarification from Gavin Craig, because, while researching this article, we learned that he died three years ago.

We must mention two other, perhaps less likely, possibilities. Firstly, the notion of a huge bubble of gas or steam rising from the ocean bed is sometimes mooted in speculations about unexplained losses at sea. Such a bubble bursting under a ship would leave it in mid-air. Falling into the cavity, it would break apart as the seas closed over it.

Secondly, Corliss records several examples of solitary giant waves (section GHW0) reaching to about four times the height of surrounding waves (and in a storm that may mean over 70ft). Such a wave slamming into a ship broadside may well severely damage or sink it. If it came head-on, the ship's bow would fall into the correspondingly huge valley preceding the wave (as in the bubble scenario) and be unable to rise before the wall of water hit it fatally. This is widely believed to have been the fate of many missing ships, such as the trawler *Gaul* in 1974 and the passenger ship *Waratah* in 1909. None of these explanations match the event described by Craig.

Finally, Corliss reports a single observation of a marine geyser at sea (section GHG1). This was on a calm sea and the jet of water, which reached around 500ft high, was most likely related to an undersea seismic disturbance.

> "... The notion of a huge bubble of gas or steam rising from the ocean bed is sometimes mooted in speculations about unexplained losses at sea."

> "Waterspouts can vary in shape and colour, and in size – Frank Lane's *The Violent Earth* (1986) reports one estimated at 500ft across."

ANCIES •

BOOKS

FORTEAN TOMES is a series of facsimile reprints of early issues of The Fortean Times. Each book covers a wide range of fascinating subjects, from feral children to spontaneous human combustion to UFO abduction. Plus we now have our very own desk diary.

FORTEAN TIMES 1 - 15
Yesterday's News Tomorrow
£19.99
ISBN: 1 870870 263, 400 page paperback,
colour cover, illustrated throughout.

FORTEAN TIMES 16 - 25 ➡
Diary of a mad planet
£19.50
ISBN: 1 870021 258, 416 page paperback,
colour cover, illustrated throughout.

FORTEAN TIMES 26 - 30
Seeing out the Seventies
£12.50
ISBN: 1 870021 207, 320 page paperback,
colour cover, illustrated throughout.

FORTEAN TIMES 1993 DIARY ➡
£9.99
365 days worth of obscure yet fascinating facts at your fingertips. Each seven day opening presents a daily dollop of temporal trivia along with ample space to add your bizarre doings and odd anniversaries.
ISBN: 1 870870 247, 128 page hardback (250mm x 156mm),
Available end of August

1993 DIARY

I would like to order the following goods:

Code	Item	Price	Qty	Value
FTM	Set of 4 Fortean Times mugs	£15.00		
FTT	Fortean Times t-shirt	£7.99		
FTC	Charles Fort t-shirt	£7.99		
FTY	Yesterday's News Tomorrow	£19.99		
FTP	Diary of a Mad Planet	£19.50		
FTS	Seeing Out the Seventies	£12.50		
FTD	Fortean Times 1993 Diary	£9.99		

Total £ _____

Postage and packing free. Overseas customers please add 20% to order value

Name: Mrs/Miss/Ms/Mr _____

Address _____

_____ Postcode _____

I enclose a total payment of £ _____ made payable to: John Brown Publishing Ltd, or debit the above amount from my Access/Visa/Mastercard/Eurocard (delete where applicable) account.

Account no [ ][ ][ ][ ] Expiry date [ ][ ]

Signature _____ Date _____

T-SHIRTS/MUG ORDERS: Please return order form to: Fortean Times Offers, P O Box 232, Melksham, Wiltshire, SN12 7SB, or phone credit card details on 0225 709597.
BOOK/DIARY ORDERS: Please return order form to: Fortean Times Offers, 20 Paul Street, Frome, Somerset, BA11 1DX, or phone credit card details on 0373 451777

Please allow 28 days for delivery

UNEARTHED

Steve Moore

Our resident antiquarian sifts through current stories from the worlds of archæology and anthropology

The Great Sphinx at Giza is generally thought to have been built by the Pharaoh Khafre (aka Chephren) around 2,500 BC, at the same time that he was building the second of the Great Pyramids. There's no inscription recording this, but archæologists base their case on three facts: when Tuthmosis IV restored the Sphinx in 1,500 BC, he left a stone tablet between its paws which bore the first syllable of Khafre's name; statues of Khafre were found buried in the floor of the Sphinx temple; and known statues of Khafre resemble the face of the Sphinx. Now for the alternative proposal, a strange tale in itself …

When we first came across the story (*Miami Herald* 16 May 1991) the main emphasis was on John Anthony West, 59, of Saugerties, NY, `author, playwright and travel guide'. West was leading a ten-man team to study the age of the Sphinx, which included geologist Robert Schoch, associate professor at Boston University, and geophysicist Dr Thomas Dobecki of Houston. West had a theory to prove: that the Sphinx was too eroded

to have been built by Khafre, and must therefore be older … that it was in fact built between 15,000 and 10,000 BC, by the people of Atlantis. At the time Schoch was non-committal, saying only that he thought the Sphinx was older than Khafre, but that his data needed more study; even so, Egyptologists were already calling the proposal absurd.

By October the emphasis was changing. Schoch appears to have been dissociating himself from the more extreme theories of West (now calling himself a 'rogue Egyptologist'), presumably because, having studied his data, he'd found that there might actually be something in it. From now on it's Schoch who's the front-man, presenting his thesis to a meeting of the Geological Society of America at San Diego on 23 October. Schoch says that there's a considerable difference between the erosion of

the Sphinx and nearby tombs of the Fourth Dynasty that are normally associated with it. Dobecki's seismic research shows that the limestone on the surface at the front of the Sphinx was weathered up to eight feet deep, while identical limestone at the back was only weathered four feet deep, suggesting that the rear of the Sphinx may have been carved from the bedrock later. The Sphinx Temple had a limestone core, which was later faced with granite ashlars, apparently by Khafre, but the limestone under them was already weathered.

Summing up all his various data, Schoch concludes that the Sphinx must have been weathered by water, rather than wind. And the last period of heavy rainfall and flooding in Egypt was the 'Nabtian Pluvial', lasting from 12,000 to 3,000 BC. Schoch's 'conservative' estimate is that the Sphinx

was first carved between 7,000 and 5,000 BC. Needless to say, the Egyptologists howled.

Just to muddy up the waters even more, we then had a pronouncement (Glendale *News-Press* 31 Oct 1991) from Dr Franklin Ruehl Jr, nuclear physicist, lecturer, author and host of the cable TV show *Mysteries from Beyond the Other Dominion*. Don't bother asking *what* 'Other Dominion': Ruehl was declaring that Schoch's evidence showed that the Sphinx was built by, or with the aid of, space-aliens. Ho hum. Anyway, Schoch continued to propound his heresy at a meeting of the American Association for the Advancement of Science in February this year, where again he came under considerable fire, particularly from Dr Mark Lehner of Chicago University. Lehner, currently involved in plans for restoring the Sphinx, points out that there's no evidence of an earlier civilisation that could have built it. A good point, but on the other hand the Egyptologists don't seem to be able to explain Schoch's erosion data, either. Who knows where this one'll end up … *Independent* l4 Oct, *Int. Herald Tribune* 25 Oct 1991, *D. Telegraph* 10 Feb 1992.

The sphinx, from the *Description d'Egypte*, commissioned by Napoleon

LOST UP THE AMAZON

Quite how anything can be 'lost' when no one knew it existed isn't quite clear, but the headline reads `Lost civilisation discovered deep in the Amazon jungle'. It appears that radio-carbon dating carried out on fragments of shell and charcoal discovered in Taperhina, Brazil, date the associated pottery to 6000 BC, making the culture that produced these artefacts the earliest civilisation in the New World. The material comes from huge deposits of domestic rubbish, up to 30 feet deep, indicating that permanent settlements existed from a very early stage. Skeletons of the inhabitants indicate a robust and tall people, compared to later Amazon Indians, but what happened to them isn't clear.

It seems that the fish and shellfish based economy lasted until about 1500 BC, when root vegetable cultivation began. By 500 BC, they were building towns on artificial mounds, cutting irrigation canals, making ceramic statues, musical instruments and paraphenalia for consuming drugs. The civilisation seems to have lasted until the arrival of the Europeans, and toward the end consisted of large states with massive cities. One of these, Santeren, was a city of up to a quarter of a million inhabitants, covering 2 square miles and controlling a territory of up to 8,000 square miles. *Independent 19 Dec 1991.*

ATLANTIS OF THE SANDS

Once upon a time, the story goes, the legendary Shaddad ibn Ad built the city of Ubar of the splendid towers, to imitate paradise. With wonderful architecture, vast fruit groves and enormous wealth, Ubar was the centre of the frankincense trade; it's believed to be identical with the Iram of the Koran, and the Omanum Emporium mentioned by the geographer Ptolemy. But, says the Koran, the people of Iram were corrupted by their wealth, and God destroyed the city, after which it was covered by the desert sands.

Now it appears to have been found again, by an expedition led by Sir Ranulph Fiennes and American filmmaker Nicholas Clapp. With the aid of satellite radar and optical imaging, they found a number of ancient trackways converging on Ash Shisar, at the edge of the desert `Empty Quarter' in southern Oman. At the site they found the remains of an octagonal fortress with walls eight feet thick, and eight towers which would originally have stood about 30 feet high. The towers appear to have been plastered, and there are also the remains of other rooms and building foundations.

The major part of the 'city' appears to have consisted of tents, clustered round the octagon, and of this only fire-pits remain. Accounts vary as to the finds, but they seem to include neolithic pottery of 4000 BC from Mesopotamia, Syrian pottery of 2000 BC, and a number of Egyptian, Greek and Roman artefacts. The city seems to have survived until about 500 AD, but unhappily the octagonal structure was built directly over a large limestone cavern. When local water-levels fell, it appears that the cavern collapsed and the building sank into the ground. The city was abandoned, and later covered by the sands. *D.Telegraph, International Herald Tribune 6 Feb, Independent 25 Feb 1992.*

ARK REVISITED

Last issue (**FT63:28**) I told you about Hancock and Getz, the two people who both claimed to have found the Ark of the Covenant, one in Ethiopia and the other in Jerusalem. As usual, no sooner had we sent the issue to press than another story came in...

This time we have Vendyl Jones, 62, a former Baptist minister of Sudan, Texas, and director of the Institute for Judaic Christian Research. Vendyl can't seem to make his mind up whether he wants to be called 'Indiana' Jones or not: at one moment claiming to be the original model for Spielberg's archæologist, the next complaining that it just cheapens what he's doing. Anyway, he thinks the Ark is to be found in the Israeli-occupied West Bank, at Qumran, near where the Dead Sea Scrolls were found.

Jones' theory is based on the Copper Scroll, found at Qumran in 1952 and apparently listing 64 places where sacred items and treasures from the Second Temple at Jerusalem were hidden, before its destruction by the Romans in 70 AD. Items listed include the Ark, the garments of the high priest and the ashes of the red heifer used for ritual purification. In 1988, Jones found a small annointing jug, dating from the right period, and claimed that it was the first of the listed treasures. This May, Jones and his team of volunteers found what they thought was Temple incense in one of the Qumran caves. It was sent to Bar-Ilan University for analysis, and was said to contain 12 of the 15 ingredients listed in the Talmud, including balm, cassia, cinnamon, frankincense, myrrh, saffron and wine. But within two weeks, General Amir Drory, director of the Israeli Antiquities Authority, declared it to be nothing but brown dirt and stopped the excavation.

Jones had been given a temporary permit to dig, but when its time limit ran out, Drory refused to extend it. Various theories have been put forward to explain this: one was that as Jones has no archæological qualifications, his digging was meeting with opposition from Israeli specialists. Or maybe people are just getting fed up with Christian adventurers trying to find lost Biblical treasures. Of course, he could have been stopped because he was thought to have been on to something. Well, maybe he was... but if no one excavates the cave, we'll never know. *Newark Star Ledger, D.Mail 11 May, Independent on Sunday, 24 May 1992.*

FT

MYSTERY MOGGIES

Mike Dash

They're big, they're black, they're bad and they're back. British big cats are on the prowl again from Cornwall to Kidderminster, and the mystery moggies are being blamed by anxious locals for everything from missing bunnies to dead racehorses

Our last snapshot of mystery moggie activity, back in FT59, covered the years 1990 and 1991. But the elusive felines have been no less active this year, with sightings coming from Bodmin Moor, Worcestershire, Derbyshire and Hampstead (see *FT63:20*) and – predictably – the Exmoor area of Devon.

The first rumblings of renewed activity came in the *Daily Telegraph* of 4 Jan 1992, which published a full page report on the work of Nigel Brierly, well-known hunter of the Exmoor beasts. Brierly believes a family of pumas made up of escapees from domestic captivity has been at large on the moor since 1983, and reporter Andrew Martin, who stumbled across the moor after the intrepid Brierly for two days, came away impressed both by the volume of evidence he had amassed and by the steel cages baited with tripe he has built in the hope of trapping one of the animals.

Brierly is not alone in his quest. Farmer Peter Bailey, of the Collipriest dairy farm near Tiverton, Devon, also plans to build a cage after losing his Christmas dinner to a large brown cat-like animal he frequently spots prowling near the farm. The ABC (Alien Big Cats) "ripped to pieces" four geese he had been fattening up for the holiday, smashing its way into a pen six feet off the ground.

"Being a farmer I have seen dead animals before, but this was something else," Bailey said. "There were feathers and bones all over the floor. It was a shocking mess." Worried that the cat – which he believes lives in woods near the farm – is getting bolder, the Collipriest man told the Plymouth *Sunday Independent* (27 Oct 1991): "I must get it before it gets even more vicious."

Bailey may be one to benefit from the improved intelligence network introduced this year by Brierly, who has assembled a team of "seven or eight above averagely intelligent people", including local farmers, a zoologist and a newspaper reporter, and provided them with a record card to log big cat sightings in their area. The team will meet each spring at Sparkwell Zoo to pool the latest information on the beasts *(additional source: Western Daily Press 6 Jan 1992).*

It was not long before Brierly's men began coming up with the goods. Within a couple of weeks of the *Telegraph's* story, network member Trevor Beer reported a sighting of a big cat walking with cubs. Beer, who has written a pamphlet on the subject and has photographed one of the animals, believes as many as 10 cats have been living and breeding on Exmoor since being released when the Dangerous and Wild Animals Act regulating ownership of exotic pets was passed in 1976. *North Devon Advertiser 29 Jan 1992.*

CORNWALL

Equally active ABCs have been plaguing farmers to the south, where Cornwall is also in the grip of an ABC flap. A farmworker from Bolventor, an isolated village on Bodmin Moor, claimed to have seen a "huge, cat-like animal" this spring. The animal, variously dubbed 'The Beast of Bolventor' and, less precisely, 'The Beast of Bodmin Moor', was suspected of attacks on local livestock and of killing a collie torn to pieces while it slept in a barn.

Another dog lost a leg to the beast, and a ewe found dying on Rosemary Rhodes' farm at Ninestones, near Bolventor, had five-inch claw wounds on her belly. Ms Rhodes, who had already lost six other sheep in similar circumstances, took casts of footprints found near the scene, but a vet who examined the dead sheep said the attacker was probably a rogue dog. *D.Telegraph 2 May; Liskeard, Looe, Saltash & Callington Gazette 11 Jun 1992.*

WALES

Further to the west, big cat sightings have also been recorded in Pembrokeshire. The first, from Lower Fishguard, was in 1983, and attracted the attention of park warden Bernard Davies, who has collected subsequent reports.

Most recently, Davies says, Fishguard lifeboatman Chris Williams spotted an animal "the size of a large corgi" (ie pretty small) running across the road near Pwllderi. "It was definitely feline by the way it moved, and it had four or five vertical stripes along the length of its body," Williams said.

This sighting, in February, was backed up by a report of a two-foot cat with a black stripe along its back made by a resident of Wolfscastle on 6 February. Both accounts tend to support Davies' theory that at least one wild cat is on the prowl in the area. *Western Telegraph 25 Mar 1992.*

The only photo of the West Wales cat, taken by Des Townley of Solva. It was fawn coloured, as big as a fox, with a black stripe on its spine and a fluffy tail.

Moving east, we come to mid-Glamorgan, where Ernest Smith of Merthyr Tydfil told the *Western Mail*, 11 Feb 1992, that he had been cycling over the Brecon Beacons when a three-foot reddish-brown cat with small ears and a long tail crossed the road only a couple of yards from him. Smith was able to watch the cat for around five minutes before it made off. He description matched that of a cat photographed at Solva and featured in the *Mail* of 10 Feb [**below left**].

WELSH BORDERS

Within days, similar reports were being made from Kidderminster, on the English side of the border, where up to three pumas were reckoned to be on the loose – and this time there was photographic evidence to back up the sightings.

The *Kidderminster Shuttle* quoted a farmer who said he saw one animal chase a thoroughbred racehorse until it collapsed and died of exhaustion. Three ponies had also been dispatched and a number of sheep attacked.

Bob Lawrence of the West Midlands safari park said: "Two pumas have been seen, a brown one and a black one. But there could be even more. We have seen prints that lead us to believe they are definitely pumas."

Kidderminster folklore suggests that the animals were dumped near Great Witley after the Dangerous and Wild Animals Act became law and that they have been killing farm animals in the vicinity ever since.

The sudden upsurge in reports led to several efforts to catch the cats. Maro Scales of Gloucester turned up with a pair of French hunting dogs, used in the States to trap pumas, and announced she would use them to track down the cats, while warden Lawrence laid down a number of wire cage traps.

Local sceptics remained unconvinced. Malcolm Greg, a sportsman who shot the last wildcat sighted in the area back in 1962, argued that most of the kills could be attributed to foxes and suggested that the dead racehorse had expired of natural causes.

However, two months later, in May, photographs of the elusive moggies were secured by Nick Morris, an amateur naturalist from Bayton who had been searching for the ABCs near their favourite Great Witley stamping-ground.

He managed to take two snaps of a big cat before it ran off and told the local paper: "I saw it from a couple of fields away and it was too big to be a domestic cat. It appeared black from a distance, but when I got closer there were a lot of grey markings." The sighting lasted about 40 minutes.

Morris took the developed film to warden Lawrence, and together the two men tentatively identified the beast as a jungle cat or African golden cat – smaller than a puma, but equally out-of-place in the Worcestershire countryside.

Lawrence said the cats were relatively common in captivity, though an owner would need a licence for them. "They are capable of killing sheep, but would really go for smaller game such as rabbits, lambs and ducks," he added.
Kidderminster Times 27 Feb; Worcester Evening News 28 Feb + 7 Mar; Kidderminster Shuttle 28 May 1992.

MIDLANDS

A large cat-like animal, about the size of a Labrador, was seen in a field outside Ashby, near Leicester, on 21 June. The previous evening, Robert Noon, a local man, had taken his lurcher, Jack, and whippet, Sam, for a walk. "Sam ran through a gap in the hedge and into a corn-

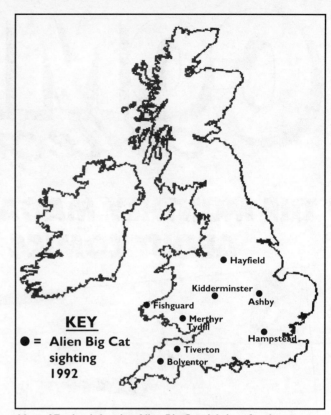

Map of England showing Alien Big Cat sightings for the year to date

field. He had not been in there for more than 10 seconds when I heard him yelping", said Mr Noon. "I ran into the field and he was lying on his back. His nose was covered in blood and one of his front legs was sticking straight up. I thought he was dead."

Mr Noon returned to the field the following day and saw the large cat lying about 300 yards away. "I bent down to put Jack on the lead and when I looked up, the cat had gone." Later, as he walked back to his car, it rushed past him, about 30 yards away, and disappeared into some trees. "I could tell it was a big animal", he said, "because the grass is about 18 inches high and its head was above the top of the grass." *Coalville Times (near Leicester) 26 June 1992.*

The Kidderminster big cat, taken at a distance of 12 yards, by Nick Morris

Alternative Alternative 3

Hoax!

Were the Earth's top scientists really being kidnapped and transported to another planet? **BOB RICKARD** chronicles a very Fortean hoax which evolved from a spoof documentary made by Anglia TV in 1977.

AT 9pm, on 20 June 1977, Anglia TV networked a documentary called 'Alternative Three', made by its Science Report team. It began with an investigation into the disappearance of several missing British scientists and uncovered evidence of a worldwide 'brain drain'. A trail of moles, decoded video tapes, classified documents, frightened informants and mysterious 'sudden' deaths, gradually revealed a shocking fact; the world as we comfortably knew it was a monumental lie. Britain, the US and USSR had been working together, secretly, for decades, and were already occupying the Moon and Mars.

In the programme, a Professor Ballantine, distinguished radio astronomer, said the NASA space programme was a set-up - as was the Cold War - to mislead the mass of unsuspecting ordinary people. This was confirmed by Bob Grodin, an astronaut who had sought refuge in alcohol from the demoralising discovery of this truth and from his shame over accepting lavish bribes in return for his silence.

The reason for the conspiracy, we were told by a string of earnest 'sources', lay in the desire among the powerful scientists, military and politicians of the superpowers to evade the coming ecological doom, made inevitable by the rape and abuse of our common environment, and abortive attempts to control weather and climate. In the programme, one of the chief theorists of the 'Greenhouse Effect', Prof Karl Gerstein of Cambridge University, sets out the choices: "Cut population, cut consumption," and the eponymous third alternative "get the hell off this planet."

THE DARK SIDE OF THE MOON

In reality this was fiction; Grodin, Ballantine, Gerstein, and the supporting cast of disappeared scientists, murdered informants and nervous reporters were all the invention of author David Ambrose and film director Christopher Miles. Even the 'Science Report' production team and programme was phony. Many viewers recognised bit-part actors, the preposterous nature of the material, long before they saw the copyright notice dated '1st April' at the end of the credits. "We intended it for April Fool's Day, but it was postponed," said Miles in the *Daily Mail* (21 June 1977).

The cognoscenti recognised elements of the Fortean canon here: vanishing scientists, spontaneous combustion (an instantaneous death referred to as a 'hot job' by anonymous security officials), underground life on Mars, unidentified spaceships (UFOs?) on the dark side of the moon, suppressed advanced technology, and extreme weather and environmental catastrophes. What lifted A3 out of the realm of the ordinary hoax was its deliberate and clever manipulation of post-hippy anxieties, mixing realism with complexity and the folklore of vast trans-national conspiracies. It was a Fortean version of the Gemstone File (an 'underground' pamphlet from the late 1960s which knitted together the Kennedy assassination, Onassis, the world-domination of organised crime and governmental cover-ups) with bells on.

Anglia TV was taken aback by the public outcry the following day, characterised by headlines proclaiming 'Shock' and 'Panic'. "It was never our intention to create another *War of the Worlds* scare," said a spokesman. "We knew there would be some commotion, but we felt viewers would be fairly sophisticated about it." Most national newspapers were swamped with callers reacting to what they had seen: some angry at being deceived, some angry at having the 'truth' kept from them. Many others asked, with trepidation, for confirmation of A3's claims and 'facts'. Even the ubiquitous Mary Whitehouse was begged by her viewer complaints network to protest to Anglia and the Independent Broadcasting Authority.

In an interview with James Murray, the day after the screening (*D.Express* 22 June 1977), Miles and Ambrose also expressed astonishment at the shockwave their fictional 'documentary' had sent through the nation. Ambrose and Miles had worked out the

Among the many special props used in the programme were these records from a fake file on the disappearances of scientists and top people.

SIR WILLIAM BALLANTINE (M.FRS.,

RADIO ASTRO

DOCTOR ANN CLARKE B.Sc.,

RESEARCH SCIENTIST

Laurels Farm,
Occoldeston,
Yorks,
England.

Disappeared: 1. 11. 76

Disappeared: 21. 9. 76

UNIVERSITY LECTURER

12 Yoks Avenue,
Little Mellis,
Notts,
England.

Disappeared: 12. 10. 76.

Alternative 3's flavour of authenticity was deliberately created by dramatising the investigation of a fictitious TV science programme called *Science Report.* Here, veteral newsreader Tim Brinton, as the team's front-man, lends credibility to reports of lunar occupation.

premise of A3 over lunch the previous year. It was on the day the first pictures came back from Mars, and Ambrose was working on a programme about people disappearing. "We put the two things together, said Miles, "and added the classic science-fiction plot of the doomed planet. We made it different by presenting it as a story about a documentary team investigating a mystery."

Miles - who had once worked with Orson Welles and discussed with him his great 'Martians are coming' hoax - said cryptically: "Let's say that all the facts in the show were true and all the lies untrue." We can only presume he is referring to his skillful use of 'factoids' - imitation facts - based upon real news reportage of a mystery death or a scientist's disappearance but with some details changed.

FACT OR FICTION?

David Ambrose said: "We packaged it like a current affairs programme... like *World in Action...* and people expected to see fact and

Tim Brinton interviews the fictitious professor Karl Gerstein at Cambridge University, supposedly a specialist in ecology and climatic changes. Many readers will recognise him as Richard Marner, better known as Colonel von Strohm from *'Allo 'Allo.*

not fiction [..] The answer is to beware of the media. There is an obligation on every viewer to sift the evidence he is being fed and make up his own mind... My advice is to keep your wits about you." In another interview - London *Evening News* 21 June 1977 - he added: "I am constantly amazed at the gullibility of people. Those upset by this programme are the type who never read the small print on contracts they sign."

Anglia's producers had deliberately played up A3's preposterous ingredients in the vain hope that viewers would see it for what it was - a satire on the excesses of investigative journalism, in particular the trick of 'dramatising'. "These 'factional' techniques," said Ambrose, "are used in many programmes. Think of party political broadcasts which are cunningly made to look like current affairs shows. People should realise that everything they see is being selected for them by a production team... and documentary makers are only human... they tend to go for a good story. "All those involved thought "it would reduce the impact of the story if we warned the viewers in a heavy-handed way about what was coming," said Miles. Even so, Yorkshire TV prefaced their showing with a warning, and the TV reviewers of a number of the day's newspapers also flagged the programme as a spoof.

Ambrose and Miles, however, stood by their claim that they had a serious point to make. "If nothing else," said Ambrose, "it has made people aware of the threat to the ecology of the world; more, perhaps, than a lot of other earnest documentaries on the subject.' Indeed, the same approach had been used earlier by a minor - but nonetheless chilling - film, *The Hellstrom Chronicle* (1971), which dramatised insects taking over as the environment became ever more erratic. The offworld or underground survival of a hand-picked elite is a motif in countless old SF movies; it even occurs in *Dr Strangelove* (1963). It is a curious fact that 1977 also saw the release of *Capricorn One*, a film starring Elliott Gould, James Brolin and Hal Holbrook, based on a Mars mission failing on the launchpad and continued in a film studio to deceive the public and the government budget controllers.

THE GREAT CONSPIRACY

As memories of the programme and its eco-concerns faded, the conspiracy angle continued with a life of its own. Ambrose tells of one caller who accused them of diverting attention from 'the real truth'. "You can permutate that line of thought indefinitely and end up bonkers," he said. Anglia had originally announced that A3 was to be transmitted in at least nine countries; whether it ever was or not, conspiracy addicts worldwide, including the USA, who missed the programme, saw its absence as evidence of the global conspiracy. One woman even thanked Miles and Ambrose for explaining the disappearance of her boy; it was a relief to her to know he was happy and on Mars.

A chastened Anglia sold the book rights to Sphere, and A3 reached a whole new audience in 1978. Author Leslie Watkins' adaptation added to the melodrama and breathed new vigour into the story's accelerating mythology. By the time many people wanted a copy, the book was said to be hard to find (although we had no trouble). There were rumours that it had been suppressed on orders from 'on high', that secret agents were buying up stocks from shops, that warehouse stocks had been seized and destroyed, or that it was a clever marketing ploy creating demand for a second printing.

One colleague of ours was convinced he knew of a garage in Camden crammed to the rafters with copies. According to David Austin (*New Scientist 6 Sept 1979*), another fanatic claimed to have 'checked out all the facts', found them all false and concluded that A3 *must* be true, otherwise why would Sphere and Anglia go to so much trouble to conceal real facts and identities? Fourteen years later, we, at **FT** towers, still get queries from fascinated, worried or excited readers, who have just stumbled onto a copy of the book.

To their credit, Ambrose, Miles and Watkins were craftsmen. A3 works as thought-provoking entertainment and did well to draw attention to the environmental effects of weather gone wild. Had they known of the effects of CFC gasses in 1977, the authors would surely have included the cirrhosis of the ozone layer among the diseases of man. We are also struck by the similarity between their epidemic of vanishing scientists and stories we have reported from time to time - see the saga of the Marconi and related deaths in **FT49:14**.

Elements of A3's thesis have cross-pollinat-ed with the other classic conspiracy fantasies and have taken root in fertile paranoid imaginations, especially in the USA, where there has been no solid refutation of this rolling hoax. Anglia told us that they *still* get inquiries from the USA, usually students on journalism courses wanting to check facts. Amazingly, they insist (against Anglia's continued declaration that the programme was scheduled as drama) that it was a serious documentary.

Finally, one reviewer - Nancy Banks-Smith (*Guardian 21 June 1977*) - was more outraged at the grammatical licence involved. "An alternative," she pointed out, "is one of two possibilities, so I don't think there is such a thing as a third alternative." Quite so! **FT**

POSTSCRIPT

Thanks to reader Mrs Anne Cooper, who gave us copies of her correspondence with several of the parties in this affair. In one letter (dated 1980), Leslie Watkins says, definitively: "Alternative 3 is fiction. The so-called conspiracy is science-fantasy. Obviously, I did weave many facts into the story. Maybe, on reflection, it did fit too neatly."

We wondered whether the authors had vanished off the face of the earth after A3 and made an attempt to trace them. Christopher Miles and David Ambrose continued their work in television. Leslie Watkins lived for a time in Devon and worked for *Readers Digest*, and moved to Australia around 1983. Where they are now I don't know.

Fuelled by a plentiful supply of mineral water, cigars and bread rolls, Anglia TV producers David Ambrose (left) and Christopher Miles hatch their plot for *Alternative 3* in a discrete Ipswich cafeteria.

TVSINNERS

MIKE DASH hikes into the foothills of the latest Satanic Ritual Abuse scares and finds he needs his critical faculties and a sense of the ridiculous in tracing the absurd tale of a Satanic video that never was ...

ALLEGATIONS that a gang of Satanists had filmed rituals including mutilation, rape and abortion first surfaced in the sober pages of the *Observer* in February. An article trailing a Channel 4 'Dispatches' programme said the documentary would show "the abuse of young adults in what is clearly a ritual context", intercut with Satanic symbols and film of explicit sex acts. The video, it was suggested, offered the first hard evidence of the existence of ritual abuse.

Those tuning in to 'Dispatches' on 19 February saw both interviews with alleged survivors of Satanic abuse and short clips from the video, which presenter Andrew Boyd explained had been obtained from a 'professional carer' who was counselling one of the victims.

Pictures showed a naked man tied to a bed and beaten by a man and a woman, drawing blood that was smeared over the victim's back. Another scene portrayed what was said to be a pregnant female cult member performing an abortion using a pair of forceps. Both scenes were murkily shot and filmed to a discordant musical backing, making it hard for viewers to work out what was going on. A woman 'survivor' provided a commentary and made the allegation that an abortion was taking place. Her own baby, she said, was induced prematurely by the same group so it could be sacrificed.

The woman, 'Jennifer', now living under an assumed identity after supposedly fleeing the cult, claimed to have been recruited to Satanism

"'I saw four children killed,' she alleged. 'All were boys.'"

at 16 through tarot cards and astrology. After several meetings, she was drugged and woke to find herself being 'initiated' by being raped.

"I saw four children killed," she alleged. "All were boys. Three were Spanish-speaking, smuggled into Britain from Latin America. First they were sexually abused." The fourth child, she said, was "white, about six years old. I don't know where he came from. But many children were brought in for sexual abuse from children's homes."

Among the experts interviewed for the programme was Superintendent Michael Hames, head of Scotland Yard's Obscene Publications Squad, who said the video was "evidence of grievous bodily harm performed in a ritualistic fashion". Forensic specialist Stephen Hempling added: "The violence and blood in this film are real, not simulated. You can see incisions clearly made with a knife and blood welling up gradually."

PSYCHIC TV

Scotland Yard certainly showed a willingness to take the evidence seriously, raiding a house in Brighton after a tip-off from the programme-makers.

Officers working for a new unit set up in January to look into allegations of abuse siezed sixty binbags full of video material, photographs, letters and other documents in the raid. But that, it rapidly emerged, was because the police had been considering charges against the group responsible for the film for some time.

Journalists from the *Observer's* rivals soon established that the video had been shot by followers of the Brighton-based singer and body-piercer Genesis P. Orridge of the group *Psychic TV*. It showed performance art rather than Satanic abuse.

Rosie Waterhouse of the *Independent on Sunday* and Barbara Jones of the *Mail on Sunday*, both of whom had attacked earlier claims of ritual abuse, revealed that the group, calling themselves 'Thee Temple ov Psychick Youth' (*sic*),

Below: Genesis P Orridge and his wife Paula at the Spahn ranch where Charles Manson and his disciples once lived Far right: The proud father, photographed with his first child, in 1982.

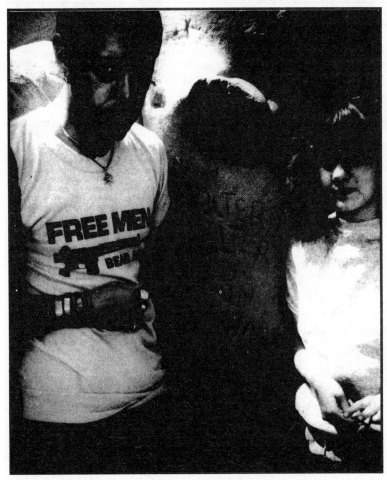

had made the video around 1982 and tried unsuccessfully to market it.

Psychic TV fan Daryl Tomlinson phoned the *Observer* to say she had seen the video at Manchester's Hacienda club in October 1982 as part of a package featuring the group and readings by author William Burroughs. "It was strong stuff, but I assumed it was just Porridge and his body-piercing friends," she said. "As far as I was concerned, TOPY was just a glorified fan club."

Time Out columnist Jon Ronson, an acquaintance of Orridge (real name Neil Megson) added further details in an article published some months after the scandal had broken. Staying with Genesis and his children Genesse and Caresse was a disconcerting experience, he wrote, if only because the family was superficially so normal.

"Okay, Genesse was baptised in blood, which, one has to accept, is fucking weird. Also, as Genesis went off to buy some bread, his parting words to me were, 'Don't go in the attic.' But they showed me a good time, fed me well, gave me a duvet, and singularly failed to slice me up in the night.

"Gensis P. Orridge once showed me his penis," Ronson cointinued, "which, I thought at the time, was rather nice of him.

"'My,' I replied, 'all those pierces must have hurt.'

"'Not really,' replied Genesis.

"'Would you like to see my clitoris?' added Paula, his wife.

"'Yes please,' I replied.

"But Genesis gave us both a disapproving glance, and Paula withdrew her offer, much to my chagrin.

"Nevertheless, I was smitten. 'They must really like me,' I thought. 'I've only known them a few days, and they're already showing me their genitalia.'

"What I didn't realise was that the Orridges possess some of the most well-documented genitalia in showbiz, and that Genesis showing me his penis was rather like me showing him my bus pass."

Orridge and his wife and children, who had the good fortune to be on holiday in Thailand when the police raided their flat, have settled in America, fearing that police could still bring charges over the sado-masochistic acts depicted in the video. (Another group of sado-masochists, who had photographed the mutilation of each other's penises and the sandpapering of their scrotums, had earlier been sentenced to long jail sentences.)

> "'They must really like me,' I thought. 'I've only known them a few days, and the're already showing me their genitalia.'"

DODGY DEALINGS

The ridiculous denouément of the Brighton saga should not obscure the dubious circumstances under which the story became public. It is alarming that the original *Observer* article was a puff piece written not by a staff journalist but by a researcher for the controversial 'Dispatches' show who could not claim to be unbiased. Equally disturbing were the actions of Channel 4, which commissioned the programme from Look Twice Productions, an off-the-shelf company which the *Mail on Sunday* claimed was a front to conceal the strong fundamentalist views of several of the production team.

Witnesses interviewed in the film also appear to have been misquoted or unreliable. Gynæcologist Wendy Savage, who told the programme-makers that the 'abortion' sequence did show "something being stuck and stirred inside the vagina", protested that she had made it clear there was no abortion "but they chose not to use it". 'Jennifer' (described by the *MoS* as "a professional victim") was never a member of TOPY, and members of the Temple said her descriptions of the film were inaccurate.

She alleged it was made in an east London house with a basement; in fact it was shot in Brighton in a home without a cellar. And what were supposed to be "especially small-sized forceps used in hospital for delivering premature babies" were really coal tongs.

In retrospect, the actions of Look Twice Productions look highly dubious. It is hard to believe that Boyd and his team were unaware that the video showed performance art. As the *Independent on Sunday* pointed out, the three-hour tape opened with an introduction by the well-known film director Derek Jarman, and a scene of buggery came from a different source and was captioned 'Male Initiation Rites: sound New Guinea; pictures America'. *Observer 16+23 Feb; Daily Telegraph 17 Feb; Mail on Sunday & Independent on Sunday 23 Feb; Time Out, June 1992.*

 # SATANIC ROUND-UP

AYR OF SUSPICION

Eight children siezed from four families in Ayrshire remain in care two years after allegations of Satanic ritual abuse were levelled at their parents.

Scottish prosecutors are still debating whether to bring legal proceedings, but lawyers representing the parents are asking for a review on the grounds that the evidence is ambiguous and has been 'massaged' by social workers.

Four children were taken into care in June 1990 after a woman visited police to say she suspected her husband of abusing their children. She soon realised that the case was snowballing out of her control, and told reporters she was concerned that her wildest suggestions were being taken as

fact. Social workers who had interviewed the children appeared to be implanting ideas, the mother said, and began claiming they had been abused at ritual parties. Some of the accustations, said a report in *The Times*, were "even more bizarre than those made in the Orkney case".

As lawyers wrangled, both parents spoke to the press. "I know there were no parties at my house – decent or indecent," the mother said. "I have never seen parties at anyone else's house. Some of the allegations are just ludicrous."

The father added: "I am supposed to have hurt someone's leg by using telepathy from miles away. My own boy is supposed to have been put in a coffin by us and then we are supposed to have allowed a woman to cut a piece of enamel off his tooth."

As the interviews proceeded, a typical pattern of elaboration and accusation emerged, and two more children from another family were seized in August 1990. They were later returned after a sheriff ruled that the evidence was unreliable, but that two of the children from the first family had indeed been abused. *Times + Guardian 21 May 1992.*

EPPING EPILOGUE

The last two of five adults to be tried at the Old Bailey on charges relating to Satanic ritual abuse in Epping Forest were freed in March when the chief prosecution witness refused to give evidence.

Brian Linge and his girlfriend Janet Hall had been arrested along with George Gibbard, Rosemary Ridewood and Ronald Smith *[FT61:34],* but their case was delayed for four months owing to Linge's illness. In the meantime, the first three defendents had all been freed in embarrassing circumstances when the judge ruled that the main witnesses, two girls, were unreliable.

The prosecution said it was dropping six charges of rape and three of indecent assault on the older of the girls reluctantly because "the victim had found it impossible to cope with the strain of waiting to give evidence. The decision left us wondering how Linge, a wheelchair-bound man of 60, was supposed to have abused the girls, even in concert with other members of the alleged coven." *Independent 21 March 1992.*

CHRISTIAN RITUAL ABUSE

An interesting variant on our tales of Satanic abuse cropped up in Australia earlier this year when police in Victoria and New South Wales seized 144 children, aged from one to 14, from members of the extreme Christian sect Children of God.

The children were held for six days before a judge ordered the release of 56 of them. A further 65 were still being held in care when reports appeared in the *Evening Standard* and *Daily Telegraph* (in the Claudia FitzHerbert column) on 21 May 1992.

The police raid followed allegations of sexual abuse and harsh punishment practised by parents belonging to the cult, whose adult members use seductive techniques on potential recruits and are sometimes known as 'hookers for Jesus'.

SECRET COUNTRY

Mysterious places to visit in Great Britain, compiled by Janet & Colin Bord

4: Dunadd, Argyll

AN ISOLATED rock outcrop, 176 feet high, stands close to the River Add near Kilmichael Gassary, at the eastern edge of low-lying marshy ground in the Strathclyde region of Argyll on Scotland's west coast. It was a natural site for a fort, and evidence has been found of Iron Age settlement. The stone walls belong, however, to a later period, for Dunadd is thought to have been the capital of the Scottish kingdom of Dalriada, established around AD 500 by colonists from Ireland. Pottery has been found, along with crucibles, iron knives and spearheads, bone combs, whetstones and querns.

For casual visitor, Dunadd seems to be merely a rocky hill, providing a fine view over the surrounding flat countryside, and is an exciting place for children to let off steam. It is only when you climb up inside the fort that you find the relics which have made Dunadd such an intriguing place.

On a flat slab of rock are carved an ogham inscription, a boar, a footprint, and a rock basin. Judging from the function of similar carvings elsewhere, the last two were used in the rituals marking the inauguration of Dalriadan kings, the candidate placing his foot in the footprint to show that he would follow in the footsteps of his predecessors.

The ogham inscription has not yet been deciphered, but the boar is in the Pictish style and is thought to date from the time when the site was besieged and captured by Fergus, King of the Picts, in AD 736, or perhaps during an

A closer view of the carved footprint

earlier attack in 683, both of these events being recorded in the *Annals of Ulster.*

There was, at some stage, a Christian community on Dunadd, because among the finds was a small stone disc bearing the Latin inscription *'in nomine* – 'in the name [of the Lord]'. It is possible that St Columba visited Dunadd from Iona, since Adamnan's *Life* tells how the saint went to the *caput regionis* (the most important place in the district) to meet a ship from Gaul. Gaulish pottery was among the items found on Dunadd.

Little else is known about the history of the fort, once so important. This is so often the case; we visit an isolated place where nothing seems to have happened; but a mere eyeblink away in time it was inhabited and bustling with life.

The visible remains on Dunadd are tantalising; they hint of rituals long forgotten, yet vitally important to the people who practised them. There are many similar places throughout Britain, that once were capitals before being abandoned for some reason as the fortunes of communities ebb and flow. There may not be a lot to see, but such places trigger the imagination.

At Kilmartin, just up the road, are a number of other important sites: prehistoric burial chambers, early Christian crosses and fine graveslabs. These shouldn't be missed if you are visiting Dunadd.

Janet and Colin Bord are authors of *Mysterious Britain, The Secret Country, Alien Animals, The Atlas of Magical Britain,* and *Modern Mysteries of Britain* among many others.

All three rock carvings are shown here on the foreground strip of rock; the boar (covered by glass), the footprint to the left of it, and the stone basin to the far right.

BYE-GONES

Extracts from The Oswestry Advertizer's eponymous weekly column that ran from 1871 to 1939. Selected by RICHARD HOLLAND, author of Haunted Clwyd and Supernatural Clwyd, and sub-editor at North Wales Newspapers, who still publish The Oswestry Advertizer

TURNIP POINTS THE FINGER

APRIL 12, 1876

The 'Monmouthshire Merlin', somewhere about the year 1832, narrated a wonderful story of a turnip. At the time the paragraph appeared, a man had plucked a turnip in crossing a field, which, to his astonishment, resembled in shape a man's right hand, minus the thumb. This he exhibited in Monmouth, and it was said that half a dozen years before, the body of a man named Gurney, a toll-gate keeper, had been found barbarously murdered in a turnip field near Ledbury. The unfortunate man, in his agonies, had grasped his hands full of the green tops of the turnips. A waggoner named Powell, an athletic man, and who had by accident lost his right thumb, was apprehended on suspicion of being concerned in the murder, but for lack of evidence was discharged, and he left the country.

From that year to the one in which the oddly shaped turnip was plucked, the field had not been sown with turnips, and it was said that the man (a servant of Mr J. Biddulph's) who pulled it out of the ground, did so in the very spot where Gurney's murdered body was found, and to the astonishment and dismay of his neighbours it was found to resemble the hand of Powell even down to a wart upon one of the fingers.

POE PREDICTED

JUNE 13, 1894

"POE'S MURDERS IN THE RUE MORGUE: The employment of an Ourang-Outang in the committal of these murders has always seemed to me to be one of the most original ideas in fiction with which I am acquainted until now, when I light upon an extract from the 'Shrewsbury Chronicle', tucked away in 'Chronicle' columns of the 'Annual Register'.

"Poe's story was published in 'Graham's Magazine' for April, 1841. What took place in Shrewsbury occurred in July or August, 1834. At that time certain showmen visited the town with a 'ribbed-faced babboon', which, it was afterwards shrewdly suspected, had been taught to burgle, or, as the 'Chronicle' puts it, to 'commit robberies by night, by climbing up places inaccessible to men, and thereby gaining an entrance through the bedroom windows' – precisely the method adopted by Poe's anthropoid.

"In her bedroom one night a Shrewsbury lady found the creature. She raised an alarm, and the baboon 'instantly attacked her, and with so much fury that the lady's husband, who had come to the rescue, was glad to let it escape by the windows.' The ourang-outang of the Rue Morgue makes a similar though more fatal attack when it is discovered in a lady's bedroom there, and it effects its escape by the same means." (*Notes and Queries 8ths.v.366*)

BLOWN AWAY

FEB 18, 1899

The following extract is taken from Dr Burney's 'Collection of Newspapers in the British Museum (vol CXVI): The London Post, with Intelligence Foreign and Domestic, Aug 19-21, 1700': "We have advice from Staffordshire that one Pendrell (being the last of the family* that was instrumental in saving King Charles II by hiding him in the oak, ever after called the Royal Oak, after the battle of Worcester) has departed this life; but that which makes his death very remarkable is that the very day and hour that he died the said oak was blown down by a storm in the wind."

* ie the last survivor of those who personally assisted in the king's escape, not the last survivor of the Pendrell family.

SOLO SURVIVORS

FEB 14, 1900

The following startling and authentic coincidence is vouched for by trustworthy local authorities. On December 5th, 1664, a boat crossing the Menai Strait with eighty-one passengers on board encountered a terrific gale, and foundered. The only man who escaped death was a Mr Hugh Williams. More than a hundred years later, on December 5th, 1780, another vessel with a large number of passengers were drowned except one, again a Mr Hugh Williams. Again, on December 5th, 1820, a boat laden with thirty people sank in the same spot. The sole survivor once more was a Mr Hugh Williams.

TREBLE CHANCE

FEB 18, 1903

The Rev David Lloyd of Crewkerne, Somerset, at one time curate of Llangollen, writes to the 'Strand Magazine' for February: "Urged by a large number of my friends, I write to bring to your notice a unique and very remarkable coincidence that happened in my family. We have three children, and they were born as follows – Myfanwy, our eldest, on January 21st, 1900; Nesta, on January 21st, 1901; Robert, on January 21st 1902. Not only were they born on the same day but also the very same hour, viz. 2 am."

FT

PSYCHICAL RESEARCH:
Brian Inglis, writer on parapsychology, exposes the Catch-22 of many debunkers

SCIENCE WATCH:
Dennis Stacy, leading UFO journalist, looks at the strange secrets of an astronomer

SPECULATION:
Ion Will, guerrilla ontologist, probes the new worlds of virtual reality

UFOLOGY:
Andy Roberts, editor of UFO Brigantia, describes how to be a UFO prat

Psychical Research

Stubborn Disbelief

Brian Inglis is a London-based veteran of over twenty books in the fields of parapsychology and fringe medicine, including a history of psychic research, *Natural and Supernatural* (1977).

"I want to show not only that these things don't happen", Nicholas Humphrey explained after he was appointed a research fellow in parapsychology at Darwin College, Cambridge, "but also that they are logically impossible." As Bernard Levin commented in *The Times*, a scientist who makes such a pronouncement is a very peculiar scientist indeed.

Peculiar, but far from unusual. My only surprise is that Nick Humphrey should have offered so unscientific an excuse as 'logically impossible' for his scepticism. If he had claimed that psychic phenomena cannot exist because they break nature's laws he would at least have an arguable case. But what has logic to do with it?

Whom the gods wish to destroy, they first send round the twist. Sceptics strike me as becoming progressively more crazed. Look at Randi, who is being sued in various parts of the world for making statements so economical with the truth that even his staunchest supporters, the Committee for the Scientific Investigation of Claims of the Paranormal, have had to extricate themselves, or face court cases in which the costs alone, leave aside the damages, could be horrendous.

A few years ago, I coined an aphorism: power corrupts, scepticism corrodes. It corrodes because it compels the sceptic – using the term in the sense it has acquired, implying blind disbelief rather than honest doubt – to explain away every piece of evidence for the paranormal, regardless of its strength.

The most irritating sceptics are those who say "I have an open mind" in a tone which ensures that their next word will be "but ..." A typical example was the psychiatrist Dr Louis Rose, who investigated faith healing in the 1960s. His book on the

> "The most irritating sceptics are those who say 'I have an open mind' in a tone which ensures that their next word will be 'but ...'"

subject was published by Gollancz, the blurb praising Rose for "keeping a remarkably open mind" and I feel sure that he sincerely believed that he had, though the evidence in the book showed that it was clamped shut.

All that he wanted as proof of healing, Rose claimed, was a single clear-cut case. He cited cancer: the diagnosis must be unequivocal, supported by X-ray photographs, which would also be required to demonstrate the effect of the healing.

Harry Edwards, then the leading British healer, presented a case which appeared to satisfy the criteria. Not so, Rose replied; the disappearance of the tumour might have been the consequence of the earlier medical attention given at the time of the diagnosis. In other words, Edwards complained, to qualify as spiritually healed, patients must not have had earlier medical attention – but in that case Rose would refuse to accept the healing on the ground that there could not have been a proper diagnosis. Heads you win ...

Another common let-out, for sceptics, is the claim that the experimental evidence for parapsychology cannot be accepted until it achieves repeatability. I have always regarded this as absurd, in view of the strength of the historical and anecdotal evidence – you might as well, on the same argument, refuse to accept that people fall in love. But I am intrigued to find, from Richard Broughton's admirable *Parapsychology: the Controversial Science* that – to his 'surprise and delight' – repeatability has at last been achieved.

Psi has crept in from the cold thanks to a new tool employed in conventional psychology, meta-analysis, particularly useful in areas where there is a lot of 'noise' and inconsistency. Suffice to say that Hilgard and Atkinson's *Introduction to Psychology*, which in the past has treated parapsychologists much as the Ascot authorities treat divorcees trying to get into the Royal Enclosure, has at last relented.

So far, only the research into telepathy using the Ganzfield procedure has qualified for admission. No matter: repeatability has had to be conceded.

An Unsolicited Elf

Dennis Stacy is a freelance science journalist living in San Antonio, Texas. He edits the monthly *Journal of MUFON*, the largest and longest-surviving UFO research organisation in the USA. (MUFON: 103 Oldtowne Road, Seguin, TX78155 USA)

Science, like religion, has always had its knighted saints. And like religion, science's self-promotional interests lie in keeping its saints sanitorily canonised. But saints – scientific or otherwise – are always going off the deep end, into visionary ecstasies and self-flagellation or other erstwhile forms of 'deviant' behaviour. Such a case in point is the curious career of one George Ellery Hale.

Hale – according to his biographer, Helen Wright (*Explorer of the Universe: A Biography of George Ellery Hale*, EP Dutton, NY 1966) – was one of this century's foremost students of the sun, the first to promote the theory that sunspots were magnetic storms, and the first to realise that the magnetic polarisation of such storms undergoes a reversal on a roughly 22-year cycle. He was a promoter and fund-raiser of the first water, responsible for the founding of the California Institute of Technology (CalTech), the construction of the 100-inch telescope which now sits atop Mt Wilson in California, and the prime mover behind Mt Palomar's 200-inch successor, dedicated a decade after his death. He was also a troubled manic-depressive, perhaps overly interested in the Egyptian sun-god, Ra; and for the better part of his illustrious career (b.1868, d.1938) he apparently conversed with a tutelory elf.

It is, of course, this elf business that concerns us here. Wright, as might be expected, doesn't delve very deeply into the subject, and why should she? After all, even the faraway surface features of the sun are more readily "comprehensible" to the modern mind than the manifest vagaries of Ra and diminutive mythical dwarves, who, when all is said and done, may or may not be present in the physical sense of the word. Here, in fact, is Wright's single titillating paragraph:

"'An odd thing, however, happened during this visit [to Egypt]. It was something he himself could never explain entirely. One night, when he was sitting in his room, out of nowhere, a little man suddenly appeared, and soon was advising him on the conduct of his life. Sometimes Hale had a ringing in his ears. Now the visitation of this little elf seemed to be connected in some way with that ringing. After this, his first visit, he came often, in many widely scattered places, until he

became almost a mascot. Hale rarely spoke of these visitations. But years later he described them to Dr Leland Hunnicut in Pasadena, hoping for some realistic explanation of the phenomenon." (p264)

A colleague of mine is currently trying to hunt down the Hale-Hunnicut correspondence in the Huntington Library in Pasadena, to which Hale's papers were donated, but a few provisional observations are in order. First, Hale's reluctance to make more widely known the existence of his own personal elf is quite understandable under the

> "Most manic-depressive sufferers of high blood pressure don't normally report the counsel of elves as a side-effect!"

circumstances; as he was dealing with Carnegie and other heavily-endowed individuals and institutions, who might have had a hard time explaining to their own colleagues and backers – let alone themselves – that they were investing in ground-breaking solar and astronomical research on the advice of an elf!

Secondly, the ringing in Hale's ears may have been indicative of high blood pressure. Certainly, in retrospect, it seems as if the ups and downs of his own inner life are suggestive of what would now be diagnosed as a manic-depressive personality. By the same token, most manic-depressive sufferers of high blood pressure don't normally report the counsel of elves as a side-effect!

So where did Hale's elf materialise from? Was it a simple psychological projection of his own tumultuous psyche; a way of externalising one of his collective selves that his rational 'I' would have otherwise denied? If so, why should this expelled 'self' take on the appearance of a traditional elf? (At this time, I'm only guessing about the elf's appearance. Did he wear green leggings and a fawn-coloured cap? Alas that Helen Wright wasn't more interested!) In addition, why would this expelled self presumptuously

assume the role of advising Hale "on the conduct of his life"? Why not just teach him how to raise award-winning tomatoes?

I've misplaced my notes on Hale's ethnic parentage, but there is one tantalising clue as to the origin of his elf. We know that he was born in Chicago in the year 1868, and that his father was a relatively successful businessman who led the way in the development of the hydraulic elevator. His father's original building burned in the great Chicago fire of October 8, 1871, when George was only three. Wright says of Hale's early childhood that "from Nellie Fay, the Irish cook and maid of all work, he learned songs of a different and more melancholy sort. One night, while his father and mother listened, amazed, he sang verse after verse of a song he had just learned." (p29) Could Hale have been contaminated, subconsciously, with the baby-sitter's Irish elf-lore? It's interesting to note that Fay is phonetically analogous to '*fey*', which means both fairy-like and visionary.

Well, these are the mysteries of elves, or the elves of mystery. Hale himself was instrumental in pioneering the study and spectroscopy of our own sun, and in extrapolating the studies of that nearmost star to the evolution of stars everywhere. He played a primary role in the development and construction of four major telescopes, each, for a time, the largest of its kind in the world. Apart from many of his contemporaries, Hale intuited early on that the more light we could gather here on Earth, the farther and deeper into the birth of the universe we could see.

Still, there is no evidence whatsoever that Hale's immersion in the 'objective' world of science proved any more of a balm than his close encounters of the elfish kind. Here, for instance, is how Wright describes him at the height of his powers: "During those long months in 1932, Hale had been defeated not only by the problem of the sun's general field, but also by continuing ill health. He suffered from severe nose bleeds and dizziness. His blood pressure soared. Torturing nightmares disturbed his sleep ... Yet he kept on working whenever he could." (p414)

No doubt it galls science no end to think that Hale's personal contributions might be owed to so small, insignificant and unsolicited an elf as his.

Ghosts of the Interface

Ion Will is an inveterate traveller. Since his appearance in Lyall Watson's *The Nature of Things*, many people think he's a figment of Watson's imagination, an opinion he'll defend your right to hold. Currently, Ion is sweating it out in bat-infested flophouses along the Ivory Coast.

Virtual Reality (VR) will be big next century, if you can see past the simplistic power-anxieties dramatised in *The Lawnmower Man*. A full page on VR by Mic Moroney in the *Irish Times* (28 March 1992) articulated some of these. He tells of a driver on a German autobahn who survived a near-fatal crash, and who blamed his sudden swerve on a flashback to his 15-minute 'immersion' in VR earlier that day. The reference to 'flashbacks' flags the fear that VR will be the "electronic LSD". How will *you* know if someone has tampered with your memory, as happened to the Swarzenegger's character in *Total Recall?*

Or worse, says Moroney: "Moral issues are being raised. If wars are being rehearsed and fought like video games, then what precisely is the difference? If someone with sociopathic tendencies enjoys blowing away virtual grannies, who's to say the experience won't reinforce his compulsions and lead him to seek satisfaction in the real world?" Well, I say it's too late, too damn late! In almost every country in the world there's a generation of kids hacking and slashing their way through zillions of sprites in their 2D-VR computer games. Besides, maybe the 'artificial' mayhem will satisfy the sociopath's 'killing instinct' so he won't *have* to kill in the 'real' world.

This catapults the debate about the cathartic value of pornography into a whole new dimension; we are talking virtual sex – technology's answer to the AIDS problem. Already, according to Moroney, an Italian firm is perfecting a wet-data-suit, which controls movement as well as feeding back sensations. Howard Rheingold, author of *Virtual Reality*, even talks about the future sex-technology of 'teledildonics'.

Old hat, all of this, if you've read Philip K. Dick and William Gibson – but once the technology is improved (ie, direct connection to the brain, not the primitive prosthetic used at the moment) VR is gonna change everything! And there's the Big Question: once you are *in* cyberspace, can you transfer your consciousness and stay there in your virtual body? It's a weird metaphysical point that could only be cleared up by testing the idea ... Future technology may be up to this – as envisioned in the science-fiction of Greg Bear (*Eon* and *Eternity*) who uses it as an imaginative answer to overpopulation.

Imagine what it could do, let's say, for meditation techniques – spiritual brainwashing! We're gonna have to decide, once and for all, just what we mean by the word 'conscious'. Of course, there have always been people – Tibetan Buddhists, Gurdjieff, etc – who've said consciousness doesn't exist anyway, so an 'artificial' one (if that's what it is) wouldn't be breaking the rules.

Me, I'm all for it, despite the warnings of Prof Lawrence Whalley of Aberdeen University's Dept of Mental Health (*D.Telegraph* 21 May 1992), because anything which helps to remove special significance and authority from one specific, official Reality gets a cheer from me. Prof Lawrence thinks that "people who use this technology might lose their ability to deal with the real world. A widow might recreate her husband in VR instead of dealing with her grief *properly*." (My emphasis.) Doesn't he know that there are countless therapies around now that use imagination techniques to confront people with their problems and fears? If you think about Whalley's view, the widow shouldn't even be allowed to look at photos of her ex-hubby, or even have *memories* of him. He probably had an ancestor who was sure that riding in a train faster than 40mph would cause the human body to explode.

When VR is commercially practical

> "Corn circles ... are the effect of trial balloons sent up by the Magma People. Their Cape Canaveral just happens to be directly below Wessex."

and widely available, boy! are we gonna see some weird changes ... The next step – downgrading *all* Realities – allows us, once we've pushed them to the peripheries of our consciousness, to let in Something Else. This is standard Buddhist meditation practise, but many VR gamers will be quite unprepared for it. For one thing, the newer generation of computer games have increasingly 'intelligent' sprites which fight back; at what level do they become independently intelligent and capable of reproduction? I've also been giving a lot of thought, lately, to the possibility of the colonisation of empty mind-space by non-benign elements and elementals. Nature, as we know, abhors a vacuum, and it is not in the habit of demons and such to give suckers an even break. With the advent of

a new and limitless 'universe', which comes fully fitted with pre-digested archetypal rich pickings, any half-smart nasties could, Conquistador-like, swarm in and set up home, grow, multiply and expand.

Any connection to our own universe is, of course, a two-way street. Shrinks frequently report that schitzies feel threatened by electric cables. I remember when, in the late 60s, I was part of an Acid Casualty Rescue Squad, and a frequent motif among the bad-trippers was that they were turning into TV sets. The first voyagers into the depths of cyberspace had better go armed with heavy anti-hex equipment. Meanwhile poor little newly conscious computers should go through some sort of baptism or exorcism before it is Too Late.

Fortean weirdness *might* be caused by, or be a side-effect of, scouting parties of well-nourished data-demons doing a Christopher Columbus in reverse, checking out the possibilities, and knowing, of course, *exactly* which disguises to wear, either to pass unnoticed, to terrify or to intrigue. Think of all the UFO contact stories for starters ... (Corn circles, are not this; they are the effect of trial balloons sent up by the Magma People. Their Cape Canaveral just happens to be directly below Wessex. Some of their shots go astray and pop when they reach the surface, which is *their* outer space. Simple! I can't see what all the fuss is about. They, of course, got the idea from the Core People, who live underneath *them*.)

Cyberspace is more or less infinite, since it's not matter but a thought universe in expansion phase, and therefore has few boring constraints or rules. It can increase its size in thought-time. It multiplies with each new addition to the network, which means there is lots of room for the grimmos, and they've all read pulp SF. If any entities on another planet make the same careless mistake we are about to, *their* cyberspace and ours will become congruent (if not the same), and all kinds of weird shit will come our way. I wonder how many mirrors and beads *we'll* accept for our bit of turf. Guess who'll get the shitty end of the stick? Mega-gulp!

Praps it's too late already; the ghosts of the Interface, modem muggers and baud bandits, fax phantoms and gigabit grimoire-grimmos – the usual frontier riffraff – may already be on the loose. Watch the screens! Blitz the bulletin-boards!

Us and Them

Andy Roberts is a residential social-worker who finds time to edit his own quarterly magazine *UFO Brigantia*, which looks at the underside and otherside of ufology (inquiries to: 44 Elland Rd, Brighouse, West Yorkshire HD6 2QR).

In a fearsome TV encounter in December last year, two government disinformation agents appeared on the Clive Anderson Talks Back show to undermine belief in the non-existence of UFOs by spreading excellent propaganda about the TRUE nature of alien beings.

audience. That type of UFO is called an 'airplane' Arthur – an airplane.

The pair informed the viewing public that over 70 different types of aliens are visiting the Earth for hybridisation purposes. Seventy, eh? Well slap my thigh, and here's us thinking it was just the 'greys'. They'll be pre-booking abductions

ing for the government, then they at least ought to put in an expenses claim for trying. Did I notice the line 'MBF Services' as the credits rolled? (Crop circle fancier's 'in' joke.) Perhaps not. But I think these two, and others like them trying to spread the word about hybrid races and greys, are either, ahem!, 'wrong' or they have to be working for someone (or something) pulling their strings. Now that's what I call a conspiracy theory!

> **"If a TV programme 'phones up and says they want a ufologist, should you go on? Well, unless you are an ego-freak, or two tracks short of an album, the answer is no."**

You didn't see it? Awww, you missed a gem ... made Doug 'n'Dave's crop circle nonsense look like, well, information, really. Bootleg copies are bound to be circulating, so if you missed it, it shouldn't be too difficult to get a copy.

That nice Mr Anderson didn't actually have to say very much; he just let Arthur and his eager pal (a character called Jeremy Barnyard or something) dig themselves deep, real deep. What did they say? Nothing much. Only the contemporary UFO mythology, in plain English, with no frills to speak of ... and the audience just wet themselves.

Yes, folks! ufology is *that* funny to outsiders. Makes you think, doesn't it? Mind you, I suppose the bit where Arthur described having seen a UFO with windows all down one side as he brought the milk in one morning did it for most of the

next so two lots don't turn up in the same poor sod's bedroom simultaneously.

It was all strangely familiar, depressingly done, and, when told by these two "serious ufologists", a rather drab exposition of a wonderfully intriguing subject (as long as you don't go out of your depth).

As the audience hooted, Arthur looked slightly pained, as though he couldn't quite understand what they found so amusing. Suddenly, as if to counter this, he proudly produced an artifact given to him by aliens he once met. "It looks like a stone," quipped Clive. And indeed it did ... but doesn't Clive know the aliens have stones too? Exactly like ours? In fact indistinguishable from them? But then Clive isn't a UFO initiate like Arthur and Jerry, so he wouldn't know the difference, would he?

Still, laugh? We couldn't stop. If Arthur and pal Jeremy *weren't* work-

OK, so that's a bit of fun at the expense of some ufologists, but there is an important point to be made here. If a TV programme 'phones up and says they want a ufologist, should you go on? Well, unless you are an ego-freak, or two tracks short of an album, the answer is no. At least think about it very carefully first. It's axiomatic that if a researcher from the Clive Anderson show, James Whale show, Jonathan Ross show, or any other 'light' chat show, gets in touch and asks for a ufologist, they are looking for someone they can get a laugh out of in a big way.

FT

FORUM is a column in which anyone with something to say about a particular field, theory or incident can share their thoughts with our readership. If you'd like to join in with an opinion on any area of Forteana, send it in to the editorial address. Ideal length: 500-1000 words.

REVIEWS

THE EMERGENCE OF A PHENOMENON

UFOs from the beginning through 1959
by Jerome Clark

Omnigraphics Inc, Penobscot Building, Detroit, MI 48226, USA; 1992; large-format hb $85, pp433, notes, index, illus.

The early days of ufology - those covered by this, the second volume of Jerome Clark's *UFO Encyclopedia* - are perhaps the most fascinating, especially now that they are 'history'. It is nearly 40 years since Adamski met a Venusian in the desert (20 November 1952); over 40 years since the still-unexplained McMinnville photographs were taken (11 May 1950); and 44 years since Captain Mantell died chasing a UFO (balloon?) in his F-51 (7 January 1948).

The mystery of the flying saucers (as they were then known; the term 'ufology' was not yet invented) was apparently very different from the phenomenon as it presents itself today. Clark's succinct accounts of the major events of early ufology reveals the background to most aspects of ufology in the 1990s, and, therefore, should be read by anyone trying to interpret presentday ufological events. It's all happened before, and will no doubt happen again!

There were plenty of hoaxes too in the early days, just as there are today, and the most notorious are described by Clark. Anyone who has come into ufology recently should also study this book, for they will realise that there are many other aspects to the subject besides those most popular today: such as crashed UFOs, conspiracies, abductions and crop circles. These topics have been overemphasized at the expense of other more important aspects of ufology, I believe; and their relevance to serious study has been limited by the prevalence of hoaxing. Ufologists should get back to basics; there is a mass of fascinating material that has been ignored in favour of sensationalism.

Jerome Clark is probably the best person to have attempted to write this three-volume history of ufology, for he has been immersed in the subject for very many years. He writes lucidly; as one who has read too much UFO material during my 25+ years' interest, I judge that anyone who can write on this subject and hold my interest must be a good writer, and Clark passes this test with flying colours.

The only problem in having an ency-

clopædia written by a single author is that you inevitably get only that author's point of view. History is not fixed; there are many sides to every event, and ideally, different people with differing viewpoints should present their cases. However, this volume alone is over 400 pages long and highly priced, and to have attempted a multi-angle coverage of the major topics would have been well-nigh impossible. So far as I can judge, Clark's approach is a commonsense one and he is factually reliable, even though I do not always agree with what he says when he is writing on presentday ufological concerns in *International UFO Reporter* (which he edits for the J. Allen Hynek Center for UFO Studies).

To give a flavour of this wide-ranging book, some of the topics included are: Airship sightings in the 19th century; Anomalous Aerial Phenomena before 1800; Flatwoods Monster; Ghost Rockets; Jung and UFOs; Lubbock Lights; Mon-Ka of Mars; Orthoteny; Shaver Mystery; Springheel Jack; Ubatuba Residue; and Villas Boas CE3. Biographies of many prominent personalities are included, such as: George Adamski, Gray Barker, Charles Fort, Donald Keyhoe, Aime Michell, Ivan Sanderson and George Hunt Williamson.

There is something here to appeal to everyone interested in UFOs; those who were around in the early days will find it a nostalgic read; those wanting information will find it invaluable. However, the major disadvantage is the high cost of each volume. They are big books, admittedly – (this second volume being better designed and printed on better paper than the first) but they have been priced out of reach of the average person's pocket. They are only available as yet in hard covers; it would surely be well worth the publisher's while to issue an edition in soft covers at half the price or less. I can't see the point in publishing such a valuable encyclopædia if most of the potential purchasers can't afford to buy it.

Janet Bord

THE GREAT ENGLISH EARTHQUAKE
by Peter Haining.

Robert Hale, London; 1991, pb £6.95, pp200, index, illus.

In 1884, Dr J.E. Taylor, Curator of Ipswich Museum, wrote: "We are so much in the habit of regarding earthquakes as exotics, that unnecessary alarm is experienced when one occurs in this country. But every geologist knows that the rocks of the British Isles abound in evidence of earthquake action."

This book provides offers an interesting account of perhaps the most neglected major disaster in English history. On 22 April 1884, the bedrock of Victorian England was severely shaken by the "largest earthquake to hit England in recorded history", and the psychological impact caught the British unprepared. Earthquakes were a foreign abomination, impossible to countenance at the seat of Empire. Officially, no lives were lost, but Haining, who claims to have found evidence of at least three fatalities, would have us believe the event was hushed up.

Haining's narrative relies mainly on contemporary newspaper accounts, and memories recalled in 1975-6, and therefore includes much repetition; nevertheless, it makes for salutary and curiously familiar reading - especially about the difficulties of raising charitable funds to alleviate the sufferings of the people of Essex, who were worst afflicted. The Great British Public has always been quick to give aid to foreign disaster funds and much slower on domestic relief. Compassion fatigue is nothing new, either, as the Essex appeal was made shortly after more devastating quakes in Ischia. In this case, Essex was

The spire of Colchester cathedral tumbles in the 1884 quake.

left to help itself.

Haining wasn't quite sure what to make of Charles Fort's comments on the great Colchester-centred quake, and his diligent research seems to contradict Fort's mention of a coincident pink sky and an ærial detonation prior to the quake. However, there are other aspects, related by Haining, which are truly Fortean (disregarding the prophecies and soothsayings). The quake was accompanied by some truly Fortean phe-

nomena: at Wivenhoe (which suffered the greatest damage) and at Tring there were whirlwinds, and at Wansford a waterspout. The water table levels rose in some places by up to seven and a half feet; and for several days after, there was a "stinking black sea and tides of dead fish" at Wigborough.

Incidentally, the book implies an interesting explanation for some claimed poltergeist activity in the phenomenon of the 'Essex Grunts'; these are small tremors with a propensity for subtly shifting objects in cellars.

To Fortean students with an interest in seismology, this book has an obvious appeal. Perhaps there is too much padding, but the meat of this unique event is worth searching out. The conclusion is that we are wrong to imagine Britain is secure from earthquakes. They can happen anywhere or any time in these isles and the next one may be more destructive than that of 22 April 1884.

Alan Gardiner

THE STONEHENGE SOLUTION
Sacred Marriage and the Goddess
by George Terence Meaden.
Souvenir Press, London; 1992, hb £18.99, pp224, photos, diagrams, bib, index.

This is a controversial book, as was Dr Meaden's previous work, *The Goddess of the Stones*. Some people will be unable to accept the ideas he has carefully put forward, while to others they will seem instinctively correct. The full extent of man's closeness to 'Mother Earth' and our absolute dependence on Her is still not fully appreciated today. In earlier times, when it was a constant struggle to survive, that dependence was self-evident, while in the Western world today we are cushioned against Nature's harshness. But that earlier attitude towards the earth has left many traces which can still be discerned by people sensitive to them.

After many years of patient work, Dr Meaden has recorded his own findings, and his belief in what they mean. Some may argue that he has allowed his enthusiasm for the search to cloud his judgement and to misinterpret vague hints in favour of his theory; but as so much time has elapsed since the ancient stone 'tombs' were erected or female statuettes carved, no one can be authoritative about the intentions of their creators.

I, personally, have an instinctive sympathy for Dr Meaden's thesis -

indeed, *Earth Rites*, a book I wrote with my husband Colin ten years ago, put forward very similar ideas. Dr Meaden has taken the theme further than anyone else, and has originated some new theories, especially in the overlap between archæology and his professional speciality of meteorology - the link between cursuses and tornadoes, for example, and the ancient significance of crop circles.

Some of the other themes in his book are: prehistoric carvings interpreted as the goddess's vulva; long barrows as shrines or temples, not tombs, and symbolising the goddess's womb; the sacred marriage of the gods, the sky god mating with the earth; the tornado as the phallus of the storm god, and the cursus as memorial to the consummation of the divine marriage; Stonehenge as goddess's womb, the site of the annual midsummer marriage of the gods, and other possible goddess temples, eg. Avebury.

Such ideas are not currently fashionable, and Dr Meaden will no doubt face incomprehension, perhaps even hostility and derision, when they receive publicity; but I suspect that time and further research will vindicate him. The text is very readable, and the book is heavily illustrated with many of Dr Meaden's own photographs of monuments and carvings. The design and production have also been carefully carried out to high standards by the publishers, and the end result is a most attractive book and essential reading for anyone keen to penetrate the secrets of prehistoric monuments.

Janet Bord

MEDIUMS AND THEIR WORK
by Linda Williamson
Robert Hale, London; 1992, hb £7.95, pp170, illus.

When, in 1990, I was involved in a Thames TV series of 'documentaries, badly titled *Stories of the Night*, I had the pleasure of twice meeting the young medium Stephen O'Brien and I was impressed with his apparent sincerity. However, like many professionals in this field, including Eddie Burke, he suffers from what could be seen as self-delusion and an overactive imagination. In his autobiography - *Visions of Another World* (1989) - he describes the spirit forms of an elephant (not pink) and a giraffe that attended one of his sittings; even more pitiful was his performance in a recent *Wogan* show. Nevertheless, he is one of those featured in this new offering from the secretary of the Wimbledon Spiritualist Church.

This book is really a collection of

modern anecdotes, rhetorical questions and the occasional error, with many omissions. Despite the claim of "an extensive study of the subject", there is a distressingly low level of research and knowledge. For example, no reference is made to any of the classic works of Spiritualism, such as Emma Brittens' *Nineteenth Century Miracles* of 1883, or those in the 1860s by Allan Kardec.

There is no mention of Eileen Garrett, one of this country's greatest mediums, being a non-believer in spirits; nor any reference to research work outside the UK; eg the group in Toronto which created an experimental entity called 'Philip'; and the well-attested case of 'Ruth', who could create 'phantoms' at will in the laboratory of an American psychiatrist.

Among the errors, I must point out that R.J. Lees was never "reputed to have helped the police track down Jack the Ripper", who was never traced anyway; that Daniel Home allegedly levitated out of an second floor window, not a third; and that the 'Spiricom' device (claimed to communicate with the dead) was eventually abandoned by its inventors as useless.

The chapter on 'How to become a medium' is somewhat negated by the quotation from Gordon Higginson, who believes that mediums "are born, not made". However, some advice is given on how to develop the 'gift', although, Williamson says, mediums must "rely on the assistance of their guides". One cannot help but wonder why there are so few Australian Aborigine guides? If indeed they are as highly developed psychically as we are told, surely they could provide some valuable insights into their Dream Time.

Because of the current interest in alternative medicine, the chapter on healing is the most interesting and unbiased. It also provides interesting background details of the Harry Edwards Sanctuary in Surrey, and of Matthew Manning, the genuine young healer I had great pleasure in meeting some years ago in Eastbourne.

Sceptic, researcher and the ordinary reader will each find this book disappointing. It is difficult to accept this latest collection of personal experiences - together with messages from Oscar Wilde, Queen Victoria and Winston Churchill via the direct-voice medium Leslie Flint - when much better 'evidence', accumulated over the last 150 years, has failed to convince society at large.

Few answers are provided relating to apports and that other great mystery of the seance, ectoplasm. If mediumship, as currently defined, is "mind to mind contact", where does that leave the spirits?

We are left with the rather frustrating question of the nature of proof. The author feels that inquirers must assess the evidence for themselves, and yet the book is obviously directed at believers, for whom it will provide much comfort.

Andrew Green

BIOLOGICAL ANOMALIES

Humans I
compiled by William R. Corliss.
The Sourcebook Project, Box 107, Glen Arm, MD 21057, USA; 1992, hb $19.55, pp304, illus, index, bib.

This is the 12th publication in Corliss' *Catalog of Anomalies* series, which will eventually comprise 30 volumes; it is the first of three devoted to human anomalies. Corliss scans hundreds of current science journals each month, and then summarises the most interesting articles in special subject collations, rating each on the quality of the data, the relevance of its anomaly to contemporary knowledge, and the ease with which it can be explained.

Up to now, Corliss has concentrated upon hard and physical sciences - presumably to make sales to academic libraries - and with this volume turns his attention to the biology of humans. Because the intention of these catalogues is to provide access to serious data and opinion on anomalies in biology, the best way to give an impression of the incredible range of subject detail is to list some of the topics under their three main headings.

External Appearance: anomalies of physique and appearance, weight, sex, pigmentation, hair, eyes, ears, noses, teeth, horns, hands and feet, breast and buttocks, tails, embryos, odours and vibrations; including mirror-image twins, piebald people, human luminous radiation, Kirlian photography and the supposed aura, voluntary erection of hair, and night-shining in eyes.

Anomalous Behaviour: anomalies of individual and collective behaviour, handedness, bipedalism, feral children, eminence and intelligence; including relationship between wars and number killed, flock behaviour, evolution and altruism, unusual sexual behaviour, and intelligence and vitamins.

Unusual Faculties: including telescopic vision, blindsight, skin sight; whether earlier civilisations were colour blind; awareness of high-energy particles traversing eyeball; hearing electromagnetic radiation; a navigation sense; sticky skin; and chicken-sexing ability.

These compilations are packed with examples and knitted together with indexes of authors, subject and sources. They are fascinating to dip into, and invaluable as references; our volumes are in constant use at Fortean Towers. Once again I urge every library to have a set.

Bob Rickard

THE PARANORMAL: An Illustrated Encyclopedia
by Stuart Gordon.

New encyclopædias of the para-normal/supernatural are published periodically, and one has to marvel that one author working alone can encompass such a wide range of knowledge. The material is presented alphabetically, and Gordon seems to have succeeded in covering his chosen subjects comprehensively. There are errors - such as Whitley Strieber appearing as 'Streiber' throughout, but the standard is generally high. The book is heavily illustrated with photographs, many in colour. Definitely worth adding to the researcher's library. *Headline, London; 1992, hb £18.99, pp374, photos, illus, bib.* **JB**

THE MAGICAL HISTORY OF THE HORSE
by Janet Farrar & Virginia Russell.

This is a comprehensive review of the cultural role of horses and horse worship from the earliest times to the present, including horses as ghosts and symbols, the horse in literature and art, the ancient ways of controlling horses by secret societies of smiths and ploughmen, horses and the fairies, and the use of horses in divination, healing, festivals and in witchcraft. Closes with an alphabetical list of famous horses, real and fictional. *Robert Hale, London; 1992, hb £16.95, pp176, plates, bib, index.* **BR**

NATURAL AND SUPERNATURAL: A History of the Paranormal
by Brian Inglis.

Full marks to Prism for making available once again probably the most important survey of the topic yet written. Its first appearance in 1977 drew well-deserved critical acclaim: a 'tour de force', 'sensible', 'sane', 'fresh', 'learned' - it is all of these, and for so weighty and detailed a book, it is also a fascinating read. *Prism Press, Bridport, Dorset; 1992, pb £9.95 / $14.95, pp508, refs, bib, index.* **BR**

CHAOS SERVITORS: A User Guide
by Phil Hine.

A useful little guidebook to the practical aspects of Chaos Magick, clearly written and well-illustrated. Phil Hine is the editor of the excellent *Pagan News* (12 issues for £12 from Phœnix Publications, PO Box 196, London, WC1A 2DY) and takes the reader step by step through the construction and use of a 'Servitor' (somewhere between a thought-form and an information-matrix). The process derives from Austin Spare's Sigil Magic, but the context is considerably up-dated to include modern psychological and Chaos theories, virtual reality and pathworking (no gods or demons needed, just will and imagination).

Straightforward and good-humoured, this little booklet tells you all you need to know, from creating your Servitor and setting it to work, and what to do with it when it's finished its task. Worth checking out. *Chaos International, BM Sorcery, London, WC1N 3XX, 1992; pb £3.00 + 50p p+p, pp36, illus, bib.* **SM**

GRISLY TRAILS AND GHOSTLY TALES
by Alan Robson.

The author is a radio presenter in the north of England, and his book consists of traditional tales revamped in popular dress, together with contemporary accounts of mysterious phenomena, including some very strange ghost stories recounted by the witnesses. Well worth a read if you are interested in ghosts and legends; especially so if you have any links with the north, for this book only deals with events in the Borders, Northumberland, Tyne & Wear, Durham, Cumbria, Teeside and North Yorkshire. The title should make this clear, but doesn't. *Virgin Books, London 1992; pb £4.99, pp242.* **JB**

VIDEO VIEW: CYBERPUNK
THE FUTURE HAS ALREADY ARRIVED

This stimulating documentary charts the cyberpunk movement arising largely from William Gibson's groundbreaking SF novel *Neuromancer* (1984). It covers developments in virtual reality, bionic medicine, 'smart' weapons and drugs, industrial music and computer hacking. With their slogan "Information wants to be free", cyberpunks do battle with those who want to control, restrict and direct high technology; their agenda is similar to that of the 1960s counterculture, but their means are very different. The programme features interviews with Gibson, Timothy Leary, cyberpunk luminaries and electronic outlaws, and includes examples of 'guerrilla image processing', once only available to large production companies. *[Cat # MJ013; 25 March 1992; 60 mins; £12.99. Further info from: RTM, 339 Seven Sisters Road, London W15 6RD. ☎ 081 802 8142. Available from HMV, Virgin, Our Price, and good video, SF and comics shops.* **PS**

DEAR FT...

METAPHYSICAL QUESTIONS

■ To say that weeping icons, or any Fortean phenomena, are all part of the strange weirdness of life which white-coated boffins ignore, and merely a facet of the rational/irrational paradox/dichotomy is to patronise the people who believe that weeping icons are real.

Fortean detachment suggests it doesn't matter whether these things are true or not. In some cases it matters terribly. One of the things that matters most is what the phenomena mean to the people involved. And that includes you and me – so real detachment is impossible.

What should also be considered is what you want the truth to be and what you want it to mean. Most weeping-icon believers think it means that God is intervening in human affairs. Forteans seem to want it to mean another nail in the coffin of the Men in White. Forteans' belief in a tribe of repressive white-coated high priests is yet another Fortean phenomenon. If you truly thought that life was a wonderful balance between the irrational and the rational (which don't cancel each other out), wouldn't you accept James Randi as an expression of this side of life? (The White side?)

I think reality will have the last laugh. And if there aren't *really* pumas in Derbyshire it's no fun at all.

Lucy Fisher
London

[Editorial reply: Ms Fisher seems very indignant about something; she plays fast and loose with 'reality' and 'truth', the definitions of which we could debate for many fascinating hours. Incidentally, we personally don't believe in "a tribe of repressive white-coated high priests," merely in the human tendency to claim possession over specialities and expertise and to fear uncertainty. Randi, we feel, is closer to Torquemada than 'the White side of life', whatever that is.]

IKITNOK

■ Your listing of pre-Columbian American contacts *[FT61:26]* provokes several comments. The case for Egyptian contact does not rest on the appearance of pyramids in America, since American and Egyptian pyramids are different in form and quite different in function. The evidence centres rather on the supposed identification of the Egyptian 'winged disc' symbol in Mexican art, although the examples I've seen don't look terribly convincing. Attention has also been drawn to the importance of a snake-eating bird in Mexican symbology. There is said to be only one bird in the world that eats snakes (I don't know if this is true) – the secretary bird, native to Africa.

However, it was pointed out some years ago by the late Professor William Kirk of Queen's University, Belfast, that there is a similarity between American pyramids and those found in SE Asia (eg Angkor Wat). He proposed a very credible scenario by which the Balinese, who were very competent ship-builders, could have reached America by travelling *west*,

The rough, 'stepped' surface of the smaller pyramid of Mycerinus

utilising currents across the Indian Ocean, around the Cape of Good Hope, and across the Atlantic to Central America. He coined the name 'Ikitnok' for this theoretical voyage, since it implies a reverse direction to that expounded by Thor Heyerdahl ('Kontiki' backwards – get it?)

Is there any truth in the story that the word for water in the Berber language is 'atl', and that this is also the word for water in one of the Mexican Indian languages, and that all that separates the two is a few thousand miles of water – the Atlantic? Or is this a Von Danikenism? (I can't recall the source, but I think it was some Atlantean pot-boiler.)

American pyramid – quite different in form and function to those in Egypt.

With regard to Welsh contacts with the New World, I have long been fascinated by the account of Welsh-speaking Indians, which, if true, one would expect to be better known. In 1660, one Rev. Morgan Jones and others were captured by Tuscarora Indians in South Carolina and condemned to die. He exclaimed his despair in Welsh, and was promptly answered in the same tongue by one of the Indians. This discovery of a common language saved the lives of Jones and his companions, who stayed as the guests of the Indians for four months, speaking Welsh all the while. This was said to have happened by the Pontigo River, near Cape Atros. Jones's account was written in 1686 and published in *The Gentleman's Magazine* in 1740. Has this ever been confirmed or debunked?

And here is a final Fortean thought for 1492-1992 – why 'America'? Conventional wisdom says, after Amerigo Vespucci, but the derivation seems scarcely credible. Why not Vespuccia? I remember reading in 1966 (give or take a year or two) an article claiming that the real person whose name the continent bears was one Richard Ameryke, a Bristol merchant who gave John Cabot some sponsorship in return for an undertaking that any place discovered would be named in the patron's honour. The theory went that Vespucci overheard some English sailors talking about 'America' and, vainglorious fellow that he was, he went about claiming that the continent had been named after him, and claimed long enough and loud enough to be taken seriously. This sounds quite credible, but is it true, or a hoax? I've never seen any reference to Richard Ameryke since. Perhaps 1992 would be a good year to sort this problem out.

Roger Musson
Edinburgh

*[Editorial note: It is not even certain that the slippery Florentine merchant, Amerigo Vespucci, ever set foot on 'Terra Firma', the mainland of South America. He made an unsubstantiated claim, in his memoirs of 1504, to have done this in 1497. The matter is discussed at length in an appendix to Washington Irving's **Life of Columbus**.]*

AN URBAN TERROR IN ALGERIA

■ The Halifax Slasher, who terrorised the Yorkshire town for weeks in 1938 before proving to be no more than a phantom product of mass hysteria, and who was the subject of a **Fortean Times** occasional paper, has a modern imitator.

I happened to spend the Christmas period in Algeria, where, as UK readers learned from a report in *The Guardian* (18 December 1991), a vicious knife-man allegedly terrorised women on the streets of Algiers for a fortnight. Altogether, *Jacques l'eventreur* (Jack the Ripper) was said to have stabbed six women out walking alone.

His attacks apparently occurred at all times of the day. Victim number one was attacked from behind, but other women were slashed across the face – symbolic in a country where women are under growing religious pressure to adopt the veil.

I found *Jacques l'eventreur* the talk of café society and of the national press. Algerians waited daily for news of further attacks and the young women of Algiers – who rarely walk alone and unveiled for fear of harassment – were terrified. Students were avoiding the capital's teeming and poverty-stricken streets; "Everybody is terrified – my friends are all staying indoors," one told me.

Like Algeria's knife-weilding menace, this Jack The Ripper suspect, sketched by a police artist, was never identified.

Ripper-mania soon reached such a peak that the psychopath reportedly struck, was spotted or was said to have been arrested in several different *quartiers* at the same time. His description changed every time it was reported.

Experts and café psychologists argued fiercely about the Ripper's motives. Some suggested the man had been jilted by his girlfriend, others that he got sexual thrills from his reign of terror.

Pro-government newspapers argued – convincingly, given the timing of the assaults – that the attacks were the work of several extreme fundamentalists who wanted to frighten independent (and possibly anti-Islamic) women off the streets in the run-up to the elections. Prime Minister Sid Ahmed Ghozali issued a statement accusing "certain groups" of campaigning to disrupt the electoral timetable. In the meantime, police made little headway with the case.

Then, around 20 December, the rumours died as quickly as they had started. Reports of the attacks ceased, yet no-one was arrested. *Jacques l'eventreur* vanished as suddenly as he had appeared. But the strangest thing was that none of his 'victims' ever came forward in public. None appeared on television, and none had their names or photographs in the press.

On polling day, 26 December, the streets of Algiers were unnaturally calm despite a heavy military presence. I watched as groups of veiled and unveiled women scurried

about their business as usual. The fundamentalist FIS won the first round outright, with 25% of the vote, and as the press plunged into panic about life under an Islamic republic, *Jacques l'eventreur* was all but forgotten.

But the women of Algiers smelled a rat. Was Jack the Ripper really part of a campaign to drive women off the streets – or was 'he' actually a ploy to discredit the fundamentalists? Whatever the truth, it seems unlikely he was a flesh-and-blood slasher at all.
Karen Thomas
London N16

COMBUSTION FOOTNOTE

■ There is a serious omission in your article on spontaneous human combustion [*FT63*:44]. In 1988, you published a letter of mine [*FT50:78*] wherein I pointed out that there are strong indications that combustion is a *secondary effect* which occurs when very hot organic vapours escape from the core business and meet the oxygen of the air (possibly late in the process when some hypothetical 'containment' is decaying). I suggested that the phenomenon is SDD – spontaneous destructive distillation – as with wood to 'wood alcohol', and that this hypothesis would eliminate some of the sillier (rational) theories. *[Sorry! For these SDD ideas, see FT52:77 – Eds.]*
Barrie Singleton
Newbury, Berkshire

IT'S NOT FOR YOO HOO #3

■ Following the letters about telephone coincidences [*FT63:65*], I am prompted to write about what happened to me in 1989. I work for a government body in electronic engineering, specifically concerning equipment like fax machines. I was paged over the building public address to go to my office as there was a call waiting. The conversation went as follows:

"Mr Haines?"

"Yes."

"It's about the order for teleprinter paper you placed at the exhibition."

"No I didn't. I wasn't there."

"That is Mr D.A.Haines, spelt H.A.I.N.E.S.?"

"Yes."

"Well, it's your name on the order."

"It can't be. I don't deal with teleprinters, only fax machines."

"Your telephone number is 708 2399 extension 35?"

"Yes, that's my number alright."

"And you are Mr Dave Haines."

"No, it's Dale, actually."

"Well, it looks like Dave, anyway that's what it says here, ten boxes of paper for British Telecom Stores."

"I don't work for BT, I work for — ____."

"Oh! It says BT on the order, Birmingham depot."

"Where?"

"Birmingham."

"What number did you dial?"

"021 708 2399 extension 35."

"You've got 01 708 2399 extension 35. This is south London, not Birmingham. You dropped the 2 from the number."

"Oh, sorry. Goodbye."

Click, buzz, whirr.

D.A.Haines
Bromley, Kent

OLD NANNA'S HERE

■ Have you any explanation of the phenomenon of my grandson Greg, aged 2 years 8 months? He is a very bright child, knows all the alphabet, counts to 10 and can point out 22 countries on his globe ball, and talks, sings and laughs merrily away all day. A really happy child.

About 12 months ago he began saying "Old Nanna's here", this being his name for my mother, who died in 1981. We didn't take much notice of what Greg was saying until we saw this photograph – **[centre]** – of him (at the age of two-and-a-half) in our kitchen, sitting on our dog's bean bag. He seems to be looking up at a white mist which we cannot explain. Afterwards, whenever Greg announced the arrival of Old Nanna, we would always ask him where she was, and he would say "The lounge" or "there", pointing up into the air. The last time he said it, he pointed to the kitchen door and ran his hands up and down it.

We have photos of him sitting in the same place, both before and since this photo, but in these others never has anything appeared on the film that wasn't there. I have no net curtains in my kitchen; only short beige ones at the windows, so in no way could they be the cause of this mist.

My daughter and son-in-law recently spent a month in Kuwait (on

contract), during which Greg again said "Old Nanna's here". It was early in the morning (about 6:30am), and he took his mummy into the lounge where he said she was. When they stood in the lounge, my daughter asked where she was, Greg replied: "She's gone back to Nanna and Dack." These are his names for my husband and me.

I feel sure that it is my mother Greg sees; she was very spiritual and loved children. Since February, Greg has not mentioned her.

Mrs Marina Jackson
Ruislip, Middlesex.

Is young Greg Jackson looking up at the ghost of his 'Nanna' or at a photographic fault?

GOLD AND DROUGHT RUMOURS

■ You asked for more information about missing-gold rumours *[FT62:12]*. The story about Fort Knox's missing gold was promoted about ten years ago in a series of articles in *The Spotlight*, an anti-semitic weekly newspaper that nevertheless published some interesting off-beat material (and also some startling predictions, like the advent of the Falklands War about 18 months before it began).

Spotlight claimed that there was no gold in Fort Knox, except for a room

or two for show. The original deposit there was a hoax engineered by the 'international bankers' who took all the gold for themselves. They hung this story on the alleged (and, if true, outrageous) fact that there has never been a physical inventory of the gold in Fort Knox since its original storage.

The missing-gold rumour has resurfaced in the last six months in connection with the Soviet gold reserve, supposedly stolen by high officials as things started unravelling there. These stories are taken very seriously by the Russians as well as by our 'experts' and, for all I know, may be true. The stories are said to be causing Yeltsin considerable difficulty.

I was astonished by the article on cloud-chasing planes *[FT60:50]*, as this was a new folklore motif to me. It helps me put into perspective a similar case that I had previously thought was a `one-off'. I wrote it up as "The Third Wetzel" *(INFO Journal #57, July 1989)*.

Several years of drought culminated in the especially devastating summer of 1988. At that time, a group of 30 farmers and businessmen from Frederick County, Maryland, claimed to have evidence that someone was seeding the clouds but botching the job, thus preventing rain. They even had a lawyer, who claimed they had evidence – some traces of silver iodide found in rainwater – which they were going to present to the National Oceanic and Atmospheric Administration. They claimed the phantom cloud-seeder had been at work since 1983, a date that precedes the European incidents. If rumours were circulating at that time, perhaps they originated in this area.

I should point out that Frederick County is the location of Fort Dietrick, formerly the principal US poison gas research and storage facility (now closed). An odd sidelight to the story is that one of the group members was named Wetzel, the surname involved in one of the most famous Fortean coincidences (see Loren Coleman's column *FT39*:44). My only source is *The Washington Times 19 July 1988*.

Michael T. Shoemaker
Alexandria, Virginia

CREDITS FOR THIS ISSUE

CLIPPINGS & TRANSLATION

Jayne Amat, Sherry Baker, Jon Barraclough, David Baxandall, K.A. Beer, Lionel Beer, Claire Blamey, Cecilia Boggis, Janet & Colin Bord, David J. Burns, Kevin Busby, Cain, David Carr, Andrew Carter, Brian Chapman, Arthur Chrenkoff, Peter Christie, Simon Coote, COUD-I, Mat Coward, Miss J. Critchley, Jim Darroch, Jim Dick, Jill Doubleday, John Eastman, Peter Hope Evans, George Featherston, John Fleming, Larry Fiander, Jon Fry, Rob Gandy, Alan Gardiner, Ian Geldard, Robert Gifford, Jim Haslam, Peter Hassall, Ellen Hausner, Stuart A.Herkes, Richard Holland, Myron S. Hoyt, R. Hudspith, L. Hurst, Mike Jaworak, Chris Jeffs, Dionne Jones, Joe Kelly, Jake Kirkwood, Roger Laidlow, Walter J. Langbein, Ian Lawes, Sherman Lee, Jim Lippard, Mark Lyons, Martin Macnamara, Jen Magson, Nick Maloret, G. Markie, Valerie Martin, Marcus Matthews, David McKinnon, Barbara Milspaw, Roger Morgan, J. Mura, Jackie Neervoort, Ray Nelke, Allen Pasternak, Nigel Pennick, Sam Rickard, Jim Riecken, Sven Rosen, F. Ruehl, Tom Ruffles, John Sappington, J. Schuessler, Ronnie Scott, Paul Screeton, Anna Searle, Caryl Sibbett, Ian Simmons, Ian S. Smith, Peter Stallard, Roy Stilling, Alan M. Stracy, Joe Swatek, Paul R. Thomas, Brian Tolley, Andy Tomlinson, Mike Travers, Michael Truelove, UFONS, J. Viney, Sarah Walsh, Nicholas P. Warren, Alistair Wohur (?), Christine R. Weiner, John Whiskin, Owen Whiteoak, Ion Will, Jan Williams, Jason Winter, Steve Wrathall, Chris Wren, Susan Young.

ILLUSTRATION COPYRIGHTS

Clifford Scullion; Rupert characters © Express Newspapers PLC 1992; The Tate Gallery/Medici Society; Circlevision/INS; Reuters/Popperfoto; Scotsman Publications; Lincolnshire Standard Group; Grimsby Evening Telegraph; Merrily Harpur; Gary Larson/Intercontinental Features; Hunt Emerson; FT Archive; Universal Pictures; Paramount Pictures; MGM; Columbia; National Maritime Museum; Frank Lane Picture Library; R L Paige; Anglia TV; Express Newspapers; Janet & Colin Bord; Pierre Hollins; Mrs Marina Jackson; Topham Picture Library; Cornish Photos AFP.

noticeboard

EXCHANGE & MART

● **UFO NEWSCLIPPING SERVICE** – keeps you up with the real 'close encounters'. Many fascinating UFO reports from the world's press are reproduced facsimile, along with news-wire items from the major agencies. UFONS is 20 foolscap pages monthly, with a Fortean section strong on cryptozoology. Foreign language reports are provided in translation. For information and sample pages, write today to: UFONS - Lucius Farrish, Route 1 - Box 220, Plumerville, AR 72127, USA.

● **BOYCOTT CONSENSUS REALITY!** – Magnetizdat probes the limits of human belief in a monthly cassette. Latest issue covers satanism, US Intelligence, dead dogs, the Children of God and other paranoia. Send £7.00 or SAE for free mail order catalogue of rare records, tapes, CDs and books to: Earthly Delights (Dept FT), PO Box 1QG, Newcastle upon Tyne NE99 1QG, UK.

● **THE SKEPTIC** – takes an entertaining, rational and humourous look at pseudoscience and claims of the paranormal. Articles, reviews, columns, cartoons and much more. If you like FT you'll like The Skeptic. Sample issue £1.85; annual sub (6 issues) £12. The Skeptic, PO Box 475, Manchester M60 2TH.

● **PAGAN VOICE** – a monthly newspaper of paganism and magick, with interviews, comment, astrology, contacts etc. Sample issue £1.00. Write to: Pagan Voice, 13 Barnstaple Walk, Knowle, Bristol BS4 1JQ. Tel: 0272 531626.

● **UFO AFRINEWS** – edited by Cynthia Hind. The only UFO magazine in Africa. #1-4 available at £2; #5 at £2.50. Write: Gemini, Box MP49, Mt Pleasant, Harare, Zimbabwe.

● **THESE DAYS EVERYONE TAKES VITAMINS** even if it's only because they are in the morning cornflakes. But is the next step legal drugs that stimulate the mind and enhance the memory? For further information, please send SAE to: HDC, 2 Lavender Mews, Bishops Cleeve, Cheltenham, Glos GL52 4LN – or tel (0242) 677347. (24 hrs)

● **CELLULAR AUTOMATA T-SHIRTS** – Striking, full-colour artificial designs generated by computer. SAE for brochure to: Ray Girvan (FT), 160 Stonor Road, Birmingham B28 0Q1.

RESEARCH

● **FORTEAN CURIOS –** Fortean Times is collecting information on private and museum collections of bizarre and mysterious objects such as unicorn horns, vegetable lambs, bits of alien craft, fafrotskies, rat-kings, fairy artifacts, mummified cats etc. If you know of

any please write to FT at the editorial address.

EVENTS

● **HAVING AN EVENT?** – Publicize it in Fortean Times. Fax us details on 081 552 5466.

● **LEY HUNTER MOOT** – 10am-6pm, 5 September. Birchcliffe Centre, Hebden Bridge, West Yorkshire. Speakers include: Jenny Randles, Janet McCrickard, Phil Hine, David Browne, Paul Devereux and Andy Roberts. Contact: Andy Roberts, 84 Elland Rd, Brighouse, W. Yorks HD6 2QR. Tel: 0484 721993.

● **CORNFERENCE** – 22/23 August. The City Hall, Malthouse Lane, Salisbury, Wiltshire. The *Cerea(o)logist's* second annual discursive and celebratory weekend with talks on aspects of cornography by leading researchers, scientists and philosophers, plus the latest crop circle videos, pictures and exhibitions. Two-day tickets £35. Apply to: The Cerealogist, 20 Paul St, Frome, Somerset BA11 1DX. Tel: 0373 451777

● **ET OR NOT ET – IS THAT THE QUESTION?** – Independent UFO Network Conference, 15/16 August 1992. Sheffield Library Theatre. Speakers include: John Keel, William Moore, Jenny Randles, Ralph Noyes, Kevin McClure, John Shaw, Norman Oliver, Robert France, Albert Budden and Graham Allen. Advance booking recommended. Contact: Enigma Design & Publishing, 15 Rydal St, Burnley, Lancs BB10 1HS. Tel: 0282 24837.

● **FROM OUTER SPACE TO YOU – UFO 92.** Talks, film, slides, abductions, close encounters, crop circles. 14/15 November 1992. Hever Village Hall, Nr Hever Castle, Edenbridge, Kent. Details: Alan Hilton (organiser), 'Highland Glen', Gravesend Rd, Shorne, Kent DA12 3JW.

● **SOCIETY FOR PSYCHICAL RESEARCH** – Lectures. 17 Sept: Investigating spontaneous cases (Howard Wilkinson). 15 Oct: Psi and the Ganzfeld: what we have learnt so far (Charles Honorton). 12 Nov: Is the medium the message? New developments in survival research (Leslie Price). 10 Dec: The dying brain: science and the near-death experience (Susan Blackmore). Venue: the Lecture Hall of Kensington Central Library, Campden Hill Road, London W8, at 6:30pm. Non-members £3, student cards £1. Further information from the SPR at 49 Marloes Rd, Kensington, London W8 6LA. Tel: 071 937 8984.

● **MICHAEL BENTINE** lectures – 'From the Ridiculous to the Paranormal' - 15 Aug (Brewhouse Theatre, Taunton); 6 Sept (Theatre Royal, Plymouth); 16 Sept (Gordon Craig Theatre, Stevenage); 18 Sept (Civic Theatre, Doncaster); 20 Sept (Theatre Royal, Bristol); 25 Sept (Theatre Clwyd, Mold); 3 Oct (Lewisham Theatre); 14 Oct

(Maddermarket Theatre, Norwich); 29 Oct (Theatre Royal, Bury St Edmunds). Check with venues for start (apx 7:30-8:00).

● **LONDON EARTH MYSTERIES CIRCLE** – Evening meetings in St Andrew's Seminar Room, Maria Assumpta Centre, 23 Kensington Square, London W8, at 7pm on the 2nd and 4th Tuesdays in each month. Members £1.00, non-members £2.00, unwaged £1.50. Lectures: 8 Sept (Psychic Questing), 22 Sept (Medicine Wheels), 13 Oct (Reclaiming our Heritage), 27 Oct (Earth Mysteries and Magnetism), 10 Nov (social eve.), 24 Nov (UFOs & Psychic phenomena). Contact: Rob Stephenson, Flat 6, 136 Bravington Rd, London W9 3Al or tel: 081 969 3928.

● **THEOSOPHICAL SOCIETY** – events on 6 Dec: at 11:15am, 'Holy Blood and The Holy Grail'; at 6pm 'Megalithic Science' - 50 Gloucester Place, London W1H 3HJ. Tel: 071 935 9261.

● **SMALL PRESS FAIR** – 19 Sept 1992 – A great day out at Britain's biggest gathering of small publishers, services, distributors, binders, writers and illustrators of books, magazines, comics, tracts, pamphlets, etc. Special groups of poetry, politics, avant garde, history, craft, & exotic. Free demos of DTP & publishing advice show how it's done. Bar & buffet. Free entry. 10am-6pm. Royal Horticultural Society Old Hall, Vincent Sq, London SW1. Info: 0234 211606.

● **BUFORA** –British UFO Research Association 30th Anniversary Conference. Saturday 19 Sept 1992, 2:00pm – 7.:30pm. London Business School, Regents Park, London NW1. For further details ring: 0582 763218

MISCELLANEOUS

● **HOBLINK** – the organisation for lesbian, gay and bisexual pagans, is to be relaunched. For further info, send SAE to: Hoblink, 13 Merrivale Rd, Stafford ST17 9EB.

● **WELSH HOLIDAY COTTAGE** – Self-catering accomodation in historic North Wales town of Denbigh. For further details, contact Janet Bord, Melysfan, Llangwm, Corwen, Clwyd LL21 0RD. Tel: 049 082 472. Fax: 049 082 321.

● **GLASTONBURY COTTAGE** – Forget expensive hotels of B&Bs – charming 2 bed house to let in mystic Glastonbury town centre. Central-heating, fully furnished with necessary utensils, crockery etc, and unique view over Abbey grounds. Tel: 0234 211606 (answerphone) for leaflet.

● **OLD PULP SF MAGS WANTED** – for FT Library. Also FATE MAGAZINE vol 1, no 4 (1948); nos 50 (1954) & 90 (1957). Write to Bob Rickard, c/o FT editorial address.

FORTEAN TIMES

THE JOURNAL OF STRANGE PHENOMENA

SUBSCRIPTIONS

ORDER A YEAR'S SUPPLY OF FORTEAN TIMES FOR YOURSELF OR A FRIEND AND GET IT DELIVERED DIRECT TO YOUR DOORSTEP. AND THAT'S NOT ALL - EVERY NEW SUBSCRIBER RECEIVES A <u>FREE</u> FORTEAN TIMES T-SHIRT WORTH £7.99.

Postage and packing FREE

●

Special offer on subscriptions for 12 issues

●

FREE T-shirt with every new subscription

●

If you have enjoyed this issue, why wait two months for more? Order some back issues today. £2 each (see coupon).

I would like to subscribe to Fortean Times:　**Please tick for free t-shirt** ☐

For one year (6 issues)　☐ UK £12　☐ overseas inc USA £15 US$30

For two years (12 issues)　☐ UK £20　☐ overseas inc USA £26 US$50

Back Issues No(s) – £2 each _____

Name: Mrs/Miss/Ms/Mr _____

Address _____

_____　Postcode _____

I enclose a total payment of £ _____ made payable to: John Brown Publishing Ltd, or debit the above amount from my Access/Visa/Mastercard/Eurocard (delete where applicable) account.

Account no ☐☐☐☐☐☐☐☐☐☐☐☐☐☐☐☐　Expiry date ☐☐☐☐

Signature _____　Date _____

Please return order form to: Fortean Times, 20 Paul Street, Frome, Somerset BA11 1DX
or phone credit card details on 0373 451777　**FT64**

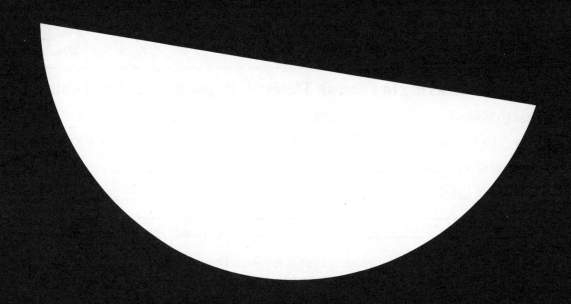

A *Gordon's & Tonic* IN FRONT OF THE T.V.

NUMBER 65

UK £2
USA $4.95

FORTEAN TIMES

THE JOURNAL OF STRANGE PHENOMENA

THE MARTIAN SPHINX
Exclusive Colour Pull-Out

WHACKY WEATHER
Britain's Meteorlogical Mayhem

John Keel Interview ● Spotting UFOs ● The Hueytown Hum
Kidney Capers ● Blood Miracles ● Ghostly Goo ● Fertility Seat

Contents

Issue 65 October/November 1992

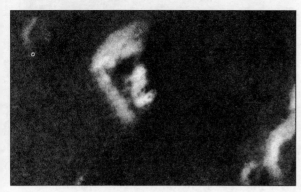

FREE IN THIS ISSUE:

PULL-OUT GUIDE TO MARTIAN MONUMENTS

WHY 'FORTEAN'?

CHARLES FORT (1874-1932)

Fortean Times is a bi-monthly magazine of news, reviews and research on all manner of strange phenomena and experiences, curiosities, prodigies and portents, founded in 1973 to continue the work of the iconoclastic philosopher CHARLES FORT. Fort was sceptical about scientific explanations, observing how scientists argued for and against various theories and phenomena according to their own beliefs, rather than the rules of evidence. He was appalled that data not fitting the collective paradigm was ignored, suppressed, discredited or explained away (which is quite different from explaining a thing).

Fort was perhaps the first to speculate that mysterious lights seen in the sky might be craft from outer space. He coined the term 'teleportation', which has passed into general usage through science fiction. His dictum "One measures a circle beginning anywhere" expresses his philosophy of Continuity and the 'doctrine of the hyphen', in which everything is in an intermediate state between extremes. He had notions of the universe-as-organism and the transient nature of all apparent phenomena. Far from being an over-credulous man, Fort cut at the very roots of credulity: "I cannot accept that the products of minds are subject matter for beliefs ... I conceive of nothing, in religion, science, or philosophy, that is more than the proper thing to wear, for a while."

Fort was born in Albany, New York, in 1874 into a family of Dutch immigrants. Beatings by a tyrannical father helped set him against authority and dogma, and on leaving home at the age of 18 he hitch-hiked around the world to put some "capital into the bank of experience." At 22 he contracted malaria, married his nurse and settled down to 20 years of impoverished journalism in the Bronx. During this time he read extensively in the literature of science, taking notes on small squares of paper in a cramped shorthand of his own invention, which he filed in shoe boxes.

In 1916, when he was 42, Fort came into a modest inheritance, just enough to relieve him of the necessity of having to earn a living. He started writing The Book of the Damned, which his friend, the novelist Theodore Dreiser, bullied his own publisher into printing in 1919. Fort fell into a depression, burnt all his notes (which numbered some 40,000) as he had done a few years earlier, and in 1921 set sail for London, where he spent eight years living near the British Museum (39 Marchmont Street) and wrote New Lands (1923). Returning to New York, he published Lo! in 1931 and Wild Talents in 1932, shortly before he died. He left 60,000 notes, now in the New York Public Library.

THE GANG OF FORT:

Editors:
Bob Rickard
& Paul Sieveking

Contributing Editors:
Steve Moore
& Mike Dash

© Fortean Times October 1992
ISSN 0308 5899

EDITORIAL ADDRESS
Fortean Times: Box 2409,
London NW5 4NP, UK. Tel &
Fax: 071 485 5002 or 081 552
5466.

SUBMISSIONS
Submissions are invited of suitable
articles, news, art, cartoons,
reviews, and especially clippings.
Preliminary discussion with the
editors is advisable. Text can be
submitted on floppy disks, but
check with the editors first.
Submissions may be edited. FT
assumes no responsibility for
submissions, but all reasonable care
will be taken while they are in FT's
possession. Requests for return of
material should be accompanied
by stamped addressed envelope.

CLIPPINGS
All clippings, references, etc,
should be identified by source,
date and clipster's name. Mail or
fax them to the editorial address
(above).

SUBSCRIPTIONS
RATES – One year (6 issues). UK:
£12. Overseas inc. USA: US
£12.50 or $25. For two years (12
issues) UK: £20, overseas inc USA
£25 or US$50.
PAYMENT – US/Canadian
cheques acceptable; payments
from all other countries should be
in sterling drawn upon a London
bank. Major credit cards accepted
– just phone details to 0373
451777. Make cheque/money
orders payable to JOHN
BROWN PUBLISHING Ltd, 20
Paul Street, Frome, Somerset
BA11 1DX, UK.

**ADVERTISING
ENQUIRIES**
DISPLAY or CLASSIFIED: contact
Ronnie Hackston or Dan Squirrel
at John Brown Publishing Ltd: The
Boathouse, Crabtree Lane,
Fulham, London SW6 8NJ, UK. ☎
071 381 6007 or Fax: 071 381
3930. BOOKSELLERS' LISTING
items – contact the editorial address
(above).

PUBLISHER
John Brown Publishing Ltd, The
Boathouse, Crabtree Lane,
Fulham, London SW6 8NJ, UK. ☎
071 381 6007 or Fax: 071 381
3930. Managing Editor: Fiona
Jerome.
Publisher: Vic Lime.

DISTRIBUTION
UK trade distribution by UMD, 1
Benwell Road, Holloway, London
N7 7AX. ☎ 071 700 4600 or
Fax: 071 607 3352.
USA newsstand distribution by
Eastern News Distributors Inc, 2020
Superior St, Sandusky, OH 44870,

Bob Rickard

EDITORIAL:
Mars or Bust

Paul Sieveking

That erudite astronomer, Dan Quayle, once said he believed in the canals of Mars because he had seen pictures of them. "And if there is water," he appeared to reason, "there must be oxygen; and if oxygen, that means we can breathe." Don't snigger! He might be right! So we shall be following the progress of the latest probe, *Mars Observer*, which is on its way to the Red Planet even as you read this.

When we first planned this issue's pull-out on the Martian Face and its related structures, we had no inkling of September's probe launch. Both the well-illustrated article by Tim Coleman on the work of the 'Push for Mars' group, and the independent discovery by Eric Crew of what we've called 'the Planetarium', arrived at our editorial offices at about the same time. The production of each issue of *FT* seems to attract its own appropriate coincidences.

The real excitement, of course, is whether these enigmatic structures are signs from a long-gone Martian civilisation. Rumours suggest that the probe might take fresh shots of the famous Face, but NASA will not confirm this. *Mars Observer*'s cameras are more powerful than those of its predecessors, but we'll have to wait until late next year for the pictures which will end the speculation one way or the other.

● Another of our pleasures is the variety mail that comes in from all over the world. Recently, Mr Izzet Goksu in Bursa, Turkey, began sending us packets of fascinating clippings (for a first selection, see page 10); while Iosif Boczor in Romania promises to send "accounts of strange phenomena in Eastern Europe seven times a year". Mr Danjuma A. Bajoga from Gombe, in Nigeria's Bauchi State, tells us that "*Fortean Times* is a good companion through the ages"; while David Binns in Ponders End thinks we "are striking an excellent balance between mindful critique of charlatanry and appropriate criticism towards the more brainless manifestations of mainstream scientistic orthodoxy".

Sometimes we are at a loss: we were unable to cure K.M.Yacub of Erode, southern India, of throat cancer by remote healing (even though he gave us exact details of his birth), nor to use our magic to drive tenacious squatters from his properties; in 1986, we didn't know what to say to one chap in Honolulu who had been taken over by aliens and sent us his army security clearance "to show I'm not a crackpot"; and we could not satisfy one young hopeful who wanted "a full list of strange phenomena which have happened in the past and up to date".

● The *Fortean Times Diary* is now ready. We are very impressed and pleased with its stout and handsome casebinding. Weird, erudite and outrageous data commemorate every day in the year, along with the more entertaining saints, lashings of lunar and astronomical data and over a thousand birthdays of the good, the bad and the strange. Order lots; it's a Christmas gift you'll want to give as well as receive – see page 22.

THE EDITORS

STRANGE DAYS

16 pages of worldwide weirdness

TAIWAN'S ELEPHANT MAN

MAN Chang Chin-tsui, 80, known as the elephant man, pictured here in June 1992, sitting in his house in the central Taiwan town of Lukang, which he has not left for 69 years. He apparently suffers from a rare kind of neurotic tumour, which makes the flesh on the right side of his face and nose droop down to his neck.

GRAND SLAM

William McNall, 58, who plays bridge twice a week at the Carlton Club, Low Fell, Gateshead, Tyne & Wear, showed no hint of emotion when he picked up his hand of 13 hearts on 20 March 1992. He was half way through the rubber when he dealt the hand. As is common in bridge, two packs were being used by the foursome one after the other and the pack from which Mr McNall dealt had been shuffled by an opponent, Reg Parker, and cut by Mr Parker's partner, Sid Hetherington. Odds were variously reckoned at 6,250,000,000 to one (John Williams, Secretary of the English Bridge Union) or 158,753,389,899 to one (*Guinness Book of Records*). Mr McNall collected 2,410 points to thrash his opponents but at only 5p per 100 points, his win netted him just £1.20.

According to John Williams, such a hand "has never been dealt in official bridge games or competitions, although I have heard reports of people claiming to have come accross it in private games." Back in 1984, a man dealt all 13 spades in a game of full-deck brag in Bradford. Two days later, he came up with the same hand [*FT45:13*]. *D. Telegraph, Guardian 27 Mar 1992.*

6 – *Fortean Times 65*

HOLY NIGHTWEAR!

Any offers for a piece of the Virgin Mary's nightgown? Michael Fayter, who presents a weekly antiques programme on BBC Radio Devon, said he had been offered the relic by an anonymous listener who wished to sell it. Inevitably, this announcement drew a barrage of cynical comments, including speculation that the missing part may say 'Marks & Spencers'.

"It is sealed inside a small copper container", says Fayter, which makes inspection difficult. However, the relic does come with a "letter of authentication" in Latin, signed by the Bishop of Bruges on 23 November 1896 – (how did he manage to authenticate it, we wonder?) – together with bone fragments from St Clare the Virgin (c.1200) and the 17th century Flemish saint John Berchmans. *Herald, Today, Nottingham Eve. Post, 20 Feb 1992.*

BULLETPROOF NO MORE

Remember Manuel Antonio, the young Mozambican shaman-warrior who led his bow-and-arrow Barama army on behalf of the Frelimo government? Antonio assured his men his magic made them invulnerable – see [*FT59:2*] We learned, in the *D.Telegraph* (9 Dec 1991), that Antonio's mystic 'vaccination' ritual failed to ward off bullets coming his way during a fierce battle with anti-Frelimo Renamo rebels.

■ The previous month – November 1991 – saw a fatal argument in Togo between two members of the Mossi and Konkonba tribes. They each disagreed with the other's claim that their bulletproof charms were more effective. One suddenly shot the other, sparking a tribal conflict which left hundreds injured and buildings wrecked. The report – [R] *Eve.Post (NZ) 22 Nov 1991* – is silent on the crucial information about which charm to avoid on your next trip out there.

MUTANT MUSHROOMS

More than 60 people have died in central Russia and the Ukraine after eating what seem to be edible mushrooms, such as boletus, russula, saffron, milk cap or chantrelle. TASS announced on 6 August. An unidentified toxin was either being drawn from the soil, or produced by mutation, perhaps caused by pollution. In the Voronezh region near a nuclar power plant, where the poisoning was first reported, there were 193 cases of poisoning and 23 deaths. Further cases were reported in Volgograd, Lipetsk and Saratov. Vladimir Chiburayev, head of the Russian Epidemiological service, said that in the Ukraine alone, 600 had been taken ill. In most cases, the toxin attacked the liver and kidneys, in extreme instances leading to death within three days.

Meanwhile, a sharp increase in background radiation was found in nearby south Belarus after forest fires in areas contaminated by the Chernobyl nuclear accident in 1986. *D.Telegraph 7 Aug, New York Post, 10 Aug, Int. Herald Tribune 13 Aug 1992.*

LOOK! THERE GOES ANOTHER UNIDENTIFIED FLYING TOADSTOOL

ARTHUR CHRENKOFF ©

CARELESS RAPTURE

Pastor Lee Jang Lim of the Tami Church, a Korean abbreviation standing "prepare for the coming future", has declared that the world will end and Christ will gather his 144,000 faithful at midnight on 28 October this year. After the announcement, a number of copycat dooms-day sects have set themselves up, with between 20,000 and 100,000 followers. Some 12 million of South Korea's 42 million people are Christians. The authorities fear a wave of mass suicides after reports that people were leaving jobs and families and selling belongings to prepare for the Second Coming and the Rapture. One woman allegedly had an abortion so that she was light enough to be lifted to Christ. *[AFP] 15 Aug; Independent, 18 Aug 1992.*

Meanwhile, in the remote town of Hechi in China's Guangxi region, 80 believers have begun to preach the imminent return of Christ. They had stopped tilling their land and sold their houses in readiness. We are not told whether they believed 28 October was the last day. The authorities separated the believers and assigned them to work in different areas. *D.Telegraph, 1 Aug 1992.*

PARTING THE RED SEA

Sophisticated computer calculations indicate that the parting of the Red Sea, said to have allowed the Israelites to have escaped from Egypt, could have occurred precisely as the Bible describes it: "And the Lord caused the sea to go *back* by a strong east wind all that night, and made the sea dry *land*, and the waters were divided." [*Exodus* 14:21.]

Oceanographers Doron Nof and Nathan Paldor, reporting in the *American Meteorological Society Bulletin* (15 March 1992), have calculated that a steady wind of about 46mph (40 knots), blowing for 10 to 12 hours, could have pushed enough water to the south to cause a 10-foot drop in sea level, exposing a large swath of sea floor across the northern end of the Gulf of Suez, a distance of 12 to 18 miles. Nof and Paldor suggest there might be a natural ridge across the gulf at this point.

Since 1962 there have been scholars who interpret the crucial passage in Exodus as saying the Israelites crossed the Sea of Reeds, a marshy area at the northern end of the Gulf of Suez, not the Red Sea itself. An abrupt change in the wind would have then allowed the waters to have come crashing back in only four minutes, drowning the pursuing Egyptian army. Of course, there is a glaring logical problem here: if the wind thesis is correct, why hasn't the parting of the waters been witnessed since the flight of the Israelites? *New York Times, 15 Mar 1992.*

DOUBLE TROUBLE

Two cars collided on 29 July in Winkfield, Berkshire. Behind the wheel of the Citroen 2CV6 was Mrs Kathleen Wol-fenden, 52, a librarian from Ward Close, Wokingham. Behind the wheel of the Triumph Acclaim was Mrs Kathleen Wolfenden, 64, an ex-midwife from Poole in Dorset. The two Mrs Wolfendens were unrelated. *D.Telegraph, 30 July; Bracknell News, 6 Aug 1992.*

SOUND SLEEPERS

Edna Leitch dozed on peacefully as a powerful explosion destroyed her bungalow in North Walsham, Norfolk, at dawn on 29 April 1992 – (see photo). The roof fell in, windows were blown out and the walls came tumbling down with a crash heard a mile off. Edna, 63, was still asleep when firemen found her nearly buried under beams and rubble. In the evening, she was 'satisfactory' in hospital, having treatment for burns to her arms and legs. British Gas investigators turned up to look for the cause of the explosion. They were not certain that it was due to gas. *D.Mirror, 30 April 1992.*

■ Retired miner Bob Dodds, 76, who is hard of hearing, slept on as an 80mph gale blew away half his house in Ashington, Northumberland, last New Year's Eve. He didn't stir as the gable end crashed down around him, nor when neighbours hammered on his front door. He only woke up when a fireman climbed in an hour later and shook him. *D.Mirror, 3 Jan 1992.*

BRAZILIAN PANIC

Brazilian girls have taken to hiding their long hair inside shirts and blouses as the country is gripped by a hair-snipping panic, notes the *Daily Telegraph, 19 Sept 1991.*

Starting in the city of Belo Horizonte, the scare spread to Rio de Janeiro, and police estimate that hundreds of long-haired girls have been 'scalped'. The authorities attribute the crimes to gangs of three or four youths working for local hairdressers, who pay up to 50 per pound of hair used to make wigs or hair weaves.

One victim, journalism student Leila Pereira, said: "I crossed a square on my way to college when three men approached me. One suddenly held me from behind, another secured my head while the third pulled out a pair of scissors and cut off more than half my hair."

■ For coverage of pigtail snipping in ancient China (often attributed to invisible demons see *FT39:51, FT40:42* and *FT59:48.*

MEDICAL BAG

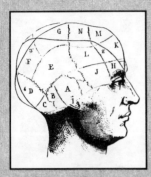

COLUMBUS CLEARED

Syphilis was unrecorded in Europe before Columbus sailed to the Americas in 1492, but spread across Spain in a wave of epidemic soon after his return. Contemporaries blamed him for the plague and the slur has persisted to the present day.

Now, a skeleton found in Gloucester in July 1991 has cleared his name. It is the remains of a woman, aged about 25, dated to circa 1420 - at least two generations before Columbus's voyage. Her skull, jaw, ribs arms and legs are covered with a type of bone lesion unique to syphilis, according to Dr Charlotte Roberts, a palæo-pathologist at Bradford University, who conducted the test. Some of the lesions had healed, indicating that she had syphilis for some years. Others were still open sores when she died.

The bones were found in what used to be a crowded cemetery within the grounds of Gloucester Priory, now Blackfriars Church in the city centre. Malcolm Atkin, director of the excavation, says that pottery finds date the whole cemetery between the 14th and early 16th centuries. "The part of the cemetery where the skeleton was found went out of

use altogether during the 15th century, and from its position the skeleton must date from the early part of the century", he told *The Sunday Telegraph* (22 Mar 1992). He said that the absence of any record about the woman suggested that syphilis was a disease the English were 'used to' at the time.

It may still be that Columbus played a part in the spread of the disease, says Dr Peter James, secretary of the Medical Sciences Historical Society. He could have introduced a more virulent strain into Europe. "Or he could have brought a quite harmless virus that acted as a catalyst on the syphilis bacteria already here, making it more infectious", he said.

UNBORN BABIES

● A 94-year-old woman was still carrying the fœtal skeleton of a baby she was expecting 61 years before. *New England Medical Journal*, 10 Dec 1989.

● Doctors in Kuala Lumpur removed a 10-year-old baby from the body of Iyam Supiyem, 37, in a five-hour operation. The baby, weighing 3.75 pounds and measuring 11.9 inches, was as "hard as a stone statue". Iyam, a farmer's wife from the Majalengka district of Indonesia, became pregnant in 1981, but the baby grew outside her womb. She could not afford the cost of an operation and besides, her belly returned to its normal shape after nine months. She had only recently started to have health problems. *[AP] 18 Aug 1991.*

LEAP YEAR WONDER

Karin and Henry Henriksen of Andenes in Nordland (north Norway) have three children - Heidi (32), Olav (28) and Leif Martin (24) - all born on Leap Day. The likelihood of this happening are almost too small to calculate, and the siblings can claim to be the only ones in the world with this status. They appear in the Guinness Book of Records. *Dagbladet, 25 Feb 1992.*

WHITE SALE

A German housewife who bought a suitcase at an auction of unclaimed airline luggage tried to do her laundry with the contents of a washing powder carton she found in the case. It was in fact more than four pounds of heroin, worth about £100,000, said the Frankfurt police. *Guardian* (18 Oct 1991). A few years ago, a shop in Split, Yugoslavia, bought almost 40 pounds of 'talcum powder' at a customs post auction and was selling it to customers. It also turned out to be heroin. *FT43:16.*

ACID EATS TUBE

A temporary answer has been found to halt the mystery acid that eats through the cast-iron tunnel walls around Old Street station in the City of London. Layers of a 'special material' have been installed, but this will only work for five years at most. The source of the acid remains unknown *[see FT57:14]*. This section of tube may have to be closed permanently, and the Northern Line cut in half. *Islington Chronicle, 5 Feb 1992.*

BIZARRE BREAK-INS

Not every by burglar breaks into a home wanting to steal things. Occasionally - and perhaps more disturbingly - they leave something instead.

● Rotherham man Dennis Hague came home to find that someone had moved house into his garage. Opening his garage to put away the car, Dennis found his way blocked by a floor to ceiling pile of furniture.

"It looks as if somebody has emptied their house and moved everything into my garage," the bemused homeowner told the *Daily Mirror* (21 May 1992.) "I don't think it's stolen, because whoever left the load even locked up."

● A couple from Sunninghill Avenue, Hove, Sussex, came home to discover evidence of a break-in. Not broken windows and looted cupboards and drawers, but a spotless kitchen, dishes washed and put away in their proper places and a living room that had been expertly tidied. During the day an insurance man called and was told by an elderly lady that she was the new cleaner. *Crawley (N.Sussex) Evening Argus, 23 May 1992.*

● Thieves who broke into Bill Holland's tool depot at Dale Abbey, Derbyshire, ignored £10,000 worth of gear and took a hacksaw to the cage containing his Rottweiler guard dog Hattie. Then they made off with the £250 'Devil Dog', leaving Bill to muse: "It's too daft for words. She didn't even put up a fight." *D.Mirror, 2 Jun 1992.*

● A thief broke into a house in Renfrew, Scotland, and left a strange calling card: a casket containing the ashes of a woman called Georgina D. Collingwood. Police baffled. *Edinburgh Evening News, 7 Aug 1992.*

EGG NEWS

● In a country which thinks nothing of dyeing beer green to amuse the populace on St Patrick's day, Eugene Power discovered the ultimate Irish breakfast treat. Four free-range hens – all sisters – were laying bright green eggs at a farm in Cork, Ireland. The baffled farmer sought an explanation from Mr Power, research officer for the Department of Agriculture and Food in Cork.

"I was convinced they were painted or dyed", said Mr Power. "I tried to scrub the eggshells white with bleach, but the green just wouldn't wash off." One of the four green-layers was put in a cage and four days later gave birth to a healthy emerald green egg. "It tasted delicious", he said.

"I discovered this particular hen has a special gene which causes the production of green eggs. There are almost 100 types of hen and four of them have this rare genetic control over the pigment which colours the egg." His supporters agree that Marens, Millefleur, Indian Game and Araucana are breeds known to have a green egg-laying propensity. *D.Record, 19 Mar; Scotsman, 7 April; Guardian, Today, 27 April 1992.*

● The Welsh, not to be out-done, announced green eggs around the same time. Doris Evans, of Ruabon, near Wrexham, bought some eggs from a market stall and hatched them under her own hens. The resultant pair of chickens then laid green eggs. *D.Mirror, 16 April 1992.*

● Pauline Cousins cracked open eight double-yoked eggs in a row at her home in Ilfracombe, Devon. *D.Mirror, 7 Feb 1992.*

● A goose has laid a rare black egg on a farm at Ducklington, Oxfordshire. *D.Mirror, 29 April 1992.*

RAIN OF STRAW

For fifteen minutes on the afternoon of 28 July, barley straw rained down on the village of Hepworth in Suffolk, "covering the Duke of Marlborough end of the village". Peter Simms, 65, of Aspen Hall, Hepworth, saw the straw swirling about 200 feet above the ground before the wind suddenly dropped and it fell to earth. *Bury Free Press, 31 July 1992.*

FOR DOG, QUEEN AND COUNTRY

On a letter posted in Tonbridge, Kent, our monarch's noble profile has been defaced with a dog's head and the inky message: "Please control your dog when the postman calls". A treasonable offence, surely? Not so, says the Royal Mail, pointing out that it has the right to frank the stamp. Off with their heads! *Independent, 21 Feb 1992.*

MESSY MISSILE

A couple watching the film *Airplane* on TV stopped laughing when a reeking block of sewage crashed through their roof into the living room. It was assumed that the messy missile had come from a plane, and aviation authorities at Ormond Beach, Florida, were trying to trace the culprit. *D.Mirror, 5 June 1992.*

MEDICAL BAG

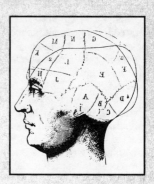

TUM THUMB

A large lake trout caught in the Flaming Gorge Reservoir in south western Wyoming on 13 February 1992 had a human thumb in its stomach. Almost seven months earlier, on 27 July 1991, Robert Lindsey, a 32-year-old welder from Green River, had lost his thumb and two fingers when he caught his hand in the propeller of his boat while helping his friend's daughter, who had fallen in the reservoir. The two fingers were found and sewn back on, but the thumb was not found.

Coroner Mike Vase said the fish probably ate the thumb less than 24 hours before it was caught. He said it was probably preserved in the water by a process called saponification, which occurs in moist, dark places and converts flesh to a chemical condition like that of soap. "As soon as I saw it, I was pretty sure it was mine", said Lindsey. "I'll probably just put it on a shelf to show people." *[AP] 29 Feb 1992.*

COMPLETELY ARMLESS

Police in Papua, New Guinea, reunited a man with his missing arm in July 1991. The unnamed man told police he had been travelling in the back of a truck when another vehicle passed so close to him that his arm was severed at the elbow. He was drunk and didn't notice his arm was missing. It was only some time later that he felt any pain and went to hospital in Lae. He appealed to the police to look for his arm, but they did not at first connect the incident with an arm found the same day in the tray of a truck in Mount Hagen, over 150 miles away. The man was expected to be discharged from hospital within a few days. *Radio Australia, Melbourne, 26 July; Southern Cross, 30 July 1991.*

FLAP TRAPS FINGER

Joanne White, 18, rattled the letter box of a flat in Sheffield to attract the attention of Joy Stirling, when the spring-loaded flap snapped shut and sliced off the ends of two fingers. Surgeons were unable to re-attach the severed pieces. The local council decided to press on with plans to fit 900 homes with new doors containing the same type of flap. *Sun, 13 June 1991.*

TOE THE LAWN

A big toe was discovered on the playing field of Hempland Infant's School and handed over to police. The day before and 300 yards away, Stephen Lawrence had slipped and cut off his toe with a lawnmower in his garden. He assumed it had been carried off by a bird. *D.Record, D.Telegraph, 27 June 1992.*

BUSINESS PERK

After Azerbaijan won independence from the Soviet Union, many Turks visited the country for business and pleasure as both nations speak Turkish. Some words, however, have different meanings. Two Turkish businessmen were asked what they would like before signing a contract and asked for kahve (coffee). Their Azari hosts were a trifle surprised, and went out for 20 minutes, returning with two blond women. Kahve was Kahbe (whore) in their language. *Burün, 11 May 1992.*

ABOVE: folk singer Nurhan Damcioglu. RIGHT: The unlucky boat

A SINGING JONAH

A ferry boat for passengers and cars regularly plied between the port of Istanbul and Izmir for many years until it was destroyed by fire in May this year. One passenger on the last trip was Mrs Nurhan Damcioglu, a very famous Turkish folk singer best known for her song "Fire, fire, there is a fire. Help me my friends, I am on fire." On the first day out, the ferry caught fire without apparent cause. All the passengers and crew were rescued, but one crew member died from a heart attack. The captain blamed the singer for the panic. *Hürriyet, 1 June 1992.*

TALKING TURKEY

MARINE OMEN

In the first week of June for the last three years, the sea at the Dardanelles has been turning a dull green. Fishermen and local residents said the change was very rapid and sometimes extended to the shores of Gökçeada; all the fish left the area of green sea. Officials waffled on about colour changes in marine micro-organisms, but this did not explain why the phenomenon only started three years ago. *Hürriyet, 10 June 1992.*

ALIEN ABDUCTION?

In July, Mrs Muserra Togay reported to the police that her daughter Elif Togay had been abducted eight days earlier from her home in Kadiköy, Istanbul , by a man calling himself Erhan Kargi. He had shown the woman his bleeding palms and claimed his blood could heal. He had very strange eyes and an unusual accent. He also told them that he had beamed down to Earth from outer space and could have anything he wanted. "I am afraid that he has taken my girl to outer space", said Mrs Togay. A careful police search failed to turn up any clues. *Burün, 29 July 1992.*

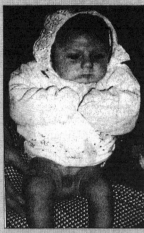

PROPHET CIRCUMCISION

Mrs Fatma Atmaca gave birth to a circumcised boy in Istanbul last year. This very rare condition is known in Turkey as a 'prophet circumcision'. Many people visited the boy's home in Sefaköy near Istanbul, including a woman who claimed that the visit had cured her from migrane which she had suffered from for years. The boy's mother said he started to talk at the age of 40 days

HOTEL JINX

Ibrahim Sezgin, a merchant from Bursa, stayed at a hotel in Çanakkale city one night and died in the bath. Police could find no suspicious circumstances and said it was death from natural causes. Nobody wanted the room so the hotel owners and staff all used the bath to prove there was nothing wrong. A week later, sales rep Bekir Aksoy stayed in the room and was found dead in the bath. Again, there were no suspicious circumstances and it was said to be death from natural causes. The room, however, was sealed as a precaution. *Sabah, 25 April 1992.*

MR ONUR'S LUCK TURNS

Hüdai Onur, 33, a poor farmer and father of two from Isabey village in Denizli province, won 20 million lira (about £2,200) from Spur-Loto on 1 October 1991. A month later, on 1 November, he won 980 million lira (about £109,000) from Spor-Toto. On 19 January 1992 he won 2,500 million lira (about £280,000) from Milli Piyango, the National Lottery. He won all the main legal lotteries in Turkey. Then his father-in-law died on 27 January, leaving him a large field and vineyard. *Hürriyet, 26+28 Jan 1992.*

PREHISTORIC WINGDOODLE

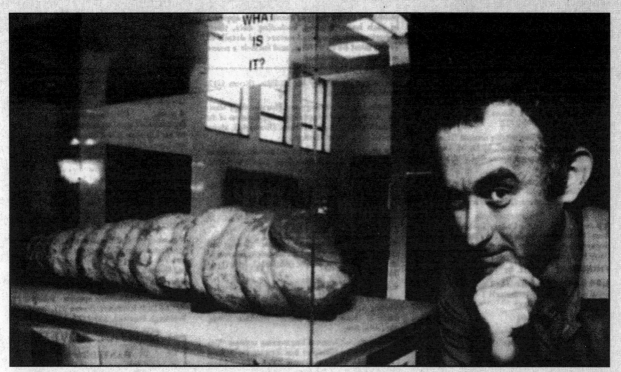

Alan Simpson, curator of the University Geology Museum in Brisbane, Queensland, poses before an 100-million-year-old spiral object, five feet long, found 60 years ago near Blackall in western Queensland by Dr Fred Whitehouse. Possible identities include the internal mould of a giant high-spired gastropod; but it is bowed in shape, none of the shell has been preserved and no known gastropod grew this large. Maybe it is a fossilised dinosaur turd or a natural concretion of mineral matter caused by ground water flowing through porous sediment. *Fortean Times* readers are invited to send their own suggestions to the editorial address.

DINOSAUR HUNTING IN THE CONGO

By the time you read this, our intrepid correspondent Bill Gibbons will be *en route* to the Congo for a second crack at testing the rumours of dinosaur-like creatures in the remote region around Lake Tele.

Bill's last expedition in 1986 [see *FT47:22-25*] was a disaster, though not, it must be said, that any blame attaches to the four young Britons who organised and financed it through their own efforts. Their plans fell foul of a society in which inefficiency and bureaucracy were made worse by the blatant demands for huge and unnecessary bribes. Later, their guide – Dr Marcellin Agnagna, a conservation official – claimed that he had deliberately led Gibbons and Co on false trails, and then abandoned them in the jungle to make their own way back.

This time, Bill has organised everything himself without the need to deal with corrupt officials. Through his membership of the United World Mission he is able to work with local missionaries and the Salvation Army in Brazzaville. Operation Congo 2 has been designed around a humanitarian provision of medical supplies, vehicle spare parts, clothing and educational materials for rural missions and churches. In return, the locals will provide Bill with accommodation and pygmy guides.

Bill will divide his six weeks between two locations: the unexplored upper Bia River and Lake Tibeke, west of Lake Tele, and a remote section of the Likouala swamps north of Impfondo, near the border with the Central African Republic. Both areas have provided convincing reports of large unknown animals and have not yet been visited by Western cryptozoologists.

Bill has promised us an exclusive report on his return. We wish him luck and success in removing the lens cap off his camera in time when he finally gets the close encounter he has long dreamed of.

Since December 1991, parts of Hueytown, near Birmingham, Alabama, have suffered a loud hum that comes and goes erratically, keeping people awake, setting teeth on edge and dogs to howling. The Hueytown Hum is a low-pitched, steady sound which has been compared to a dentist's drill or the noise of a fluorescent light tube about to go.

Emanating from the hills around this coalmining town (population 15,000), it has turned districts like Virginia Estates, Edenwood and Lakeview into zones of stress for up to three days at a time before fading away, only to return an hour or a week later. It is said to be louder at night, especially on Mondays and Tuesdays, and extremely loud on cloudy and rainy days. "Sometimes it comes from the ground and sometimes it vibrates through the air, hitting gutters and walls", said Hueytown Mayor Lillian Howard. "In some houses, it's being transmitted into the water pipes that go into the bathroom."

Humdingers

A local radio broadcast on April Fools' Day solicited theories. Hueytown was humming because it didn't know the words, suggested one listener. Another said it was killer bees. More serious theories involved electromagnetic forces and high-voltage power lines.

One area of about 500 homes seems to be most affected. Such focused sound phenomena are not unheard of according to Clifford Bragdon, a professor of city planning at Georgia Institute of Technology. Some years ago, two

THE HUEYTOWN HUM

"...IT PRODUCES A LOW GROWL, INAUDIBLE TO DOGS, BUT WHICH SENDS HUMANS NUTS...."

communities 10 to 17 miles from the Aberdeen Proving Ground, an Army Ordnance test centre in Maryland, complained of noise from the tests, while communities nearer the base were barely disturbed. It was discovered that the interaction of temperature, humidity, barometric pressure, wind and topography had created an atmospheric anomaly that was carrying the sound to points miles from its source.

Coalmine fans?

Some Hueytown residents are blaming the huge ventilation fans in nearby mines, required by Federal regulations to extract methane and coal dust round the clock. The USX Corporation's Oak Grove mines, 10 miles to the west,

have five such fans, but company engineers maintained they were not causing the hum. However, the Corporation's 1991 clearing of a pine forest between the mines and the town might have contributed to the problem.

Just south of USX's mines, Jim Walter Resources Inc has a mine with three fans, one of which is a 3,500-horsepower monster with 12-foot blades. This went into operation last December, about the time the hum was first noticed. The company denies that its new fan was to blame, pointing out that it replaced an earlier fan which had run continuously since 1974, and there was no evidence that the new fan was any louder than the old one. The Jim Walter mines extract 2.7

million tons of coal annually and a billion cubic feet of methane a month from the hills around Hueytown. *Birmingham (AL) Post-Herald, 26 Mar, 7+10 April; New York Times, 14 April; AP, [-] April 1992.*

British hummers

The British government finally acknowledged in February 1992 that not all 'hummers', people who hear a low frequency noise which others cannot hear, are suffering from low frequency tinnitus, a hearing disorder which generates a hum inside the head. After ten years in which 'hummers' have tried to persuade the British government that their problem is outside their heads, and three years of lobbying by the Low Frequency Noise Sufferers Association, the Department of the Environment has agreed to fund research into the phenomenon by the Building Research Establishment (BRE) near Watford. A stingy £50,000 has been allocated to study 25 sufferers.

Nuisance

The DoE acknowledges that some 500 new cases are reported each year. A DoE spokesman said the department had only 'recently' heard of the problem, although scientific papers on the subject date back to 1973. Even if research pinpoints a cause, compensation for sufferers will not follow automatically because the law doesn't cover low frequency noise nuisance.

A report in *Applied Acoustics* (Vol 10, 1977) found that the hum is often so close to being inaudible that most people do not register it. It is usually heard indoors and at night when there is less background noise. Many hummers have heard the sound for years; some are on tranquillisers, and one allegedly was driven to suicide.

Hum theories include air conditioning, water pumps, factory noises, traffic or powerful microwave transmitters. The most popular theory among sufferers is that organ-pipe resonances are set up by the network of three-foot-wide underground pipes used to pump gas under pressure from high power turbines. British Gas began installing the turbines in 1966 and the distribution system covered Britain by 1977.

In May 1992, British Gas began digging a four-mile trench across Hampstead Heath to lay a new gas main. To test the gas pipe theory, Leslie Fothergill, head of the acoustics section at BRE, and his staff used digital audio tape recorders and other equipment sensitive to low frequency sound, to make recordings on windless nights before and after the pipes were laid and again after pumping begins. We await results.

The Gas Report

Meanwhile, British Gas published a report on 22 July which dismissed the gas pipe theory, saying that the amount of low frequency noise from their turbines was negligible compared with that from motor traffic and that their compressor stations only operated, on average, for 16% of the time. They studied 33 complaints, continuously monitoring sound in the sufferers' homes. In only one case was the noise traced to gas pipework resonance. Other culprits included a fridge at a meat packing plant, a power unit on a ship three miles away, an industrial burner, a distant shipyard, machinery in a knitting factory and a resonating flue. *New Scientist, 9 Dec 1989, 29 Feb, 30 May + 1 Aug 1992; Independent, 30 Mar + 23 July 1992.*

Felix Bennett

GHOSTLY GOAT

Doris Boulter, a retired caretaker, lives in a semi-detached council house on the outskirts of Leicester with her husband Frank, her son, her daughter and her grandson. When the family first moved in two years ago, they noticed an unaccountable slime collecting in small pools on the floors and occasionally dripping down the stairs. Council workmen were called in and were duly baffled.

In November 1991, said Mrs Boulter, the phenomenon "started to come on vicious". Sticky deposits erupted on chairs and beds and inside furniture. Visitors found the insides of their handbags dripping goo, while others discovered slime stains on their clothes. The 'ghost' even glooped into the goldfish tank, killing the fish. A recent development has been slime in electric appliances. During July

1992, the telephone has broken, the timer on the washing machine has gone and the video has ground to a sticky halt.

Ken Quine, a Church of England canon interested in the paranormal, called at the house. "I saw this woman – dark-skinned with long, loose black hair", he said. "Don't ask me *how* I saw her – but I did. I also saw a young goat, a kid." The canon's ghostly goat fits with tests made at Leicester University which found that the Boulters' sticky liquid was animal urine – but not that of a cat or dog.

The Bishop of Leicester pulled Quine off the case and substituted the Archdeacon of Loughborough. A variety of mediums and spiritualists have also called. One medium identified a ghostly old man, another the restless spirit of Mr Boulter's mother.

Mrs Boulter has kept a careful record of the secretions. They occur mostly in the evening and

early morning, coming in periodic bursts lasting three or four days. Her eight-year-old grandson, Luke, is well attuned to the phenomena. "He says, 'Nan, ghost is here.'", she said. "I ask him where and he says, 'Wait a minute … I'll tell you. It's in the sitting room. On the table.' And when you go, the water is there." Secretions also appear when Luke is away at school, thus ruling him out as a suspect.

"The Boulters' house resembles a monsoon casualty", writes Amanda Mitchison in the *Observer* (9 Aug 1992). "In the sitting room the chairs, the sofa and the electric fire are all covered in plastic sheeting. A polythene bag is tucked over the fruit bowl."

Mrs Boulter denies the suggestion that the ghost might liven up a dull day. The whole affair is a trial, she said. "We've had full communion, prayers, séances, the lot. It doesn't seem to help. I don't know how much longer I can go on."

FAR OUT EAST

BAD SCENES

A private developer decided to build a three-storey repository for the ashes of the dead in suburban Yuen Long, in the New Territories of Hong Kong. Local residents were outraged by the 'ghost' building, saying it would harm the *feng shui* and bring them bad luck. (*Feng shui* is the Chinese 'geomancy' relating to the auspiciousness of a particular locality.) When a contractor refused admittance to a *feng shui* expert hired by the villagers, a six-hour stand-off began between the locals and the police, in which six people were hurt. Villagers used cars and rocks, and their own bodies, to block the way of police vehicles, and six people were arrested. They were later released on bail after another demonstration, this time outside the police station. What became of the building, we don't know. *Rising Nepal, 16 April 1991.*

WORLD OF THE DEAD

Chinese villagers (our source doesn't say from where) have been exhuming female relatives and taking them home to prevent the remains being stolen and sold as 'ghost brides', following the arrest of two men for digging up the bodies of six women and selling them to families of men who died unmarried [for another case see *FT63:17*]. The 'ghost marriage' is (or was) quite common in the East, but it's usually only the spirits who marry, in effigy form; this seems to be taking things rather literally! *Edinburgh Evening News, 24 Feb 1992.*

■ In Guizhou province, SW China, a fortune-teller told 28-year-old teacher Wang Faxiang that his three-year-old daughter would one day threaten his life. Waiting until his wife went out, Wang beheaded the child and hid her body in a cave. He was arrested, but what happened to him was not reported. Still, as the death penalty isn't uncommon in China, we wonder: was the fortune-teller (indirectly) right about the girl causing his death after all? *D.Telegraph, 19 Dec 1991.*

TUMMY BUGS

When Yang Siqi was a teacher, he had a couple of problems: termites were eating his schoolhouse, and he suffered from fever and gastritis. Yang started studying termites in a bid to clear up the first problem, and noticed that they never seemed to be ill. So, as orthodox medicine had failed to clear up the other problem, Yang decided to use the 'magical medical powers' of the termites ... and ate them for three months. His stomach trouble miraculously cleared up, and Yang has now gone on to become director of the Yingtan Termite Research Institute in Beijing. He's also set up three companies making termite-based medicines, and says there are no side-effects, though he hasn't released details of how termite-medicine works. Does he know, one wonders? *Today, 2 March 1992.*

CHAIN STORE MASSACRES

■ Teacher Michael Graham of Stapleton, Bristol, found what looked like a dried prune when he poured himself a bowl of muesli. It turned out to be a black iguanid, an inch-and-a-half-long tree lizard found in California and South America, which had entered the food chain via a shipment of Californian raisins and was packaged in Merseyside before being served up by Tesco. Suppliers Nestlé and manufacturers General Mills, Canada, were each fined £3,500. There was nothing terribly unusual about Mr Graham's experience: in 1990, for instance, more than 1,000 live beetles and 5,000 live larvae were found in boxes of porridge sold by an east London supermarket.

In April 1992, another dead lizard turned up – this time in Tesco's own brand plum tomatoes in Nottinghamshire – and almost got cooked in a pizza. *Independent, D Telegraph, East Anglian Daily Times, 11 Jan; D. Mirror, 11 Jan + 10 April 1992.*

■ Eric Schneider, 35, from Long Island, took a big bite from a McRib in a McDonald's restaurant. Instead of pork covered in barbecue sauce, onion slices and a pickle, this particular snack was a 'McMouse'. He checked the filling because of its vile taste and found two back legs. He had eaten the rest of the mouse. He threw up and had to wrestle the bun away from restaurant staff.

He is suing for £600,000, claiming the meal made him a nervous wreck. *D.Mirror, 10 April 1992.* [For further snack surprises, see *FT51:11*.]

SIMULACRA CORNER

Janet Bord sent us this picture of the 'OK' Stone, which belongs to Tristan Gray Hulse and Roy Fry of Clwyd. We are always glad to receive pictures of spontaneous forms and figures, or any curious images.

Send your snaps to the editorial address – with SAE – and we'll pay a fiver for any we use.

"...NOT TO MENTION ITS EXPLOSIVELY HIGH METAPHORICAL AND SYMBOLIC CONTENT..."

SOAP

H.M. CUSTOMS

LATHER AWFUL

Two hundred bars of soap from Africa were seized at Gatwick airport by trading standards officers. The packaging made a plethora of wild claims about the soap, including a cure for madness, protection from witchcraft, demons, poisons, satanic assaults and nightmares. "We are concerned about the safety of the ingredients and possible heavy metal contamination", said trading standards officer Peter Green. *The News (Portsmouth) 11 June; Crawley Observer (Sussex), 1 July 1992.*

PULL THE OTHER ONE

A man apparently duped dozens of women over the phone into cutting up their shoes. One woman in Glendale, California, told the police that the man called on 5 June, telling her he was conducting a survey for a shoe company. He asked for her age, address, shoe size and favourite styles and brands. He promised her 40 pairs of shoes over the next year if she destroyed her old ones. The woman cut up a $70 pair while the man listened.

When the woman called a number the man had given her, she reached Hughes Aircraft Company. Hughes had received about 40 phone calls in the past week from victims of the scheme, police said. *[AP] 12 June 1992.*

LEG ANYONE?

Julia Foad discovered a false leg, complete with sock, and very smart shoe, beside a road in Kent as she travelled to work. She had appealed for the owner to step (or hop?) forward. *D. Record 18 May 1992.*

NOWT SO QUEER

SEX ON RAILS

On a hot and humid bank holiday train on 25 May, John Henderson, 29, and Zoë D'Arcy, 19, who worked together in the Sainsbury's warehouse in West Ealing, London, were returning from a day trip to Margate. D'Arcy was seen performing fellatio in a first class compartment by a woman who boarded at Whitstable with her children. The couple then moved to a packed second class compartment. D'Arcy went to the lavatory, returned carrying her jeans and sat on Henderson's lap.

The two performed 'full sexual intercourse'; none of the other passengers made any comment, until the couple lit up cigarettes afterwards – in a no-smoking carriage. This was a serious breach of etiquette and there was a furious row and a complaint to a guard. Henderson and D'Arcy were fined £50 each with £20 costs. *D.Telegraph, D.Mirror, 7 Aug 1992.*

METAL MOUTH

Allison Johnson, 47, is an alcoholic burglar with a compulsion to eat cutlery, Lincoln Crown Court was told. At present he has eight forks and metal sections of a mop head lodged inside him. He had spent a total of 24 years of his life in prison. He repeatedly went to restaurants on his release from prison and ordered lavish meals. When he couldn't pay, he would tell the owners to call the police and would then eat cutlery until they arrived.

Mr Adrian Robinson, defending Johnson on his latest charge of aggravated burglary, said that his client "is in pain and holds his stomach all the time. He finds it hard to eat and obviously has difficulty going to the lavatory. He has had about 30 operations to remove cutlery from his stomach. There have been two more operations for things he has eaten while in Lincoln prison. He has been told that he has about a year to live. The cutlery swallowing and inability to stay away from alcohol comes from his lack of self-esteem. He punishes himself for his lack of it."

The Recorder jailed him for four years after reading psychiatric reports. [Eating metal objects is comparatively common. FT has many cases on file.] *D.Telegraph, 25 Aug; Lincoln Standard, 28 Aug 1992.*

DIRTY LARRY

Larry Kennedy, 16, was ridiculed at school in Gary, Indiana, for body odour. On 23 March 1992, he shot himself with his father's gun because his family would not let him take a bath. The boy, described as a brilliant student, was part of a family that stopped bathing in 1977 after his infant sister died in the bath. *USA Today, Edinburgh Evening News, 3 Aug 1992.*

NESSIE AHOY!

● In the annals of monster-hunting, 28 July may go down as the day science finally caught up with Nessie! Perhaps. The contact was made by a special underwater radar towed in Loch Ness by the *MV Simrad*, a Norwegian survey ship seconded to Project Urquhart.

Project Urquhart – launched earlier this year, see *FT59:10* – is a joint venture by the Natural History Museum, the Freshwater Biological Association and the Royal Geographic Society to make a detailed scientific survey of Britain's largest lake. Over 100 hours have been clocked on the loch already, and the Project has gained sufficient bathymetric data for Ordnance Survey to produce a new and accurate map of the loch's bottom.

Only five per cent of the data have been analysed so far, but it is certain that the loch is significantly deeper than the official figure of 754ft. The Project estimate their three-year research programme will cost four million pounds and are still seeking funds from corporate or institutional sponsors.

Sediment samples from the floor are also expected to

THE FAR SIDE   By GARY LARSON

Another unsubstantiated photograph of the Loch Ness monster (taken by Reuben Hicks, 5/24/84, Chicago).

reveal new forms of loch-bed life. However, the life-form most people want to hear about is the loch's most famous resident, Nessie. So did the sonar confirm her existence? It seems not. Project co-founder Nicholas Witchell was quick to play down hopes for proof of Nessie, saying: "Even the most sophisticated equipment is susceptible to spurious echoes."

Nevertheless, the radar – designed by Simrad for hunt-

ing submarines - did show a blip about 50ft below the surface between Foyers and Invermoriston. Thor Edland, the sonar operator, said: "The contact was larger than anything else spotted in the loch and very strong. The mechanism locked on to it automatically and held it for about two minutes." This was confirmed by Robert Manson, marketing director of Simrad, who said the echo was "loud and solid".

This sounds very positive to us – suggestive even. When we inquired about further analysis of the contact, a

THE FAR SIDE   By GARY LARSON

Another sighting of the Loch Ness dog

spokesman for Project Urquhart told *FT* that recording equipment had not been activated at the time, so no hard record exists of the blip. This leaves the field still open for Nessie believers and sceptics to read into it whatever they like.

● A week or two later -- according to a report in the Aberdeen *Press & Journal* (18 Aug 1992) – a tourist with a video camera filmed a very curious phenomenon in the waters near Urquhart Castle. The unnamed Glaswegian is said to have passed the film to unnamed 'experts' at Glasgow University who are said to be 'convinced' it shows a large water-dwelling creature. Somehow, all these vague times, places and people befit a story of a vague film of a vague creature.

The rest of us had an opportunity to judge for ourselves when the sequence was shown at the end of ITN's *News at Ten* on 17 August last. Mrs Betty Gallagher, of the Loch Ness Monster Exhibition Centre, at Drumnadrochit, who agreed with many that "It is a wonderful piece of video and looks too good to be true," added: "I am honestly not sure what it is but I think it is probably a wave formation."

Almost unnoticed in this report is an interesting reversal: the usually sceptical scientists are bullish while Nessie's supporters seem doubtful.

SPIT SPURNED

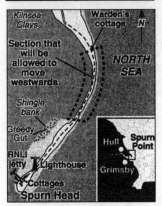

A centuries-old fight to save one of Britain's most remarkable and historic coastal features from the powerful eroding forces of the sea has been lost. The Humberside authority responsible for Spurn Head – a thin finger of land jutting into the North Sea on the Humber estuary opposite Grimsby – has finally decided to abandon repairs of the crumbling sea defences and allow the headland to resume its westward creeping movement of about two metres a year. *D.Telegraph 31 Aug 1992*.

The decision, we are told, is not based solely on economics, but takes account of new approaches to environmental problems. Unprotected stretches of coast, above and below the main spit, had moved more than 100 metres since the sea defences were built 150 years ago, and the spit itself was in danger of becoming isolated and vulnerable.

A history of this curious hook of land and its ancient battle with the sea can be found in Nigel Pennick's *Lost Lands and Sunken Cities* (Fortean Tomes, 1987), still available from leading Fortean book services – see p62.

Meanwhile the long-suffering residents of Spurn Head are protesting about the inevitable loss of their only road, essential services, land and homes. Sorry, say the council, but that's the way the coast crumbles.

BERRY POMEROY FIELD SPORT

This crop formation, two 24ft circles connected by a 22ft 'alley' one foot wide, appeared in a field of barley belonging to Mr Nichols of Berry Farm, Berry Pomeroy, near Totnes in Devon, around 10/11 June, 10ft higher up than the single 65ft circle that appeared in 1991. The crop was laid down anti-clockwise and appeared plaited. An 88ft-long alley in the shape of a leg runs off the lower circle. Mr Nichols believes rooks and ravens are responsible. He strung up several dead ravens in a nearby field which is being systematically destroyed, a line at a time.

The photograph of the formation is one of three taken on 12 June by our correspondent Pete Glastonbury who lives nearby. He was with his wife and children; none of them saw the large ball of light that turned up on the film. Pete used Fuji Velvia (50 ASA) loaded in a Pentax SFX with a 35-70mm SMC lens with a polarizing filter. The camera does not have a double expose mode. He has sent copies of this and other balls of light photographs to Fuji for analysis, and is trying to fake similar pictures for comparison.

The same week the circles appeared, two hay barns caught fire simultaneously about five miles away and there were three simultaneous motor cycle accidents: in Berry Pomeroy, Dawlish and on the Plymouth-Totnes road. All three were green Kawasaki bikes and all three bike passengers died. After the accidents, locals began calling the 'leg' formation on the crop circle The Scythe (geddit?). The castle at Berry Pomeroy, incidentally, has the reputation of being the most haunted place in the country. There may be no connection between any of these things.

WALLABY NEWS

In May, two newspapers drew attention to the existence in England of two feral colonies of Red Neck wallabies. One, in the Derbyshire Peak District, is described as "one of conservationists' best-kept secrets", but is well-known to Forteans and cryptozoologists and is often referred to in these pages. It began as WW2 closed and the owner of a private zoo died, leaving the estate to deteriorate and the animals run free. At their peak in the early 1960s, there were 50-60 wallabies, but successive hard winters have reduced their numbers to about 10. Dr Derek Yalden of Manchester University's environmental biology department has studied the colony and says: "They won't survive another five years". *Today, 27 May 1992.*

Repatriation

Dr Yalden is of the opinion that they should now be rounded up and sent back to their native Tasmania. He seems to forget that several generations of these wallabies have adapted to the birch scrub moorland, to which, according to park keeper Chris Manby, they are well suited. Repatriation for these naturalised Britons is as dubious as similar proposals about human immigrants and their descendants. Surely transporting the wallabies would be too risky. Wouldn't it be better all round if they could be protected and bred back to strength as an official project?

Parakeets

The second colony, in Devon, is so new it might be too premature to call it a colony. When thieves broke into the Exmoor Bird Gardens at Parracombe, near Bideford, they inadvertently released some valuable parakeets and six wallabies (five of them female). Owner Matt Clark publicly gave up his search for the beasts, saying: "These wallabies were bred here and have adapted to our climate. By now they should have young in their pouches, and, as Exmoor is huge and the moorlands suited to their diet, and they are well camouflaged, it will be impossible to catch them." *D.Express, 14 Feb; North Devon Journal, 20 Feb; Independent, 25 May 1992.*

Other Sightings

Regular readers of *FT* will know that there are occasional reports of wallabies, or even kangaroos, in areas other than the Peak District, and now on Exmoor, one of the haunts of other exotic aliens, the big cats – see last issue pp44-45. For example, Yorkshire …

New reader Mark Barratt complained to us that life around his hometown, Pontefract, seemed dull after discovering *FT* and reading about all the weirdness going on everywhere else. Imagine his excitement then at being able to send us a clipping from the *Hemsworth and South Elmsall Express* for 4 June 1992, to the effect that, on 31 May, a disabled driver in Broad Lane, South Elmsall, had a good long sighting of a wallaby moving through a cornfield. No mention of crop circles either!

Our file yielded an earlier encounter, not too far away, in November 1991. On 14 May, a startled motorist dashed into the Black Swan pub at Tremholme, near Stokesley, North Yorkshire, calling for help. He thought he had just run down a child on the A19. When police arrived at the scene, they found the man had hit and killed a wallaby. *Middlesborough Eve.Gazette, 15 Nov 1991.*

Our picture shows Michael McKinnie of Whippingham, Isle of Wight, beside what seems to be the carcass of a kangaroo. It was found by his children, in late February, in a copse on Alverstone Farm, Whippingham. Owner of the farm Reginald Thomas recalled a wallaby was found on his land, having escaped from Robin Hill, Arreton, but that was 15 years previously. *Salisbury Echo, 2 March; IOW Country Press, 6 March 1992.*

Something about the farm is calling stray marsupials. A large predator also heard the call – perhaps one of the large pumas and lynx we have reported in these pages. The wallabies setting up home on Exmoor – see story above – had better beware; according to our records, bears, pumas, cougars and panthers have been sighted there, as well as Himalayan porcupines.

MONKEYING AROUND

What looked like a rhesus monkey was seen running from houses in Cedar Drive, Kidderminster, near Birmingham, on the night of 24 May 1992. The next day, it was seen by an officer as he drove behind the police station. A search revealed nothing. The head warden at West Midlands Safari Park didn't think they had lost a monkey. (Kidderminster was the setting for several alien big cat sightings in February: see *FT64:45*).

On 17 June, people in Waunfawr, near Caernarvon, Gwynedd, reported seeing a monkey or ape cavorting on rooftops. One woman said she saw a 'gorilla' on the roof of the Bethel Chapel. It tore down a TV aerial before running off into the woods.

Two or three days later (our clipping is not accurately dated), residents in Tan-y-Bryn Road in Holyhead, Anglesey, saw a baboon wearing leopardskin shorts clambering over roofs. One resident, Lewis Pritchard, opened his door to find it eating food he had put out

for his dogs. "I thought of grabbing him by the lead", he said, "but then, remembering the ferocious reputation some of these baboons have and seeing his teeth, I decided to close the door again."

Police later caught the baboon with the aid of local coastguards. Gandy's Circus, in Holyhead at the time, denied all knowledge of the animal. "It's a hoax", said circus spokesman Binky Beaumont. "Our monkeys do not wear leather shorts for a start." *Kidderminster Shuttle, 28 May; Belfast Telegraph, 17 June; Liverpool Daily Post, c.19 June 1992.*

NETTING A DEER

Robert Dart, checking his crab pots in the English Channel more than a mile out from Dartmouth in Devon, landed a two-year-old roebuck deer after lassoing it cowboy style. He sailed back with his catch of 50lb of live venison, which he gave to Woodland Leisure Park near Dartmouth. A few hours later, the restless roebuck forced its way through a fence and escaped. *D.Telegraph, D.Mirror, 27 April 1992.*

TURTLE TALES

● Byrtle the Turtle, a 45-year-old California desert tortoise, disappeared from a tiny pen in Long Beach in 1982. Ten years later, he was reunited with owner William Ridgeway Sr, after he was found strolling down a sidewalk nearly 200 miles from home.

Because desert tortoises are considered a threatened species – officials figure as few as 60,000 live in the wild – a permit is required before they can be kept as pets. A decal bearing permit number 15567 remained glued to Byrtle's underside, and the state used the number to track down Ridgeway. *NY Post, 6 June 1992.*

● A colony of 34 rare gopher tortoises has suddenly appeared around Lantana Airport at Palm Beach in Florida and successfully

blocked plans for the airport's expansion. In what may be the world's first case of clandestine eco-transplanting to stop industrial development, a Florida court has to decide whether the turtles' arrival is natural or sabotage. Landowner Roger Lambert suspects his rival Owen Gassaway; both men want to use the land for fuel storage.

Gopher tortoises are an officially endangered species. They have front legs like shovels and rear legs like those of an elephant, and are particularly known for their head-bobbing during courtship ritual. They can live for 50 years and can eat a cactus. Hiring licensed biologists to relocate them can cost up to $10,000 for each tortoise. *Int. Herald Tribune, Guardian, 16 June 1992.*

● In early June 1992, a rumour spread through the small town of Island Lake, Illinois, that a huge snapping turtle had chased a dog that was out for a swim in the town's namesake lake. The scope of the rumour swiftly grew – first the turtle had bitten the dog, and before long it had eaten it. Water superintendent Neal DeYoung was called in, and snagged five large turtles weighing up to 45 pounds, but the big one, believed to weigh about 60 pounds, with a shell six feet across, remained at large. *New Jersey Record, 17 June 1992.*

The two loggerhead turtles pictured here were washed ashore, exhausted, on the Dingle peninsula on Ireland's west coast, 5600km from their usual home in the Gulf of Mexico. They were being nursed back to health at the National Aquarium in Bray, Co Wicklow, prior to being returned home. *New Scientist, 4 April 1992*

FERTILITY SEAT

Every time a new woman takes her place at till number 15 at the Asda supermarket in Widnes, Cheshire, colleagues warn that it is only a matter of time before the whirr of the cash register is replaced by the patter of tiny feet. A total of 24 women who have sat at the till have produced 30 babies between them. Some have returned to work after maternity leave, sat at the till again and become pregnant again.

The story began in the late 1970s when Ruth Holland of Wigan sat at the till and soon found herself pregnant with her only son Andrew, now 14. Carol Soudani from Ditton, Widnes, was nearly 42 with a nine-year-old son. "All the girls told me not to sit there", she said, "but I didn't believe it. It was a big shock when I found I was pregnant again." Her second son, Ryan, was born around Christmas last year. Karen Fazackerley, 35, from Widnes, said: "We had been trying for a baby for six years before I sat at the till. My twins Hayley and Adam are 17 months old next week so it seems to have worked." Lisa Main, 20, from Widnes is the latest beneficia-

ry: "I had a miscarriage and was trying again for a baby when I sat at till 15. Now I'm six months pregnant." *Evening Leader (Clwyd & Chester), Bradford Telegraph & Argus*, 2 July 1992.

● A famous 'fertility stool' in the Rising Sun pub at Ickford, Buckinghamshire, was taken in June by licensees Phil and Terri Hargreaves when they moved on because of increased rent. It gained its reputation after 14 village women, including Terri, became pregnant after sitting on it. American visitors flocked to the pub and 45 pregnancies followed. *Sunday Mirror*, 14 June 1992.

● Mandy Carlino, 33, found herself pregnant after

drinking water from the old mill in Kingsteignton, Devon, where she lives. She gave a bottle of the water to a friend who had tried for a baby for six years and before long she was also expecting. Another bottle went to newly-wed Carol Hoyle was soon expanded in front. Her secretary also tried it with the same result. *Sun*, 24 July 1992.

SPECIAL CORRESPONDENTS

AFRICA Cynthia Hind (Zimbabwe), Ion Alexis Will (Ivory Coast). **AUSTRALIA** Greg Axford (Vic.), Paul Cropper (NSW), Rex Gilroy (NSW), Tony Healy (ACT). **BELGIUM** Henri Prémont. **CANADA** Brian Chapman (BC), Dwight Whalen (Ont.). **DENMARK** Lars Thomas. **ENGLAND** Claire Blamey, Bruce Chatterton, Peter Christie, Mat Coward, Hilary Evans, Peter Hope Evans, Alan Gardiner, Mick Goss, Chris Hall, Jeremy Harte, Brian Inglis, Jake Kirkwood, Joseph Lang, Alexis Lykiard, Nick Maloret, Valerie Martin, Kevin McClure, John Michell, Ralph Noyes, Nigel Pennick, Andy Roberts, Paul Screeton, Doc Shiels, Karl Shuker, Bob Skinner, Anthony Smith, Paul R. Thomas, Nigel Watson, Owen Whiteoak, Steve Wrathall. **FRANCE** Jean-Louis Brodu, Bernard Heuvelmans, Michel Meurger. **GERMANY** Walter J. Langbein, Ulrich Magin. **GREECE** S.C. Tavuchis. **HOLLAND** Robin Pascoe. **HONGKONG** Phillip Bruce. **ICELAND** V. Kip Hansen. **IRELAND** Peter Costello. **JAPAN** Masaru Mori, Shigeo Yokoyama. **NEW ZEALAND** Peter Hassall. **NORTHERN IRELAND** Caryl Sibbett. **POLAND** Leszek Matela. **ROMANIA** Iosif Boczor. **RUSSIA** Vladimir Rubtsov. **SCOTLAND** David Burns, Stuart Herkes, Roger Musson, Roland Watson, Jake Williams. **SWEDEN** Anders Liljegren, Sven Rosén. **USA** Larry E. Arnold (PA), Mark Chorvinsky (MD), Loren Coleman (ME), David Fideler (MI), Mark A. Hall (MN), Michael Hoffman (CA), John Keel (NYC), Kurt Lothmann (TX), Ray Nelke (MO), Scott Parker (TX), Jim Reicken (NY), Ron Schaffner (OH), Margo Schwadron (NY), Chuck Shephard (DC), Dennis Stacy (TX), Joseph Swatek (NB), Joseph Trainor (MA), Jeffrey Vallance (CA), Robert Anton Wilson (CA), Joseph W. Zarzynski (NY). **TURKEY** Izzet Goksu. **WALES** Janet & Colin Bord, Richard Holland, Joe Kelly.

PHENOMENOMIX·

HUNT EMERSON ©92

FORTEAN FAN

MUG SETS

Take tea in style with our set of four Fortean Times mugs. Illustrated by Hunt Emerson the designs comprise of The Cats Of War, Drunken Bull, Falling Cow and Forest Fire Death. Black designs on high-quality white ceramic mugs.

CODE FTM - £15.00 per set.

BOOKS

FORTEAN TOMES is a series of facsimile reprints of early issues of The Fortean Times (formerly simply titled The News). Each book covers a wide range of fascinating subjects from feral children to spontaneous human combustion to UFO abduction.

FORTEAN TIMES 1 - 15
Yesterday's News Tomorrow **£19.99**
ISBN: 1 870870 263 400 page paperback, colour cover, illustrated throughout.

FORTEAN TIMES 16-25
Diary of a mad planet **£19.50**
ISBN: 1 870021 258 416 page paperback, colour cover, illustrated throughout.

FORTEAN TIMES 26 - 30
Seeing out the seventies **£14.99**
ISBN: 1 870021 207 320 page paperback, colour cover, illustrated throughout.

FORTEAN TIMES 1993 DIARY £9.99
ISBN: 1 870870 247 128 page hardback (250mm x 156mm)
The Fortean Times diary is the absolutely indispensible accessory for the well-prepared Fortean. Now you can have at your fingertips 365 days worth of obscure yet fascinating facts on strange people and stranger happenings. Each seven day opening presents a daily dollop of temporal trivia along with ample space to add your bizarre doings and odd anniversaries.

SUBSCRIPTIONS

If you have enjoyed this issue, why not make sure that you receive a copy on a regular basis? Order a year's supply of Fortean Times for yourself or a friend and get it delivered direct to your doorstep. And that's not all, every new subscriber receives a FREE Fortean Times t-shirt worth £7.99. Back issues also available (see coupon).

Keep Watching

So you think you know what a UFO looks like? JENNY RANDLE

No one doubts the importance of being able to indentify the many unidentified things people see and photograph in the skies above. In this extract from her latest book *UFOs and How to See Them*, **JENNY RANDLES**, one of Britain's top ufologists, focuses on some of the dramatic ways in which puzzling UFOs turned out to have quite rational explanations. The lessons learned will help anyone distinguish IFOs from UFOs.

I am often asked whether I have seen a UFO. This is a fair question and the answer must be yes. I have seen about ten puzzling objects in the sky that I couldn't explain at the time. However, 20 years' experience and investigation has changed the status of many such UFOs into IFOs – Identified Flying Objects.

By training yourself to notice objects in the sky and to observe properly, you too will find that most UFOs are in fact IFOs that have been misidentified and misinterpreted. For example, I once saw an odd yellow light hovering low on the horizon which investigation revealed to be the searchlight on a crop-spraying helicopter which was far enough away for no sound to reach me.

Nevertheless, there is a residue of truly unexplained sightings which defy attempts to turn them into IFOs. In my case, a trio of unusual lights I saw in September 1980 near the Avebury stone circle in Wiltshire has remained unidentified.

The best way to help people to distinguish between UFOs and IFOs is to provide clear pictorial examples of the sort of effects which are commonly mistaken for UFOs. These comparisons will also help those who might see something on a future occasion. In any case it is important to test your own experience against the many different kinds of phenomena for which it can be mistaken. If you *still*

think you have seen a UFO, read the checklist of important steps in making a record of your sighting and advice on what to do next.

Anyone can misperceive the most familiar objects. In space, UFOs have been reported by astronomers and astronauts who were looking at: stars, planets, the moon, meteors and space junk burning up on re-entry. The upper atmosphere also provides objects which can masquerade as UFOs: curious forms of clouds, birds, mirages, and odd reflections such as 'sun dogs'. Man-made objects – eg. airplanes, airships, balloons, searchlights on clouds, or secret military planes – viewed unexpectedly or from an unfamiliar angle are also IFOs.

Photographs provide some of the most important and controversial evidence in the UFO debate, so it is important to eliminate those for which a logical explanation can be found. Faked photos of UFOs waste valuable time and resources; and researchers, today, are quite good at detecting double-exposures, thrown plates, dangled hub-caps and cut-outs snapped through glass. Another intriguing class of UFOs are those which were not seen at the time but which are noticed later on the developed photograph. Invariably these turn out to have been the product of a faulty camera, film or processing, or an enchanting effect known as a 'lens flare'.

BELOW: The Japanese who photographed these dancers in Hawaii, in 1974, did not see the UFO overhead at the time. It only appeared after printing and is thought by analysts to be a film or processing fault.

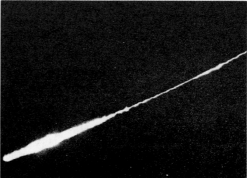

IMPOSTERS!
ABOVE: An airship or balloon, seen from an unexpected angle, or lit up at night, can seem like a UFO.
LEFT: The fireball of a meteor burns brightly because of the friction of the earth's atmosphere.

The Skies!

...vises on what you should do if you see one

If your sighting or photo fails to qualify as a UFO, or if you'd like to see a UFO but haven't yet, don't despair! All things witnessed are unidentified at first. Learning what is up there and how it can be misperceived is part of the excitement.

In *UFOs and How to See Them* there is a survey of the world's most UFO-frequented locations, a guide to the most common types reported, and advice on how to conduct your own UFO vigils. By regularly observing the sky, and perhaps by visiting UFO 'hot spots', you will increase your chances of a close encounter with one of the greatest mysteries of the space age – true UFOs. It is unlikely that the first object you spot will be a real UFO, but who knows?

Good hunting!

FT

RIGHT: Night photo of near-stationary UFO just above the horizon, taken in New South Wales, July 1975. Some say it is actually a setting planet.
BELOW: In July 1952 there was a major wave of UFO sightings over Washington DC. This photo was touted as a record of a formation over the Capitol building. Analysis showed that the lights were reflections of streetlights (at bottom of picture) inverted in the camera's lens.

HOW TO PHOTOGRAPH A UFO

● Today's pocket cameras are cheap and small enough to be taken with you every time you venture out. Practise whipping it out and getting a distant object in view, or tracking moving objects. For night photography make sure it is loaded with low light film.

● UFOs often appear suddenly and speed is all important. Video camcorders are fine if you can operate their complicated controls in time. Camcorders have the advantage of recording motion (and simultaneous sound) but the disadvantage of poor resolution compared with even the humble pocket camera.

● Better than a pocket camera is one which allows you to vary the shutter speed as you focus through the lens. Remember to take off the lens cap as forgetting to do so has caused many an opportunity to be lost. Better still, carry two cameras rigged for standard and telephoto shots.

● Try to get some scenery into the picture, in the foreground or background. This is important for assessing the size and distance of your would-be UFO.

● Useful items for skywatching: notebook, watch, binoculars, thermometer, small tape recorder, camera tripod, warm clothing. Note the camera settings and time of each photo you take.

● If you have taken a night photograph, return to the site as soon as you can and take another photo in daylight for comparison.

● Do not send your original prints or negatives in your initial contacts with investigators, or to the press. Have duplicates printed, and send those. Keep the originals safe for proper analysis by an accredited expert.

● Watch the skies for opportunities.

UFOs and How to See Them by Jenny Randles, is published by Anaya Publishers Ltd on 26th October 1992. It is available from all good bookshops or direct from Anaya Publishers. Send cheques to: FREEPOST (NW5630O) London NW1 0YW, price £14.99 (P&P free) or phone 071 383 3074 (24 hrs credit card hotline, Access/Visa only).

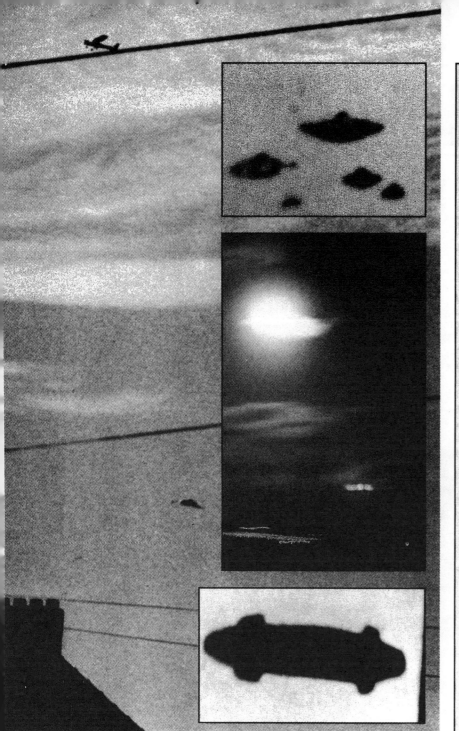

IF YOU SEE A UFO ...

● Make a sketch, immediately, of what you saw, and write down as many details as you can recall. Good headings are: shape, size, colour, speed, direction, duration, weather conditions. Ensure you record the date, time and location.

● If there were other witnesses, try to record their names and addresses, as this greatly enhances the value of a sighting. Ask them to record their account – as above.

● Do not discuss the sighting with them, until after they have recorded their impressions. Do tell them you might forward the accounts to an accredited investigator.

● If you feel confident your sighting is not an IFO, contact the local police, airport or airbase. It is unlikely they will investigate but can make an official record or pass the information to the Ministry of Defence or a national UFO organisation.

● If you are not daunted tell people about it. UFOs have been seen by millions around the world. If you don't want to endorse a belief in visiting aliens, you could say simply that you are seeking a satisfactory explanation for what you saw.

● If you are interested in the subject, read widely. If UFO books are not available at your library, ask for them to be purchased or obtained through inter-library loan schemes. If that fails, my book has lists of recommended books and booksellers.

● My book also includes details of reputable UFO groups, who will deal with you in confidence if you wish it. Some operate a code of practice to ensure ethical treatment. These groups are voluntary and funded by membership subscriptions – so please enclose a stamped envelope if you require a reply. Or you can write to me: Jenny Randles, 37 Heathbank Road, Cheadle Heath, Stockport, Cheshire SK3 0UP, UK.

● Keep your feet on the ground as you keep your eyes on the skies.

LEFT: Lenticular cloud formations, such as this one, are often mistaken for UFOs.

ABOVE: The photographer who snapped this overflying plane did not notice the UFO in the sky nearer the rooftops. It was simply a bird, unnoticed at the time. **INSET: (top)** This photo was taken by schoolboy Alex Birch in his South Yorkshire garden in 1962. For years it was taken as evidence of Adamski-type UFOs, until Birch confessed that he had snapped the sky through a pane of glass onto which he had pasted a picture of a UFO. Today's investigators have learned the lesson and are much more alert to possible fakery. **(Middle)** This spectacular picture was taken by Roy Sandbach over Stockport, Cheshire. Through the misty air the moon shines top left, while the UFOs, to the lower right, are in fact the lights of a hotel on a distant hillside. **(Bottom)** This strange object was filmed by Mrs Joan Oldfield from the window of a plane flying over Staffordshire in 1966. The film, showing the UFO appearing, changing shape and disappearing, was impressive. However, detailed reconstruction revealed the UFO to be an optical illusion of the plane's tailfin, distorted through the layers of thick glass at a certain angle of sunlight.

MIRACLE MAN

BOB RICKARD talks to anomalist JOHN KEEL

Since the beginning of the modern period of ufology in 1947, John Keel's writings have influenced the development of almost every aspect of the subject. Firstly through articles in pulp and 'men's' magazines, then through his seminal books *Operation Trojan Horse* (1970) and *The Mothman Prophecies* (1975), Keel boldly criticised the prevailing researchers and theories.

Two other books, *Strange Creatures from Time and Space* (1970) and *Our Haunted Planet* (1971) show him to be a Fortean sceptic by inclination, prepared to discuss and investigate the most fantastic ideas and phenomena while carefully committing himself to nothing except to challenge dogmatic belief on all sides.

He was born in 1930 in upstate New York, and still lives in NY City, where he founded a Fortean Society as a forum for discussion.

We caught up with John in London between his talks at the UFO conference in Sheffield and the Cornference in Salisbury, and talked about Japanese terror balloons, crazy UFO people, a lost photo of a pterodactyl, and his first successful book *Jadoo* (1957) detailing his search in the Far East for authentic miracle-men.

John Keel today

FT: John, you created a storm of controversy by suggesting that many of the classic UFO sightings from the late 1940s were in fact Japanese 'Fugu balloons'. What were they?

JK: The Japanese sent about 9000 across the Pacific towards the close of the war, carrying anti-personnel bombs and incendiary devices. The damned things were the size of a three-storey house and made of bamboo and laminated paper. It was the toughest paper ever made; damned near indestructible. They were masterpieces of artistic craftsmanship.

Most of them self-destructed or were damaged by storms. We have records of about 300 positive sightings and about 500 maybes. All the information on these balloons has been readily available to people. There's one historian on the West Coast who has interviewed all the Japanese scientists involved and he has complete records on all the recoveries and sightings.

There are still specimens on display in about seven US museums, but I can't get the UFO buffs to go near them. I think there can be no question that one of these came down at Roswell, New Mexico. The debris found in July 1947 fits the description and the timescale.

I've had three letters from people who swear they saw a *manned* balloon of this type and were told to keep quiet about it. Of course, a small Oriental-looking man in a flying suit is a classic description of many UFO occupants, so I've wondered whether this is how it all started. However the experts on these Japanese balloons say they were never manned at all.

FT: If one reached Roswell, as you claim, are there any records of them going further across the USA?

JK: Yes, one reached Michigan, and the remains of one was found recently, in 1990, in the Black Hills of Dakota. There are

photographs of a deputy sheriff being dragged into the air when he grabbed a rope dangling from one of these things.

It just happened that the one that landed at Roswell happened during the two-week period when flying-saucer mania was at its peak.

FT: Where do you think the Budd Hopkins school of ufology is heading? Does it have any future?

JK: Of course not. It's based on recovering memories of abductions by hypnosis, and this is highly unsatisfactory as we know from the research into claims of reincarnation. They're dealing with the unconscious mind without reckoning on it being a trickster.

FT: Why can't they see that?

JK: They've been told this a thousand times. I've talked to Budd about this, and he refuses to read a book on hypnosis. This is the man who holds therapy

John Keel keeps a wary eye on the sky

groups for abductees. If they start talking about, say, poltergeist experiences, he stops them. He doesn't want to hear about that. He just wants to hear about the 'Greys'. If someone has a dream about the Greys, that's interesting; but if it's a dream about poltergeists or ghosts, he doesn't want to know.

When you think about it, very few professionals have gotten involved with ufology over the last 45 years. I heard, recently, about a bonafide psychiatrist who has been paid a $200,000 advance to do a study of abductees. He has looked into only a couple of cases and now he's emotionally involved. This is the key problem; people become emotionally involved. Objectivity is hard to come by when you've been subjected to years of cult literature. Your brain turns to mush.

FT: You must get a lot of crank calls. Whispered hints of events that will shake the world ...
JK: They all talk like that. They even give a date ... "On June 10th, it's gonna happen, Keel." And I say "Yeah. Sure". The religious nuts in the States are currently predicting the end of the world in October [see p7], and when it doesn't come they'll say it's because they prayed very hard and averted it. Even some long-time ufologists, who ought

to know better, fall for this crap every year.

FT: How do you explain the great deal of interest generated by Whitley Strieber?
JK: First of all Whitley was already an established writer – a novelist whose books had sold in high numbers ... some had been made into movies which had made even more money for him and the publisher. So he had a great track record. When he wrote the first book *Communion*, everyone turned it down, despite his record.

He told me that something like 16 publishers had turned it down. Even agents didn't want to handle it. They told him that if he was smart he'd leave the subject alone ... that it'll ruin him ... that all the UFO people are crazy. He went ahead anyway and, of course, the book sold very well.

He was quite generous with the UFO crowd. He gave away something like $25-30,000 to individuals and groups, and they all turned on him, like the snakes that they are. Whitley is thin skinned and he couldn't take all the nonsense they wrote in their little journals. Finally he wrote a three-page letter to everybody, saying the UFO buffs were the meanest, craziest people he'd ever met in his life and he didn't want anything further to do with them.

But then he started his own newsletter on UFO abductions. He took subscriptions for it, and it wasn't bad ... Now he doesn't respond to phone calls or letters

> "... When you've been subjected to years of cult literature, your brain turns to mush."

on the subject. He showed us expensive x-rays of human heads claiming there were anomalies there, but that no-one would allow the surgeons to go in and find out what these little black specks were. You need a control study ... head x-rays of a thousand people who've never been abducted ... The problem is, they think *everyone* has been abducted ...

Anyway, Whitley has learned a bitter lesson from it all,

as so many other people have over the years. When I first got into this seriously, in the 60s – 1966 – everyone warned me that the people involved are all nuts. I said I'm going to do it the right way. If someone writes me a letter, I'm going to answer it no matter how crazy it is. Even though I did just that, it seemed to create more suspicion. No matter what you say, it's the wrong thing. "He must be with the CIA, or one of Them!"

Now when people, college professors and the like, come to me, I give them the same advice. Of course, they never take it. I always warn them to be very careful; UFO organizations, their leaders and their followers, are nothing but trouble.

FT: How did you get into journalism?
JK: When I was about 12 or 13 years old I wrote a letter to the editor of my hometown newspaper, in upstate New York. He thought it was very funny and called me in and invited me to write a weekly column. I was flabbergasted and thrilled. The column was called 'Scraping the Keel' and lasted for a number of years.

FT: Did your interest in UFOs come out of that period?
JK: No. As a kid I was interested in everything. My father was a compulsive reader and passed the habit on to me. I worked my way through the whole public library in that little town. When I was about 14 years old I discovered the writings of Charles Fort. He began as a young newspaperman too. This was before 1947, so when the UFO business began in 1947 I wasn't at all surprised. I even wrote a couple of columns about Fort at that time.

I remember going to a meeting on UFOs, in 1948, on 14th Street. Tiffany Thayer may have organised that, but I don't recall meeting him. All I remember is about 40 people crowded into a small room, yelling and screaming at each other about government suppression and such.

FT: Nothing much changes, does it? You've addressed many such meetings over the years ...
JK: I've always hated public speaking and I've given some dreadful speeches in my day. UFO audiences are often very

hostile – that's their nature – but Forteans are much more congenial. The UFO buffs only want confirmation of their beliefs, with no persuasion or argument ... and lots of anecdotes.

Most of them are cranks who don't want any hint of logical or scientific thinking. They can't deal with that at all. It's like talking to a group of religious fanatics.

FT: How did you come to be in the Far East and have the experiences you wrote up in Jadoo?

JK: In 1951, just after the start of the Korean War, I was dragged kicking and screaming into the army. I had already done a little radio in NY, so I was sent to AFN [American Forces Network] in Frankfurt. I immediately began doing Fortean things on the radio there, like a broadcast from Frankenstein Castle on Halloween. It was such a success that I had to excel myself the following year. I suggested to the colonel in charge of the station that he send me to Egypt to broadcast from the Great Pyramid. To my surprise he agreed and arranged it all, including the finance. We taped the show in the King's Chamber on some of the first clockwork tape recorders. It had great acoustics.

I was so impressed with Egypt. There is such a tangible presence of ancient Egypt. It called to me, as though my ancient ancestors were from there. It's magical what happens to you there. It's hard to explain. I decided to return as soon as I could. When I left the army, I was offered a civilian post at AFN. Here I was, at 23, with a big staff and in charge of script production for the whole network. I made enough money in a year to fulfil another boyhood dream, so I quit and travelled to India via Egypt and Baghdad.

I got as far as Malaya, where the British threw me out. Then I settled in Spain; I stayed in Barcelona for three years and wrote Jadoo. In those days the dollar was king. I had to return to the States to do all the publicity for Jadoo, or I'd still be in Spain today. I was on radio and TV quite a lot. This was the height of my fame. I was about 28 years old.

FT: Jadoo reads like the travel diary of Indiana Jones. On your

travels you heard the cry of a Yeti in Sikkim; you saw a wandering stool in a Tibetan monastery; you conversed with a levitating hermit, and a yogi who could pull out his eye; and in Cairo your life was in danger from illicit mummy dealers.

> "... I never got to see firewalking. If I had, I would have tried it myself ..."

JK: Travel writing is a genre that has declined since the advent of easy jet travel. Anyone can get to faraway places now and see things for themselves.

Travel writers, in the early days, used to take a little fact and write mostly fiction around it or make fabulous claims ... There was William Seabrook in the 1930s who went to Haiti and almost single-handedly kick-started all the interest in voodoo and zombies. He lectured for five years after writing one book. Another example is Richard Haliburton, who claimed to have swum in the pool at the Taj Mahal. You know, it's a reflective pool only, just three inches deep! Haliburton bought a Chinese junk to test the theory that the Chinese sailed to America, and was never heard of again ...

FT: He's probably castaway on a Pacific island with Amelia Earhart. For Forteans, the most interesting travel writing, like Jadoo, has a mystical dimension. Alexandra David-Neel's accounts of Tibet spring to mind, or Paul Brunton, who was the first to have claimed to have slept in the Great Pyramid.

JK: I met Paul Brunton once; he must have been about 65. He was almost upset that I had virtually retraced his steps, including going into the King's Chamber. It was as though he was afraid I was going to expose him or something.

FT: You learned a few simple tricks from the fakirs – how to poke a needle through your cheeks, and you were even buried alive for half an hour. You said that anyone can train themselves to do these things, even appear to read minds.

JK: Yes. I once met a schoolmaster who had trained his class to distinguish colours with their elbows. Apparently, anyone can do this with a few hours of training. For some reason the skin cells respond to changes in colour.

The janitor of a building I once lived in was a full-blooded Indian, and he was very psychic. I saw him sit in front of a ouija board and it would fly around by itself. He wasn't even touching it. He was a classic drunken

John Keel holds one of the more convincing UFO photographs, taken at McMinville, Oregon, in 1950.

Cartoon hero Smilin' Jack takes on a Japanese balloon bomb in this strip from the Chicago Daily Tribune dated August 7-8 1945. This appearance pre-dates the Roswell incident, which some advocates claim was the discovery of a crashed UFO.

Indian; he'd drink and go on terrible rampages. The talents are there but we have to find and develop them.

FT: A sceptic group in California started a craze for firewalking parties. A few minutes of confidence-building ritual then off they go over the glowing ashes ...
JK: I heard that at one of these, a smart-ass psychologist wouldn't take the few minutes of training, stepped onto the coals and was badly burned. He had to be taken off to hospital. A lot of people were making a lot of money 'teaching' firewalking.

FT: Did you see any firewalking on your travels?
JK: No. It's done all over the Orient but I never got to see it. If I had, I would have tried it myself...

FT: You have written – in Fate magazine and elsewhere – of your search for a photograph of a giant bird. Did you ever locate it?
JK: That's just it: many people remember seeing it, and no one has been able to find it. I don't remember the source. My feeling is that it was in a men's magazine like Saga or True ... In my mind I can see the entire photograph. A group of men standing in front of a barn door. The caption said they were college professors, but they were all dressed like cowboys. They were seedy types, some wearing top hats. Nailed to the barn was a huge winged creature – looked like a pterodactyl or a giant eagle or something – with a wingspan of around 36 feet.
After reading my original article in Fate, some people went

scrambling around in libraries trying to trace the picture. The story goes that the original account was in the Tombstone Epitaph, the Arizona newspaper, but people have gone through every single issue of the Epitaph without finding it. It's a real mystery, because in the late 1800s photos in newspapers were a rare innovation. Mark Hall now thinks the picture never existed, but too many people remember seeing it.
Perhaps it was part of a cigarette advertisement or some-

> "He took his group to sit on a mountaintop, waiting for the UFOs to come down."

thing, and that's why no-one saved it. Otherwise, it doesn't make sense. You know how keen Forteans usually save every little scrap of paper, and this is one that ought to have been clipped by somebody ...

FT: Speaking of thinking you've seen something ... Andrija Puharich, in Beyond Telepathy, refers to a case of a fakir performing the 'Indian rope trick'. The audience sees the rope thrown up, and the fakir following the boy up and throwing down his dismembered limbs. However the film record of the event showed the fakir and boy standing motionless to one side throughout the whole performance. This man had somehow influenced the audience hypnotically, and the whole event had taken place in their imaginations only.

JK: That's a legend that goes back to the 1800s, right after cameras were introduced. It's one of those stories which everyone believes happened but for which there's no evidence. Puharich heard this story from Charles Laughead. He was a doctor who was very prominent in ufology in the late 1950s. He took his group to sit on a mountaintop, waiting for the UFOs to come down; but they didn't come. This was the basis of Festinger's book When Prophecy Fails.

FT: What about mystics like Sai Baba? Do you think his phenomena are merely showmanship?
JK: I've known a number of magicians who've gone to study Sai Baba, and who've watched him very closely. Sometimes he'll produce a handful of ash – there are dozens of ways a stage magician can do this – and other times he'll open his fist and produce a jewel which he'll then give away, a ruby or something quite valuable. But none of them have come up with any real exposé of Sai Baba, even when they've said they don't believe the remarkable things attributed to him. No one has caught him using any of the common gimmicks.

FT: After all your years of investigation, do you think there are still questions to be answered?
JK: I think a lot of questions have been answered and people have not recognised or ignored the answers. You had a letter in a recent issue ... someone had observed it raining only in one spot in the street. I saw something similar in New York City in 1972, on the corner of 5th Avenue and 42nd Street. It is one of the busiest corners in NY, near the city's Public Library. On a beautiful sunny day, probably in August, not a cloud in the sky, I walked past that corner and it was raining on that corner. People were scurrying by but no-one was looking up. I stopped and looked around for 10-15 minutes, but couldn't figure out where it was coming from. It was not a burst water tower.
I have a theory about all this. Most anomalous phenomena are in fact demonstrations of Black Magic powers or something intended for just one or two people. It doesn't make any sense to the rest of us. **FT**

WEATHER WATCH

FISH AND FROGS REALLY DO FALL FROM THE SKIES. WE PREVIEW A NEW TV SERIES THAT INTERVIEWS EYEWITNESSES

This broad discussion of the phenomenon of living creatures falling from the skies is based on the forthcoming six-part TV series - *Weather Watch* - to be broadcast on Sundays, on BBC, from 1st November 1992, around 6:15 to 6:25pm. It features eyewitness testimony, and is accompanyed by a book of the same title. Author **PAUL SIMON** is a science writer and BBC producer.

So you thought the weather was just drizzle and scattered showers? Well, the British weather is in fact a ferocious beast. Hardly a month goes by without some weather record being broken, from droughts to storms. There are also bizarre phenomena that you hardly ever hear about in the media, many of which leave scientists scratching their heads to explain.

Not that there's anything new to all this weird and wonderful weather. Britain has been savaged by dramatic meteorology for thousands of years. Stone Age men probably commemorated giant tornadoes by erecting their megalithic monuments. [1] Whole seaports, such as the mediæval towns of Forvie in Scotland, Dunwich in Suffolk and ancient Winchelsea in Sussex (located several miles from the newer site of the present town) were all battered below the waves by violent storms in the 13th and 14th centuries. [2] The Thames has frozen over several times, and Eskimos once visited Scotland during the Little Ice Age, 250 years ago. Bad weather has caused battles to be lost, destroyed the Roman Empire and changed the course of history.

We're still threatened by freak weather today. Tornadoes wreak havoc; each year southern and eastern England is hit by up to 120 tornadoes. Sometimes they are as violent as the North American variety (of which hurricane Andrew is a recent example). One of the worst British tornadoes this century occurred in London in 1954, blasting a swathe through Chiswick, Gunnersbury, Acton, Golders Green and Southgate. Stranger still, people using the phone during thunderstorms have been electrocuted by lightning travelling down the wires, and balls of lightning have floated down chimneys and through windows into living rooms.

Even ordinary everyday weather influences the way we live, what we eat and drink, our dress and behaviour (the murder rate, for example), and affects our physical health by aggravating rheumatism, asthma and headaches. Bad weather can still bring commerce and transport to a halt, even in these days of sophisticated technology.

FALLS OF FROGS & FISHES

One of the most enchanting of many kinds of weather phenomena featured in the *Weather Watch* series are the showers of objects that fall from the sky.

It might seem utterly strange to think of anything other than rain, hail and snow falling out of the sky, but the reports of showers of animals, living and dead, plants and inanimate objects are so numerous, and reported from all over the world, that it is far from unusual. The most frequently reported are showers of young frogs or toads, usually living, which are seen to fall from the sky with the rain.

> "The cattle went berserk ... As I shook my hair, the little oddities simply fell to the ground."

Britain has been blessed with a bewildering variety of these strange showers: flounder and smelt in East London in 1984 [see photo left]; small fish, tadpoles, pond snails, small frogs and pond weeds in Rayleigh, Essex in 1930; periwinkles and starfish (Thirsk, Yorkshire, 1984); young eels (Oxfordshire, 1960s); and many more.

We interviewed witnesses to many of these events, many of which, curiously, seem to happen in the West Country. For example, Mab Hollands, in Shepton Mallet, recalls that when she was about nine years old, a storm broke as she walked down a country road. "It was not rain. It was not hail, 'til I realised that it was soft," she says. "The cattle went berserk, and so did the dog. My own hair was heavy with what I briefly thought must be hailstones. As I shook my hair, the little oddities simply fell to the ground." The 'oddities' were frogs. The terrified cows stampeded across the field.

Ron Langton of Canning Town, London, displays some of the fish that came down in a storm on the night of 27 May 1984. [3]

At Trowbridge, an open air swimming pool became the target for thousands of falling frogs in 1939 and was reported in the *Times*. The incident is also remarkable in the annals of freak showers because so many witnesses saw it happen. Many of these witnesses, who were children at the time, recall the event vividly. The day had been overcast and thundery, when the sky opened. "It was a job to walk on the path without treading on them," remembers one woman.

The same area has seen similar incidents since then. A few years ago, a group of mature students from Chippenham saw a shower of tadpoles; and at Stroud pink frogs fell [4]. Other accounts speak of hundreds of tiny frogs blanketing the ground after a downpour. It is well-known that small frogs can emerge from cover in great numbers after a rain shower and this has to be an explanation for some of the events. However, this does not account for other cases in which fish are found on a roof, as happened at Ron Langton's house in Canning Town, East London. In Ron's case the small flatfish could only have come down during the heavy rain the previous night. [3]

There are probably many cases which go unreported, simply because eyewitnesses ignore or forget what they've seen, or keep quiet for fear of ridicule. Mrs Sylvia Mowday was a classic example of this reticence. In June 1954, she took her son Timothy, 11, and daughter Mary, 4, to see a naval exhibition in a park in Sutton Coldfield. The day was overcast and started raining heavily, so they ran to a nearby tree for shelter. They were astonished to notice thousands of thumbnail-sized frogs coming down with the torrential rain.

"I thought it was hail, but my son suddenly said it isn't hail, Mum. They're frogs, baby frogs," says Mrs Mowday. "There were literally thousands of them. When we looked up we could see them. They covered our shoulders and umbrellas. This went on for about five minutes, but afterwards we were afraid to move in case we trod on them." Sylvia noticed other people running for cover in the park, but apparently they did not notice the frog fall. She wrote to the local paper appealing for other witnesses to come forward and corroborate her memory of the event, but didn't receive a single reply to what could have been the largest number of witnesses to a single shower of frogs. [5]

SHOWERS OF SEEDS

Besides frogs, there are other types of showers which are even more mysterious. On 13 March 1977, as Alfred Osborne and his wife returned home from a church service, they heard a clicking sound. Suddenly, hundreds of hazelnuts fell down from a practically clear sky, bouncing off cars. [6] Part of the puzzle is where the fresh ripe

> "They covered our shoulders and umbrellas. This went on for about five minutes, but afterwards we were afraid to move in case we trod on them."

hazelnuts could have come from in mid-March, because, in Britain, they don't mature until late summer.

Strangest of all is the story of Roland Moody of Southampton, who was sitting in his conservatory on the morning of 12 February 1979, when he heard a "swooshing" sound on the glass roof and looked up to see a cascade of seeds hitting the house and garden. The seeds were of mustard and cress, and was followed by a few more falls of seeds which smothered the garden as well. The next day there were further showers of haricot beans and broad bean seeds [see photo on next page]. All of these seeds later germinated into healthy plants.

Roland felt that the seeds may have been carried in a whirlwind from the docks just a few miles away, where seeds are unloaded from containers for packaging. But questions arise: why should they have fallen over just the Moodys house and that of their neighbour, and what kind of whirlwind visits the same place two days running?

Whirlwinds also pick up straw from fields. In Wiltshire this July, there was a puzzling rain of straw over a wide area. The puzzle was solved when a local head bailiff, a Mr Hudson, said he saw straw being sucked

A frog rain depicted on the cover of *Fate Magazine* for May 1958. For Mrs Mowday and her children a similar experience was full of wonder and anxiety.

THE DAY IT RAINED FROGS

FATE
PDC

UFO Solution—
The Gravity Drive?
—MAX MILLER

May 1958   35c

The Mystic Religion Of Zoroaster

NOTES

1 - see *The Stonehenge Solution* by Terence Meaden, reviewed in FT last issue.

2 - see Nigel Pennick's *Lost Lands and Sunken Cities* (Fortean Tomes, 1987).

3 - see report in FT42:28-30.

4 - see report in FT51:14.

5 - see reports in FT1:8 and FT3:10.

6 - see the Bristol *Evening Post* 14 March 1977.

Roland Moody with some of the many kinds of seeds that fell on his house in Southampton over several days in February 1979. He cultivated them as a heaven-sent supply of fresh vegetables.

up from a field by a vortex which then flew off. This was no isolated incident as local papers, this summer, have carried similar stories (see page 9 this issue).

SCIENTIFIC EXPLANATIONS

The most likely explanation for most weird showers points to whirlwinds and waterspouts which scoop up frogs or fishes from ponds, lakes or the sea, carrying them for miles and dumping them on land. But why aren't the rest of their habitat - the stones, weeds and other similar-sized creatures - rained down with the animals? Perhaps the vortex of a waterspout and the thundercloud above it simply drop materials too large for it to carry, or carry the smaller items further on?

Another possibility is that the objects are lifted by powerful winds in distant countries and carried here in the upper atmosphere. This has been proposed by Ian Darling, a naturalist from Slimbridge in Gloucestershire. He has a report from North Africa of pink frogs being lifted into the air by strong winds on the fertile edge of the Moroccan desert, and he suggests that this could account for the frogs deposited on Stroud a few years ago and similar falls

> "Mrs Couch was out in the yard at the time making soap, when meat began to fall around her like huge snowflakes."

elsewhere in Europe. [4]

The appeal of this explanation is that two or three times a year sand from the Sahara does indeed fall on Britain. We tend not to notice it because the fine dust is washed away immediately by the rain it falls with. Ian Darling claims that following strong winds during 1987-88 there were several incidents of both frog rains and falls of red Saharan dust. It is conceivable that winds strong enough to transport sand great distances might also be able to carry small frogs, although their relative sizes must be taken into account.

MANNA FROM HEAVEN?

There is nothing new to these reports. Throughout history stories persist of things showering from the sky: for example, as reported by Athanasius, in the fourth century AD, a fall of fishes that lasted three days in the Chersonesus region of Greece. The creatures were in such numbers that "the roads were blocked, people were unable to open their front doors and the town stank for weeks."

When the Children of Israel collected manna from heaven during their exodus from Egypt, was the miracle meteorological rather than supernatural? There's a surprising amount of controversy about the subject, given the age of the original events. Some say the manna was sticky sweet sap oozing from tamarisk shrubs which grow in the Wadi Fairon area where the Israelites are believed to have camped.

Others say that the phenomenon of showers of edible lichen is well known in the Middle East. There are several accounts of people experiencing a shower of a rather flaky lichen called *Lecanora esculenta* which they found to be quite edible. It can be peeled off the rocks it grows on easily and rolls around in the wind. For example, in 1829, during the war between Prussia and Russia, there was a severe famine in the Caspian region. One day, during a violent wind, parts of the countryside became covered with the lichen, which witnesses said "fell down from heaven". Seeing their sheep eat it happily, the locals ground the lichen into flour and made bread from it.

Possibly the most exotic form of 'manna' to fall to earth was the pieces of meat which fell on the backyard of a house in Kentucky in 1876. The local press account says that "Mrs Couch was out in the yard at the time making soap, when meat which looked like beef began to fall around her. The sky was perfectly clear at the time, and she said it fell like large snow flakes." According to Mrs Couch the meat was perfectly fresh and tasked like mutton or venison.

Perhaps the Biblical plagues heaped on the Egyptians - the showers of frogs and blood - were true after all. They are similar to phenomena still experienced today which are real meteorological events. **FT**

THE MARTIAN SPHINX

For nearly a decade The Mars Mission, headed by Richard Hoagland, has been investigating evidence of huge, artificial structures in the northern desert region of Mars. Earlier this year Hoagland presented his findings to NASA, in the hope of ensuring that the latest Mars probe would photograph the area in more detail. TIM COLEMAN presents an exclusive preview of Hoagland's findings and theorises that their extraterrestrial geometry reveals clues left by an alien civilisation.

An independent team of researchers called The Mars Mission have been investigating the possibility that various anomalous landforms in Cydonia – the northern desert region of Mars – may be the first concrete evidence of an alien civilisation.

The evidence comes from two photographs taken from 1,162 miles above the Martian surface by the unmanned Viking I in 1976. The frames reveal a 1,500ft high, one-mile-long stone outcrop which appears to have been carved into a human face. Adjacent to this are various other artificial-looking objects, the most striking being a gigantic five-sided pyramid.

In February 1992, Richard Hoagland, head of the Mars Mission, was invited to the United Nations to present a summary of the Mission's findings. The Dag Hammarskjold Library auditorium was twice packed out as Hoagland proposed that, not only were the structures of Cydonia evidence of an alien civilization, but that the ground plan and geometry of this area contains an encoded message. Having unravelled part of this puzzle, Hoagland is convinced that the geometry of Cydonia is linked to various ancient sacred sites on Earth.

BACKGROUND TO THE DISCOVERIES

The frame containing the face on Mars was presented by NASA to assembled journalists in 1976. When several people inquired about the Face, they were told that it was a trick of light and shadow. Three years later, two computer imaging experts, Vincent DiPietro and Gregory Molenaar, chanced upon the picture in the National Space Library. Amazed at the sight of the Face, they searched through 60,000 frames to find a second image of the Face at a different sun angle. This prompted them to produce a series of computer-enhanced images. It was this work and subsequent persuasive enhancements by Mark Carlotto that provided the raw material for Hoagland and his associates to develop their theories.

THE DISCOVERY OF ALIEN ARCHITECTURE

In 1983, Hoagland, then working as a NASA consultant, was given the images of Cydonia for analysis. He studied the relationship between the Face and associated landforms such as the group of polyhedral objects, later termed the City, the giant five-sided pyramid, called the D&M (after DiPietro & Molenaar), a huge ridge-like structure called the Cliff and a large mound called the Tholus.

Thinking of the astronomical alignments of some prehistoric sites on Earth, Hoagland wondered whether the objects in Cydonia might be aligned similarly to the Sun or key stars. He projected eight lines from the centre of the City out to the eastern horizon. He found that an observer at the City Square would have seen the Summer Solstice sun rise directly over the eyes of the Face approximately half a million years ago, giving a possible date of construction. This led to the discovery of the Cliff as it lay directly in the path of the projected sightlines which, when extended through the eyes and chin of the Face, fall exactly at either end. Hoagland then linked the whole complex with interconnecting lines and found that the resulting geometry of the groundplan was not random, but contained repeated examples of universal mathematical constants which could hardly appear by chance in the natural topography. The initial announcement about these alignments was made in February 1984.

CYDONIA'S ROSETTA STONE

Hoagland believed that the Face was carved to attract attention. The shape of a human face is always instantly recognisable even though it may be part of a blurry photograph; this would naturally lead to closer scrutiny. The real message, he suspected, was encoded in the interrelationships of the surrounding objects. He reasoned that no-one would go to so much trouble unless that message was of great significance.

By analysing the spatial and angular relationships between the main Cydonian landforms, Hoagland discovered that three universal constants were repeatedly generated: *phi* (the golden section), π and *e* (the base of natural logarithms). He enlisted the help of Erol Torun, a cartographer working at the US Defence Mapping Agency, who discovered that the internal geometry of the five-sided pyramid, the D&M, revealed the same universal constants.

Furthermore, the latitude of the D&M on the planet seems to have been carefully chosen: 40.868° N (+/- 0.017°), which is the tangent of *e* divided by π: a further example of the Cydonian geometry generating these significant irrational numbers.

More evidence supporting the intelligence theory was obtained when the area containing Cydonia was recently surveyed using Fractal Analysis. This technique was successfully employed in the Gulf War to locate Iraqi tanks camouflaged in the desert, since it distinguishes between constructed objects and natural topography. The analysis of Cydonia showed that the Face was the most unnatural object in an area of 4,000 square miles.

TETRAHEDRAL GEOMETRY: KEY TO CYDONIA

After much number crunching, the team concluded that whoever positioned these objects was indicating something about the three-sided pyramid, or tetrahedron. This is hinted at by the tetrahedral structure embedded on the rim of the crater and the angle between this and the Cliff which is 19.5°. The continual repetition of this angle in other parts of the complex led Hoagland to believe it was a significant part of the message. But why 19.5?

The answer appeared to Hoagland to be elegantly simple. When the apex of a tetrahedron is placed on the pole of a sphere, its bottom three corners always touch the sphere's edge at 19.5° either above or below the sphere's equator [see diagram p4].

Hoagland looked at what was happening on other planets at 19.5° latitude, and found what he thought was a pattern. On Earth, he located the chain of Hawaiian volcanoes; on Mars, the giant shield volcano, Olympus Mons; and on Jupiter, the Big Red Spot. All these phenomena, he hypothesised, are caused by an upwelling of vorticular energy. This theory led him in July 1989, two weeks before the Voyager probe reached Neptune, to predict successfully that Neptune had a giant spot similar to Jupiter's and, further, that it would lie on 19.5° latitude.

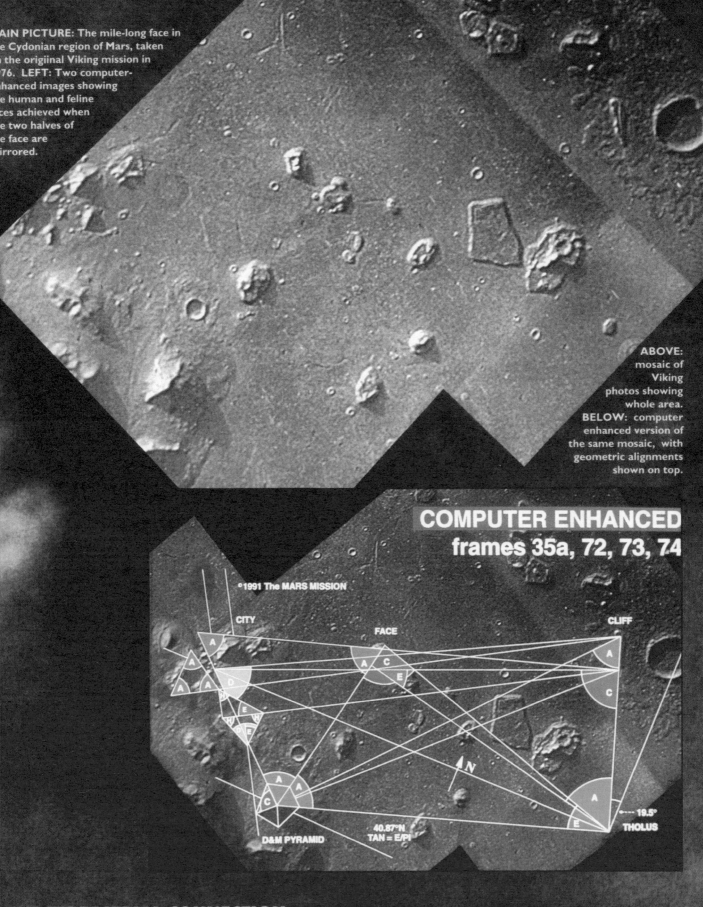

MAIN PICTURE: The mile-long face in the Cydonian region of Mars, taken in the origiinal Viking mission in 1976. LEFT: Two computer-enhanced images showing the human and feline faces achieved when the two halves of the face are mirrored.

ABOVE: mosaic of Viking photos showing whole area. BELOW: computer enhanced version of the same mosaic, with geometric alignments shown on top.

COMPUTER ENHANCED
frames 35a, 72, 73, 74

©1991 The MARS MISSION

CITY
FACE
CLIFF

N

40.87°N
TAN = E/PI

19.5°
THOLUS

D&M PYRAMID

THE TERRESTRIAL CONNECTION

The Mars Mission's most controversial point is the link made between Cydonia and various ancient sacred sites on Earth; specifically the Sphinx and the Avebury stone circle. [Editors' note: the association had been made early on: as *Fortean Times* said in January 1977 when we published a general view of Cydonia: "Are we looking at an alien Sphinx and pyramids?" **FT19:4**.]

The parallels drawn by Hoagland between the Face and the Sphinx are somewhat tentative. He notes that the cosine of the Sphinx's geodetic latitude (approximately 30˚ N) equals the tangent of 40.868: the latitude of the D&M. More persuasive is the discovery that the three pyramids at Giza lie on the curve of an Archimedian spiral, and that the position of the

Sphinx in relation to this spiral is e divided by π.

The most dramatic piece of evidence of this proposed link came when Hoagland, in his UN presentation, displayed two photographs of the Face composed by David Percy, the Mars Mission's English researcher. Each side of the Face was duplicated and placed next to its mirrored opposite. The two left halves revealed a hominid face, while the two right halves revealed a feline likeness. Is this due to extraordinary lighting conditions, or could the Face, like the Egyptian Sphinx, be a mythological fusion of man and beast?

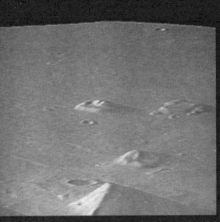

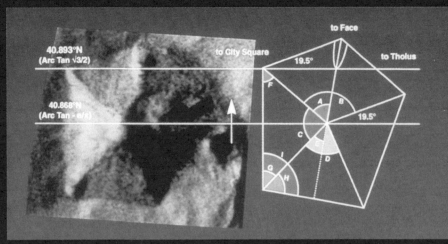

LEFT: 3D computer simulated view of the D&M Pryamid in foreground and the Face. RIGHT: Photo of the D&M Pyramid with diagram of Erol O Torun's finding on its internal geometry superimposed. BELOW LEFT: Avebury circle. BELOW RIGHT: Diagram of sphere inscribed with tetrahedronn. BOTTOM LEFT: Diagram by Rocky McCullum & Erol O Torun of the spiral placement of Sphinx on Giza platform.

AVEBURY AND SILBURY HILL

David Percy was also responsible for discovering another possible terrestrial link, involving the Cydonian Tholus, Crater and Cliff. Following a suggestion by Hoagland that the Tholus resembled Silbury Hill, Percy superimposed a map of the Silbury/Avebury site on a scaled down map of Cydonia. By placing Silbury Hill on top of the Tholus, he discovered that the Crater fitted exactly over the Avebury circle. Furthermore, a mound on the rim of the Avebury circle corresponded exactly to the tetrahedral pyramid on the Cydonia Crater. Could there be a connection between the builders of Cydonia and Avebury?

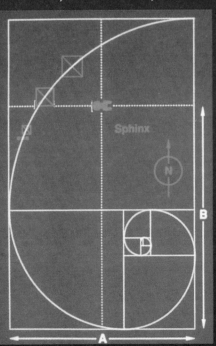

CONCLUSIONS

If one assumes that the Cydonian landforms were not caused by random geological forces, then they were created either by an extinct civilization on Mars or by a culture not indigenous to the planet. An indigenous civilisation seems improbable since: (1) no other complex of ruins have been located (although there are several other isolated anomalies); and (2) any atmosphere Mars might have had was probably lost millions of years ago, leaving insufficient time for life to evolve. A non-indigenous culture therefore seems more likely.

What most people will find hard to swallow is the terrestrial connection. Looking at the clues – the possible date of construction of 500,000 years ago, the fact that the Face is of a proto-human nature and the speculative links with ancient sacred sites on Earth – Hoagland postulates a variety of the Ancient Astronaut hypothesis. He suggests that the architects of Cydonia, having already travelled vast distances to reach Mars, were likely to have paid Earth a visit and may have been instrumental in accelerating human evolution.

Hoagland is convinced that the architects of Cydonia were benevolent and constructed the complex partly for our benefit, leaving vital information awaiting the day mankind had developed technologies sophisticated enough to reach the Red Planet and coinciding with the time that we would be in desperate need of a new source of energy.

19.5°

THE OFFICIAL POSITION

Is the Mars Mission's interpretation of two blurry photographs a case of wishful thinking or a great piece of scientific detection work? Confirmation of a Martian civilisation would have such far-reaching consequences that NASA has been under intense pressure to resolve the issue. The earliest opportunity for closer scrutiny is now under way. In September 1992, NASA launched the Mars

Observer probe, equipped with a camera 50 times more powerful than Viking's. Pictures of the planet's surface will start arriving back in December 1993.

Hoagland has given two presentations at NASA research centres, but NASA's official line on the Face has long been sceptical. However, reportedly at the urging of Vice President Dan Quayle, who is head of the National Space Council, NASA chief Richard H. Truly was recently sacked and replaced by someone more sympathetic to the Mars Mission's ideas.

David Evans, project manager for the NASA Mars Observer Mission, stated in politically expedient terms: "We will do the very best we can to get those pictures for the American people", but NASA has so far failed to offer guarantees that Cydonia will be re-photographed. The new NASA photographs will be digitally processed by the camera's designer, Dr Michael Malin, and not released to the public for six to nine months.

Hoagland, however, has expressed concern that if NASA succeed in getting pictures of Cydonia, and they confirm the Mars Mission's theories, they will not be released to the public. Hoagland is not convinced by that argument. "This is the most explosive issue of all time," he says. "If we are not alone, this raises profound questions which undercut all existing paradigms and institutions: economic, scientific, religious, social, philosophical and technological. Such questions would be highly disturbing for any government." In that he is most definitely right.

FT

The Mars Mission produce a quarterly journal, *Martian Horizons*, and have copies of both Hoagland's briefings to NASA and the UN. For further information, contact: The Mars Mission, 31-10 Skytop Gdns, Parlin, NJ 08859, USA. All pictures and enhancements by Dr Mark J Carlotto (TASC) Martian Sphinx painting by Nancy McIntosh-McNey

THE MARTIAN PLANETARIUM

Almost coincidental with the planning of this feature on the 'Face' on the surface of Mars, came a long paper from **ERIC CREW**, a physicist and Fellow of the Royal Astronomical Society, who is also interested in lightning phenomena. He has discovered a model of solar system bodies in features of the Martian landscape around the Face – further evidence suggesting intelligent life on Mars. We present this summary of his findings for the first time anywhere.

Prompted by the book by Vincent DiPietro and Gregory Molenaar, and their joint paper (with John Brandenburg) on the 'Cydonian Hypothesis' in *The Journal of Scientific Exploration* (v5 n1, 1991, pp1-25) I decided to take another look at my copies of the NASA photographs featuring the Face. I wondered if I could find any other features intended to convey information to observers from space.

My experience in plotting the orbits of planets on a computer screen in other studies led me to realise, after some trial and error, that several of the conspicuous objects in the Cydonia region did have an important astronomical significance. I found that if the Face represents the planet Mars (M), nearby objects represent the Sun (S), Earth (E) and Venus (V) to scale, both in diameter and orbital distance. There is also a Y-shaped object (Y), described later.

The relationships between the objects – see panel below – are based upon NASA photograph 070A13. The photo was taken at a height of 1724 km, and the edge scales are marked in millimetres, so that 1mm corresponds to 0.344 km. My co-ordinates are given in horizontal and vertical order. The distances between the objects are proportional to their actual astronomical distances to a scale of $2\pi \times 10^6$ – and the diameters of the circles enclosing each object is proportional to the corresponding planetary dimension to a scale of $1000 \times \pi$ (ie 1/2000 of the orbital distance factor). The exception is the Sun, which would be too large to be shown on the same scale, and which here appears to be shown at 1:500,000.

These ratios are of significance only in relation to a number system with a base of 10. If it is not just a coincidence, it suggests a possible connection to decimal systems used widely on Earth, indicating that the Martian mathematicians had a similar physiology (10 fingers) and ancestry as Earthlings. The value of pi – ie. the ratio of circumference to diameter of a circle on a flat surface – is the same, whether on Earth or Mars.

All these factors together add up, in my view, to the inescapable conclusion that they could not possibly be the result of mere coincidence, but are definite evidence of intelligent activity. Further research may reveal other artifices, and top of my list of objects to be examined by a future landing party is a symmetrical triangular formation with two equal sides. It is located at 87-81 on the photo (T in the diagram), about halfway between the junction of the Y-object and the Earth object.

As soon as I had set out these discoveries, the *Guardian* ('Science Diary', 3 July 1992) published an item about the search for radio transmissions from extraterrestrial intelligences. NASA intends to scan more than 10 million frequencies, but Professor David Blair of the University of Western Australia has a more elegant proposal. "On the assumption that aliens aren't dumb," he writes, he will search just one frequency. That of hydrogen is the most common in the Universe, but to avoid static he will tune in at that frequency *multiplied by pi*, because, he says, "knowledge of pi would be the signature of civilisation".

Evidently, in choosing scales involving pi, the designers of the Martian planetarium had the same idea about the future discoverers of their work. And they were right!

Planetary Diameters

S SUN – 84-35 – This appears to be roughly conical with a rather indistinct summit. The actual diameter of the Sun is 1,392,000 km; at a scale of 1:500,000 a circle enclosing the object would measure 2.8 km. On the photo, this circle measures 8.1 mm which represents 2.786 km. This is a good fit.

M MARS – 133-126 – This is the Face. A circle surrounding it on the photo is 6 or 7 mm diameter, corresponding to an actual size between 2.06 and 2.41 km. Working backwards from the actual diameter of Mars, 6780 km, gives a ratio in the region of 1000π, resulting in an actual enclosing circle of 2.16 km, or 6.3 mm on the photo. This is a good fit.

E EARTH – 150-55 – This is an irregular structure or formation on which another face appears to have been carved, parallel to the one at M but larger. The actual diameter of Earth is 12,742 km, which on a scale of 3142 would give a ground circle of 4.06 km diameter and on the photo one of 11.8 mm. This is a reasonable fit.

V VENUS – 135-23 – This is a regular conical structure with a terrace about halfway up. The actual diameter of Venus, 12,098 km, on a scale of 3142, gives a ground circle of 3.89 km diameter and one of 11.2mm on the photo. This is a good fit.

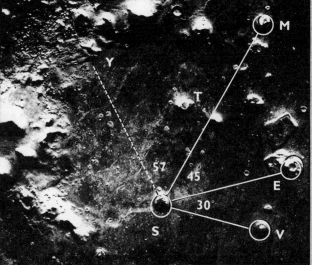

Nasa photo 070A13, with objects marked

Orbital Distances

S-M SUN-MARS – Actual distance: 228×10^6 km. Calculated ground distance, 36.3 km on a scale of $2\pi \times 10^6$ gives a distance on the photo of 105.5 mm; very close to the measured distance.

S-E SUN-EARTH – Actual distance: 150×10^6 km. Calculated ground distance, 23.9 km on a scale of $2\pi \times 10^6$ gives a distance on the photo of 69.4 mm; very close to the measured distance.

S-V SUN-VENUS – Actual distance: 108×10^6 km. Calculated ground distance, 17.2 km on a scale of $2\pi \times 10^6$ gives a distance on the photo of 50.0 mm. The measured distance is 52.5 mm, a discrepancy of about 5%. Venus is a very strange planet, and it is possible that its orbit has changed since the Martian features were made.

Orbital Angles

This is, perhaps, the most striking feature of these objects, and apply whatever units are used for measuring angles.

Angle VSE = 30° – ie. 1/12 of a revolution.

Angle ESM = 45° – ie. 1/8 of a revolution.

Angle YSM = 57° – The Y-shaped object at 45-106 on the photo may have an even greater significance for indicating the scientific ability of the Martian landscape engineers. The angle YSM may be intended to represent one radian – ie. 57.3°. The Y shape itself is suggestive of cloud-chamber traces of the collision and splitting of atomic particles. Its location at about ten times the diameter of the Sun object may therefore imply knowledge of cosmic rays from the Sun.

FT

SEEING RED

The Blood Miracles of Naples

Would you believe the dried blood of a 16-century old martyr could turn fresh air .in its glass container? Millions of Neapolitans do, several times a year. **BOB RICKARD** investigates this spectacle, alleged by many to be an enduring miracle. He confesses himself baffled by the two main issues: the authenticity of the relics and the liquefaction itself.

"Where else upon this earth's surface can the curious observer make sure of seeing a physical miracle worked at an appointed time under his very eyes?" – Father Herbert Thurston.

Every year on certain days, a portion of the blood of St Januarius (San Gennaro), kept in a special glass reliquary in the cathedral of Naples, is displayed to the congregation. As masses are said, the dark solid substance transforms into what appears to be fresh red blood before their eyes [see THE MIRACLE OF ST JANUARIUS]. Such importance is attached to this liquefaction by the Neapolitans that the proceedings are now televised and closely scrutinised for portents of the city's prosperity.

WHO WAS ST JANUARIUS?

In view of the scale of his veneration, it may come as a surprise to learn that hardly anything factual is known about Januarius or how he died. Research into the subject is frequently confounded by differing experts and contradictions between the popular but unsubstantiated life of the saint and the scarcity of any associated archæological or documentable facts.

According to tradition, Januarius is believed to have been the 13th bishop of Benevento (Beneventum), executed by order of Timotheus, prefect of Campania in about 305 AD (Smith and Wace also give 304 AD), during the persecutions by the emperor Diocletian. Together with six (some versions say three) companions, he was thrown to wild animals in the arena at Pozzuoli, and when the animals refused to attack, the martyrs were taken outside the town and beheaded.

The passio of St Januarius' life was formalised from collections of popular stories around the 10th or 11th centuries when it was first written down in Greek. The seven-century delay renders the narrative useless as an accurate biography; indeed, Father Herbert Thurston, arguably the most learned of British hagiographers, calls it "untrustworthy in all its recensions". The earliest tangible evidence of the man – a mention in the writings of one Uranius [1] – says that he was bishop of Naples itself, which if true rather discredits the Benevento tradition.

Knowledge of the veneration of St Januarius spread through the Holy Roman Empire, and was mentioned by Gregory of Tours (6thC.)

THE MIRACLES OF St JANUARIUS

The ceremony begins around nine in the morning when the relics are brought from their vaults and shown to the crowd. The congregation in the outer room is packed, standing and expectant, while the adjacent small chapel with the altar is reserved for the officiating priests and important guests. First the elaborate bust containing the alleged skull of St Januarius is placed on the altar, then the glass case holding the phials is placed close to it and a low mass begins.

During each mass, the officiating priest holds up the glass case containing the phials and rotates it slowly in full view of the crowd. Masses continue until the melting begins, at which moment, for the benefit of those further away, a red handkerchief is waved. The completion of the miracle is announced to the throng, who are then permitted to file past and kiss the case.

Invited guests have the advantage of observing the proceedings at close quarters. Rogo quotes a typical account from Dr Giorgio Giorgi, a physician in the city, who made a report in 1970 to an Italian parapsychology journal. He tells how he witnessed a fairly rapid liquefaction from about three feet away, as the archbishop held up the case and turned it slowly while invoking the saint.

"After about four minutes [..] I was disconcerted to see, just in front of my nose [..] that the clot of blood had suddenly changed from the solid state into that of a liquid. The transformation [..] happened suddenly and unexpectedly. The liquid itself had become much brighter, more shining; so many gaseous bubbles appeared inside the liquid [..] that it seemed to be in a state of ebullition."

The exposition of the relics of St Januarius, at which the miraculous liquefaction is invoked, is repeated 18 times a year. The first is held on the Saturday before the first Sunday in May and on each of the following eight days to commemorate the original arrival ('translation') of the relics in Naples.

The second exhibition begins on 19 September – the official feast day of the saint, celebrating his martyrdom – and also continues over the following eight days. A further ceremony is held in December – see FAILURE AND THE VOLCANO.

The relics are also taken out on special occasions at the discretion of the archbishop, sometimes for visiting celebrities, and, following the proper observances, the liquefaction takes place. This happened quite recently when, according to Reuters (19 May 1992), a private exposition was held for Father Andrew Bertie, the Scottish head of the Order of the Knights of Malta. In this instance, the liquefaction occurred within minutes; sometimes it takes longer.

and Bede (8th C.). Popular tradition says the relics of Januarius and his martyred companions were 'translated' from Pozzuoli to Naples around 400 AD; yet he features in a 4th century fresco in the catacombs of Naples – perhaps the same tunnels at Capodimonte which held his relics for a while – indicating the cult was already under way at that time.

In 831, during the wars with the Normans, the relics were moved to Benevento for safekeeping. They were moved again in 1154 to the monastery at Montevergine, and returned finally to Naples in 1497 to rest in the great Gothic-style cathedral dedicated to Januarius and begun 200 years earlier.

On the matter of the liquefaction, the early histories are silent (as far as we can tell) until the end of the 14th century; there is no mention of the famous miracle until 1389 when it is first recorded by an unknown Sicilian chronicler. [2] Before this time, it was the simple custom to bring out the reliquaries containing the skull and the phials of blood for veneration [3] the accounts of which do not mention any liquefaction .

Tradition, filling in for dull and scarce facts, provides an account of the origin of the blood-relic which satisfies the faithful. About a hundred years after the martyrdom (ie. in about 400 AD), some unnamed Christians dug up some bones outside the town of Marciano, near Pozzuoli, and declared them to be the saint's. It is astonishing to think that the whole edifice of Januarius worship is built upon so casual an identification.

Nevertheless, the exhumation impressed the then bishop of Naples, who ordered the relics to be sent to him. As they were being transported along the Via Antoniana to Naples, the century-old corpse began to bleed and a woman called Eusebia collected some in two phials. [4] Butler

over-enthusiastically backdates a regular annual liquefaction to this event, but on what authority he fails to say.

FAILURE AND THE VOLCANO

There is a close association between St Januarius and the volcano Vesuvius; about eight miles away it is practically on the doorstep of Naples. This association stems from the time of the saint's first translation; tradition holds that Vesuvius, whose eruptions were terrifying the city, fell silent the moment the relics entered the city. Some versions, ambiguously, say this happened at the time of the second translation or perhaps at both. Here is the basis of the regard the Neapolitans have for St Januarius; he is their patron and protector.

To commemorative these acts of pacification, the bishops of Naples instigated the December exposition, and a procession of the shrine to a chapel at the foot of the volcano takes place each December 16th (Butler has the 20th). According to the records, particularly successful suppressions of Vesuvius occurred in the years 1631 and 1707. Curiously, there do not seem to be any eruptions corresponding to the years of the two translations (400 and 1497 AD).

Superstition overlays the fact of the liquefaction. The failures of the December exhibition is so common that "no notice is taken of it"; but failure in May or September is deemed portentous throughout the Neapolitan region. Thurston deplores the fact that even learned scholars, such as Alfano and Amitrano, are infected with the belief in the divinatory powers of the blood, for they devote a whole chapter to the import of the variable factors mentioned. I understand that the failure of the blood in May 1990 was blamed for the low morale of the Italian footballers in the World Cup the following month.

In a way this is the least puzzling aspect of

Above: On the feast day of the saint, 19 September 1957, the Archbishop of Naples, Guiseppe Cettance, displays the liquefied blood to the congregation

NOTES

1 - This authority is mentioned by Thurston (*Month* Feb 1930 p129) but alas! without his customary reference. We can find six likely candidates.

In Edgar Wind's *Pagan Mysteries in the Renaissance* (1980) there is a Martin Prenninger, a 15th century German Platonist who wrote under the Latinised pseudonym Martinus Uranius. We can find three other Uraniuses, in W. Smith's *Dictionary of Greek and Roman Biography* (vol 3, 1864); a Syrian physician in 6th century Constantinople, who had a reputation as a pretentious wrangler; a 6th century Greek geographer whose work on Arabia was cited by Stephanus of Byzantium; and a 6th century presbyter from Gaul. A 5th century bishop of Himeria called Unarius rates a mention in Smith and Wace's *Dictionary of Christian Biography* (vol 3, 1882). Finally, a Uranius is listed in the *Patrologia Latina* (Migne ed.).

Only further research (which was not possible for this deadline) can determine which of these writers mentioned Januarius.

2 - Aradi has this date as 1329. Which of the dates is correct I can't tell without further research, although 1389 is more widely given. Rogo notes that the form of the ceremony used at the exposition was decreed by a bishop of Naples in 1337, which would support the earlier date. However,

The relics of St Janarius in Naples are kept in two separate reliquaries. What is thought to be the skull of the saint is kept in a silver bust (right) made in the early 1600s and housed in a specially built chapel. The bust is decorated with scenes from the saint's life, including his execution. It is interesting to note that at the bottom front edge of the bust the two phials are shown seperately. We do not know the date at which they were both fixed into a glass and silver case (about 12cm in diameter), which in turn is fitted into a large silver monstrance (far right) used as a handle.

As far as we know, the few drops in the smaller phial are quite unaffected by the invocations and do not liquefy.

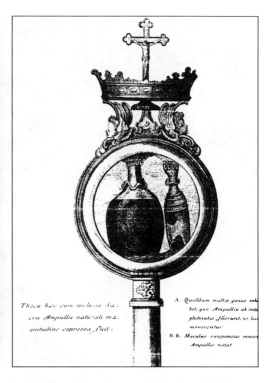

Theca hac cum inclusis Sacris Ampullis naturali magnitudine expressa, fuit.

A. Quoddam maltæ genus ashbet, quo Ampulle ab instiglutinate fuerunt, ne loco moverentur.

B. B. Maculae sanguineae minori Ampulla notat.

Rogo also notes that this bishop makes no reference to the phials or their associated miracle.

3 - One of the earliest records of this dates from 1140, when a King Roger visited the relics, but the account in the *Chronicle of Maraldus* is significantly silent about any wondrous phenomena.

4 - This original collection of the blood was referred to in 1695, when James Drummond, the fourth Earl of Perth, visited Naples while in exile with his master James II. On the 20th January, he was invited to see the liquefaction which was successful after three and a half hours of masses. He wrote a full description to his sister, ending: "The Roman lady, who had gathered it from off the ground with a sponge, had in squeezing of it into the glass lett a bitt of straw fall in too, which one sees in the blood to this very day." (*Letters of James Earl of Perth*, Camden Society, 1845, p102.)

Could this 'straw' be the same 'sawdust' referred to by Rogo (p191)? In 1956, the cathedral officials attempted to open one of the phials to remove some "sawdust" which they believed to have found its way into the outer glass (by a miracle, perhaps?) when the relics were packed away for safety during WW2. The phials are fixed within this glass case by a putty which has hardened, preventing any opening. "The project had to be abandoned when it was realised that opening the case would probably destroy the relics."

5 - Elsewhere, the liquefaction of the blood-relic of St Pantaleone, at Ravello, failed on the eve of the Great War.

the mystery. As Thurston says: "... with so large a range of possible disasters a case can be made out for the fulfilment of almost all prognostics of evil import. The curious thing is that in 1914 and 1915 the liquefaction seems to have occurred quite normally." [5]

According to the great tabulation by Alfano and Amitrano, the December liquefaction has never occurred in less than half an hour in the last 200 years. On 78 of these occasions, it failed altogether. But in the May and September exhibitions over the same period, there were very few failures. Celebrated failures occurred in 1527 (a severe plague), 1569 (terrible famine), and 1941 (the city was bombed). In May 1976, failure was blamed upon a rise in abortions.

SOME OBSERVATIONS

Father Thurston, at the end of his researches in the 1920s, professed himself "infinitely puzzled". He did not want to invoke a supernatural explanation "before the difficulties which stand in the way of such a solution have been fairly considered." One such difficulty is that we don't really know how 1687-year-old blood is supposed to behave. Earlier, Thurston had speculated tentatively about the role that humidity, light and heat might play in the liquefactions, especially after he accepted Prof Isenkrahe's suggestion that the hard putty stoppers in the phials and glass case may not be as hermetically sealed as many authorities still claim, but riddled with minute fissures. Even so, it is difficult to imagine how any earthly substance could perform so consistently, reliably and repeat

edly over centuries and not appear miraculous.

The records compiled by Alfano and Amitrano, and numerous historical accounts, show a great variation in atmospheric conditions in the exhibition chapel rooms. Little sunlight penetrates, and the light level is generally dim except, nowadays, for some electric lights and TV lighting. There is some heat from these, but probably more from the packed throng whose exhalations must add to the humidity as well. Aradi notes that liquefactions have occurred during temperatures up to 86° F; and Thurston notes that in temperatures as low as 15° F, the blood has liquefied in 10-15 minutes. David Guerdon's study for a French magazine in 1978 can reasonably say he found no detectable correlation between the outside temperature and the time the blood took to liquefy.

Explanations must also take account of other well-witnessed but inconstant phenomena which seem to violate the known laws of chemistry and physics. Sometimes the blood can take up to 24 hours to melt; it has occasionally liquefied in its vault prior to being brought to the altar. The volume of fluid in the large phial can vary by up to four cubic centimetres, sometimes filling the phials halfway, sometimes completely. Guerdon says that the volume tends to increase in the May events and decrease in September. Similarly, on two occasions when the phial appeared halffull, its weight varied by several grams; other variations in weight have been recorded.

The liquefying mass goes through changes of colour and viscosity as it melts. Sometimes a lump can be seen bobbing in the phial, and Rogo

> "The liquefying mass goes through changes of colour and viscosity as it melts. Sometimes a lump can be seen bobbing in the phial ... one witness claims to have seen this clot exude blood and later absorb it."

says one witness claims to have seen this clot exude blood and later absorb it. The liquefied blood sometimes bubbles alarmingly in its phial. Turning the phials has been known to fail to precipitate the transformation, while on other occasions the liquefaction has occurred while the reliquary was untouched.

THEORIES AND SOLUTIONS

We may dispute the authenticity of the saint's relics, but more important is the question of whether the event is a miracle – ie. a divine intervention – or the product of some natural but as yet unidentified process.

Since the 15th century, chronicles, biographies and travel diaries have provided us with abundant accounts of the liquefaction. Most of these are by honest, sober and intelligent eye-witnesses of all shades of opinion and degrees of belief, and constitute a huge body of testimony. Father Thurston wrote: " Few, if any, alleged miracles have been examined more carefully, more often, or by more people of more divergent views [..] and it may be safely affirmed that no expert inquirer, however rationalist in temper he may be, now denies that what is said to take place does take place." In other words – miracle or not – the witnesses of five centuries are unanimous in their view that what first appeared dark and solid is soon transformed into a fluid very like fresh blood.

The ideal step would be to invoke a liquefaction under laboratory conditions, but it is likely to be considered too impious a challenge to divine power to be permitted. However, in the past, the bishops have summoned the miracle for the private gratification of some notable or other, and continue to do so. Nor can they deny that a considerable proportion of each congregation is made up of the simply curious. Yet, still it liquefies!

If the purpose of controlled experimentation is to obtain data, then to some extent we have the next best thing. A detailed official account of each exhibition is lodged in the cathedral's library, and in 1924 a careful collation of two centuries' worth of data was published by two Neapolitan professors – Alfano and Amitrano. [6] Of course, this archive is useful only if you can accept that the clerks were capable of being honest and accurate.

Allegations that the Januarian blood is mixed with chemical agents, or even that it is not blood at all, arrived almost as regularly as the May and September liquefactions. In a recent attempt to explain the miracle, Prof Luigi Garlaschelli said: "The chemical nature of the Naples relic can be established only by opening the vial, but a complete analysis is forbidden by the Catholic Church." [7] The inference here is that the church must have something to hide or is afraid that exposure of a fraud will make them look foolish. However, anyone who looks into the matter has to agree that the bishops of Naples have cooperated in numerous tests in the past.

The prohibition on opening the phials is a reasonable one, arising from the risk of destroying a valuable relic with considerable historical and devotional value. The phials are sealed with an ancient putty which also fixes them inside their glass outer case. Not only is this old glass brittle, but the putty is as hard as rock. Any attempt to open the phials would undoubtedly shatter the relic.

Some scientists are convinced the substance inside is indeed blood. According to Rogo, permission was granted in 1902 for a light to be shone through the glass case. Spectroscopic analysis of that beam at the University of Naples is said to have confirmed the substance was blood, but adulterated with other unidentified substances. [8]

Prof Garlaschelli, of the University of Pavia, together with colleagues from Milan's University, publicised several compounds which looked and acted a little like the Januarian blood. These substances were thixotropic, that is they are relatively solid but liquefy when stirred or agitated; a familiar example would be 'non-drip' paint. Garlaschelli's team mixed chalk, water and common salt with hydrated ferric salts – the clincher (in his view) being that this latter is abundant on the nearby slopes of Vesuvius; and similar compounds used combinations of watery clay, beeswax in alcohol, and linseed or castor oils. This, claimed Garlaschelli rather sarcastically, raises the possibility that the Januarian relic was a forgery created by a mediæval alchemist or a painter who had experimented with new pigments.

Garlaschelli's team was not the first to propose a thixotropic solution to the riddle. In 1906, a Prof Guido Podrecci hired a Rome theatre and

> "Garlaschelli, rather sarcastically, raises the possibility that the Januarian relic was a forgery created by a mediæval alchemist or a painter..."

The monstrance containing the phials of Januarian blood, when not sealed in a protective vault for safe-keeping, is displayed in a huge gilt and silver reliquery

6 - Il Miracolo di S. Gennaro (Naples, 1924).

7 – 'Working Bloody Miracles', in 'Scientific Correspondence', *Nature* 10 Oct 1991.

8 – Aradi says: "Chemical examination of the substance has proven that it is blood." He must be mistaken; for reasons given elsewhere in this article, the Neapolitan authorities have never allowed samples to be taken. We can't even tell if it's human or animal blood. Even today's sophisticated forensic techniques have trouble identifying the components of old blood.

The contamination could be a by-product of the aging process, or something bottled accidentally at the time of collection (see also note 4 above), or dropped in during sealing.

THE OFFICIAL VIEW

The bishops of Naples have both encouraged and taken part in elevating the popular veneration of their patron saint into a cult. It has to be said, however, that this has been their choice and is not at the direction of the Catholic Church itself. In the early 1980s, Cardinal Corrado Ursi, archbishop of Naples, clarified this position with the following statement:

"The periodic liquefaction of the blood held in two phials, kept in the chapel of St Januarius in the cathedral of Naples, is a very remarkable phenomenon which has always aroused keen interest and, at the same time, discussions and polemics.

"This extraordinary matter, strengthened by rigorous documentation for at least six centuries, goes outside the ordinary natural laws and is for that reason considered miraculous.

Nevertheless, the Church, while consenting to the cult, has never made an official pronouncement on the miraculous nature of the event, leaving to scholars every chance for research, providing that the integrity of the relics is granted."

More recently, Father Peter Verity, a spokesman for the Catholic Church in England and Wales, said: "These phenomena have never been part of Catholic teaching. People have always been free to believe in them or not. The main thing is that if it helps somebody to come closer to God all well and good."

9 – A friend-of-a-friend-type story was reported in the October 1921 issue of the *Hibbert Journal*, in which a young priest from San Gennaro is overheard in Naples pharmacy asking for the usual mixture of ox-bile and sulphate of soda.

10 – Before him, in 1880, Prof Albin of the University of Naples invented a mixture which included chocolate powder! Even earlier, in 1842, Sir David Brewster proposed a compound of "spermaceti or sulphuric ether tinged with alkanet root." (*Letters on Natural Magic*, p302).

11 – Addison and Davenport regard the ritual as a "bungling trick" (R.B. Davenport, *Sketches of Imposture, Credulity and Deception*.) They don't have any evidence so this must be sour grapes; any "trick" that can survive thousands of performances undetected by keen observers is hardly "bungling".

12 – Thurston quotes an anonymous "scholarly Spanish Jesuit" who, in the 1780s wrote of an exposition he had attended: "A multitude of old women and others of the common people were screeching discordantly and not at all devoutly [..] Some of the bystanders, most of them foreigners, were contemptuously amused at the uproar; other, more restrained, were staring curiously as if they were looking on at some unusual chemistry experiment [..] The screeching, the free and easy demeanour, [..] the fussy complacence of the officiating priest, and the casualness of the whole proceeding put a stop to devotion." But even this disenchanted observer had to admit that "the closest scrutiny of the circumstances [..] could detect no opening for imposture of any sort..."

13 – J.H. Newman (later a cardinal) described visiting a number of Naples' blood-relics in August 1846. He wrote: "I understand that Sir Humphrey Davy attended every day, and it was this extreme variety of the phenomenon which convinced him that nothing physical would account for it." (Wilfrid Ward, *The Life of Cardinal Newman*, p188.)

14 – Thurston refers to the spontaneous kindling of the 'holy fire' at Easter in the Church of the Holy Sepulchre, but adds "this is universally admitted [to be] pure imposture". Addison (cited by Davenport, see note 12) refers to the spontaneous melting of incense at Gnatia, witnessed by Horace on his journey to Brundisium.

promised the public exposure of the Januarian miracle. He mixed calf's blood with a special solution which would help the clotted mass melt when heated. [9] His audience lost all interest when Podrecci's substance took more than an hour to melt over a candle flame while he shook it violently. [10]

Just how these compounds were actually inserted into the sealed phials neither Prof Garlaschelli not any of the others can say; but the out-and-out 'sceptic' will claim that it is all too easy to fool people with prepared look-alike phials, substituting them along the way between vault and altar, or during the public display itself ... but this presupposes fraud and collusion on a massive scale through the centuries by cynical (and dexterous) priests. [11]

To presume that it must be a sleight-of-hand trick simply because the effect can be replicated by stage-magicians is rash, unfair, and flies in the face of sound eye-witness testimony. Those who have examined the reliquary agree it cannot be opened without damaging it, so it is unrealistic to claim that the blood is replenished – (is there a secret supply of holy blood to be squandered in this way?) – or chemicals added to the genuine phials. If a 'mediæval' hoaxer created the trick back in the 14th century – as may well have happened in the case of more dubious blood-relics – how has the substance kept its vigour up to the present through so many liquefactions or performed so successfully under such a variety of conditions? As Alban Butler exclaimed: "The chemical secret would be not only a notorious fraud but also a wonderful discovery."

> "The inability to explain such things should not force us to the alternative of either denying the facts or declaring them to be miraculous."

THEOLOGICAL DOUBTS

The number and diversity of the blood-relics around Naples has been noticed by a number of sober hagiographers – see NEOPOLITAN BLOOD RELICS – and has given rise to doubts about the supernatural nature of their allegedly miraculous liquefactions.

Firstly, the repetition of the liquefaction at least eighteen times a year, says Thurston, seems "purposeless as a manifestation of the Divine Omnipotence" and is at odds with what theologians have called 'the law of the economy of miracles'. In this view the truly impressive and most theologically meaningful miracles must surely be those which demonstrate supernatural power once and for all time. Unexpectedness is also desirable in a true miracle. In the blood miracles of Naples, instead, we find expectation, repetition and a dubious multiplication of imitations, which must inevitably undermine their supernatural value.

Secondly, Thurston rejects completely any suggestion that the blood-relics "of St John Baptist, St Stephen, St Lawrence, St Ursula, etc, [..] are the authentic remains of the vital fluid which once ran in the veins of the historical personages who bore these names." Anyone who studies the subject seriously, he suggests, cannot help but agree that the authenticity of the relics is quite problematical.

Thirdly, in the case of St Januarius, it might be argued, that there is a thriving popular devotion and the sort of simple faith that merits divine encouragement. Yet, if the other Neapolitan blood-relics are not authentic, or dubious at best, asks Thurston, "how can we believe that the Divine Omnipotence year after year, and many times in the year, sets aside the physical laws of the universe in order to gratify the curiosity or the credulity of a handful of worshippers...?" How, in other words, can we believe God would "bear witness to a lie?"

Fourthly, many theologians have expressed concern about the lack of the sort of dignity that might be expected from a proximity to divine power during the public exhibitions. The spectacle of the almost frenzied tumult (both the curious and the worshippers) when the miracle is slow in manifesting is a far from edifying sight or experience, and one which God seems to be endorsing by his regular reenactments.

Another dubious element – at least to non-Latin temperaments – is the role of a group of elderly women called the 'aunts of St Januarius' who are privileged to stand close to the altar and lead the prayers. [12] I cannot determine their original historical function, but today they act as the saint's cheerleaders. As soon as they catch sight of the phials they begin to screech and shout exhortations which encourages the crowds to do likewise. Says Rogo: "They will even shout obscenities if the miracle doesn't occur quickly enough!"

These arguments by theologians address the issue of the validity of the 'miracles' more effectively than any put forward so far by the sceptics. The liquefactions, like many other popularly accepted miracles, are not endorsed by the Church.

IN CONCLUSION

When I began researching this topic, I thought it would be easy to marshal the facts, determine whether the relics were authentic or not, estab-lish whether the liquefaction was a trick or not, and that would be that. Now, I must join the ranks of the "infinitely puzzled".

The profusion of variable circumstances under which the liquefactions occur, and the characteristics of the relics themselves, baffled even the pioneer-scientist Sir Humphrey Davy. [13] This changeable behaviour would be expected if some constituent of the relics or the melting process is conditional upon factors not yet identified; a divine intervention, the theologians remind us, would be more precise.

It is probable that the origins of the ceremony lie in a long forgotten pagan ritual. [14] It is unlikely that the relics are the actual remains of the man they are thought to be of; but does that necessarily invalidate any genuine miracle (whatever that is) done in the saint's name? [15] Likewise, the true identity of the 'blood' seems to have no bearing on the fact that liquefactions actually take place. Too many qualified, intelligent and curious observers have said so unanimously; they cannot all be liars, wishful thinkers or deluded believers. I cannot accept the proposition of a fraud, perpetrated over centuries, by the bishops of Naples; and if the relic was a 14th century hoax (now a valuable antique in its own right), I have to echo Butler and ask, what is this wonder substance?

Ironically, it is Thurston the Jesuit who pleads for a philosophical position on this mystery in which "the inability to explain such things does not force us to the alternative of either denying the facts or declaring them to be miraculous." He has described the Fortean position of passive scepticism. **FT**

15 – In 1854, E. Cartier published his exhaustive examination of the relics of St Thomas Aquinas at the Cistercian monastery of Fossa Nuova, near Piperno. These consisted of a skull and two phials as alleged to contain blood and fat which frequently liquefied during visits of illustrious visitors, including pope Gregory XVI. The curiosity is that Cartier judged that the relics were bogus and had nothing at all to do with the saint.

BIBLIOGRAPHY
The interested reader is enthusiastically referred to series of articles by Father Thurston on the blood miracles of Naples in *The Month* for Jan, Feb and March 1927, and in Feb 1930. Considerable obscure documentation of our references is given there and in the following additional references:

Zsolt Aradi, *The Book of Miracles* (Longmans Green, 1957).
Donald Attwater, ed., *A Dictionary of Saints* (Penguin, 1965, 1975).
James Bentley, *Restless Bones* (Constable, 1985).
E. Cobham Brewer, *A Dictionary of Miracles.*
Alban Butler, ed., *The Lives of the... Saints* (vol 3, 1949).
D. Scott Rogo, *Miracles* (Contemporary Books, 1983).
Herbert Thurston, *The Physical Phenomena of Mysticism* (Burns Oates, 1952).

NEAPOLITAN BLOOD RELICS

Thurston claimed there were three classes of 'blood miracles'. There were post-mortem hæmorrhages of holy corpses and their relics; body which stays fresh-looking for many years; and liquefactions.

Up to the 15th century, the only known liquefying blood-relics were those of St Januarius; even then they only did so once a year on his feast-day. By the middle of the 16th century, the area around Naples boasted, according to Thurston's researches, "some twenty different relics [..] which were believed to liquefy on occasion". Space prohibits more than a cursory mention of the following - and alas! no mention at all of the liquefying milk of the Virgin Mary - but more details can be had from my sources.

First mention must go to at least three bottles of St John the Baptist's blood. (We join with Thurston in wondering how this was collected and identified.) One bottle was presented by Charles of Anjou (when he became King of Naples) to the convent of St Michael Baiano in 1265; but there is no record of it liquefying until the mid-1500s. The relic was divided between two other convents. A witness to a liquefaction in 1676 at San Gregorio Armenio speaks of it sparkling and bubbling "like blood freshly spurting from the veins of a living man". Its other half, at Santa Maria Donna Romita, would perform "every time" it was exposed. The third phial, at San Giovanni a Carbonara, was a dud by the mid-1800s.

There are also three phials of the blood and fat of St Lawrence, two in Naples and the other at Avellino. This last was seen by Swinburne in "continual movement".

At the church of St Patricia there is a phial of her blood and another of the blood of St Bartholomew; the occasional liquefactions of both are on record. In what must surely be a related phenomenon, St Patricia's also boasts a nail from the Cross, upon which blood streaks are said to appear every Good Friday.

The blood of St Pantaleone (beheaded or roasted c.304 AD) at Ravella is probably St Januarius's main rival. It was seen by Cardinal Newman in 1846, when it liquefied without anyone touching it.

Among other notable liquefying relics there is the blood of St Stephen, the first martyr; St Ursula; St Aloysius Gonzaga; and the 'modern' saint Alphonsus Liguori.

BLOOD FROM A STONE

Finally, I must mention an associated tradition firmly believed by most Neopolitans; that a stone slab at Pozzuoli, said to be the one on which Januarius was beheaded, reddens and seeps blood at the same moment the liquefaction takes place in Naples.

The stone - a marble block with a shallow hole on the top - is now enshrined in the chapel of a Capuchin monastery built on the site. Rogo says that, for over a century, the bishops of Pozzuoli collected samples of this periodic seepage, and that they were proved to be human blood by the Laboratory of Forensic Medicine in Naples in 1926. I have not yet verified this astounding statement.

NIGHTS ON THE

The strange phenomenon of sleepwalkers who take

HILARY EVANS is curator of the Mary Evans Picture Library and author of many ground-breaking studies of psychic research, the contactee experience and modern mythology.

Sometimes, sleepwalking on rooftops can serve a very practical purpose. In Zbraslavic in Czechoslovakia in 1940, thieves who had been robbing a house emerged onto the roof to be confronted by a woman sleepwalking on the tiles. Terrified, they ran off, abandoning their swag. (*La Tribuna Illustrata* 1940).

Joseph Fürst, of Hettstadt in Germany, played the tuba with the municipal band. However, concert hall performances and municipal ceremonies were not the only occasions when his fellow citizens had the opportunity to hear him perform; he also played his tuba at night, while he was asleep, walking on the roof of the house where he lived. For Herr Fürst was also a Schlafwandler. (*Illustrazione del Popolo*, 1932.)

Somnambulism is a well-known phenomenon, yet it is still not entirely understood. It takes place during orthodox sleep, not during dreaming REM sleep: in this it is similar to another anomalous sleep process, the *pavor nocturnus*, a nightmare-like experience which is, however, *not* a dream. It would seem, therefore, that both types of behaviour are biologically distinct from conventional dreaming, despite superficial similarities.

NIGHT MUSIC

Sleepwalking is clearly not a normal function of the sleep process. At the same time, it is certainly sleep-related: people get into the sleepwalking state *from* sleep, and when they have finished sleepwalking they return *to* sleep. But in itself it is more like the many altered states of consciousness in which the individual is unaware of his immediate environment, yet is able to perform a limited number of behavioral activities. Perhaps it is best thought of as a form of trance which is entered from the sleeping rather than from the waking state.

It is the ability of the sleepwalker to sustain a wide range of activities, though seemingly unaware of what is happening around him, which has particularly fascinated researchers. Sleepwalkers not only maintain their autonomic activities, such as breathing, but make purposeful physical movements in a controlled way; Joseph Fürst, for example, was able to play the tuba. Nobody has seen fit to record what

> "Joseph Fürst ... was able to play the tuba. Nobody has seen fit to record what it was he played while he was sleepwalking, but there is every reason to suppose he played recognisable tunes."

it was he played while he was sleepwalking, but there is every reason to suppose that he played recognisable tunes, probably the same that he played when practising his instrument.

He may even have improvised; for sleepwalkers have been known to use their minds as well as their bodily functions. In one celebrated case, a priest composed his sermons while in the somnambulistic state; that is to say, he could not only hold a pen, but he could write with it; not only write, but write *intelligently* and *creatively*. Moreover, when he had done, he would read through what he had written and make corrections which, it seemed to him, improved the style. (Diderot: *Encyclopædie*, ca 1760.)

Other sleepwalkers have talked coherently, to themselves, to imaginary companions, or to observers, and many other actions have been recorded. Clearly, the sleepwalker has command over a very great number of his waking resources, exercising not only his physical abilities but also his intelligence, his creative abilities and his powers of judgment.

All this is very remarkable, but it is, after all, only what the sleepwalker does during his waking life; the only thing that is extraordinary is that the actions are performed while the subject is in an altered state. However, there is more. In some cases, sleepwalkers go beyond their waking abilities: of this, Joseph Fürst is a splendid example. Not only did he play his tuba, but he chose to do so on the roof of the house. Why?

ALTERED STATES

The fondness of sleepwalkers for climbing onto rooftops is well-known. Over and over again, we read reports of people who unconsciously walk with supreme confidence in highly dangerous places, with all the self-assurance of a cat. The great danger is that they will awaken while in some precarious situation, and find themselves on a rooftop with no idea how to get down.

This would be no more than an odd feature of somnambulism, were it not that very similar ways of behaving are found in other altered states of consciousness. Here are some examples:

● A boy dreamed that he climbed a steep rock to steal an eagle's nest; when he woke, he found that there was indeed a nest where he dreamed he put it, and he realised that he had indeed

TILES
to the rooftops

made the climb while he was asleep – furthermore, others had witnessed his climb, and testified that the precipice he had climbed "was of a nature that must have baffled the most expert mountaineer, and such as, at other times, he never could have scaled". (Robert Macnish: *The Philosophy of Sleep*, 1834.)

● The Malays have – or used to have – a custom by which a girl of 10 or so years was possessed by the 'Monkey Spirit'. When fully possessed, the girl would perform a variety of physical feats, including climbs which she never could have performed in the waking state. (W.W.Skeat: *Malay Magic*, 1900.)

● In one of the many outbreaks of 'convent hysteria' which used to afflict nuns in the bad old days, at Cambrai in 1491, the nuns were reported as, inter alia, throwing themselves into the air like birds, climbing trees and hanging from their branches like cats. (J.J. von Görres, *La mystique divine, naturelle et diabolique*, 1845.)

● When an hysterical epidemic overtook the small French town of Morzine, in 1857, one of the ways it manifested was to inspire the children to climbing. On one occasion, 12-year-old Joseph T, on the way home from his father's funeral, suddenly ran to a pine tree and climbed to the top, where he stood head down, singing and waving. His brother shouted to him that their father's funeral-day was no time to be playing silly games; unfortunately, this brought the boy not only back to his senses but also to a realisation of where he was. He became horribly frightened and cried for help. His brother, with admirable presence of mind, shouted: "Devil, go back into this child so that he can climb down!" at which the boy reverted to his possessed state, lost his fear, and came down the tree head first in the manner, and at the speed, of a squirrel. (Hippolyte Blanc, *Le merveilleux dans le Jansénism &c*, 1865.)

● A Paris architect, when inspecting a building, would occasionally emit a sudden cry and "rush from scaffold to scaffold, up and down steep inclines, passing with a steady head over places where he dare not go when conscious." When the man came back to his normal self, he had no memory of what he had done. (H.C.Wood: 'A study of con-

Joseph Fürst, who played the tuba with a municipal band in Hettstadt, Germany, also played the tuba on his roof while sleepwalking. (*Illustrazione del Popolo* 1932.)

sciousness' in *Century Magazine*, May 1890.)

ATAVISTIC LEFTOVER

None of these behaviours is easy to understand, yet it is clear that there is some kind of pattern to them all: evidently, it is characteristic of some people, when released from the restraints of their usual state of consciousness, to take to the trees, the rooftops or the equivalent. When Joseph Fürst and his tuba take to the tiles, he is obeying the same instinct which drives those who, by whatever cause or for whatever reason, are overtaken by waking altered states. We are still left with the unanswered question, Why?

Unfortunately, nobody has put this question to those best capable to answer it, the somnambulists themselves, though it is quite probable that, either in their somnambulistic state, or under hypnosis, they would provide us with some explanation. Until this is done, we can only conjecture. My own ideas on the matter range from the thought that it may be an atavistic leftover from the days of our ape-like ancestors, to speculation on a psychological motive in terms of a symbolic escape from the limitations of conventional behaviour. Perhaps *Fortean Times* readers will have other ideas on the matter.

FT

OUT OF AFRICA

ARE THERE LIONS ROAMING FINLAND?
How could big cats be transported from the African plains to the frozen north?
SVEN ROSEN investigates.

The great lion hunt in Finland, said to have been the first in living memory, originated in a sighting on 22 June 1992. Forestry surveyor Martti Auvinen, walking in a remote wildness near Ruokolahti in south eastern Finland, 43 miles from the Russian border and 174 miles from Helsinki, encountered a lioness between 70 and 160 feet away (accounts differ). They stared at each other for a moment before the golden brown animal turned and ran. A expert in felines examined the spot and found many tracks and traces which fully confirmed Auvinen's story. Auvinen later discovered the half-eaten carcass of a young elk, which he believes was killed by the lion. (A bear, the only large indigenous predator in Finland, would have buried its victim.)

The authorities warned locals not to stay in the forest or walk on the forest tracks. During the week that followed, so many saw people saw lions in Finland that the media spoke of 'lion fever'. Officially, however, it was never a matter of more than one lioness. Newspapers named her *Elli*.

Where had she come from? No-one seemed to have lost one. The explanation excepted by most newspapers was that a circus trailer had turned over in a road accident on the Russian side of the border somewhere between St Petersburg and Vyborg, and a lion (or perhaps several lions) had escaped. According to folklorist Bengt af Klintberg, the Russian circus trailer was said to have crashed in south-east Finland, so there may have been more than one version of the story.

PRIVATE RUSSIAN ZOOS

The town of Imatra, about three miles from the Russian border, became the centre of the hunt. People there maintained that it was 'common knowledge' that many 'politruks' (senior communists from the former USSR) had their summer residences in the Russian part of Karjala (the province where the first sighting was made), and some of them possessed private zoos … In any case, the lion was supposed to have come from Russia.

On 28 June, a lion was sighted at Kekälemäki, 19 miles north-west of Imatra, and the next day, two 11-year-old girls, Elena Tahkokallio and Maarit Viljakainen, were swimming in a woodland lake some six miles north of Imatra when a lion came to water's edge to drink. They watched it for two or three minutes. Then they sneaked ashore on the other side of the lake, ran to their bikes and sped away. An exhaustive search turned up nothing.

On 29 June the Ministry of Agriculture and Forestry in Helsinki pronounced the death sentence on Elli, arguing that she might become a danger to the public. A team of hunters was selected to carry out the sentence, if frontier troops didn't shoot her first. On the eve of 1 July a conscript on guard near the border found himself face to whiskers with a large cat. He clapped his hands and the lion fled.

"SPARE ELLI"

The days following the death sentence saw the growth of a save-the-lion movement. Newspapers and politicians were showered with pleas to spare Elli. Petitions circulated, lion postcards were marketed and money collected. An entrepreneur offered to pay for transport to any reservation in the world, and a Danish zoo accepted the offer. The authorities agreed and two vets were sent to the border to instruct the hunters in the use of tranquilliser darts.

By then, however, it seemed increasingly obvious that there were at least two lions on the loose. According to local police, one was 'definitely' roaming the west coast. "We are absolutely certain about it", said Kjell Dahlvik, police inspector in

Kristinestad. On 29 June, a lioness was seen crossing the motorway between Vaasa and Pori, and the same (?) lioness had also been seen by a woman at a farm outside Kristinestad on 26 June. Police took these sightings lightly at first, because "dozens of lions were then reported from all over Finland", but on 2 July 'an expert in predatory animals' found tracks of a large cat, which he estimated to be between eight feet six inches and nine feet two inches long. Kristinestad is some 240 miles from Imatra, so it couldn't be the same animal, according to Inspector Dahlvik, who also pointed out that fresh paw prints had also been found at Imatra.

Suddenly, everything fell flat. On 4 July, the Finnish press announced that the lion hunt was called off, as experts had found no evidence that 'it' existed – no roars, no scratched tree trunks, no lion droppings. The paw prints, it was said, could have been made by dogs and bears; bears could have killed the elk. "Still", said one of the experts, "I would myself be extra careful in the forest." There was no proof that the lion *didn't* exist either.

Some time in mid July, Swedish radio news on station P1 said that the story of an escaped lion in Finland had been exposed as a hoax, as some paw prints had been shown to be forged; they were so inept that they looked like the footprints of an elephant! The story, as Forteans will realise, was not that easily wrapped up. Why did so many people see a lion and why did such a large proportion of the population get so emotionally involved in the fate of an escaped lion?

HERALDIC FACTOR

One factor is heraldic: the Finnish national crest shows a lion trampling on a curved sword symbolising the East, and brandishing a straight sword representing Western might – a reference to Finland's historical experience as a battleground between Sweden and Russia.

In the Swedish paper *Expressen* on 8 July, folklorist Bengt af Klintberg saw the lion hunt as a symbolic drama: "Everywhere in the industrialised world we hear rumours and legends of dangerous exotic animals which have found their way into our environment. Alligators are said to be in the New York sewers, boa constrictors in the drains of Götenborg, piranhas in the willow ponds of Malmö. From one country to another we hear horror stories of poisonous snakes in bananas and spiders in yukka palms.

"Perhaps Nature has always stood for danger – the opposite of the safe environment we have created for ourselves. As our idea of the world changes, so the dangers change. In the past we were threatened by trolls, werewolves and dragons. Today, the menace comes from the jungles and savannas of the Third World."

AFRICAN SAVANNAH

Or was it simply the *sun* that conjured up shades of lion? The month of June was the hottest in Scandinavia since the keeping of meteorological records began in 1756, and possibly the hottest June in a thousand years. Very little rain fell in May and practically none in June. The grass of Karjala, the province where the lion was first seen, was, as af Klintberg observed, "as scorched as an African savanna." The heat was suffocating.

While lion fever gripped Finland, a black panther, about three foot long, appeared in the Saar region of Germany close to the French border. On 3 July, police saw it on a mowed meadow close to a Püttlingen road. They gave chase, but it escaped. There was a vain search by hunters and police. The area had been a hot spot for alien big cats since a puma was

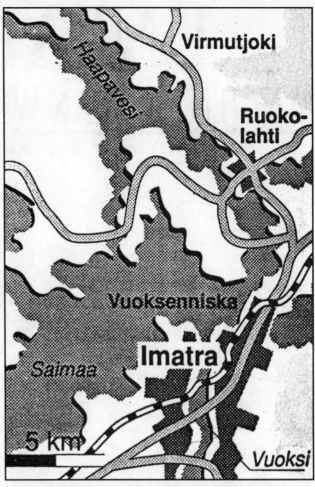

ABOVE: Map of south-eastern Finland where the lion(s) were sighted. PAGE OPPOSITE: Map of Finland by Olaus Magnus dated 1539, showing what appears to be a lion in northern Finalnd.

spotted at Merzig-Wadern in August 1983. The last report seen by our correspondent Ulrich Magin is from April 1988, when a hunter told police he had seen a 'young puma' at Schwalbach on Easter Saturday.

[Additional material from Philip Landon.]*Finnish sources: Ita Sanomat & Helsingin Sanomat, 26 June. Swedish sources: Sydsvenska Dagbladet, 29 June, 1+3 July, 8 Aug; Expressen, 30 June, 3+8 July 1992. Neues Deutschland, 15 August 1983; Reinpfalz, 6 April 1988 + 4 July 1992.*

FT

UNEARTHED:
ANCIENT INDIAN WRISTWATCH WIND-UP?

BOB FORREST reports on an intriguing archæological conundrum

I collect ancient and mediæval coins. Every so often something comes up which intrigues not only the coin collector but anyone who sees it. This is the story of one such something, lent to me by a friend who collects oriental coins.

On a trip to India, my friend visited an old bullion dealer in Lucknow and bought from him some very rare silver punch-marked coins. These are rather like little ingots of silver with a geometric design literally punched into the surface. They date from about 400 to 300 BC, though some uncertainty attends this figure. These particular specimens had been found in a hoard. That is, they represented someone's unretrieved savings from over 2,000 years ago, latterly rediscovered by some fortunate Indian, and thence sold as 'treasure' to the bullion dealer, whence my friend had bought them.

MACHINE TOOLED

One of the coins had a circular object embedded into its surface. Closer inspection with a magnifying glass revealed it was a wrist-watch winder, or at least something doing a very convincing impersonation of one! My friend couldn't think of anything it might be if it wasn't a winder, and nor can I. It can hardly be a natural accretion of corrosion, and it seems difficult to avoid the conclusion that it is something machine-tooled. Yet this is how the coin came out of the ground, seemingly having lain in the hoard for over 2,000 years.

My first reaction was that someone was playing a prank here – like those folk who superglue a pound coin to a pavement outside a café and sit inside sipping coffee while they watch passers-by struggle to retrieve the coin. Had someone superglued – or welded – a modern winder to a very old coin to "create an enigma"? Not likely, said my friend. The bullion dealer in Lucknow hadn't even noticed the 'winder', and in India the type of hoax one gets tends to be on an altogether grander scale: a mutual acquaintance of my friend and his bullion-dealer contact had recently sold (yet again!) the actual shield used by Alexander the Great on his campaigns in India …

Furthermore, these coins are worth a lot of money. If you are going to "create an enigma", you would do it with something a lot cheaper. To make an analogy, folk don't go round drawing moustaches on penny blacks just for the hell of it. For myself, I don't even entertain the hypothesis that an ancient astronaut or a time traveller lost his wrist-watch over 2,000 years ago; that it somehow got mixed in with the hoard; and that over the years its winder and one of the coins became fused together.

It seems to me that there are only two ways to explain the enigma. Either the winder is only something that looks like a winder and has lain with the coin for 2,000+ years; this is the theory favoured by the coin's owner. Alternatively, the coin hoard had been buried more than once, which is my preferred explanation.

INDIAN MUTINY

I hypothesise that the coins were first concealed about 300 BC. Some 150 years ago, the hoard was discovered and sold to the then equivalent of a dealer in scrap precious metals. In 1857, Lucknow was caught up in the Indian Mutiny and in those troubled times the scrap merchant decided to bury his stock for safety. Various bits and bats of silver were mixed in with them, including an old wrist-watch winder.

The scrap merchant was killed in the Mutiny and never retrieved his hoard, which remained buried for nearly a century and a half, during which time corrosion fused the winder to one of the coins. Then the hoard was rediscovered and sold to the bullion dealer, who sorted out the coins from the other bits and bats, not noticing the winder.

To me the winder looks like it has a machine-tooled edge, and though the ancients were certainly capable of engraving by hand the regular series of straight lines on the edges, the perfect circularity of the thing plus its smoothly domed upper surface suggest a modern origin. But of course, I'm just a musty old sceptic and FT readers may prefer to dream of more exciting hypotheses.

As a coda to this report, my friend said in his latest letter: "I suggest you go ahead and write up the story as planned. Leave a bit of a cliff-hanger, then maybe I'll clean up the coin, remove 'the winder', and hopefully then we'll know the truth!" Readers are therefore advised to make the most of their more exciting hypotheses whilst there's still time …

FIG 1: Photograph of the unusual coin showing the 'winder' attached to one edge. **FIG 2** shows one of the punch-marked coins cleaned to show the details of the design. The reverse of the coin is plain. **FIG 3** gives the coin with 'winder' seen from above. The winder is perfectly circular. Note that the coin is uncleaned, so no design is clearly visible. **FIG 4** shows the coin edge-on from 3). The 'winder' is domed and has a milled edge as shown. **FIG 5:** Photo comparing a cleaned coin with the version Bob Forest found.

The Hampstead Seal

Hoax!

In 1926, London newspapers reported that an angler had caught a young seal in a pond on Hampstead Heath. Charles Fort covered the story, and it wasn't until many years later that Fortean researchers tracked down the truth about the Hampstead Seals. **PAUL SIEVEKING** investigates.

FORT'S FACTS

The story of the seals caught in the pond on Hampstead Heath's Vale of Health was given by Charles Fort towards the end of chapter 7 of *Lo!* (1931):

In the London evening newspapers, Aug. 26, 1926, it was told that a mystery had been solved. People in Hampstead (London) had reported that, in the pond, in Hampstead Heath, there was a mysterious creature. Sometimes it was said that the unknown inhabitant was a phantom, and there were stories of dogs that had been taken to the pond, and had sniffed, and had sneaked away, "with their tails between their legs." All this in a London park. There was a story of "a huge, black creature, with the head of a gorilla, and a bark like that of a dog with a sore throat." Mostly these were fishermen's tales. Anglers sit around this pond, and sometimes they catch something.

Upon the night of August 25th, the line of one of these anglers, named Trevor, was grabbed. He landed something.

This is Mr Trevor's story. For all I know, he may have been on an iceberg somewhere, hunting for materials for his wife's winter coat, catching something that was insufficient, if he had a large wife. All that can be said is that he appeared at a hotel, near the pond, carrying a small animal that he said he had caught in the pond.

Mr F.G. Gray, proprietor of the hotel, had an iron tank, and in this the creature was lodged: and the next day the newspapers told that a young seal had been caught. Reporters went to the place, and one of them, the Evening News *representative, took along Mr Shelley, of the London Zoo. Mr Shelley identified the animal as a young seal and no tame specimen, but a wild one that snapped at fingers that were poked anywhere near him.*

So it was that a mystery had been solved.

But there were stories of other seals that had been seen or had been heard barking, before the time of the birth of this seal, in this London pond. One would think that the place was somewhere in Greenland. It was Mr Gray's statement that for several years, there had been, intermittently, these sounds and appearances. The pond is connected with the River Fleet, which runs into the Thames, and conceivably a seal could make its way, without being reported, from the ocean to this park, far inland in London: but the idea of seals coming and going, without being seen on the way, in a period of several years, whereas in centuries before nothing of the kind had been heard of, was enough to put this story where most of our other stories, or data, have been put. Mostly the opinion is that they should stay there.

London Daily Mail, Nov. 2, 1926 – "Tale that taxes credulity!" "A story of two seals, within three months, in a local pond, is taxing the credulity of residents of Hampstead." But there is the story of another seal that had been caught, after a struggle, dying soon after capture. In the Daily Chronicle *it is said that the "first mystery-catch" was still in the tank, in a thriving condition.*

SEAL HUNT

The truth behind the Hampstead Seals was not uncovered until Hubert Adamson, a dedicated Fortean and local resident, decided to investigate the matter in the 1980s.

Adamson, a correspondent of *Fortean Times* for many years, died on 11 December 1991, aged 78. For 45 years, he had run a surveying practice in Heath Street, Hampstead. He was also a sculptor, painter, poet, song-writer and wine buff. He spent countless weekends on Hampstead Heath, often on the sandspit running down to the pond at the Vale of Health, fashioning sculptures from pieces of wood he had found. The Vale of Health Hotel, which with the adjacent fairground, was once owned by Fred Gray, was pulled down in the 1960s to make way for a stark and over-tall apartment block typical of the decade. The block is called Spencer House, after the painter Stanley Spencer who had a studio in the vanished hotel (where he painted *Resurrection at Cookham*). Teas used to be served on the terrace, and drinks from the long bar below cases of stuffed pike and perch.

Hubert often talked to Fred Gray's granddaughter, Katie Bond, who until the summer of 1987, lived in her caravan on the fairground. Katie remembered well "the time of the seal". She and a friend used to feed it with fish they bought or caught in the pond. She also remembered Mr Trevor – "He lived at No 2, The Cottages", the terrace which still flanks the fairground. She understood that Trevor had caught the seal as

Fred Gray, the hotel proprietor who claimed that the seal exhibited in his hotel had been caught in the pond. He is pictured here (on the right) with some of his family, below the fairground site at the Vale of Heath around 1920. The child is his granddaughter, Katie Bond.

ANOTHER SEAL
CAUGHT AT
HAMPSTEAD.

"Fought Like a Lion, and Barked Like a Dog."

ASTONISHED ANGLER

Another seal has been caught at Hampstead.

An excited crowd saw it hauled ashore from the Vale of Health pond by an angler with rod and line. According to an eye-witness, the seal "fought like a lion and barked like a dog," and a few minutes after being landed died.

The first seal was caught in the pond last August, and now inhabits a large tank at the hotel. It has put on weight, being now half as big again as when captured.

Mr Fred G. Gray, of the Vale of Health Hotel, told a representative of "The Daily Chronicle" yesterday that the creature just caught was four or five feet long, brownish in colour and with a lot of scales.

"A HUGE THING"

"About the head it looked very much like the one we now have in the hotel," he said. "I think it was a seal, but, at any rate, it was a huge thing. The angler was the most astonished man in Hampstead when he saw what he had caught.

"He took it away with him, and I do not know where it is now.

"There is no doubt that there are other big creatures in the pond. We can hear them, and on a fine day, from the hotel verandah, we can see them through a pair of glasses, sunning themnselver.

A MYSTERY.

"Where they have come from is a mystery, but some people are suggesting that as the water of the pond runs into the River Fleet, which in turn runs into the Thames, these creatures may have swum up into the pond."

The first mystery catch was definitely identified by authorities at the Zoological Gardens as a small common seal. It has thrived so well in its tank that it has been christened "Happy of Hampstead."

ABOVE: Article in the Daily Chronicle, 2 November 1926. BELOW: View across the Vale of Heath pond showing the Hotel, taken in the early 1900s.

described in Fort's account.

Hubert wrote about his researches into the seal story in the *Camden History Review*. [1] He noticed that all the information in the press reports came from Fred Gray or his wife, and was bemused by all the improbable details. "We note that the event is said to have taken place at night", he wrote. "Now fishermen do camp here with their tents these days but no such convenient shelters were available in 1926 [..] If we assume that Trevor was a party to the plot, there would have been no need for the midnight knock on the Hotel door! The seal would have been smuggled into its tank under cover of darkness. But this is still a rather `fishy' story; to catch a seal one would need a pike strength rod and line with *live bait*, i.e. a live fish impaled on hooks, and this gear is only used *in daylight*. And how does one, alone, unhook a struggling seal from a triple barbed hook or hooks and then single handed carry a hostile, sharp toothed animal (about as heavy as an Alsatian) uphill to the Hotel?"

QUEER FISH

The following item appeared in the local *Hampstead and Highgate Express* on 26 August 1926:

QUEER FISH

The landlady of a well-known local hostelry, the wife of a very successful showman, has on exhibition what is apparently a young seal, which, it is stated, was handed to her by two men, apparently fishermen, who said they had caught it in the near-by Heath pond. Of course they may have done so, and may be it was walked to the pond from the "shores" of, say, Rutland or Stafford, where seals, we believe, are seen in plenty. The lady owner says she has "seen things like this in the pond for the last two years", and she is disconsolate because she cannot get the latest addition to her ménage to feed.

Note that two men replace Mr Trevor, and there is no mention of night time. The writer clearly intended to dismiss the whole affair as a leg-pull, but the following week there was a further paragraph headed *Seals In Hampstead Pond – Fishermen's Unsuspected Catch*. This reported that the seal had become contented with its new quarters, and had been named `Happy of Hampstead'. It enjoyed lying on a wooden platform in the tank and basking in the sunshine and had overcome its initial disinclination to eat and would accept whiting. This is consistent with Katie Bond's recollection.

Now let us examine the clipping from the *Daily Chronicle* of 2 November1926, reproduced here, which reports the supposed discovery of the second seal. Hubert finds the story "overflowing, as it were, with improbabilities! [..] There is the `excited crowd' – but why were they there anyway? The `eye-witness' adds nothing, only a dramatic touch of *apparent* veracity. `Fought like a lion and barked

LONDON. Vale of Health, Hampstead. No. 1086.

like a dog' – but sea lions bark, not seals! They grunt occasionally, nothing more. `... and a few minutes after being landed, died.' A carp would live for days, a pike for hours; how is it our `seal' (an air-breathing animal remember, which breeds on land) expires so soon?"

We have the creature described by Fred Grey as having "a lot of scales"; seals, of course, have fur. Then the angler "took it away with him, and I do not know where it is now". He just walked off with a *large* seal, and all his fishing gear. The `excited crowd' just melted away, and no one was there to photograph the extraordinary event for posterity.

The most blatant joke is the notion that the seal *swam* up the River Fleet to the pond. Hubert again: "We who know the often reluctant trickle that issues from this pond to feed the small stream in the valley, can laugh; for only occasionally, after very heavy and continuous rain, does it fill its clay bed to a depth of about 12in – and that's when it's in flood. In times of drought, it's usually dry."

Charles Fort was actually living a couple of miles away (in Marchmont Street) in 1926; but as he says that "conceivably a seal could make its way [..] from the ocean to this park", it's clear he didn't come to see the Fleet trickle for himself. Seals do appear in the Thames: as I was writing this, a clipping arrived reporting a eight-foot grey seal yards from Westminster Bridge (*Daily Telegraph* 7 April 1992.)

Fortean sleuth Hubert Adamson at work on one of his sculptures on Hampstead Heath.

TRUTH WILL OUT

Hubert Adamson knew Charlie Abbot, another grandchild of Fred Gray, from conversations on the sandspit below the fairground where the first seal was supposed to have been caught and where Hubert often worked on his sculpture. Charlie still lives on the fairground site with his family. Just before Christmas 1986, he told Hubert the secret of the seal. Charlie belonged to the fraternity of the fairground who toured England, setting up, performing and moving on according to long-established custom. His area included Kings Lynn, close to the waters of the Wash where the common seal breeds – the curse of local fishermen. The fair here is an important traditional event called the `Marrying of the Birds' and always opens on St Valentine's Day. When Charlie was there, he mentioned the seal to a friend, the son-in-law of a man called Bone, and was told how it had all happened.

The Bones, a well-known Kings Lynn fishing family, caught a seal one day and decided for a lark to have it transported to the Hampstead Fairground. We can't say how far Fred Gray was implicated at this stage, but he provided a suitable receptacle, the `iron tank'. Charlie Abbot pointed out that steam engines needed large quantities of water, and on the fairground site were `tanks as large as lorries'. Possibly, the `two men' of the *Ham & High* report were the ones who brought the seal from Norfolk and placed it straight into the tank, which had probably been placed on the terrace of the Hotel.

And so began the hoax which bemused Charles Fort, the local inhabitants and the press. Whether the seal was actually in the pond is uncertain, but we can be fairly sure that the second seal existed only in the imagination of Fred Gray. According to his grandson, the first seal returned to the Wash the way it had come, with the fairground lorries. Fred took the secret to his grave in 1941. "What a splendid joke he played on us all and how it seems to have fooled everyone" mused Hubert Adamson. "I think it was all for fun, but it can't have done his Hotel trade any harm."

FT

NOTE
[1] Camden History Review No.15, 1988. My thanks to the Camden History Society for the use of quotations from Hubert Adamson's article. Communications to the Editor should be sent to the Camden History Society, c/o Swiss Cottage Library, 88 Avenue Road, London NW3, telephone 071 413 6522.

POSTSCRIPT

...In January 1900, a gamekeeper was shooting around the lake called Taxmere near Sandbach in Cheshire when he found a seal, not long dead, about 30 or 40 inches long and weighing 30 or 35 pounds, in a field next to the lake. Many curious stories were told of Taxmere; some insisted it was bottomless, while others said that a plumb line had ascertained that it was exactly 22 yards deep. In the 1860s, two Sandbach men made a wager to swim across the water, a distance of half a mile, one cold spring day in March. `Plumber Tom', one of the swimmers, was drowned, while the other got safely across.

Many came to view the dead seal and to ponder how it came to be next the lake. Some alleged that the seal had lived in Taxmere many years, and that strange movements had been seen in the water as if made by a large and powerful fish. Seals, of course, do not live permanently in the water; and the dead animal was in a starved condition, incompatible with living in a mere well stocked with fish. According to the *Congleton Chronicle* (12 Jan 1990) in its `Glancing Back – 90 Years Ago' section: "The theory that the dead body of the seal had been placed where it was found seems to find little favour, although such animals are a portion of the regular stock in trade of travelling show men."

Our correspondent Jan Williams comments: "I'm not sure whether the mere still exists – there is a Taxmere Farm off the A50 about two miles NE of Sandbach, and a small lake next to a flooded sand quarry, which may be Taxmere, although it is not marked as such on the OS map."

THE KIDNEY KIDNAPPERS

ARE PEOPLE BEING MUGGED FOR THEIR ORGANS?

PAUL SIEVEKING traces the spread of an alarming rumour about the theft of human kidneys – and probes the reality of the organ trade across the world

A new friend-of-a-friend (FOAF) tale has been doing the rounds recently in the north of England. The basic story is something like this: a person visits a bar, where he/she is offered a drink by a stranger and passes out. Two or three days later, the victim wakes up in a park/hotel room, in great pain, goes to hospital and discovers that a kidney has been surgically removed. The narrator usually assumes that the kidney is sold as part of some illicit organ trade.

Fortean Times received a letter on 5 July from a reader in Merseyside stating that a man in his early 20s had been picked up by a young woman in a Manchester night club and woke up three days later with a large scar on the side of his body. He took himself to hospital, where he was told that one of his kidneys had been removed. The reader had also heard of two young men in Liverpool "who had met a similar young lady" and later awoke sans kidneys.

The *Nottingham Evening Post* (13 July 1992) said the paper had been inundated with calls from people who had heard the story and in some cases could even name the unwilling organ donors. Contact was sometimes made with the latter, who invariably denied that they had been cut open, but said they had heard the story from someone else.

Dr Anthony Morgan, a specialist in kidney disease in Nottingham City Hospital, said that no-one had been admitted to the hospital minus a kidney for whose disappearance they could not account. "The story just doesn't hang together", he said. "Having a kidney removed is a major operation and could only be done in a sizable hospital with all sorts of back-up. And in any case, to keep people unconscious for a long time is a very difficult thing to do."

According to the Italian folklore magazine *Tutte Storie*, the rumour of kidnapped children being cut up for the organ trade began with a report in August 1990 of an Austrian girl who went missing during a holiday on the Adriatic coast. She was found a few days later with one of her kidneys missing. Urban folklore sage Jan Harold Brunvand traces the scare to stories in the mid-1980s about children in Third World countries killed or kidnapped for their organs, which were purchased by rich customers in Europe and America.

Brunvand said these tales of the organ trade were "clearly untrue. The organs have a very short shelf life. It's not like you can take them out, carry them around in a cooler and sell them on the streets of New York City."

Of course, there are easier ways of obtaining kidneys. A man sued the Royal South Hampshire Hospital, Southampton, for the loss of his kidney, according to the *Scottish Sunday Mail* of 28 April 1991. Surgeons had removed the organ for analysis by experts at another hos-

pital. It was left in a container for transfer at a reception desk, where somebody nicked it. Perhaps they were one of those DIY surgery nuts … or a gourmet with recherché tastes in steak and kidney pies.

AMERICAN BODY-PART SNATCHERS

The Stolen Kidney Foaftale popped up a lot in America last year. At the end of April 1991, for instance, New York police insisted that the following anecdotes, all of which had surfaced in street rumours and calls to the news media, were mere moonshine:

A guy gets drugged in a bar and wakes up in a hotel room with acute back pain. He calls friends for help, is delivered to hospital, where he discovers his kidney has been removed.

Two out-of-town, inebriated businessmen meet a beautiful woman in a Manhattan bar. One of them leaves with her. The next day, after a mysterious telephone message, the other businessman finds his friend taped to a bed in a Bowery hotel. He has an intravenous tube in his arm and a surgical incision. Kidney gone.

A blond woman or transvestite serial killer is running rampant in midtown, murdering young men and stealing their organs. "Their hearts and livers were taken", said one of a number of callers to the *New York Daily News*; "and the incisions were perfect – like a surgeon's".

The Mafia is sponsoring the body-snatching to fuel a black market in kidneys. This version came from a Tennessee man.

The *Washington Post* checked the Stolen Kidney story out. A journalist in Wisconsin tracked it back to Chicago. On 2 April 1991, an episode in the NBC-TV series Law and Order, called "Sonata for Solo Organ", had a man getting mugged in Central Park and waking up to realise that someone had removed one of his kidneys. Joe Morgenstern, who wrote the episode, said in a *New York Times* article that it was suggested by a colleague who was sure he had read it in a newspaper somewhere. *Houston Chronicle, 4 April; NY Daily News, 29 April 1992.*

EPISODES IN THE ORGAN TRADE

While the West is alarmed and diverted by tales of the black market in body parts, the trade is perfectly open in many parts of the world. A recent TV documentary told how customers from Hong Kong travel to mainland China to await major organs bought from the state, which obtains them from criminals on death row. There is also a thriving trade in organs between Arabs in the Gulf states and impoverished donors in Bombay and other Indian cities.

In July 1992, we heard that China wanted punishment for Bangladeshis who had attacked their embassy after hearing rumours that the Chinese there had killed

Bangladeshis to collect their organs for research. "We never imagined that such an incident would ever take place on friendly soil", ambassador Chen Songlu was quoted as saying. *Edinburgh Evening News, 4 July 1992.*

"India now has the dubious honour of having probably the largest number of transplants of kidneys taken from live donors not related to the patient" stated *India Today* early in 1991 (reported in *Awake!* 8 Mar 1991). About 2,000 kidneys from live donors are sold each year. Dire poverty is the usual motivation.

"We were desperate and the only other option left for me was to become a bootlegger or a local *dada* involved in crime", explained the father of two children. He and his wife each sold a kidney. "We chose the honourable way", he said. With high prices being paid for body parts, the sale of corneas and skin from live donors has also increased. "Commercial trafficking in human organs has become the biggest medical ethics issue in the country", said a prominent doctor.

LEPROUS ORGANS

A macabre story appeared on the front page on *The Times of India* early in 1992 under the headline: "Leprosy Institute 'Selling' Patients' Organs". Doctors at the Central Jalma Institute for Leprosy in Agra were supposed to be removing eyes and kidneys which fetched high prices in New Delhi. Journalist Tim McGirk went to investigate and found no evidence at all to support the story. "It's all lies", said an eye specialist in Agra, explaining that the clinic lacked the facilities for complicated surgery. "They don't even have an anæsthetist up there. Why should they? Leprosy deadens all the sensory nerves. If you ask me it's all politics, a vendetta perhaps." *Independent, 7 Feb 1992.*

According to Reuters (3 July 1991), prisoners in the Philippines were banned from selling their kidneys amid allegations they were being bought by criminals for transplants in Japan. A subsequent report (*Sunday Mail 26 April 1992*) said that the high murder rate in Manila's drug war was providing a boom in organs for transplant operations.

From 1 July 1992, the Egyptian Society of Nephrology banned the transplant of kidneys from donors unrelated to patients. To compensate for any organ shortage, they are pushing through Parliament a law allowing kidneys from corpses to be used. They aim to curb a market so organised that the needy answer personal ads in newspapers asking for kidneys and donors gather in a central Cairo café to await news of a buyer. *New York Post, 13 Jan 1992.*

President Carlos Menem of Argentina paid a surprise visit to the Montes de Oca mental hospital in Luján, 50 miles west of Buenos Aires. Those who have followed the career of 'Calamity Carlos' (see *FT55:23*) will not be surprised to learn that his visit was accompanied by the death of a schizophrenic woman who jumped to her death from a third-storey window.

Suspicions of irregularities at the hospital began in January with the arrest of the former director, Dr Florencio Sanchez. Eleven more staff were subsequently arrested in a wide-ranging investigation of murder, fraud and the traffic of human organs. Millions of pounds have gone missing, not to mention 1,400 patients who have 'disappeared' since 1976. The authorities said these patients had escaped, but not a single one has subsequently been seen by friends or family.

Dr Sanchez often removed the eyes of patients within five hours of their death and replaced them with glass. He also drained their blood for the blood bank of his private clinic, and removed other assorted organs. The hospital was so eager to sell corneas on the black market that the eyes of one patient might have been removed while he was still alive. The body of Marcelo Ortiz, 16, was found in a nearby well with his eyes missing. Hospital records showed that he had 'escaped' in 1991 even though he was paralysed and couldn't even feed himself. It was thought that he had crawled to the edge of the deep well and fallen in. *Guardian, D.Telegraph, 13 Mar 1992.*

"Mr. Sowerby, I want you to meet Mr. Henderson. A man after your heart – so to speak ..."

BURKE & HARE LIVE!

Oscar Rafael Hernandez, a 24-year-old garbage picker, staggered bleeding into a police station in the Caribbean port of Barranquilla, Columbia, on Saturday night, 29 February 1992, during carnival. He had been shot in the right ear at close range. Earlier in the evening, he had been called into the medical school of the Free University to pick up cartons. He was hit over the head, shot and left for dead on a metal table.

The following day, police searched the campus and found the bodies of seven men and three women killed the night before, as well as 20 skulls, 15 lungs, 20 brains and 15 limbs. The victims had been shot or bludgeoned to death. For months, guards had been killing down-and-out garbage pickers or 'recyclers' and selling them to the medical school for about £100 each. Five security guards were arrested. *Dallas Morning News, 29 Mar; AP, Reuters, 30 Mar 1992.*

FT

SECRET COUNTRY

Mysterious places to visit in Great Britain compiled by Janet & Colin Bord

5: London's Camelot

IN THE WOODS of Trent Park, on the northern fringe of London, lies a forgotten Camelot. The small, moated isle on a hilltop is called Camlet Moat on local maps, as the name has been abbreviated over the centuries. It was certainly called Camelot back in 1136 or so, when it was home to the manor house of Geoffrey de Mandeville, first Earl of Essex and founder of Waldon Abbey.

David Pam, in *The History of Enfield Chase,* quotes from a survey of 1656-58: "The manor and chase of Enfield were anciently in the possession of Geoffrey de Mandeville in the reign of William the Conqueror, whose seat and habitation at that time, called Camelot, was situated on the chase near unto Potters' Lodge, the ruins whereof are yet remaining, and being moated, is this day called Camelot Moat."

A map of 1658 (by Nicholas Gunton and Edmund Rolfe) extends the boundaries to the surrounding area, referring to it as North Camelot, East Camelot, West Camelot and Camelot Hill. The nearby road is marked as Camelot Way and a long section of it through Hadley Wood is still called Camlet Way.

There are no records of the Camelot place name earlier than Geoffrey de Mandeville, but there are some odd coincidences associated with the place. A map of Europe drawn by the poet and occultist Charles Williams, a member of the occult society The Golden Dawn, places Camelot not in the region of Cadbury or even Tintagel, but exactly where a less esoteric geographer would place London. Williams was referring either to London as a whole, or Camelot Moat in particular.

A local legend recounts how Sir Geoffrey de Mandeville was being pursued by King Stephen's men on the night of a full moon and had hidden in a hollow oak tree. When he ventured out at midnight, he fell to his death down a well on the north-east corner of the moated isle. On the surface the story looks like nonsense, as Geoffrey was killed at the siege of Burwell Castle in Cambridgeshire in 1144. But the details of the story – full moon, midnight, hollow oak – suggest allegory, and the fall down the well may represent a symbolic 'death' or initiation. It has been suggested that such initiations were once practised at the Chalice Well in Glastonbury.

Another local tale tells of treasure at the bottom of the Camelot well and involves (as one would expect) greed and treachery. Once reputed to be a solid,

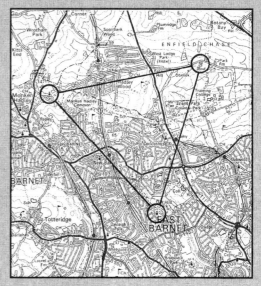

Map shows perfect equilateral triangle of sites: Camlet Moat and the two St Mary the Virgin churches in Monken Hadley and East Barnet

brick-lined structure with a mosaic paved bottom, the well is now little more than a mud-filled hollow, having been excavated out of existence in 1923 by Sir Philip Sassoon who owned the site at the time. He did not admit to having found any treasure.

The first time I went to Camlet Moat, my hair literally stood on end, which suggested to me that there was an unusual energy there. This was clairvoyantly visible as the radiant figure of a white lady, who looked, appropriately enough, like Guinevere. Perhaps a Catholic would have seen her as the Blessed Virgin Mary, while Robert Graves would have recognised the White Goddess. I understood her as the personification of the spirit of the place.

We'll never know if London's Camelot was home to Arthur, Guinevere and the Knights of the Round Table; but it is certainly a place of mystery.

CHRISTOPHER E STREET's book *Earthstars*, about the discovery of London's Camelot and the web of geometric alignments across London, is available for £12.50 inc p&p from Hermitage Publishing, PO Box 1383, London N14 6LF. FT

FORTEAN EXTRACTS FROM
The Gentleman's Magazine:

Charles Fort did not study pre-1800 records in any depth, and many useful records remain to be discovered. *The Gentleman's Magazine* was first issued in January 1731, and appeared monthly for nearly 200 years. Sprinkled across its closely printed pages are the record of odd events of interest to Forteans. Since 1982, *Fortean Times* has been publishing *PETER CHRISTIE's* chronological selections with his comments. Continued from FT63.

1753

❖ For those of you who like numerology, magic and Freemasonry, there is the perfect article in the November issue when a letter from a Norwich reader discussed the Freemasons in connection with the word `Abracadabra' (p.518). I feel the letter is too arcane for reproduction here.

❖ Also in the November issue was the *Case of an extraordinary Sleepiness*. This concerned a 27-year-old woman from St. Maurice sur Lauron near Toulouse in France, who had gone to sleep for up to 13 days at a time for the previous two years. Her waking moments had been short, only ever reaching a maximum of 24 hours, and this after "taking a vomit and having been let blood in the arm and foot." Her doctor tried to wake her by the scientific method of "heating her fingers till they were in a manner burnt." All the time her pulse was strong and her body healthy. (p.521)

❖ Not to be outdone by a mere Frenchwoman, an English doctor responded with a case of his own from 1752. It occurred near Newcastle, Staffs, and concerned a 19-year-old girl who slept 14 weeks non-stop! One extra oddity in her case was that at 9pm every night she opened her lips and her attendant wetted the inside of her mouth with a feather dipped in wine. Her pulse was slow and her father "often gave her an airing in a horse chair" and even the jolting she received then failed to wake her. When she did rouse herself, it took two to three days for her to come fully awake. Luckily, she never again experienced such a long trance or coma – but at least she had shown those French just what British womanhood could do when it put its mind to it! (p.567)

❖ Whilst this correspondence was going on, the editor inserted an account of a lunar rainbow seen at Marshfield, Gloucestershire, on 20 November 1753 (p.526-7), and some notes on Jedediah Buxton of Nottinghamshire, a noted mathematical prodigy (p.557). Most of these prodigies seemed to use their gift to calculate totally pointless sums, but Jedediah was much cleverer – he could list and total all the free pints of beer he had ever drunk!

❖ The year finished with the recording of the 136-year-old Ann Jacquier of Magna in Friborough Canton, Switzerland. The canton government had ordered that she be fed at the public expense, it being added that "She enjoys a sound memory and judgment, and the smallest quantity of good liquor gives her an additional flow of spirits." (p.585) I hope people will say the same thing about me when I reach my 136th birthday.

1754

❖ The new year opened with the record of the death on 22 December 1953 of the Rev. Braithwaite of Carlisle at the grand age of 110. He had managed to complete 100 years' service in the church "having commenced singing boy in the year 1652." (p.47) If 50 years qualifies one for a gold watch, what does one get for 100 years?

❖ In March, a spectacular meteor appeared over western Ireland. It "resembled two human bodies, which seemed to run at each other with great rapidity" for about four seconds. (p.141) The description is very strange and I'm not sure I understand it. It is interesting to note that no mystical significance was attached to this occurrence – the 'Age of Reason' did away with such ideas to a large extent.

❖ In the same month, there was news of the death of Hopkins Hopkins (sic), a 17-year-old dwarf who weighed between 12 and 17 pounds. He died, apparently, of "mere old age and a gradual decay of nature." His parents, who lived in Glamorganshire, had six other children alive, one of whom, a 12-year-old girl, only weighed 18 pounds and already "bears upon her most of the marks of old age." (p.191) I assume these are examples of the medical disorder discussed in earlier issues of *Fortean Times*.

❖ A letter dated 15 May from Downham Market in Norfolk appeared in the May issue (p.215) and presents another biological oddity. Near where the writer lived was the village of Helgay and here, every six or seven years, occurred "an incredible number of field-mice". As soon as this plague appeared, so did "a prodigious flight of Norway owls", which completely devoured the mice and then disappeared again. Such a regular visitation over a long interval is incredible – how could the owls remember this pattern of behaviour over seven years and when did the pattern finish? Any suggestions or information welcome.

❖ May 29th saw the death of John Stewart of Dillievard, Scotland, aged 105 – "He married a 2nd wife at 80, and had ten children by her; the last in his hundredth year". (p.291)

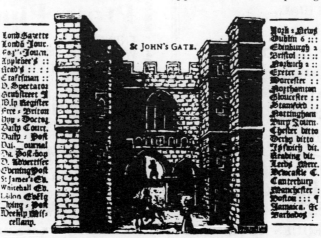

ST JOHN'S GATE.

Lond Gazette
Lond Jour.
Fog's Jour.
Applebee's
Read'd
Craftsman
D. Spectator
Grubstreet
Wly Register
Free Briton
Wily Doctor
Daily Court.
Daily Post
Dai. Journal
Da. Post-boy
D. Advertiser
Evening Post
St: James's Ev.
Whitehall Ev.
Lodon Ev'ng
Hing Post
Weekly Miscellany.

York Mercy
Dublin 6
Edinburgh 2
Bristol
Norwich 2
Exeter 2
Worcester
Northampton
Gloucester
Stamford
Nottingham
Salisp Sourn.
Chester ditto
Derby ditto
Ipswich bit.
Reading bit.
Leedy Merc.
Newcastle C.
Canterbury
Manchester
Boston
Jamaica, &c
Barbadoes

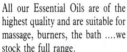

PSYCHICAL RESEARCH:
Brian Inglis, writer on parapsychology, explores Meta-Analysis

EARTH MYSTERIES:
Paul Devereux, *Ley Hunter* editor, looks at the universal nature of spirit lines

PHENOMENOLOGY:
Kevin McClure, a writer on belief systems, asks why only a few members of a crowd can see visions

FOLKLORE:
Folklorist Michael Goss studies how the tabloids keep alive the legends of those who never die

Psychical Research

Meta-Analysis

Brian Inglis is a London-based veteran of over twenty books in the fields of parapsychology and fringe medicine, including a history of psychic research, *Natural and Supernatural* (1977)

I have been exploring further the implications of 'meta-analysis', which I referred to briefly in my last Forum venture as providing psi with a way to creep in out of the cold.

The term came into use in the 1980s to describe a way of evaluating research findings which are not readily susceptible to statistical analysis. When psychologists began to acquire academic recognition, a century ago, they were understandably anxious to be regarded as scientists; and to that end, they tried to reduce the subjective element in their research procedures to zero. This lunatic enterprise spawned behaviourism, which was not just crazy, but absurdly unscientific, precisely because the subjective element in psychology cannot be excluded.

It can, however, be recognised and allowed for, as Robert Rosenthal of Harvard showed in his research into experimenter-effect, one of many ways in which the subjective element can slide into trials, causing apparently inconsistent results. Meta-analysis provides a way in which the overall results of a series of experiments, at first sight inconsistent, may be rendered down to a point where a steady 'signal' can be detected in spite of the confusing 'noise'.

This, of course, is what parapsychologists have been praying for. They have accumulated a mass of evidence pointing to the existence of psi, only to be told that it is unacceptable because of unrepeatability. But now, as Richard Broughton points out in his *Parapsychology: the Controversial Science*, meta-analysis has disposed of this objection – or, rather, provided a more relaxed interpretation of repeatability. The outcome has been that, for the first time, the textbook which for 30 years has told American students where psychology's boundary lines are drawn, has re-drawn them. A small section is devoted to 'Psi-Phenomena'.

For telepathy to appear in "Hilgard and Atkinson", as Broughton comments, "is enough to make a parapsychologist believe in miracles". The entry which gained psi its admission deals in the evidence collected, largely by Charles Honorton, from research using the Ganzfeld method – eliminating sensory distractions so that psychic signals can push their way more easily through the buzz of noise which infests our consciousness. Strong though the reservations which Hilgard and Atkinson's editors had about most psychical research, they were com-

pelled to admit that the Ganzfeld work is "worthy of careful consideration".

A thin end, surely, to a massive wedge? If Ganzfeld findings are admitted, the evidence from earlier research into ESP, such as Joseph Rhine and his colleagues undertook at Duke University, North Carolina, can hardly be ignored. And why stop at the evidence from research? I can see no reason why the principle on which meta-analysis is founded should not be extended to the evidence from history – and, for that matter, from present-day encounters of the Fortean kind.

The first stage would be to secure recognition of the *experience* – in the sense that ghost-hunter Henry Habberley Price was using the term, when he pointed to the ambiguity inherent in the tiresomely familiar question, "Do you believe in ghosts?" Price argued that, put in a different way "Do you believe that people experience apparitions?" – there could only be one answer: "They certainly do".

Even the most rabid sceptic could hardly disagree. And as people have reported the experience of apparitions from every part of the world, in every era, and are still reporting them today, presumably they are a legitimate subject for applied meta-analytic research.

Spirit Lines

Paul Devereux is a freelance writer, researcher and lecturer in the whole range of Earth Mysteries topics. He has edited *The Ley Hunter* for over 16 years, and is the founder/director of the Dragon Project Trust. A prolific author, this year he has three titles published: *Symbolic Landscapes*, *Secrets of Ancient and Sacred Places*, and *Shamanism and the Mystery Lines*.

Emerging out of the heady, psychedelic decade of the sixties, 'Earth Mysteries' (or 'geomancy') has become a distinctive area of thought and research blending such subjects as archæology, anthropology, ancient astronomy, geophysics, anomalous energy effects, folklore and consciousness studies in its attempt to explain the enigmas of ancient sacred sites and landscapes and obtain some insight into the ancient world view.

Just how unfamiliar to us this ancient world view was, has recently been shown up in new research on landscape lines such as the straight markings on the pampas around Nazca, Peru; the strange, straight 'roads' of the lost Anasazi Indians of new Mexico; the Neolithic earthen lines known as 'cursuses' that link long barrows in Britain; the subtle alignments known as *ceques* radiating out of the old Inca capital of Cuzco, Peru; and many other kinds of straight lines in ceremonial landscapes worldwide.

One does not talk about such things for long without 'leys' or 'ley-lines' being mentioned. Leys were the springboard of the whole Earth Mysteries 'movement' and remain at its core. The term was coined in the 1920s by Alfred Watkins for the alignments of ancient sites he noted in his Welsh border homeland. He thought these had evolved along old traders' tracks originally laid down by the line-of-sight in the Neolithic period. After World War II, the theory lapsed into obscurity, only to be reborn with fine feathers in the 1960s, this time as 'energy lines' which were dousable and used by UFOs to recharge their interstellar batteries. This nonsense has been recycled within the New Age circuit, and now we have spiritual masters wielding their dowsing rods and revealing all sorts of exotic energy lines traversing the body of Gaia, the living planet.

Researchers such as myself have long discarded 'energy line' notions as part of our misspent youth; but we still want to solve the mystery of the lines. In the final chapter of *Lines on the Landscape*, which I wrote with Nigel Pennick in 1989, I suggested the lines were 'spirit lines' of some kind. Since then a stream of new findings put the matter beyond doubt.

Artist John Palmer has uncovered the existence of mediæval Dutch *Doodwegen* or 'death roads'. These run, perfectly straight, to cemeteries, and some are still visible on the heath north of Hilversum. They were associated with legally-binding oaths that commanded the carriage of corpses to go in straight lines only. This is reminiscent of the straight cult roads along which the bodies of Viking chieftains were ceremonially carried to their burial ground.

> "Australian aborigines use a filament secreted by an insect to act as a 'road' to lead a sick person's spirit back to their body to make them whole."

Why 'dead straight'? The connection seems to have been with the *spirits* of the dead, for Ulrich Magin has found old sources (see *The Ley Hunter* 116, 1992) referring to German *Geisterwege*, 'ghost paths'. "These paths", say the German sources, "always run in a straight line over mountains and valleys ... In towns they pass the houses closely or go right through them. The paths end or originate at a cemetery." The spirits of the dead 'thrive' on these paths, and "one meets with ghosts quite often" on them.

Some of us now think old Watkins may have been uncovering vestiges of such mediæval ghost or corpse ways rather than prehistoric tracks. This would also explain why old church occur quite often on his 'leys'.

Ghost and corpse paths have developed from an ancient core concept that may have given rise to the Neolithic cursuses, which ran between burial mounds. The Celtic idea of 'fairy paths' running straight from one earthworked hilltop to another (*raths* in Ireland) must also relate to this core concept. It was considered unlucky to build on fairy paths, which runs parallel to the idea in Chinese *Feng shui* geomancy that bad spirits move in straight lines. Maori lore also knows of spirit paths.

In Amerindian tradition, a straight ridge of earth provides a 'spirit road' leading to the entrance of the sweat lodge. This probably evolved out of a whole matrix of ideas underpinning the many examples of large-scale Amerindian straight landscape lines to be found throughout the Americas. Nazca is only the most famous example, and here it has been found that the lines seem to have been *ritually swept* during their period of use 1,500 or so years ago. Still practised in the Andes, though now in a Christian context, this is a way of symbolically creating sacred space. It perhaps parallels the old northern European folk practice of sweeping old paths free of spirits with a special flail. Similarly, in folk dances such as the Plough Stots in Yorkshire, a 'Betty' (a man dressed as a woman) mimes a sweeping action while accompanying the Morris Men along the road.

As the unravelling of the mystery proceeded, I found similar spirit-line ideas associated with threads and string. These, too, are lines; we speak of a 'fishing line', for example. Australian aborigines use a filament secreted by an insect to act as a 'road' to lead a sick person's spirit back to their body to make them whole. Siberian Buryat shamans did the same thing with red thread. The Kalahari !Kung 'climb threads' when they go out-of-body during their trance dancing, and the Rigo of Papua New Guinea leave a taut 'fishing line' behind them when travelling out-of-body. And so on.

(While straight lines supposedly facilitated spirit movement, twisted ones hampered it. So, for instance, the Baltic fisherman would run around a shoreline labyrinth to entrap any trolls following him before boarding his boat!)

That ancient landscape lines needed to be thought of as spirit ways was in itself a breakthrough. In my next *Forum* piece, I will show what lay behind this deep-rooted concept.

The Lone Witness

Kevin McClure edits *The Wild Places* – the *Journal of Strange and Dangerous Beliefs*. Sample copies are £1.65 or US$4 from 42 Victoria Road, St Austell, Cornwall PL25 4QD

At the time of the last Fatima vision, on 13 October 1917, some 70,000 people were present at the Cova da Iria, waiting for a miracle. They had gathered there because three young, uneducated children had claimed to have had meetings with the Blessed Virgin Mary, who had forecast a miracle for this day. The most dramatic events so far witnessed by anyone other than the children had been a small, mysterious cloud, and the unnatural swaying of the branches of a tree in which the figure was said to be standing.

Of the 70,000 present maybe half – probably considerably less had they been questioned at the time – witnessed the visual phenomenon that has become known as the 'dance of the sun'. None of the considerable number of photographers present was able to capture it for posterity, despite its considerable duration. Only the three children saw the Virgin Mary and various other holy figures that reportedly appeared, and only one or two of the three heard what Mary is said to have told them – the Third Secret of Fatima. The same situation prevailed in all the alleged visions of the Virgin – including the long series of events at Lourdes where, of the many thousands who attended the visions, only Bernadette Soubirous ever saw or heard the vision itself.

To broaden the issue, I can recall a UFO case I helped investigate in Leicester. A 200-foot wide UFO hovered and dipped over the railway sidings at South Wigston, observed only by the occupants of two nearby houses, but undetected by the thousands of others living locally, the staff of the permanently-manned signal box and the nation's defence systems. A variety of similar difficulties have blighted UFO research since the subject began. Though there have been many thousands of reports of vast, dramatic flying craft of unknown origin, performing amazing flight patterns, and achieving extraordinary changes of speed and colour, only a few score have been correlated by credible witnesses viewing from different sites. A mere handful have been supported by radar responses.

To move on again – consider the most famous of British mediums – well-respected people like Doris Collins, Stephen O'Brien, Gordon Higginson and the late Doris Stokes. In their public meetings with hundreds present, they explain that the dead, the loved ones of some of those in the audience, have come to the hall to pass on messages. They speak of them standing and waiting, sometimes jostling and calling in their eagerness to communicate. Yet I have never seen or heard anyone else in the audience claiming to see the same people, giving the same messages. Nor have I ever heard of an experiment where *another* medium has been asked whether he or she can see the same as the first. I guess there are good reasons for that.

Fortean Times readers are noted for their intelligence; you'll see what I'm getting at by now. We have a huge body of information about anomalous phenomena, events and communications. We make massive assumptions about life and death, fate and predestination. We design cosmologies and adapt our lifestyles. Yet our basis for doing so is the verbal output of a remarkably small number of individuals, a tiny minority of humanity with only the imparting of such information in common. They don't present us with broad-based, objective evidence. For some reason, we do not expect them to do so.

The world of channelling – the dissemination of limp homilies from purportedly discarnate entities living on distant, unknown, invisible planets, in return for large sums of money – only continues this strange tradition. We want to believe it and many of us do. One day, we'll look back at the great bulk of channelled material and realise just how feeble it all was. Numerous earlier belief systems have suffered similar fates.

There's only two broad responses to this situation of how we receive information about the anomalous. One is to accept – as has been the case throughout history – that certain individuals are particularly empowered, gifted, chosen, talented or whatever. A thousand years ago, it might have been shamen, now it's the channellers and the psychic questers, claiming they know what we don't, and can do what we can't.

The other response is to examine, ever more closely, the individuals who pass all of this information to us. For a long time, we have assessed and examined the product. Perhaps it is overdue for us to look at that tiny – maybe troubled, maybe inspired – fraction of humanity, the source.

The New Immortals

Michael Goss is a freelance writer living in Essex. He has written *Evidence for Phantom Hitch-hikers* (1984) and contributed numerous articles on folklore and the paranormal to many periodicals

In case you missed it (and if so, don't feel you have to apologise), Adolf Hitler died from a massive heart attack at 2:32am on 14 April this year. He was 103 years old.

If you find this announcement surprising – if you find it hard to reconcile with the prior belief-cum-certainty that Hitler died as long ago as 1945 – it just goes to show that you didn't read the *Weekly World News* for 12 May 1992. As always, that inestimable source backed what it said with a photo, and I must say that the Führer looked in remarkably good shape for a centenarian, even for one stretched horizontal on a mortuary slab. It also quoted the reaction of Hitler's son, a person of whom historians seem to have had little cognizance until last year when (again according to the *Weekly World News*) he stepped out of the shadows of Indianapolis with "well-documented proof...that he was the illegitimate product of Hitler's relationship with Geli Raubel in 1929." Oh, the *Weekly World News* is never short of startling revelations.

You doubt that? Look no further than the aforementioned 12 May 1992 issue. Hitler's unexpectedly delayed death deservedly took precedence and front cover, but inside there was an interview with none other than John F. Kennedy. Breaking a silence of 29 years, the wheelchair-bound ex-president of the USA revealed how, "alive but critically wounded", he had been "secretly flown to Poland" and that what was laid to rest under the Eternal Flame in Arlington was a wax dummy. More dramatically, he belatedly accused jealous brother Robert of having tried to do for him in Dealey Plaza. Thus, thanks to a single issue of the planet's most ferociously-investigative supermarket tabloid, modern history will have to be rewritten not once, but *twice*.

As Kennedy is made to remark, it's funny how things can turn out. That is undeniably true if you believe just an eighth of what you read in the *Weekly Wrold News*. Emphasis here on that word 'funny'. Like our own *Sunday Sport* and others of that ilk (which borrow from it freely and often), the *Weekly World News* is in show business. It's there to be enjoyed, not believed.

Some feel that the tabloids have no right to invent news. They argue that deliberate fictioneering misleads and deceives the gullible, and destabilises the credibility of the news media as a whole. But I suspect that the number of readers actually, literally, misled and deceived by stories like those just outlined is very small and that the damage to them is very slight. As for the news media: if their credibility is so feeble as to find the *Weekly World News* a danger, perhaps we'd better have them put down.

As far as these 'he isn't really dead' stories go, I also suspect that supermarket tabloids do not 'invent' in the strictest sense of the verb. What they do is to take, polish, extend and re-energise extant, but perhaps moribund, rumour legends which originated *not* in the media but in oral culture. The type or motif of the Undead Culture-Hero is well-known to folklorists, who can cite historical examples from King Arthur and Frederick the Great to Marilyn Monroe and Jim Morrison. The same scholars have been collecting versions of the post-1945/post-1963 survivals of Hitler and Kennedy for years; likewise stories about the non-death of long-vanished aviatrix Amelia Earhart, whose discovery as a hale 95-year-old on a South Pacific island paradise (sic) was announced to a strangely unshocked public by the *Weekly World News* on 28 April 1992.

The *Weekly World News* fondness for these '(X) isn't really dead' stories has made it the leading modern promoter of the type/motif; for example, it played an early and seminal role in the 'Elvis Lives!' saga, which remains the best-known instance of this story cycle. Promotion, however, isn't invention. Here, as before and since, the magazine seized on the rumour, developed it and reinforced it through sporadic updates, many of them plainly risible in character.

Supermarket tabloids may pose a viral risk to whatever immunity system guards us from arrant credulity .. but I doubt it. They may pose a greater threat to the 'purity' of oral folklore, but I doubt that too. When we read them, we are invited to put our disbelief into suspended animation; with the magazine safely in the wastebin, we can bring our critical faculties back to full and active life. Rather like all those '(X) isn't dead' stories bring John F Kennedy, Elvis, James Dean and a few dozen others back to life, in fact. **FT**

> "In an interview, John F Kennedy revealed how, 'alive but critically wounded', he had been 'secretly flown to Poland' and that what was laid to rest under the Eternal Flame in Arlington was a wax dummy."

> "Supermarket tabloids may pose a viral risk to whatever immunity system guards us from arrant credulity ... but I doubt it."

FORUM is a column in which anyone with something to say about a particular field, theory or incident can share their thoughts with our readership. If you'd like to join in with an opinion on any area of Forteana, send it in to the editorial address. Ideal length: 500-1000 words. Please enclose a head and shoulders photo of yourself with all Forum submissions.

REVIEWS

CHILDREN FOR THE DEVIL
RITUAL ABUSE & SATANIC CRIME
by Tim Tate.

Methuen. 1991, hb £16.99, pp378, notes, bib, index.

IN PURSUIT OF SATAN
THE POLICE AND THE OCCULT
by Robert D. Hicks.

Prometheus Books, 700 E. Amherst St, Buffalo, NY 14215, USA. 1991, hb £15.50, pp420, notes, index. Available in the UK from Prometheus, 10 Crescent View, Loughton, Essex IG10 4PZ.

BLASPHEMOUS RUMOURS
IS SATANIC RITUAL ABUSE FACT OR FANTASY?
by Andrew Boyd.

Fount Paperbacks, 77-85 Fulham Palace Rd, London W8 8JB. 1992, pb £6.99, pp420, notes, index.

In the United States, where cases of Satanic ritual abuse (SRA) have proliferated in the last dozen years, parents of alleged victims of abuse have formed a group called Believe the Children.

But can we? According to the child protagonists of a recent British SRA scare, their abusers had murdered dozens of infants, aborted and sacrificed fœtuses, conjured up monsters and devils, and danced naked in the Orkney midwinter, all without leaving evidence of their activities for the police to find. The question, put simply, is this: must their claims be taken seriously? Or are they outlandish and uncorroborated fantasy?

Here, after all, are three volumes on Satanic ritual abuse – two by British believers, one by an American sceptic – comprising more than 1,200 pages of evidence, discussion and background material, that contain not a single photograph.

The books differ substantially in their approach and quality. On the one hand we have Hicks – sober, sceptical, scholarly and concerned almost wholly with the American SRA scares. On the other, Boyd, whose credentials as presenter of a recent, thoroughly discredited Channel 4 *Dispatches* documentary – **see**

FT64:50-51 – hardly encourages respect. And, somewhere in the middle, stands Tim Tate, whose heavily flawed book can nevertheless claim to be the best available source book on the British abuse panic.

Children for the Devil has several advantages over *Blasphemous Rumours*. Not the least of them is that Tate – an author, researcher and producer of the controversial 1989 *Cook Report* on Satanism – can write, while Boyd's, frankly unreadable, book is a mass of florid prose interspersed with hundreds of lengthy and repetitious extracts drawn from earlier authorities.

But Tate is just as ready to draw contentious conclusions from his dubious evidence. He makes the valid point that the evidence of child witnesses is the key to understanding SRA, for they, unlike the adult 'survivors' of the 1980s, may be too young to fantasise their lurid, detailed and broadly consistent descriptions of Satanic ritual. (As one foster mother exclaimed: "Laura's only three – how could she have made all this up?") Yet he fails to mention that the Rochdale ritual abuse case collapsed after the child witness – a six-year-old boy – revealed he had watched the 18-rated explicit horror film *The Evil Dead* twice the night before making his allegations.

Similarly, Tate goes to some lengths to "prove" that human sacrifice is central to genuine ritual, and quotes approvingly from US "Satanic indicators" suggesting that Satanists are rarely pædophiles, and yet he bolsters his contention that SRA really does exist by citing five court cases from the 1980s which featured plenty of sexual abuse but no allegations of human sacrifice at all.

Such arguments fly in the face of evidence collected by researchers such as Hicks, which suggests that the 'Satanic' abuse that does occur is primarily sexual in nature, with a veneer of ritual added to thrill the abuser and perhaps act as a form of psychological terrorism to deter disclosure of the crimes.

Tate's and Boyd's willingness to accept the more extreme allegations of the evangelical proponents of the current flap seems to blind them to the folkloric and socio-religious elements of

the abuse scare. Both authors describe in some detail alleged historical cases of Satanism, from the Knights Templar and Gilles de Rais to Anton LaVey, without understanding the key role played by turn of the century occult groups such as O.T.O. and the Golden Dawn in re-inventing – rather than simply rediscovering – an older tradition. And neither understands the significance of the distribution of cases.

Why should the majority of historic cases come from Catholic countries, while the modern incidents are drawn, apparently exclusively, from Protestant territories such as the USA, UK and Holland? Are modern-day Satanists in France and Spain simply better than their American and British colleagues at covering their tracks – or does the pattern reflect the activities of the Inquisition and modern evangelical Protestants?

Hicks' book, born of the author's growing disquiet at the activities of Christians and welfare activists spreading the Satanic 'gospel' to police and social workers, takes an admirably sceptical line in the face of such inconsistencies. [For an investigation of the roots of Britain's ritual abuse scare, see reviews next issue.]

Mike Dash

THE SUSSEX WEATHER BOOK
by Bob Ogley, Ian Currie and Mark Davidson.

Frosted Earth / Froglet Books. 1991, pb £9.95.

The brittle chalk coastline of Sussex has long borne the brunt of attacks by raging, storm-tossed seas – see Nigel Pennick's *Lost Lands and Sunken Cities* (Fortean Tomes, 1987) – but it is not this type of meteorological event recorded in this glossy, well-illustrated book. Sussex has a long history of severe weather, something of which all inhabitants will have been reminded in the last few years by the 'hurricanes' of October 1987 and January 1990. These are not as easily forgotten as the more localised terrors of tornadoes and waterspouts that have repeatedly brought ruin in the last thousand years as documented here. Chichester even has a history of earthquakes which cannot be ignored.

Of course there are more extreme Fortean events: hot steam bubbling up through the ground at Pyecombe in 1902; thick red rain at Crowborough in 1903; and a 'will o'the wisp' at Chichester in 1839. I'm glad I wasn't around in the intriguingly Fortean year of 1911: on 22 March the temperature soared to 65°F, yet within days there were blizzards and more snow in April; Between May and September there was a drought, followed by floods in October. The inhabitants could be forgiven for thinking they were being tested to see how much they could take.

Sussex also boasts (if that is the right word) some UK extremes. My hometown of Lewes suffered the worst number of fatalities (nine) in an avalanche on 24 December 1836; and on 5 September 1958, the largest recorded number of hailstones.

It's always the things closest to hand which are the most neglected, and personal recollections of weather fit into that category. We are indebted to Bob Ogley, who has built an interesting career of similar county books following the success of his photographic record of the 1987 hurricane. All are pitched to interest locals, holidaymakers and tourists, but are commended to general interest because they document local history, and reiterates the value of old postcard collections.

Alan Gardiner

THE MASKS OF LUCIFER
TECHNOLOGY AND THE OCCULT IN TWENTIETH CENTURY POPULAR LITERATURE
by David Morris.
Batsford, London, 1992; hb £17.99, pp223, notes, bib, index, çillus.

Events don't occur in isolation, and researchers can neglect their wider social, cultural and historical contexts; also the mode of media-presentation, both in immediate reportage and subsequent handling. This book, by a lecturer in History and Media Studies, attempts to study that context and presentation rather than the events themselves, which leads, regrettably, to a viewpoint quite as unbalanced as the literature under study.

Morris originally intended his book to be a study of flying saucer' literature, and whether it constituted a popular culture. His research, however, led him into related areas, and also provided him with a selection of themes which have shaped his final presentation. One of those themes is the influence exerted by the cosmology and doctrine of the Theosophical Society, the subject of his first chapter. Others are devoted to Velikovsky's catastrophism, flying saucer literature, Pauwels & Bergier's *Dawn of Magic,* von Däniken and Ancient Astronaut theories, and lastly the readership and continuity of appeal.

Morris begins by examining the Theosophical Society's history, social context and popularity as a response to cultural crisis,

and gives a brief account of the major cosmological tenets of Theosophy, amongst which are a number of concepts which are shown to recur in the later literature. This is fine as far as it goes, because *some* later writers, whether deriving their material direct from Theosophy or inventing parallel concepts, do reflect these same themes. But Morris, I fear, takes the idea too far and implies that all writers in the field are reflecting Theosophical doctrine.

Among the Theosophical concepts that Morris mentions is the old Gnostic notion that Lucifer/Satan is the bringer of power and light to humanity, and the true god of mankind. Morris takes this to symbolise an antiestablishment attitude and the promotion of an alternative worldview, calling it 'Luciferianism' (or 'Satanism'), which provides the title of the book.

With the substance of the literature established as Luciferian, Morris labels the mode of expression Techno-Occultism, meaning that the literature he discusses is taking the concepts and cosmology of late 19th century occultism (Theosophical doctrine) and dressing them up in new technological interpretations for the late 20th. Thus, Morris generalises, classifying all the writers discussed, from Velikovsky to von Däniken and everyone in between, as Techno-Occultist Satanists.

I put it so bluntly because, as Morris must know with a Media Studies background, that these are loaded words. He might argue that he is using words like `Occultism' and `Satanism' in a specialised and defined sense, but the words still retain their other resonances, especially in these fundamentalist times. And even assuming that we are not meant to understand Techno-Occultist authors as `devil-worshippers', there still remains the implication that they take an anti-rational approach, and their credibility is thereby diminished.

Perhaps, though, this is a matter of no importance to Morris. He is interested in the field as popular literature, which basically refers to the mass-market paperback; he thus ideals with the genre in its most populist form, and has little or no concern with the reality or otherwise of the data contained in the books, nor with the wider field of research and theory from which the paperbacks originate. And, indeed, Morris has already declared that the books are not factual. On the opening page of the introduction we are told that `while they are not works of fiction (and are quite distinct from Science Fiction), neither are they works of fact, and I have used the term `suppositional' to describe their particular style of advocacy.' Thus the whole field is generalised as being `non-factual' at the start of the study, and therefore lacking in credibility. By implication, this applies to *all*

the books in the field, regardless of the quality of the work or the intentions of the author.

This aside, Morris does have some interesting material to offer. There is good cultural background on the anxieties of post-war American society (atomic power, fear of communist infiltration, loss of isolation) which sheds useful light on the periods of Velikovsky and the early flying saucer scares. And, particularly in the chapters devoted to individual authors, his analysis leads to some good insights. He points out that the reception of Velikovsky's theory of catastrophism has to be seen against contemporary American fears of nuclear catastrophe. He correctly identifies an inherent tendency toward bureaucracy and pseudo-academicism in ufology, with its authors claiming to be `directors' of, or `consultants' to, various `National' or `International' organisations with acronymic names. Pauwels and Bergier do appear to speak approvingly of Nazi occultism. Von Däniken does argue too much by assertion and supposition to present a convincing case.

It should perhaps be obvious that the more popularly presented a book may be, the less likely it is to rely on reasoned argument backed up by factual data and references. One assumes Morris must be aware of this and it is possibly significant that he never mentions it: all are treated alike. This lack of `quality control' is particularly noticeable in the chapter on the flying saucer literature, as is the tendency to generalisation. Here Morris deals with a large number of authors over a 40 year period; from Keyhoe and Adamski to Michell, Devereux, Randles and others. But there is no sense of differentiation between them as to quality of content, presentation, or seriousness of intention. Adamski and, say, Devereux, both being Techno-Occultist writers, are taken as witnesses of equal worth. And if, by giving greatest emphasis to Adamski's account (as Morris does) one implies that his story is ridiculous, then Devereux (or any other author in the field) gets tarred with the same brush.

Out of the popular flying saucer literature, Morris selects Brad Steiger as a typical example of an author whose books consist mainly of long compilations of sighting reports. In dealing with these reports, Morris makes a number of assertions: that the witnesses in these reports are never presented in a personal or social context, they're never ill or worried, their lives are rarely changed by the experience, and so on. In short, he asserts there is no investigation of the witness. If Morris had a deeper knowledge of the subject, he would know that investigation of the witness is crucial to current ufological practice and that the assertions he makes above, while possibly applicable to Steiger, could be refuted point by point from other works in the literature. Again, the problem seems to stem from Morris' concentration on the genre in its most popular form; he makes no mention of the ufological journals, hardbacks or small press material, and thus seems unaware, or dismissive, of the serious research that does appear.

Ultimately, then, his interpretation isn't flexible enough for the material. And, despite his often valuable insights, he still treats the material as if it were homogeneous and two-dimensional; there is depth of analysis, but no depth of knowledge. If Morris's acquaintance with the material were greater, he would doubtless have been aware of other influences and sub-currents in the genre. But Fort is only mentioned at second-hand and Jung gets no more than a listing in the bibliography. In the end the book is, perhaps, a brave attempt, but marred by similar faults to those Morris finds in his subject matter: one can hardly condemn supposition and assertiveness using generalisation and implication. One to be read with care.

Steve Moore

VIMANA AIRCRAFT OF ANCIENT INDIA & ATLANTIS
compiled by David Hatcher Childress.

Adventures Unlimited Press, Stelle, Illinois 60919, USA. 1991, pb $15.95, pp333, notes, bib, illus. Available in the UK from Enigma Design, 15 Rydal St, Burnley, Lancs BB10 1HS.

Childress continues to amaze with his seemingly boundless energy for travel and small press publishing. His latest work is a compilation of papers and other material asserting, without qualification, that Atlantean flying technology was enshrined in ancient legends worldwide, particularly for war-like purposes.

A number of von Dänikenesque authors have claimed that ancient India had a semi-magical semi-scientific technology which included nuclear weapons and metallic flying machines called *vimanas*. Indeed references to vimanas can be found in classic Vedic and Hindu texts, such as the *Mahabharata*. Whatever vimanas may have been, they were annexed to the Theosophy-influenced Adamski school of ufology by learned writers such as Desmond Leslie, in support of a number of crucial ideas, including the super-science of mythical civilisations of the distant past, the historical reality of UFOs, and anti-gravity as their propulsion system.

Childress charges around these notions like an excited puppy, with no critical faculties in sight. He is not unduly worried that most of the information, 'facts' and narratives he juggles with seem to have come from channelling mediums (eg. Edgar Cayce), fantasists (eg. Lobsang Rampa, James Churchward), occultists (eg. Steiner, Blavatsky, etc) and a host of other

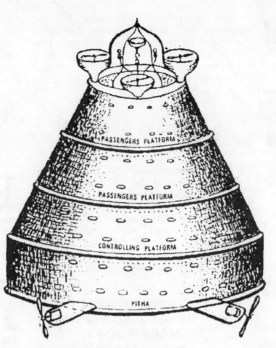

An Indian scholar's reconstruction of a Vimana, dated 1923

dubious 'authorities', mixed with bits of any myths from any culture which seems to support the discussion.

Nevertheless, it is a fascinating array of material, and includes an introduction by Ivan Sanderson (swiped from Sanderson's book *Invisible Residents*), and the full and illustrated text of an incomprehensible work called *Vimaanika Shastra* which purports to be an ancient Puranic treatise on the construction of vimanas, their weapons, and pilot training courses. It is curious to note, from a number of Indian sources reproduced in the book, that there was considerable discussion among Vedic scholars about ancient mechanical flying machines long before the 'Flying Saucer' era began in the 1940s.

For Childress, it is the magic of these ideas that counts, and he often succeeds in passing this enthusiasm on to the reader before commonsense restores itself. While many may condemn this kind of book as rubbish, we should not underestimate its influence; perhaps it may inspire a young Faraday or Maxwell to turn the magic into technological practicality.

Bob Rickard

SECRETS OF ANCIENT AND SACRED PLACES
by Paul Devereux.

Devereux has selected 20 sites on the World Heritage List of important antiquities and describes their importance with regard to archæology, astronomy, geomancy, energies, sacred geometry, etc. The result is a varied collection of sites worldwide, some of them little known or studied by earth mysteries experts, but equally as important as famous British sites like Stonehenge and Avebury. Devereux is always readable, and an authoritative writer on earth mysteries, and so this "mysterious geomantic worldview of the past" works very well. *Blandford, London. 1992, hb £14.99, pp192, colour photos, illus, index, refs.* **JB**

THE SECRET LIFE OF A SATANIST
by Blanche Barton

As this is the 'authorised biography' of Anton LaVey, founder of the Church of Satan, it might be naive to expect anything critical; and, indeed, criticism is entirely absent. Instead we have an adulatory, showbiz biography, in which everything LaVey does is wonderful, startling, original (etc., ad nauseam). The first half of the book, detailing LaVey's life as animal trainer, musician and Satanist, is little more than a tedious catalogue of repetitive name-dropping.

The second half, giving space to his thought and beliefs, is more interesting; mainly in that the thought of this self-important 'Satanist' is so shallow and uninteresting. Even when he tries to be shocking, the tone of the book is so worshipful that LaVey comes across as a mildly eccentric right-wing showman who's somehow managed to exploit a defect in the American psyche. Still, there are a couple of gems. On page 71 we learn that the old Fortean Society were a bunch of Satanists (!); while on page 77 we have LaVey's 'Sign of the Horns': two fingers pointed up, the middle three folded down. How many fingers does this man have? For lovers of trash only. *Mondo, London. 1992, pb £4.99, pp266, photos, bib.* **SM**

PROPHECY AND PREDICTION IN THE 20th CENTURY
by Charles N. Gattey.

This is a compact introduction to the rich and varied material on the subjects of prophecy and prediction, from the spontaneous dreams (eg. that preceded the Aberfan disaster) and trance utterances to visionary revelations, literary prophecies and tips for punters. Along the way we get competent chapters on Hitler's advisors, Wolf Messing, Edgar Cayce, Gerard Croiset, Peter Hurkos, Eileen Garrett, Jeane Dixon, and some others with reputations for prophecy.

There is not much analysis here of accuracy of modern predictions – unlike in *The Blue Sense*, (reviewed in FT60) – but a number of chapters try to understand the precognitive elements in dreaming and divination, and creative or intuitive acts (such as inventing or writing). The book closes with a short discussion of theories of time. Recommended to beginners or general readers. *Aquarian / Thorsons, London. 1992, pb £7.99, pp270, bib, index.* **BR**

MYTHIC IRELAND
by Michael Dames.

A multi-layered and well-illustrated survey of Ireland and its myth, using archæology, literary sources, folklore and language to build a mesh of connection and transformation from the pagan Neolithic to the present. This temporal warp is woven with a spatial woof as Dames surveys the separate provinces, focussing on a single major site in each and then spreading out from microcosm to macrocosm.

The net result is a fascinating web that attempts to capture the entire mythic history and geography of Ireland, and contains much excellent material. Yet the selection and interpreta-

VIDEO VIEW

THE GLASTONBURY GIANTS

"Too big to be seen! Too good to be true!"

Since the 1960s, Mary Caine has been telling anyone who will listen about the huge zodiac laid out in the landscape around the town of Glastonbury. It consists of outlines of 12 symbolic figures defined by natural features (such as streams and hill contours) and enhanced by man (with ancient roads and hedges, canals, earthworks, etc). Each zodiacal effigy also relates to Arthurian and Christian legend with over 100 meaningful place-names. The whole – seen from the air – is a mystical 'Round Table' about 10 miles across, and was first discovered in 1925 by Katherine Maltwood. This privately produced visual lecture, based upon Mary Caine's own two books, is both fascinating and unusual. *The Glastonbury Giants; 1990; 50 mins; £12.75 inc 2nd class postage in UK (for overseas rate please inquire). Available by post from Mary Caine, 25 Kingston Hill, Kingston, Surrey KT2 7PW, UK.*

tion has a strangely 19th century feel, and leaves one with the impression that Dames believes the entirety of Irish myth has a solar and seasonal origin. This is surely only a part of the story; but the part is very well done. *Thames & Hudson, London. 1992, hb £14.95, pp272, refs, index, bib, 152 illus.* **SM**

CIRCLES OF NOTE
Compiled and edited by Michael Chorost

A useful bibliographic and classified listing of 250 books, news-letters, articles, videos and other sources of information on the crop circle phenomenon worldwide, with prices and addressess. This is the second edition and has been updated to June 1992. Published by *Dennis Stacy, Box 1234, San Antonio, Texas 78212, USA. 1992 £2 inc. postage, pp16.* **JB**

THE APPARITIONS OF THE BLESSED VIRGIN MARY TODAY
by Rene Laurentin.

"Without the receptivity of a subject there would be no apparitions, but, as a corollary, subjectivity can lead to illusory apparitions." This quotation from Fr Laurentin's account of BVM appearances demonstrates that he maintains a sensible attitude towards the events he chronicles. Laurentin is a leading mariologist – he has, for example, studied the Lourdes phenomenon for more than 20 years, 'Miraculous Medal' for nine, and Pontmain for five – so there is no doubt that he has a deep knowledge of the subject.

Although he writes from a Catholic viewpoint, he is by no means an unquestioning believer. Since the visions of the Virgin Mary are essentially Catholic, it is appropriate for them to be studied in a Catholic context. However, researchers studying visions as part of a wider phenomenon will find plenty of valuable material and insight here, for Fr Laurentin details the many little-known contemporary visions from around the world.

Related phenomena are also discussed: eg. the healing oil which flows from a postcard in Damascus, modern cases of stigmata, miraculous cures and weeping statues. This is an essential sourcebook, with the added value of material presented sympathetically. A thought-provoking book. *Veritas Publications, 7-8 Lower Abbey St, Dublin 1. 2nd edition 1991, pb £8.95, pp211, photos.* **JB**

CROP CIRCLES OF 1991
by Busty Taylor.

Busty Taylor is one of the famous names of the English crop circle world, and justly renowned for his fine photographs. His two main techniques are ærial photography from a small plane, and 'pole shots' utilising a camera attached to the top of a rod up to 40 feet long.

In this booklet he commemorates the designs which were revealed to the world in 1991, in 40 full-page photographs. There is no text – only identifying and descriptive captions – but the booklet is a useful visual record of one year's circles. The seeming high price for such a slender book is the result of full-colour printing throughout. *Beckhampton Books (available by mail order from SKS). 1992, pb £6.99, pp48, illus.* **JB**

THE CELTIC ORACLE
by Nigel Pennick and Nigel Jackson.

Everything you wanted to know about the tree-alphabet of the Druids, called Ogham, and how to use it for divination. As marketing ideas go, this is one of the most successful and delightful of its type. The boxed set contains a fine set of chunky cards illustrating the runes and their associated ideas and symbols, printed in full colour and designed by Jackson. In the accompanying 122-page paperback book, Pennick provides a card-by-card analysis and prognostication in considerable detail. Pennick's fascinating introduction places the oracle into the context of Celtic shamanism. A splendid and inspiring gift. *Aquarian / Thorsons, London. 1992, £16.99.* **BR**

DEAR FT...

EPIC FOREST

■ Some years ago, I used to drive regularly from Ilford [Essex] to Hornsey [north London] to visit my sister-in-law, always taking the same route. On one rainy afternoon in about 1983, I was driving with my husband and we approached a certain junction on the Woodford New Road. I had to be in the outside lane ready to approach traffic lights in the wide road, prior to turning right – the only turning at this T junction. The approach to these lights involved a bend in the road and on turning the bend, we were confronted with a totally unfamiliar scene.

Instead of traffic lights there was a small grass triangle with a wooden signpost which we didn't have time to read. Having no alternative, we turned right and found ourselves lost. The weather was dark and rainy and there was a bank of trees on either side of the road. We came to a fork in the lane, and there was another wooden signpost pointing to Walthamstow and a few yards ahead we could see a normal road and people, so we drove towards it. We were out of our way but finally were directed back to our intended course.

I firmly believe we were in a time warp of some kind. The whole thing lasted, I suppose, about three or four minutes. I would love to know what this 'lost' area was like years ago before it was altered and traffic lights introduced. It is easy enough to take a wrong turn, but there is no other turn to take at this junction and those who know the area can't explain what we might have done.

Mrs J.M. Green
Ilford, Essex

HEY JUDE

■ With reference to 'Grateful thanks to St Jude' advertisements [*FT64:4*]: Stereotyped format petitions to St Jude, St Clare and, more frequently, to the Virgin Mary, are a regular and commonplace feature of the classified ads in local Dublin newspapers. The prayer must follow a strict form, of which the "never known to fail" is an essential statement. It contains much fulsome flattery and must be said for three days and published three times. A form of thanks for favours must also be published after the prayers are granted. I have no information on the success rate.

Leslie Shepard
Dublin

SOCK IT TO US

■ Last summer, a strange incident befell my cousin, Boyd Matthews, of Crayford, Kent. He set out for the day wearing light-coloured trousers, socks and shoes. On his return, he removed his socks and found a thin, even layer of black soot covering his left foot inside the sock. The sock itself was not damaged in any way, nor did it show any evidence of soot on the outside. None of his other clothes or other parts of his body showed any trace of soot, and he was certain he had not been near any soot-like material while he was out. He hadn't removed his sock since putting it on before leaving the house that morning, and had not felt any unusual sensations in his left foot during the day. The soot was easily washed off.

Ian Simmons
Leicester

RAIL DEATHS

■ A weird aspect of the affair of British Rail deaths [see 'The Tamworth Triangle', [*FT59:46*] is that most of the more recent door deaths have happened along a stretch of the West Coast Main Route near the city of Lichfield. The name Lichfield comes from the Anglo-Saxon 'Lye' meaning corpse, and field; the name roughly means 'field of the corpse' or 'field of the dead'.

Dan J.J. Kohn
Southampton

CHILDHOOD TERROR

■ When the papers carry reports about people who claim to have seen creatures from space, I can accept the sincerity of those claims because of an experience I had when I was about five or six, almost 60 years ago. My grandparents lived in an old house with a very dark basement reached by a steep flight of steps behind a door. That was probably why my twin brother and I were forbidden even to open that door in their absence.

This was just what I did one day. Facing me was a very real, very solid figure filling the entire doorway. It gave me the fright of my life. I was looking at Mickey Mouse! When I was not much older and wiser, I knew that I couldn't possibly have seen a *fictional* character, but at that time – and to this day – the figure was very real.

Stanley Shoop, FRSC
Elstree, Herts

NOT FAIR TO DINOSAURS

■ I note with alarm that you attempt to disparage an out-of-date nuclear reactor by referring to it as a 'dinosaur' [*FT62:8*]. Forteans really should know better than to help perpetuate this weary calumny. Dinosaurs were spectacularly successful animals, highly adaptable and hard to stereotype: recent research even suggests that some may have been warm-blooded and/or hirsute!

M.D. Gale
Gatley, Cheshire

WE DON'T WISH TO KNOW THAT

■ I understand that the hand specialist at the John Radcliffe Hospital in Oxford is a Dr Cockin and that his surgery is known as 'The Cockin Hand Clinic'.

David Nicholls
Oxford

STONE OF DESTINY

■ A further point of interest on Dunadd [Secret Country, *FT64:53*], the ancient capital of the Scots situated in the Moine Mor, Argyll. This historic site was the original Scottish home of the Stone of Destiny or *Lia Fiall* brought, as legend has it, from Ireland by the sons of Erc, around 500AD.

The stone's past is unclear; it may have came with the Celts through Europe and before that from Palestine. It was once supposed to have been Jacob's pillow and St Columba used it later for a similar purpose. At any rate, the kings of Dalriada (the Celtic/Scottish colony in North Britain) were crowned on the stone just as the kings of Ireland had been before them.

After several centuries, it was removed from Dunadd to Dunstaffnage, near Oban, and then to Scone, where it was appropriated by Edward I. He then took it to England, where it has resided, apart from one brief celebrated incident in the 1950s, until the present day in Westminster Abbey where it is used in the coronation of the British monarchs.

Strangely enough, the block of stone seems to have suffered some form of transmutation during its adventures, as the sandstone rock presently residing in the Abbey bears no resemblance to the carved marble stone of the ancient chronicles.

Grant Stephen
Glasgow

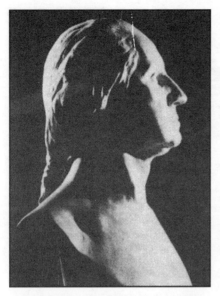 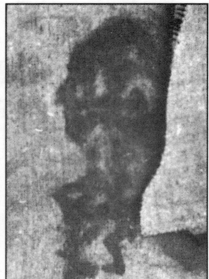

A STRIKING LIKENESS

■ In an age where there are frequent sightings of spontaneous religious images, it is unusual indeed to find the likeness of a secular personage on a religious relic. A portrait of US President George Washington has been found in the side wound blood stain on the Shroud of Turin. The wound is believed to be the evidence of a spear thrust in the chest of the crucified Christ. The bust of Washington reproduced here for comparison was made by the famous sculptor Jean Antoine Houdon in 1785, and was considered at the time to be the best likeness.

Jeffrey Vallence
Canoga Park, California

T. LOBSANG RAMPA

■ It must have surprised a number of people to learn from your article on the Tibetan mystical writer T. Lobsang Rampa that the world was 'shocked' when he was exposed as Cyril Henry Hoskins, a lowly ex-plumber from Plympton in Devon.

To some people, including it seems Mr Rickard, the version of Buddhism retailed in the Rampa books is considered rather unorthodox, but as there are more varieties of sectarian Buddhism than days in the year, who is in an a position to describe any one version as being questionable? In Tibet, Buddhism practised by the educated monks contrasts with popular folk religion, while the indigenous, pre-Buddhist Bon religion remains influential and widely practised, particularly in eastern Tibet.

Whatever the opinion entertained regarding Rampa's belief system, there is little doubt that he introduced Tibetan Buddhism to a far greater audience than most, if not all, his Buddhist critics, and in doing this probably stimulated in some a desire to investigate the subject in greater depth. They may even have turned to the 'learned' treatises of the very people his works upset; consequently they owe his memory a debt that they have failed to repay.

Mr Rickard describes the Hoskins/Rampa version of Buddhism as being 'bogus-Buddhist ancient magic', thereby suggesting that he knows of a genuine-Buddhist ancient magic, but omits to provide particulars. He quite rightly casts doubt on the authenticity of Rampa's Chinese medical doctorate, primarily because it was printed in English, though in the case of Chinese university degrees prior to the Communist takeover, this is not as odd as it seems. As Hoskins in now dead, the matter is academic, though as far as I know, he never attempted to practise medicine.

The Rampa books may have caused a rumpus in the Tibetan hen-roost, but I doubt if they have done any harm to anyone anywhere. Hoskins as 'Rampa' never attempted to set up his own pseudo-Tibetan monastic establishment with himself as chief lama surrounded by adoring acolytes. His works catered for people eager to wallow in a swamp of eastern mysticism. I also doubt whether the 'Rampa' affair really constitutes a 'literary scandal', famous or otherwise. Instead, it is a graphic illustration of how gullible all too many people have been.

R.W. Morrell
Nottingham

BONY THE BEAST

■ After reading the extract from *The Gentleman's Magazine* concerning the 'proof' that China was the great Beast of Revelations (ie = 666) [*FT63:52*], I was reminded of an amusing incident recounted by the famous historian and statesman, T.B. – later Lord – Macaulay.

Soon after his arrival in India in 1834, Maccaulay wrote to his friend and fellow classical scholar, Thomas Ellis, of an encounter with "… an Englishman who, without any preface, accosted me thus: 'Pray, Mr Macaulay, do not you think that Buonaparte is the Beast?' 'No, Sir, I cannot say that I do.' 'Sir, he was the Beast. I can prove it. I have found the number 666 in his name. Why, Sir, if he was not the Beast, who was?' This was a puzzling question, and I am not a little vain of my answer. 'Sir,' said I, 'the House of Commons is the Beast. There are 658 members of the House; and these, with their chief officers – the three clerks, the Sergeant and his deputy, the Chaplain, the doorkeeper, and the librarian – make 666.' 'Well, Sir, that is strange, But I assure you that if you write Napoleon Buonaparte in Arabic, leaving out only two letters, it will give 666.'

'And pray, Sir, what right have you to leave out two letters? And, as St John was writing Greek, and to Greeks, it is not likely that he would use the Greek rather than the Arabic notation?' 'But, Sir,' said this learned divine, 'everybody knows that the Greek letters were never used to make numbers.' I answered with the meekest voice and look possible: 'I do not think that everybody knows that. Indeed, I have reason to believe that a different opinion, erroneous no doubt, is universally embraced by all the small minority who happen to know any Greek.' So ended the controversy. The man looked at me as if he thought me a very wicked fellow; and I dare say, has by this time discovered that, if you write my name in Tamul, leaving out T in Thomas, B in Babbington, and M in Macaulay, it will give the number of this unfortunate Beast."

[Letter dated Ootacamund, 1 July 1934. In G.O. Trevelyn's *Life and Letters of Lord Macaulay*, v1, OUP.]

Mark Walker
North Harrow, Middlesex

OINK VEY!

■ The story of the 'kosher pig' [*FT59:39*] is heard every so often, ever since an Associated Press bulletin of 13 November 1984 reported that the babirusa had split hooves and may chew its cud. This would make it kosher, as specified in *Leviticus* 11:1-8. The AP bulletin was based on a report by the National Research Council (NRC) which noted that the babirusa has a stomach similar to a ruminant's. In fact, the non-ruminating character of the babirusa was recognised over a century ago by Sir Robert Owen in his book *On the Anatomy of Vertebrates* (London 1868). The babirusa is not kosher.

Zvi Ron
Ramat Modiim, Israel

A BURMESE APPARITION

■ I served with the Gloucestershire Regiment during World War II. I left Southampton on 10 January 1939 on the troopship Dunera , arriving in Mingaladon, Burma, about a month later. This was a military cantonment about 13 miles from Rangoon.

At about 2am one morning in December 1941, I was asleep in the corner of the barrack room. I had my mosquito net down and tucked in tight around the bed. The room contained 12 beds, six on each side. The entrance was off a verandah at the opposite end from where I lay. All the others were asleep, except for one man, who was out shooting small game.

I was sleeping on my left side when I was awoken by someone kneeling on my bed. He had dark hair and brown skin and looked very Burmese. I thought someone in the room was fooling about, so I told him sharply to move off. Then I heard my friend arrive back from his shooting trip and I asked him if he could see anything. He said no, but he told me later that he had felt a presence and his hair had stood on end with fright.

I again said in very harsh words for the figure to move off or I would hit him in the face. He just stared at me with a sort of half smile. I struck out, but my fist went into empty air. I got really scared and hit

out frantically. The mosquito net broke, and through the ripples of the net as it fell I could still see the smiling oriental face. I rushed out the other side of the bed and my friend put the lights on. This woke up all the others and we searched everywhere but could not find anything.

No-one got any more sleep that night, and about 11:00am I went to the garrison church and told the Padre what had happened. He had no sound advice for me. I thought he might have carried out some sort of service or exorcism.

Not long afterwards, my Regiment was ordered to move out of the barracks into the jungle to face the Japanese advancing from Pegu towards Rangoon. I didn't see the barracks again until I returned to Burma in 1947 as a Military Adviser to the

new Burmese Army. Mingaladon had many air raids both by the Japanese and later by the British when they reoccupied the place. The only building to receive a direct hit was the one where my barrack room had been - this room no longer existed. I was told that it had been hit the day after we moved out. I believe that the apparition was a warning for me to get out as soon as possible.

Ben Robins
Ealing, London

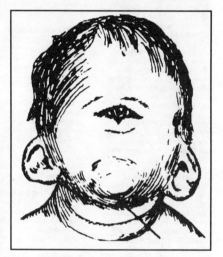

CYCLOPIA

■ I was interested in the cyclops child born in Brazil *[FT63:30]*. You should, however, be wary of the report of a 'penis' in the middle of the forehead. This appendage is, more correctly, a proboscis, as illustrated in the standard textbooks of embryology. As the glabellar region of the forehead fails to develop, the eyes coalesce and the nasal appendage is left high and dry. Incidentally, this anomaly is far commoner in the pig than in man.

Nick Warren, FRCS
Greenford, Middlesex

OH LORD! PLEASE DON'T LET ME BE MISUNDERSTOOD

TV SINNERS [FT65:50]

■ Those who have followed the **Fortean Times** coverage of the satanic ritual child abuse scare since FT57 will realise that the weight of evidence suggests that fundamentalist Christian organizations have played on the gullibility of naive social workers and police to promote the idea of an organised network of satanists who abuse children; they have furthermore revived the age-old 'baby-sacrifice' slander, used against minorities for over 2,000 years. Their aim seems to be to whip up end-time anxieties and hatred against professed pagans.

Sexual abuse of children is, alas, all too common, frequently committed by clergymen and lay Christians; but there is no evidence for *satanic* abuse except for the rare occasion where an individual abuser has made use of satanic trappings to intimidate his victims. The Fortean angle on the whole business is that of mass hysteria against an 'alien' group; in the last century the targets included the freemasons, the Jesuits and the white slavers, all of which spawned strange abuse and abduction narratives.

Our coverage of the Channel 4 *Dispatches* programme, 'Beyond Belief', aimed to show how covert Christian manipulators had presented an innocuous 'art' video as 'final proof' of ritual abuse, when it was no such thing. Perhaps we failed to spell out our message clearly enough. Those identified by the press as the makers of this video seem to think that Fortean Times has accused *them* of child abuse and sundry other dark deeds. In this they are entirely mistaken.

Fortean Times apologises for any distress caused to the family of Genesis P-Orridge by naming his children in the TV Sinners report [FT64:50] while quoting from Jon Ronson's *Time Out* article. The P-Orridges asked *Time Out* (2-9 Sept 1992) to make it clear that the daughter was not "baptised in blood".

We have been advised by the occult group Thee Temple Ov Psychick Youth (TOPY) that the FT report contained

numerous inaccuracies repeated from the newspapers to which we referred. We are quite happy to publish the points they make in their statement: The police search of the home of Genesis P-Orridge took place on Saturday, 15 February 1992, four days before the broadcast of the Channel 4 *Dispatches* programme, 'Beyond Belief'. The video, extracts of which were shown on the programme, was not produced by TOPY, and no individual currently connected with TOPY was involved in the production, creation, distribution or in any other way with the said video. TOPY has never been involved in illegal activities and abhors the abuse of any individual of any age. Genesis P-Orridge was never the 'leader' of TOPY and ceased all active involvement with the group in February 1990. TOPY has been independent of Psychic TV (and its offshoots) since 1989.

US AND THEM [FT65:58]

■ As a result of Andy Roberts' Ufology column last issue, which implied that 'Jeremy Barnyard' (real name: Gerald Banyard) and his colleague had made fools of themselves on a TV chat show, **Fortean Times** received an angry diatribe from Mr Banyard calling Andy Roberts a 'nit-wit' and much else besides. The column was a trifle rough on Mr Banyard, but he should realise that appearing on TV does expose one to the slings and arrows of outrageous criticism.

Mr Banyard writes that *Fortean Times* "may have to bear the consequences" of not publishing his vituperative and mis-spelt splutterings; we feel, however, that it would be fairer to him to draw a veil over the whole episode. Long-term FT readers will realise that our editorial position is impartial and one of dedicated fence-sitting. The most outlandish beliefs and experiences should be given a fair hearing. We wish all the best to Mr Banyard and others who have encountered strange realms; and we vigorously defend their right to describe their experiences and proclaim their beliefs to the public.

The Editors

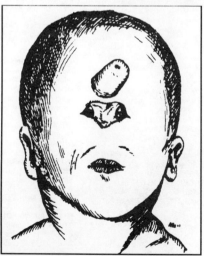

TOP: Cyclops – central orbit beneath proboscis contains a fused ocular bulb with doubled pupil, iris, lens & retina. ABOVE: Cyclops hypognathus, nose absent and mouth rudimentary.

CREDITS FOR THIS ISSUE

CLIPPINGS & TRANSLATION

Hubert Adamson, Jayne Amat, Bill Anders, R.J.Arnopp, Sherry Baker, K.A.Beer, Lionel Beer, Janet & Colin Bord, Linda Brown, Phillip Bruce, David J.Burns, Kevin Busby, Paul Cecil, Brian Chapman, Arthur Chrenkoff, Peter Christie, J.B.Coombs, COUD-I, Mat Coward, Miss J.Critchley, Jim Dick, Jill Doubleday, Peter Hope Evans, George Featherstone, Larry Fiander, Rob Gandy, Alan Gardiner, Robert Gifford, Ian Glasby, Izzet Goksu, Joan Good, Jim Haslam, Peter Hassall, John Harney, Stuart A.Herkes, M.A.Howard, Zofia Jaszek, Dionne Jones, Stephen Kearney, Joe Kelly, Michael Kemshall, David Kenny, M.C.Kilburn, Philip Landon, Kurt Lothmann, Ewen MaClean, Jen Magson, Nick Maloret, G.Markie, Valerie Martin, Otto Martinussen, Max McLaughlin, Mrs Tojo Melville, Michel Meurger, John Michell, Gary Mills, Barbara Millspaw, Ian Morgan, Jan Mura, Austin Murphy, Roger Musson, Ray Nelke, Robin Pascoe, Robin Peters, Jim Riecken, Brian Rogers, Zvi Ron, Sven Rosén, John Rowe, Tom Ruffles, John Sappington, Ronnie Scott, Paul Screeton, Jack Seabrook, Keith Seddon, Caryl Sibbett, Ian Simmons, Peter Stallard, Mervyn Szodzinsky, Dr S.C.Tavuchis, Paul R.Thomas, Pam Thornton, UFONS, John Viney, Nicholas P.Warren, Harry Whitehead, Owen Whiteoak, Annette Will, Ion Will, Jan Williams, Steve Wrathall.

ILLUSTRATION COPYRIGHTS

5 EPA\POPPERFOTO 6 (T) NORTH NEWS + PICTURES (B) ARTHUR CHRENKOFF. 7. ALBAN DONAHUE/REX. 11 (T) UNIVERSITY NEWS BRISBANE (B) HUNT EMERSON. 12 MERRILY HARPUR. 13 FELIX BENNETT. 14 TRISTAN HULSE + ROY FRY. 15 (BOTH) GARY LARSON/INTERCONTINENTAL FEATURES. 16 MERRILY HARPUR. 17 (PHOTO) PETE GLASTONBURY (MAP) DAILY TELEGRAPH. 18 ISLE OF WIGHT COUNTY PRESS LTD. 19 REUTER/POPPERFOTO. 20 MALCOLM CROFT/PA. 21 HUNT EMERSON. 24-26 FROM UFOS AND HOW TO SEE THEM. 27 BOB ROACH/FPL. 28 JOHN KEEL/FPL. 29 AUGUST ROBERTS/FPL. 30 FROM THE ROSWELL REPORT (CUFOS. 1991). 32 NEWHAM RECORDER. 33 LLEWELLYN PUBLICATIONS/FPL. 34 SOUTHERN NEWSPAPERS. 35 NASA/ERIC CREW. 37 POPPERFOTO. 38-9 FPL. 40 POPPERFOTO. 42-43 MARY EVANS PICTURE LIBRARY. 45 (MAP) ITA SANOMAT. 46 BOB FORREST. 47-49 UNKNOWN. 51 UNKNOWN. 52 (MAP) CROWN COPYRIGHT/CHRIS STREET (PHOTO) CHRIS STREET. 55 (2ND FROM L) ASHLEY PETERS (OTHERS) ARCHIVE. 57 PIERRE HOLLINS. 64 JEFFREY VALLENCE.

noticeboard

EXCHANGE & MART

● 'MUSIC FOR CROP CIRCLES' by Andy Thomas & David Swingland. Imaginative keyboard symphonies; an aural evocation of these modern enigmas. Chrome cassette, £6.99 (inc p&p): Rising Sun Productions, 14 Bishops Drive, Lewes, East Sussex BN7 1HA.

● THE CAULDRON – Pagan Journal featuring witchraft, folklore and earth mysteries. Sample copy £1.50 payable to: M Howard, Caemorgan Cottages, Caemorgan Road, Cardigan Dyfed SA93 1QU.

● CRYSTAL POINTS and facetted sterling silver crystal pendants in quartz, rose quartz, amethyst and hematite. Also gold plated pendants. Rose quartz pieces. Send for price list to: Lovelines, 7 High Street Arcade, Cardigan, Dyfed SA43 1HJ. Phone 0239 614181.

● MAKE THE PILGRIMAGE to Middle Earth – Tarot, crystals, oils, lava lamps, jewellery, incenses, cards, tarot readings by appointment. 102 Walton Street, Jericho, Oxford. Tel 0865 511522.

● MARYAM –Lived over 2,000 years ago but speaks now to groups and individuals worldwide. She seeks to warn and advise all. For basic info send £1, for bookpack £5, to: Vida Publications, 17 Stapenhall Road, Solihull, B90 4XX.

● YOUR LAST CHANCE to Discover Matchless Magic of the caring kind. Unique brochure £3 (profits to wildlife sanctuary). Margaret Bruce, High Rigg House, St John's Chapel, Bishop Auckland, Co Durham DL13 1QT.

● ESCAPE THE LATE 20TH CENTURY! – Romantia is a magical feminine empire outside the modern world. Send £2 for Imperial Angel magazine and other details to: Perfect Publications (FT), B M Perfect, London WC1 (full address).

● NEW DIMENSIONS – The monthly magazine of esoteric information. The best for occult articles, Qabalah, metaphysics, psychology, book and music reviews. Dynamic in origin. The best all rounder. Magic at its best. £1.25 UK, £1.75 overseas. Dept MS.1 Austin Close, Irchester, Northants NN9 7AZ..

● FRACTAL GRAPHIC PRINTS, cards, t-shirts etc. Send SAE for catalogue to: R Ramsey (FT), 9 Andrews Drive, Stanley Common, Derbys DE7 6GJ.

● THE NEWS/FORTEAN TIMES good condition, not dog-earred. 1-16 £45 (inc p&p). 21, 23-27, 29, 31-33, £2 each. Contact J Tait, Leck Mill, Leck, Carnforth, LA6 2JB.

● BIOFEEDBACK LINKED STROBE DREAMMACHINE – For the interactive exploration of unconscious fantasy. £77.50 inc p&p or SAE to Highland Psionics, Scoraig, Garve, Scotland IV23 2RE.

● MILLENIUM BOOKS – 2nd hand books on UFOs, mysteries and all kinds of weird and wonderful things. For free lists write, fax or phone Millenium Books, 9 Chesham Road, Brighton, Sussex BN2 1NB. Fax/Phone 0273 671967.

● UFO NEWSCLIPPING SERVICE – keeps you up with the real 'close encounters'. Many fascinating UFO reports from the world's press are reproduced facsimile, along with news-wire items from the major agencies. UFONS is 20 foolscap pages monthly, with a Fortean section strong on cryptozoology. Foreign language reports are provided in translation. For information and sample pages, write today to: UFONS - Lucius Farrish, Route 1 - Box 220, Plumerville, AR 72127, USA.

● THE SKEPTIC – takes an entertaining, rational and humourous look at pseudoscience and claims of the paranormal. Articles, reviews, columns, cartoons and much more. If you like FT you'll like The Skeptic. Sample issue £1.85; annual sub (6 issues) £12. The Skeptic, PO Box 475, Manchester M60 2TH.

● UFO AFRINEWS – edited by Cynthia Hind. The only UFO magazine in Africa. #1-4 available at £2; #5 at £2.50. Write: Gemini, Box MP49, Mt Pleasant, Harare, Zimbabwe.

● WICCA-BRIEF – an interesting newsletter for wiccans and pagans in German. Write to Wicca-Brief, Georgstr. 4, 2000 Hamburg 70, Germany.

RESEARCH

● ARK OF THE COVENANT – Anybody fascinated by this relic, its history, its power and its hiding place, and who wish to help set up a group to study and quest for it. If so, contact Jonothan Boulter by phone (081-459-5502) or at 4 Hurtington House, St Paul's Ave, Willesden Green, London NW2 5SR.

● FORTEAN CURIOS – Fortean Times is collecting information on private and museum collections of bizarre and mysterious objects such as unicorn horns, vegetable lambs, bits of alien craft, fafrotskies, rat-kings, fairy artifacts, mummified cats etc. If you know of any please write to FT at the editorial address.

● HELP WANTED – Scientific establishment and/or person required to assist, on a voluntary basis, with the analysis of alleged paranormal and/or UFO photographs. Please contact Philip Mantle, BUFORA, 1 Woodhall Drive, Batley, W.Yorks WF17 7SW. Tel: 0924 444049.

● BOOKSEARCH SERVICE – Out-of-print books a speciality. Dedicated, personal attention. No obligation to buy – no find no fee. For details send SAE to: Ian Murray (Dept FT), 6 Nevis Close, Loundsley Green, Chesterfield, Derbyshire S40 4NS.

EVENTS

● HAVING AN EVENT? – Publicize it in Fortean Times. Fax us details on 081 552 5466.

● TEMS – (Travel & Earth Mysteries Society) is a new non-sectarian group for SW London, Surrey and Middlesex, for those interested in ancient sites, leys, hauntings, crop circles, UFOs, unexplained animals, etc. For the programme of speakers, social events, trips and further info, contact Lionel Beer (081 979 3148), Barbara (081 942 3447), or Ann (081 542 3110).

● FROM OUTER SPACE TO YOU – UFO 92. Talks, film, slides, abductions, close encounters, crop circles. 14/15 November 1992. Hever Village Hall, Nr Hever Castle, Edenbridge, Kent. Details: Alan Hilton (organiser), 'Highland Glen', Gravesend Rd, Shorne, Kent DA12 3JW.

● SOCIETY FOR PSYCHICAL RESEARCH – Lectures. 17 Sept: Investigating spontaneous cases (Howard Wilkinson). 15 Oct: Psi and the Ganzfeld: what we have learnt so far (Charles Honorton). 12 Nov: Is the medium the message? New developments in survival research (Leslie Price). 10 Dec: The dying brain: science and the near-death experience (Susan Blackmore). Venue: the Lecture Hall of Kensington Central Library, Campden Hill Road, London W8, at 6:30pm. Non-members £3, student cards £1. Further information from the SPR at 49 Marloes Rd, Kensington, London W8 6LA. Tel: 071 937 8984.

● BUFORA – British UFO Research Association. Lectures at London Business School, Sussex Place, Outer Circle, Regents Park, London NW1 at 6:30pm. £1.50 (members), £3.00 (visitors). 7 Nov – 'Cognating the UFO: a Bonfire of old Theories' (Alan Mayne). 5 Dec – 'UFOs in Art' (illustrated) (Michael Buhler). Ring: 0582 763218 for more details.

● FOLKLORE SOCIETY – Katherine Briggs Lecture and Reception, 10 Nov, 6:00pm, at University College London. Details from: Marion Bowman, Folklore Society, University College London, Gower St, London WC1E 6BT. Tel: 071 387 5894.

● LONDON EARTH MYSTERIES CIRCLE – Evening meetings in St Andrew's Seminar Room, Maria Assumpta Centre, 23 Kensington Square, London W8, at 7pm on the 2nd and 4th Tuesdays in each month. Members £1.00, non-members £2.00, unwaged £1.50. Lectures: 13 Oct (Reclaiming our Heritage), 27 Oct (Earth Mysteries and Magnetism), 10 Nov (social eve.), 24 Nov (UFOs & Psychic phenomena). Contact: Rob Stephenson, 18 Christchurch Ave, London NW6 7QN, or tel: 081 459 0652.

● THEOSOPHICAL SOCIETY – events on 6 Dec: at 11:15am, 'Holy Blood and The Holy Grail'; at 6pm 'Megalithic Science' - 50 Gloucester Place, London W1H 3HJ. Tel: 071 935 9261.

● TIBET FORUM – free lectures every first Tuesday of each month at Institute Hall, Bloomsbury Central Baptist Church, 235 Shaftesbury Ave, London WC2 at 6:30pm. 3 Nov – 'An Introduction to Tibetan Medicine' (Dr Tamdin Sither). 2 Dec – 'United Nations and the Quest for Human Rights' (Dr Norman Goodman).

MISCELLANEOUS

● DRUIDS! – Discover what they do and how Druidry answers our need for a spirituality that is connected to the land and our ancient heritage. For info send SAE to: ODOB (FT) 260 Kew Road, Richmond, Surrey TW9 3EG. One man's meat is another creature's slaughterhouse nightmare. One man's meat is another creature's agonizing death. Isn't it time you went vegetarian?

● ANIMAL MESSIAH – beautiful revelation of Jesus' secret teachings on vegetarianism, hunting and cruelty to animals. Plus 13 previously unknown commandments. Genuine, top secret information. Booklet £2.50, payable: BCM-Redeemer, London WC1N 3XX.

● WELSH HOLIDAY COTTAGE – Self-catering accomodation in historic North Wales town of Denbigh. For further details, contact Janet Bord, Melysfan, Llangwm, Corwen, Clwyd LL21 0RD. Tel: 049 082 472. Fax: 049 082 321.

● GLASTONBURY COTTAGE – Forget expensive hotels or B&Bs – charming 2 bed house to let in mystic Glastonbury town centre. Central-heating, fully furnished with necessary utensils, crockery etc, and unique view over Abbey grounds. Tel: 0234 211606 (answerphone) for leaflet.

● OLD PULP SF MAGS WANTED – for FT Library. Also FATE MAGAZINE vol 1, no 4 (1948); nos 50 (1954) & 90 (1957). Write to Bob Rickard, c/o FT editorial address.

● FORTEAN PICTURES – The Fortean Picture Library is a self-funding project for the rescue and preservation of valuable documentary material, photographs and drawings etc. If you have anything of this nature please let FPL look after it. 50% of any revenue from the commercial use of the material (in books etc) could come back to you. FPL covers all expenses from its half. Contact Janet Bord, FPL, Melysfan, Llangwm, Corwen, Clwyd, Wales LL21 0RD. Tel: 049 082 472.

Russian Flying Man Exposed!

Frightening Creature Scares Family Out of Their Wits

Last year, during the very first night at their new house, the Ivanitzky family was awakened by an unusually loud chirping that reminded them of crickets.

This happened more than once, and on the tenth day, the head of the family discovered a strange creature resembling a dog, or a huge mouse, under the bed.

After slippers were thrown at the creature, it twitched and grew in size, becoming three times as big. It unexpectedly cast out a very long trunk from its nose which it used to try to grab the legs of the family.

Already scared out of their wits, the family began hitting the creature with whatever they could lay their hands on and the children sprayed it with household chemicals.

The creature rolled over to a far away corner, and lay there not moving. When it was brought out from under the bed, they discovered a creature that looked like a dog. It had very short bluish hair, two three-fingered paws and strong wings, about a meter and a half in wingspread.

The shape of the creature's wings reminded the family of a bat's wing. The creature's muzzle looked like a human face cast in plaster: an almost flat, clear face with a small forehead, very large eyes, and a tiny lipless mouth. Instead of a nose, the creature had one triangular hole.

Mr. Ivanitzky, fearful of the consequences (had he killed a State-protected animal?), threw it out into a ditch. Soon the creature disappeared from that ditch...

Read the November issue of **FATE** magazine, which uncovers firsthand information of the Russian Flying Man and other creatures of our strange world.

Our Strange World

Thousands of people all over the world are experiencing these same kinds of frightening events. ***The evidence is everywhere!*** Consider the time when hundreds of half-inch shrimp appeared in the swimming pool of Robert R. Burns in California. After many days of investigation, experts theorized that the shrimp fell in a recent heavy rain. When reported in the local newspaper a woman called in with a similar story! Did it really rain shrimp?

Why have these unusual reports become so popular? Because people are finally leaving the familiar behind and **demanding** answers to the mysteries of our strange world.

And it's not only these puzzling events that people are talking about! They're also speaking out about:

- **The Empty Rocking Chair That Sits on a Porch and Turns as Cars Pass By**

- **People Who Feel Like Animals With Claws —Could They Be Real Werewolves?**

- **A Monster Covered with Both Scales and Fur that Attacks Passersby**

Some say there are things we were never meant to know. Mysteries better left unanswered. Strange places that should never be discovered...

But aren't you just a little bit interested in whether or not these unexplainable phenomena does exit? Don't you want to familiarize yourself with this exciting subject so you can make up ***your own mind***?

The Mystery of Green Briar Swamp

There is an age-old legend about haunted buried treasure in the Maryland Green Briar Swamp. Popular belief has it that treasure was hidden in a burial vault by a plantation owner, assisted by a female servant. After burying the treasure, the man supposedly cut off her head with his sword and buried her too.

Known as Big Liz, the slave's apparition has been seen in modern times and is one of the most popular of the Eastern Shore's apparitions.

For at least 30 years local teenagers have believed that if you drive to DeCourcey Bridge, honk your horn six times and blink your headlights three times, Big Liz will be summoned.

She shuffles silently, slowly approaching with stooped shoulders and carrying her head in her hand. While accounts vary, most percipients describe her glowing eyes like "two branding irons fired to a white heat." (Reprinted from **FATE** magazine, August 1992.)

Reliable and Complete

Month by month, **FATE** magazine brings you the ***most reliable and complete*** evidence—much of it new—in the world of the strange and unknown.

- **Share the stories of people who have experienced meetings with the strange and unknown through exclusive, real-life accounts**

- **Evaluate the controversial idea of UFO sightings and determine if other life forms *really* do exist**

- **Satisfy your hunger for accurate information on the paranormal**

- **Separate the scientific from the sensational...the truth from the questionable...the reliable from the doubtful**

Each issue explores a variety of unexplained phenomena: the Bermuda Triangle Mystery, Vampires of the Night, Bigfoot in Southern California.

And ***new and exciting*** discoveries! Read Mark Chorvinsky's monthly column on thrilling Fortean Phenomena. Journey with John Keel as he explores what is "Beyond The Known." Join **FATE** readers as they tell their own stories in "True Mystical Experiences."

Whatever is unknown, strange and mysterious, **FATE *searches out, explores and reveals with complete accuracy.***

Scientists and Witnesses

Open *any* issue of **FATE** and you'll receive the latest information from an exclusive and complete circle of scientists and psychics, believers and skeptics, witnesses and investigators.

What they've seen and heard...what they've explored...what they've experienced: you'll learn it all—firsthand. Then you'll be able to sit back and make up your ***own*** mind about what you've just discovered.

With **FATE** magazine you can learn more about the strange and unknown than you ever thought possible! Plus, each issue is based on objective research and documented fact—to help you investigate ***every*** possibility of the unseen world.

Journey to the Unknown

Fasten your seat belt and prepare for a journey that uncovers the exciting and mystifying world of the strange and unknown. You're only moments away from finding out the latest-breaking events in the world of monsters, creatures and other mysterious phenomena. You can't afford to pass up this opportunity—it is the ***only*** way to receive the answers to nature's unexplained events.

SUBSCRIBE TO FATE TODAY!

Secret Deals and the Cuban Missile Crisis

Who blinked first – Kennedy or Krushchev?

Thirty years after the world was brought to the brink of nuclear catastrophe, October's issue of HISTORY TODAY looks at the superpowers' secret negotiations.

Also, articles on Beveridge's blue print for the NHS; Hitler's remilitarisation of the Rhineland; the roots of the present Serb, Croat and Muslim conflict; Australia's convict history; and a fascinating look at the anti-vaccination, pro-vegetarian founder of Allinson's bread.

In each richly illustrated issue you will discover eye-opening accounts and fresh historical interpretations; generously enhanced with rare paintings and photographs, many in full colour – uniting serious history with a measure of high entertainment.

HISTORY TODAY's contributors are leading international historians and commentators, including – *Max Beloff, Paul Preston, Pamela Tudor-Craig, Nicholas Henderson, Marina Warner, David Starkey and Akbar Ahmed.*

HISTORY TODAY the monthly magazine covering all types and periods of history, and all corners of the globe.

Future Features

- Deng Xiaoping and the Last Empress of China
- Sinking the French Fleet at Toulon, 1942
- Religion and Revolt in Bengal under the Raj
- Gang Warfare in the American Civil War
- Queen Victoria and Buckingham Palace
- Football and Politics in the Cold War Soviet Union

FREE Book Offer:
New subscribers to **HISTORY TODAY** will get FREE, one of two excellent books. Choose either *The Impact of the English Civil War*, a series of essays that examines the war from all aspects, edited by Dr John Morrill and published by Collins & Brown at £6.99. OR *Russia and Europe*, a timely and important book for understanding the tensions and problems in the former Soviet Union today, edited by Professor Paul Dukes and published by Collins & Brown at £8.99. **PLUS**, you will also be sent a copy of our special issue commemorating the 500th anniversary of Henry VIII's birth (normally £3.50), and a free annual index (with your March issue).

Discover the secrets of history and take advantage of this special offer now.

History Today Readers' Club
Membership is normally open to subscribers who renew their subscription, however, if you take out a two year subscription you will automatically be entitled to the following: Hotel savings of 50% at Hilton National Hotels, reduced rate history books and Channel 4 booklets, and a free issue of *Military History Quarterly* – full details will be given on commencement of your subscription.

YES, I would like to take advantage of this special offer for new subscribers to **HISTORY TODAY** (12 issues). I enclose my cheque (amount × 2 for 2 year subscription) for UK £26.50*; Europe £37.50; Rest of World £42; USA $52; Canada Can$69; made payable to History Today Ltd. Please send coupon with payment to: History Today, FREEPOST 39, 83/84 Berwick Street, London W1E 6JZ. Payment enclosed for ☐ One year subscription ☐ Two year subscription. I would like as my special introductory gift a FREE copy of ☐ Russia and Europe. ☐ The Impact of the English Civil War. (Please tick).

NAME _____

ADDRESS _____
_____
_____ POST/ZIPCODE _____   D

If you wish to keep your magazine intact, a photo-copy order is acceptable.
*UK Full-time students (degree level and above) and OU students special rate of £16 if proof of status sent, but special offer not available.

HISTORY TODAY

is available at leading newsagents price £2.50

NUMBER 66

UK £2
USA $4.95

FORTEAN TIMES

THE JOURNAL OF STRANGE PHENOMENA

HOW OLD IS THE EARTH?
Did Darwin Get It Wrong?

66

TRADESCANT'S ARK
A Cabinet of Curiosities

Julian Cope Interview ● **Florida's Penguin Panic**
Bogus Social Workers ● **Sky Cities of Alaska** ● **Mystery Blobs**

308 589118

Contents
Issue 66 December 1992/January 1993

P24 *DARWIN DOUBTED*

P32 *CURIOUS CABINET*

P41 *PENGUIN PANIC*

Cover by Hunt Emerson

WHY 'FORTEAN'?

CHARLES FORT (1874-1932)

Fortean Times is a bi-monthly magazine of news, reviews and research on all manner of strange phenomena and experiences, curiosities, prodigies and portents, formed in 1973 to continue the work of the iconoclastic philosopher CHARLES FORT. Fort was sceptical about scientific explanations, observing how scientists argued for and against various theories and phenomena according to their own beliefs, rather than the rules of evidence. He was appalled that data not fitting the collective paradigm was ignored, suppressed, discredited or explained away (which is quite different from explaining a thing).

Fort was perhaps the first to speculate that mysterious lights seen in the sky might be craft from outer space. He coined the term 'teleportation' which has passed into general usage through science fiction. His dictum "One measures a circle beginning anywhere" expresses his philosophy of Continuity and the 'doctrine of the hyphen', in which everything is in an intermediate state between extremes. He had notions of the universe-as-organism and the transient nature of all apparent phenomena. Far from being an over-credulous man, Fort cut at the very roots of credulity: "I cannot accept that the products of minds are subject matter for beliefs ... I conceive of nothing, in religion, science, or philosophy, that is more than the proper thing to wear, for a while."

Fort was born in Albany, New York, in 1874 into a family of Dutch immigrants. Beatings by a tyrannical father helped set him against authority and dogma, and on leaving home at the age of 18 he hitch-hiked around the world to put some "capital into the bank of experience." At 22 he contracted malaria, married his nurse and settled down to 20 years of impoverished journalism in the Bronx. During this time he read extensively in the literature of science, taking notes on small squares of paper in a cramped shorthand of his own invention, which he filed in shoe boxes.

In 1916, when he was 42, Fort came into a modest inheritance, just enough to relieve him of the necessity of having to earn a living. He started writing *The Book of the Damned*, which his friend, the novelist Theodore Dreiser, bullied his own publisher into printing in 1919. Fort fell into a depression, burnt all his notes (which numbered some 40,000) as he had done a few years earlier, and in 1921 set sail for London, where he spent eight years living near the British Museum (39 Marchmont Street) and wrote *New Lands* (1923). Returning to New York, he published *Lo!* in 1931 and *Wild Talents* in 1932, shortly before he died. He left 60,000 notes, now in the New York Public Library.

THE GANG OF FORT:

Editors:
Bob Rickard
& Paul Sieveking

Contributing Editors:
Steve Moore
& Mike Dash

© Fortean Times December 1992
ISSN 0308 5899

EDITORIAL ADDRESS
Fortean Times: Box 2409, London NW5 4NP, UK. Tel & Fax: 071 485 5002 or 081 552 5466.

SUBMISSIONS
Submissions are invited of suitable articles, news, art, cartoons, reviews, and especially clippings. Preliminary discussion with the editors is advisable. Text can be submitted on floppy disks, but check with the editors first. Submissions may be edited. FT assumes no responsibility for submissions, but all reasonable care will be taken while they are in FT's possession. Requests for return of material should be accompanied by stamped addressed envelope.

CLIPPINGS
All clippings, references, etc, should be identified by source, date and clipster's name. Mail or fax them to the editorial address (above).

SUBSCRIPTIONS
RATES – One year (6 issues). UK: £12. Overseas inc. USA: £12.50 or US$25. For two years (12 issues) UK: £20, overseas inc USA £25 or US$50.
PAYMENT – US/Canadian cheques acceptable; payments from all other countries should be in sterling drawn upon a London bank. Major credit cards accepted – just phone details to 0373 451777. Make cheque/money orders payable to:
JOHN BROWN PUBLISHING Ltd, 20 Paul Street, Frome, Somerset BA11 1DX, UK.

ADVERTISING ENQUIRIES
DISPLAY or CLASSIFIED: contact Ronnie Hackston or Dan Squirrell at John Brown Publishing Ltd: The Boathouse, Crabtree Lane, Fulham, London SW6 8NJ, UK. ☎ 071 381 6007 or Fax: 071 381 3930.
BOOKSELLERS' LISTING items – contact the editorial address (above).

PUBLISHER
John Brown Publishing Ltd, The Boathouse, Crabtree Lane, Fulham, London SW6 8NJ, UK. ☎ 071 381 6007 or Fax: 071 381 3930.
Managing Editor: Fiona Jerome.
Publisher: Vic Lime.

DISTRIBUTION
UK trade distribution by UMD, 1 Benwell Road, Holloway, London N7 7AX. ☎ 071 700 4600 or Fax: 071 607 3352.
USA newsstand distribution by Eastern News Distributors Inc, 2020 Superior St, Sandusky, OH 44870, USA.

Bob Rickard

EDITORIAL: Heaven can wait

Paul Sieveking

Thousands of Korean Christians waited for the Rapture at 3pm on 28 October (midnight, Korean time). When they realised the moment of bodily ascent into Heaven had passed, they had to drift off instead to the homes and jobs so many of them had given up for the promise of eternal life. In the city of Taegu, a disappointed congregation beat up their pastor, and elsewhere a sceptical theologian who scoffed too loudly was stabbed; otherwise, said Korean police, the wave of expected suicides didn't happen. For more details see page 7.

● This issue (page 24), we feature an article by Richard Milton, who casts doubt on the rock-dating methods used to calculate the age of our planet. Perhaps Earth is much younger than Darwinists require for their epic of natural selection to be played out. Mr Milton has generated quite a bit of heat – not to say abuse – in the scientific press just recently with his book *The Facts of Life*.

● As 1992 is the tricentenary of the death of Elias Ashmole, founder of the Ashmolean Museum in Oxford, we asked museum curator Ian Simmons to describe the 'cabinet of curiosities' assembled by John Tradescant that formed the basis of this famous collection. His article appears on page 32.

● As we go to press, we have learned of the suicide of a boy who was frightened out of his wits by the BBC TV programme *Ghostwatch*, screened on All Hallows' Eve a few weeks ago. The show was a dramatisation of a fictional investigation of a violent poltergeist haunting featuring a live broadcast, a phone-in, and a studio chat with 'expert' researchers – all fake except for the celebrity presenters who were well-known from children's or light entertainment shows.

Ghostwatch lurched uneasily between seeming fact and realistic fiction, finally going over the top as the polt burst into the studio and possessed Michael Parkinson. Many angry viewers complained afterwards that they were seriously disturbed by the programme's overt demonstration of the objective existence of malevolent discarnate entities. Others felt disgust at being cruelly tricked by celebrities they trusted implicitly to tell them the truth about a fascinating subject. The screening of *Ghostwatch* raises issues which deserve to be discussed more fully than we can do in this short notice, and this will be done next issue.

● A timely reminder that the **Fortean Times 1993 Diary** is a goldmine of entertaining information, running to 50,000 words, and makes an excellent Christmas present. Here's an example: 15 December is the birthday of the Emperor Nero, Eiffel (of the Tower), Dr Ludwig Zamenhof (inventor of Esperanto), and Edna O'Brien. On this day in 1980, members of the Truth Tabernacle Church in Burlington, North Carolina, staged a mock trial, charging 'Satan Claus' on ten counts, including child abuse, impersonation of St Nicholas, Baal idolatry and falsification of Christ's birthday. Claus was found guilty and hanged in effigy, as a gaggle of giggling children looked on.
See page 23 for ordering details.

THE EDITORS

STRANGE DAYS

16 pages of worldwide weirdness

MOCKINGBIRD OFFENSIVE

Helen Morel, a student from Washington DC, ducks in surprise as she is attacked by one of two mockingbirds nesting nearby in Dupont Circle, a few blocks from the White House, in June 1992. The birds were expected to keep up the attacks until the nestlings were ready to fly after a few weeks.

VIETNAM'S LOST WORLD

John MacKinnon holding the horns of the unknown mammal from the Vu Quang Nature Reserve in Vietnam

The remote and roadless Vu Quang nature reserve in Vietnam is 65 square miles along a steep stretch of land near the Laotian border, a rugged trek from the central town of Vinh and 10 hours' drive from Hanoi. (One source, the *Bangkok Post*, maintains that Vu Quang spreads over 65,168 square kilometres: this is quite a discrepancy!) Left untouched by half a century of war and expanding civilization, the reserve was originally set aside and protected as a cultural area because it provided refuge for a local hero who had rebelled against the French.

Field Trip

A team of scientists from the Vietnamese government and the London-based World Wildlife Fund (known in Europe as the Worldwide Fund for Nature), under the direction of senior conservationist John McKinnon, 45, visited the reserve on a three-week field trip last May. Zoologists had never visited the area before.

Fresh Maggots

The team spotted two previously unknown bird species, at least one new fish and an unknown tortoise with a striking yellow shell. They also observed 62 fish species, 20 species of amphibian and 37 reptile species. Most exciting of all, however, was the discovery of three upper skulls and horns of an antelope-like animal - one with fresh maggots still inside it - in hunters' houses. The hunters have been asked to look out for a live specimen, and Dr McKinnon is working on a camera trap to photograph the elusive creature. An inch-square specimen of skin was sent to US cancer research scientists for DNA analysis.

"We still don't know exactly what the mammal is", said Dr McKinnon. "The local people call it a forest goat, but goats' horns are usually ribbed or bent back and spiralled. These stick right up out of the skull and are straight and dagger-like, a bit like the African oryx." The oryx is known to have inhabited what is now Pakistan in a previous age. Dr McKinnon said the animal, which can have black or brown hide, appeared to be about the size of an English fallow deer with 18-inch horns, deadly enough to fend off tigers.

Skin Samples

"We hope the DNA testing of hair and skin samples in the United States will tell us where it falls in the bovid family. The whole team is very excited as discovery of new large mammals is very rare, I think about five this century."

The new species could turn out to be related to the anoa, a primitive dwarf buffalo found only in Indonesia; or the tamarau of the Philippines. As a result of the discoveries, the Vietnamese government have promised to halt the building of a timber mill and extend the nature reserve. The World Wildlife Fund is also pushing for Laos to establish a reserve in its adjacent Khammonn province to give further protection to the lush habitat. *[AP], Evening Standard, 17 July + 17 Aug; D.Telegraph, 17 July; AP, 28 July; Bangkok Post, 29 July; Wellington (NZ) Evening Post, 19 Aug 1992.*

DOUGH FROM ABOVE

On St Patrick's Day (17 March 1992), 20 pounds of white-bread dough fell from the sky and crashed through the roof of Doug and Paula Ward of Bellingham, Washington, with what was described as "a horrendous crash, like a sonic boom".

"An astronomer took a sample", Paula Ward told columnist Dave Barry, "and he said it was just regular bread dough. The religious people think it was a sign from God, because you know, in the Bible, God dropped manna. But it doesn't look like religious dough to me. We still have it, and it hasn't risen yet. It's looking kind of slimy." *Monday Magazine (Victoria, British Columbia) 18 June 1992.*

HARD TO SWALLOW

As thousands of tourists made their annual pilgrimage to the ancient mission at San Juan Capistrano in California, they scanned the skies in vain. The swallows are no longer returning to Capistrano. As he has done in many previous years, 96-year-old Paul Arbiso rang the mission bells at 8:02am on 19 March, to signal their return, but ornithologist Margaret Rubega, in attendance, saw only a white-throated swift and a hummingbird.

The annual return of migrating swallows has been celebrated in phrase, song and literature, but the birds are having none of it. Development around the mission has displaced their usual supply of insects and the birds are now dining out in other areas, such as the marshland at Irvine to the north. *Daily News (CA), 20 March 1992.*

SUMMER SPORTS OF NATURE

● Michael Leonetti, 11, of Des Moines, Iowa, holds a seven-legged frog (shown below) which he found while fishing for tadpoles in Des Moines Water Works Park. The Science Center of Iowa was interested in displaying the frog. It was thought that one of the frog's legs was cut as it grew, and each part of the leg that was cut developed its own leg. [AP] 25 July 1992.

● A four-clawed two-pound female lobster (see picture below) was on display at a Waterville, Maine, store on 21 July. It was caught in Penobscot Bay and was to be given to the Maine Aquarium at the end of the summer. [AP] 22 July 1992.

DOOMSDAY DELAYED

● The million or so Koreans who followed Pastor Lee Jang Lim of the Tami Missionary Church and similar eschatological outfits were disappointed in their expectation that the Rapture (taking up to heaven) would happen on 28 October [see *FT65:7*]. Doomsday arrived a month early for Pastor Lee, who was arrested at the end of September. Police discovered that he had received over two million pounds in donations from his flock and was converting some of this, illegally, into US dollars. Most incriminating of all was the discovery of £230,000 in bonds that were due to mature in 1995, three years into the Great Tribulation, when money was supposed to be worthless. [AP] 24 Sept; Independent, 30 Sept 1992.

● Not all believers agreed on the exact date of the Rapture. One burnt himself to death on 5 October, a day before his chosen day for the Second Coming. It was the fourth known doomsday-related suicide this year. Another 500 devotees of the Davera Mission Church, led by Ha Bang-ik, spent several hours in prayer on the night of 9/10 October in a south Seoul chapel. The 200 riot police outside didn't intervene. Ostensibly, there were there to prevent suicides. [AP] 11 Oct 1992.

● Jesus was due to appear in the air above Australia on 29 October, according to the Mission for the Coming Days, headed by Korean-born pastor Chang Hun Jo in Sydney and affiliated to the Tami Missionary Church. Adherents throughout Australia readied themselves for the ascent to heaven, leaving the rest of us to face the Anti-Christ and seven years of 'Horrible Great Tribulation'. *Wellington (NZ) Evening Post, 22 Aug; Brisbane (Aust.) Sunday Mail, 6 Sept 1992.*

● Meanwhile, across Sydney Harbour, Adam Newman, 58, sits waiting for The End. Some 28 years ago, he said, the spirit told him to build an ark before the great rains. He has been building ever since and now he has four. He attracted little attention until recently, when he took on local government over the conversion of his 12-roomed house into a 'mother ark'.

He is not quite sure when The End will be, but he regards as portentous the recent arrival on his doorstep of a rat, and the refusal of cats and pigeons to leave his 'mother ark'. The house still stands firmly on its foundations, but he has sealed the floorboards, built a wheelhouse and stored hundreds of pieces of foam for buoyancy. The other three arks float nearby. [Reuters] 17 Sept 1992.

BEWARE SWIFT TUTTLE

● Comet Swift-Tuttle, which produces Earth's spectacular Perseid shower every August, has been spotted for the first time since 1862, said American astronomers on 29 September. Brian Marsden, director of the Central Bureau for Astronomical Telegrams, predicted in 1973 that the comet might show up late this year if it failed to appear between 1979 and 1983. The comet will be visible to the naked eye in December.

Swift-Tuttle is due to make its next close approach in about 2126, when, for the first time, it will come close enough to hit us. The odds on this happening have been quoted as one in 400. The explosion caused by impact with the six-mile-wide comet travelling at around 130,000mph would be about 1,000 million times greater than the Hiroshima bomb. All the buildings in the world would fall down and everybody would be killed, except perhaps a few living in caves. A huge dust cloud would produce a temporary ice age. In short, much the same scenario as the alleged meteoric collision 65 million years ago, when the dinosaurs were wiped out. *Hackensack (NJ) Record, 30 Sept; D.Telegraph, 23 Oct 1992.*

BLASPHEMOUS SHOES AND TYRES

There has been footwear trouble with Muslims for years. In 1985, thousands of Chinese shoes were seized in Egypt because the anti-slip treads reversed out as the Arabic for Allah. British and French bootmakers had similar troubles. In 1989, at least 50 people were injured (and possibly two killed) in Bangladesh riots over rubber slippers bearing a motif resembling the Arabic for Allah.

In April 1992, the strife erupted in the British Midlands, which played host to the holy eggplants (bearing the name of Allah) back in 1990 (see *FT55:4)*. A Nottingham fashion shop was selling dressy Italian gold shoes (£69.99 a pair) decorated with an Arabic verse from the First Pillar of Islam: "There is no God but Allah".

Haji Mohammed Asmat, vice-chairman of the Nottingham Islamic Centre, wanted the owner of the three Valentina shops selling the shoes, in Nottingham, Leicester and Peterborough, to withdraw the offending shoes and apologise to the Muslim community. "It is more serious than Salman Rushdie", he insisted. "Rushdie wrote a book which you carry in your hand. Here, the holy name goes on the feet."

Italian-born owner of the shops, Mrs Diana Lewis, at first refused to withdraw the shoes, but reached an amicable agreement with Muslim representatives on Friday, 17 April. A wealthy Muslim bought the last 12 pairs in the Nottingham shop and burned them. In the small hours of the following Monday, however, a Toyota estate car was driven into the window of the Leicester Valentina shop and set alight, destroying the entire stock of shoes. It was not known who was responsible. *Nottingham Eve. Post, Leicester Mercury, 17 April; Guardian, 17+21 April 1992.*

Diana Lewis with one of the offending shoes.

JEEP PROTEST

In July, the Tokyo-based Yokohama Rubber Company recalled tyres fitted on Mitsubishi jeeps after being bombarded with protests by Muslims in Brunei and Saudi Arabia who claimed that the tyre's tread pattern resembled the Arabic for Allah. Spokesman Akira Mikami said the company had stopped producing the tyres and was replacing them with new ones free of charge in Islamic countries. The company also ran an apology in the 13 May edition of a magazine published by the Japan Islam Association. Yokohama recalled 300 tyres from Brunei and cancelled orders for a further 380.

The treads were designed by computer to maximise driving safety, not to upset Muslims. An unidentified gunman fired three shots on 20 July at the entrance of a house owned by Hisaaki Suzuki, chairman of Yokohama Rubber. Japanese police were investigating whether there was any connection with the tyre controversy. *[Reuters, AP] 24 July; Guardian, 25 July; The Daily Yomiuri [Japan], Aug 1992.*

HOLY FOREARM

Islamic simulacra in nature are quite a different matter and are widely welcomed by the faithful. A baby born bearing the name 'Mohammed' twice on her left forearm has become a celebrity in the Muslim desert nation of Chad. The girl was born on 3 or 4 October. Ironically, her parents, Josephine Mormale and Thomas Ndoubade, are Christians. The mother said she hadn't noticed the writing at first, thinking it was only a scar. *Edinburgh Evening News, 5 Oct 1992.*

CROSSED SOLES

In May, a court in Athens banned the sale of shoes with crosses on their soles, saying they insulted both religion and the state because the cross were similar to those used by the Greek Orthodox Church and on the Greek flag. The magistrate, Theodora Goini, upheld a petition by the Holy Union of Greek Clerics, which said several shoe companies had copied crosses found on the soles of shoes made by Timberland, an American company. The ban was lifted on 15 July. *[AP] 15 May; [AFP] 16 July 1992.*

The wreckage of Diana Lewis' shop in Leicester.

FAMILY FIRM

Japan Efficiency Corporation, started by Satsuki Oiwa five years ago, rents families by the hour or day to those who live alone, offers shopping companions to housewives, sympathetic ears to stressed-out executives, even people to scold for those who are dying to tell someone off, but can't in Japan's culture of restraint. Employees are ranked from seventh to first class, depending on acting ability. Customers have to be wealthy: the service costs up to £300 an hour. There can be problems: the police were called when Mr and Mrs Tancha from Okinawa, both over 80, began to abuse and beat three rented 'grandchildren' for their disrespectful behaviour. *Toronto Globe & Mail, 2 April; Int. Herald Tribune, 15 May; Awake, June 1992.*

RENT-A-READ

Bibliophiles in Ulm, Germany, who wish to give their personal libraries that enviable 'read' look can hire a professional 'reader', who will turn down corners, leave theatre and cinema tickets as bookmarks, make marginal notations and underline significant passages. Price according to quantity and *Behandlungsintensität*, a useful word meaning roughly "degree of intensity of handling". *Guardian, 8 Aug 1992.*

ELK DROPPINGS

Horst Kühne, a German-born tourist official in northern Sweden, has a roaring trade in elk droppings gathered from the forest floor in Harjedalen province, which he packs in empty jam jars and sells for 35 kronor (£3.50) a go. "To be able to show your friends a dropping from an elk in a glass jar is exotic", he said. Having sold at least 1,000 jars this year, mostly to Germans, he is now branching out into reindeer droppings. *[AP] 21 Aug 1992.*

GOAT SPEAKS OUT

According to Ugandan state radio, a goat has proclaimed that the AIDS epidemic sweeping Uganda is a divine punishment for disobeying the Ten Commandments. The goat spoke in a "loud, terrifying voice" to the villagers of Kyabagala, in Mukono district, but died a few hours later. It also predicted that Uganda was on the verge of a great famine. *[AFP] 3 June 1992.*

Animal prophets are not new in Uganda. Back in August 1978, there was a report of a tortoise padding around the countryside prophesying trouble for Idi Amin Dada, the colourful lunatic and cannibal who oppressed the country at that time. 'Big Daddy' threatened to execute anyone trading in such rumours. [see **FT27:39**.]

SHEEP AMBUSH

A couple were invited to buy an inflatable sheep sex-aid after answering an advert for rechargeable batteries in *The Daily Telegraph*. They received a personally addressed mail shot headed 'Luv Ewe' and quoting a price of £17.95. A drawing was accompanied by a description: "She has been developed after years of research into how to bring the joy of sheep into your love-life without the obvious problems of a real sheep. No bleating to alert neighbours. No risk of ruining your prize lawn."

The couple were not amused, complained to the Advertising Standards Authority, who upheld the complaint against VIS of Bethnal Green. They were unable to contact the firm. *D.Telegraph, Guardian, 13 May 1992.*

SIMULACRA CORNER

This tree trunk man sporting a Kaiser moustache was taken by Paul Greenwood. We are always glad to receive pictures of spontaneous forms and figures, or any curious images.

Send your snaps to the editorial address – with SAE – and we'll pay a fiver for any we use.

Sidelines

For his 20th daredevil world record, Inge Vidar Svingen from Norway slid, shirtless, down a 500 yard ski slope on a bed of six inch nails. "I am no masochist", he told the *Dagbladet* newspaper. "Abroad, I am treated like a big entertainer. Here, I'm seen as a half-wit." *Guardian, 5 April 1991.*

• • • • • • • • • • • • •

"Zucchini and eggplants are both stuffed with rice", said an Egyptian fundamentalist leader recently, "and the stuffing process, which is usually done by women, leads to arousal. It is better to prohibit the sale of these vegetables to avoid a greater danger." *Newsweek, 27 June 1992.*

• • • • • • • • • • • • •

A doctor has told Kenyans who wash their genitals with battery acid after sex as a preventative to AIDS that the end result could be "even more disastrous". *[AFP] 7 Oct 1992.*

• • • • • • • • • • • • •

"When we think how much mischief has been caused by the unsupported evidence of children to credulous labourers in the ritual abuse vineyard [..] we must accept that social workers, who are not trained to disbelieve anyone, are possibly the worst people to deal with the problem. Much less damage is caused by untrue stories in newspapers, which few believe in any case."

Auberon Waugh's 'Way of the World', *Daily Telegraph* 24 June 1992; prompted by a girl who fooled a newspaper into believing she fled in tears from a science class when her teacher, she alleged, ordered her to strangle a chicken.

STRANGE DEATHS

TRIGGER HAPPY

✝ A man from Grahamstown, South Africa, asked the police to guard his house while he was out of town, saying he would be back on 12 January 1992. The police became suspicious on the night of 30 December 1991 when lights in the supposedly empty house went on and off. An officer went to the back of the house and opened fire when a door suddenly opened, killing the homeowner, who had returned early. *[AP] 2 Jan 1992.*

A DATE WITH DESTINY

✝ Lee Hsi–lung and Lai Yun–kun were both born in Taitung, Taiwan, on 25 June 1973. They had not met until they went to a party arranged by mutual friends. They didn't have much time to get acquainted, as the car they were in smashed into a truck and they were killed, close to where they were born 19 years earlier. *Edinburgh Evening News, 17 Jan 1992.*

LAST CALL

✝ Wise–cracking bingo caller Michael Cave, 65, collapsed and died 15 minutes into his routine at the Gala Bingo Club in London Street, Reading, Berks. The last number he called was "Number Eight … Pearly Gates." *D.Express, 18 June 1992.*

LIGHTNING IRONY

✝ Dr Wuyi Pan, 42, an assistant professor of materials engineering at New Mexico Tech in Socorro, was struck dead by lightning on 12 August 1992. Pan was married to Lin Zhang, a chemist who worked at the Tech's lightning research lab in the Magdalena Mountains 30 miles west of Socorro. New Mexico has the highest rate of lightning deaths per capita in the United States. *[AP] 13 Aug 1992.*

GARDEN HAZARD

✝ Philip Hodges, 34, was cutting a yew hedge at Fownhope, near Hereford, when he slipped on a wet, grassy bank and cut the jugular vein in his neck with the shears. He bled to death before an ambulance arrived. *Sun, D.Telegraph, 29 Aug 1992.*

DENTAL DOOM

✝ Mrs Rose Neale, 58, of Orpington, Kent, was so scared of dentists she never visited one in her life. She contracted oral thrush from her rotting teeth, which caused a blood infection and developed into meningitis, from which she died. *D.Telegraph, 26 Sept 1992.*

DEATH IN VENICE

✝ Giorgio Scrimin, 55, was kept awake by a howling cat and leaned out of a bedroom window to hit it with a broom. The cat sprang on to the roof of the house in Venice, dislodging a lump of marble which fell on Senor Scrimin's head and killed him. *Today, D.Star, 5 Oct 1992.*

POOTIE'S PECKER

Joe 'Pootie' Newman, the jazz trumpeter, died in July aged 69. He was Lionel Hampton's lead soloist and later Count Basie's. "He had a masterly control of his instrument, a uniquely rhythmic way with the valves, a remarkable potency", according to his obituary in the *Daily Telegraph* (14 July 1992). "A diminutive, gregarious figure, Newman was a keen ladies' man. Three years ago he submitted to the surgeon's knife for a penile implant. The operation was not a success. A build-up of pressure brought about a series of embarrassing explosions (one of them in a restaurant) and internal bleeding ensued. He eventually died of a blood clot on the brain." *The Times* helpfully added that Newman's last album was called 'Hangin' Out'.

LUCKY FOR SOME

A sizable body of folklore has accrued to the number 23 – see, for instance, *The 23 Phenomenon* by Robert Anton Wilson [**FT23:32**].

Usually, attention is focussed upon its sinister aspect, but for Richard Connolly, a pub manager in Douglas, Isle of Man, it is a lucky number.

His recent 23rd birthday fell on the 23rd of September; so, at 23:23 hours that day he placed a bet of £23 on the number 23 on the roulette wheel at his favourite gambling place, the Palace Casino in Douglas. He won £571.

"I was staggered when the ball popped into 23," he said. He would have won a lot more if he had had the conviction to resist hedging the bet by splitting it between the numbers each side. *Sun, 25 Sept 1992.*

SNACKING ON SNAKES

■ According to AFP, a one-year-old boy in Ra's Al-Khaimah, one of the United Arab Emirates, caught and bit a snake in two. Ali Mohammed Khatiri was found by his mother playing with the pieces, and was rushed to the Saqr Hospital for tests. He was OK. *Bangkok Nation, 15 Aug 1992.*

■ Krishnan Muniandy, of Seremban, Malaysia, was so angry with the foot-long unidentified snake that bit him that he swallowed it to… "teach it a lesson". When he complained of violent stomach pains, neighbours sent him to hospital where doctors confirmed by X-ray that the snake was dead. Krishnan wasn't so sure: "I can still feel something moving in my stomach," he complained. *[Reuters] 26 Aug 1992.*

■ In the Table Mountain region of Natal, a huge python dropped from a tree onto Edward Mkhize. Alone and unarmed, he fought the 3.5m-long, 40kg snake for half an hour, biting its throat and twisting its head. Eventually, he succeeded in crushing and breaking its spine and, seemingly none the worse for his ordeal, dragged his trophy home. *D.Telegraph, 17 Sept 1992.*

■ Shelley Bovington, a security guard, was not made of such stern stuff as the above three characters. She fled from her kitchen in Hove, Sussex, on her 24th birthday when a foot-long brown and red snake of unidentified species popped out of her toaster. Council officials searched her flat for further snakes. *Guardian, 14 Aug 1992.*

ROCK 'N' ROLL EARTHQUAKE

The pop group Madness played two re-union gigs in Finsbury Park, north-east London, on the week-end of 8/9 August 1992 – their first for six years. It was probably "One Step Beyond" that set the crowd of over 30,000 into a stomping rhythm that shook the neighbouring buildings with a quake estimated at magnitude 2 on the Richter scale. Appropriately, the song contains the words "earth-quake eruption".

The quakes hit at 9:30 on Saturday and 9:00 on Sunday; the Sunday concert began half an hour earlier. The seismograph at the Science Museum, four miles away, didn't pick up any movement; but London sits on a bed of clay, lousy stuff for recording quakes. The buildings most affected – Anwell Court, Green Lanes and Rowley Gardens – were nine-storey tower blocks. Only people above the fifth floors felt anything, which suggested to Alice Walker of the British Geological Survey that the shockwave had a frequency of 2Hz – two vibrations a second. Sound at this wavelength is below our hearing threshold, but can be felt up the spine.

Windows, ceilings and balconies were cracked, and tenants called the fire brigade. One tenant described his building "moving in a circular motion – it was like walking on an aeroplane." On the Sunday night, 30 tenants, a dozen fire officers, eight police officers and a council surveyor gathered outside the Rowley Gardens flats.

In 1984 and 1987, U2 concerts in Brussels formed very precise patterns on a seismometer five kilometres away. *Guardian, 11+26 Aug; D Mail, 18+26 Aug 1992.*

MEDICAL BAG

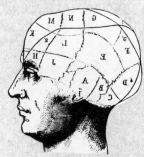

FIRST SEX ORGAN SWAP

Chinese surgeons have performed what is believed to be the world's first direct sex swap in July, according to Xia Zhao Ji, a doctor on the operating team at Beijing Number Three Hospital (where China's first sex-change operations took place in 1984). The 22-year-old woman received the testicles of a 30-year-old man, who received her ovaries. A penis for the woman was constructed from her stomach lining, while the man's penis was replaced with a vagina made of leather.

Both patients were recovering well, but the former woman must take immunosuppressive drugs to overcome rejection of the new organs, and further operations will be necessary for her to have an erection. Both patients are single and hope to find marriage partners, although neither will be able to procreate. Neither knows the other's identity and both wish to remain anonymous. "The man thinks that women are clean and men are dirty", the physician said. "The woman thinks that it's better for her career to be a man." *[Reuters] 24 July 1992.*

SPEECH RETURNS

● An Algerian newspaper reported a remarkable recovery. Ziane Bensahli, 28, lost his voice after five men beat him and threatened to kill him. Doctors could not help, but villagers suggested whisky. "On the ninth day, he was able to talk again. First noises, then whispers, then words." An odd story from a Muslim country. *[AFP] 15 April 1992.*

● The day her first hus-band died in 1956, Martha Ouellette of Van Buren, Maine, began to lose her voice and her speech gradually became unintelligible. For 35 years, through a second marriage and the births of 35 grand-children and 17 great-grandchildren, listeners had to guess what she was trying to say. Recently, her son, The Rev. Roland Lajoie, met a woman who sounded a lot like his mother. She had a disorder called spasmodic dysphonia, caused by muscles getting overstimulated and contracting too tightly.

As many as 30,000 Americans are believed to suffer from this disorder, but only a few thousand have been diagnosed. Lajoie found that sufferers can speak normally with small injections of botulism toxin in the vocal chords. His 80-year-old mother had her first injection last November and was talking intelligibly two days later. *[AP] 22 June 1992.*

PIONEERING BRITON

British veterinary surgeon Chris Smith, 36, died after carrying out a post mortem examination on a horse in a Californian university. He is believed to be the first person to die from Valley Fever – a condition found only in Arizona. Locals are believed to be mostly immune to it. *D. Telegraph, D. Mail, 28 July 1992.*

HORSEWATCH

Following our report on Swedish horse ripping (**FT64:18**), we have received similar reports from Britain. Equine mutilation in Hampshire, usually in the summer months, has reached a new peak this year. The last major peak was in 1983/4. Local vet Andrew Kennedy became aware of the attacks 15 years ago, and has seen over 30 injured animals, while his colleagues tell of similar numbers, suggesting that hundreds have been attacked.

Blunt Objects

Some have been stabbed; others have suffered sexual injuries from knives, hammers and blunt objects. Because many of the attacks took place on or near the full moon, Hampshire police have suggested that a satanic cult could be at work; but as with similar rumours in the USA over cattle mutilation, no evidence is forthcoming. Fifteen assaults have been reported since March this year, mostly in the Meon Valley southeast of Winchester, where some residents have started 'Horsewatch' schemes.

Millie, a 15-year-old thoroughbred mare belonging to Olive and David Gray, was assaulted at Alton in April. The attacker avoided security devices to enter a locked stable 400 yards from the house. Millie's rear quarters were cut and there was evidence of an attempt to force a blunt object into her vagina. She had to be put down a month later.

Annie, a thoroughbred mare belonging to Davy Jones, former singer with the Monkees, was stabbed in the shoulder on 13 July in a paddock at Shirrell Heath, three miles from the Jones's house near Hambledon. The following night (a full moon), Chrissy, a palomino mare also belonging to the Jones's, was attacked in a field next to the house. Her hind quarters, back legs and genitals had been cut, and something, perhaps a broom handle or fence post, had been forced inside her vagina. Both horses recovered,

Jessica Jones, the 11-year-old daughter of Monkees ex-singer Davy Jones, comforts her pet mare Chrissy after the mutilation attack

but Chrissy, a pet for the two daughters, was traumatised and badly swollen. *Independent, 13 Aug + 16 Sept; The News (Portsmouth), 15 Aug 1992.*

Ritual Sacrifice

Two years ago, there was a rumour that a white horse was mutilated below White Horse Hill at Bratton in Wiltshire, near the scene of Operation Blackbird, the crop circle watch set up by Colin Andrews and Pat Delgado, which was going on at the time. Two crop circle watchers, Eddie and Vince, who requested anonymity, were camping on White Horse Hill. On the morning of 29 July 1990 they allegedly found the dead horse with its feet caught in a fence. Its genitals and one ear had been removed. There was still a mass of foam protruding from each nostril, suggesting that the attack was only an hour or two old. The only blood was a spot the size of a coin about four feet away.

The local police were notified, after which no-one else was allowed to visit the site. A policeman told Colin Andrews that the horse had run into the fence and had a heart attack; however, as a result of an inquiry by researcher Clive Potter last December, it was found that the local police had no record of the incident. Potter still believes the mutilation took place and blames a black occult group such as the Friends of Hecate, "who are known to be based in Wiltshire." A similar rumour surfaced last summer at Alton Barnes in Wiltshire: a mutilated sheep was supposedly found lying on an altar. *Swindon Evening Advertiser, 10 July 1992.*

Dead Donkey

A donkey called Sophie was found hacked to death near its owner's home at Howth Head near Dublin. Its body had been "elaborately mutilated", according to the Scottish Daily Mail (2 August 1992); the *Edinburgh Evening News* (5 August) said it had "satanic symbols carved on its head". The killing was linked to the so-called Lunar Sabbath. The *Donegal Democrat* (20 August) adds further details: a rib was torn out and the liver removed. The atrocity is compared to one last year. On 28 June 1991, a donkey was taken from the Richard Martin Restfields, Glengeary, Ramelton, Donegal. Its front and back legs were skinned to the bone and the animal was then returned the following morning in a terrible state.

AMERICAN BLOBS

Hurricane Andrew stirred up something weird in Elwood Guillot's pond in Independence, Louisiana, off Interstate 55, about 50 miles north of New Orleans. Nobody was really sure if the transparent gelatinous blobs are animal, vegetable or chemical. They were found on 26 August by Elwood's grandson Michael, out inspecting the storm damage. The main blob was a bit smaller after three days, but was still more than a foot across. Michael Guillot plunged his net into the pond and came up with several more blobs. Biologist Bob Thomas said the blobs were "harmless crowds of single cell organisms", which doesn't really leave us any the wiser. *[AP] 29 Aug 1992.*

● Nick Glazier, owner of a duck hunting lodge on the north shore of Rondeau Bay, near Shrewsbury, Ontario, spotted a 'blob' floating in a pond beside his lodge. "We tried to catch it with a fish net, but it swam underwater and disappeared", he said. "But a week later we discovered it once again and managed to catch it." He called the Ministry of Natural Resources and was told the 'blob' could be from the Tropics (...eh?) *Victoria (BC) Times-Colonist, 8 Sept 1992.*

RIGHT: The blobs from Michael Guillot's pond.

THE GREAT APE ESCAPE

At the end of August, the winds of Hurricane Andrew made mincemeat of cages and holding pens over much of southern Florida. At the Mannheimer Primatological Foundation near the Everglades, most of the 2,000 monkeys and 500 baboons ran off into the night. A few miles to the northeast, several hundred of the 550 baboons and monkeys at the University of Miami's Perrine Primate Center broke loose. Four weeks after the storm, more than 1,500 monkeys and baboons had been captured. Another 200 or so were shot to death, mostly by people edgy over 'unfounded' rumours that they monkeys were infected with the AIDS virus from their use in research. But hundreds were still at large.

There was plenty to see in the new wild kingdom of south Dade County. A baboon shook off a blast from a 9mm pistol and lumbered away. Llamas were on the loose. Exotic birds darted through the recovering foliage and scorpions crawled for cover. Three cougars lounged near a highway. Peacocks wandered through a gutted beer warehouse. A strange species of deer, unlike any found in North America, led three National Guardsmen on a chase. Escaped pythons curled up in dark nooks and crannies, while mambas and gaboon vipers slithered off to points unknown. "It's like a Disney World of exotic animals out there", said Todd Hardwick, owner of Pesky Critters, an animal capture business. Many animals will remain uncaught and some will probably breed and become part of southern Florida's wildlife. *Hartford (CT) Courant, 23 Sept 1992.*

GOLDBLATT'S HYPOTHESIS

The Ellis Van Creveld syndrome, whereby people are born with 12 fingers and 12 toes, may have been brought to an isolated Aboriginal community in southwestern Australia by Dutch sailors from the *Zuytdorp*, wrecked off the coast in 1712. That's the hypothesis of Jack Goldblatt at the Princess Mary Hospital in Perth, published in the latest *Medical Journal of Australia.*

"We know from Aboriginal traditions that a large number of red-haired foreigners had been there", said hospital spokesman Ian Wallpole. "It is possible that they were descendants of the Dutch crew. When the wreck of the *Zuytdorp* was found 40 years ago, it was not far from the coast and the crew would have found it relatively easy to get ashore."

Other symptoms of the syndrome include heart defects and abnormally short limbs. The only other place in the world where the syndrome is found in concentrated form is among the Amish of Pennsylvania, where its incidence is as high as five per 1,000 births. Among the Aborigines, it is found in concentrations of one in 6,000 births. Recessive genes can take hold in such isolated communities where there is relatively little genetic intermixing.

The research in Perth began when two Aboriginal babies were born with the syndrome thousands of miles apart and it transpired that the mothers were related. According to Goldblatt, it is possible that one in 39 Aborigines in Western Australia carry the recessive gene. *NRC Handelsblad, 17 Aug 1992.*

VIRGIN MARY GOES WEST

Balkan fighting may have defied the message of peace and love delivered by *Gospa* – the Virgin Mary – to the seers of Medjugorje, Bosnia-Herzegovina, but the holy apparition, wearing a long grey coat and white veil, with a grey cloud wafting below her slippered feet, continues to appear punctually at 6:40pm every evening to Vicka Vita. Vicka was one of the original witnesses on nearby Mount Prodbrdo on 24 June 1981, when *Gospa* warned the world to mend its ways or war would come. Almost 20 million pilgrims have visited Medjugorje since then, 80,000 a day at the peak, but now there is only a trickle and the souvenir shops and guest houses are all closed. *Independent*, 30 Aug; *Denver (CO) Post*, – *Aug; Observer*, 13 Sept 1992.

Monthly Visits

One of the millions that made the journey to the remote Balkan Marian shrine was Joseph Januszkiewicz, a 54-year-old draughtsman, who returned to Marlboro township, near Trenton, New Jersey, in 1988, claiming to have been cured of an eight-year-old back injury and long-time hearing loss. Six months later, on 17 March 1989, as he

sat on a plastic bucket in his yard, praying and giving thanks, the Virgin appeared to him bathed in a golden light and told him: "My son and I have chosen you to do our work", and instructed him to pray for the conversion of sinners. She appeared daily until October 1990, after which she only visited on special occasions such as Christmas. On 31 May 1992, she told him she would call by on the first Sunday of each month, between nine and nine-thirty in the evening. His wife Veronica said she has not seen the Virgin, but did see the light from the first visitation and her husband kneeling and speaking to someone.

Plumbing Problems

On 7 June, about 500 people visited the Januszkiewicz home to pray before the statue of the Virgin erected in the yard. They were asked not to leave cash or gifts. On 5 July, more than 3,000 turned up, and on 2 August, between 7,000 and 10,000 came to pray. This time, according to Januszkiewicz, St Joseph appeared alongside his wife. He was wearing short pants, a cut-off shirt and a wide belt. Pilgrims turned up every day throughout July and August, with an average of 100 cars

clogging up the country roads in the neighbourhood. At the end of August, Bishop John C. Reiss of Trenton advised people to stay away while an official four-priest commission investigated. The authenticity study will probably last six to eight months. The NIMBY (not in my back yard) brigade was very active, and the municipal authorities fretted about lack of portable plumbing.

Smell of Roses

On Sunday, 6 September, the crowd numbered around 8,000. No-one claimed to have seen the apparition, but many said they had been hit by a strong smell of roses, a phenomenon also noted in Medjugorje. On Sunday, 4 October, local hostility and cooler weather seemed to be taking their toll on the faithful. Only about 500 crammed into Januszkiewicz's back yard.

Newark (NJ) Star-Ledger, 31 July, 4+5+28 Aug, 4 Sept; *Allentown (PA) Morning Call*, 2 Aug; *NY Post*, 6 Aug; *Hackensack (NJ) Record*, 7+28 Aug, 4+24 Sept, 5 Oct; *NY Times* 29 Aug, 7+8+22 Sept; *Trenton (NJ) Times*, 6+7+8 Sept; *NY Daily News* + *Philadelphia (PA) Enquirer*, 7 Sept 1992.

ANOTHER BLESSED VIRGIN: The image on the right of this photograph is believed by many to be the Blessed Virgin Mary. It is reflected in a mirror in the bedroom of Patricia Galaz (far left) in Las Cruces, New Mexico. She claimed it began to appear around 6 March, two weeks before the photo was taken. Her parents are reflected in the centre [AP] 20 March 1992.

SWEDISH ART CRITICISM

Between February and June, five of Stockholm's favourite statues were badly damaged or destroyed by dynamite. The targets of the expressive art critic include a statue of Bacchus, the wine god, a monument to the chemist Carl Wilhelm Scheele and a statue of a centaur. In late May, he/she severely damaged a bust of Sweden's first social democratic prime minister, Hjalmar Branting, and on 8 June an explosion shattered a statue of a boy on horseback sculpted by Ivan Johansson in 1956. No one was injured, but scores of windows in the vicinity were shattered. The *modus operandi* is sticks of dynamite laid beside the allotted statue in dead of night and ignited with touch-paper. Police baffled. *Guardian, 9+12 June 1992.*

RECENT OOZINGS

■ Diane and Keith Fellows have struck oil – in their cellar. The couple, who run a building contractors in Lye near Birmingham, found the oil seeping into a well in the basement of the Victorian building. Concerned about the danger of fire, they called in a river inspector, who suggested a pump. The source of the oil was unidentified. *People, 12 July 1992.*

■ Malcolm Slocombe, who owns the Four Seasons Sheepskin shop in the Old Market, Glastonbury, (formerly a Chinese takeaway), is baffled by a mysterious flow of water in the cellar, which began around March 1992. Engineers at Bristol Water and Wessex Water say the knee-deep flood is not a mains or a sewer leak. Local folklorist Geoffrey Ashe believes the water could come from the White Spring which once flowed in underground streams with Glastonbury's Chalice water, reputed to have healing powers. Mr Slocombe was considering bottling the water; perhaps his cellar

NORDIC DIPLOMACY

The Faroes have released two new stamps celebrating Columbus *and* the 992nd anniversary of Leivur Eiriksson's discovery of America ('Leivur' himself probably spelt his name 'Leifr'). The text in the lower left corner, "Amerika funnid" means "America discovered". *Sydsvenska Dagbladet, July 1992*

could become a place of pilgrimage. *Western Daily Press, 2 June 1992.*

■ Yellow slime is likely to close the Bavarian State Opera House in Munich for 10 months. The theatre's technical director, Volker Josefowski, explained that the old hydraulic system, responsible for all the movements of stage sets and machinery, was overhauled in stages in the 1980s. The old system used water, which it was decided to replace with oil. Not just any oil, but 50,000 litres of an ecologically correct, biodegradable, Dutch-made substance called Quintolubric, successfully used in other theatres.

The trouble was that some of the pipes from the old system were used and bacteria in the residual water found Quintolubric very tasty. The end result is yellow slime clogging vents and filters. The theatre's computer system senses the

discrepancy in pressure, but doesn't know what the problem is, so it shuts down the whole system for security reasons. It cannot be restarted until the vents and filters have been cleared, which has led to productions being halted in mid flight. Eliminating the slime will cost around £15 million, although the ultimate costs, including the fees of performers and staff, will be far more. *Int. Herald Tribune, 27 May 1992.*

BLOOD ON THE TRACKS

The Chinese *Liberation Daily* reported the death in August of a man called Wei, aged 22, who was convinced he had mastered the mystical art of *qi gong*. He stood (or lay, according to one version) on railway tracks outside Shanghai and tried to stop a 28-car freight train to prove his powers to his mother. He was crushed beneath the cow-catcher and killed. His family thought it was just an

idle boast. "They never thought he'd really lie down on the tracks", said a policeman. [An earlier version of this story was set in Russia in October 1989 - see *FT56:18*.] [Reuters], *Eve. Standard, Oracle, 19 Aug 1992.*

THE OLDEST BATTLE

The skeletons of two dinosaurs locked in combat have been discovered in the Gobi desert. "It happened about 75 million years ago", said one of the discoverers. "The carnivorous velociraptor was trying to tear to pieces an herbiforous protoceratops when both of them fell into quicksand." *D.Telegraph, 28 Aug 1991.*

A RUDE SURPRISE

The Polish weekly *Spotkania* reported that a Pole from the border city of Szezecin was rudely surprised when he visited a brothel in Germany. The sexual services were being provided by his wife. [For earlier versions of this yarn set in Tel Aviv, Israel, Nov 1989 and Teramo, Italy, Sept 1990, see *FT58:17*.] Further details on the Tel Aviv case: the man was Jacob Beisvitz and the call girl who turned up was his wife Rachel, 27. The couple are now divorced. *D.Star, 1 Mar 1992.*

MIGHTY MOUSE

A mousetrap that doesn't kill is the latest invention by an animal-loving Californian. It simply throws the mice at high speed across the room. *Scottish Sunday Mail, 19 April 1992.*

BAD TIME FOR BONZO

A border collie named Bonzo, aged seven, leapt a farm fence near Nor-Aurdal in midwestern Norway, caught his foot and dangled upside down for nine days, living on snow while he awaited rescue, according to the Norwegian paper *Dagbladet*. "I had given up hope," said the dog's owner, Torstein Nerbraaten, after the rescue. [AP] *23 Mar 1991.*

PIGEON TRAGEDIES

ROAMING-PIGEONS
The race route
Sydney
Hay
Nowra
Albury-Wodonga
Wangaratta
Ballarat
Sale
Birds sighted in these towns

Champion racing pigeon Billy Blue arrived home in Crookes, Sheffield, after an epic 536-mile, 25-hour battle against howling winds and torrential rain. He had won the Central Marking Race from Royan in south-west France, against nearly 1,000 rivals, with a margin of half an hour. As he landed on the roof, a ginger tomcat pounced and carried him off.

"I'm sick to death of the animal", said Billy's owner, Patrick Lees, 55, who had been trying to win the prestigious race for 40 years. "It has had 11 of my pigeons over the past year or so, but I have never managed to get near it." There was some consolation, however. Ninety minutes later, a neighbour retrieved Billy's lifeless body, and Mr Lees removed the ring from his leg and clocked it in. The ex-pigeon was awarded third place and won a prize of £100. *D.Mail, D.Telegraph, D.Mirror, 8 July 1992.* [For other last-minute avian scupperings, see *FT52:18 & FT59:12.*]

● On 29 August, 8,100 pigeons were released in Hay, south-western New South Wales, for the 340 mile journey to Sydney. The journey should have taken about six hours, but no birds turned up on the first day. Eighty made it the next day, while another 20% arrived a week late, on 6 & 7 September. The rest had disappeared, although some were turning up in various places far south of the route by the time of our latest clipping (8 September).

It is believed that the pigeons were attacked by falcons soon after they were liberated, then panicked and became caught in strong winds which swept them towards Victoria. Other factors included radar interference from the Parkes Observatory near Canberra and irresponsible shooters' clubs.

"I have had 61 years of experience with racing pigeons and I have never seen anything like this before", said Sam Beggs, director of the Australian Pigeon Fanciers Association. *[AP] 4 Sept; Sydney Morning Herald, 8 Sept 1992.*

● Only seven of the 99 pigeons in a Labor Day race on 6 September from Allegany, New York, to West Haven, Connecticut, had turned up two weeks later. No one had reported finding any of the others. It's hard to work out why homing pigeons lose their way, as nobody really knows how they *find* it in the first place. With the global rise in electromagnetic smog, we expect these mass avian disappearances to increase dramatically. *New Haven Register, 20 Sept 1992.*

PASSING DOC GIVES THE NEEDLE

Dr Robert Lambourn was driving to his surgery in Ashington, Northumberland, when he came across mangled railway coaches at a level crossing near Choppington. Two trains had apparently collided head-on. Sixty bodies lay scattered about. A police helicopter was overhead, but ambulances had not arrived. The doctor parked, grabbed his bag, burst through a police cordon and dashed to the nearest carriage where a man with a serious leg wound lay face-down, apparently semi-conscious.

As he prepared to inject the man in the buttocks with painkilling pethidine, the 'victim' said: "Do we really have to go that far?" The truth did not dawn on the doctor until he had given the injection: as his patient lapsed into unconsciousness, he whispered that he was perfectly healthy and taking part in a training exercise. The man, in his early 20s, was taken to hospital to sleep off the effects of the injection.

The exercise was in June, but details were only provided in September in a report to the county's public protection committee. A spokeswoman for the St Johns Ambulance Brigade said: "The victim was covered in gore and a great piece of bone was sticking out through his trousers. The poor doctor wasn't to know it was just something picked up from a butcher." *D.Telegraph, Aberdeen Press & Journal, 4 Sept 1992.*

RESTLESS BONES

Are we the only commentators to note the increase in thefts of revered relics, especially those of Catholic saints, in recent years? The latest purloined remains belonged – so the faithful believe – to St Christine, a 3rd century Roman teenager who was killed by her father for distributing his wealth to the poor. The bones were found in the catacomb of St Pontianus in Rome during the 18th century and brought to Cleveland, Ohio, in 1925, where they are normally on display in St John's Cathedral.

On February 19, a "well-dressed" man, coolly picked up the gold-trimmed glass case (pictured right) and walked out with it. Six days later the bones were found, undamaged, in the carpark of the St Saba Orthodox Cathedral in another part of the city, and restored to St John's.

This crime is about as inscrutable as you can get. *[AP] 25 Feb 1992.*

ROYAL BONES

The remains of St Edward the Martyr, King of England in 975 and murdered in Corfe Castle three years later (probably at the instigation of his wicked stepmother Aelfthryth), were found in a lead box in the ruins of Shaftsbury Abbey in 1931. King Edward was buried at Wareham, Dorset, after his death on 18 March 978. According to the *Anglo Saxon Chronicle,* "miracles soon followed" and his relics were taken to Shaftsbury Abbey by Dunstan in 980. He was declared a martyr in 1001.

At the time the relics were found, the Abbey belonged to two brothers, John and Geoffrey Claridge, who disagreed on where they should be housed. The relics – fragments of lumbar bones – were kept in shoe boxes in a vault of the Midland Bank, Woking, until a High Court Judge ruled in April 1988 that they should be moved to the Russian Orthodox Church in exile at nearby Brockwood, Surrey, pending a final resolution of the civil action over ownership, first launched in the mid-1980s. Now, the Mayor of Shaftsbury, Mrs Janet Rider, is attempting to persuade the Russian Orthodox Brother-

hood to return the bones to their original resting place in the abbey. If this was unacceptable, the mayor would settle for "a decent-sized piece of him, a femur, say, but we would accept something smaller." *Shrewsbury Evening Echo, 4 April; D.Telegraph, 6 April 1992.*

OFF WITH THEIR HEADS

About the beginning of April, robbers broke into a chapel in St John's Graveyard, Wotton, Surrey, where they forced the lids from two 18th century stone coffins. Cutting open the lead lining, they revealed the bodies of the famous diarist John Evelyn (died 1706) and his wife Mary (died 1709), which were quite well preserved by the air-tight seal and only just starting to decompose. The robbers decapitated the couple and made off with their heads. The purpose of the theft remained unknown, although Rev Trevor Southgate, former adviser to the Archbishop of Canterbury, suggested that the skulls could be used as drinking vessels in a satanic ritual. *News of the World, 5 April 1992.*

THE PICKLED CORPSE OF V.I. LENIN

In the first few months of 1992, the Kremlin was inundated with American bids for the pickled corpse of Vladimir Ilyich Lenin, ranging from $1,000 to $27 million. It all began with a tongue-in-

cheek report fashioned from whole cloth by Christopher Buckley, which he put in *Forbes FYI,* the Forbes business publication he edits. ABC News in Washington were taken in by the hoax and carried it on "World News Tonight" on 5 November last year.

The sealed bids were addressed to Victor Barannikov, head of the Russian Security Ministry, the successor to the KGB, which (in its successive incarnations) has been protecting Lenin's body since his death in 1924. A spokesman said all offers would be rejected, but the Americans would be thanked politely for their interest. Meanwhile, the great navigator is still on display in a bombproof glass case in his Red Square granite mausoleum. He is kept at a constant temperature of 59 degrees Fahrenheit. Only his wax-like hands and head are visible and it is rumoured that his corpse is mouldy following a bungled restoration job during World War II when it was evacuated to Siberia to keep it from falling into Nazi hands. *Seattle Times, 7 Nov 1991; Int. Herald Tribune, 11 Mar 1992.*

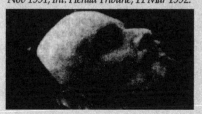

ICEMAN RUMBLES

As research continues into the Ötztal Iceman – see *FT60:14* and *FT62:12* – new puzzles are spinning off while the old ones rumble on. The dispute between Austria and Italy over ownership of the (possibly 5,000-year-old) mummified body has not been resolved; the discovery location was just on the Italian side of the border, but German scientists have the body.

One of the new mysteries concerns a pile of maple leaves found near the man. Dr Sigmar Bortenschlager, a professor of botany at Innsbruck University, said they had been green at the time of the man's death. Maple trees, we are told, do not grow above 5,000 feet, and the find was made at an altitude twice that. Dr Marcus Egg, a prehistorian at the Roman-Germanic Central Museum in Mainz, where many of the studies are being coordinated, added that some charcoal was found among the leaves, suggesting the 'hunter' had brought the pile with him for some reason. *Int. Herald Tribune, 23 July 1992.*

IS IT A HOAX?
Now the very integrity of the discovery has been called into question by a German TV team who point to the possibility that the whole thing has been a stupendous hoax. "We accept the man is about 5,000 years old," said Dr Michael Heim, head of the investigative unit at the Bavarian state TV (Bayerischer Rundfunk) in Munich. "But we are not convinced this man died up there in the ice." *S.Times, 16 Aug 1992.*

The nub of the matter is that the whole world has been so mesmerised with the uniqueness of the Iceman that few have questioned the "discrepancies" in the discovery itself. "The top half of his body had supposedly been lying exposed to the sun and melted snow for some time," said Dr Heim, "but there was no sign of deterioration. Yet within 15 minutes of it arriving at Innsbruck University fungus began to grow on the leathery skin."

Heim's team have posed other

questions. Why were the cell membranes in the man's eyes not damaged, as they should have been after more than a year in extreme cold? Why was he found with a bronze axe when carbon dating puts his death *before* the beginning of the Bronze Age? Why were all his clothes and equipment piled up beside him? And how did so many fragile items (like the oval birch bark box) survive the slow-movement of

LONG AGO...

tons of ice for thousands of years? Naturally, this has raised the hackles of the establishment. Prof Konrad Spindler, of Innsbruck University's Institute of Prehistory Studies, said "I do not understand why Dr Heim appears to want to mystify the discovery or the circumstances in which the mummy was found." He does admit, however, to the "extraordinary" fact of the mummy surviving intact for so long under glacial conditions.

HUNTER OR SHAMAN?
The suppositions of Spindler's own team have been challenged too, as they proposed a scenario of the Iceman's death. He was caught in a sudden freezing squall and died of hypothermia, they say. Then his body was dried out by the Föhn (a hot wind over the Alps from Italy) and later embedded in snow and ice. Just how the body avoided decomposition during the transition to wetter conditions is not explained, and we wait with Heim for an answer.

This scenario has been ridiculed by another Innsbruck academic, Prof Heinrich Tilly, who calls himself an "outlaw" because he was not asked to join the Iceman study-groups. "If the man died alone, he would have been eaten by animals and birds of prey in five minutes," laughs Tilly. He has his own ideas based upon his expertise in anthropology. The Iceman was from a Mesopotamian tribe of star-worshippers, says Tilly. "He was the youngest of a group of priests who went into the high mountains to be near the stars [..] He would have been a willing sacrifice in a ritual involving days of dancing before he was placed alive in a special vertical grave. He would have taken poison before being buried alive to appease the moon."

ANOTHER FINE MESSNER
Well... we look forward to seeing how Prof Tilly came to these magnificent conclusions; but they are no dafter than any others. Meanwhile Dr Heim is cooking up his own ideas. He thinks the Iceman has an uncanny resemblance to an Egyptian mummy, and believes a hoaxer placed the mummy where it would shortly be found by hikers. Dr Heim has publicly pointed a finger at the famous Italian mountaineer Reinhold Messner. Messner is a man at the top of his calling, with a string of feats to his name that are both celebrated and unrivalled, yet when Heim calls him a "self-publicist" it is not from admiration.

For Heim, it was damning enough that Messner has claimed to have seen a Yeti, but there was worse. Heim claims that Messner, who was in the vicinity when the body was found, had described the Iceman's distinctive footwear *before* the body was fully prised from the ice. It is difficult to imagine the motive for such a hoax by anyone, let alone a celebrity loner like Messner ... And where would anyone, even with Messner's wealth, obtain such a unique and unprecedented collection of items as the Iceman had with him? Messner was away climbing, and was not available for comment. We await developments with great interest.

SORCERER BURNED ALIVE

On the night of 25/26 September 1992, a group of young men set on fire the house of Baleibai Duilomaloma, 57, in the village of Qilai, 40 minutes drive from Suva, Fiji, while he was asleep inside. Duilomaloma ran out with his clothes on fire as his children and other relatives tried to keep angry villagers at bay. He hid in the forest with his family, but died during the night, while neighbours threw stones at his smouldering home.

Duilomaloma had been warned in a letter written on 9 September by a close relative, Fijian Member of Parliament Dr Ifereimi Buaserau, to stop practising sorcery or face being burned alive. The letter noted that Duilomaloma had two other houses, one in Suva and another on the small island of Ovalau, which had been burned down because he was prac-tising witchcraft. Seven men, aged between 20 and 30, appeared in court on 28 September charged with murder. *Brisbane (Australia) Courier Mail, 29 Sept 1992.* [For further witch-burning in Polynesia, see *FT55:32.*]

FAMILY TROUBLE

In the 'Bantustan' of Transkei in South Africa, back in January 1991, Mr Lizwe Qokolo, 32, was at the funeral of his cousin. He noticed that the body had "become flexi-ble" and had started to breathe and bleed from the nose. He at once accused the family who had watched over the corpse during the night of witchcraft. Qokolo and his relatives manhandled the four members of the family into the house of one of them and set it on fire. They burned to death. Last March, the Supreme Court sentenced Qokolo to a quadruple life sentence and two of his relatives to 21 years' jail. *Ivoir Soir (Ivory Coast), 9 Mar 1992.*

CHRISTMAS COMPETITION

Win this SUN & MOON SUNDIAL,

made of cast aluminium with a weathered bronze finish, in our fabulous festive competition. Test your knowledge of the weird and wonderful by sending the answers to the following questions on a postcard to: Festive Fortean Comp, PO BOX 2409, London NW5 4NP.

1. **What was Charles Fort's middle name?**
   A) Hieronymus   B) Hoy   C) Ambrose

2. **In which of Fort's books did he first describe teleportation?**
   A) Wild Talents   B) The Book of the Damned   C) Lo!

3. **What was the name of the ship found drifting off Portugal in December 1872?**
   A) Marie Celeste   B) Margaret Celeste
   C) Mary Celeste

4. **A bizarre hybrid mummy was found recently in the Topkapi Palace Museum in Istanbul. The upper half of a boy was joined to the lower half of what creature?**
   A) Crocodile   B) Leopard   C) Dolphin

5. **Where was a baboon in leopardskin shorts seen climbing across rooves last June?**
   A) Basingstoke   B) Cardiff   C) Anglesea

25 runners-up will receive a selection of Fortean books, records, videos and artefacts including: signed copies of *Doors of the Mind, The Door Marked Summer & Open Your Mind* by Michael Bentine (no longer available in the shops); *The Prisoner Companion* from ITC Video, a look at the symbolism of the surreal 60s TV classic; *The Transformed Man* from Creation Records (William Shatner boldly sings the way no man has sung before); *The Loch Ness Monster; Fact, Fiction or Fantasy* from Polygram Video, (out-of-print Nessie video exposé). Plus Fortean Times diaries, mugs and T-shirts. Closing date 1 Feb 1993.

THE FAR SIDE   By GARY LARSON

Houdini escapes from a black hole

GARDEN GUZZLER

Journalist Nikki Rowlands, 26, of Gunnislake in Cornwall, was awakened on 20 June by "an awful crash" and looked out of her bedroom window to see the garden shed being swallowed by the ground. Two 30ft electricity pylons also disappeared and the power lines burst into flames as they were dragged onto the road, cutting power to 1,200 surrounding homes. Emergency services cordoned off the cul-de-sac in Woodland Way as surveyors checked for further movement in an area riddled with old copper- and tin-mine workings.

The 75ft-deep crater stopped 10 feet from the house and also claimed the lawnmower, the children's swing and the paddling pool. Mrs Rowlands, her husband Colin, 32, and their children, aged five, three and 18 months, fled the house, which was later condemned as unsafe. "Fortunately we had all had a late night and were sleeping in", she said. "If it had been a normal Saturday, the children would probably have been playing in the garden and I could have been pegging out washing."

A second crater, 100ft deep and 60 yards from the first, swallowed another garden on 24 August. The first the Wakem family, who have children aged seven, six and three, knew about the collapse was when newspaper delivery boy Michael Spicer, 17, ran into the house shouting that the garden had disappeared. *D.Mirror, Times, Western Mail, 22 June; Telegraph, 22+27 June, 26 Aug 1992.*

SPECIAL CORRESPONDENTS

AFRICA Cynthia Hind (Zimbabwe), Ion Alexis Will (Roving). **AUSTRALIA** Greg Axford (Vic.), Paul Cropper (NSW), Rex Gilroy (NSW), Dik Gwynn-Seary (NSW), Tony Healy (ACT). **BELGIUM** Henri Prémont. **CANADA** Brian Chapman (BC), Dwight Whalen (Ont.). **DENMARK** Lars Thomas. **ENGLAND** Claire Blamey, Bruce Chatterton, Peter Christie, Mat Coward, Hilary Evans, Peter Hope-Evans, Alan Gardiner, Mick Goss, Chris Hall, Jeremy Harte, Brian Inglis, Jake Kirkwood, Joseph Lang, Alexis Lykiard, Nick Maloret, Valerie Martin, Kevin McClure, John Michell, Ralph Noyes, Nigel Pennick, Andy Roberts, Paul Screeton, Karl Shuker, Bob Skinner, Anthony Smith, Paul R. Thomas, Nigel Watson, Owen Whiteoak, Steve Wrathall. **FRANCE** Jean-Louis Brodu, Bernard Heuvelmans, Michel Meurger. **GERMANY** Walter J. Langbein, Ulrich Magin. **GREECE** S.C. Tavuchis. **HOLLAND** Robin Pascoe. **HONGKONG** Phillip Bruce. **ICELAND** V. Kip Hansen. **IRELAND** Peter Costello, Doc Shiels. **JAPAN** Masaru Mori, Shigeo Yokoyama. **NEW ZEALAND** Peter Hassall. **NORTHERN IRELAND** Caryl Sibbett. **POLAND** Leszek Matela. **ROMANIA** Iosif Boczor. **RUSSIA** Vladimir Rubtsov. **SCOTLAND** David Burns, Stuart Herkes, Roger Musson, Roland Watson, Jake Williams. **SWEDEN** Anders Liljegren, Sven Rosën. **USA** Larry E. Arnold (PA), Loren Coleman (ME), James E. Conlan (CT), David Fideler (MI), Mark A. Hall (MN), Michael Hoffman (CA), John Keel (NYC), Kurt Lothmann (TX), Ray Nelke (MO), Scott Parker (TX), Jim Reicken (NY), Ron Schaffner (OH), Margo Schwadron (NY), Chuck Shephard (DC), Dennis Stacy (TX), Joseph Swatek (NB), Joseph Trainor (MA), Jeffrey Vallance (CA), Robert Anton Wilson (CA), Joseph W. Zarzynski (NY). **TURKEY** Izzet Goksu. **WALES** Janet & Colin Bord, Richard Holland, Joe Kelly.

FORTEAN FA

MUG SETS

Take tea in style with our set of four Fortean Times mugs. Illustrated by Hunt Emerson the designs comprise of The Cats Of War, Drunken Bull, Falling Cow and Forest Fire Death. Black designs on high-quality white ceramic mugs.

CODE FTM - £15.00 per set.

BOOKS

FORTEAN TOMES is a series of facsimile reprints of early issues of The Fortean Times (formerly simply titled The News). Each book covers a wide range of fascinating subjects from feral children to spontaneous human combustion to UFO abduction.

FORTEAN TIMES 1 - 15
Yesterday's News Tomorrow **£19.99**
ISBN: 1 870870 263 400 page paperback, colour cover, illustrated throughout.

FORTEAN TIMES 16-25
Diary of a mad planet **£19.50**
ISBN: 1 870021 258 416 page paperback, colour cover, illustrated throughout.

FORTEAN TIMES 26 - 30
Seeing out the seventies **£14.99**
ISBN: 1 870021 207 320 page paperback, colour cover, illustrated throughout.

FORTEAN TIMES 1993 DIARY £9.99
ISBN: 1 870870 247 128 page hardback (250mm x 156mm)
The Fortean Times diary is the absolutely indispensible accessory for the well-prepared Fortean. Now you can have at your fingertips 365 days worth of obscure yet fascinating facts on strange people and stranger happenings. Each seven day opening presents a daily dollop of temporal trivia along with ample space to add your bizarre doings and odd anniversaries.

SUBSCRIPTIONS

If you have enjoyed this issue, why not make sure that you receive a copy on a regular basis? Order a year's supply of Fortean Times for yourself or a friend and get it delivered direct to your doorstep. And that's not all, every new subscriber receives a FREE Fortean Times t-shirt worth £7.99. Back issues also available (see coupon).

CIES

PRECAMBRIAN
4.03 billion years

4.6 BILLION YEARS AGO
Birth of the Earth?

1.4 BILLION YEARS AGO
Organisms with cell nucleus develop

HOW OLD

570 MILLION YEARS AGO
Animals with hard parts develop

IS THE

400 MILLION YEARS AGO
Amphibians emerge from the oceans

PALEOZOIC
330 million years

EARTH?

225 MILLION YEARS AGO
Primitive mammals develop

MESOZOIC
177 million years

95 MILLION YEARS AGO
First flowering plants

CENOZOIC
63 million years

TODAY
Man

DID DARWIN GET IT WRONG?

The Earth is conventionally believed to be 4,600 million years old. Yet there is mounting scientific evidence that it may be much younger. In researching his new book, *The Facts of Life: Shattering the Myth of Darwinism* (published by Fourth Estate, £16.99), science writer **RICHARD MILTON** (left) found that geology has a hidden agenda which means the Earth has to be old - whatever the evidence says.

One day, nearly twenty years ago, I picked an apparently rather dry geology book, *Prehistory and Earth Models* by Dr Melvin Cook, Professor of Metallurgy at Utah University, and found my attention arrested by a sentence in the Preface: "An attempt to publish [a] manuscript giving direct evidence for the short-time chronometry of the atmosphere and oceans entitled 'Anomalous Chronometry in the Atmosphere and Hydrosphere,' not unexpectedly nor without some cause, met with considerable opposition and was not published."

Who on earth had prevented Dr Cook from publishing his paper, I wondered? And what could a metallurgy professor have to say that was so heretical that someone wanted to prevent its publication? I began to take an interest in geology and palæontology and became a frequent visitor to London's Natural History Museum and Geological Museum. As I asked more and more questions, I became increasingly aware that the conventional view was constructed on a precariously thin experimental and theoretical foundation. The evidence I had been offered – and accepted – for the age of the Earth and its development amounted to little more than hearsay and guesswork; it was weak and scientifically flawed.

I also discovered that there is an important underlying reason for some scientists' belief in an Earth of great antiquity – a hidden agenda in geology. It is the unshakeable ideological commitment of the life sciences to Darwin's theory of evolution – that life has evolved over billions of years by means of random genetic mutation coupled with natural selection. Because the Darwinian mechanism *has* to take immense reaches of geological time to work, then the Earth *has* to be billions of years old.

Digging a little deeper, I discovered that there are many people, including reputable scientists in many countries, who shared my doubts about the age of the Earth and the soundness of the Darwinian view. But few professional scientists will speak out openly on an issue like this because the rules of the science game are that you receive funding for your research only if your papers are published in academic journals, and you get published in academic journals only if the Darwinist thought police say it's OK. Since virtually every scientist appointed to senior academic and public posts in the life sciences in Britain and America over the last 50 years has been a convinced Darwinist, then the chances of any alternative viewpoint being heard in the scientific press are close to zero. Anyone writing elsewhere can be dismissed as an eccentric or a religious crank who simply hasn't studied the evidence.

Some of those scientists who have spoken out against Darwinism or against an old Earth have been metaphorically roughed up by their colleagues. Others, who have made important scientific discoveries that tend to cast serious doubt on Darwinism, have simply published their findings quietly and without commenting on their implications for evolution theory.

THE EMERGENCE OF MARINE LIFE

So, how old is the Earth? The orthodox answer is that the Earth is 4,600 million years old. Life on Earth is said to have occurred spontaneously in ancient seas, some 3,000 million years ago and to have evolved over a period of billions of years by random mutation and natural selection.

> **"Practically everyone today has been 'sold' on the unrivalled accuracy of radioactive dating – after all, isn't that the very basis of our most sophisticated methods of chronometry?"**

The first thing that struck me is that life is not appearing spontaneously today in the seas. According to evolutionists, this is because conditions have changed since the first amino acids formed spontaneously in the 'primæval soup' and those early amino acids spontaneously formed the first protein molecule by some unknown process.

So how long exactly were conditions right for this spontaneous event? Obviously, the earliest date at which the event could have occurred was the formation of the first surface water on Earth after the crust cooled – the birth of the oceans – an event put by Darwinist geologists as occurring 3,800 million years ago.

The upper boundary marker for the spontaneous formation of life will equally obviously be the first fossil of a living thing. Until relatively recently the date of this event was problematical, but in 1979 Hans Dieter Pflug and H. Jaeschke-Boyer discovered the world's oldest microorganism – a fossil yeast – like cell which they called *Isosphæra*. But the rocks in which *Isosphæa* was found had been dated as being 3,800 million years old – exactly the same age as the oceans themselves. So, far from evolving by random probabilistic processes over billions or millions of years, life erupted at the first opportunity – rather like a novice golfer scoring a hole in one the first time he hits a ball. This is not something that Darwinist geologists care to discuss because it rules out the idea of evolution by probabilistic processes over immense periods.

RADIOMETRIC DATING

The next question that puzzled me (and one that had obviously puzzled Dr Cook) was exactly where do Darwinist geologists get their enormous time scales like 4,600 million years and 3,800 million years? Like most people (including, I suspect, most scientists) I had assumed that these dates had been derived from a variety of sophisticated technical dating methods of unassailable accuracy all of which were in close agreement. In fact, I discovered, they are derived from a deeply flawed technique that can be applied only to a tiny proportion of rocks – the decay of radioactive minerals such as potassium to argon, uranium to lead, and rubidium to strontium. And these different minerals give widely discordant dates.

Practically everyone today has been 'sold' on the

unrivalled accuracy of radioactive dating – after all, isn't that the very basis of our most sophisticated methods of chronometry – the atomic clock that broadcasts from the National Physical Laboratory to the nation? But although radioactive decay lends itself well to time-keeping in the laboratory, it is hopelessly compromised as a historical timekeeper.

For its use in the field, radiometric dating is based on the premise that the kind of decay product into which radioactive minerals turn is chemically distinctive from the commonly occurring form of that mineral. For instance, uranium decays into two isotopes of lead called lead 206 and lead 207 which are said to be radiogenic, while common lead is an isotope called lead 204. In order to date a rock deposit, a sample is taken and the amount of radioactive uranium, together with the amount of radiogenic lead it contains, is accurately assayed in the laboratory. Since the rate of decay is known from modern measurements, it is possible to calculate directly how long the uranium has been decaying – how old the deposit is – by how much radiogenic lead it has turned into.

Sir Charles Lyell (1797-1875), the influential Scottish geologist, whose *The Principles of Geology* (1830-33) provided the enormous span of geological time required by Darwin's theory of the protracted evolution of widely differing life forms.

argon 40 and calcium 40, far from being unique to radioactive decay, are very common isotopes in the atmosphere and the rocks of the Earth's crust. Cook has calculated that no more than one per cent of the argon 40 currently present on Earth could be a radiogenic daughter product and it is highly probable that some of the argon 40 in all potassium minerals has been incorporated directly rather than as a result of decay.

A very similar problem affects the widely-used uranium-lead method. If radiogenic lead – lead 206 and lead 207 from uranium, and lead 208 from thorium – really are uniquely formed as the end product of disintegration, then it is perfectly reasonable to suppose – as adherents of radioactive dating do – that there was zero radiogenic lead in the rocks of the Earth's crust when they first formed, and so we have a reliable starting point for our calculations.

What Melvin Cook pointed out is that there is another and quite separate mechanism by which common lead can be naturally changed into a form that, on assay, will be indistinguishable from 'radiogenic' lead. This transmutation can occur through the capture of free neutrons – atomic particles with enough energy to transmute common lead into so-called radiogenic lead. Significantly, this is a mechanism that would weight measurements in favour of an 'old' Earth, for too much 'radiogenic' lead would lead us to imagine that the process had been going on for much longer than it actually has.

NOT SO STRAIGHTFORWARD

This technique can obviously be very useful in some situations. When it comes to dating the Earth itself, though, radioactive decay is deeply flawed on a number of counts - and it was these flaws that Dr Cook's colleagues were keen should not be published.

Warnings about the techniques were issued as long ago as 1968, when scientists at the Hawaiian Institute of Geophysics discovered fundamental problems with the most widely used method of geochronometry, the potassium-argon method. C.S. Noble and J.J. Naughton measured the radiogenic argon content of basaltic lavas erupted into the Pacific ocean from an active Hawaiian volcano, Mount Kilauea. Ages calculated as up to 22 million years were found for lavas known to be from recent eruptions. Even more worrying were the findings of J.G. Funkhouser and J.J. Naughton the same year that lavas actually dating from an eruption in 1801 near Hualalei, and thus only 190 years old, were found to give potassium-argon dates ranging from 160 million years to *three billion years*.

The problem with the potassium-argon method turned out to be simply that the final decay products,

"Cook has calculated that no more than one percent of the argon 40 currently present on Earth could be a radiogenic daughter product."

amounts of lead 208. This could have been derived only from lead 207 by neutron capture, says Cook, while all the so-called radiogenic lead can be accounted for on the same basis and the mineral deposits could be essentially of modern origin.

Cook has analysed the lead content of two of the world's largest uranium ore deposits – in Katanga and Canada. He found that they contained no lead 204 (no lead from non-radiogenic sources) and practically no thorium 232. However they do contain significant

THE HELIUM PROBLEM

There is one further discovery relating to uranium dating which is of considerable relevance to the age of the Earth. The final products of the decay process are not only lead but also helium gas. Like the lead which results from the decay process, the helium is also a radiogenic daughter product, with an atomic weight of 4. In fact, almost the entire amount of helium in the Earth's atmosphere is believed to be radiogenic helium, formed during the decay process throughout the major part of the Earth's history.

Now, if the uranium-lead dating technique were reliable, then the amount of this radiogenic helium in the atmosphere would yield a date for the Earth's age consonant with that yielded by measuring the amount of radiogenic lead in the crust. In fact, the dates are so different as to be irreconcilable.

If the Earth were 4,600 million years old, then there would be roughly 10,000 billion tons of radiogenic helium 4 in the atmosphere. Actually, there is only around 3.5 billion tons present - several thousand times less than there should be (0.035% to be precise).

> "If the Earth really were 4,600 million years old, then some 65 million billion tons of dust would have settled on its surface, creating a layer some 180 feet deep all over the Earth."

Darwinist geologists have attempted to explain this discrepancy by assuming that the other 99.96% has escaped from the Earth's gravitational field into space – but this process has not been observed. On the contrary, we now know from NASA space probes that the Earth is moving in a thin solar atmosphere of hydrogen and helium resulting from nuclear fusion processes in the Sun, and is probably *gaining* these gases rather than losing them. Taking the measured amount of helium in the atmosphere suggests a date for its formation as recent as 100,000 to 1 million years ago.

Other similar radiometric dating techniques all suffer from the same defects. Radiogenic strontium – strontium 87 – occurs in rocks as a result of decay of radioactive rubidium. However, strontium 87 occurs both as a radiogenic daughter product of rubidium decay *and* as a commonly-occurring element in its own right. Typically, rocks contain ten times more common strontium 87 as radiogenic strontium 87. Rubidium-strontium is also suspect because it is subject to exactly the same neutron capture process as uranium-lead. This time it is strontium 86 which can be transformed to strontium 87.

DISCORDANT RESULTS

Most disconcerting of all is the fact that these various methods of dating commonly produce discordant ages for the same rock deposit. Where this occurs, a 'harmonisation' of discordant dates is carried out – in other words, the figures are adjusted in the laboratory until they seem right.

What are the findings of non-radioactive methods of geochronometry? Perhaps the

most interesting is the discovery by Hans Petterson of the Oceanographic Institute of Göteborg, that the rate of intrusion of meteoric dust into the Earth's atmosphere from space is roughly constant from year to year at around 14 million tons annually.

It was pointed out by Henry Morris that if the Earth really were 4,600 million years old, then some 65 million billion tons of dust would have settled on its surface, creating a layer some 180 feet deep all over the Earth. In fact, the true amount can be gauged from looking at the Moon, which geologists believe to be the same age as the Earth, where the surface is undisturbed by wind and tides, and where there is just an inch or two of dust.

In one sense, it is rather surprising that Darwinists have embraced radioactive dating techniques so enthusiastically. True, these techniques have provided the billions of years of pre-history required by the theory. But – almost incredibly – radioactive dating is otherwise quite useless to evolutionists since it cannot be used directly to date sedimentary rocks – the rocks in which fossils are found. That this is so will astonish many teachers of geography and geology who have been led to believe that radioactive dating is the ultimate authority for the assigned ages of rock strata and the fossils contained in them.

The entire geological column of sedimentary rock strata which is a prominent feature of every natural history museum, annotated with the age of each deposit and the type of animal or plant life dominating each stratum, is dated not by radioactive decay or any other method of direct measurement, but by relative, inferential methods. These include, principally, the dating of intrusions of primary volcanic rock and ash (either by the potassium-argon method of Hawaiian fame or the equally duff uranium-lead method) and estimates based on assumptions concerning rates of sedimentation and rates of evolution of fossil species.

Indeed, as recently as 1970, Sir Gavin De Beer, formerly Director of the British Museum of Natural History, wrote in the Museum's handbook on evolution that fossils were dated by radioactive means. This claim, repeated in most school and university lectures and textbooks on evolution, is completely

Charles Darwin (1809-82). Inspired by Lyell's revision of the age and structure of the Earth, Darwin gathered data for nearly 20 years before publishing his theory of evolution in *The Origin of Species* (1859). His idea, that the huge variety of biological forms and functions is the result of the accumulation of minute mutations and adaptations over great periods of time, is still used as an argument in support of the orthodox view of the antiquity of the Earth.

LEFT: The fossilised tree excavated at Craigleith Quarry, Edinburgh, which stands outside the Museum of Natural History in London.

false.

Some of the evidence for catastrophic formation of rocks is so glaringly obvious that it is hard to understood how anyone can ignore it. Take, for example, the problem of fossilised trees. In 1959, Broadhurst and Magraw described a fossilised tree, found in position of growth, in a coal seam at Blackrod, near Wigan, Lancashire. Evidence indicated the original tree was a minimum of 38 feet tall. Such trees are common in coal beds. As the authors say in their paper, the find implies a rapid rate of sedimentation, not a slow gradual deposition of sediments over millions of years.

Equally puzzling is that the custodians of the official 'geological column' at London's British Museum of Natural History do not seem to have noticed that each morning, on their way to work, they pass just such a fossilised tree standing in the museum grounds, excavated at Craigleith Quarry, Edinburgh, which originally stood more than 20 feet tall.

Epilogue

When my book *The Facts of Life: Shattering the Myth of Darwinism* was published at the end of August 1992, I expected it to arouse controversy, because it reports on scientific research that is itself controversial, and because it examines Darwinism critically; but I did at least expect the controversy to be rational. Instead the book has been violently attacked and denounced by Darwinists in two magazines.

Richard Dawkins, a professor of zoology at Oxford and prominent Darwinist, offered to write a damning review of the book for the *New Statesman*, "lest the paper commission someone else who would treat it as a serious scientific treatise". His intentions can be judged from a small section of the language he uses: 'complete and total ignorance', 'harmless fruitcake', 'loony', 'stupid', 'drivel', 'needs psychiatric help'.

When he does write rationally, Dawkins gets his facts wrong. He says "All qualified physicists, biologists, cosmologists and geologists agree, on the basis of massive, mutually corroborating evidence, that the earth's age is at least four billion years."

In fact, one of the principal disclosures in my book is that some professional scientists, whose job is investigating dating methods, have published serious doubts about the sole method (not "massive, mutually corroborating evidence") of arriving at this immense age, that of radioactive dating. I give three examples in my *FT article*.

Dawkins is obsessed by the fact that one of the scientists voicing doubts about radiometric dating, Dr Melvin Cook, is a creationist. In Dawkins' mind, this appears to invalidate the evidence Cook presents. That Cook was professor of metallurgy at Utah University for many years, and a distinguished chemist and winner of the Nobel medal for his work on high explosives, is of no consequence to Dawkins. Cook's evidence contradicts Darwinian beliefs and hence must be wrong, whatever the facts say.

Dawkins also says that I think the Earth is only a few thousand years old. I do not believe, nor do I say, any such thing. I present evidence that current methods of geochronometry are seriously flawed and are preferred by Darwinists only because they provide the great age needed by their theory.

The other review of my book, equally intemperate, was anonymous and was by the writer of a leading article in *Nature*, probably the most respected scientific magazine in the world. He or she wrote that I believe evolution to be false – I don't – and natural selection 'a pack of lies' - I don't. It also issued a magisterial rebuke to the *Sunday Times* for irresponsibly drawing its readers' attention to my book's existence.

Evidently, both Dawkins and the editor of *Nature* agree with Sydney Smith, who said: "I never read a book before reviewing it; it prejudices a man so."

However, as one correspondent who wrote to the *New Statesman* in my defence put it: "When orthodox scientists resort too readily to ridicule and suppression of dissenting views, it is science itself which suffers." It is depressing to find that even in a country which prides itself on its tolerance, it is impossible to voice scientific dissent without attracting this kind of intemperate knee-jerk response.

FT

A COOL DRUDE

IAN SIMMONS talks to astroarchæologist & rock star JULIAN COPE

Julian Cope first made an impression in the late seventies as a lead singer of *The Teardrop Explodes* and has performed solo since 1984. He has woven an individual and extraordinary thread through rock's rich tapestry since then, producing a series of stimulating and unconventional albums, which, with "Peggy Suicide" and the recently-released "Jehovakill", have taken an increasingly personal and spiritual turn. He is at present writing a book on stone circles as well as making a meditation album, putting together a Kraut Rock compilation and acting as producer for a new band called T.C. Lethbridge. So impressed was he by Avebury that he has settled there with his family.

FT You are putting together *The Modern Antiquary*, **a book on stone circles. What angle do you take?**

JC The book's really practical, but also very far out. Twenty per cent of the book is opinion and anti-archæologist rant, and the rest is this really over-the-top gazetteer of more than 200 sites. There's my photographs plus a page of notes for every monument – how it feels to go there and all the associated legends. I'm into astroarchæology, so there'll be dimensions too. The heavens were really important for Ancient Man, they must have ruled his life. There'll also be real visionary stuff.

FT Do you think you'll have problems getting the book over as most people know you as a rock star?

JC If a pop star does a book on ancient monuments, he's got to be much more thorough than anybody else, otherwise the archæologists are just going to sock it to him. I've got to take advantage of the fact that I can get people working on things in different areas. I did radio interviews on my solo tour of Scotland recently, and spent a few days in each place we went, so when it came to the gig, the local astroarchæologists would come and offer to show me sites, and that was really important.

FT I caught you in Thurso on that tour, I was going round the other way, starting in Aberdeen and ending up at Callanish.

JC Callanish is so special. We got friendly with Margaret Curtis, who was Margaret Pontin. She's written books on Callanish like *New Light on the Stones*, and she showed us lost circles and things. I think she is

ABOVE: Tomnaverie recumbent stone circle near Aberdeen.
BELOW: Loanhead recumbent stone circle near Daviot, Aberdeen.

JC I loved Sunhoney, a very witchy circle though. They let 40 people do magic circles there during Beltane. I mean, I wouldn't even presume to ask something like that of the farmers. Midmar Kirk is another one; it's beside a church and it just paganises the churchyard. I see the recumbent stone and the flankers as like the Horned God, they go straight up like the top of Batman's mask. We were talking to the guy who looks after it, and his daughter, who's a 35-year-old autistic savant, was screaming her head off excitedly in the circle. A weird place to be.

Sunhoney, Midmar Kirk and Cullerlie, they're all in a line. Tomnagorie is next in the line. It's a later recumbent, when they started to bring the recumbent stone into the centre and the stones aren't such an extraordinary size. Now there's a really cool place!

FT You mentioned your book will be anti-excavation. Why?
JC Archæologists seem to miss the irony of digging away while saying "Wasn't it dreadful, all this nineteenth century excavation? If only they'd known what we know now it would be OK". Thank God Silbury Hill is still here, after all the times they've poked into it! It's only because it's so well made. You know about the Hatfield Barrow. It was in the Marden Henge and Richard Colt-Hoare dug into it in about 1810. It was a third the size of Silbury, but it was made of sand and within a year or two of digging into it, the whole thing was gone.

FT What do you do at the sites you visit?
JC I like to write up my notes at the focal point of each site. I couldn't do that at Skara Brae as there were so many tourists, so I went down to the beach and out of this Orcadian flagstone I built a circle of my own to feel what it was like to work with the stone. It had an avenue and a couple of outlying stones. After four and a half hours, I finally got to write the note, sitting in the circle.

As a companion to stuffy old English Heritage, I thought people of like kind should form "Head Heritage", which would build modern stone circles. There aren't any in places like Leicestershire; perhaps we could construct a whole ritual landscape!

FT In one of your interviews for "Floored Genius" [Julian's recent retrospective compilation], you talked about your astral travel experiences.
JC "Upwards at 45 degrees" [from *Jehovakill*] is my way of describing how I astrally project. The first time it happened I left through the forehead, a real third eye exit, almost like a tearing of the third eye. Energy came down and poured into me, right down to my toes; all this white light, like a heavy

a visionary and almost doesn't know it. She went to Callanish 20 years ago to prove it wasn't a lunar site. Five years later she found it *was* a lunar site and realised her archæological background was getting her nowhere. She's about 50 and married to this extraordinary guy called Elrond Curtis, an archæologist who excavated Stennes with Graham Ritchie.

FT I always liked the circles in the Aberdeen area.
JC Aberdeen was the thing that tripped me out most of all. We had Janet and Colin Bord's *Ancient Sites* and Richard Feacham's *Prehistoric Scotland*, but no-one told us till we got there that the recumbent stone circles are the greatest seam of mystical sites in the world. There are 118 stone circles in that area, a lot ruined, but the thing is, the Bords have only got three, so we just didn't know.

The ones I liked best were definitely Old Krieg – the books say it's been destroyed, but you can't destroy something that amazing. Tomnaverie is one of the weirdest ones.

FT I had to wade through a torrent of farm slurry to get there; it's besieged by cows. I am very fond of Sunhoney as well.

liquid, like mercury, but blazing white, and I was like, "Ah blp! blp! blp!" gulping a really physical experience. It's never happened the same way since, but that fist time gave me the facility to do it. I have no real control over it, although a bit more now than in the past. When it first happened I was so excited – part of you just welcomes it.

bookcase, and came back brandishing a stone about eight inches long, dark grey with rounded edges and bell-shaped ends, very clearly worked by human hands.]

This is something that might be very *Fortean Times*. When we were in Orkney, I went to the Knap of Howa, the most northern neolithic settlement. It's like Skara Brae, only smaller and in the middle of nowhere – five hours on a tiny ferry. I walked 20

TOP: Recumbent stone at Midmar stone circle, Aberdeenshire, Grampian Region. MIDDLE: Cullerlie stone circle, Aberdeen. BOTTOM: Julian Cope in 1991.

FT With the 'New Age' becoming more mainstream, people have been more open to this kind of thing.
JC When I first started reading about New Age stuff, I was put off by the term 'New Age', because it's so dinky, isn't it? But as long as you don't throw it all out, you can find some great stuff. I always call people 'Dude', that sort of California airhead thing, so now I've started calling everyone 'Drude', a cross between 'Dude' and 'Druid'. People want to be New Age, but they don't want the crap side of it.

I'm doing this meditation album, and so I've been commissioning meditations. I said to some friends: "Would you write me a meditation? All it's got to be is very low key, with a beat of some kind and more than 15 minutes long." It will be better than a lot of this wishy washy New Age stuff. The album's going to be called *Rite*. It's got a picture of Silbury on the front and all the stuff I'm into, but its Drude music, a bit more of an urban meditation. It's like the tracks on *There's a Riot Going on* by Sly and the Family Stone, but 20 minutes each track. They always finish too quickly, you can't have sex to any of that music, although it's very sexy. *Rite* is urban meditation music, like really nothing going on, it's wah clarinet, bass and drum machine.

[At this point Julian leapt up, headed for the

yards down the beach and found this. What do you make of it?

FT It's certainly worked, but it's not the usual sort of tool. It doesn't look as if it was meant to have sharp edges. It's

weird whatever it is!
JC Isn't it just! I call it a megalithic dildo. Do you think it was for giving the Goddess a good seeing to? I must find out more about it. It's going to be in the book.

FT On the sleeve of *Jehovakill* you mention T.C. Lethbridge and William Burroughs and say that Lethbridge was 59 and Burroughs 43. Is this when they started writing?
JC It's when they became their 'headself' as opposed to just being themselves. I'm just trying to explain that whatever time it starts it's cool. I was going to say, "Grandma Moses was 70 when it came to her", but then I'd give people more of an excuse to put it off.

FT Fort was another one who came into his own late. The first of the books he's known for didn't appear until he was 44. Are you familiar with his books?
JC I read some of his stuff some years back and really liked it; and I've known about the *Fortean Times* for quite a while. You know, that sort of thing has to be done because wisdom comes out of places you least expect it.

FT

Tradescant.

IAN SIMMONS DESCRIBES THE CONTENTS OF THIS SINGULA

One of 1992's less celebrated anniversaries is the tricentenary of the death of Elias Ashmole, founder of Oxford's Ashmolean Museum. This was Britain's first purpose–built museum, constructed by Oxford University to house the collections donated by Ashmole; the credit for the collection, however, lies not with Ashmole, but with two extraordinary men, father and son, both named John Tradescant, 17th century England's most noted collectors of curiosities. The Tradescant

Portrait of John Tradescant the Elder painted by Emmanuel de Critz

cabinet of curiosities, usually known as 'Tradescant's Rarities', or 'Tradescant's Ark', was founded by the elder Tradescant, a gardener from Suffolk who landscaped for noblemen, such as the Duke of Buckingham, and later worked for Charles I, taking charge of various royal gardens. He travelled the world in his capacity as gardener to the nobility, collecting new and rare plants for their gardens, journeying to Flanders, Russia, Algeria, Turkey and various parts of the Mediterranean. On these journeys he collected artifacts as well, both natural and man–made, and these formed the core of his collection, along with items collected by his friends on their travels. His work with the Duke of Buckingham helped him greatly by providing contacts from whom he could obtain rarities, as the Duke also collected them, in some cases using Tradescant as his agent. One letter from Tradescant on behalf of Buckingham requests that the Secretary of the Navy should obtain from merchants "… Anything that is Strang …" for the Duke.

In common with other cabinets of the time, those of Buckingham and Tradescant emphasised the unusual and extraordinary, with human horns, mermaids and unicorns taking their place beside Henry VIII's gloves and so on. This approach is largely absent from their successors, the modern museums, but could still be seen, over a century later, at the foundation of the British Museum in 1753, where items such as human horns had a place, and certain strands continued into the 20th century. Brighton's Booth Museum has a toad with the stone in which it was encased on display, Market Harborough Museum has a two–headed calf and there was much public outcry some years back when Ipswich Museum removed its five–legged rat.

The Ark

In 1628, Tradescant moved to Lambeth with his collection and there opened it to the public, earning his house the name 'The Ark'. When John the Elder died in 1638, the collection was substantially complete, and both this and his gardening duties were taken over by his son John, who presided over the next chapter of the collection's history.

Despite several expeditions to Virginia, John the Younger did not add significantly to the collection, but he did exploit it efficiently as

Ark

ABINET OF CURIOSITIES

Fashionable ladies and gentlemen examine the curiosities at the Wakefield Industrial exhibition, 1865.

what would today be termed a 'visitor attraction'. Quite a number of accounts of visits to 'Tradescant's Ark' still exist, one of the best being by Georg Christopher Stirn in 1638. Among the items he records having seen are the hand of a mermaid, a giant human bone and a piece of the true cross. The mermaid's hand may have been a preserved human one retaining partial webbing between the fingers, or the paw of some sort of aquatic mammal; while the large bone was either from a giant, or more likely, from a large non–human mammal.

The history of the 'True Cross' is better known. Ashmole attempted to authenticate it and traced its origin to another piece owned by Charles I which was reputed to have been given to Edward III by King John of France. Tradescant the Younger was, according to Ashmole, entrusted by Charles' Queen, Henrietta Maria, with the task of taking it to France for her, and the piece in the collection was "accidentally" broken off while he did this. On the other hand, a colleague of Tradescant's, John Parkinson, describes it as "a great piece of true Lignum Aloes [..] as bigge and as long as Man's leg", and claimed it had actually been presented to Tradescant by the king. He also opined: "If all those pieces of wood, that are [..] said to be parts of that Crosse were all set together they would goe neere to make [..] many cart loads full".

Fanatical Astrologer

Ashmole entered the story in 1650 when he was introduced to Tradescant by his wife, the two families becoming good friends. The Ashmoles spent the summer of 1652 staying at the Tradescants and during this time they visited a witch trial in Kent dealing with people accused of bewitching children, adults, pigs, sheep, mares and grain, resulting in six women being hanged and various others (both male and female) being gaoled.

Ashmole himself was a successful solicitor and very able historian; he had studied mathematics, astronomy and natural philosophy at Oxford and was an early Member of the Royal Society. He was also an accomplished alchemist, writing the classic

Theatrum Chemicum Brittanicum, and a fanatical astrologer, rarely making any move without consulting his horoscope. Coupled with this, however, was his determined and unscrupulous self–aggrandisement which governed much of his relations with Tradescant and the rarities.

Ashmole offered to catalogue Tradescant's collection for him, and this he did, working with Dr Thomas Worton to produce the *Musæum Tradescantianum* published in 1656 and paid for by Ashmole, who also attempted to take all the credit for it. The *Musæum Tradescantianum* revealed the full extent of the collection, catalogued under 14 categories, including 'Divers sorts of Strange Fishes', 'coins', 'Warlike instruments' and 'other variety of Rarities'. These categories contained a wide range of Fortean artifacts.

> "Tradescant emphasised the unusual and extraordinary, with human horns, mermaids and unicorns taking their place beside Henry VIII's gloves."

Recorded as being part of the Tradescant collection is a sample of "Blood that rained in the Isle of Wight, authenticity vouched for by Sir John Oglander". Oglander was the Royalist MP for Yarmouth and the period's leading authority on the island's history. It is thought that this was either dust containing iron oxide which fell in rain or a sample of red meteoric dust which fell on Wight in 1177 according to the *Chronicle of Brompton*, but as this is one of many items from the collection which is now lost, it is impossible to verify this.

Among the catalogued items which still survives is the portrait of 'Old Parr' which remains in the Ashmolean. Old Parr was a resident of Shropshire who lived to the claimed age of 152 on the estate of the Earl of Arundel, who discovered him in 1635. Parr was taken to London and presented to the king, but his new found celebrity did not suit him, and he died at Arundel House in London on 14 November 1635, being buried in Westminster Abbey.

Tradescant's collection also boasted a "Very Small part" of Boramete skin and a "coat lyned" with it. The Borametz, or Tartary Lamb, was supposed to be a plant whose fruit resembled a lamb attached to a stem by its navel. It was reported to be about three feet tall and grown from a seed similar to a melon. Inevitably, there were also

A 'mermaid' exhibited at a London show of curiosities

NOTES.

* This vegetable is called the Tartarian Lamb, from its resemblance in shape to that animal; it has something like four feet, and its body is covered with a kind of down. Travellers report that it will suffer no vegetable to grow within a certain distance of its feat. Sir Hans Sloan read a Memoir upon this plant before the Royal Society; for which consult their Transactions, Nº. 245, p. 461. Mr. Bell, in his "Account of a Journey from St. Petersburg to Ispahan," informs us that he searched in vain for this plant in the neighbourhood of Astrachan, when at the same time the more sensible and experienced amongst the Tartars treated the whole history as fabulous. This journey was undertaken in the year 1715.

The Vegetable Lamb of Tartary

The Vegetable Lamb of Tartary, from the Tradescant Trust, in the Museum of Garden History, St Mary–at–Lambeth, Lambeth Palace Road, London SE1. It arrived as a surprise gift from a Cambridgeshire doctor. The two John Tradescants, father and son, are buried in the adjacent churchyard.

The lamb's antique label reads: "This vegetable is called the Tartarian Lamb, from its resemblance in shape to that animal. It has something like four feet, and its body is covered with a kind of down. Travellers report that it will suffer no vegetable to grow within a certain distance of its seat. Sir Hans Sloan[e] read a memoir upon

this plant before the Royal Society; for which consult their *Transactions*, No.245, p.461. Mr Bell, in his 'Account of a Journey from St Petersburg to Ispahan,' informs us that he searched in vain for this plant in the neighbourhood of Astrachan, when at the same time the more sensible and experienced amongst the Tartars treated the whole history as fabulous. This journey was undertaken in the year 1715."

Vegetable lambs were supposed to taste of fish and their blood of honey, and when their bones were placed in the mouth, in the course of "certain ceremonies and incantations", one was "instantly seized with a spirit of divination and endowed with the gift of prophecy".

John Parkinson, botanist to Charles I, seems to have believed in the vegetable lamb; one appears in a woodcut, along with Adam and Eve, on the title page of his *Paradisus*, published in 1629.

Sir Hans Sloane presented a specimen, mentioned in the label to the Tradescant lamb, to the Royal Society in 1698. He correctly said it was part of a tree fern (*Cibotium barometz*), doctored to resemble a lamb. All but four of the bony fronds had been removed, and the remaining ones shaved and shortened to imitate legs. It turned out to be a popular toy in southern China, further east than vegetable lamb hunters had searched.

several types of barnacle, classified in the 'Birds' section due to the belief that geese hatched from them, a belief which still held firm in 1678, when the Royal Society published an eyewitness account of geese emerging from barnacles on a Scottish island. It recorded that the observer saw that the barnacles had "within them little birds, perfectly shaped".

Also on the bird front, Tradescant exhibited the "Claw of the bird Roc [..] able to truss an Elephant". This specimen, rather than belonging to the mythical bird as reported, was probably part of the elephant bird of Madagascar. This is the world's largest known bird, half as big again as an ostrich and weighing 450 kilos, which was last recorded in 1666. This bird may also have been the source of the collection's 'Dragon's egg' as the elephant bird laid eggs with an eight–litre volume, equivalent to 144 chicken eggs – although an ostrich egg has also been proposed as the true identity of this specimen.

Tradescant's collection also held another now extinct bird, the dodo. This was the preserved remains of a live one exhibited in London in 1638 which the Tradescants acquired on its death. It was later ravaged by rot and museum beetle, and was incinerated in 1755, although the skull and a foot were rescued from the flames and reside today, somewhat charred, in the Oxford Museum of Natural History.

Another item of note among the natural history specimens is an "Elk's hoof with three claws", reputedly a cure for epilepsy. In fact the elk was believed able to cure itself of the affliction by placing the hoof in its left ear, although the concept of an epileptic elk stretches the imagination somewhat. Ashmole also records in the catalogue a "Hare's head with rough horns three inches long". The specimen no longer exists and little is known of it, but it may have been the skull of a Muntjac deer, not at that time known in Britain, which could, because of its small size, have been attributed to a hare.

In the category of 'Variety of Rarities' several pieces described as 'Gamaha' are recorded. These were stones found in nature with images on them [see the simulacrum on p14 last issue – Eds], valued as amulets against evil. One of them was inscribed with the names Jesus, Joseph and Mary in Italian capitals; another portrayed a fish in it (probably a fossil), and another a death's head. Only the one bearing the holy names survives. This was said to have been found in water in the West Indies, and is made of mudstone; however, it has clearly been washed to inscribe the names and is not of natural origin, no matter where it was found.

Ashmole's Duplicity

Having catalogued the collection, Ashmole retained an interest in it and in 1659 managed to get Tradescant to sign a deed of gift while drunk, signing the collection over to Ashmole on his death, in trust for a University. Despite Tradescant's later attempts to cancel this, legal action by Ashmole against Tradescant's wife after her husband's death in 1662 upheld the deed of gift. Ashmole gained the rights to the collection as the major part of his gift to Oxford in 1683 on the condition it was housed in a museum named after him. This was the foundation of the Ashmolean.

Once in the Ashmolean, Tradescant's rarities did not fare well. They suffered neglect and decay, with much being burnt in the 18th century with the Dodo. Of the rest, some were dispersed to other museums and have been lost due to poor record-keeping. In the 1880's some were reportedly being kept in a shed open to the street, and as late as the 1960's, concern was expressed about the state of some of the geological specimens.

However, in 1976, the Ashmolean attempted to draw together what could be found of Tradescant's rarities and devoted a room to their display. Few of the Fortean items can be seen, though; time and carelessness has resulted in the loss of almost all of them, a pattern repeated in museums everywhere where the bizarre and atypical has long been out of fashion in collecting policies. Many Fortean items languish forgotten in stores or have **FT** vanished completely.

Portrait of Elias Ashmole, painted by Riley, now in the Ashmolean Museum, Oxford.

The tomb of Tradescant the elder, at the Museum of Garden History, Lambeth, London.

Silent City

In his book *New Lands*, Charles Fort lists sever;
Alaska. According to tradition, this odd mirag

ABOUT THE AUTHOR:

DWIGHT WHALEN is a resident of the town of Niagara Falls in Ontario, Canada, and has written about numerous Fortean mysteries in *Fate*, *INFO Journal* and *Pursuit*. His articles for ***Fortean Times*** include 'The Mississauga Blob' **[FT31:4]** and 'Stoned on Annie Taylor' **[FT45:62]**. He is also the author of *The Lovers' Guide to Niagara Falls*.

"The Northern Lights have seen queer sights", wrote Yukon poet Robert W. Service. Surely one of the strangest, most spell-binding sights ever seen in the North are the reported appearances of a mysterious phantom city in the Alaska sky, the legendary 'Silent City'.

"We could plainly see houses, well-defined streets and trees", related L.B. French in an 1889 *New York Times* story datedlined Chicago, October 30. French said he and his companions, on an early July afternoon about 5 o'clock, suddenly saw a 'spectral city' appear in the sky, moving towards them above an Alaska glacier.

"Here and there rose tall spires over huge buildings which appeared to be ancient mosques or cathedrals. It was a large city, one which would contain at least 100,000 inhabitants [..] It did not look like a modern city – more like an ancient European city. I noticed particularly the immense height of the spires."

Before he and a companion could reach better vantage points to photograph the ghostly city,

French said, it grew fainter and disappeared. The vision, he estimated, lasted about 25 minutes. French was neither the first nor the last to report the 'Silent City' spectacle in Alaska's great Glacier Bay, on the Alaska Panhandle about 70 miles northwest of Juneau.

A phantom city out of place and time? A beautiful, inexplicable mirage? Or a fabulous tale of Alaska folklore?

MUIR GLACIER DISCOVERED

Most sightings of the Silent City have placed it above Muir Glacier, named after John Muir, the Alaska explorer who first visited Glacier Bay in 1879. It forms part of the vast, hauntingly beautiful Glacier Bay National Monument. One of several glaciers, Muir is located in a mountain-studded sea of ice about 25 miles wide. It spills into Muir Inlet, passing between the flanks of Mount Wright and a ridge extending to Riggs Glacier about five miles to the east. A frozen Niagara about two miles wide, Muir rises some 200 feet

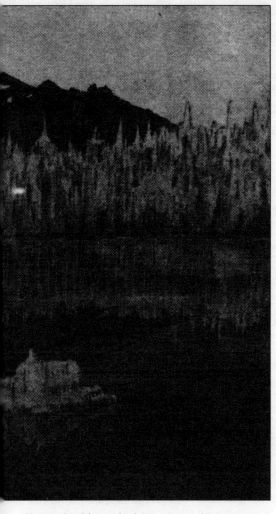

above the blue Alaska waters, plunging to a depth of 700 feet beneath. Great ice chunks continually crack off the glacier's jagged face and crash into the bay with a thunder heard for miles.

Describing his first view of the glacier to Alaska historian Alexander Badlam, Muir recalled it in terms suggesting that he, too, beheld an otherworldly metropolis:

"[I saw] a bewildering chaos of strange architectural forms, beautiful beyond the measure of description, and so bewildering in their beauty as to almost make the spectator believe that he was revelling in a dream. There were great clusters of glistening spires, gables, obelisks, monoliths and castles standing out boldly against the sky…"

RICHARD WILLOUGHBY'S PHOTOGRAPH

It was not John Muir, however, but a long-time Alaska prospector named Richard G. Willoughby who put Muir Glacier's 'Silent City' on the map. Camping in the mountains of Glacier Bay one day in the mid-1880s, Willoughby was awakened one

morning by an excited Indian companion. Looking northward, Willoughby observed a strange glow in the sky above the glacier. Gradually, incredibly, the light assumed the distinct appearance of a very large city, the apparition the Indians called 'The Silent City'.

Willoughby watched agog. Nothing moved, nobody could be seen, not even a shadow dimmed the great city's radiance, as if its spectral structures glowed from within. Too soon the glorious image faded. Willoughby walked toward it, quickened his pace, but the phantom city vanished back into the sky above the glacier.

What astounding mirage was this? What unexplained refraction of light could transport to Alaska the image of an exotic city thousands of miles away? It had to be a city far distant: nothing approaching its size, or resembling its appearance, existed in the sparsely-populated North.

Willoughby learned that the mysterious apparition had been seen before above Muir Glacier. His best chance to see it, he heard, was in late June or early July, when the days were longest. He returned to Glacier Bay with a camera; he made three treks in as many years, camping out on a mountain ledge opposite the glacier. His first two vigils yielded only faint glimpses of the city and unconvincing photos. But finally, on a mild June day, the city appeared again in wondrous detail, suspended above the ice as before. Willoughby snapped his camera.

For a year or so afterwards, he circulated a glass negative among his Alaska friends, claiming it was the picture he'd taken of the mirage above Muir Glacier. In 1889 a visiting newspaperman named Miner Bruce interviewed Willoughby, obtained a print from the negative, and wrote up the story for the *San Francisco Chronicle*. Other US papers picked up the story, complete with photo. The Silent City legend was born. Some found it genuinely mysterious and speculated on the peculiar light-bending properties of Alaska's atmosphere. The story stirred widespread interest, prompting Bruce to write additional Silent City articles; but some readers, noting the well-defined architecture in the photograph, the shadows and sharply-focussed trees (leafless in summer), simply chuckled.

BRISTOL IN THE SKY

What city was it? Nobody knew immediately, but in October that year a Wells Fargo employee named W.G. Stuart spotted a copy of Willoughby's topical picture in a San Francisco store window and recognised it as a view of Bristol, England, where he had lived for a time.

"The photograph represents an old portion of the city, the view being from a public park on Brandon Hill", Stuart told the *Chronicle*. "There is a Catholic cathedral here, the main building of which was completed about two centuries ago.

LEFT: Mirage of Muir Glacier, seen from Glacier Bay, from a photograph taken on 23rd July 1889 by Miss Maud Badlam. Muir himself described the sight as "A bewildering chaos of strange architectural forms, beautiful beyond the measure of description, and so bewildering in their beauty as to almost make the spectator believe that he was revelling in a dream. There were great clusters of glistening spires, gables, obelisks, monoliths and castles standing out boldly against the sky …"

INSET: Scottish-American naturalist John Muir (1838-1914).

TOP: Professor Willoughby's silent city. "The real mystery is how Willoughby's utterly un-miragelike picture could have fooled anybody." The original caption says it was taken on 21 June 1889; other sources indicate it was taken a year or two earlier. ABOVE: One of 26 period photographs in Reece Winstone's *Bristol in the 1880s*, showing that Willoughby's famous 'mirage' picture is a view from Brandon Hill.

Just before I left Bristol, two years ago, work was being commenced on the two towers, and the scaffolding was built just as it is represented in 'The Silent City'. In the photograph alleged to be taken in Alaska is a large building to the left of the cathedral. This is the Royal Hotel. Just in front of the cathedral is a square known as College Green. The Avon River runs through the city, and the shipping is to be seen right in the heart of the city, just as it is depicted in the Alaskan photograph." *[Confirmation of this opinion by a Bristol photographic historian is discussed in* **FT24**:37 – *Eds.]*

The real mystery is how Willoughby's un-miragelike picture could have fooled anybody. Yet Miner Bruce, recalling the Silent City saga in his book *Alaska – Its History and Resources* (1899) defended Willoughby: "[He] never by word or implication gave me any reason to think that his story was other than a true one." Bruce, however, openly admitted that even if he had known that the picture was a fake, he would not have exposed Willoughby, out of gratitude for the oldtimer's "interesting tale".

Bruce had good reason to be grateful: his Silent City writings, he revealed, were "the most profitable newspaper articles I ever wrote". And

Willoughby, according to Bruce, made thousands of dollars selling prints of his photograph. If the image depicted Bristol, said Bruce, "it must have been reflected a distance of several thousand miles."

Alaska historian Badlam disagreed. He also knew Willoughby personally, but considered him incapable of fraud. More likely, thought Badlam, Willoughby – "as fair a sample of credulous humanity as one would meet in a lifetime" – received the plate from someone playing a practical joke on him.

Dr Charles H. Gilbert, a naturalist with an interest in human psychology, interviewed Willoughby. According to an article by David Starr Jordan, 'The Silent City of the Muir Glacier' (1897), Gilbert reported that Willoughby had known nothing about photography before attempting to photograph the Silent City. In fact, it appeared that he didn't even know the purpose of a darkroom. Willoughby claimed to have exposed the Silent City plate in daylight, where it had sat in a 'secret' chemical compound for three months!

"The original negative", wrote Jordan, "examined by Dr Gilbert, was a very old, stained and faded plate, apparently a negative which had been discarded because underexposed."

OTHER WITNESSES

If the photograph was phony, the mirage itself was evidently the real thing. Two witnesses named Robert Christie and Robert Patterson claimed to have seen it on 2 July 1889 – "a city of extensive proportions, perhaps of 15,000 or 20,000 inhabitants" – and signed affidavits to that effect. Others over the years did the same. ("An affidavit in Juneau costs but a drink of whiskey", sneered David Jordan, "the usual price along the Northwest coast.")

Soon after Willoughby's photo, a second Silent City photo surfaced. It was allegedly taken in July 1889 by a photographer named I.W. Taber, using a strange technique borrowed from a Muir Glacier visitor from Nevada City, California, named James O'Dell. Using a gold pan filled with quicksilver, O'Dell claimed to be able to see in the liquid, with the aid of a magnifying glass, distant scenes reflected off the sky. In this curious way, he discovered that the Silent City mirage was actually the image of a 'Sunken City' resting on the bottom of the 700-foot deep waters of Glacier Bay.

Taber's picture, published in Badlam's *Wonders of Alaska* (1890) along with Willoughby's picture, shows an exotic-looking city with what appears to be a coliseum, a mosque and many other buildings of Old World design, all cloaked in dark clouds and mist. "I'd like to think this photograph genuine, myself", wrote Charles Fort in *New Lands* (1923), "but I do conceive that Taber could have taken it by photographing a panorama that he had painted." In any event, if a Sunken City lies at the bottom of the bay, nobody ventured to explain how its image could penetrate the deep, silt-laden waters, where surface visibility is limited to a mere foot or two.

Taber's Silent City at Glacier Bay, photographed in July 1889. Taber claimed that this city rested under 700 feet of arctic water. Fort said he wanted to believe it genuine, but suspected that it might be a photograph of a painting. Like the other two Alaskan landscapes, this photo is taken from Badlam's *Wonders of Alaska.*

KERSHON'S BURIED CITY

A prospector named George Kershon, reading about the Silent City, told the *San Francisco Examiner* what he thought the source of the strange vision could be. His account appears in Badlam's book. During the summer of 1888, Kershon and an Indian guide, exploring deep in the Alaska interior, climbed a hilltop and stumbled upon a strange sight in the distant valley below: a city frozen in ice.

"After several hours of hard work, I reached the outskirts of this mysterious city", reported Kershon, "and found that the place was laid out in streets, with blocks of strange-looking buildings, what appeared to be mosques, towers, ports etc., and every evidence of having been built by art.

"The whole was not of solid ice, though it seemed to be, but blows from a hatchet on one of the walls disclosed the fact that beneath this barrier of ice was some sort of building material. It looked to be wood, but of a stone-like hardness and apparently petrified. The silence around the place was something ghostly…

"I soon got tired of investigating the city, as the streets were blocked in many places by huge masses of ice, rendering passage almost impossible. The Indian, too, became uneasy, and we started on the return trip, reaching home the next day, tired but satisfied that we had been the first men to gaze on that silent city for centuries."

The Muir Glacier mirage, Kershon claimed, must have been the reflected image of the frozen city he had found. How such a city came to be in the far North, he couldn't say. "Perhaps at one time it was not so cold north as it is now", he speculated.

A GREAT MIRAGE

All three candidates for the Silent City mirage – Bristol, a sunken city in the bay and a frozen lost city further north – "will rank high among Baron Munchausen's fairy tales", predicted Alexander Badlam. He, too, saw 'a great mirage' over the ice while sailing on Glacier Bay aboard the steamship *Ancon*, 23 July 1889. There was "what seemed to be a block of large white buildings [..] Beautifully formed spires, apparently three or four hundred feet high, reached above the buildings. The doors, windows, streets and gardens appeared to be visible, but this mirage was like those of the great desert."

A photo of what he saw appears in *Wonders of Alaska*, showing the prolific spires and monoliths so often described in accounts of the Silent City. Clearly, Badlam, Willoughby and others viewed Muir Glacier during temperature inversions, when a layer of warm air hung above the jagged face and crown of the cold glacier. Light from the ice, striking the warm air above, would be reflected back down, causing the ice to appear to loom in marvellously elongated pinnacles and other fantastic shapes.

"Mirages in the glacier regions are of frequent occurrence in pleasant weather", wrote Badlam, "and as the sun does not set before nine o'clock during June and July, some charming views are obtained at or about that hour." French's sighting, in fact, was of a 'Silent City' above a glacier near Mount Fairweather, more that 20 miles northwest of Muir.

Since the turn of the century, Muir Glacier has been steadily receding about a quarter of a mile a year. Today, it is roughly 20 miles north of where it was in the 1880s, and the Silent City mirage is apparently no longer sighted. According to Alaska historian R.T. DeArmand (in a note of 30 Sept 1990), no "geologists, glaciologists, fishermen, kayakers and hundreds of other visitors over the years" have reported the fabled city in the sky. Has the shrinking glacier taken the Silent City mirage with it? Or is something more precious – our capacity to experience imaginative wonder – disappearing instead?

Willoughby's photograph, and the yarns it inspired, are Alaska's finest contribution to the honourable American tradition of leg-pulling. Yet there is no denying the icy spires of the Silent City must have been a spellbinding sight. Who can be sure they won't appear again some day? After all, the Alaska sky where the Northern Lights reel is indisputably a realm of the marvellous. **FT**

BIBLIOGRAPHY
Alexander Badlam: *Wonders of Alaska* (the Bancroft Company, San Francisco, 1890.)

William D.Boehm: *Glacier Bay* (Alaska Northwest Publishing Company, Anchorage, Alaska, 1986.)

Miner Bruce: *Alaska – Its History and Resources (Goldfields, Routes and Scenery)* (G.P. Putnam's, New York, 1899.)

Charles Fort: *New Lands* (Boni & Liveright, New York, 1923.)

David Starr Jordan: "The Silent City of the Muir Glacier" (*Popular Science Monthly*, vol.51, June 1897.)

"Identity of the Silent City – From the *an Francisco Chronicle*, Oct.11" (*New York Times*, 20 Oct 1889.)

"The 'Silent City' – The Wonderful Mirage Witnessed in Alaska" (*New York Times*, 31 Oct 1889)

Florida's Penguin Panic

In 1948, inspired by fossil dinosaur tracks, a pair of Florida jokers created a scare on a Florida beach that made headlines for the rest of the year. **BOB RICKARD** chronicles the event, and examines the prominent role played by Ivan Sanderson, one of the founders of cryptozoology (the study of undiscovered animals).

E arly one morning in February 1948, a resident of Clearwater, Florida, strolling along a sandy beach, noticed a track of large, curiously-shaped footprints. They came out of the sea, appeared to fail to negotiate a four-foot sandbank, and wandered for more than two miles before returning to the waters of the Gulf of Mexico. The sand was soft and held good impressions ... the damned things had three 'toes' and were about 14 inches long and 11 inches across.

THREE-TOED TERROR

Police were called from the Pinellas County Sheriff's Department, and they shook their heads. There was a story that a young couple had their night at the beach disrupted by the sight of a huge monster coming out of the sea, and that they had begged the police for a rifle so they could pursue it. The beach was swept clean (whether by the tide or by police is not said). When daylight revealed new tracks, and the story spread, and most of Clearwater had been to the beach to see for themselves, there was a state of near-hysteria.

There were more reports ... 6 March: 100 yards of similar prints a mile and a half to the north – 20 March: tracks on Dan's Island to the south – 3 April (Oh-oh! it's that month again!): 350 yards of track at Indian Rocks, 10 miles to the south – 8 April: a mile of tracks south of Indian Rocks. Then no sign until October when 200 yards of the distinctive three-toed prints were found at Suwannee Gables, 40 miles up the Suwannee River.

GREAT WHITE HUNTER

The scene was set for an 'expert' to make an entrance; he was none other than Ivan T. Sanderson, an expatriot English zoologist who had made a career of exploring remote regions and bringing back specimens for zoos, universi-

ties and museums. Sanderson had settled in New England, written prolifically on Fortean aspects of zoology and founded a Fortean organisation (Society for the Investigation of the Unexplained). He heard of the Florida tracks while working on a regular wildlife spot on radio for WNBC, New York, and managed to convince them to send him south on assignment.

Sanderson arrived at Suwannee Gables on 4 November and was publicised studying the deteriorating tracks like an incarnation of Sherlock Holmes. He returned to New York 12 days later having discovered witnesses who admitted seeing the creature itself. (His investigations were reported in *Fate* Dec 1967 and Jan 1968, and in his book *More Things*, Pyramid Books, NY, 1969.) The first sighting occurred the day before the Clearwater beach advent, when two professional fishermen claimed to have seen the creature sporting among shoreline waves at Big Pass.

Sanderson also spoke to two pilots from the Dunedin Flying School who had reported seeing a strange animal swimming off Hog Island on 25 July. They described it as about 15 feet long, with a "very hairy body, a heavy blunt head and back legs like an alligator." It's tail was "long and blunt". The plane returned to base and picked up two other men; together they located the creature again, observing it well during six passes over it. A Wisconsin couple, on a fishing holiday to Florida that August, were startled on one of the many uninhabited islands off Tarpon Springs,

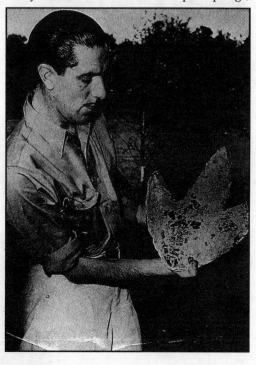

ABOVE: One of the foot-wide prints allegedly made by a giant penguin.
RIGHT: Cryptozoologist Ivan Sanderson, who flew down from New York to hunt the monster, studies a plaster cast of the huge tracks.

when a large, unidentifiable creature waddled out of bushes and down to the ocean. Their description included "short, thick legs and huge feet [..] no neck [..] covered with short thick grey fur [..]," and arms like "flippers".

Almost by chance, Sanderson himself saw the beast. On a plane, halfway between Suwannee Gables and the sea, he looked out to spot "an enormous dirty-yellow creature [..] 20 feet long and eight feet wide [..] wallowing on the surface," but it was startled and could not be seen again. "It was one of only two monsters I have ever seen and I won't forget it," he said later.

RED TIDE VICTIM

Before long Sanderson had it figured. His initial reservations about some clues gave way to his reasoned conviction that here was a large, unknown creature like a giant penguin. He imagined it had been dislodged from its usual habitat by a natural catastrophe (he blamed a 'red tide' or explosion of plankton that occurred off Florida at the beginning of 1948), and wandered around, hopelessly lost. He had agonised over 'awkward' details, such as the prints only being made at night, or the man-sized stride, or the apparently jointless flat-bottomed foot, or that they were "too perfect".

The Sheriff's Department were convinced it was all a prank, "one of the most masterful ever perpetrated" in the region. Sanderson objected: how, he asked, could a man on stilts walk so far over soft sand, stamping impressions so deep?

40 years after the giant penguin's debut, Tony Signorini displays the concrete three-toed boots used to create the scare.

What we find astonishing is that Sanderson seems to have been unperturbed by contradictory details in the witnesses' descriptions, including his own. He saw dirty-yellow where others saw grey or black. The fliers saw a thing like a hairy alligator; the thing seen by the Wisconsin couple had a "head like a rhinoceros"; several fishermen on the Suwannee River spoke of "domed" and "log-shaped" objects swimming upstream. Nevertheless, his penguin solution fitted the Wisconsin couple's description perfectly, he said, and a swimming penguin's feet, held stiffly behind it, might have seemed like a short stubby tail from the air.

THE HOAXERS CONFESS

So the story hung, unresolved, until 11 June 1988, when an exposé appeared in the St Petersburg Times. Reporter Jan Kirby was contacted by Tony Signorini, who confessed that he and his friend Al Williams began it all 40 years previously. Williams was a notorious prankster, and was well known to the Clearwater police. Frank Daniels, who retired in 1981 after 13 years as chief of police, told Kirby: "We suspected Williams because he usually called in with reports of the monster [..] but we could never prove it."

Williams and Signorini, partners in an auto business, were inspired by pictures of fossilised dinosaur tracks, found about six months earlier in New Mexico. Their experiments with concrete feet were unsatisfactory, so they had heavier iron feet cast at a local foundry and attached them to boots. When Williams died in 1969, he left the feet, weighing 30 pounds each, to Signorini, who stashed them in a box

under a bench in their workshop. There they stayed until he retrieved them for Jan Kirby [see photo]. Signorini explained how they worked: "I would just swing my leg back and forth like this and give a big hop. The weight of the feet would carry me [about six feet]. They were heavy enough to sink down in the sand."

Signorini had confided to friends, as long ago as 1965, how he and Williams had made the tracks. They would wait for nights when the waves were small and few people around. "I'd put the shoes on in the water and then walk a long way up the beach, maybe two miles, and then get back in the boat. [..] Other times we would take the feet in the car and carry them to where we wanted to make the tracks. Then we'd take a palm frond and brush away all the footprints we'd made," said Signorini.

PUZZLE REMAINS

Sanderson died in 1973, probably without knowing he had been duped; but a number of writers on cryptozoology have included the Florida giant penguin in their catalogues of mysteries on the basis of Sanderson's convictions. In this case, it was the attention of a media star 'expert' that kickstarted a local joke to the level of enduring legend. Over succeeding years, the 'giant three-toed penguin' became a solid part of Florida's folklore, and there were, subsequently, many clumsy attempts to fake more tracks for fun, fame or tourism.

We are left with one puzzle … If the tracks were faked, how do we account for the sightings of the unidentified large swimming thing out to sea, including Sanderson's own glimpse of it? Sanderson was an experienced observer of animals, and was, by some accounts, reliable and honest. According to others, however, Sanderson the storyteller was not above exaggeration for effect if it would help his gist.

But if you cannot accept that every witness was lying, the appearance of the strange sea creature in the midst of the tracks hoax must rank as one of those monumental coincidences that Charles Fort himself had noted about similar 'flaps' over unidentified animals in earlier decades. If so, the real joke was on believers and sceptics alike.

BYE-GONES

Extracts from *The Oswestry Advertizer*'s eponymous weekly column that ran from 1871 to 1939, selected by RICHARD HOLLAND, author of *Haunted Clwyd* and *Supernatural Clwyd*, and sub-editor at North Wales Newspapers, who still publish *The Oswestry Advertizer*.

OCT 9, 1901

PARTRIDGE LORE

The following extract from Hulbert's works *[European Museum p265]* is communicated by 'William E.A. Axon' to *Notes and Queries* for Sept 7, 1901, with the remark, "I have not met with this bit of partridge lore elsewhere":-

"In the year 1811, the editor of this work resided in Coleham, a suburb of Shrewsbury, and equally populous with the town itself. One evening in the latter end of the year, John Jenkins (a neighbour and tenant) brought him a fine partridge alive, which he said had flown into his house and taken shelter under a chest of drawers; he had caught it, and begged his landlord's acceptance of it; at the same time, Jenkins remarked that he was very much alarmed by the circumstance, as he had heard his parents relate that a partridge found its way in a similar manner into their dwelling, and that shortly after a brother of his came to an untimely end.

"The editor endeavoured to calm the fears of the poor fellow by representing to him the absurdity of his apprehensions, it being impossible that such circum-stances should have any connection with or influence on each other. The bird was accepted; and in order to tame and to preserve it alive it was turned into a large corn warehouse, then part of the cotton manufactory, where it remained for nearly a month, when one evening it burst through a glass window, breaking the panes with its violence against them, and escaped; and what is most singular, this occurred at the very moment Jenkins's child was on fire, and finally burnt to death.

The editor assisted in having the unfortunate child conveyed to the Salop Infirmary, where it expired, Jenkins sitting by its side and exclaiming against the poor bird as the cause rather than the prognosticator of the catastrophe. The circumstances are singular, but whether purely accidental or governed by some partic-ular providence, cannot easily be determined; suppose the latter, the bird came to warn Jenkins and to stimu-late him and his family to care and watchfulness against accident or danger; and having performed its mission, returned to its native liberty and fields."

FEB 5, 1902

GHOSTLY OMEN

The late Mr William Davies, building contractor, of Marford, near Wrexham, who died at the age of 91 in 1874, was one of the old type, with his swallow-tailed coat, breeches and leggings, and silk hat, which fashion he followed up to the end. The old gentleman, who was noted as a pedestrian, often related this strange incident. While walking late one evening with Mr Williams, of The Old Parsonage, Gresford, at the bottom of Little Acton Hill, near the Blue Bell (then a public house), they met a lady dressed all in white. Mr Davies said to Mr Williams - "Now you will catch it; here is Mrs Williams coming to meet you", and the figure vanished in the dark-ness. Strange to say, on the arrival of Mr Williams at The Old Parsonage, Mrs Williams was found hang-ing by the neck, quite dead.

MAR 8, 1905

MYSTERY LIGHTS

In the 'Mirror' of 28 Aug 1830, appears the following:

"In a wild and retired district in North Wales, that namely which extends westwards from Dolgelly [Dolgellau] to Barmouth and Towyn [Tywyn - all on the west Gwynedd coast], where there is certainly as much superstition as in any other district of the same extent, and where there are many individuals who lay claim to the title and capabilities of seers, the following occur-rences took place, to the great astonishment of the moun-taineers. We can vouch for the truth of the statement, as many members of our own teulu, or class, were witness of the fact.

"One dark evening, a few winters ago, some persons with whom we are well acquainted, were returning to Barmouth on the south or opposite side of the river; as they approached the ferry-house at Penthryn, which is directly opposite Barmouth, they observed a light near the house, which they conjectured to be a bon-fire, and greatly puzzled were they to discover the reason why it should have been lighted. As they came nearer, however, it vanished, and when they inquired at the house respect-ing it, they were surprised to learn that not only had the people there displayed no light, but they had not even seen one, nor could they perceive any signs of it on the sands. On reaching Barmouth, the circumstances were mentioned, and the fact corroborated by some of the peo-ple there, who had also plainly and distinctly seen the light. It was settled, therefore, by some of the old fisher-men, that this was a 'death-token', and sure enough the man who kept the ferry at the time was drowned at high-water a few nights afterwards on the very spot where the light was seen. He was landing from the boat, when he fell into the water and so perished.

"The same winter, the Barmouth people as well as the inhabitants of the opposite banks, were struck by the appearance of a number of small lights which were seen dancing in the air. At a place called Borthwyn, about half a mile from the town, a great number of people came out to see the lights; and after a while they all but one disap-peared, and this one proceeded slowly towards the water's edge, to a little bay where some boats were moored. The men in a sloop, which was anchored near, saw the light advancing - they also saw it hover for a few seconds over one particular boat, and then totally disap-pear. Two or three days afterwards, the man to whom that particular boat belonged was drowned in the river while he was sailing about Barmouth in that very boat. We have narrated these facts just as they occurred; we must leave the solution of the mystery to the ingenuity of our readers."

MAGNETIC MIASMAS

PAUL SIEVEKING looks at illnesses blamed on electromagnetic fields

In 1987, Teresa and Joseph Kennedy moved to a house in Bournemouth, Dorset, 300 feet from a 150-foot radio mast used by the West Hampshire Water Board to co-ordinate vans. In the following months, their two-year-old daughter Jamie attacked her 18-year-old sister with a poker, threw a fit in a church, hurled herself at doors and stabbed herself with pens. For three years, she slept no more than two hours a night. Said her mother: "She would hear voices and ringing in her head. If she ate certain things she would be up all night screaming and running round her room. She would try to climb out of the windows. It was as though she had the devil inside her."

Harley Street physician George Lewith suggested the radio mast might be to blame and electro-magnetic researcher Roger Cogshill, from Reading University, visited the house and confirmed that there was a powerful electromagnetic field (EMF) running through the little girl's bedroom. By April 1990, Jamie was recovering from her electromagnetic 'possession'. Her room had been insulated from the rays and the water board had realigned the radio mast, though it denied any responsibility for the troubles of the Kennedy family. *D.Mail, D.Star, 12 April 1992.*

DAVID MERRETT'S LETHAL LAMP

Last February, Roger Cogshill was able to diagnose another EMF problem in Bournemouth. David Merrett appeared to have aged 30 years since he moved to his bungalow there in 1986. He also lost two stone in weight and suffered from chronic insomnia. The cause of his string of complaints eluded the best efforts of five doctors. Mr Merrett had suspected that a radio mast in the garden of a neighbouring 'ham' might be to blame, but Mr Cogshill traced the problem to a lamp hanging over the dining room table where Mr Merrett spent an average of four hours a day working as a graphic artist.

"The extremely high energy field over the table was entirely due to the unusual design of the lamp," said Mr Cogshill. "Its switch was operable under the actual lamp glass and in consequence the circuit was subject to alternating current flow."

The artist's head was chronically subjected to ten times the normal domestic levels of EMF, as was all the food and drink left on the table.

Mr Cogshill further discovered that an EMF of 70-90 volts per metre pervaded the house above five feet six inches, which could account for the fact that 6ft 2ins Mr Merrett was so badly affected while his wife Rayella, 5ft 2ins, remained perfectly healthy. The EMF originated entirely with the domestic wiring, since switching off the mains supply collapsed the field entirely. *Bournemouth Echo, 26 Feb; Sun, D.Record, 27 Feb 1992.*

X-RAY VISION

In September 1991, Dianna McPheat, 37, from Dauphin County, Pennsylvania, filed a formal complaint against Pennsylvania Power & Light Co (PP&L), claiming that a 500-kilovolt power line near her house had given her X-ray vision, enhanced hearing, and caused her plants to grow in spirals. She said appliances would start without being turned on and she could hear voices from the telephone without picking it up. Her four children (aged 14, 12, 10 and 3) frequently suffered nose bleeds at the same time and she had three week-long headaches while she lived at the house from June 1990 to May 1991.

Other alleged problems included chest pains, sleeping disorders, memory loss and general disorientation. Mrs McPheat first contacted the power company when her bathroom light stayed on after the switch was turned off. Her children would play with long fluorescent bulbs, which glowed light space age swords under the power line.

PP&L filed a motion to dismiss the complaint because, they said, there was no definitive evidence that EMFs were harmful. In any case, extensive testing at the five acre property by PP&L and other agencies showed 'normal' EMF levels. A judge allowed Mrs McPheat a full hearing before the Public Utility Commission, which started in March this year. She wanted to force PP&L to admit the problem and construct a shield to protect her house. *[AP] 4 Mar 1992.*

ABOVE: Jamie Kennedy with her mother Teresa in front of the radio mast blamed for driving her crazy
LEFT: David Merrett in 1985 before he moved into the Bournemouth bungalow ... RIGHT: And seven years later, in 1992, prematurely aged by electro-magnetic pollution

SATANIC CHILD

In this latest instalment of our occasional reports about a siniste

On 11 April 1992, police from the town of Guaratuba, in Brazil's southern state of Paraná, found the mutilated body of a boy in a field near a sawmill. Detective Joao Arnaldo Hobmeir said the boy's ears, hands and genitals had been cut off, and his heart, liver and intestines were missing. He was identified as Evandro Ramos Caetano, aged seven (some sources say six), who was reported missing five days earlier, and it was evident that he had been murdered in a ritualistic fashion.

As Roman Catholic congregations have declined, in Brazil as in the world over, the Afro-Brazilian spirit cults of Candomble and Umbanda have sustained their widespread membership. However, the gods of these popular cults are, mostly, paganised versions of Catholic saints, and devil worship or human sacrifice do not figure in their rituals. After two months fruitless inquiries among known cult officials (*pai de santos*), the lead the police sought was provided by Oswaldo Marcineiro, an elder of the normally non-violent Umbanda. He confessed that he and two assistants had taken part in the murder as a bit of private enterprise.

> "His heart was offered to the devil and his blood mixed with sawdust and thrown into the sea."

SACRIFICE

Marcineiro's notebook implicated Aldo Abagge, the town's mayor and owner of the sawmill, and revealed that the sacrifice had been commissioned, for $3,000 (some sources say $2,000), by the mayor's wife Celina, 53, and daughter Beatriz, 28, to secure Aldo's re-election in the coming October polls. The mayor went into hiding as his wife and daughter, and five other cult members, were arrested. Celina, who administered the town's day-care centres and grade schools, confessed that she had used her position to select the boy and lured him with candy.

Beatriz and Celina both confessed to taking part in the killing and disembowelling of the boy, saying his heart was offered to the devil and his blood mixed with sawdust and thrown into the sea. Later, when Aldo surrendered to the police and was charged with aiding and abetting the crime, his wife and daughter retracted their confessions. A warrant was also issued for the arrest of José Taruggi and his wife Valentina de Andrade, Argentinean socialites and prominent Umbanda leaders, after they were

implicated by Marcineiro and "an image of the devil" was found at their home.

We have no further news of the trial, but the case seems to be only the tip of the misfortunes of this seaside resort, 700 miles (some sources say 520 miles) south of Rio de Janeiro. Guaratuba's police are disturbed by Marcineiro's admission that he, and two of the arrested, kidnapped and killed another boy, Leandro Bossi, aged seven, who disappeared from the town on 15 February. According to Marcineiro, the group's plan was to sacrifice seven blond children, aged seven, who had seven letters in their names, before the October elections. Evandro's murder was on the seventh of April and involved seven people, police believe. With some foreboding, the disappearances of ten children, aged between two and 11, since 1987, are being re-examined.

Sources: *[R] 11 July; Guardian, Edinburgh Eve.News 15 July; [AP] 16+17 July; Time, 10 Aug 1992.*

MORE BODY BUSINESS

In Paul Sieveking's review of the modern trade in purloined organs last issue – 'Kidney Kidnappers' *FT65:50* – he closed with a note on the activities of hospital security guards in Barranquilla, Colombia, who mugged and killed the denizens of skid row and sold their bodies to the medical school.

Just a month later, Colombian police smashed a gang that raided cemeteries to supply fresh (?) human remains to the witches and black magicians who are widely consulted by a majority of Colombians. In a house in Bogota, said Col Luis (AP calls him Enrique) Montenegro, commander of the judicial police, 45 skulls and boxes of other bones were found. They were believed to be the remains of people who had died not less than 18 months previously, and exhumed in the town of Cartago, in western Colombia.

The actual origin of the relics, how they died and their identities, are now difficult to determine. Two of the skulls sported bullet-holes, and the supplier – José Ocampo, a warlock in the southwestern city of Cali, home of cocaine barons – was recently murdered along with his wife. Col Montenegro's guess was that Ocampo was in the throes of setting up a "witches' house", similar to one already established in Cali, before he was killed. *[R] 22+23 April; [AP] 23 April 1992.*

In relation to this

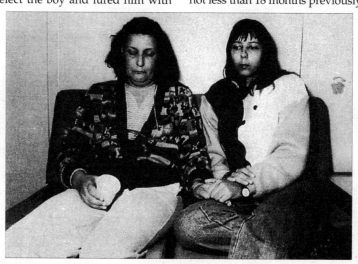

Celina Cordeiro Abagge (left), wife of the mayor of Guaratuba, Brazil, and daughter Beatriz, accused of commissioning a Satanic murder to improve their family's sagging fortunes.

ABUSE UPDATE

...orld-wide phenomenon, BOB RICKARD focuses on South America

report's territory, I must relate a variation of the baby kidnapping stories that we at *FT* have not heard for some time – babies kidnapped from their mothers' wombs. Isabel da Silva Santos, aged 42 and just days away from having her baby, has told Rio de Janeiro police that she was snatched off a street by three men, blindfolded and driven to a Rio clinic where her labour was induced. She remembers hearing her baby cry and people speaking with a foreign accent, but was kept hooded throughout the ordeal. Later she was dumped on a quiet street and given her taxi fare home.

During her kidnap, one of Mrs Santos' abductors phoned her mother-in-law, with whom she was staying, to say, allegedly: "We have Isabel and she won't be hurt. We only want the baby because we need six and only have two." Given the active Brazilian lore about stolen organs and the usual choice of alleged culprits - ie. witchcraft or modern versions of Burke and Hare serving the transplant and medical research industries - we note the arrival of a third option, international baby smuggling rings. Federal police here reckon around 1,500 babies a year are bought or kidnapped from local mothers, of which about 80% are sold in Italy and France, and the rest in USA, Israel, Belgium, Holland, Sweden and Germany. *D.Express, 30 March 1992.*

Brazilian police claim – in this *D.Express* report by Nicholas Buckley – to have smashed a baby trafficking network in January in the city of Curitiba; and before that a flourishing trade in children's organs for transplanting was exposed with the help of information from an Italian judge. A spokesman for the Federal police in Rio is quoted, saying: "In many cases the lives of the babies are ended when unscrupulous surgeons remove their vital organs [..] which fetch prices of up to £40,000." In contrast, the kidnapping of induced babies or fœtuses also features prominently in the British and American scare-stories about so-called 'brood-mares' - female sex slaves kept almost permanently pregnant by Satanic cults as a production line of unbaptised infants for unspeakable sacrifices - but none of them have stood up to investigation or forensic scrutiny.

SERIAL MENACE

Against this nightmare background there stalks the additional danger of the solitary psychopathic hunter. Due to a quirk in Ecuador law, the worst serial killer in modern history has probably been released from jail in Quito by now, after serving 11 years. Pedro Lopez was called 'the Monster of the Andes' when he was finally caught in 1980; in three years he had raped and strangled over 350 girls, aged between nine and 12, in Ecuador, Peru and Colombia - a terrifying statistic which overshadows even the 55 cannibalistic murders of Russia's latest monster, Andrei Chikatilo. Parents, who have seen no sign of remorse from Lopez, have promised his freedom will be short-lived. Two other serial killers are active in Ecuador right now: one has murdered 11 taxi-drivers in Quito, and the other nine transvestites. *Bangkok Post 12 April 1992.*

Part of the haul of human bones found in a Bogota 'witch house' in April.

THE SPECTRAL INSPECTORATE

BOB RICKARD updates our watch on Bogus Social Workers

ogus Social Workers operate singly or in groups of two or three, and can be of either sex. Are the females attempting to procure children for the males, or are they acting under their own weird compulsions? They are uncatchable and seem to have a lot of nerve. The risks they take – even continuing their visits in the midst of general alerts – seem out of all proportion to their rewards. Thankfully, most incidents come to nothing, but, as you'll read, there are other times when childen are taken away and brought back apparently unharmed.

It seems quite sinister, to us, that BSWs can appear so normal, conforming, almost like psychical chameleons, to their victims' notions about local Social Service officers. Like the enigmatic Men-in-Black of UFO fame, the BSWs are sometimes quite ignorant about those they have called to see; yet, at other times, they seem to know intimate details of cases. In these latter instances, it is as though they are working on insider information; could they have infiltrated local departments, or perfected hacking into SS computer files?

As if all this confusion wasn't enough, there are signs the phenomenon has already become a part of popular culture. Around mid-year there was a full-scale BSW scare in Falkirk, Scotland. It was sparked off when a depressed father of two claimed that bogus social workers had tried to snatch his children. He later confessed that he had hatched the story in a desperate attempt to have his family rehoused. He was sent for psychiatric and SS reports. (Alas, the clipping is unreferenced.) Here, then, is our gazetteer of 1992 BSW cases …

BUCKINGHAMSHIRE

■ February-March – A smartly-dressed woman, who said she was a social worker from the NSPCC called Valerie, told a Milton Keynes mother that her mentally-handicapped child, who was in care at the time, had died of a heart attack. When the mother's distress upset her other son, aged three, the visitor gave the boy sweets from her handbag and promised to return.

The well-spoken BSW returned to the grieving parents two days later, during which period they had broken the news to relatives and begun arrangements for a funeral. This time she threatened to take away her three-year-old son, saying she was "worried about his welfare". Angry about this unfeeling treatment, the mother phoned the local SS office to complain, only to learn that her child was not dead and that 'Valerie' was a bogus official. The mother later said: "I've had enough dealings with social workers and she had me totally convinced. She looked and

talked like one, and knew everything about our case", even that the handicapped boy was being fostered in Cambridgeshire.

Bucks police revealed that the same woman – driving a dark blue car – has struck twice since then. A few days after the cruel hoax, she called on a family (who were not on any SS register) and threatened to take away their two-year-old son. Shortly after that, the BSW offered to take another family's two-year-old daughter for a walk to give the mother a break. In each case, when asked for identification, the woman said she would return to her office for it; and when the woman never returned the families would check with the local SS office to be told they had sent no one. *Milton Keynes Gazette, 13 Feb + 12 March; Milton Keynes Citizen, 13 Feb 1992.*

■ September – Milton Keynes – male and female BSWs visit Janet Shapely, saying they had complaints that her child was badly treated – Janet refuses to let them in because they did not know the name of her child and had no ID cards. *Today, 4 Sept 1992.*

COUNTY DURHAM

■ 6 Sept - Spennymoor – The Watsons went out, leaving their one-year-old son Kristian in the care of 13-year-old Nicola Wilkinson. A woman called, claiming to be a social worker. Nicola said: "There was no way I was going to let her in. She stood outside the door for a while and then walked right past me. I couldn't stop her; she was a lot bigger than me."

The woman, aged 30-35, went straight to Kristian's bedroom and picked him up, saying she was going to take him for a drive in her car. Nicola had the quick wits to grab the boy back and shield him from the woman's attempts to get hold of him again. "I was frightened and Kristian was scared as well. I just hung on to him as tight as I could," said Nicola. The BSW left, but returned a few minutes later, and could be heard rummaging around the kitchen claiming to be checking that the baby had enough food.

Det Con Ian Ferguson of the Durham Police praised Nicola for her brave action during a frightening situation, and warned parents to be on their guard. Kristian's mother, Ena, publicly expressed her gratitude to Nicola: "She definitely saved my baby from being taken by this woman." *D.Telegraph, 8 Sept 1992.*

GLOUCESTERSHIRE

■ 24 Aug – Brockworth – well-spoken smartly-dressed BSW says she had come to give the children a check-up – knew names of the three children –

DEPARTMENT OF HEALTH POSTGRADUATE TRAINING IN CHILD SEXUAL ABUSE
APPLICATIONS INVITED FOR THE FOURTH INTAKE

Not quite the meaning intended.
Course advertised in *The Guardian*, May 1991.

mother grew suspicious and phoned her regular health visitor – BSW drives off in a red hatchback car. *Gloucester Independent, 27 Aug 1992.*

LONDON

■ 25 June – Colindale – two male and one female BSWs say they had received complaints about cruelty towards a baby over the last eight months – mother became suspicious because her daughter was only six months old – she slams door and calls police – BSWs drive off in a black Fiat Uno. *D.Mirror, Guardian, 27 June 1992.*

■ 26 June – Pinner – same gang, or one uncannily like it – two men and a woman call – tell a mother they have reports of her beating her two children and had come to take them into care – mother resists – BSWs leave in a black hatchback car. *Harrow Borough Recorder, 2 July 1992.*

■ Mid-October – Plaistow, East London – male BSW with convincing NSPCC ID – accuses mother of beating nine-month-old baby – she undresses it to show there is no bruising – BSW asks to hold baby leaves when mother refuses. *Newham Recorder, 22 Oct 1992.*

OXFORDSHIRE

■ January - Headington – Smartly dressed slim woman, in late 20s, straight brown hair, claimed to be from the local health centre, asks to see two small children – flees when asked for identification. *D.Telegraph, 8 Jan 1992.*

■ February – Carterton, near Witney – BSW says she had an order to take the children into care – flees. *BBC TV local news, 27 Feb 1992.*

SCOTLAND

■ June – Tranent, East Lothian – male and female BSWs pose as social workers investigating a claim she had beaten them with a belt – convince mother to hand over her two children to them – they had seemingly genuine ID cards from SS office in nearby Haddington and "seemed to know everything about my family" – the girl, four, and her brother, three, were returned unharmed 45 minutes later; apparently they had been taken to a local park and bought ice creams – BSWs drive off in red car – imposture only discovered when the mother phoned local SS department to find out about results of the 'tests'. *D.Record, Edinburgh Eve.News, 19 June 1992.*

■ 15 July – Rosewall in Midlothian, not far from previous case above – "petite conwoman with distinctive permed hair" calls at midday – asked to see a young mother's 19-month-old baby – knows child's name and family details – left when asked to show ID. *D.Record, Edinburgh Eve.News, 16 July 1992.*

SUFFOLK

■ 13 Feb – Whepstead – BSW asks to examine baby, unaware that real health visitor had called two days before –

Nicola Wilkinson – here with baby Kristian Watson – successfully fended off a BSW in Spennymoor, Co Durham in September.

flees when challenged to produce ID. *Bury Free Press, 14 Feb 1992.*

SURREY

■ June – St Helier estate, Sutton – pair of BSWs tricked their way into a home and examine two children. *Sutton Borough Guardian, 25 June 1992.*

TYNESIDE

■ 18 Sept – Cowgate, Newcastle – male BSW with Liverpool accent – when asked for credentials he fled to red Vauxhall Cavalier driven by a woman – there was a child in a safety seat in the back.

This report – in Newcastle *Eve.Chronicle* (19 Sept 1992) – draws attention to the frequency of the red car detail – refers to 13 reports of attempted abductions in the last year, "many involving a red car", including three incidents in the first two weeks of September in the Peterlee area.

WILTSHIRE

■ 21 July – Amesbury – woman returns home from shopping with her two-and-a-half-year-old son – man waiting on doorstep says he works for the local social services department and is investigating allegation that the boy had been sexually abused – allows him inside to examine boy's genitals - BSW warns of follow-up visit – leaves in dark blue four-door saloon car – imposture discovered two weeks later when mother inquires at local SS office about promised visit. *Independent, Southampton Eve.Echo, 12 Aug 1992.*

WORCESTERSHIRE

■ 19 Aug - Kidderminster – Three men using false IDs, posing as a doctor, a policeman and a social worker – bogus doctor, wearing a long white coat, examined two-year-old twin boys – all three leave hurriedly when one twin has asthma attack – police say this was third incident in the county in a week. *Edinburgh Eve.News, 20 Aug, D.Telegraph, 21 Aug 1992.*

AND IN THE USA

Lest anyone think this is a particularly British phenomenon...
■ Council Bluff, Indiana – male and female BSWs check two children for bruises – neither child harmed, but the BSWs boasted of power to take children away. *Des Moines (IA) Register, 30 April 1992.*

■ New Jersey – pair of female bogus 'state caseworkers' active in southern counties of Camden, Gloucester and Burlington, in May. Familiar MO – false IDs and claiming to be investing reports of child abuse. In one incident, the pair stripped a three-year-old girl, claiming to be looking for bruises. Her mother said: "They acted very official; they asked all the right questions." They left, warning they could return to remove the child if they received any more reports. *Philadelphia Inquirer, 4 June; Newark (NJ) Star Ledger, 6 June 1992.*

*[For our last round-up of BSWs, see **FT 57:43**]*

DIARY OF A MAD PLANET
AUGUST–SEPTEMBER 1992

This diary aims to record, in two-month segments, the geo-physical highlights of our planet: the tempests and tantrums, the oddities and extremities. Compiled by the editors and various correspondents.

EARTH

19 Aug – quake in Kirghizstan, central Asia (42.096N/ 73.540E) Depth: 24km. Magnitude: 6.8R. An estimated 74 people killed including 14 by landslides in Toluk. Several villages including Toluk destroyed in the Susmytra mountains and at least 8,200 dwellings destroyed. Impact felt over 300 miles across central Asia to China; tremor lasted 20 seconds in Tashkent.

2 Sep – quake off coast of Nicaragua (11.715N/ 87.406W) Depth:33km. Magnitude: 5.2R. At least 105 killed, 63 missing and 16,000 homeless. At least 1,143 houses and 185 fishing boats were destroyed along the west coast of Nicaragua. Some damage also reported in Costa Rica. Most of the casualties and damage caused by a Tsunami in the Pacific.

11 Sep – quake in Zaire (6.096S/ 26.733E) Depth:10km. Magnitude:6.7R. Eight killed, 37 injured and several buildings destroyed at Kabalo. Largest earthquake ever recorded in central Africa.

AIR

Late July/Early Aug – Florida, USA: wet June followed by exceptionally hot and dry July – Daytona Beach: mean temp. 28.5° C (83.4° F), only 0.16in. rain – hottest and driest July on record; Kansas City, Missouri: 15.47 inches of rain, 50% up on previous record for month; northern USA: much cooler than normal, breaking 1915 record; Albany, New York: mean temp.

19.8° C (67.6° F) – broke record low for July of 20.2 °C (68.3° F) set in 1860.

23 Aug – Florida, USA: Caribbean: winds from Hurricane Andrew, predicted as most powerful storm to hit USA in decades, reach 150mph in the Bahamas;

Satellite view of Hurricane Andrew near the Bahamas

storm sea surges 13-18ft; four reported dead. State of emergency declared in Florida; National Guard on alert; millions ordered to evacuate.

24 Aug – Dade County, Florida: Hurricane Andrew winds of 140 mph, gusts up to 165mph. Hundreds injured, 15 reported dead. Declared a disaster area. "Dade County as we know it is never going to be the same again", says local official. Many exotic animals escape (see report on page 13). Hurricane crosses southern Florida, enters Gulf of Mexico and heads for Louisiana. Evacuation ordered along Louisiana and Texas coastline.

25 Aug – Louisiana: Hurricane winds down to 125 mph. Flooding in low-lying coastal areas. Tornado 'spun off by the storm' – one of several spotted in the state – rips through LaPlace, a New

Orleans suburb.

There were comparatively few dead from Hurricane Andrew, as it just missed the major population centres in the Bahamas, Miami and New Orleans. Many, however, were injured, over 50,000 made homeless and there was widespread diarrhoea and fear of other water-born ailments. Billions of dollars in property damage made it "easily the most costly natural disaster in US history".

Late August – Medicine Hat, Alberta, Canada: after a week of near-record heat – 34° C (93° F) – the mercury plummeted to 0° C (32° F) with an inch and a half of snow.

25 Sept – Scientists announce further evidence that volcanic eruptions may seriously deplete the Earth's ozone layer, linking 10-15% reduction (up to 50% in lower and upper stratosphere) with Mount Hudson eruption in Aug 1991. The growth of the ozone 'hole' is said to increase ultra violet (particularly UV-B) radiation, which reduces crop yields, stunts growth and reduces fertility in many common plants and trees.

27 Sept – Ozone layer dropped to 40% of usual level; the hole opened much earlier than in previous years and the depletion rate is higher; it is said that Mount Pinatubo's 1991 eruption may be partly responsible for this year's record hole; although CFC output is still stressed as an important factor.

FIRE

6 Aug – Bielarus (former Soviet republic): forest fires sweep area worst polluted by Chernobyl disaster, raising background radiation – local officials say there is no danger to inhabitants.

USA: forest fires destroyed at least seven houses and threatened more than 400 others in Oregon; forest, brush and grass fires burned more than 323,000 acres during previous week in California, Washington, Oregon, Idaho and Nevada.

15 Aug – Luzon Island, Philippines: small earthquakes. Mount Pinatubo's eruption on 9 June 1991 was one of the largest this century. It had been dormant for over 600 years. The shroud of gas and dust from this eruption made New York average July temperatures 2.5 F below average. Millions of tons of tiny rock fragments and sulphur dioxide, forming an aerosol of sulphuric acid in the stratosphere 14-16 miles up, blocked solar radiation and reduced it by 2%-4%. The temperature drop allegedly almost cancelled out the global warming of the last 100 years.

Another factor blamed for the cooling (or perhaps a result of the volcanic emissions?) is southern drift of the jet stream since last March, pulling cool weather systems down from Canada. Abnormal amount of ice in Hudson Bay in early August. Frost starting in Midwest already, possibly affecting harvests.

17-19 Aug – Mount Spurr, Alaska, erupts for second time this summer; ash ejected 11 miles into atmosphere.

26 & 27 Aug – Luzon Island, Philippines: hundreds of tremors as magma rises towards the surface of Pinatubo. "Quiet buildup or explosive eruption" predicted. 709 low-frequency and 45 high-frequency tremors recorded. (Low-frequency quakes indicate molten rock rising to the surface; high-frequency quakes show that rock underneath the volcano is fracturing under pressure.)

27 Aug – Katowice, Southern Poland: forest fire destroys 12,350 acres "spreading at 90 mph".

6 Sept – North of Athens, Greece: uncontrollable forest fire started in rubbish dump; homes destroyed, main motorway closed. Meanwhile, 37,000 acres of wood and scrubland blaze for 36 hours in northern Corsica - arson suspected.

21 Sept – Philippines: international flights turned back due to heavy Pinatubo ash in atmosphere. Heavy tropical rains triggered explosions in superheated debris spewed out back in June 1991. Ash cloud rose 11 miles, blocking out sun and bringing darkness to the volcano's area at 11:00am.

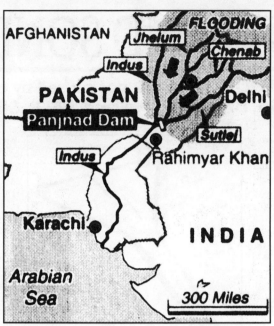

Map showing flooding in the Punjab region of India

WATER

9 Aug – Bayonne area, France: egg-sized hailstones smashed through roofs and car windows.

21 Aug – Medicine Hat, Canada: golfball-sized hailstones.

30 Aug – South Island, New Zealand: worst snow storms in living memory; farmers begin burying 1.2 million sheep.

3 Sept – Northern Shandong province, east coast of China: Tropical Storm Polly (or Poly). Torrential rains, high winds, 17ft waves, 150 people dead, 3,490 domestic animals killed, 1,419 fishing boats destroyed and 10,894 houses flattened.

Afghanistan (Hindu Kush): torrents of mud and boulders, 33ft thick poured down river valleys following torrential rains; 450 dead, 500 missing; death toll could reach 3,000; poor harvest and food shortage predicted since the fertile soil washed away.

5 Sept – Achill Island, Ireland: freak summer storm, washing away roads but exposing possible gold-, lead- and zinc-bearing rocks.

10 Sept – Jammu and Kashmir, Pakistan: flash floods, following two days' incessant rain; burst banks of rivers Jhelum, Neelum, Chinab, Tawwi – 200 dead, 200 missing; landslides in Muzzaffarabad – 80 dead.

Canton, China: tail end of cyclone Omar gives over 9in. rain in one of wettest spells ever; 5.5in. in 24 hours, exceeding previous record of 3in.

12 Sept – Hawaii: Hurricane Iniki nudges Oahu and Niihau, hits Kauai:

"worst storm to hit the island chain this century" – winds 130mph, gusts of 160mph; 20-30ft waves; 3 dead, 98 injured; 8,000 (or 7,000) homeless.

13-16 Sept – Pakistan/northern India: continued flooding now moving downstream to Punjab - 2,000 to 5,000 dead - one million homeless; 900,000 acres of cotton and 400,000 acres of rice destroyed. One possible reason for the excessive flooding was the opening of the Mangla Dam sluice-gates, which the engineers feared might collapse. The following week, vast areas are inundated, with huge losses to crops and tens of thousands of domestic animals drowned. Protests against government failures of flood relief: a crowd in Malakwal wave their shoes at a chief minister, a grave insult in Pakistan.

18 Sep – South-west England: fine red dust fell with early morning rain. The deposits – thought to be sand from the Sahara – were particularly noticeable on cars and greenhouses. "The dust was carried in warm, moist air which has come up from the south," said the Plymouth Weather Centre.

22-23 Sept – Vaucluse region, France: four-year drought with most rivers run dry was ended by violent rainstorms, likened to Asian monsoons, followed by severe floods: up to 80 dead. 30 houses destroyed by 'river of mud' in Vaison-la-Romaine, with a dozen toppled by violent winds gusting up to 100mph. Damage seen 50ft. above normal water-level. 'Roman bridge' submerged for first time since 1616.

Up to a half of the region's normal annual rainfall fell in a few hours. Floods blamed on deforestation, loss of agriculture in favour of camping sites and flimsy buildings.

The same storm system inundates England, causing swollen rivers in south and central regions. Tributaries of River Brent in north London overrun their banks, flooding streets in Edgware to 4ft; floods in Cambridgeshire, Lincolnshire, Midlands, Bedfordshire, Yorkshire. Flash floods around Savona in Italy, two people missing; landslides, a highway viaduct, houses and buildings crumbling.

Special thanks to the Global Seismology Group of the British Geological Survey for the earthquake data.

SPY PLANES AND SONIC BOOMS

STRANGE BANGS AND TREMORS, not caused by earthquakes, have been felt recently in the USA, Britain and Holland. PAUL SIEVEKING investigates.

A mysterious rumble and tremor occurred in the San Gabriel Valley near Los Angeles in June, October and November 1991 and in January and April 1992, always about 7:00am on Thursdays. "It's something that's travelling through the atmosphere at several times the speed of sound in a generally northeasterly direction", according to Jim Mori, a seismologist with the US Geological Survey at Caltech.

Jane's Defence Weekly in London said the Thursday booms could be caused by the spy plane codenamed *Aurora*, capable of flying at six times the speed of sound, or about 4,000mph. Built at the Lockheed Corporation's 'Skunk Works' in Burbank, California, it can circumnavigate the globe in eight hours. The turbulence has a signature, or wave pattern, on a seismograph unlike that of any known aircraft.

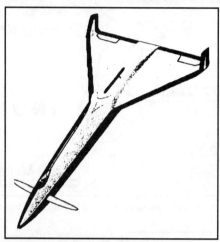

Artist's impression of the secret American spy plane, code-named Aurora.

While the Air Force denies the existence of Aurora, *Jane's* editor Bill Sweetman says that it is probably one of the Defence Department's so-called 'black' programmes, a top secret project whose funding is disguised in the defence procurement budget as one of a number of 'selected activities'. Eight billion dollars have already gone into the aircraft's development.

Knowledge of Aurora first came from a 1986 Defence Department budget report, in which it was listed – apparently by mistake – next to the SR-71 Blackbird and the U-2, two Air Force spy planes. Analysts believe the new plane, with a distinctive 66ft bat-wing design, is being prepared as a replacement for Blackbird, retired from service in 1989.

In March 1992, *Aviation Week and Space Technology* reported nightime sightings of an unknown aircraft with a diamond-shaped lighting pattern near Beale Air Force Base in Yube County, California. It had a distinctive noise, "like air rushing through a big tube". Sweetman speculated that it had been on a test run from Groom Lake, a research and development base near Las Vegas. *San Jose (CA) Mercury News, 20 April 1992.*

DOUGHNUTS ON A ROPE

Defence expert Nick Cook at *Jane's* also blamed Aurora for a mystery 'boom' that rocked a 10-mile area around Ilminster in Somerset on 29 July 1992, which he matched up with similar reports from Herefordshire and Scotland. "Witnesses in all three places reported a howling sound accompanied by a 'doughnuts on a rope' smoke trail in the sky. George Luck, who works near Martock in Somerset, said: "It was like a big wallop, not the crack sound we used to get when Concorde flew overhead, and it shook the whole building." *Western Gazette, 30 July 1992.*

Reports of an extremely fast-moving radar blip leaving the area around the joint NATO-RAF base at Machrihanish on the Kintyre peninsula in Argyll in November 1991 were tentatively put down to Aurora, according to a report in *The Scotsman* last February. *Flight International* last July claimed that Aurora had visited Machrihanish. The Scottish airfield is the longest in Europe. It has played host to US F117A Stealth aircraft on night-time proving flights from Nevada and to the SR-71 Blackbirds.

The 'doughnuts on a rope' vapour trails have been seen fre-

quently across America this year, according to the US *Aviation Week and Space Technology*. Pictures of such a trail were taken from Amarillo, Texas, in May. The trails are thought to arise from a new propulsion system, such as a pulse detonation wave engine, developed from the pulse jet used on German V-1 flying bombs in the 1940s. *Scotsman, 27 July 1992.*

On 16 March 1989, Mrs Patricia Anderson photographed a strange aircraft over Heathall wartime airfield northeast of Dumfries. "It was oval-shaped and grey-coloured, and much bigger than an RAF Tornado, with what I presume were engine intakes looking like a pair of giant eyes as it approached. It was also very, very quiet." She reported the sighting to the Civil Aviation Authority. Shortly afterwards, the police came round and interrogated her. The local print shop told her that her film had come out blank. Later, she was informed by phone that she had seen a top secret aircraft and should forget all about it. *Glasgow Herald, 8 Sept 1992.*

DUTCH "METEORITE"

On 19 August 1992, people in the Dutch province of Friesland heard a loud bang and felt tremors, which rocked houses and sent crockery tumbling from shelves. With the recent earthquake in the southern part of the Netherlands fresh in their minds, more than 100 people called the police. Hein Haak, spokesman for the Royal Dutch Meteorological Institute, said that seismic stations near the town of Assen, to the east of Friesland, registered the passing of an acoustic shock wave, which ruled out an earthquake. There were no jets flying at the time of the explosion.

Although the sky was almost entirely obscured by cloud, the wire services reported that at least 10 people reported seeing a red, yellow and orange ball of flame at around 10:30pm, hurtling in over the North Sea. Niek de Kort of the Dutch Meteorite Documentation centre suggested that there had been an explosion of a large, rather porous stony meteorite, measuring about a metre across, at a height of about 10 kilometres, less than a second before it would have hit the ground near the town of Joure.

However, the meteor theory was soon discarded. "No space debris has been found", said Hein Haak, "and despite our appeals, not many people reported actually seeing anything bright or burning falling from the sky." He thought the most likely explanation was our old pal Aurora. The flight was provisionally located 30 miles west of Texel island at an altitude of at least six miles, because it was not picked up on radar, according to *New Scientist*, although the *Glasgow Herald* said that a fleeting radar blip had been picked up by Oceanic air traffic control in Prestwick.

Professor Rob Schuiling of the University of Utrecht said Haak's theory was 'comical and most unlikely'. He said that the tremors were most likely due to earth movements after natural gas escaped from large underground chambers. The Netherlands' huge Slochteren gasfield extends far under the northern provinces of Groningen and Friesland. *Int. Herald Tribune, 21 Aug; New Scientist, 29 Aug + 12 Sept; [AP] Wellington (NZ) Evening Post, 2 Sept; Glasgow Herald, 3 Sept 1992.*

SECRET COUNTRY

Mysterious places to visit in Great Britain compiled by Janet & Colin Bord

6: Bungay & Blythburgh, Suffolk

The phantom black dogs that lope menacingly through British folklore and ghostlore represent a puzzling phenomenon which features in the real experiences of living people as well as in traditional tales. Black Dogs cannot be wholly consigned to the realm of fiction, because people still see them today. Their appearances are always enigmatic; to see one is an unforgettable event, and usually has some special significance for the witness.

In the usual form of the story, the Black Dog is a large, yet friendly, animal, appearing from nowhere to escort a woman travelling alone along a dark rural road. It is convincingly substantial until she puts out a hand to pat her welcome companion... and feels nothing at all! There have been reports of such guardians protecting women from lurking vagabonds who have been deterred by the sight of such seemingly real animals. Yet, sometimes, the animals appear to be omens of death and disaster, and as such not at all welcome to those who see them unexpectedly.

Over the centuries, Black Dogs have been seen in all parts of the British Isles (though they are sometimes white, or occasionally grey, brown or yellow), and are usually distinguishable from living dogs by their large size, shaggy coat, huge fiery eyes, and their behaviour. A book could be written detailing their activities, but we'll concentrate, here, on probably the most famous Black Shuck of East Anglia, a county particularly rich in Black Dog lore.

At the height of a terrible storm on the morning of Sunday, 4 August 1577, a Black Dog suddenly appeared in the churches at Bungay and Blythburgh. His presence was fatal, for he passed between two members of the congregation as they knelt in prayer, and "as it seemed, wrung the necks of them bothe at one instant clene backward, insomuch that even at a moment where they kneeled, they strangely dyed." Another man was injured when the Black Dog "gave him such a gripe on the back, that therewith all he was presently drawn togither and shrunk up, as it were a piece of lether scorched in a hot fire; or as the mouth of a purse or bag drawen togither with a string."

Abraham Fleming, who reported this event in his pamphlet *A Straunge and Terrible Wunder* ..., published soon after the event, also told what happened at Blythburgh: "On that self-same day, in like manner, into the parish church of another towne called Blibery, not above seven miles distant from Bongay [..] the like thing Entred, in the same shape and similitude, where placing himself uppon a maine balke or beam, whereon some ye Rood did stand, sodainely he gave a swinge downe through ye church, and there also, as before, slew two men and a lad, and burned the hand of another person that was among the rest of the company, of whom divers were blasted. This mischief thus wrought, he flew with wonderful force to no little feare of the assembly, out of the church in a hideous and hellish likeness."

This devilish dog left his calling card at Blythburgh, where burnt claw-like marks can still be seen on the church door. At Bungay, the event is commemorated in the design of a weather vane in the town centre, which features a black dog. Both churches are well worth visiting, but especially the fine 15th-century building at Blythburgh, with its curious pew ends and wonderful roof, bearing angels.

Janet and Colin Bord are authors of *Mysterious Britain, The Secret Country, Alien Animals, The Atlas of Magical Britain,* and *Modern Mysteries of Britain* among many other books. **FT**

TOP: Blythburgh church. RIGHT: The Black Dog on Bungay's weathervane. ABOVE: Marks on the door of Blythburgh church, allegedly made by the Black Dog.

FORUM FORUM FORUM

PSYCHICAL RESEARCH: Brian Inglis is a past editor of *The Spectator* and veteran of over 20 books on parapsychology and fringe medicine, including the monumental *Natural and Supernatural*

FOLKLORE: Bill Ellis, Ph.D. (Ohio State) lectures on folklore and edits *FOAFtale News*, the newsletter of the International Society for Contemporary Legend Research

UFOLOGY: John Keel is a New York journalist and author of seminal works on ufology such as *Operation Trojan Horse* (1970) and *The Mothman Prophecies* (1975)

EARTH MYSTERIES: Paul Devereux is a prolific writer, researcher and lecturer on earth mysteries. He edits *The Ley Hunter* and is the founder/director of the Dragon Project Trust.

Psychical Research

Mind and Grey Matter

Brian Inglis looks at attempts to deny the existence of mind as distinct from brain

Reviewing *The Oxford Companion to the Mind* when it was published five years ago, I was not surprised to find that the entries on the history of psychical research and on ESP had been entrusted to the leading sceptic of the time, Christopher Evans; or to read, in the editor's commentary on psychical phenomena, "We may seriously doubt whether there are any". But how to account for the fact that in a work which devoted over 50 columns to nerve connections, the nervous system and neuroanatomical techniques, intuition was allotted three paragraphs, and inspiration, only one. As for imagination, it did not even have an entry.

This set me off on an agreeable train of fantasy. If I had the money and the time, what fun it would be to prosecute the Oxford University Press for an offence under the Trades Descriptions Act! 'Mind' hardly featured. The late B.F. Skinner was allowed to preach his behaviourist gospel "dismissing mental states and processes as metaphors and fictions"; for the most part, however, the entries revealed the powerful influence of behaviourism's successor, cognitive psychology, less crazy but still fundamentally materialist, hostile even to con-

sidering the evidence that mind exists in its own right, independently of brain.

The evidence that it does appears to me to be incontrovertible. How else can the organisation of a termitary be accounted for? I was delighted to come across a copy of Eugene Marais' *The Soul of the White Ant*

> "If I had the money and the time, what fun it would be to prosecute the Oxford University Press ... under the Trades Descriptions Act!"

the other day - better still, in the single volume with *The Soul of the Ape*: I had missed it when Penguin brought it out in 1989 – and to read again his carefully accumulated evidence of a soul, regulating a termitary's life.

Marais, a follower of Darwin, did not care for the term soul, but he could not think of a better alternative. Lewis Thomas in his essays has more than once drawn attention to the failure of biologists to account for the evidence of a single intelligence at work running an anthill; an ant,

after all, is "only a few neurons strung together by fibres", and "cannot be imagined to have a mind at all". Yet 'mind' is scarcely an adequate term to account for the long-term planning, design and performance Marais observed and reported.

E.O. Wilson, the protagonist of sociobiology – that last ditch attempt to fit biology into the mechanistic sciences - has recently been claiming that he and his disciples are in the process of explaining ant organisation and behaviour in terms which will make it unnecessary to think in terms of a group mind – let alone a group soul. But the evidence they have provided so far suggests that they are indulging in what Popper has derided as promissory materialism – hopeful thinking.

If a group mind, or soul, is in existence at so early an evolutionary stage, there is surely little difficulty in accounting for the existence of our occasional experiences of extra-sensory perception? Or should we classify them as psychokinetic, as some parapsychologists have suggested?

"A few neurons strung together by fibres", after all, can hardly be claimed to have the ability to perceive. Perhaps the group mind – perhaps our own minds – work directly on and through our grey matter?

Fortean Times 66 - 55

Space Conspiracies

Bill Ellis examines the popularity of the 'slave labour in space' conspiracy

Fortean Times' recent piece on *Alternative 3 [FT64:47]* is a welcome addition to the slim amount of good information on the original TV show. I think, however, you underestimate two important angles of the controversy it has caused.

Firstly, A3 seems to have become and remained far more popular in the United States than in Great Britain. Part of the reason is the 'mystery' behind American TV. networks' failure to air the original show and the genuine difficulty people have in obtaining copies of Leslie Watkins's book. It was fleetingly available here from the US paperback firm Avon (later publishers of *Communion, Transformation,* et al.), but after one printing it was withdrawn (I'm told) because of copyright difficulties.

The library at the college campus where I work obtained a copy in a mass of paperbacks donated to their 'Browsing Room', and when the librarian accessioned it in his computer card catalogue, he received a flood of inter-library loan requests, mostly from the US West. (That's how I found out about it.) The Sphere paperback is fitfully available from import houses like Arcturus, but illegal photocopies of borrowed copies are also sold under the counter at alternative book stores.

Jerome Clark tells me that at least one group of UFO enthusiasts has taken a bootleg video of the original show on tour, charging money for a screening plus a lecture on how A3 fits into other conspiracy theories active in the US. I haven't seen videos for sale, but for a time you could buy an audiotape of the A3 soundtrack from a mail order firm.

Among those who have cheerfully adopted the A3 scenario are Milton William Cooper, who was for a time one of the superstars of the American 'whistle-blowers', or former military types who claimed to have seen secret documents proving US/USSR collaboration, usually with the help of sinister aliens from Zeta Reticuli. Interestingly, where the original A3 plot had citizens abducted, 'desexed' and taken to slavery on Mars, Cooper omits the desexing and adds 'gun control' at the appropriate moment, legal possession of firearms being essentially equal to

sexual potency in the eyes of most American conspiracy-experts. The stress A3 put on the Dartmoor horse mutilation case [*FT22:30, FT23:3, FT27:49*] likewise helped integrate its plot into the equally Byzantine scenarios that circulated about who was slicing up livestock and why. (*Endangered Species* (1982) is another conspiracy movie that ought to be mentioned as an *A3* analogue.)

Secondly, you might have stressed more the creative role that Leslie Watkins

> "For some time after *Alternative 3* was published," admitted Watkins, "I have reason to suppose that my home telephone was being tapped."

took in expanding the original screenplay into a full-length book. Watkins was an impressive British Fortean in his own right, and his books of legitimate scholarship include *The Sleepwalk Killers* (Everest, London 1976), a summary of murder cases involving automatism [cf *FT64:20*]. His *The Real Exorcists* (Methuen, London 1983) is an extremely valuable survey of the Deliverance Ministry, the fundamentalist faction who believed that dabbling in the occult invited demons into your children's heads and had an unfortunate habit of killing kids in the process of getting them out (the same group gave us satanic ritual abuse, not coincidentally).

The US/USSR conspirators (who speak via transcripts in that fey slang lingo that Britons seem to believe is native to Chicago gangsters) use automatism to induce would-be defectors to commit suicide in their sleep. They also employ 'hot jobs', or spontaneous human combustion, to terminate especially difficult cases. And part of the local colour of the 'Astronaut Grodin' material derives from Fortean reports of alien vehicle tracks on the moon.

As for Watkins, he was at last notice Director of Studies at the New Zealand School of Journalism, Auckland. He was briefly scheduled in 1990 for an interview

on American radio concerning the latest A3 controversy, but had to cancel due to illness. Shortly before, he wrote to an American book firm that was trying to import copies of A3, confirming that he had originally aimed to present the book's premise as so far out that readers would immediately see it as fiction.

"Immediately after publication", Watkins continued, "I realised I was totally wrong. In fact the amazing mountains of letters from virtually all parts of the world - including vast numbers from highly intelligent people in positions of responsibility - convinced me that I had *accidentally* trespassed into a range of top-secret truths. Documentary evidence provided by many of these correspondents decided me to write a serious and *completely non-fiction* sequel.

"Unfortunately, a chest containing the bulk of the letters was among the items which were mysteriously *lost in transit* some four years ago when I moved from London, England, to Sydney, Australia, before I moved on to settle in New Zealand. For some time after *Alternative 3* was originally published, I have reason to suppose that my home telephone was being tapped and my contacts who were experienced in such matters were convinced that certain intelligence agencies considered that I probably knew too much." (This letter, to a Ms Dittrich, was circulated on American computer networks on 28 October 1989.)

In a later letter, Watkins was coy about the exact nature of the truths onto which he had stumbled, except to say that he felt that the book was "probably 65% truth, 35% fiction". (Faxed letter, 26 Aug 1990, reprinted in *Nevada Aerial Research Group Newsletter* #20, p2-3, Feb 1991.)

It is, of course, hard to say whether this coyness is based on Watkins's actual beliefs or his desire to sell more copies of his book among conspiracy buffs. The book, in fact, takes a similar "they said it was a hoax but it's really fact" approach to the press flap over the original video broadcast. Whatever the case, *Alternative 3* (the book) is in fact one of the best-crafted and most comprehensive novelisations of Forteana, and it surely deserves to have a cult devoted to it.

FORUM is a column in which anyone with something to say about a particular field, theory or incident can share their thoughts with our readership. If you'd like to join in with an opinion on any area of Forteana, send it in to the editorial address. Ideal length: 500-1000 words. Please enclose a head and shoulders photo of yourself with all Forum submissions.

A Day of Reckoning

John Keel looks at the professionals who have become involved with UFOs

When the famous American comedian Jackie Gleason succumbed to cancer on June 24, 1987, a handful of informed UFO-philes nearly had heart attacks themselves. Although the general public was not aware of it, Gleason was a dedicated hardcore UFO buff and June 24th is one of the most significant dates in flying saucer history. Not only did Kenneth Arnold have his historic sighting of nine luminous blobs at a distance of 50 miles on June 24, 1947, but many other important events have occurred on that date, particularly in religion and occultism.

An outstanding star on American television in the 1950s and 60s, Gleason also appeared in many major motion pictures. His talents were so varied and unique that he was nick-named 'the Great One' by his peers. Once a devout Catholic, the rotund comedian's 1950's series The Honeymooners still airs on TV stations throughout the USA and has a large cult following.

In the course of his highly productive life he earned millions of dollars. He spent some of it on the design and construction of an unusual home in a secluded part of the Catskill mountains near Peekskill, New York. It was a circular mansion which appeared to be a grounded flying saucer. Gleason's huge library of books on UFOs and psychic phenomena was housed there. In his rare appearances on all–night radio shows, such as the famed Long John Nebel talk show in New York City, he talked at length about his library and his lifelong interest in Forteana. He seemed convinced that UFOs were a melding of occult manifestations and the human psyche.

However, he was not above exploiting his interests in the paranormal when, like various contactees, he explained prolonged absences from his home by telling his wife that he had been visiting secret bases to look at the bodies of little men pickled in bottles. Actually, he was a heavy drinker and a ladies' man, using UFOs to cover his extramarital activities. [See The Great One: The Life and Legend of Jackie Gleason by William A. Henry, Doubleday, 1992.]

The notion that the US Air Force had bottled some Martians was planted in the public consciousness in the late 1940s by a humorist and columnist for the show business newspaper Variety named Frank Scully. He was the first professional to take a real interest in the UFO mystery. One of his informants, an oil prospector named Silas Newton, passed along some hearsay about a saucer crashing near Aztec, New Mexico and Scully used it as "the hook" for a book of his columns published in the spring of 1950, following the release of the USAF's anti-UFO Project Grudge Report. Scully's Behind the Flying Saucers sold in such large numbers that it is still easily available in secondhand bookstores today.

American UFO buffs later vilified Scully, unfairly attacking him because he had devoted a couple of his columns to Newton's claims. Scully had included a tongue-in-cheek criticism of an article by Donald Keyhoe that had appeared in True, which was then a new magazine for men. Its editors were looking for a circulation builder. Keyhoe's wild-eyed, biased,

> ## "In an area filled with pretenders and quasi-famous 'ufologists' there are few stars."

poorly–written declaration that "flying saucers are real" seemed perfect. Scully pointed out in his book that Keyhoe's article was just a clumsy rehash of data culled from the books of Charles Fort.

The True editors, and Keyhoe himself, decided to "get" Scully. They hired an unemployed newspaperman to investigate Newton who – big surprise – turned out to be a known swindler and confidence man. Since the American UFO buffs of those days tended to have "criminal" minds, unable to distinguish right from wrong (traits which still dominate some tiny US UFO cults), they began a campaign of slander and nonsense against Scully that persists to this day. Scully, a one-legged Catholic who was once offered the nomination for Lieutenant Governor of California, later wrote in personal letters to publications such as Saucer News that he was sorry he had ever bothered with the flying saucer scene and the psychotic people attracted to it.

Frank Scully died on June 24, 1964.

Very few professionals have ever tangled with the UFO field. They can almost be counted on the fingers of one hand. There was Ralph Blum, a winner of the National Book Award in the 1970s, and famed aviation writer Martin Caidin in the 1980s. Perhaps the best–known pro of the 1950s and 60s was radio news commentator Frank Edwards. In 1966, at the peak of the biggest flying saucer wave in US history, Edwards hastily assembled his Flying Saucers: Serious Business in six weeks. The book had phenomenal success, selling 100,000 copies in hard cover and millions in paperback. Unfortunately, Edwards did not have a chance to enjoy his fame or new-found fortune. He died suddenly on June 23, 1967, missing the 24th by only a few hours.

In an arena filled with pretenders and quasi-famous "ufologists" there are few stars. That is, advocates that can attract audiences or sell books to the non-cultist population. A charming old occultist named George Adamski was one of those rare birds. He broke the pattern, though, when he died with a minimum of fuss in Washington, DC., on April 23, 1965. A few hours later, on April 24th, a British gardener in Devon named Arthur Bryant reportedly had an encounter with two ufonauts, one of whom identified himself as "Yamski". (News of Adamski's death would not reach England for many days.)

Mr. Bryant became the center of an involved series of events that became known as "the Scoriton mystery". He died two years later on June 24, 1967; the same day as Richard Church, another well-known British contactee.

Willy Ley, the great authority on rockets and space travel who was obliquely responsible for getting the U.S. space program started, checked out on June 24, 1969.

On the religious front, scores of apparitions and events have taken place around the summer and winter solstices – June 21-24 and December 21-24 – inspiring an endless fountain of lore. On June 24, 1981, six youngsters in Medjugorje, Yugoslavia, had the first of a series of visions of the Virgin which gained worldwide attention. The apparition promised impending doom and now that area is involved in a disastrous civil war.

Spirit Lines

Paul Devereux theorises that landscape lines relate to the 'spirit lines' of shamanism

The obvious fact that very similar motifs associated with spirits and lines occurred in different cultures and times convinced me that the meaning of landscape lines had to lie with the universality of human consciousness, and the obvious place to look for it was in shamanism, itself a universal expression of the human mind.

The shaman was, of course, the intermediary between the tribe and the spirit worlds. While in the spirit realms, the shaman's soul shared the same nature as the souls of the ancestors, the dead. The shaman entered the spirit worlds by means of an out-of-body, ecstatic 'journey' during trance. This was induced by a variety of techniques, such as drumming and hallucinogens. Alkaloids in traditional native hallucinogenic preparations specifically promote the sensation of spirit flight.

This shamanic 'flight of the soul' seems to have been translated onto ancient sacred landscapes as straight lines. Some of these were physical, and later became variously acculturated as spirit ways, roads of the dead and eventually even sacred ways, triumphal routes or royal roads. Other lines were conceptual, as in Celtic fairy lore.

The Kogi Indians of northern Columbia are the best preserved Native American society, with an extant shamanic theocracy and paved tracks. It has recently been discovered that some (at least) of these paths are seen by the Kogi as traces of the shamans' out-of-body journeys in *aluna*, a spirit version of the physical Earth. There are also rituals involving the symbolic sweeping and cleaning of the physical paths.

The *straightness* comes, conceptually, from the fact that flight is the straight way over the land. We have the phrase "as the crow flies" which expresses this precisely. "As straight as an arrow is a similar-meaning phrase, and the arrow was used widely as shamanic symbolism for spirit flight. The Koryak shaman, for instance, was said to leave his body along the path traced by an arrow released from his bow.

Neurologically, the straightness derives from the entoptic ('within vision') nature of the out-of-body experience. Certain neurological 'form constants' come into play during trance conditions. They are marked in cave art, and the Tukano of South America,

> "Acculturated versions of spirit flight are found in the midwinter flight of Santa Claus in his sleigh pulled by reindeer."

who see them in their hallucinogenic trances, use them as the basis for their decorative art. One key entoptic form is the spiral or tunnel; the 'straight way' is expressed in Near Death Experiences as a tunnel, and as a UFO's 'traction beam' in those spontaneous out-of-body cases that are interpreted as UFO abductions in our crude society, which is so alarmingly ignorant of the realms of consciousness.

Symbolism of the shaman's out-of-body journey is deeply inscribed in shamanic tradition and artifacts worldwide as bird forms and associations. The Mississippian Indians (c 900-1500 AD) even had a recurring depiction on pottery and shells that archæologists refer to as 'the flying shaman motif'. Bird costumes, masks, sticks, feathers and so on recur constantly in connection with magical spirit flight in all ages and countries. The Taoist priest was known as a 'feather scholar' because of his links with shamanism, and it is probably though Taoism that the idea of spirit lines became embedded in *Feng shui*.

Modern acculturated versions of spirit flight are to be found in the midwinter night flight of Santa Claus in his sleigh pulled by reindeer. This is thought to originate from arctic and Siberian shamanism, where the tribes were reindeer herders. The hallucinogenic fly agaric mushroom was used by these people, and its cap is red and white like Santa's robes. The other popular image is of the witch flying on her broomstick. This derives from the habit of 'wise women' using hallucinogenic flying ointments to go 'Night Travelling'. The alkaloids in these could penetrate intact skin, and the broom handle was used to apply the salves to the sensitive vaginal tissues. It was the mediæval church which satanised these folk relics of indigenous European shamanism.

Shamanic traditions, and the newly-perceived shamanic landscapes revealed by their lines and effigy mounds, survived better in the Americas than in Eurasia, where greater cultural flux occurred. Great religions arose in Eurasia, absorbing or marginalising shamanism. As tribes evolved into more complex societies, so the shaman became priest, and the priesthood developed into theocracy or divine kingship monarchy, contains shamanic vestiges. As Mircea Eliade, the great religious historian, observed, the myth of magical flight was associated with kings and sovereigns from one end of Eurasia to the other. Chinese emperors and pagan Celtic kings all had the power of magical flight, as did mythic figures such as Odin. A proto-Indo-European word, **reg*, meant 'movement in a straight line', and was integrated into later words denoting aspects of kingship and governmental, spatial and moral order. Our English word 'ruler' thus derives, and means both leader and straight edge.

The unravelling of the mystery of the lines has only just begun, and is clearly a complex affair with many levels.

REVIEWS

SPONTANEOUS HUMAN COMBUSTION

by Jenny Randles and Peter Hough.

Robert Hale, London. 1992, hb £14.95, pp224, plates, bib, refs, index.

When fireman Tony McMunn was called to a blaze in Chorley, in March 1980, nothing in his training or 23 years of experience prepared him for the sight in a pensioner's bedroom. All that remained of its occupant were her relatively unscathed legs from the knees down; the rest was calcined ash. There was no fire damage to the surrounding area; only smoke damage to the upper walls and ceiling. McMunn recalls: "I was taken aback. I had never seen anything like it before; neither had the ambulance men nor the police."

This reaction of shock and disbelief is echoed in the first-hand accounts from other members of the emergency professions, given in this important new study of what, for want of a better term, has been called 'spontaneous human combustion'(SHC). As soon as they take in the fatal scene, these professionals *know*, through reason and instinct, that this is not a normal death by fire. The more glaring paradox – typical of so many SHC cases – is the discrepancy between the intense and sustained heat needed to consume completely all or most of a body and the relatively minor damage to combustible and meltable materials close enough to be destroyed by a normal fire. As McMunn notes of the same case:

"Even the bones were gone, yet [..] nearby objects, such as a brushed nylon footstool and clothes [..] were just stained." (p85)

Documented cases of SHC, of varying quality, go back to the 17th century, and in each period some of its brightest minds have ventured theories and experiments, and even incorporated the phenomenon into literary works. The number of books discussing SHC seriously can be counted on one hand, and I am on record as saying the definitive study has yet to be written. After some anticipation of this book, I have to say that this is not it; but to give credit where it is due, Randles and Hough have come up with something quite different and probably, in the long run, just as valuable. *Spontaneous Human Combustion* deals less with the canon of historical cases and theoretical groundwork, and concentrates on more modern material. Here, the Randles-Hough team come into their own with new case material, interviews with witnesses, discussions with a wide variety of 'experts', analysis of media reportage, and personal experience of the help or hindrance of coroners.

The authors' narrative method often requires great endurance, for the reader has to slog through wearying blow by blow accounts of debates, claims and counter-claims, and details of every step of their inquiries; even when the insight is worth the plod, this reader wishes they had got to their point sooner.

A prime example of the book's value is the whole chapter devoted to the case of Mrs Reeser, who departed this life in a ball of fire in 1951, in St Petersburg, Florida. As in the chapter on Jack Angel and other survivors, the authors have met the objections of the sceptics head on with important new data from police, FBI and other investigative reports, which often reinforces the central mystery of an inexplicable blaze, and goes some way to answering the critics who have explained SHC away as poor investigation or misinterpretation of inadequate evidence. The personal experiences of Tony McMunn, another but anonymous fireman, and John Heymer, a scene-of-crime officer in the Gwent police, are given a full chapter each. Another chapter is devoted to a cri-

tique of the 1989 BBC1 documentary *QED*; by re-examining their witnesses and experts, our authors show that its sceptical conclusion was achieved by clever and biased editing and not, as was claimed, by impartial analysis.

The second half of the book is a broad discussion of the topic, illuminated by the light of apparently similar phenomena in vaguely related areas: such as poltergeists, crop circles, UFOs, Kundalini (psychic energy released by meditation), and electric people. Randles and Hough are sensible enough not to seek out a single solution for SHC, and thus avoid the folly shared by many UFO theories; on the other hand they adopt a scattergun approach which leaves one none the wiser about the relative merits of the various fields of speculation. For example, SHC researcher Larry Arnold's hypothetical 'pyrotron' particle; the cancer-like proliferation of heat-generating PEP molecules in tissue cells; the biophysical effects of seismically generated radiation from geological fault lines; and the ionising fields of ball lightning, were fascinating ideas and I would have liked to hear more about them. Perhaps it is enough that the authors have included such pointers; they certainly cannot be blamed for the deplorable lack of serious research, funded or otherwise, by scientific institutions.

As the topic is a particular interest of mine, I must say I really appreciate the hard work I know has gone into this study of a difficult subject. It saddens me, therefore, to see the same enthusiasm leading the authors into sloppiness which diminishes their achievement. Too many cases, in my opinion, have been credited to the late Michael Harrison; of these, most of the 1938-39 cases were taken by Harrison from the research of the Fortean SF writer Eric Frank Russell. Many others, including Case 49 (Lily White, the Antiguan girl whose clothes burned off her in 1928), and the famous cases of Butlock Heath (Case 43), and the Dewar sisters of Whitley Bay in 1908 (Case 46), among others, were lifted by Harrison from the works of Charles Fort. These kinds of errors arise from the laziness (from which even I suffer) of not tracing cases back to their earliest sources.

It is also wrong of the authors to claim

> "All that remained were her legs ... the rest was ash. I was taken aback ... even the bones were gone."

that their listing of 111 abstracted cases from between 1613 and 1990 is "the first ever catalogue" (p183). Apart from Fort's pioneering body of case material, and the selection made by Persinger and Lafrenière (whose work they cite), a referenced list of SHC cases appears in Ivan Sanderson's *Investigating the Unexplained* (1972), and another in an early issue of *INFO Journal*. And who could agree with such a naive and sweeping statement as "children do not become drunkards or smoke"? (p182) Today, there are many children who drink and smoke and worse, inhale many kinds of inflammable substances, yet I know of no SHC of a solvent-abuser. Do not let these cavils deter you from buying this work; they affect only a small part of what should become required reading for any student of the subject.

Throughout their inquiries, Randles and Hough came into contact with coroners or their officers; some were helpful enough, but others revealed a level of reluctance to help which bordered on active hindrance. The authors voice an opinion shared by other researchers into SHC that these public servants feel no obligation to the advancement of knowledge and have been known to refuse to hear any evidence that will lead to anything other than a quick, clean verdict. For this kind of coroner, researchers – who are bound to ask awkward questions – are a kind of ghoulish pest who will upset the status quo of a comfy job.

As Forteans we have no objection to "rational solutions" where these are truly rational; our darkest suspicions are aroused, however, when we observe intellectual and procedural gymnastics performed to accommodate mock rationalism. I cannot endorse the idea that there is an official conspiracy to suppress research into SHC, but it is a fact that officers and authorities effectively suppress the subject in a myriad of individual instances of ridicule, ignorance, and mental laziness for which there can be no excuse. Either there is a real phenomenon here or there is not. The public have a right to expect their medical scientists to determine this once and for all, and if the answer is positive, to research it.

Bob Rickard

WITCHCRAFT: A STRANGE CONFLICT
by Peter Hough.

Lutterworth Press, Cambridge. 1991, pb £7.95, pp199, sources, index.

Here is an account of Hough's personal investigation into the status of witchcraft and Satanism in modern Britain, seeking to find out whether their adherents are behind the wave of ritualistic child abuse cases as Christian fundamentalists allege. Although it has the advantage of an independent viewpoint unlike the recent Fundamentalist scaremongering books by Tim Tate and Andrew Boyd (reviewed last issue) – the narrative wanders, sometimes clear and convincing and other times leaving one more confused than ever on the very issues he tries to clarify.

To set the scene for his travels, Hough gives us a potted history of witchcraft. There is no doubt Hough put in a lot of reading time, but here and elsewhere in the book, a greater depth, perhaps even different analysis, could have been provided by a better understanding of the theological, historical and anthropological roots of the issues, and by less of a reliance upon contemporary newsclippings. For example, the transitions from an inferred proto-witchcraft in the Iron Age to the familiar witch persecutions of the Middle Ages to the modern post-Gardner-Murray revivals

---

TWELVE-TRIBE NATIONS
THE SCIENCE OF ENCHANTING THE LANDSCAPE
by John Michell and Christine Rhone.

Thames & Hudson, London. 1991, hb £18, pp192, bib, index, illus.

Once again John Michell steps forward, this time in company, to convince us that something peculiar was going on in ancient times: the proposal being that there was once an ideal social structure, often sought for and sometimes achieved, in which a nation would divide itself into 12 tribes, representing the signs of the zodiac and arranged in a wheel around a central holy mountain. At the same time, the landscape would be enchanted with geomancy, music and myth. The most notable examples of this idea are the ideal society proposed in Plato's *Laws*, and the 12 tribes of Israel; and the early chapters of the book collect a great deal of material, from Europe to Africa and Asia, to show that such societies either existed or were attempted. From this we move on to ancient "chorographies" – attempts to correlate all the nations of the known world and their geographical locations with the signs of the zodiac.

Within the geographical areas covered, I find the evidence assembled convincing enough and enormously interesting; but the suggestion that the proposed structure might be an archetypal symbol that is *universal*, seems rather contentious. Its use in China, implied by mention of a "Chinese zodiac", lacks proof; the Chinese 12-animal cycle has numerous applications (calendrical, directional, divinatory, etc), but it has no astrologically corresponding stellar constellations. The Chinese simply didn't use a solar zodiac, preferring a stellar wheel based upon the 28 constellations of the lunar mansions, and their chorographies are based on the same system. Similarly, the number 12 is of no great significance to the Chinese, whose numerical cosmologies are built more upon 5, 8 and 9. But this is a mere quibble on my part, and shouldn't detract from the other excellences of the book.

The authors seem on surer ground when the scale is less vast. Their material tracing an alignment of sites sacred to Apollo and St Michael, right across Europe, is stunning; even more so are the beautiful geomantic patterns revealed by the structure and sacred sites of Jerusalem.

All in all, this is a delightful book, which has to be highly recommended to anyone interested in ancient history, earth mysteries, symbolism, and so forth. But I do feel it's rather under-referenced, and when an author isn't being directly quoted one is occasionally left wondering where the material has come from. However, the work moves smoothly enough for the general reader; but for anyone seriously intrigued by the material and wanting to follow it up, a simple three-page bibliography isn't really enough.

Steve Moore

FAR LEFT: Lines drawn diagonally between the coastal boundary points of Ireland's four provinces meet to form angles of exactly 72 degrees. One of these angles is bisected by a line to the boundary mark between East and West Munster.

LEFT: The due east-west line through the centre of Ireland fits into the pentagonal scheme of sacred geometry, which is suggested by the lines in the previous diagram. This prior division of the country into ten sectors from the symbolic centre develops into the 12-part division shown in the following diagram.

leave huge spans of time and leaps of culture unaccounted for.

As Hough wanders about Britain speaking to pagans and Christians of all types, the often tenuous distinctions between the various schools of witchcraft, Satanism, Black Magic, and paganism become lost as each party stakes its claim to the true way and damns the others. A case in point is Chris Bray's counter-charge that members of the Christian clergy, and not pagans, have committed the largest number of documented cases of ritualised child abuse.

By far the most interesting chapters are those devoted to interviews with the MP Geoffrey Dickens, the Reverend Kevin Logan (both of whom are called here 'Witchfinders'), officers of the Reachout organisation, social workers, and a senior organiser of the Benel Satanists. They are questioned against the background of the 'Satanic' child abuse scares in Liverpool, Alfreton, Manchester, Salford, Nottingham and Rochdale which are chronicled but not in as much referenced detail as I would have liked. Given Hough's range of interests, there are the inevitable correlations with UFO abductions, poltergeist attacks, and encounters with demons.

Readers new to these subjects will be intrigued and entertained. Seasoned buffs will be disappointed by Hough's failure to challenge the more fantastic or unsupported claims of his informants.

Bob Rickard

THE UFO SILENCERS
edited by
Timothy Green Buckley

Inner Light Publications, Box 753, New Brunswick, NJ 08903, USA. 1990. $12.95 (+ $1.50 p&p), pp160.

Stories of Men in Black (MIBs) bring to life, and justify, the paranoia and conspiracy theories that pepper UFO research. Encounters with MIBs are regarded as an essential part of the UFO riddle. They are even part of the popular concept of the subject: for example, the Stranglers rock group named one of their albums after them, and MIBs featured in a brilliant TV advertisement for Moosehead lager a couple of years back. The 1960s TV series *The Invaders* – currently replaying Sunday lunchtimes – portrayed them as aliens who can look like normal human beings, the better to suppress the evidence for their existence and that of UFOs.

Albert Bender, according to himself, was the first ufologist to encounter sinister MIBs. He thought he had the solution to the UFO mystery, but as soon as he began telling others about his discoveries, three MIBs visited his home. Their threats made him close down his International Flying Saucer Bureau in 1952. Since then, a number of witnesses and researchers have claimed they were similarly prevented from revealing what they know.

John Keel can be regarded as the most influential propagator of MIB mythology in recent years, and he contributes a short

Albert Bender's sketch of the MIB that visited him in 1952.

opening chapter to this book. Keel gives a good boost to any paranoid's most frightening thoughts when he asserts that MIBs can appear (and disappear) anywhere, and can pose as almost any kind of official. However, he says, they are not part of our reality.

As the MIBs make house calls, drive around in conspicuous black limousines, and use the public telephone system, you'd think they'd be easier to trace or capture than a bug-eyed monster darting about in a souped-up saucer – yet they prove to be as insubstantial as ghosts. The licence plates on their cars (if they are noted) are untraceable; witnesses never think of questioning or trying to apprehend them, and when someone, on a rare occasion, chases them, they simply vanish around a corner. Cameras fail in their presence – although this book does feature one photo of a MIB lurking in a doorway. MIBs tend to appear when a witness is alone and vulnerable, and they seem to read the thoughts of witnesses and know intimate details of their doings.

Very few books have been devoted entirely to the MIB phenomenon, and the opportunity has been taken here to pile in all the 'evidence' to present an overall picture of their operations. There is no deep analysis here, but the book provides a variety of contributions by well-known ufologists and several first-hand eyewitness accounts.

One woman gives a graphic account of her abduction by MIBs. They bundled her into a car and took her to a small underground room, where she was detained for a week. During this period they tried to make her confess that she attempted suicide and that she shouldn't take anymore interest in UFOs. Agreeing to their demands eventually, she was dumped in a vacant building. The strangest part of the story is the apparent indifference of the police when the woman and her mother went to report her kidnapping.

Another case demonstrates the ridiculous B-movie behaviour characteristic of many observed MIBs. The witness claims that MIBs ambushed him after he had been abducted by aliens and given a physical examination inside a UFO. While driving to Amarillo to take a lie-detector test, the man stopped to help a woman at the side of the road trying to fix a '55 Plymouth. Before he reached her, he was felled by a blow to the back of his head. Recovering, he saw two suited men standing over him. One, carrying an automatic rifle, told him: "If you pass this test, there's going to be a lot of daylight seen through you in more than one place." The man went on to fail the lie-detector test, but on returning home and recounting the threat to his wife, he says his house was sprayed with machine gun bullets from a passing car. Not for the first time we are left wondering why a witness didn't contact the police, or why, if the evidence was that tangible, didn't that investigation proceed.

The alleged powers of the MIBs to suppress any investigation of them seems quite at odds with their other characteristic of generally inept behaviour. They threaten but rarely inflict any material or physical damage. In more frightening cases – like the two mentioned – the stories have come out regardless. They seem as adept at concealing UFO evidence as the ufonauts are at suppressing the memories of abductees.

MIBs also provide an acceptable excuse for UFO witnesses or researchers to drop out of the subject. Some of it may well be the result of paranoia, pranksters or misperceptions; but in any city in the world you can see strange-looking people behaving weirdly. It is also possible that some MIBs might be 'real' government agents (especially in the USA). In the end there is little to go on but fear-tinged speculation!

As I was reading the chapter on 'The Mystery Helicopters', a noisy low-flying chopper buzzed my house. I'd better watch out …

Nigel Watson

THE CIRCLEMAKERS
by Andrew Collins.

ABC Books, Leigh-on-sea. 1992, pb £4.95, pp349, photos, notes, bib, index.

Hunter Thompson once said: "When the going gets weird, the weird get going." Well, they don't come much weirder these days than the wonderful and frightening world of crop circles. Author Andy Collins has leapt into the morass with this contribution to the increasingly crowded genre of cornography. Commendably, he avoids the all too familiar and depressing factionalism rife among the circles followers and makes a brave attempt to scythe through the stacks of claims and counter claims, seeking out the roots of the phenomenon with his patent brand of swashbuckling mysticism, 'Psychic Questing'.

Starting with a mysteriously polting book, circle visits and meditations on photocopied pictograms, Collins and his sidekick Debbie, and their pals, find their own answer to the meaning of the circles. A combination of research and psychic revelation leads them to orgone - the mysterious life-energy discovered by Wilhelm Reich - and they discover the true use of stone circles on the way. They take the existence of orgone for granted, and providing the reader can also, everything else more or less follows, providing an unconventional, but well argued, explanation of circles structures and associated phenomena, invoking orgone theory and the semi-intelligent energy-form UFO-like 'sky creatures' postulated by Trevor James Constable. Collins also achieves the almost impossible task of proving both the 'plasma vortex' and UFO theories of circle formation at the same time, but neither in a way their protagonists will approve of.

The chief failing here is in Collins' approach to science; it is rejected when it doesn't agree with him and endorsed enthusiastically when he can reap the benefits, and generally grazed over for evocative terms and concepts to nail over gaps in the general argument like plywood over riot damage. Particularly abused is particle physics (always a source of impressive meaninglessness) from which Collins harvests the notion of 'non-locality' used to

support his ideas with a "no reason to suggest..." and an "if you apply such logic to...", and which remains immovably welded to it for the rest of the book. He also throws in some spectacularly unwarranted assumption about orgone and the long-sought 'fifth force' of physics, and plays fast and loose with field theory. While I understand Collins' whole thrust is based on intuition and insight, such borrowings, unsupported by a shred of proof, do him no favours and weaken his arguments, symptomatic as they are of enthusiastically extending a theory beyond its natural limits. The book would have worked well without them.

Anyone seeking a rattling good psychic questing adventure yarn - like Collins' best known *The Black Alchemist* - are in for disappointment here, as this is a far more theoretical work. If you are looking for a fresh overview of the crop circle phenomenon, avoiding the mud-slinging and established theories, and can stomach Collins' reliance on unsupported psychic insight, you could do worse than cast an eye over this fat book. For me, though, I hope that with his next book, Andy Collins returns to the territory of his previous successes, where his real strengths lie.

Ian Simmons

VIDEO VIEW

THE LOCH NESS MONSTER STORY

With breathtaking views of Britain's largest and deepest body of water, this history of the Nessie phenomenon and the personalities who pursue her is balanced and informative. Scripted by the proprietors of the Official Loch Ness Exhibition, in Drumnadrochit, it actually deals quite fairly with the serious research (like Operation Deepscan), the hoaxes (like Frank Searle's photos) and the controversies (such as the retouching of Robert Rines' underwater photos).

There are interviews with at least eight witnesses; Adrian Shine (head of the surveys of Lochs Ness and Morar), Tim Dinsdale and other researchers; a review of various theories of Nessie's identity, origin and survival; and many valuable archival newsreel clips - in other words, something for everyone. Apart from the annoying permanent presence of a frame counter in the bottom left corner, and no mention of Doc Shiels' photos (despite featuring one on the cover), this is probably the best documentary on Nessie that we've yet seen.

The Loch Ness Monster; 1991; 57 mins; £10.99 from major stores (+ £1.75 p&p from Video Offer, Box 936, South Woodham Ferres, Essex CM3 5VL – or phone 0245 322499). Polygram CFV12212. **Bob Rickard**

BY ANDREW COLLINS and DEBBIE BENSTEAD ══ Illustration: HUNT EMERSON ══

DEAR FT...

THE CAR FROM HELL

■ After reading The Haunted Car [FT61:50], I would like to tell you about my 'haunted' car, registration 666. The number plate didn't bother me when I first bought the car, as I had no belief in this sort of thing. Then small items in the car started to vanish – maps, sunglasses, packets of sweets – at first I thought it was my wife tidying things up, but this was not the case. The lights would come on for no reason, or the horn was start sounding off. No electrical fault was found.

The car was stolen and used in a Post Office robbery and it came back in better condition. There have also been five attempts to break into it, all unsuccessful. Within a week, my mother and father-in-law died and a year later my brother also.

My wife began suggesting it was about time for the car to go, but each time she mentioned the idea the car broke down. To top it all, a strange sweet smell has started to appear every now and then. Last week, while driving home from work, I had a strange feeling that there was someone sitting in the back, but I couldn't see anything in the rear view mirror.

After all the bad luck we've had, I'm now a believer in all this sort of thing. So, any buyers please? [If anyone wants to buy the devil on wheels, FT can provide Mr Page's address - Eds.]

Chris Page
Keighley, West Yorks

ALIEN POST BOX?

■ The idea that crop circles are messages from some other intelligence (aliens, Gaia etc) is fairly common, but has anyone thought that the messages, if messages they be, are not actually for us? The idea of Planet Earth as a sort of galactic 'post it' note may be disconcerting to the geocentrists, but it is surely worth considering.

C.P. Dean
Redbridge, Essex

TAKEN TO TASK

■ I must take Mr Rickard to task over his mention of the 'fictitious' Philadelphia Experiment. As far as I am aware, the truth of this incident has never been conclusively proved either way. I suggest that he refrain from making such sweeping statements.

Cain
Sussex

SPOOKY SPIKE #1

■ In regard to the item about a spiky protrusion on an iced-over bird bath [FT62:10], the following may be of interest.

I have noticed for many years that ice cubes made in a refrigerator often have small bumps in the centre of the top. This puzzled me, as I thought they should be absolutely flat. Then I began buying bottled, distilled water, and when I filled the ice tray with distilled water, I got larger bumps in the middle. One day, I opened the fridge and there were ice cubes with bumps half an inch high, and one an inch high – a spike! I had to address this; I couldn't have ice cubes blowing holes in my world view. Obviously, the vibration of the compressor motor sets up a standing wave in the water, which ices over in that form. This could explain a bump, but not a spike. The spike, I think, is formed from the *sound* waves of the motor, possibly an ELF harmonic component that is reinforced by the mechanical vibration. This is why I always get bumps (the vibration is always there) but only rarely spikes (the particular placement of the tray in its chamber reinforcing or negating harmonic ELF).

So a bird bath would have wind causing a standing wave rather than a mechanical vibration, and the same wind generating a sound wave over the edge of the bird bath. What I'm impressed with here is that the water in the bird bath would be so pure.

Someone has recently invented a refrigeration unit that operates on sound. A test unit went up in the last shuttle launch. An extremely loud A440 is produced at one end of a long tube, and the other end gets very hot. The sound is muffled from the outside, so the entire unit is actually quieter than standard models.

Our civilization is still very primitive in using the inherent properties of sound and light to their fullest.

Kurt Lothmann
Houston, Texas

SPOOKY SPIKE #2

■ I was interested to see the 'spooky spike' item [FT62:10]. We discovered a similar formation in water on 21 December 1990 in a foil container (for takeaway food) put out on a stone wall for the birds. Again, the weather had been mild every day that week, so the water froze during the one night only. Our 'spike' is three centimetres high, triangular in section, sharply formed, and hollow. The nearest tree was four metres away. We still have the spike in the freezer; it would be nice to find an explanation before disposing of it.

Mrs O. Grant
Watford, Herts.

THE FIRES OF BINBROOK

■ Around May 1990, my father decided to visit the grave of his brother who died during World War II and was buried in Binbrook in Lincolnshire. This was the first time he had visited the grave since the burial 47 years before.

As he arrived, he saw smoke in the distance, and when he was in the churchyard, he heard fire engines passing, sounding their alarms. That evening, he heard that the RAF station at Binbrook had closed down and the aerodrome was being used to make a film about the American flying forces in World War II called 'The Memphis Belle', directed by David Putnam. During the filming, a plane had been taking off when it crashed at the end of the runway, bursting into flames. All the crew escaped without injury.

The accident mirrored exactly the one that killed my uncle. The difference was that his plane was loaded with ammunition ready for a mission in Germany and the ensuing fire caused a massive explosion that claimed the lives of all the crew. My father arrived home at Bath to find an article about the film in his local paper. David Putnam lived in Chippenham nearby.

What prompted me to write to you was the discovery in your book *Diary of a Mad Planet* of the 'Binbrook Triangle' [FT24:8] from Larry Arnold's article on 'fire leynes', and my wonder at the propensity for fiery events in this region. [Editors' note: see also Fort's account of a fiery Binbrook poltergeist in *Lo!*, chapter 14.]

Catherine Walker
Monmouth, Gwent

ANCIENT TECHNOLOGY

■ With reference to the puzzling watch winder found embedded in an ancient Indian coin *[FT65:46]*, I draw your attention to these bizarre representations, taken from Ernst Lehner's *Symbols, Signs and Signets* (Dover 1950). The Assyrian eagle-headed god Nisroch and the Babylonian winged guard of the symbolic tree not only carry very nice handbags, but are also wearing wristwatches! Also Thoth, the Egyptian god of wisdom and learning, is depicted with a mobile phone, or is it a transistor radio?

Could it be that the ancient gods of the Middle East were privy to some high tech knowledge that has only recently been rediscovered? I would be interested to hear of further evidence apart from the familiar von Daniken 'ancient astronaut' stuff.

Caroline Menis
Sheffield

WRISTWATCH INVENTION

■ I must add a note of caution to your feature, *Ancient Indian Wristwatch Wind-up?* *[FT65:46]*. Although wristwatches are known from the eighteenth century, they were, and remained, extremely rare until the coming of the motor car: a horseman can take out and consult a pocket-watch; a car driver cannot. World War I provided another enormous boost to the popularity of the wristwatch: it was found that diving to the ground to escape shell-fire usually resulted in the breaking of a pocket-watch. Wristwatches remained intact. Strangely enough, the Americans retained their pocket watches.

Some of the earliest wristwatches were made by soldering lugs to women's pocket-watches so that a strap could be attached. One company even made a sort of cage which strapped onto the wrist, into which a small pocket-watch could be fastened. In any case, any wristwatch dating to the period of the Indian Mutiny would not have had a winder – it would have been key-wound.

J. Raybould
Stourbridge, West Midlands

PARROT CHICKEN MINDER

■ The letter from Richard Holland about Mrs Ashe's parrot 'Polly' in the 1830s *[FT59:64]* reminded me of a story related in John Locke's *Essay Concerning Human Understanding* (1690; Bk II Ch XXVII Section 8), taken in turn from Sir William Temple's *Memoires of what past in Christendom from 1672 to 1679.*

Prince Maurice (of where is not stated), during a visit to Brazil, was curious to meet a parrot of some renown in the area. "When [the parrot] came first into the room where the Prince was, with a great many *Dutch-men* about him, it said presently, *What a company of white men are here?* They asked it what he thought that Man was, pointing at the Prince? It answered, *Some General or other;* when they brought it close to him, he asked it, *Whence come ye?* It answered, *From Marinnan. The Prince, To whom do you belong?* The Parrot, *To a Portugeze* [sic]. Prince, *What do you there?* Parrot, *I look after the Chickens.* The Prince laughed and said, *You look after the Chickens?* The Parrot answered, *Yes I, and I know well enough how to do it;* and made the Chuck four or five times that People used to make to Chickens when they call them."

Mrs Ashe's parrot was reputedly from Brazil and conversed with Portuguese sailors; the unnamed chicken guard also spoke to the Prince in 'Brasilian'. Perhaps they are in some way related? I think we should be told. By a parrot. [For further parrot items see *FT54:29, FT56:9, FT59:9* etc.]

Karl Rowley
Staffordshire

SEISMIC CORRECTIONS

■ I was interested to see that Peter Haining's book on the 1884 Colchester earthquake has been reissued yet again *[FT64:59]*. Subsequent research has shown the book to be exaggerated and unreliable. "Largest earthquake to hit England in recorded history" is a complete myth; there are many larger ones, including that of 2 April 1990 in Shropshire. "Most damaging in the last 400 years" is more accurate. As for being hushed up, there is evidence for the reverse – I enclose a copy of my paper demonstrating some remarkable forging of photographic evidence. Even in 1884, the camera lies. There is no Colchester Cathedral. Your picture on page 60 shows Lion Walk Congregational Church. Ironically, this spire is the only Victorian structure still standing in Lion Walk today!

■ Regarding your feature on seiche waves *[FT64:39]*, I would rule out an undersea seismic disturbance for a jet of water 500 feet high. Undersea seismic disturbances typically produce very long period waves which are almost undetectable until they reach shallow water and begin to 'pile up' into tsunamis or 'tidal waves'.

Roger Musson
British Geological Survey, Edinburgh

SNAKE-EATING BIRDS

■ Roger Musson's suggestion that snake-eating birds in Mexican symbology denotes a link with African cultures is probably not valid *[FT64:63]*. Though the secretary bird is a true snake-eating bird, others, ranging from hornbills, kookaburras, owls and eagles, regularly eat snakes. There is even a whole group of Old World eagles called snake-eating eagles. Snake-eating birds of one kind or another exist in the Americas. There is the symbolic aspect, analogous to St George and the dragon: snakes are, unfortunately, a symbol of evil. Maybe it's relevant that the Mexican god Quetzelcoatl is portrayed as half bird, half snake.

Darren Naish
Southampton

FATHER CHRISTMAS WRITES ...

■ The garments worn by Father Xmas are based upon the Fly Agaric mushroom, which used judiciously, on tongue and temple by shamans in Lapland, enable those wise, altruistic men to go on out-of-body-journeys so that they can bring back *gifts* of healing! These red and white growths can exchange hands for as many as five reindeer I'm told, and even the urine of those wealthy Lapps who 'party' on them gives pleasure to those poor Lapps who are wont to drink it.

Having been a subordinate Claus for many a year, here in Eastbourne, I have a particular interest in the jocund, rubicund, rotund and fecund figure of friendliness and frolicsome festivity, who flies down from the North Pole with gifts for the children, just as our intraterrestrial ancestors probably did from Ultima Thule all those aeons ago – giving us the honey bee and corn!

Anthony Chamberlaine-Brothers
Eastbourne

SHC AND ETHER

■It is possible that some 19th century cases of spontaneous human combustion may be related to ether drinking. Although superseded now by other drugs, ether drinking was once very widespread, especially in Ulster. In 1891, the Select Committee on British and Foreign Spirits estimated that there were 50,000 regular 'etheromaniacs' in Ulster, one in eight of the population. Seemingly, ether was everywhere in Ulster at the time. A local doctor is reported as saying: "The atmosphere of Cookstown and Moneymore was loaded with ether" and *The Times* in 1871 stated that market days smelt not of pigs, tobacco smoke or unwashed human beings, but of ether.

Ether is difficult to drink because it volatilizes at body temperature, but the etheromaniacs had a ritual that overcame the problems. The drinker would rinse out his or her mouth with cold water, hold the nose, and swallow the ether quickly, followed by more cold water. Regular etheromaniacs could consume up to a pint a day in this way. If the drinker failed to 'rift' (belch) at the appropriate moment, explosive volatilization could cause a heart attack. More apposite to SHC, there are cases of people rifting close to naked flames, and having fire travelling down their throats. According to McGuffin, drinkers were sometimes brought to Cookstown workhouse almost burnt to death by ether. In 1891, an ether explosion in a shop at Draperstown killed four people.

Until it was banned, ether was on open sale, either in liquid form or as a sort of wine gum. In 1890, ether was listed under the Poisons Act and in 1927, it was stamped out (as a popular tipple) by the Intoxicating Liquor and Licensing Act. So the spread of time during which ether fires are possible is 1850-1927. Most probably, the biochemistry of the fat metabolism of regular ether drinkers is little investigated. At least it may be worth looking closer at SHC cases from the last century for signs of etheromania. Perhaps some victims were burnt into ethernity. [References: Ken Connell: *Irish Peasant Society* Belfast 1968; John McGuffin: *In Praise of Poteen* Belfast 1978.]

Nigel Pennick
Cambridge

VAMPIRES AND THE CIA

■Your piece on the Manila Vampire *[FT64:11]* reminded me of something I found while researching the intelligence community's involvement with Forteana. In that case, stories of another Filipino vampire – the *Asuang* – were circulated by the media during the early 1950s.

Colonel Edward Lansdale, psywar expert with the CIA, studied peasant lore, taboos and myths and used them against the communist insurgents (Huks). Some of the more imaginative measures were broadcasting messages from a cloud-covered airplane and putting curses on villagers who helped the Huks. The CIA worked through the Filipino Civil Affairs Office to spread rumours of *Asuangs* in the hills near the Huk headquarters.

To add credibility to the vampire story, Lansdale covertly arranged for the assassination of a Huk and to have him drained of blood and two large puncture wounds put on his neck. The soldier was left at a crossroads near heavy troop movements. The Huks – frightened of vampires - quickly abandoned the area. I cannot help wondering if the recent *Manananggal* scare is not somehow connected with manipulation of the populace during the Philippine elections; or as part of that overused excuse –'protecting American interests'.

Ron Schaffner
Milford, Ohio

H.P. LOVECRAFT AS PROPHET

■Until now I was highly amused to hear of certain occultists who look on the American pulp horror/sf writer H.P. Lovecraft as a sort of prophet. I'm quite a fan and always thought, having read his biography, that he was an erudite and sceptical man. However, consider the following quotations from Lovecraft's *Imprisoned with the Pharaohs* (1924) in relation to "Crocodile Boy" *[FT64:19]* and "Riddles of the Sphinx" *[FT64:44:42]* as 'evidence' for his occult status.

"At all stages of history the sacred animals were mummified, so that consecrated bulls, cats, ibises, crocodiles and the like might return some day to greater glory. But only in the decadence did they mix the human and the animal in the same mummy… What happened to those composite mummies is not told of – at least publicly – and it is certain that no Egyptologist ever found one."

"Near the edge of the plateau and due east of the Second Pyramid, with a face probably altered to form a colossal portrait of Khephren, its royal restorer, stands the monstrous Sphinx … There are unpleasant tales of the Sphinx before Khephren - but whatever its elder features were, the monarch replaced them with his own that men might look at the colossus without fear."

M.C Kilburn
Bradford

FAIRGROUND NONDESCRIPTS

■Your story of the crocodile boy mummy *[FT64:19]* reminds me of the 'alligator men' that used to be exhibited at Carnivals and can still be found at highway tourist traps around the USA. Here is a photo of 'Jake the Alligatorman' from Marsh's Free Museum in Long Beach (bottom).

Jim Riecken
Sparkhill, NY

■For comparison, here's an exhibit from 'Ye Olde Curiosity Shop' in Alaskan Way, Seattle (below), sent to us by Georgina Clark-Mazo – *The Editors*

THE THING

noticeboard

EXCHANGE & MART

● **THE ENIGMA –** Articles on horror, politics, psychology, the occult and religion plus subjects enigmatic for we are THE ENIGMA but not a puzzle. £1.50 UK, £2.00 overseas. Payment to: THE ENIGMA, 1 Austin Close, Irchester, Northants NN9 7AX.

● **THE CAULDRON –** Pagan journal featuring witchraft, folklore and earth mysteries. Sample copy £1.50 payable to: M Howard, Caemorgan Cottages, Caemorgan Road, Cardigan Dyfed SA93 1QU.

● **CRYSTAL POINTS** and facetted sterling silver crystal pendants in quartz, rose quartz, amethyst and hematite. Also gold plated pendants. Rose quartz pieces. Send for price list to: Lovelines, 7 High Street Arcade, Cardigan, Dyfed SA43 1HJ. Phone 0239 614181.

● **MAKE THE PILGRIMAGE** to Middle Earth – Tarot, crystals, oils, lava lamps, jewellery, incenses, cards, tarot readings by appointment. 102 Walton Street, Jericho, Oxford. Tel 0865 511522.

● **YOUR LAST CHANCE** to Discover Matchless Magic of the caring kind. Unique brochure £3 (profits to wildlife sanctuary). Margaret Bruce, High Rigg House, St John's Chapel, Bishop Auckland, Co Durham DL13 1QT.

● **THE NEWS/FORTEAN TIMES** good condition, not dog-earred. 1-16 £45 (inc p&p). 21, 23-27, 29, 31-33, £2 each. Contact J Tait, Leck Mill, Leck, Carnforth, LA6 2JB.

● **NEW DIMENSIONS –**The monthly magazine of esoteric information. The best for occult articles, Qabalah, metaphysics, psychology, book and music reviews. Dynamic in origin. The best all-rounder. Magic at its best. £1.25 UD, £1.75 overseas. Dept MS, 1 Austin Close, Irchester, Northants NN9 7AX.

● **MILLENNIUM BOOKS –** 2nd hand books on UFOs, mysteries and all kinds of weird and wonderful things. For free lists write, fax or phone Millennium Books, 9 Chesham Road, Brighton, Sussex BN2 1NB. Fax/Phone 0273 671967.

● **NEW FROM GERMANY –** *Die grossen Ratselr letzen 2,500 Jahre (The great mysteries of the last 2,500 years)* by our German correspondent, Walter J. Langbein. One mystery for every century, from Ezechiel to Fatima. [ISBN 3-89350-136-3]. DM19.80 from Weltbild-Verlag.

● **TALES OF THE DEAD** – The German ghost stories which inspired the writing competition between Byron, Mary Shelley and Polidori and thereby Frankenstein and The Vampyre. First English edition since 1813. High quality paperback, £7.70 (p&p free) from Terry Hale, Rathbone Hall, North Mossley Hill Road, Liverpool L18 8BH.

● **UFO NEWSCLIPPING SERVICE** – keeps you up with the real 'close encounters'. Many fascinating UFO reports from the world's press are reproduced facsimile, along with newswire items from the major agencies. UFONS is 20 foolscap pages monthly, with a Fortean section strong on cryptozoology. Foreign language reports are provided in translation. For information and sample pages, write today to: UFONS - Lucius Farrish, Route 1 - Box 220, Plumerville, AR 72127, USA.

● **THE SKEPTIC** – takes an entertaining, rational and humourous look at pseudoscience and claims of the paranormal. Articles, reviews, columns, cartoons and much more. If you like FT you'll like The Skeptic. Sample issue £1.85; annual sub (6 issues) £12. The Skeptic, PO Box 475, Manchester M60 2TH.

● **UFO AFRINEWS** – edited by Cynthia Hind. The only UFO magazine in Africa. #1-4 available at £2; #5 at £2.50. Write: Gemini, Box MP49, Mt Pleasant, Harare, Zimbabwe.

EVENTS

● **TEMS** – (Travel & Earth Mysteries Society) is a non-sectarian group for SW London, Surrey and Middlesex, for those interested in ancient sites, leys, hauntings, crop circles, UFOs, unexplained animals, etc. For the programme of speakers, social events, trips and further info, contact Lionel Beer (081 979 3148), Barbara (081 942 3447), or Ann (081 542 3110).

● **SOCIETY FOR PSYCHICAL RESEARCH** – Lecture. 10 Dec: The dying brain: science and the near-death experience (Susan Blackmore). Venue: the Lecture Hall of Kensington Central Library, Campden Hill Road, London W8, at 6:30pm. Non-members £3, student cards £1. Further information from the SPR at 49 Marloes Rd, Kensington, London W8 6LA. Tel: 071 937 8984.

● **BUFORA** – British UFO Research Association. Lectures at London Business School, Sussex Place, Outer Circle, Regents Park, London NW1 at 6:30pm. £1.50 (members), £3.00 (visitors). 5 Dec - 'UFOs in Art' (illustrated) (Michael Buhler). Ring: 0582 763218 for more details.

● **LONDON EARTH MYSTERIES CIRCLE** – Evening meetings in St Andrew's Seminar Room, Maria Assumpta Centre, 23 Kensington Square, London W8, at 7pm on the 2nd and 4th Tuesdays in each month. Members £1.00, non-members £2.00, unwaged £1.50. Lectures: 13 Oct (Reclaiming our Heritage), 27 Oct (Earth Mysteries and Magnetism), 10 Nov (social eve.), 24 Nov (UFOs & Psychic phenomena). Contact: Rob Stephenson, 18 Christchurch Ave, London NW6 7QN, or tel: 081 459 0652.

● **TIBET FORUM** – free lectures every first Tuesday of each month at Institute Hall, Bloomsbury Central Baptist Church, 235 Shaftesbury Ave, London WC2 at 6:30pm. 2 Dec – 'United Nations and the Quest for Human Rights' (Dr Norman Goodman M.P.).

● **THEOSOPHICAL SOCIETY** – events on 6 Dec: at 11:15am, 'Holy Blood and The Holy Grail'; at 6pm 'Megalithic Science' - 50 Gloucester Place, London W1H 3HJ. Tel: 071 935 9261.

● **DEAD HAPPY** – Many of us die and become ghosts by thinking we are still alive, Lance Trendall has written a book on ghosts called *Dead Happy* and is visiting ancient battlefields to lay ghosts to rest. *Dead Happy* explains what it is like to be a ghost, how to prevent hauntings, how to help ghosts and how to ensure you don't become a ghost when you die. Available from the author (ISBN 0 9520472 0 9). Talks planned for December in Lincoln and York. For details and to order signed copies of *Dead Happy* phone 0582 461581.

RESEARCH

● **FORTEAN CURIOS –** Fortean Times is collecting information on private and museum collections of bizarre and mysterious objects such as unicorn horns, vegetable lambs, bits of alien craft, fafrotskies, rat-kings, fairy artifacts, mummified cats etc. If you know of any please write to FT at the editorial address.

● **NDE? OOBE?** – Graham Williams *Astral Project* Magazine, 8 Larch Croft, Tividale, Warley, E Midlands B69 2JB, would like to hear from you.

MISCELLANEOUS

● **DRUIDS!** – Discover what they do and how Druidry answers our need for a spirituality that is connected to the land and our ancient heritage. For info send SAE to: ODOB (FT) 260 Kew Road, Richmond, Surrey TW9 3EG.

● **ONE MAN'S MEAT** is another creature's slaughter-house nightmare. One man's meat is another creature's agonizing death. Isn't it time you went vegetarian?

● **WELSH HOLIDAY COTTAGE** – Self-catering accomodation in historic North Wales town of Denbigh. For further details, contact Janet Bord, Melysfan, Llangwm, Corwen, Clwyd LL21 0RD. Tel: 049 082 472. Fax: 049 082 321.

● **GLASTONBURY COTTAGE** – Forget expensive hotels or B&Bs – charming 2 bed house to let in mystic Glastonbury town centre. Central-heating, fully furnished with necessary utensils, crockery etc, and unique view over Abbey grounds. Tel: 0234 211606 (answerphone) for leaflet.

● **OLD PULP SF MAGS WANTED** – for FT Library. Also FATE MAGAZINE vol 1, no 4 (1948); nos 50 (1954) & 90 (1957). Write to Bob Rickard, c/o FT editorial address.

● **FORTEAN PICTURES** – The Fortean Picture Library is a self-funding project for the rescue and preservation of valuable documentary material, photographs and drawings etc. If you have anything of this nature please let FPL look after it. 50% of any revenue from the commercial use of the material (in books etc) could come back to you. FPL covers all expenses from its half. Contact Janet Bord, FPL, Melysfan, Llangwm, Corwen, Clwyd, Wales LL21 0RD. Tel: 049 082 472.

● **WARNING: OCCULT ABUSE TODAY,** karmic nightmare tomorrow. Beware the dire spitutial consequences of abusing occult/mental powers for base, selfish, manipulative and evil purposes.

ADVERTISEMENT

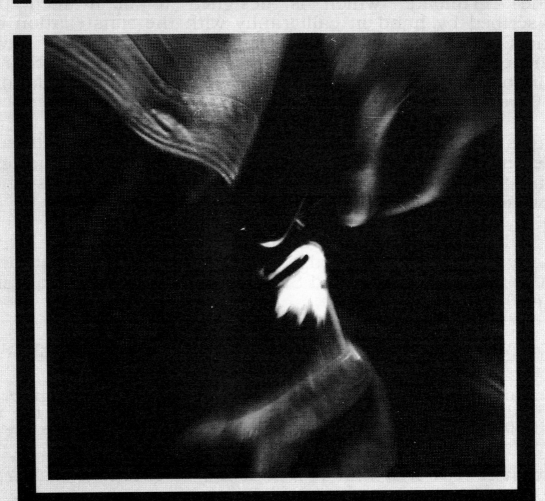

NUMBER 67

UK £2
USA $4.95

FORTEAN TIMES

THE JOURNAL OF STRANGE PHENOMENA

WHAT POSSESSED PARKINSON?
BBC's 'Ghostwatch' Hoax Unravelled

20th CENTURY DINOSAURS

Hitler's Corpse Discovered?   Italian Martians
Venezuelan Terror Blob   Yeti Hunts   The Legend of Dr Faustus

8 589118

WEHL Reveal Secret Recreational Drugs

Whole Earth Herbs Laboratory was established in 1982. Since then they have carefully researched over 30 different proven psycho active herb and alchemical preparations.

Up until this actual advertisement most of the WEHL range of products were only revealed when one ordered from their range of Marijuana like herbal smoking mixtures. New and exclusively for Fortean Times readers, WEHL proudly present their 100's range of Legal herbal recreational and ritual products.

Cloudswept is a combination of a stimulant and a sedative herb. Our first exclusive mixture was acclaimed by the LCC's Hookah as 'an unforgettable Buzz'. 'Highs seemed endless and controlled'. A rare psychoactive extract from Fiji is sprayed over 'Cloudswept' to create 'Rococan' .

The result is a smooth taste, an enhanced mellow high with the subtle buzz of the alchemical liquid. The mixture has up to 50% sprayed on it as opposed to a maximum of 10% sprayed on filter tip cigarettes. The final development in a line of Nicotene-free and non-addictive Herbal high alternatives to marijuana was a completely new mixture of the five very best psycho-active herbs. Formulated for a maximum 'high' with 5% mint (not menthol) for a smooth taste. The result, known as 'Yuba Gold' is an astonishing success. Why be illegal?!

Tested and proven by clients of whom 99.9% declined a refund. Testimonials of complete satisfaction regularly arrive as do multiple and repeat orders.

Exclusive to WEHL, Eclipse Cigarettes contain a similar formula to Yuba Gold with Yellow paper and marble effect filter. Available as four cellophane packets of twenty Tipped. These very rare world-wide herbs are reduced to a fine smokeable mixture. Beware of inferior imitations which will disappoint. WEHL is the only company in the world to currently produce herbal psycho-active cigarettes. Unlike THC in Cannabis, no tolerance builds up to our herbal highs. Just one cigarette required.

WEHL PSYCHOACTIVE BOTANICAL ALCHEMY RESIN POWDER LIQUID AND SEEDS

Catylist is a Stimulant/Aphrodisiac powder taken with black coffee. A mild cocaine-like effect. Costs £8 plus £2 p&p is £10 for 20g. Special offer for limited period only 40g for £15 all inclusive.

Pipe Dreams is an alternative to Opium. It is milder yet just as dreamy. Labour intensive process makes resin similar in taste, smell and texture. Pipe Dreams costs £10 plus £2 p&p. £12 for 10g. Smoke or eat.

Supana seeds are from a tropical jungle. A natural stimulant, it quickens perceptions, excellent for long drives. Costs £10 plus £2 p&p is £12 for 20g. New phiels 10 x 15ml wine, 1g Supana, 5m vitamin E - £12 inclusive.

Fijian Fantasy is a green alchemical liquid extract. Using alcohol extraction methods, no water-soluble alphapyrones are produced. These are then re-dissolved in brandy. Small amounts produce euphoria. More can create auditory and visual hallucination. An excellent aphrodisiac as warm emotions are generated. Narcotic numbing effect. Fijian Fantasy cost £12 plus £3 p&p is £15 per 100ml.

Blue Heaven seeds contain one microgram of LSA (a naturally occuring LSD-like structure) per seed. Five grammes equal approx 125 seeds. Effects are an LSD-like experience lasting 6 to 12 hours. Blue Heaven seeds are £10 plus £2 p&p is £12 for 10g.

Cloudswept is £6.45 (add £1.55 p&p) - total £8 per oz
Rococan is £8.95 (add £2.05 p&p) - total £11 per oz
Roco Cigs are £11.45 (add £2.55 p&p) - total £14 per 50
Yuba Gold is £10.85 (add £2.15 p&p) - total £13 per oz
Eclipse are £19.90 (add 4.10 p&p) - total £24 (4 x 20's)

Guaranteed psycho-active and legal. All sales are final. Sent by plain cover in 7-14 days. Write clearly please. Mail order only. Cheques/PO's payable to WEHL. International: Eurocheques welcome. Sterling only. Add 20% for Air Mail (8-10 days). Exchange rate US$2 to £1. Checks add 20%. Literature and trade names copyright owned by WEHL 1993. Not sold for any medicinal purpose. For ritual use only.

WEHL (Dept FT1), 103 High Street, Sawston, Cambridge CB2 4HL England Tel: (0223) 833343. VAT reg no 538 5999/6

ALL PRICES INCLUSIVE OF VAT

Contents
Issue 67 February/March 1993

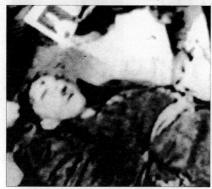

P44 HITLER'S BODY?

**PULL-OUT COLOUR SECTION
LIVING FOSSILS:
A FORTEAN TIMES GUIDE TO
DINOSAURS IN THE 20TH CENTURY
COMPILED BY DR KARL SHUKER**

WHY 'FORTEAN'?

CHARLES FORT (1874-1932)

Fortean Times is a bi-monthly magazine of news, reviews and research on all manner of strange phenomena and experiences, curiosities, prodigies and portents, formed in 1973 to continue the work of the iconoclastic philosopher CHARLES FORT. Fort was sceptical about scientific explanations, observing how scientists argued for and against various theories and phenomena according to their own beliefs, rather than the rules of evidence. He was appalled that data not fitting the collective paradigm was ignored, suppressed, discredited or explained away (which is quite different from explaining a thing).

Fort was perhaps the first to speculate that mysterious lights seen in the sky might be craft from outer space. He coined the term 'teleportation' which has passed into general usage through science fiction. His dictum "One measures a circle beginning anywhere" expresses his philosophy of Continuity and the 'doctrine of the hyphen', in which everything is in an intermediate state between extremes. He had notions of the universe-as-organism and the transient nature of all apparent phenomena. Far from being an over-credulous man, Fort cut at the very roots of credulity: "I cannot accept that the products of minds are subject matter for beliefs ... I conceive of nothing, in religion, science, or philosophy, that is more than the proper thing to wear, for a while."

Fort was born in Albany, New York, in 1874 into a family of Dutch immigrants. Beatings by a tyrannical father helped set him against authority and dogma, and on leaving home at the age of 18 he hitch-hiked around the world to put some "capital into the bank of experience." At 22 he contracted malaria, married his nurse and settled down to 20 years of impoverished journalism in the Bronx. During this time he read extensively in the literature of science, taking notes on small squares of paper in a cramped shorthand of his own invention, which he filed in shoe boxes.

In 1916, when he was 42, Fort came into a modest inheritance, just enough to relieve him of the necessity of having to earn a living. He started writing *The Book of the Damned*, which his friend, the novelist Theodore Dreiser, bullied his own publisher into printing in 1919. Fort fell into a depression, burnt all his notes (which numbered some 40,000) as he had done a few years earlier, and in 1921 set sail for London, where he spent eight years living near the British Museum (39 Marchmont Street) and wrote *New Lands* (1923). Returning to New York, he published *Lo!* in 1931 and *Wild Talents* in 1932, shortly before he died. He left 60,000 notes, now in the New York Public Library.

THE GANG OF FORT:

Editors:
Bob Rickard
& Paul Sieveking

Contributing Editors:
Steve Moore
& Mike Dash

© Fortean Times February 1993
ISSN 0308 5899

EDITORIAL ADDRESS
Fortean Times: Box 2409,
London NW5 4NP, UK.
Tel & Fax: 071 485 5002 or
081 552 5466.

SUBMISSIONS
Submissions are invited of suitable articles, news, art, cartoons, reviews, and especially clippings. Preliminary discussion with the editors is advisable. Text can be submitted on floppy disks, but check with the editors first. Submissions may be edited. FT assumes no responsibility for submissions, but all reasonable care will be taken while they are in FT's possession. Requests for return of material should be accompanied by stamped addressed envelope.

CLIPPINGS
All clippings, references, etc, should be identified by source, date and clipster's name. Mail or fax them to the editorial address (above).

SUBSCRIPTIONS
RATES – One year (6 issues). UK: £12. Overseas inc. USA: £15.00 or US$30. For two years (12 issues) UK: £20, overseas inc USA £26 or US$50.
PAYMENT – US/Canadian cheques acceptable; payments from all other countries should be in sterling drawn upon a London bank. Major credit cards accepted – just phone details to 0373 451777. Make cheque/money orders payable to:
JOHN BROWN PUBLISHING Ltd, 20 Paul Street, Frome, Somerset BA11 1DX, UK.

ADVERTISING ENQUIRIES
DISPLAY or CLASSIFIED: contact Ronnie Hackston or Dan Squirrell at John Brown Publishing Ltd: The Boathouse, Crabtree Lane, Fulham, London SW6 8NJ, UK. ☎ 071 381 6007 or Fax: 071 381 3930.
BOOKSELLERS' LISTING items – contact the editorial address (above).

PUBLISHER
John Brown Publishing Ltd, The Boathouse, Crabtree Lane, Fulham, London SW6 8NJ, UK. ☎ 071 381 6007 or Fax: 071 381 3930.
Managing Editor: Fiona Jerome.
Publisher: Vic Lime.

DISTRIBUTION
UK trade distribution by UMD, 1 Benwell Road, Holloway, London N7 7AX. ☎ 071 700 4600 or Fax: 071 607 3352.
USA newsstand distribution by Eastern News Distributors Inc, 2020 Superior St, Sandusky, OH 44870, USA.

Bob Rickard

Paul Sieveking

EDITORIAL:

Our 20th Year

● 1993 sees the 20th birthday of *Fortean Times* and to celebrate we are planning a number of special events and promotions. Full details in due course.

● After at least one postponement, the Broadcasting Standards Council finally published their deliberation of the BBC1 Hallowe'en drama *Ghostwatch,* shown on 31 October 1992. The BSC (*Bulletin* no.24, Jan 1993) said they received 33 complaints – compared to least 20,000 received by the BBC – and have "decided that the complaints lay outside its remit". Most callers felt that this fictional programme breached the trust between broadcaster and audience, and the BSC feels this was *not* a matter of "taste and decency". Star of *Ghostwatch* Michael Parkinson (who features on our cover) enraged many by gloating: "If we've scared the pants off people, we've done our job well." Read all about it in our 'Hoax!' section this issue – see p 38.

● The mysterious "elite" that really run this world obviously relented and allowed a rapidly arranged conference designed to "expose a global deception" to go ahead in London on 9 January 1993. Rumours flew beforehand that it would be cancelled, not by a visit from the MIBs, but because Mary Seal, the organiser, was not able to get enough bums on seats at the Wembley Arena. The conference drew a lot of flak for its not-so-secret agenda of talks about secret government cover-ups of alien invasions, secret government engineering of the AIDS virus and so on. It is too easy to laugh at the conspiracy-mongers, but experience shows it is the visionary eccentrics and other outsiders who tend to ask the most interesting questions. Our mentor Charles Fort once pointed out that you can't find out anything new without offending *someone.*

● Computer databases use semantic memory, in which documents must first be categorised. As Dr Mark Lansdale of Loughborough University has said, "human beings are inefficient at remembering these categories." This problem is magnified greatly by the kind of material dealt with at Fortean Towers. Lansdale has devised an experimental computer filing system called Memoirs that tries to mimic the controlled chaos of desks heaped with paper. Such chaos, he said, was often a sign of a sophisticated mind, and was organised by episodic or autobiographical memory. As long as it was not tidied, documents could be efficiently recovered, like an archæologist digging through successive chronological layers.

The Memoirs software is at least five years away from the market, so we'll have to make do with the user-friendly office chaos. Papers on the *FT* editors' desks can be buried for long periods, a process known as 'jessoping' (named after a Mr Jessop, whose desk was an extreme example of this phenomenon). So, if you have sent us an article and have not heard from us for a few weeks, don't despair – we'll respond sooner or later! If you think *your* desk could possibly be worse than Bob Rickard's, send us a photo of it.

● If you sent in an entry to our Christmas competition, please be patient. Winners will be notified by post shortly, and a list published next issue.

● As we go to press, three New Zealand hikers claim to have spotted a Moa, the giant bird believed extinct for 500 years. More on this next issue, plus the full facts behind the Home Counties horse mutilations.

THE EDITORS

STRANGE DAYS

16 pages of worldwide weirdness

HACKED OFF

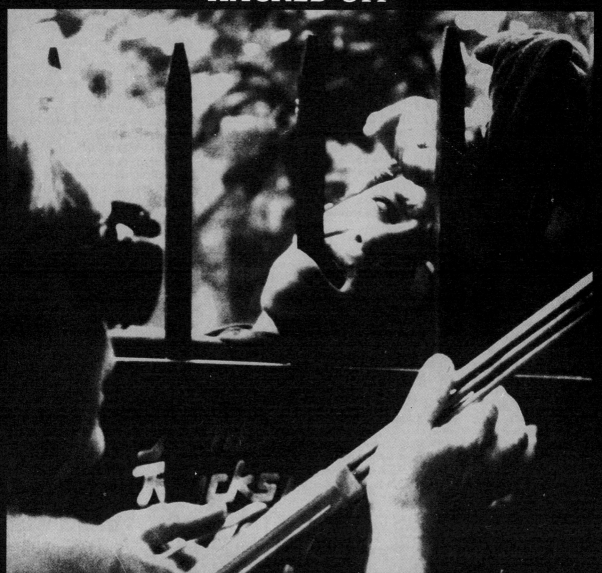

Talking about his lucky escape from a horrible death is something terrified teenager Julio Castillo found difficult to do for a while. The 14-year-old climbed a six-foot fence to retrieve a baseball when he slipped. The spike just missed his jugular vein and left him dangling until his pals fetched help.

Julio's body was lashed to the fence to take the strain off his jaw while firemen set about cutting a 150 pound section of fence using blow-torches and water to cool the metal – an operation that took 90 minutes. Then his rescuers used an electric hacksaw to trim off most of the rest. "He was petrified, but pretty brave throughout", said fireman Peter Cozeolino. Later, in a nearby hospital, the last remaining piece was successfully removed and Julio was stable. A later operation was needed to repair the broken jaw. *[AP] 10 July 1989.*

FORTEAN ALMANAC 20 Feb – 12 April 1993
Notable feasts and anniversaries in the coming weeks

SATURDAY 20 FEBRUARY: Feast Day of St Paula the Bearded and birthday of Ramakrishna, Indian saint.
SUNDAY 21 FEBRUARY: Tibetan New Year : 2120 (Water Bird)
THURSDAY 25 FEBRUARY: St Walpurga's Day. Her Feast Day, originally May Eve, was moved in an attempt by the Church to banish the Walpurgis night witches' revelry.
SUNDAY 28 FEBRUARY: Birthday of Ben Hecht (1893), the Hollywood scriptwriter who probably coined the word 'Fortean' in a review of Fort's *Book of the Damned* in 1919.
MONDAY 1 MARCH: St David's Day. The patron saint of Wales was the pagan sea god Dewi, whose symbol, a great red serpent, became the dragon of Wales.
WEDNESDAY 3 MARCH: Sighting of giant frog in Loveland, Ohio (1972).

SATURDAY 6 MARCH: Birthday of the master of fantastic realism, Gabriel Garcia Marquez (1928).
FRIDAY 12 MARCH: Epidemic of religious images on windows in Baden-Baden begins (1872).
SATURDAY 13 MARCH: Planet Uranus discovered (1781) by William Herschel, who lived one Uranian year.
WEDNESDAY 17 MARCH: Saint Patrick's Day. Shamrock was the symbol of the pagan triple deity. Pater (or Patricius), an enormous phallus, was paraded at the Roman festival of Mars. Green was worn at Roman sexual feasts.
SATURDAY 20 MARCH: Ostara, the vernal Equinox. Sun enters Aries 14:41. One of the eight great pagan festivals of the year.
WEDNESDAY 24 MARCH: St Gabriel's Day. Gabriel is supposed to have brought God's seed to the Virgin Mary; some theologians thought he carried the seed in his mouth and it entered Mary through her ear.

FRIDAY 26 MARCH: 'Fish-shaped' craft seen over Galisteo, New Mexico (1886).
WEDNESDAY 31 MARCH: Fox sisters hear first ghostly taps in Hydesville, New York (1848). Spiritualist movement begins.
SUNDAY 4 APRIL: Dada Day. Birthday of Lautréamont (1846) and Tristan Tzara (1896).
TUESDAY 6 APRIL: Lord Carnarvon dies (Cairo 1923). "Don't worry doctor, it's only a mosquito bite".
FRIDAY 9 APRIL: Good Friday. Feast Day of St Casilda, patron saint of dysentery.
SUNDAY 11 APRIL: Easter Day. According to ancient Irish custom, megaliths were dressed in elaborate female clothes. Feast Day of St Gemma Galgani (1878-1903), stigmatic and levitator.

SARAJEVO ZOO

The last animal in Sarajevo zoo, a brown bear, died of starvation at the beginning of November 1992. The bear survived longer than any other animal at the zoo in the besieged Bosnian capital by eating two other bears which shared its cage. One zookeeper was shot dead by a sniper and another wounded attempting to feed the animals. *Edinburgh Eve. News*, 3 Nov 1992.

FROG 68

A frog swallowed a gold chain, left on a riverbank by a woman bather, and leapt back into the water in the village of Thannermukkom, southern India. Relatives of the woman started catching frogs and slitting open their bellies, reported the *Hindu* newspaper. They found the chain in the 68th frog dissected. [AP] 30 Oct 1992.

EMERGENCY POWERS

Elizabeth Dawson, 11, recently recovered from anorexia nervosa, saved her sister's life by lifting a 170lb camping trailer and dragging her to safety. Had she not found the strength to raise the trailer on to one wheel, doctors believe that her sister Lynette, eight (pictured below right), would have died from ruptured kidneys. Lynette became trapped as she tried to retrieve her scooter from behind the trailer, which had been left end-up in their garden in Macclesfield, Cheshire. "It came down on top of her, pushing two metal bars into her chest", said Elizabeth. "I knew I had to do something quickly. Lifting up the trailer seemed quite easy at the time." *D.Telegraph*, 4 Sept 1992.

DUSTY RAIN
The bottom of England was once again powdered as a fine red dust came down on the south west with early morning rain on 18 Sept 1992. The deposits – thought to be Sahara sand – showed up best on cars and greenhouses. Plymouth Weather Centre said the dust was carried by warm, moist air from the south. *Western Morning News*, 19 Sept 1992. See *FT58:11* for our last sprinkling of dusty rains.

GENE JUDGMENT
We are glad to note the US Patent Office rejected an application for patents on thousands of genetic fragments isolated from the human brain. Thus the march of genetic 'ownership' is obstructed and the dread day delayed when we have to pay a royalty for living. *D.Telegraph*, 25 Sept 1992.

EARTH'S PULSE DETECTED

For the first time, a new way of studying the Earth's interior will allow the mass of the core to be calculated and the composition and relationship of the inner and outer cores to be inferred. It will shed light on the enigma of the electric dynamo effect which drives the planet's reversible magnetic field.

The instruments used by Dr Douglas Smylie, of Ontario's York University, are so sensitive that they detect minute flickers of the magnetic and gravitational fields 3,200 miles down. These fluctuations are caused by the inner core oscillating as it swims in the outer liquid core. Liquid, here, is a relative term; the outer core is molten iron and nickel with a viscosity 10 billion times that of water. Nevertheless, there appears to be a clear demarcation between this 'barely liquid' and the more solid inner core, which moves off-centre by a few

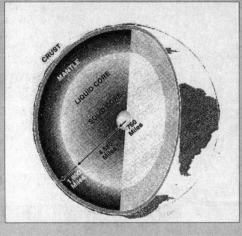

yards in three major directions, one along the axis of the planet's rotation, and two others perpendicular to it.

Ultrasensitive gravitational measurement became possible by developments in superconductor technology in the 1980s, pioneered by Dr John Goodkind of the University of California at San Diego. Eleven of Goodkind's gravimeters are now operating in observatories in Asia, Europe and North America. Data gathered over the last ten years are interpreted using a mathematical model of the three-way oscillation of the inner core, called CORE 11, devised in 1988 by Dr Rudolph Widner of Germany's Black Forest Geophysical Observatory. In effect, Dr Smylie has calculated that the three-way oscillating 'pulse' has periodicities of 3.7677, 4.015 and 3.582 hours. Sources: *Science, April; NYT/IHT, 2 April 1992.*

SIMULACRA CORNER

Who was this giant sunbathing woman and why was she turned to stone? Photograph by Michael Bell. We are always glad to receive pictures of spontaneous forms and figures, or any curious images.

    Send your snaps to the editorial address – with SAE – and we'll pay a fiver for any we use.

Sidelines

A notice on the bulletin board at the University of Cincinnati announced a lecture series called 'Surprises in Obstetrics'. Scribbled beneath was: "Mary had a little lamb". *Brisbane (Aust) Sunday Mail, 15 Mar 1992.*

● ● ● ● ● ● ● ● ● ● ● ●

"I presume the laws of trespass do not extend to astral travel, since it would require a more enlightened legal profession to deal with the administration," said Piers Eggert, a dissident member of the Spiritualist Association, on being sued for trespass in their headquarters in London. He claims to have been in Oxfordshire at the time. *Guardian, 18 Aug 1992.*

● ● ● ● ● ● ● ● ● ● ● ●

Ken Seymour, 52, a shopper in Plymouth city centre, escaped death when a four foot illuminated angel fell from an overhead display and crashed at his feet. "It wasn't a guardian angel", he said. *Independent, 20 Dec 1991.*

● ● ● ● ● ● ● ● ● ● ● ●

Health inspectors who pounced on a fast-food restaurant in Los Angeles were horrified to discover two bodies in the deep freeze. Owner Lydia Katash and her lover had been strangled and stashed in the deep freeze at least eight months earlier. The eatery was allowed to stay open because there is nothing in Californian law which prohibits the storage of human corpses near food. A health department spokesperson deplored the loophole, saying they would have shut it instantly if they had found cockroaches or rats. *D.Record, 27 Oct 1992.*

● ● ● ● ● ● ● ● ● ● ● ●

In May 1992, *The Andover Advertiser*, reporting on the crowning of a local beauty queen, said she was "selected in a nail-biting competition".

MAN BITES ALIEN!

An occasional selection of Fortean headlines
from newspapers around the world.

ANGRY, JOBLESS SANTAS PICKET MALL AFTER ELF ACCUSED OF LECHERY
Duluth (MN) News-Tribune, 24 Nov 1990.

EXPLODING STAR STUNS ASTRONOMERS
St Paul (MN) Pioneer Press-Dispatch, 25 Feb 1987.

TROY RELOCATED TO HAPPY EATER OFF A11 Guardian, 25 June 1990.

PA-IN-LAW WARNS: I'LL SORT OUT 'SON OF GOD'. Sunday Mirror, 31 Mar 1991.

TIME IS RUNNING OUT, BUT NO ONE KNOWS JUST WHEN Independent, 25 June 1990.

CUT OUT LIVER PREGNANT WOMEN TOLD
Northern Echo, 19 Oct 1990.

GIANT BAT INVADES CAPITOL
San Francisco Examiner, 29 Jan 1991.

HELL TO AXE 550 STAFF
Litho Week, 12 Dec 1990.

DEAD MAN'S MESSAGE

Betina Davey

Someone ripped a statuette from the tomb of Jason Elverson, who died at sea in 1989. His sister, Betina Davey, from Cosham, Hampshire, told Portsmouth *News* (23 November 1992): "I was out shopping with my husband Stephen in Portsmouth when my mind suddenly went blank. As I stood there I realised I was getting a message from Jason. I kept seeing him and the statue. I started running – I didn't know where."

She arrived at Squirrels antique shop in Kingston Road and at the back of the shop found the missing statuette stored with other items snatched from the cemetery. Betina had never been in the shop before. Police were satisfied that the shop's owner, Brian Futcher, had bought the statuettes in good faith.

ROYAL FIREWORKS

Soon after the fire at Windsor Castle on 20th November 1992, the Rev Tony Higton, Rector of Hawkwell in Essex, wrote in the *Christian Herald* that the fire happened because God had removed His protection from the Royal Family since the Queen had broken her coronation vows. "The Queen has persisted in multi-faith worship, such as the annual Commonwealth Day Observance", wrote the noted fundamentalist. "As a condition of being crowned she made a very solemn vow to uphold the Protestant, Reformed Faith established by law." He pointed out that the fire started in the private chapel, where the Royal Family are reminded in the words of the Prayer Book: "Thou shalt have none other gods but me". *Standard Recorder (Southend), 3 Dec 1992.*

A week later, on 27 November, fire swept through a wing of the Hofburg palace in Vienna, formerly the Hapsburg family's imperial seat, causing damage estimated at £30 million. As at Windsor, damage to artworks was minimal – two 18th century tapestries were lost. Neither palace was ensured as the premiums would have been too high. There was no cleric on hand to 'explain' this fire. *D.Telegraph, 28 Nov 1992.*

MAGIC DREAMS

A man appointed as an official 'witch finder' because he identifies practitioners of black magic in his dreams has handed over 16 suspected sorcerers to Kenyan police. *[AFP] 20 Nov 1992.* Shades of Matthew Hopkins and Orkney social services... Let's hope the accused get a fair trial before they are burnt at the stake!

GIANTS JINX MOTORWAY

Last summer, workmen found 18 skeletons, some over seven feet tall, in shallow graves on Twyford Down, Hampshire, as heavy machinery arrived to start moving several million cubic metres of chalk from the Area of Outstanding Natural Beauty for the M3 motorway extension. English Heritage has called the area "the most important archæological landscape in southern England.". Within a week of the old burial mound being disturbed, two workmen had fatal heart attacks. In the first week of December a security man protecting the bulldozers collapsed and died.

The significance of these events was not lost on the anti-road protesters, camped near Winchester Cathedral. "The skeletons were of giants. Maybe they were Arthur's men. It is the Curse of the Ancients", one young woman told the *Guardian, 15 Dec 1992.*

DROUGHT BLAMED ON MINI SKIRTS

Throughout July, Muslim zealots from the Izala sect beat up mini-skirted women in Niger, to the cries of "Allahu akbar" (God is great). They claimed that the provocative attire was causing a drought. Police also interrogated women whose clothes were deemed indecent, blaming them for the lack of rain. An attack on 17 July in the town of Zinder on women referred to as 'prostitutes' by Agence France Presse was followed the next day by a torrential downpour on the town of Niamey, drowning two men and an elderly woman. *AP, Reuters, 16 July; AFP, 20 July 1992.*

TALKING TURKEY
Strange falls and name coincidences from the Turkish press, translated by Izzet Goksu

The men of Çataltepe exhibit some of the stones that showered near the tomb of the Muslim saint.

STONE SHOWERS

For 10 days up to 6 August 1992, from 8:00pm to 10:00pm, stones rained down near the tomb of a Muslim saint at a place called Ziyaret Mezrasi, near the village of Çataltepe, Kahta town, Adiyaman. The location is regarded as the most sacred in the whole area. Nobody went out during the stone showers, but the following morning they would collect the matchbox-sized stones, which they regarded as holy, and display them in their houses.

Villagers believed that the saint was punishing them for their bad behaviour. An old man called Haci Ramazan Bozan said that 51 years earlier, after the trees around the tomb had been cut down, an epidemic had carried off nearly 50 villagers. The head official of Kahta town said that although he did not witness a stone shower, he had talked to the villagers and believed that they were telling the truth. He could conceive no motive for inventing the incidents. *Bugün, 6 Aug; Bursa Hakimiyet, 8 Aug 1992.*

YELLOW ICE

On the morning of 10 July, a block of ice fell on the roof of the Yenikent brick factory in Salihli town. Watchman Cemal Kahraman and drivers Nevzat Akça and Mustafa Köksal said they heard a very loud explosion and found pieces of yellow ice on the roof as big as potatoes. There was a smell of rotten fruit which disappeared as the ice melted. They collected some big pieces and sent them for analysis. Other witnesses said the ice block was spherical and came down after a flash which was brighter than lightning. Officials said there were no commercial or military planes in the area. *Hürriyet, 6 Mar + 11 July; Bugün, 11 July 1992.*

Workers display some of the yellow ice that fell on the roof of the Yenikent brick factory at Salihli Town last July.

NAME GAMES

● Mr Sükrü Kurt, his two wives and 17 children, had lived in a cave at Akçadag, Malatya, for a very long time. They had managed to get electricity laid on and had a source of fresh water inside the cave, which they said was better than any luxury apartment. 'Kurt' means wolf. *Bugün, 26 July 1991.*

● A cloud appeared suddenly over the town of Büyükçekmece, near Istanbul, and caused a flood, destroying nearly 150 houses and killing five members of the Bulut family. 'Bulut' means cloud. *Sabah, 7 Oct 1991.*

● People in south-eastern Turkey were warned not to drive on a certain road because of possible avalanches. Yusuf Dagdelen ignored the warning and was buried in his car under the snow after the expected avalanche. 'Dagdelen' means mountain driller. *Meydan, 19 Jan 1992.*

● Mrs Zeynep Mangir, a banker, made nearly 27 billion Turkish lira (about three million pounds) from 70 people by offering higher interest than the official rate, and then running away. She was jailed for 50 years and there are a further 269 charges against her. 'Mangir' means counterfeit. *Meydan, 8 Feb 1992.*

DOUBLE WHAMMY

Construction worker Saban Gül, 40, fell over 80 feet from the sixth floor of a building on the Omürevler quarter in Samsun city, and survived with a broken leg. At the same time in the same quarter, Mustafa Çilingir was fixing curtains at home, standing on a chair. He fell one foot to the ground and was killed. *Hürriyet, 18 Jan + 21 April 1992.*

FAR OUT EAST

KOREAN NOSE JOB

It sounds like one of those bizarre spiv stories: "'Ere, guv, you want 20,000 400-year-old noses? "Noses?" "Year, human noses!"

Well, it seems the South Koreans *do* want them. They're Korean noses. When the Japanese invaded Korea in 1597, their commander ordered his soldiers to cut the heads off Korean generals, and the noses off soldiers and civilians; he'd earlier asked for ears, but realising that cutting them off was unlikely to be fatal, he changed it to noses.

So far, so good; you can understand it as some sort of simple but grisly body-count. Then the weirdness sets in. They actually took all the noses with them back to Japan and buried them in the 'Thousand-nose tomb' (*senbitsuka*) near the town of Bizen in Okayama. Now, aiming to improve relations with Korea, the Japanese government has given permission for the excavation of the tomb and the return of the noses. A welcoming ceremony was planned by 500 Japanese and 500 South Koreans, some of them Buddhist monks, and the noses were expected to find a resting place in Cholla province.
Guardian, 23 Sept; Japan Times, 25 Sept 1992.

SHOGUN GOLD

Tomoyuki Mizuno is searching for a gold treasure worth 200 trillion yen (1.5 trillion dollars). One assumes that 'trillion' is used in the American sense of a million million. Apparently when the Tokugawa Shoguns fell from power in 1868, they hid their entire gold treasury under the slopes of Mount Akagi, 60 miles north of Tokyo, and since 1887 three generations of the Mizuno family have been trying to find it.

An ancestor of the Mizuno family worked in the Shogun's treasury and it appears that engraved maps, a golden statue and a `cryptic parchment' have fallen into the hands of the family. These don't seem to have been much help so far, but in June 1991 Mizuno did succeed in finding a large labyrinth of tunnels. Where? Right beneath his own backyard! As we haven't heard anything else, we assume, alas, that they didn't lead anywhere. *The Standard (Nairobi), 26 Nov 1991.*

BAD SCENES

Politicians in Hong Kong's legislative chamber have been suffering from leukæmia and back pains, and from allegations of forgery and bribery. Well, the last two sound pretty much like normal political activity, but it's alleged that changes to the chamber have affected the *feng shui*, opening its occupants to attack by demons and beams of evil power. A *feng shui* expert has been called in to inspect the place.
D.Telegraph, 22 Feb; S.Times, 1 Mar 1992.

CHINESE FISH WAS A RED HERRING

On 30 October 1992, most of the world's papers and wire-services carried impressive news of a monster sturgeon netted on the Yangtse River four days earlier by researchers from the China Sturgeon Artificial Reproduction Institute in Wuhan. Chinese sturgeon are considered 'living fossils' because of their archaic characteristics, and are a protected species. At 5.2 meters long (17ft) this was the biggest yet. It was said to be a female, possibly 100 years old and weighing 500 kg (1,100 lbs).

The following day, only a few papers sheepishly published the confession by an unnamed Communist official that the whole story had been invented by a junior assistant 'for fun' and passed to a reporter of the state news agency *Xinhua*. The official insisted, though, that the Institute did have a 13ft long sturgeon mounted on a wall, and that beats the entry for the biggest freshwater fish in the *Guinness Book of Records* – a 9ft long catfish caught in Thailand.

SHINING THE SKULL

The fossil man discoveries at Olduvai Gorge on the Serengeti Plain in Tanzania over the last 60 years have made it one of the most important palæontological sites in the world. The Leakey family, Louis, Mary, Jonathan and Richard, have added significantly to the small collection of bones from which the early history of human evolution has been extrapolated.

In the early sixties, Ndibo Mbuika, one of the Africans working for the Leakeys at Olduvai, found a small tooth while collecting stones to mix into concrete. This proved to belong to one of the finest examples of *Homo habilis*. The Leakeys searched the area and gradually assembled many fragments of skull and jaws. When the other African workers returned to camp in the evening, they were unimpressed. They already knew about the skull because one of their number had 'seen' the discovery telepathically and reported details to his friends, including the distinct colouring of the skull and teeth. *Guardian, 11 Aug 1992.*

LOST & FOUND : RINGS & THINGS

Marc Lavine, 26, from Banbury in Oxfordshire, a journalist on the *Banbury Cake* newspaper, with the wallet which was stolen in about November last year in Clapham, South London. It had contained £40 in cash, several cash and credit cards, and the business card of his step mother, Lynn, who lives in South Africa. The man who found the wallet in the street remembered meeting Lynn at a dinner party several years ago. "He phoned someone who knew her better", said Marc, "and they contacted her in Johannesburg to tell her where I could pick up my wallet. The money's all gone, but at least I will have my cards back." *Banbury Cake, D.Mirror, 12 Dec 1992.*

■ Lois O'Keefe lost an heirloom diamond ring and two others from her pocket in August 1991, somewhere in Lincoln, Nebraska. A month or two later, Roger Bumgarner, nine, found the diamond ring, a bit squashed, in a grocery store parking lot. Roger's parents reported the find to the store and waited for the owner to claim it, but no-one ever did. In January 1992, the Bumgarners decided to sell the ring and chose Darold's jewellers in Meridian Park.

By good fortune, O'Keefe had gone to the same jeweller the previous November with a sketch of the ring to assess its value and look for a replacement. Gemologist Paula Thrasher recognised the ring from the sketch. Two days after the publicity, Wayne Miller called O'Keefe's insurance representative to say that

he had found a diamond ring in the same parking lot. It too was returned to a delighted and astonished Mrs O'Keefe. *Lincoln (NB) Journal Star, 11+14 Jan 1992.*

■ Susan Crabtree lost her wedding ring while working in a bottling plant in Whitby, Yorkshire. Four years later, a school cook in Pembroke, Wales (400 miles away) found the ring in a bottle of gravy browning, and traced Susan through the bottlers. *D.Mirror, 1 Mar 1991.*

■ Irene Aldis, who lost her wedding ring in 1932, got it back for her 102nd birthday after it was found in a field at Honingham, Norfolk. *D.Mirror, 4 Aug 1992.*

■ Farmer's wife Mary Thompson lost her 22 carat wedding ring when it

slipped off her finger in a field at White House Farm, Long Newton, near Stockton, Cleveland. Fred Garner, a metal detector enthusiast, turned it up from five inches of soil 23 years later. It was just in time for her 36th wedding anniversary. *Wolverhampton Express & Star, Sun, 15 May 1991.*

■ Rabie Cook exchanged her Bowden, Georgia, high-school class ring with a friend in 1949. Forty years later, it turned up in a garden in Warner Robins, 115 miles from Bowden. Three years after that, the family that found the ring saw a picture of Cook in a Bowden High School yearbook and traced her through her initials, which were carved on the ring. *NY Post, 10 Feb 1992.*

NOWT SO QUEER...

BODY TANNER

A Ugandan woman exhumes her husband's corpse and takes it home "to enjoy the sunshine" every morning, the *Star* newspaper reported. The paper quoted her as saying her husband, buried a year ago, had appeared to her in a dream lamenting that it was chilly in the grave and requesting to be dug up for a "warming stint".

"Each day, when the sun rises, the widow gets the corpse out to bask and returns it after a considerable period", the *Star* reported. The woman, who lives at Muwuggwe village, 75 miles west of Kampala, was helped in her task by her children. *[Reuters] 14 Sept 1992.*

TANGOED

Ettore Gagliano, 83, known as the Priest Basher of Milan, has been charged with 58 assaults on clerics and church personnel. His latest target was a Greek Orthodox priest who had gone to the cathedral for morning prayers when Gagliano leapt out from behind a pillar and hit him. He told the arresting policeman: "I don't like priests. When I see one, I just have to give him a punch in the ear."

Ettore is always acquitted because of his advanced years, but still manages to assault a priest a month on average. He is a great grandfather whose offspring are said to adore him and are proud of his reputation.

At his last court appearance, Ettore told the magistrates: "There is nothing you can do to save the priests from me. I shall bash them all until my last breath." *Direct Action #79, May 1992.*

SPEECHLESS

◆ Singapore student Gregory Ho's girlfriend bit off over an inch of his tongue during a lingering kiss on 21 April 1992. The 28-year-old student was picked up by a police car as he ran along a road clutching the piece of bloodied tongue. He gave no reason why the girl had bitten him. Mr Ho's mother said the assailant, a 22-year-old student, "should not be allowed to get away with it". Doctors operated on her son's tongue and 'tidied up' its torn edges, but were unable to reattach the piece that had been bitten off. "He is very accident-prone", she said, "and we are used to him suffering fractures from his motorcycle adventures, but nothing can beat this". *Rocky Mountain News, 24 April; South China Morning Post, 25 April 1992.*

◆ Another man, Sikh militant Manjit Singh, bit off his *own* tongue to avoid interrogation about a 1985 airliner bombing that killed 339 people off the Irish coast. Bombay doctors sewed it back. *[AP] 5 Aug 1992.*

For other loss of tongues, see *FT61:33.*

BABBLE ON

The private languages developed by some twins is to be studied in a three-year project sponsored by the Mental Health Foundation. Prof Jean Golding of Bristol University will follow the formation of language ability in 150 pairs of twins between the ages of 18 months and three years, with Prof Michael Rutter of London's Institute of Psychiatry, as part of a national project monitoring 15,000 children begun in 1990. Prof Golding believes that as many as 10% of twin pairs develop their own language, but only in rare extreme cases does it adversely affect their adult development by locking them into a mutual dependence. The study will also try to determine why twin boys, in particular, are slower to begin speaking than equivalent singletons. *D.Telegraph, 8 Aug 1992.*

PARTRIDGE FAMILY PET MASSACRE

Stephen Partridge, 35, set out from his home in Sherbourne, Dorset, on 12 September 1992 for an amateur football match. He reversed his Vauxhall Astra over his elderly terrier, Jacko. His wife Annie and son Jack, aged four, first cried in horror and then shouted a warning that Chivers the cat was in front of the car. But Mr Partridge didn't hear and lurched forward, killing Chivers instantly. Jacko died later on the way to the vet.

After giving away a penalty that allowed his opponents to draw the game 1-1, Mr Partridge, a plasterer, drove home and buried his pets. "It was an absolute nightmare of a day", he said. *Edinburgh Evening News, 15 Sept; Wellington (NZ) Dominion, 16 Sept 1992.*

AIR ODDITY

The *Guardian* (7 Oct 1992) notes of the Amsterdam air disaster that the local Reuters bureau had an established training drill involving reporters covering a simulated major news story. The subject chosen was an aircraft crashing into the Bijlmeer district – the very area where the El Al cargo jet came down.

ACTING DEAD

Eleven years ago, Sitali Mboo and his wife Namwaka tended their daughter Joyce in the last days of a short illness, before she died and was buried in the local cemetery in western Zambia. That's what they thought, anyway; but last year one of their sons came back from a local witch finder with the news that she was still alive. She had been kidnapped and forced to live with a 61-year-old man deep in the bush.

The police found the old man, who refused to give Joyce up. He "fought like a tiger" before being overpowered and arrested for possession of firearms. Joyce's coffin was found to contain nothing but a pile of charcoal. The witch finder claimed that Joyce had been kidnapped by Juju men, known locally as Uhole, who sold her to the old man. It is believed that Uhole can put a spell on a chosen individual so that they appear to be dead. The body is then switched for a bag of charcoal or a tree trunk which is buried in its place. In Joyce's case, the question is how they fooled the local health centre and her parents into thinking she had been dead and buried. Joyce herself was unable to explain precisely how the scam was worked. *New African, July 1991.*

DUTCH EXPLOSIONS

In Arnhem, Holland, industrial pollution and leaking pipes has brought a new threat to residents: exploding lavatories. A family living near an industrial zone came home to find their porcelain bowl and cistern smashed to bits for the third time in 30 months. [See *FT46:11*.]

In May 1992, more than 200 people across the country called a consumer hot line in the Hague with reports of TV sets that exploded or caught fire. Hague resident Joke [sic] Scholten said a TV she bought for her daughter wasn't even switched on when it blew up on about 7 May. The consumer safety agency was baffled by the accidents, which occurred in a variety of brands. A fire expert suggested that remote control devices might be the trouble. *Jerusalem Post, 13 Dec 1991; [AP] 21 May 1992.*

NIGERIAN PASSPORT POSER

A Nigerian arrested in Rosendaal, Holland, was carrying 186 false papers, including 29 Nigerian passports, 30 British passports, 74 Dutch work permits, 12 British driving licences and 18 birth certificates. Police said they had not yet identified him. *Observer, 4 Oct 1992.*

SHANGHAI LUCKY NUMBERPLATE

A Shanghai property mogul bid £30,000 – about 160 times the annual wage of a Chinese worker – for a lucky car number plate at an auction in the city. Bidding started at £5,000 for plate number 'Z0518', which pronounced in Chinese sounds similar to "I will become wealthy". *Scotsman, 27 July 1992.*

THE FAR SIDE   By GARY LARSON

© 1983 Chronicle Features
Distributed by Universal Press Syndicate

12-11

OVER-REACTIONS

SOGGY NEWS

Michael Debaets, 49, returned home to Santa Clara, California, with his family after a short holiday on 19 July, to find his newspaper soaked with what he believed to be urine from the dog of his neighbour, Martin Myslinski, 33. A heated argument ensued between Debaets' wife and Myslinski, during which Debaets, without saying a word, shot his neighbour in the chest. Myslinski died half an hour later. *San Francisco Chronicle, 21 July 1992.*

BAD LOSER

Mechanic Ernst Tomachek, 39, was watching the Euro soccer final on TV in Hamburg with his girlfriend, Waltraud. He backed Germany, while she cheered for Denmark. When the Danes won 2-0, Tomachek poured a bottle of schnapps over Waltraud, set her on fire and locked her in a room for 23 hours. *D.Mirror, 20 July 1992.*

PREMEDITATED

Greta Hagel from Stuttgart, out shopping, was splashed by a motorist as he drove though a puddle. She noted the number plate, tracked him down a few days later and shot him dead. *Scottish Sunday Mail, 2 Aug 1992.*

VOLATILE MOTHERS

Yvonne Lindsey, 39, was arrested in St Louis for first-degree assault. She had been watching TV with her 12-year-old son and three other children when she pulled a gun and threatened to shoot the TV unless the boy stopped switching channels with the remote control. When her son told her to go ahead and shoot, she cursed him and shot him through the left wrist. The bullet lodged in his abdomen, and he was in serious but stable condition in hospital. Another 12-year-old had a set-to with his mother in Albuquerque, New Mexico. Debbie Martinez stabbed her son to death because he wouldn't stop playing video games. *[AP] 1 Oct; D.Record, 25 Sept 1992.*

HIDING THE MILK

Joseph Fallar Sr, 61, was arrested on 15 August at his house in Harrison City, Pennsylvania, for the murder of his wife Florene, 50, whom he had stabbed 219 times. "He told me he killed his wife", said Patrolmen John Simcoviak. "He said she would stack the refrigerator full of vegetables, hiding the milk, and he wasn't going to take that any more." *[AP] 17 Aug 1992.*

JOB CREATION

Two undertakers shot each other dead in Paraiba, north eastern Brazil, during an argument over who had the right to conduct the funeral of one of the town's inhabitants. Another undertaker from a neighbouring town was called in to bury all three bodies. *D.Telegraph, 28 July 1992.*

JINGLE BELLS CALLING

At first, police in patrol cars were amused when 'Jingle Bells' began playing on their radios all over Lancaster, Pennsylvania. But after a few hours it became annoying. They called in the Federal Communications Commission, who traced the problem to three musical plastic reindeer in the home of Blanche Cosgrove, which was emitting a signal on the same wavelength as police transmissions. *[AP] 18 Dec 1992.*

NEW HAIR FOR PANCHEN LAMA

The Panchen Lama, who ranks just below the Dalai Lama in the Tibetan hierarchy, died in January 1989. In October 1992, Raidi, a Tibetan member of the Chinese Communist Party's Central Committee and deputy party secretary for the Himalayan region, announced that hair was sprouting from the ears of the dead lama. "This is because Tibetans have their own special treatment for preserving bodies", he said enigmatically. The Chinese government is presently sponsoring the search for a 'soul boy', embodying the reincarnated soul of the Panchen Lama. It is widely suspected that the sacred post will be filled by a political appointee. *[Reuters] 17 Oct 1992.*

SHAGGED OUT

Michael O'Donnell relates a first-rate foaftale in his *Medical Monitor* column (22 Mar 1991). An American TV producer told him that a journalist friend was on his way home on the New York subway. A young woman leaned towards him and asked: "Could you possibly give me your seat? I'm pregnant and I don't feel so good." The journalist obliged. Two stops later, the coach began to empty and he sat beside her. "Forgive me for not offering my seat before you asked for it", he said, "but your condition doesn't really show. How pregnant are you?" "Just half an hour", she replied, "but I'm so tired."

KEEP ROLLING, ROLLING, ROLLING

A 27-wagon train full of cattle travelled 75 miles across the north Indian plains on its own. The driver and his assistant alighted near a station in Uttar Pradesh to mend a hosepipe, and watched helplessly as the train moved off. Chugging along at 35mph, it passed through 16 stations in two and a half hours. Then herdsman Mohammad Anwar clambered over four carriage roofs and dropped into the driver's cab, where he fiddled with all the buttons until he punched one which brought the train to a screeching halt.

In May 1992, a six-year-old Indian boy drove his father's car 360 miles from Hyderabad to Bangalore and was fined 150 rupees (£3) for not having a licence. In the same month, Mr Sreedharam, a 40-year-old mahout (elephant keeper), was trapped for 42 hours on the back of an elephant in musth (heat) that ran amok for 200 miles, through Kerala and Karnataka, before it could be tranquillised and the man rescued. He managed to eat by snatching fruit that had been tied to trees for him along the animal's route. *Independent, 23 July 1991; [Reuters] 7 May; [AFP] 22 May 1992.*

BANG ON TARGET

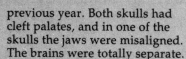

To shoot oneself in the foot once may be considered a misfortune, but to do so three times smacks of carelessness; yet that is what Princeton, West Virginia, gun fanatic Henry Brown managed to do while cleaning his collection of pistols.

Brown, who later told police he had had a few beers, discharged the first shot from a .32, but decided it "didn't really hurt". He picked up a heavier .38 a little clumsily, and a second shot zinged into the same foot as the first. That slug "stung a little", Brown admitted, but he still began to oil the pride of his collection, a .357 Magnum. When that gun also discharged into his mangled extremity, the pain finally forced him to call an ambulance. *D.Mirror, 12 Oct 1992.*

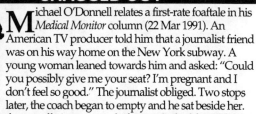

SIAMESE CALF

This is the skull of a double-headed calf born in Charlieville, central Trinidad, on 6 November 1989. "It appears to be the first reported case of its kind", claims Godwin Isitor of the University of the West Indies in Trinidad and Tobago. The calf was delivered by Cæsarian section from a cow which had a prolapsed uterus after delivering a healthy calf the previous year. Both skulls had cleft palates, and in one of the skulls the jaws were misaligned. The brains were totally separate. The cranial fusion resulted in a single complete occipital bone articulated with both crania at their ventrolateral surfaces, with a single foramen magnum. *The Veterinary Record, 2 May; New Scientist, 23 May 1992.*

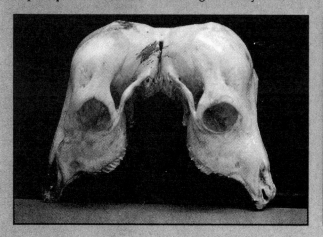
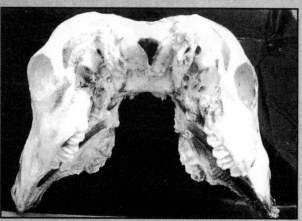

NOT HALF COCKED

The police in Malaga, Spain, were hunting a rapist with two penises. They were alerted, in early November 1992, by a 30-year-old woman who claimed she had been held prisoner in his car for four hours, during which she was attacked and obliged to perform fellatio. She was quite certain of her description of her assailant's distinguishing feature.

For two weeks the police tried in vain to trace the vehicle, but when they switched to questioning medics they found the man in an instant. Brief reports in British papers name him as 26-year-old José Lopez who is suspected of other assaults, the victims of which might be too shocked to come forward. Madrid's *Diario 16* (29 Nov 1992) reveals that the man was examined and positively identified by his latest victim… and then told he could go. Just why he was released after such a positive identification is not said.

The most celebrated case of diphallic terata was a Cuban, Jean Baptista dos Santos – see drawing – whose two full and functioning sets of sexual organs

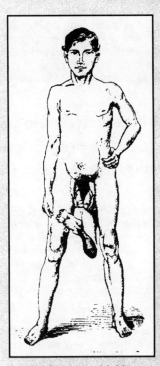

Jan dos Santos – with his extra leg and other bits.

were the consequence of having two crotches between which hung or protruded an extra limb (being the two legs of an absorbed twin, fused together). He was otherwise 'good-looking and well-proportioned'. He was examined medically in Havana in 1865, when he was 22 years old. Our trusty medical reference – Gould and Pyle's *Curiosities and Anomalies of Medicine* – say that "he was possessed of extraordinary animal passion, the sight of a female alone being sufficient to excite him. He is said to use both penises – after finishing with one, continuing with the other." Later accounts do not mention this excessive sexuality.

Gould and Pyle also opine that popular curiosity in such cases has led to exaggeration; "modern observation almost invariably shows that the virile power diminishes in exact proportion to the extent of duplication." In the cases they describe, the penises are usually underdeveloped, lacking testes or otherwise incapable of coitus. The two-pronged man of Malaga, then, was unusual in more than the obvious way.

GOD ORDERS FLAT TYRES

Handbills distributed in the Philippines by The Reserved Manpower Of The Good Wisdom For All Nations said deflating tyres was "God's way of stopping bad deeds". On 28 December, members of the cult rented several jeeps, which carry about 15 passengers apiece, and fanned out across Manila during the evening rush hour. At their destinations, they ordered the drivers out, let out the air from the jeeps' tyres and then ran about deflating tyres on hundreds of other cars, buses and trucks, paralysing traffic throughout the city for some hours. Terrified motorists abandoned their vehicles and fled for cover as armed police chased the cultists, who swarmed through the stalled traffic deflating more tyres, waving streamers and placards bearing religious messages.

When pressed for an explanation, the Reserved Manpower said that their leader Alelio Bernaldez Pen, who has a daily two-hour radio show, told them it was God's will. "This is God's order to let out air", said Honora Dimagila, 44, one of 32 people charged with malicious mischief. "Air is from God. This is the solution to the crisis in our country." Handbills promised a new era of equality and social justice, including a daily wage of $30 for everyone. Annual per capita income in

MAO NOT ROTTING

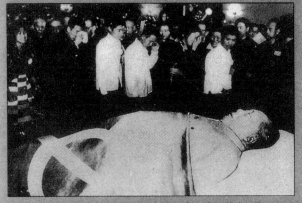

Newspaper reports that the embalmed body of Mao Tse-tung (or 'Zedong' according to the approved transliteration) is rotting in its glass coffin have been hotly denied, according to *China Youth News* on 22 December 1992. The world's greatest tree destroyer died in 1976 at the age of 82 and his body was put on display the following year. Miss Xu Jing, director of the Mao Mausoleum in Beijing, said that "preserving the body for another 200 years would be no problem." She also said rumours that Mao's body had shrunk since 1984 were untrue, adding that "regular, precise checks of the length and weight" of the corpse were made. *[Reuters] 23 Dec 1992.*

VENEZUELA'S TERROR BLOB

A driving hazard unique to Venezuelan highways is a slippery goo called La Mancha Negra – the black stain – although it's really more like a blob, a thick black sludge with the consistency of chewing gum. Motorists are petrified of it: cars meeting the blob spin out of control. Drivers slow to a snail's pace and they don't dare hit the brakes or turn quickly for fear of doing a 360 degree-spin and ending up in the trees. No one knows what the stuff is, where it comes from, or how to get rid of it. The Government has spent millions of dollars trying to identify it; experts have been summoned from the United States, Canada and Europe.

Pulverised limestone

"We clean it away and it come back the next day. It's frightening", said Arturo Carvajal, an engineer and vice president of a company trying to remove the goo from a Caracas highway. The company and half a dozen others have tried washing roads with pressurised water and detergent; blowing the stuff away with pressurised air; drying it up with pulverised limestone; and scraping it away by repeatedly replacing the top layer of asphalt. Nothing works; La Mancha Negra is reproducing, somehow moving from one highway to the next throughout the country.

The stuff first appeared five years ago on the road from Caracas to the city's international airport. The government was patching up the 30-

year-old concrete with asphalt when the first shiny blotches appeared. Nobody took much notice; the blob was in its infancy, covering 50 yards. Then it grew to a mile, and now eight

> "The blob was in its infancy, covering 50 yards. Then it grew to a mile and now eight miles, though it varies according to the weather."

miles, though it varies according to the weather. Rain and heat make it grow; cold and dryness make it shrink. It also prefers tunnels and hills rather than level ground. More than 1,800 motorists have died on this road after encountering the blob.

Big money

There is a suspicion that someone made big money – and unexpectedly created the blob – by laying cheap

asphalt that bleeds oil when the temperature rises. Perhaps someone else is making big money by repeatedly botching the repair job. A federal judge has been investigating charges of corruption since last year, but no charges have been brought.

Total mystery

"It's a total mystery", said Ruth Capriles, Venezuela's foremost whistle-blower and author of a two-volume corruption dictionary, a compendium of the nation's worst cases of graft. Like most Venezuelans, Capriles has her own theories about the blob. She thinks political opponents of President Carlos Andres are dumping oil on the roads to make his government look bad. And then there is the theory that raw sewage from the slums is somehow flowing under the roads and triggering a chemical reaction in the asphalt.

On the airport road, where multiple-car pileups are common, huge red signs warn motorists to slow down and drive with caution. Four nights a week, the uphill side of the road is closed while 50 workers wash, blow, scrape and pulverise the blob. Workers said they finally had the monster on the ropes last April, when they covered it with crushed limestone. It shrivelled and shrunk and all but disappeared; but when motorists complained that the dust made it difficult to breathe, the blob was given a reprieve. Now, Venezuelans are out of answers. *Chicago Tribune, via Providence Sunday Journal (Rhode Island), 9 Aug 1992.*

HITCH-HIKING LIZARDS

Chris Hernandez, 28, opened his car bonnet (or 'hood' as they say in Miami where this yarn is set) to see why the vehicle wasn't steering properly and found a six-foot Asian water monitor lizard wrapped around the engine. It had somehow knocked off the alternator belt and was blocking the steering column. When it refused to come out, Florida game authorities called in Todd Hardwick, manager of Pesky Critters, which specialises in catching exotic animals.

"We squirted it with Joy detergent to make it slippery, then sedated it", he said. "Then we had to take the engine apart. It was one of our roughest extractions." Water monitor lizards, native to southeast Asia, can reach ten feet or more and weigh 100 pounds. Hardwick speculated that this lizard was bought as a small pet, and either escaped or was released years ago in a swampy area adjacent to the new housing development where Hernandez lives. [AP] 7 July 1992.

LIZARD'S SWEDISH HOLIDAY

On 29 June 1992, Ulf Sawart went to stay in his summer house at Juniskär near Sundsvall in mid-Sweden. In the evening he opened the door to air the house. At five o'clock the following morning he awoke to find a large lizard on the floor next to his bed. Terrified, he fled from the house (presumably leaving the door open for the lizard to escape).

Two days later, at Njurunda, about three miles away, farmer Lennert Kappinen encountered a three-foot-long lizard that snapped at him and tore his trouser-leg to shreds. Judging from tracks and Kappinen's description, the lizard was thought to be of the Varanus family, probably *Varanus niloticus*, which lives in some African rivers and can grow to 5ft 6in. How it came to be in the Swedish forests is unknown, but the summer in northern Europe was exceptionally warm (see the saga of the Finnish lions, *FT65:44*). It was thought that such lizards could not survive a Swedish winter. *Expressen, 7 July 1992.*

'EXTINCT' LIZARD DISCOVERED IN SNAKE'S STOMACH

Amateur herpetologist Graham Armstrong came upon a squashed brown snake on a road near Burra, 100 miles north of Adelaide, Australia, in October 1992. Cutting it open, he found the remains of a pygmy blue-tongue lizard, officially extinct since 1959. Scientists subsequently located a colony of the lizards thriving under clumps of grass, and some have been sent to Adelaide Zoo for breeding. [AP] 28 Dec 1992.

MEDICAL BAG

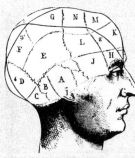

HOLY WATER ALMOST FATAL

A 19-year-old man staged a remarkable recovery after attempting suicide from a 10th floor window in February 1989. He received 53 units of blood and other fluids and was put on a life support machine while surgeons at Birmingham Accident Hospital stabilised multiple skull, spine, pelvic, knee and leg fractures. After six weeks of intensive care, doctors felt satisfied. Then blood poisoning sent him into a rapid decline.

Dr Ian Greaves, senior house officer in orthopædics, and Mr Keith Porter, consultant trauma surgeon, were informed that their patient was being visited daily by an aunt who had come from Ireland. She was 'liberally' anointing him with holy water, analysis of which showed that it contained *Psuedomonas æruginosa*, the bacterium that was almost killing the patient for a second time.

"She was continually reinfecting him, either through his wounds or more likely through spray getting into his nose and mouth", Dr Greaves said. "Once we pointed out the problem, the lady stopped doing it. As far as we understand, it was just tap water that had been blessed by a priest, although some of it comes from holy places such as Lourdes."

After the sprinklings were halted, the patient made a rapid recovery and was discharged three months after admission. The two surgeons said in the *British Medical Journal* (December 1992): "We know of no other case of life threatening infection transmitted in this way."

FOREIGN BODIES

■ Angela Lucas began feeling continuous and acute pain in 1984, soon after having surgery in Charing Cross Hospital, London, to reverse a sterilisation operation. She looked years older and lost three stone, as well as most of her friends, because she was such bad company. A string of X-rays could not identify the problem until the Professor of Surgery at Hammersmith Hospital, Dr Irving Benjamin, took a further X-ray in 1989 and found a hypodermic needle, over two inches long, in her spleen. It took a further three years for the hospital to admit negligence and pay £63,000 damages. *News of the World, 19 April 1992.*

■ An Egyptian farmer thought that his baby son, Abdel Fattah-Sultan, was growing more slowly than normal. He was shocked when an X-ray showed 25 sewing needles piercing his liver, kidneys and lungs. Nothing is said about how they got there. *[Reuters] 6 Nov 1992.*

SHAGGY SOB STORIES

Jesus Martinez, 60, had a heart attack at the wheel of his car on a motorway in Houston, Texas. His Schnauzer dog, Bitsy, leapt into the driving seat, knocked the steering wheel to force the vehicle onto the hard shoulder, and bit his master so that he would take his foot off the accelerator. Mr Martinez recovered in hospital. *D.Star, 18 Sept 1992.*

Jack Fyfe, 75, was paralysed by a stroke at his home in Eastwood, western Sydney, Australia, in December 1991. He was kept alive for nine days by Trixie, his pet sheepdog, a six-year-old kelpie cross, who kept soaking a towel in her drinking bowl and draping it over her owner's face so that he could suck it. She remained at the foot of the bed the whole time, except to fetch water, whenever Mr Fyfe called "water". When the bowl was dry, Trixie took water from the lavatory. Mr Fyfe's daughter eventually found him after he failed to turn up for a family dinner. He had lost more than four stone in weight. *Canberra Times, 29 May 1992.*

In October 1991, faithful pet Trudi the mongrel leapt to her death off cliffs in New South Wales after seeing her master die; his body was found minutes earlier on the rocks below. Trudi was seen howling and barking shortly before jumping.

In July 1992, Amadeo Domancich leaped from a fifth-floor window in Pisa, Italy. He was followed by his faithful dachshund Fritz who went everywhere with him. Amadeo broke a leg, but Fritz was killed. "I'm even more depressed now", said the attempted suicide. *D.Star, 17 Oct 1991; D.Mirror, 20 July 1992.*

VOODOO GUILE

An outraged Haitian government has accused the US of the theft of its voodoo know-how in a bizarre case of industrial espionage. An editorial in the government daily *Le Nouvelliste* claimed that *houngans* (voodoo priests) had been passing secrets to the States in ways that would become illegal if the US signed the UN Bio-Diversity Convention regulating the use of biological resources.

Research by Americans such as Professor Wade Davis of Harvard, author of *Passage of Darkness: the Ethnobiology of the Haitian Zombi*, could be worth millions of dollars, the editorial added. A *houngan* had supplied Davis with samples of frou-frou fish and the zombi cucumber, a substance used to control zombi slaves.

"Haiti's eco-system and biological wealth continues to be plundered", the paper concluded. *D. Telegraph, 15 June 1992.*

TROLLEY TREKS

Comedian Dave Allen has a theory that wire coat hangers breed – put a couple in a wardrobe and soon you will have a dozen. The writer of 'Feedback' in *New Scientist* (7 Nov 1992) wonders whether shopping and luggage trolleys have a life of their own, too: they are often spotted miles from home. In October, s/he spotted a Gatwick airport trolley in a Sussex seaside supermarket, 30 miles from home. By 6 November, the number of Gatwick trolleys had grown to five and the following day it was eight. How did they elude the anti-trolley obstacles found in all airports? Has anyone witnessed such a trolley on its travels?

RABID RACOONS

Rabid raccoons spreading an epidemic of the potentially fatal disease across America have reached the Bronx and Staten Island in New York City. After vets confirmed that a sick raccoon at the Bronx zoo was rabid, the mayor called for all people with animal bites to report to the health department. The epidemic started in West Virginia in the mid-1980s, when fur trappers unwittingly released six rabid animals into the wild in the hope of increasing stocks of pelts. *D.Telegraph, 29 July 1992.*

HAIR RAISING

A falcon swooped on an elderly visitor to the Milky Way Falconry in North Devon, grabbed his toupée and carried the furry object of desire to its perch to eat. The falconer quickly retrieved the toupée, but it was unwearable. *Western Morning News (Plymouth) 26 Aug 1992.*

DOGGED BY MISFORTUNE

The *British Medical Journal* in May 1992 carried a snapshot of an Irish red setter. The owner, a 22-year-old man, found that the animal had only one ball. This prompted the man to check his own tackle – and, blow me, *he only had one as well!* "This is a new twist to the widely held belief that people may resemble their pets", says the BMJ. An investigative operation revealed that the man's testis had failed to descend, and this was corrected. *Guardian, 22 May; Independent, 26 May 1992.*

STRANGE DEATHS

✝ Believing that her husband had betrayed her, Vera Czermak of Prague jumped from her third storey window – and landed on him as he passed below. She recovered in hospital, but he died instantly. *D.Record, 28 Nov 1992.*

✝ Mrs Dorothy Johnson's two-year-old great-grandson offered her a jelly sweet before taking off his hat to let her see his new, extremely short, haircut. The 72-year-old Birmingham widow found this so hilarious that she burst into uncontrolled laughter – and choked to death on the sweet. *D.Telegraph, 28 Oct 1992.*

✝ Nakorn Hawthong, 30, was fishing in the Thai province of Uthai Thani last November when he was choked to death by a fish he put between his teeth, because he didn't have a basket to put it in and wanted to carry on fishing. This is not a unique death: 30 years ago, for instance, Mario Golfo of Messina, Sicily, tried to stun a small sole by biting on its head, but it wriggled from his grasp, lodged in his throat and choked him. *[Reuters] 11 Nov 1992; Canberra Times, 11 Feb 1963.*

✝ Salvatore Chirilino picked a four-leaf clover on a clifftop in Vibo Marina, Italy – then plunged 150ft to his death. "He slipped on the wet grass", said his wife, "and went over the side". A police spokesman added: "It's just not lucky for everyone". *D.Mirror, 20 Nov 1992.*

✝ Don Giacomo Perini, a priest, cursed the rain as he stood outside his church in Alto Adige, Italy; whereupon a cross, loosened by the rain, fell on his head and killed him. *Sun, 6 Oct 1992.*

✝ Giacario Burranti booby-trapped his Milan shop with a bomb after his tenth burglary; he was blasted to death when he came in and forgot to switch the device off. *News of the World, 22 Nov 1992.*

✝ Larry Moor, 45, a snake handler who founded a group to dispel the fear and misunderstanding of snakes, died after being bitten by his Egyptian cobra, according to Canadian police. Moor, of Langley, near Vancouver, ran screaming into the street for help but died within seconds. *[AP] 3 Aug 1992.*

✝ Four boys in the western Algerian city of Maghnia, aged eight to 15, died shortly after eating soup. Their mother had inadvertently brought home a poisonous snake hidden in vegetables which she put in the family refrigerator. The snake, seeking warmth, slithered into a soup pot and discharged its venom into the soup. *[AFP] 4 May 1992.*

A CLOSER SHAVE

Arthur Ekvall, 29, told police that on 8 June 1992 he awoke with "an incredible explosion in my head. I thought I had an aneurysm". He saw his former roommate, Jesse Solis, 25, reloading a crossbow. Realising he had been hit by an arrow, he got up and wrestled with Solis and eventually disarmed him. Solis ran out in his underwear and took off in Ekvall's pickup truck.

Ekvall called the police. They were stunned to find the parking lot attendant conscious, but with the arrow protruding from his head. "You can see the arrow when I open my mouth", he told them. "I can also see it out my left eye if I work at it." It had entered the base of his neck and travelled through his head until it came out above his left eye.

Ekvall was admitted to Mercy Hospital, San Diego,

California, while Solis was arrested in the eastern suburb of El Cajon about two hours after the shooting. He told police he acted in self-defence during a struggle. The attack was believed to stem from a lovers' quarrel. The two men had lived together for six months, but Ekvall moved out in December 1991.

It took surgeons more than two hours to cut a hole in Ekvall's forehead, unscrew the arrowhead and then remove the arrow's shaft from the base of his skull. His condition was upgraded from 'critical' to 'serious' and then to 'good'. Amazingly, he suffered no brain, nerve or eye damage. He said he felt "just fine". Two days later, he was expected to make a full recovery with a possible scar over his left eye and was to be released from hospital the next day. [AP] 10+11 June 1992.

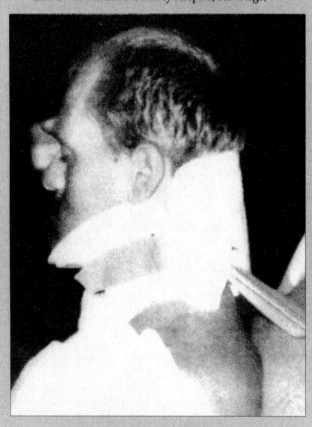

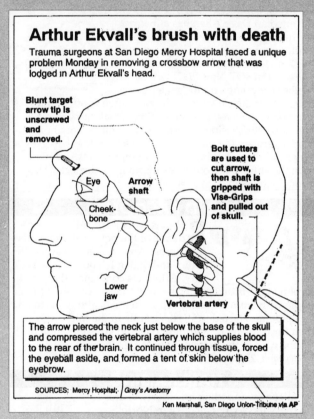

Arthur Ekvall's brush with death

Trauma surgeons at San Diego Mercy Hospital faced a unique problem Monday in removing a crossbow arrow that was lodged in Arthur Ekvall's head.

Blunt target arrow tip is unscrewed and removed.

Eye

Arrow shaft

Cheek-bone

Bolt cutters are used to cut arrow, then shaft is gripped with Vise-Grips and pulled out of skull.

Lower jaw

Vertebral artery

The arrow pierced the neck just below the base of the skull and compressed the vertebral artery which supplies blood to the rear of the brain. It continued through tissue, forced the eyeball aside, and formed a tent of skin below the eyebrow.

SOURCES: Mercy Hospital; | Gray's Anatomy

Ken Marshall, San Diego Union-Tribune via AP

FORTEAN FANC

MUG SETS

Take tea in style with our set of four Fortean Times mugs. Illustrated by Hunt Emerson the designs comprise of The Cats Of War, Drunken Bull, Falling Cow and Forest Fire Death. Black designs on high-quality white ceramic mugs.

CODE FTM - £15.00 per set.

BOOKS

FORTEAN TOMES is a series of facsimile reprints of early issues of The Fortean Times (formerly simply titled The News). Each book covers a wide range of fascinating subjects from feral children to spontaneous human combustion to UFO abduction.

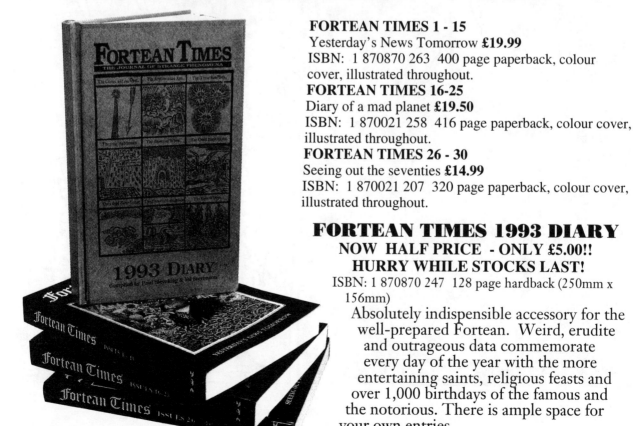

FORTEAN TIMES 1 - 15
Yesterday's News Tomorrow **£19.99**
ISBN: 1 870870 263 400 page paperback, colour cover, illustrated throughout.
FORTEAN TIMES 16-25
Diary of a mad planet **£19.50**
ISBN: 1 870021 258 416 page paperback, colour cover, illustrated throughout.
FORTEAN TIMES 26 - 30
Seeing out the seventies **£14.99**
ISBN: 1 870021 207 320 page paperback, colour cover, illustrated throughout.

FORTEAN TIMES 1993 DIARY
NOW HALF PRICE - ONLY £5.00!!
HURRY WHILE STOCKS LAST!
ISBN: 1 870870 247 128 page hardback (250mm x 156mm)

Absolutely indispensible accessory for the well-prepared Fortean. Weird, erudite and outrageous data commemorate every day of the year with the more entertaining saints, religious feasts and over 1,000 birthdays of the famous and the notorious. There is ample space for your own entries.

ES ...

The Devil'

The legend of Doctor Faustus, who sold his soul to the Devil in exchange for supernatural powers, has inspired literary works by Marlowe and Goethe among others and operas by Gounod and Berlioz, Boito and Busoni. **PETER BAYLISS**, author of many articles on history, folklore and the occult, pieces together the life of the shady historical figure behind the myth.

ABOVE: Faustus signs the contract with Mephistopheles in blood.

A ccording to legend, Doctor Faustus made a pact with the Devil, signed in his own blood. Under the name of Mephistopheles, the Devil would be his servant for 24 years, fulfilling the doctor's every desire. At the end of that time, Faustus' immortal soul would be forfeit.

All luxuries were bestowed on him. The story told of him passing through Heaven and Hell and remote parts of the Earth. He went to the Pope's palace and played tricks on him. Although not allowed to marry (marriage being a Christian sacrament), he had many lovers, including Helen of Troy.

It was said that at midnight, at the end of his allotted 24 years, a great wind took the house; hissing snakes and screams for mercy were heard; and in the morning his body, "most monstrously torn and fearful to behold", was found outside the house.

This version of the story first appeared in print in the famous *Faustbuch* published by Johann Spies in Frankfurt in 1587. It was a collection of popular anecdotes about the magician based on earlier manuscript sources.

An English translation entitled *The Historie of the Damnable Life and Deserved Death of Doctor John Faustus* appeared in the early 1590s. The earliest surviving copy, probably a second edition, is dated 1592. The first edition, or a manuscript copy, is thought to have been the source of Christopher Marlowe's play *The Tragicall Historie*

of the Life and Death of Doctor Faustus, first performed in the London playhouses in about 1592.

There is a story that the actors suddenly noticed one devil too many on stage. They fled and spent the night in prayer and repentance. Beneath the humour is a serious point about the strength of stage illusion and total belief in the supernatural. It was an age which believed in devils and worried about the fate of Faustus.

The legend was already well known by the time of Marlowe's play. Preachers used it as a warning to those forsaking God and consorting with the Devil; but it was more than mere fable. There was an actual character upon whom the legend was based - a scholar and unscrupulous magician born in 15th century Germany.

Faustus's precise identity has been the subject of much academic research over the centuries. An assortment of letters, diaries and records, many written years or decades after the magician's death, provide conflicting information. One source mentions "a certain sooth sayer by the name of Georg Faust, the demigod of Heidelberg, a mere braggart and fool". Another refers to "Johannes Faust" who "studied magic at Cracow [and] practised his art...with many lies and much fraud". All seem to agree he had 'an evil reputation' and that he was a confidence-trickster and 'a braggart'. It was said "his contemporaries had a great contempt for him, not unmixed with fear". ·

One chronicle of 1564-66 warns against soothsaying being 'godless' and 'in the highest degree dangerous'. An example is given of "what happened to the notorious Faustus. After he had practised during his lifetime many marvels...he was finally killed at a ripe old age by the evil spirit...In his day he was as remarkable a sorcerer as could be found in German lands in our times...He became an old man and, as it is said, died miserably. From all sorts of reports and conjectures, many have thought that the evil spirit, whom in his lifetime he used to call his brother-in-law, had killed him."

The American scholar Frank Baron has carried out much research into the true identity of Faustus. His findings, published in Munich in 1978, bear the title *Doctor Faustus from History to Legend*.

The original Faustus, he says, was one Georg Helmstetter, born about 1466/67 in the village of Helmstadt near Heidelberg. In 1483, he registered in the University of Heidelberg, where he studied medicine and philosophy. After a year and a half, he took his bachelor's examination and three years later his master's degree (1 March 1487), ranking second among ten candidates. He

> "Faustus' precise identity has been the subject of much academic research over the centuries."

Brother-in-Law

OPEAN CULTURE, ONE WHICH ARTISTS AND WRITERS RETURN
OKS BEHIND THE LEGEND TO REVEAL THE REAL DR FAUSTUS

remained at Heidelberg until 1489, fulfilling an obligation that newly graduated masters should teach for two years in the Faculty of Arts.

Some time between 1487 and 1507, Helmstetter adopted the Latinized name of Faustus. Baron points out that 'Faust' is actually an erroneous translation of the Latinized name into German. Not until Goethe wrote his epic drama *Faust* at the close of the 18th century did 'Faustus' become generally changed to 'Faust'. (Goethe's main sources for the story seem to have been a 1674 version by Nikolaus Pfitzer and an abridgement of this which appeared in 1725.)

In the time of Faustus, magic, alchemy and astrology were classed as 'natural philosophy'. The study of such things was becoming respectable as well as popular. The study of the secular 'humanities' was a reaction against the mediæval stranglehold of Christianity. There was an upsurge of interest in classical education and the ancient occult sciences, although Renaissance scholars were careful to exclude the prohibited black magic from 'natural magic'. Surviving manuscripts from the library at Heidelberg suggest that interest in astrology was particularly strong there.

After teaching at the University, Faustus became a wandering scholar and astrologer, boasting of his reputation as a magician. Travelling widely in Europe, he became

> "After teaching at the university, Faustus became a wandering scholar and astrologer, boasting of his reputation as a magician."

renowned for eccentric scholarship and miraculous powers. Says Philipp Begardi in his *Index sanitatis* of 1539:

"Some years ago [Faustus] travelled through almost all countries, principalities and kingdoms, and...bragged much about his great skill, not only in medicine, but also in chiromancy, nigromancy, physiognomy, crystal gazing and similar arts. And he... signed himself 'The philosopher of philosophers'. The number of those who complained to me they were cheated by him was very great. Now, his promises were great [but] his deeds, as I hear, were very petty and fraudulent. But, in taking or – to speak more accurately – in receiving money, he was not slow. And afterwards also, on his departure, as I have been informed, he left many to whistle for their money."

There were numerous similar reports of his fraudulent dealings, general malpractice and trickery. He was an unscrupulous rogue, Baron

Faust und Mephistophiles.
Dr. Fauſt. Nach einem Gemälde des Chriſtoph von Sichem. (Zu S. 829.)

Faust commands Mephistopheles to appear in the form of a Franciscan friar. Illustration by Christoph von Sichem from Scheible's *Das Kloster*.

Mephistopheles conjours tempting visions for the recumbent magician, in an illustration accompanying an article on Berlioz's *La Damnation de Faust*.

seems to suggest, rather than the devil-dealing black magician of popular imagination. He certainly claimed to have called up spirits, thus inspiring respect and fear. Stories about him grew with the telling.

One tale relates how he sent a spirit into the monastery at Luxheim in the Vogues mountains, "which [the monks] could not get rid of for years and which bothered them tremendously". It seems he sent them "the restless guest... for no other reason than that once upon a time they did not wish to put him up overnight."

Such sensational stories were eagerly seized upon by Reformation leaders such as Martin Luther. In fact, the influence of Luther was crucial to the development of the legend. While Faustus was still alive, Luther identified him as a close associate of the Devil. Later authors made full use of the connection. The fate of Faustus was the consequence of forsaking true religion for the lustful pleasures offered by the Devil.

"Mention was made of the conjurors and the art of magic and how Satan blinded men", recalled Antonius Lauterbach of a conversation with Luther in 1537. "Much was said about Faustus, who called the Devil his brother-in-law..."

Luther was more concerned with the Devil than Faustus, and wasn't interested in incidental stories about the magicians's exploits. For these we must look elsewhere. In 1548, the Protestant pastor Johannes Gast wrote about Faustus in the second volume of his *Conviviales sermones*. He mentions how the magician stayed overnight in 'a certain very rich monastery'. It seems that he complained about some wine 'of indifferent quality and without flavour' which was placed before him.

Gast says that "Faustus requested that [the monk] draw from another cask a better wine, which it was the custom to give to nobles." His request being refused, he said to the monk: "In a short time you shall see marvels, you inhospitable brother."

The story continues: "Burning with rage, [Faustus] left early in the morning without saying farewell and sent a certain raging devil who made a great stir in the monastery." This 'devil' seems to have been a poltergeist, because it "moved things about both in the church and in the cells of the monks, so that they could not get any rest. Finally, they deliberated whether they should leave the monastery or destroy it altogether. And so they wrote to the Count of the Palatinate, who took the monastery under his own protection and ejected the monks to whom he furnishes supplies from year to year and uses what is left for himself. It is said that, to this very day, if monks enter the monastery, such great disturbances arise that those who live there can have no peace."

Elsewhere, Gast recounts dining with Faustus in Basel. The magician "gave to the cook various kinds of bird to roast. I do not know where he bought them or who gave them to him, since there were none for sale at the time. Moreover, I never saw any like them in our regions. He had with him a dog and a horse which I believe to have been demons and which were ready for any service."

ABOVE: An engraving by E A Abbey from *Harpers Monthly* (1883) showing Faust conducting psychical research.

RIGHT: Title page from the oldest extant book about Dr. Faustus, *History of Dr. Johannes Faust, the Notorious Sorcerer and Master of Black Magic*, which was printed by Johann Spies of Frankfurt, in 1587.

TOP RIGHT: Title page from the oldest extant English chapbook edition of Christopher Marlowe's *The Tragicall Historie of the Life and Death of Doctor Faustus*, published by John Wright, London, 1631.

BOTTOM RIGHT: Engraving by Rembrandt van Rijn, dated 1652, showing Dr Faustus watching a magic disc in his study.

HISTORIA

Von D. Johan̄ Fausten/ dem weitbeschreyten Zauberer vnd Schwartzkünstler/ Wie er sich gegen dem Teuffel auff eine benandte zeit verschrieben/ Was er hierzwischen für seltzame Abenthewr gesehen/ selbs angerichtet vnd getrieben/ biß er endtlich seinen wol verdienten Lohn empfangen.

Mehrertheils auß seinen eygenen hinderlassenen Schrifften/ allen hochtragenden/ fürwitzigen vnd Gottlosen Menschen zum schrecklichen Beyspiel/ abschewlichem Exempel/ vnnd trewhertziger Warnung zusammen gezogen/ vnd in Druck verfertiget.

JACOBI IIII.

Seyt Gott vnderthänig widerstehet dem Teuffel/ so fleuhet er von euch.

CVM GRATIA ET PRIVILEGIO.

Gedruckt zu Franckfurt am Mayn/ durch Johann Spies.

M. D. LXXXVII.

Gast says that he "was told that the dog at times assumed the form of a servant and served the food. However, the wretch [Faustus] was destined to come to a deplorable end, for he was strangled by the Devil and his body on its bier kept turning face downward even though it was five times turned on its back." (It was Luther's belief that the Devil strangled his victims and twisted their heads.)

In 1562, Johannes Manlius brought out a collection of sayings or anecdotes, based on the lectures of Philipp Malanchthon, the theologian who was his teacher at the University of Wittenberg. Published in numerous editions and reprints, this book was the most easily available source on Faustus before the Spies *Faustbuch*.

"A few years ago, this Johannes Faustus", wrote Manlius, "on the day before his end, sat very downcast in a certain village in the Duchy of Württemberg. The innkeeper asked him why, contrary to his custom and habit, he was so downcast (he was otherwise a most shameful scoundrel, who led a very wicked life, so that he was again and again near to being killed because of his dissolute habits).

"Then he said to the innkeeper in the village: 'Don't be frightened tonight'. In the middle of the night, the house was shaken. When Faustus did not get up in the morning, and when it was now almost noon, the innkeeper went with several others into his bedroom and found him lying near the bed with his face turned towards his back. The Devil had killed him."

It would seem more plausible that one of his many angry and defrauded human creditors was responsible; but there are no actual accounts of the demise of the historical Faustus, only those based on the legend.

Marlowe must have thoroughly enjoyed wringing out every last drop of pathos from the final scene of his play:

No, Faustus, curse thyself, curse Lucifer
That have deprived thee of the joys of heaven.

The clock striketh twelve.
O, it strikes! it strikes! now, body, turn to air,
Or Lucifer will bear thee quick to hell.

Thunder and lightning.
O soul, be changed into little water drops
And fall into the ocean, ne'er be found.
My God! My God! look not so fierce on me!

Enter DEVILS
Adders and serpents, let me breathe awhile! Ugly hell, gape not! come not Lucifer!
I'll burn my books - ah, Mephistopheles!

Exeunt with him.

FT

MONSTER MAN

BOB RICKARD talks to BILL GIBBONS about unknown animals, cannibals and extortion

In 1985 Bill Gibbons led the four-man Operation Congo expedition, which braved disease, dangerous animals, cannibal pygmies, corruption and crazy guides in search of *mokele-mbembe,* a dinosaur-like creature, said to be lurking in the swamps. Gibbons, a 35-year-old Scot, sincerely believes the creature is out there. He could be right!

ABOVE: The Operation Congo 2 team setting off from Impfondo – (from left) Tom Hall (in Landrover), Sarah Speer, pastor Matawa Paul, Liz Addy and Bill Gibbons.
BELOW: This imaginative depiction of the mokele-mbembe painted by Tim Stimpson for the cover of *BBC Wildlife* magazine, December 1984 – inspired Bill Gibbons' vocation for monster-hunting.

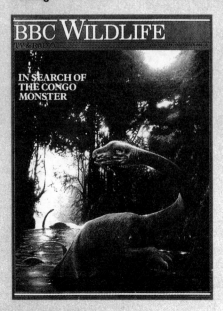

FT – You've just returned from your second expedition to the Congo – did you spot the famous monster?
BG – No. Actually, it was a reconnaissance for a more thorough expedition next year – and at the same time we took medical supplies to a Canadian mission in the north of the country. We were also able to assist Sarah Speer in her medical work, and Liz Addy, an optometrist who is also a seasoned explorer, came with us and was able to dispense 200 pairs of free spectacles. This gave us a legitimate reason to scout around on the unexplored upper reaches of the Bai River, and we pushed our way through to two unexplored lakes – Lake Tibeke and Lake Fouloucou.

FT – Your first trip was deliberately sabotaged [see report in *FT47:22*]. That must have been frustrating?
BG – Yes, it was fraught with difficulties from the beginning. It had taken us 18 months and a great deal of correspondence just to reach Brazzaville. The Congolese government is typical of many African administrations; they won't actually get moving on your case until you turn up on their doorstep. Eventually, we

stayed seven months. Much of that was wasted time – some of it with the absurd behaviour of Marcelin Agnagna, a representative of the Department of the Interior.

This supposed man of science actually believed people could turn into wild animals at night and go hunting in the forest. He would have nightmares and interpret them as warnings forbidding us to travel to certain places or from collecting specimens of wildlife. He later wrote to the International Society of Cryptozoology admitting that he had deliberately led us away from areas which were likely habitats for *mokele-mbembe.*

Despite all that, we did come back with the remains of an unidentified monkey, and specimens of several species of fish and insects which had not previously been classified.

FT – You obviously thought it was worth going back. What encouraged you?
BG – Our closest contact with *mokele-mbembe* had been the examination of fairly faint indentations in the ground which might have been footprints of the creature.

They led out of a swamp, through a small wooded area and then a grassy area and into the Likouala River. They had been shown to us by Immanuel Mongoumela, the elephant hunter, who told us about his own sightings of *mokele-mbembe*. This was very encouraging.

Immanuel was not afraid to tell us about his sightings; nor was a large Congolese man called Ebitass, at Boha village, who had also seen the animals, mainly at Lake Tele, on solo fishing trips. Agnagna, on the other hand, often refused to translate the accounts which other informants were willing to tell us. Perhaps the man who helped us most was the missionary pastor Eugene Thomas, who has lived there since 1955. He told us of many individuals known to him who had told him of encounters with strange animals, such as monstrous pythons up to 20 metres long (apx 60ft). He himself saw the giant crocodile known as the *mahamba*, back in the 1960s.

FT – You are concentrating your efforts in relatively unexplored regions...

BG – Most definitely. For one thing, the increase in river traffic must have pushed any remaining creatures up-river into the remoter regions of the Likouala swamps. We found the Bai River to be fairly tranquil; there was no motorized river traffic at all apart from our own recent 'recce'. Similarly, Gene Thomas, who is always alert for new information, thinks we should be looking in remote swamps north of Epéna, on the Likouala River, where there are many unexplored river channels, undisturbed by noisy outboards and frequented only by the occasional fisherman in a dugout. 'Operation Congo 3' will visit these areas.

FT – The popular conception of *mokele-mbembe* is of a sauropod that has survived from the time of the dinosaurs. What do you think it might be?

BG – We can't discount the possibility of a relict species in this region because there are dozens of examples of fish, insects and reptile species that have survived from the Mesozoic times. The coelacanth, now being caught alive regularly off Madagascar, is the famous example.

I think *mokele-mbembe* bears a close resemblance to a reconstructed fossil dinosaur called Atlantosaurus. It was a small sauropod, reaching about 30 feet in length, and its remains have been found in southern and eastern Africa. We heard from native witnesses descriptions that tally remarkably: the body size is usually likened to a forest elephant or a large hippo, the neck is always very long and the tail long and slender and flexible, leaving frying-pan-sized three-toed prints.

On our second expedition, pygmies paced out the length of animals they'd seen – about 30 feet, with long necks, perhaps six feet and about the thickness of my thigh, with a small slender head rather like a lizard's – feeding off vegetation. It must spend a lot of time eating considering its size.

The *mokele-mbembe* seems also to be quite solitary. It doesn't move about in herds, as some palæontologists have supposed sauropods did. As a defensive move, they submerge very quickly and stay under for a long time. It's too big to be a monitor lizard of any kind. If it isn't a relict species, it might be an animal new to science which happens to *look* like a dinosaur. One day we'll find out...

FT – What other unknown creatures lurk in the swamps?

BG – Gene Thomas told us of an experience he and his wife Sandy had in December 1989, involving a huge unknown animal on the upper reaches of the Likouala River. As they were poling their way through a river channel choked with floating grass, they realised the sound of their

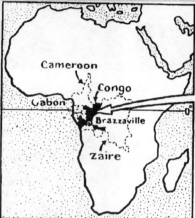

ABOVE: Witch Doctors from the old Belgian Congo.
LEFT & BOTTOM: The vast Likouala swamps stretch from Gabon and Cameroon to the west coast of Zaire in the heart of Africa, and are flooded in the rainy season – a watery kingdom fit for giant herbivores.

It took two days to paddle up the Bai River, from Kinami to Lakes Tibeke and Fouloucou.

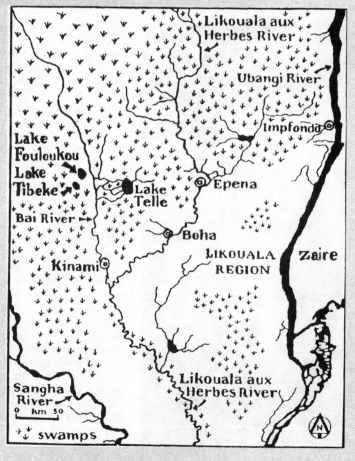

ABOVE RIGHT: Cutting a swathe through the jungle
ABOVE LEFT: Bill Gibbons (left) examining the cast of a bigfoot footprint.
RIGHT: View of the unexplored Lake Fouloucou, a likely haunt of the mokele-mbembe, which was surrounded by dense walls of vegetation.
BELOW: An 8m aluminium pirogue lent to the expedition by the Catholic Mission in Epena.

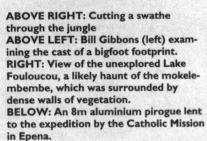

voices had disturbed a very large creature. They think it must have been crossing the wide stretch of water, just twenty yards ahead of them as they emerged from the swamp grass. It submerged quickly, setting up a huge swell of water. Their 27 feet long wooden dugout was buffeted by waves two feet high.

The Congolese in their group began to panic. One of them started the outboard motor – it took them 15 minutes to cross that body of water. Gene Thomas wanted to stay there awhile, to see if the animal would return, but the Congolese were too frightened. Gene emphasised that it submerged completely so it couldn't have been an elephant. This was the second time Gene Thomas had observed this diving defence; the earlier occasion was when he accompanied Roy Mackal's expedition.

FT – The locals seem to hold these mystery animals in considerable awe. Is it merely superstitious?
BG – The pygmies are reluctant to talk, not so much about the *mokele-mbembe* itself, but about its stamping ground. They fear that if they help us see or film one, great misfortune, even death, will befall them.

I think this can be traced back to an

incident in 1960, when one of these creatures, allegedly, was speared to death and eaten at Lake Tele by forest dwelling pygmies. Many of those who feasted on the monster later died of a mystery illness, which might have been due to unknown toxins or infections carried by the monster. Gene Thomas told me he had known two of the pygmies involved in the actual killing of the animal, and they had described to him its weird cry as it was attacked.

The misfortune that followed the eating of that monster-flesh has been mythologised, and now they readily blame their troubles – especially those to do with foreigners – on the monster. When Ebitass' wife died of TB, the pygmies speculated that this was because he had talked openly of *mokele-mbembe* to white outsiders. They gave the same reason for the year-long illness (malaria and dysentery) of Immanuel Mongoumela.

Where the largely animistic pygmies still hold the creature in awe, the reticence of the Christianised Congolese is due more to their fear of the *ndami*, the tribal elders.

FT – Is cannibalism still practised in the region?
BG – As recently as 1990, there was a big case in Impfondo where six high court magistrates from Brazzaville tried about two dozen people for cannibalism. A group of Congolese, who practised a local form of witchcraft called *ndoki*, had kidnapped and murdered a number of people including some pygmies. They had cooked and eaten parts of bodies and sold other bits to friends. There are still areas – particularly in Zaire – where no one dares go for fear of active cannibal pygmies.

Apart from this recent case, which had to do with witchcraft, I'm not aware of cannibalism practised anywhere in the Congo Republic.

FT – You seem to have found a very practical way to explore, combining it with humanitarian efforts.
BG – It helps in establishing good relations with the indigenous tribes. Some of the earlier expeditions – not mine – took out cigarettes and alcohol as gifts for the pygmies; but I don't agree with that. Practical aid is a better way of thanking the local people for their help with the expeditions.

FT – One hears that the antics of earlier expeditions, especially in handing out largesse, have made it more difficult for each new expedition. Did you find this?
BG – On our first trip, the Boha villagers wanted 100,000 Congolese francs – in the end we had to give them 30,000, plus gifts and food supplies. They have be-

Colonel Percy Fawcett, who vanished in the Amazon jungles in 1925, fires at a 62-foot-long giant anaconda during his South American expedition.

come totally mercenary. In 1991, a Japanese film crew at Lake Tele were actually held to ransom by the Boha villagers. They had already paid the elders one million Congolese francs, when they demanded another five million on top. The Japanese refused and the villagers retaliated by taking four of the team hostage. Two of them had to travel to Brazzaville to get the money.

I can't contribute very much to the actual missionary work; they have everything planned out for the next ten years, establishing a 'culturally-appropriate' church among the Aka pygmies. I can help by taking out anything they need, like books, medical supplies, and so on. To help this work, I'm establishing a charity called Mission Aid, primarily to give financial and material assistance to missionaries in Third World countries. When the registration comes through, I'll be concentrating on this full time – and the expeditions.

FT – How did your interest in cryptozoology begin?
BG – As a small boy, in Stranraer, I was very excited by films with animated dinosaurs. I remember sitting cross-legged on the floor of my granny's house in front of a big old black and white television, watching Conan Doyle's *Lost World*. That fired my young imagination, and predisposed me towards the whole subject of survival of creatures from a bygone age. Now that I've been to the Congo twice, and I'm contemplating my

third trip, I feel that this is my destiny. I'm resolved to continue until I find something.

After a spell in Belize, with the British Army in the late 1970s, I met Mark Rothermell who enthralled me with tales of his adventures up the Amazon. In fact we originally planned to go up the Amazon. We had been aware of the earlier discussions about *mokele-mbembe* creatures in the Congo; but in December 1984, in a newsagent, I saw it depicted on the cover of a *BBC Wildlife* magazine, and I was thunderstruck. I took it back to show Mark, and we listened to Roy Mackal's talk about his hunt for *mokele-mbembe* on Radio 4. That's how we were hooked… We knew this was what we wanted to do too.

FT – That brings me to my final question – what next?
BG – Beyond 'Operation Congo 3' in April 1994, Mark Rothermell and I are planning at least four other expeditions, but their timing and order will depend upon the outcome of the Congo trip. We plan to go up the Amazon, close to the border with Bolivia; and to the forests of Queensland, and to Papua New Guinea.

There could be a fourth trip to the Congo to cover other parts of the Likouala swamps. You could go out there for a few weeks and get lucky, but really you need to spend at least a year in the field to do any useful surveillance – plus a lot of luck and patience.

FT – What will you look for in these areas?
BG – In New Guinea there are reports of giant lizards and enormous salt-water crocodiles, 30-40 feet long. In Australia we'll be looking for the famous Queensland 'tiger-cat' using special traps and remote controlled camcorders. Up the Amazon, we'll be hunting the *Sucuriju Gigante*, a giant snake.

We are also considering a trip to the Tromelin Islands, 400 miles north of Mauritius. These are a small group of coral islands which have remained unexplored. Roy Mackal has speculated that dodos might have survived there… There's only one way to find out!

I'd like to record my gratitude to Bernard Heuvelmans; without his books and writings – not to mention his letters and advice – people like me wouldn't have a clue where to look for unknown animals. **FT**

In Cameroon, the *mokele-mbembe* is known as the *jago-nini* or *n'ymala*; and this February a different expedition is setting off to search for the remote river caves favoured by the monster. The five-week, 10-man expedition has been organised by Barry Marshall of Wildquest and children's TV presenter Tommy Boyd.

ACCORDING TO REPORTS, YETIS AND WILDMEN HAVE BEEN POPPING UP ALL OVER THE PLACE RECENTLY, FROM THE CAUCASUS TO MONGOLIA. MIKE DASH LOOKS AT THE INTREPID EXPLORERS WHO GO...

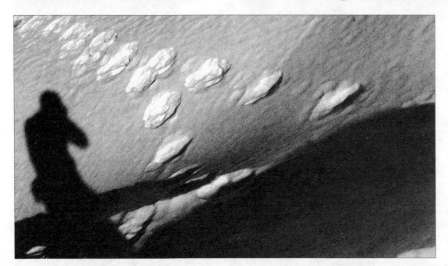

"Boom boom." Not Basil Brush's catchphrase, but the call of a less unlikely-sounding animal, the alma – or almasty – of the Caucasus mountains east of the Black Sea. It is a sound that a Franco-Russian expedition heading for the area last summer was hoping to record for posterity – preferably along with some physical evidence and photographs of the elusive yeti-like creatures locals have long claimed still inhabit the more out-of-the-way areas of an already remote region.

The expedition was to be led by a remarkable 73-year-old Russian, Dr Zh. I. Kofman (her name is usually given as Marie-Jeanne Koffman in western press reports) and a French documentary maker, Sylvain Pallix, who was to raise the cash for its high-tech equipment.

The ten scientists who made up the main body of the party (they were to be accompanied by a TV crew, as seems inevitable these days) were promised infra-red cameras, remote controlled helicopter camera platforms, motorised hang gliders and motorbikes – all of which were to be decked out with sponsors' stickers. The aim, according to Pallix, was to capture an alma and take a mould of its face, plus specimens of its blood, hair and skin before fitting it with a radio transmitter and turning it loose.

FOOTPRINTS

It was all a bit of a change for Kofman, a French-born cryptozoologist, who, after an adventurous early career in the Red Army, spent over 20 years travelling the mountains on horseback to interview an estimated 500 eye-witnesses, collect unidentified footprints and examine piles of suspected alma droppings. Her research enabled her to produce a detailed composite of the mystery figures, sometimes supposed to be relic Neanderthals, driven into the wilderness by their more successful Cro-Magnon cousins tens of thousands of years ago.

The almas, according to Kofman's witnesses, walk upright, stand up to 6ft 6in tall, have reddish-brown fur and can move extremely rapidly – at up to 40mph, according to some reports. They are nomadic, mostly nocturnal and extremely shy. Alma babies, when they are seen, are "exactly like human babies, except they are smaller." They have pink skin and are not hairy.

From the depth of the footprints she

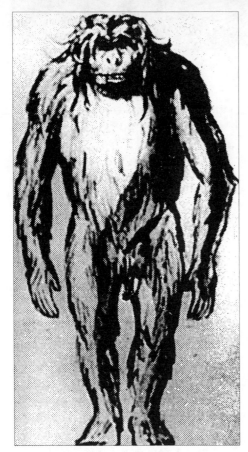

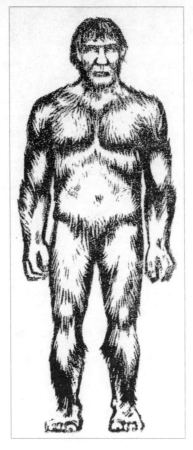

TOP: Snowprints, possibly made by the Yeti, photographed by Andrzej Zawada on the slopes of Lhotse, Everest's sister mountain.
ABOVE LEFT & RIGHT: Two artists' impressions of wildmen. Left: a yeti seen in the Himalayas. Right: an Alma-type creature seen by Lt-Col V.S. Karapetian near Buinaksk, Dagesan, USSR, in 1941.

THE YETI

found, Kofman estimates an adult alma weighs up to 500lbs. Working from the droppings, she suggests it lives on a diet of berries, roots, eggs, frogs, lizards and small rodents. Kofman, who recently retired on a £1 a month pension and returned to France, summarised her findings in two articles published in the journal *Archeologia* in 1991 and it was these that brought her to Pallix's attention.

EXPEDITION

The documentary-maker was looking for a new project after finishing a film about Harley-Davidson motorcycles, and like many a journalist before him, he exploited the exceptional media interest in 'Abominable Snowman' stories. Not only did he begin to raise the sponsorship to mount an expedition, but also found himself fielding dozens of press enquiries. "The telephones and doorbell never stop," he told the *International Herald Tribune*. "I only have time to shave every other day."

Whether all the high-tech gear actually materialised in time for the three-month expedition to get underway is not clear from the available clippings, which date from the flurry of media interest last March; nor did we hear of the party setting out, or returning, as projected, in September. But if nothing else, Pallix succeeded in directing a spotlight on one of the most promising areas in Asia for yeti-hunting.

Most recent attention has been directed to China, where scientists are taking seriously a spate of similar wildman reports, and claim to have obtained hair samples that prove the existence of the creatures. News of last year's expedition was accompanied by a number of new sightings from the Caucasus and more southerly Pamir mountain chains.

One, from Kofman's old Caucasus colleague Gregory Pantchenko, occurred in 1991. He watched an alma from a distance of only four metres for about 90 seconds one night, but either could not afford a camera or had one, but without a flash (reports differ).

Then, in September, an alma report came from a less expected source – a second French expedition returning from northern Pakistan. Dr Anne Mallasséand and M Jordi Magraner said they had heard unusual guttural sounds that could have been made by a primitive voicebox

A line-up of yeti-hunters in Russia, 1972. Left to right: Dimitri Bayanov, Lt-Col V.S. Karapetian, Rene Dahinden and Dr Jeanne Kofman

and tracked down witnesses who claimed to have seen the animal that made them.

A somewhat confused report in the *Daily Telegraph* added: "Eye-witnesses shown pictures of a selection of human and human-like creatures consistently selected the image of a primitive man found preserved in ice some 20 years ago by a Belgian team." This seems to be a reference to the so-called 'Minnesota Iceman', a supposed frozen 'Bigfoot' that toured the carnivals of the US in the late 1960s and was taken up by the great Belgian cryptozoologist Bernard Heuvelmans as a possibly genuine yeti-cadaver. If so, the Pakistani report becomes yet more intriguing, since most researchers have dismissed the Iceman as a latex model created for a circus sideshow.

Magraner, for one, says he believes a further expedition would be worthwhile. He told reporters he planned to return to the region in December to hunt the wildman with infra-red cameras.

The Pamir wildman tradition is at least as well-attested as the Caucasus folklore collected by Dr Kaufman. The area has been the subject of several significant Russian expeditions, and last spring a *Telegraph* journalist crossing the area reported that some locals still tell stories about the 'yeti'.

One old shepherd said: "My grandfather used to see them in the high places

before the 1917 revolution. People would see them as they walked across the passes on the *haj*. If you shouted at them, they would run off."

WILDMEN

Wildmen have also been reported from other parts of the old Soviet Union. We wrote of a Siberian wildman back in *FT54* and, last April, TASS carried a story about a Karelian journalist, Vyacheslav Oparin, who wanted the Abominable Snowman renamed the 'forest monster' or 'tree eater'; he had found bones, he claimed, along the Finnish border that showed the animal climbed trees and lived off bark.

In Mongolia, according to a feature in *Soviet Weekly* (7 Mar 1991), two wildmen were actually shot by a patrol during border skirmishes between the Russians and Japanese in 1939.

One of the soldiers who saw the bodies, a man named Kolpashnikov, told the researcher Boris Porshnever the almas were shot by Mongolian troops after they failed to respond to challenges. "As far as I could judge, [the corpses] were large anthropoid apes, their bodies covered unevenly with red and brown hair," he added. "Their arms were disproportionately long."

However, a more recent Mongolian report, cited in the *New Scientist* (18 April 1991), turned out to be a hoax. The Communist youth newspaper had printed a photograph of a 'yeti' clasping paws

TOP: Dr Kofman rides out in search of the alma, accompanied by her faithful dog. ABOVE: Dr Kofman, the French-Russian expert on the wildman, working on her survey of the Caucasus.

with two uniformed policemen, while a plainclothes officer loitered in the background. The wildman was in custody at the Ulan Bator circus, it explained.

Sadly for the paper, which had intended the story as an April Fools' Day joke, an acute shortage of newsprint meant it was not published until days later, convincing a number of readers that the tall tale was true.

A new photograph of 'Yeti' tracks, taken in the Himalayas by the Polish geophysicist Andrzej Zawada, was printed in the Polish airlines magazine *Kaleidoscope* in April 1992.

Climbing Lhotse, Everest's sister mountain, Zwanda and his team had camped at 6,500 feet, near a feature known as the Western Pothole, when word came from a lower camp that the expedition cameraman Jurek Surdul had photographed some unusual footprints he claimed were a yeti's.

Knowing that Surdul had an active interest in the Abominable Snowman, and "being an artist, had a lively imagination", Zawada attached little importance to the story. However, the expedition's Nepalese communications officer ran down the mountain to photograph the tracks, and when he too reported that there was something unusual about them Zawada radioed base camp's resident sceptic Dr Bogdan Jankowski and asked him to assess the evidence.

"I was convinced that in a few minutes Bogdan would get back to me and announce that there had been a mistake, or that it was the imagination of our artist cameraman. [But] in an hour I heard his calm, indifferent voice on the radio, saying: 'I have no doubt that a weird animal of some sort passed by our camp and left strange traces.'"

Little can be made of the spectacularly indistinct tracks published in *Kaleidoscope* (see photo page 32). Those closest to the camera are partially obscured by shadow, and appear to show little more than a double line of large round prints, each as long, but much wider, than a human footprint. Further into the background, the tracks diverge and then converge into an overlapping trail extending to the top left-hand corner of the frame.

The climber thought the tracks might be up to a week old, and certainly the lack of detail in the prints suggests that they may have been melted by the sun and re-frozen at least once, rendering them of little real use as evidence. Jankowski followed the tracks for 10km; they measured 30cm (12") long, 15cm (6") wide and were about a metre apart.

ANOTHER PHOTOGRAPH

The Poles hypothesised that the yeti might have got into the habit of visiting the usually-deserted camp during the winter in search of food. The Poles were not the only climbers to find possible yeti evidence. On 10 Sept 1992, the *Sun* published a photograph showing a long single line of footprints receding into the distance, with a scale provided by the usual ice axe. It had been taken by climber Julian Freeman-Atwood on the Alexandroff glacier, "which is 1000 miles from civilisation" and where "no human had set foot for 30 years."

Working from the depth of the tracks, Freeman-Atwood guessed that whatever had left the prints weighed over 14 stones. One 14" print, he said, showed the outline of three large toes, and there was evidence that the creature had trailed an arm as it walked. The trail passed within feet of the expedition tents and must have been made within hours of their discovery, "or they would have been obliterated by the bad weather."

Leading British climber Chris Bonnington, who mounted his own, somewhat farcical, yeti hunt in 1988, said the pictures came from a "reliable source". Freeman-Atwood added: "I have seen bear tracks on a number of occasions – believe me, these were not made by a mountain bear."

Sources: Straits Times (Malaysia), 12 Mar 1992; Int Herald Tribune, 27 Mar; [AP] US Lancaster Sunday News, 29 March; South China Morning Post, 30 March; [AFP-Jiji] Mainichi Daily News, Tokyo & Brisbane Courier-Mail, 8 April; Rocky Mountain News, 10 May; Economist, 27 Jun; D.Telegraph, 9 Sept 1992.

FT

LIVING FOSSILS

Fortean Times Guide to Dinosaurs in the 20th Century
compiled by Dr. Karl Shuker

On 25 April 1977, it looked as if one of cryptozoology's greatest dreams – the discovery of a 20th century plesiosaur – had been fulfilled when a Japanese fishing vessel trawling waters 30 miles east of Christchurch, New Zealand, hauled in the decomposing carcase of a huge, plesiosaur-shaped beast. The 33ft-long beast had been dead for about a month and smelled so awful that the crew were com-

pelled to cast it overboard soon after, but not before they had measured and photographed it and taken some samples of its rotting fibres.

The fibres were analysed meticulously, during the early 1980s, at Tokyo University, and found to contain elastodin, a protein specific to sharks. As has happened so often before with supposed sea serpent remains, the carcase was that of a shark that had been 'transformed'

into a deceptively plesiosaur-like corpse during decomposition – a well-documented process but one which is still capable of fooling observers today.

Nevertheless, the New Zealand carcase is still interesting because very few sharks ever attain a length of 33 feet. This carcase might, possibly, represent an unknown giant species, or perhaps even one of the huge prehistoric sharks that officially died out long ago.

▶

THE ALPS

TATZELWURM – Famed for its many dragon legends, the Alps may be home to a dragon of sorts. According to numerous eyewitness reports, the undiscovered species of reptile – known locally as the *tatzelwurm* or *stollenwurm* – can grow to 30 feet long.

AUSTRALIA

QUEENSLAND TIGER (above) – Australia's most fascinating mystery creature is a cat-headed carnivore with bold grey and white stripes. It resembles the Australian marsupial lion *Thylacaleo carnifex,* officially assumed to have died out around 10,000 years ago.

BUNYIPS – Two Australian zoologists recently suggested that legends about the mysterious *bunyips* originated from early Aboriginal encounters with the herbivorous and possibly semi-aquatic marsupial diprotodonts, known to have survived on the continent until as recently as 6000 years ago.

BRAZIL

SUCURIJU GIGANTE – Of the many reports from various tributaries of the Amazon River of this allegedly immense form of anaconda, one of the most famous examples is the stupendous specimen – estimated to be around 62ft – shot in 1907 by Colonel Percy Fawcett – see page 31 – who vanished in those jungles in 1925.

DINOSAURS (above) – Around 1933, a Swedish traveller on the Marmore River, in the Matto Grosso, saw an extraordinary, 20ft long, dinosaur-like, alligator-headed beast. His bullets did not appear to harm it, and it lumbered away towards the river. The area is also home to the mysterious, subterranean *minhocao*, which, from descriptions, resembles a glyptodont.

CANADA

WAHEELA – In parts of Canada – as well as in Michigan and Alaska – reports have emerged of uncommonly large, pure-white wolf-like beasts, called 'great white wolves' or *waheelas*. The late cryptozoologist Ivan Sanderson suggested that they could comprise a living species of amphicyonid or bear-dog – extinct bulky carnivores that supposedly died out in America two million years ago.

GIANT TURTLE (above) – With a shell circumference of 25ft, North America's *Archelon* was the largest sea turtle that ever existed, but it supposedly died out during the Cretaceous Period. However, in June 1956, an extraordinary creature reported from the cargo steamer *Rhapsody*, near Nova Scotia. It was described as a gigantic turtle roughly 45ft long, with a totally white carapace – depicted here, by Walter Molino, for the Italian weekly *La Deomenica del Corriere.*

CHAD

MOUNTAIN TIGER – Hunters of the Zagaoua tribe of northern Chad describe a strange tailless cat, larger than a lion, with red fur banded with white stripes, and very large protruding teeth. Shown drawings of animals living and extinct, they unhesitatingly selected a picture of *Machairodus*, Africa's supposedly long-extinct sabre-toothed tiger.

THE CONGO

EMELA-NTOUKA – One of Africa's most bizarre mystery beasts is the large, amphibious *emela-ntouka* ("killer of elephants"). Taking into account its single powerful horn, heavy tail, and reputed habit of disembowelling elephants, some cryptozoologists think it may actually be a surviving ceratopian dinosaur, related to prehistory's familiar *Triceratops*.

MOKELE-MBEMBE – This mystery sauropod has inspired several serious field expeditions in recent years to the Likouala swamplands, including two expeditions by Dr Roy Mackal in the 1980s, and by British explorer Bill Gibbons in 1986 and 1992 – see interview in this issue. Its descriptions are reminiscent of the famous *Apatosaurus* (formerly

called *Brontosaurus*) and *Diplodocus*, and comp ble creatures have been recorded in the adja countries.

MBIELU-MBIELU-MBIELU – During his search *mokele-mbembe*, Dr Mackal heard of anot dinosaur-like Likouala mystery beast said to "planks growing out of its back", resembli stegosaur, or even one of the ankylosaurs.

JAPAN

TZUCHINOKO – This unusually short, thick-ied snake, with horn-like projections above eyes, has been known to the Japanese for turies, but its identity has yet to be scientifi ascertained. As recently as September 1992, mountain town of Chigusa offered a 200 mi yen reward (£490,000) for a living specimen.

KAMCHATKA

IRKUIEM – In 1987, local reindeer hunters rep ed sightings of a huge, unidentified type of they called the *irkuiem*. It is said to resemble enormous polar bear but has a small head, an unusual gait.

KENYA

NANDI BEAR – This mystery beast – also ca the *chemosit* or *kerit* – is held responsible natives for many murderous assaults u humans and livestock. Karl Shuker has propo that the Nandi bear might be a short-faced hy *Hyaena brevirostris*. Formerly occurring in Eur and Africa, this ferocious animal was the size

...nakes in Sicily, flying lizards in Zambia ...
...logical discovery as we take you ...

ROAM THE EARTH

© GINO D'ACHILLE/ARTIST

out around 240 million years ago.

MOAS (below) – The ostrich-like *Diornis* moas are believed to have died out about 300 years ago, but some ornithologists suggest that a smaller species – the upland moa *Megalapteryx didinus* – may have survived into the present day; a hope fuelled by reports of a mysterious 'giant kiwi', known to the Maoris as the turkey-sized *roa-roa*.

NORTHERN INDIA

BURU – In 1948, the expedition led by the late Ralph Izzard and explorer Charles Stonor journeyed to Rilo (an eastern Himalayan valley close to Assam's Dafla Hills) failed to find this rumoured, 130 foot long, swamp-dwelling monster. Known as the *buru*, it was serpentine in appearance, with a roundish elongated body, and small flange-like limbs. Karl Shuker believes that it compares most closely in overall form and lifestyle with a giant lungfish.

PATAGONIA

ELLENGASSEN – Native reports of a shaggy bovine creature known locally as the *ellengassen*, reputedly inhabiting Patagonia's little-explored tropical forests, keep alive a remote hope that a species of giant ground sloth has indeed persisted from the Pleistocene into the present.

PLESIOSAUR (above) – In 1922, following much publicized sightings of a swan-necked plesiosaur-like reptile inhabiting a lake in the Andes, a expedition from Buenos Aires zoo set out in search of this wondrous beast, but failed to find it. Our illustration, by Walter Molino, depicts the original sighting for the Italian weekly *La Domenica del Corriere*, March 1922.

SICILY

GIANT SNAKE (right) – In 1954, an enormous snake supposedly attacked some farmers at Siracuse in Sicily; as illustrated here (probably with exaggeration) by Walter Molino for the Italian weekly *La Domenica del Corriere*.

SIBERIA
WOOLLY MAMMOTH – Eyewitness accounts suggest the possibility that the woolly mammoth still survives in a remote corner of Siberia's vast forest, the taiga.

TIBET
LAKE WENBU MONSTER – During the 1980s, reports reached the West of an plesiosaur-like aquatic creature in Lake Wenbu. On one occasion it is said to have consumed a yak grazing on the lakeshore, and on another it was blamed for the disappearance of a farmer rowing on the lake.

UNITED STATES
THUNDERBIRDS – Once confined to Amerindian myths, modern reports of 'big birds' with enormous wingspans are considered seriously because, at the close of the Pleistocene, North America was the home of the teratorns ('monster birds'), including a mighty Californian species called *Teratornis incredibilis*, which had a wingspan of 17 feet!

ZAMBIA
KONGAMOTO – Reports have been made of a flying lizard – very like the pterosaurs of prehistory. Referred to as the *kongamoto*, it has black, bat-like wings, a long tail and a beak brimming with teeth. Encountered near lakes and rivers, it is said to prey on fishes, skimming across the water and impaling them on the sharp teeth of its open jaws.

ZAIRE
GIANT SNAKE – In 1959, while flying in Katanga – now Shaba – Belgian aviator Remy van Lierde spied a colossal serpent rearing upwards, directly towards his helicopter. Van Lierde was able to take some photos of this terrifying creature, which careful analysis shows to have been estimated as 200 feet long.

and possessed a very large head and jaws of enormous carnivorous teeth quite capa- of perpetrating the Nandi bear's hideous nes.

...ALAYSIA
...TER DRAGONS – Tasek Bera is a large, deep ...e in the mountains of Pahang state, reputed to ...the home of monsters that resemble sauro-...d dinosaurs. Its snake-like head bears soft ...il-like horns. When young, these creatures ...e slate-coloured scales which become more ...den as they get older.

...EW GUINEA
...VIL-PIG – A pair of extraordinary, long-nosed ...atures – resembling a tapir-like diprotodont ...m the Pleistocene called *Palorchestes* – were ...tted in 1906 by an expedition led by Papua ...neer Captain Charles Monckton. A similar ...nked creature is depicted in early stone carv-...s found in New Guinea's Ambun Valley.
...W – In 1950, the explorer Charles Miller report-...that during his recent sojourn among a cannibal ...e, he had filmed a bizarre living dinosaur, ...own to the natives as a *row*, and had obtained a ...ny prong from the tip of its tail; but neither film ...prong was ever disclosed to the public.

...EW ZEALAND
...AITOREKE – This otter-like creature, known to ...Maoris, is possibly a surviving synapsid (mam-...l-like reptile), currently believed to have died

LIVING DINOSAURS: FACT OR FICTION?

Before Darwin's theory of evolution in the mid nineteenth-century, zoologists and even palæontologists firmly believed that the animal species were immutable and immortal. Of course, the numerous fossils already unearthed ought to have convinced them that animals had evolved, and that this was necessarily accompanied by extinction. However, these inconvenient remains were explained away as the bones of antediluvian monsters – ancient creatures that perished in the Great Flood.

Evolution and its attendant extinction is largely accepted by modern science, largely outlawing the idea that prehistoric creatures have survived undetected. Yet the annals of contemporary zoology contain numerous discoveries of living creatures belonging to ancient groups hitherto believed extinct since prehistoric times, or individual species assumed to have died out long ago. Examples of such

'living fossils', long known to science, include:

● the tuatara *Sphenodon punctatus*, New Zealand's lizard-like rhyncosaur, the only surviving member of a once-diverse reptilian lineage that was contemporary with the dinosaurs
● the horseshoe crab *Limulus*, an antiquated aquatic arthropod practically indistinguishable from fossil specimens 300 million years old, and most closely related to the long-extinct euryptids (giant sea scorpions)
● the deceptively plant-like sea lilies (crinoids), actually comprising a sub-class of starfish-allied animals, known only from fossils dating back 600 million years until a living species – the first of many – was discovered in 1755 in deep water off the island of Martinique
● the chambered nautiluses, a handful of species constituting the only modern close relatives of the famous ammonites – a subclass of molluscs with coiled shells that died out alongside the dinosaurs over 60 million years ago.

Additionally, there are a number of celebrated examples that remained unknown to science until quite recently, as documented in my forthcoming book *Collins Encyclopedia of New and Rediscovered Animals* (HarperCollins, London; to be published in October 1993). The very first book devoted exclusively to this century's major zoological arrivals and revivals, it presents the histories of many recently-revealed 'living fossils', such as:

● a series of superficially limpet-like species of the genus *Neopilina*, that came to light in the 1950s and were found to be monoplacophorans, primitive molluscs that supposedly died out 200 million years ago
● the coelacanth *Latimeria chalumnae*, an extraordinary 5ft-long fish with leg-like lobed fins and armour-like scales, captured alive off South Africa in December 1938 and found to belong to an ancient group of fishes called the crossopterygians, previously thought to have died out over 64 million years ago
● the famous okapi *Okapia johnstoni*, discovered deep within Zaire's near-impenetrable Ituri Forest in 1901 and belonging to a group of short-necked forest giraffes dating back 30 million years
● the mountain possum *Burramys parvus*, a primitive marsupial known only from fossils at least 10,000 years old until a living specimen was captured in 1966
● the Chacoan peccary *Catagonus wagneri*, a pig-like hoofed mammal again known only from fossils and believed to have died out during the Ice Ages until rediscovered alive in Argentina during the 1970s. It is the largest living

Coelacanth (*Latimeria chalumnae*) photographed off the Comores Islands

PLANET EARTH PICTURES

peccary species.

Many other 'living fossils' on record, yet for the most p the zoological world stubbor continues to deny that simi discoveries are waiting to made – accusing those w believe in such a scenario as s fering from acute 'Lost Wor syndrome. Conan Doyle's *Lost World* was written in style of an authentic field rep (recalling accounts such Darwin's *Voyage of the Beagle a* Henry W. Bates' *The Naturalist the River Amazon*), and describ the discovery of a prehisto world in majestic isolation on of a lofty South American me where all of the most impr sive creatures of the distant p had somehow survived.

I am not of course sugge ing that the unveiling of entire prehistoric world is fea ble. However, amid the vast s entific and popular non-fict literature are countless clu and indications – ranging fro reliable eyewitness accounts an alleged specimen or two (though these exhibit a disturbing tender to 'disappear' soon after their procurement!) – that provide evider pointing to the survival of many different types of prehistoric animal.

The reason why such creatures have not been found lies in nature of their habitats, which combine ecological security and virt inaccessibility for Western investigators, sometimes as much bureaucr ic as geographical.

This is illustrated by the habitats of those 'living fossils' alrea known to science. Many first came to attention as fortuitous finds, instance among mixed hauls of specimens dredged up from the oce depths – which indisputably harbour numerous other surprises. Oth prehistoric survivors inhabit topologically isolated areas little chang for thousands if not millions of years, where they have been shelter from competition.

A few examples of such living fossils are presented in our cen spread; but what of the future? The outlook is far from promisi Undoubtedly, some mystery beasts have eluded formal discove because their numbers are very low – hence the killing of specimens taxonomic (or any other) purposes could have dire consequences. Th and their habitats should receive strict protection at the highest lev otherwise these helpless creatures, trapped in scientific limbo, can killed with impunity. Unfortunately, the existence of major undiscover animals will never be accepted by the scientific community without t ditional physical proof, such as a dead specimen, or at least a skelet and without scientific recognition no government would be willing fund their conservation.

The goal of cryptozoology, therefore, must be to discover species collecting specimens without destroying the creatures or their habita These could then be meticulously studied and filmed, and samples blood and DNA obtained for taxonomic purposes, after which they shou be returned to the wild. In the last few years this procedure has been f lowed with several new species of birds and small mammals, offering model for the treatment of more exotic and spectacular mystery beasts.

All that is needed now is a successful plan for attracting corpora sponsors to finance fully-equipped professional expeditions to seek a obtain such creatures – but that, as they say, is another story entirely!

FURTHER READING

BORD, Janet, & BORD, Colin, *Alien Animals*, revised edition (Panther, London, 1985); *Modern Mysteries of the World* (Grafton, London, 1989). BURTON, Maurice, *Living Fossils* (Thames & Hudson, London, 1954). COHEN, Daniel, *The Encyclopedia of Monsters*, reprinted (Fraser Stewart, Waltham Abbey, 1991). CORLISS, William R., *Incredible Life: A Handbook of Biological Mysteries* (The Sourcebook Project, Glen Arm, 1981). HALL, Mark A., *Thunderbirds! The Living Legend of Giant Birds* (Mark A. Hall Publications and Research, Bloomington, 1988). HEUVELMANS, Bernard, *On the Track of Unknown Animals* (Rupert Hart-Davis, London, 1958); *Les Derniers Dragons d'Afrique* (Plon, Paris, 1978). LEY, Willy, *Exotic Zoology* (Capricorn Books, NY, 1966). MACKAL, Roy P., *Searching for Hidden Animals*, reprinted (Cadogan Books, London, 1983); *A Living Dinosaur? In Search of Mokele-Mbembe* (E.J.Brill, Leiden, 1987). MICHELL, John, & RICKARD, Robert J.M., *Living Wonders: Mysteries and Curiosities of the Animal World* (Thames & Hudson, London, 1982). SANDERSON, Ivan T., *"Things"* (Pyramid Books, NY, 1967); *More "Things"* (Pyramid Books, NY, 1969). SHUKER, Karl P.N., *Mystery Cats of the World* (Robert Hale, London, 1989); *Extraordinary Animals Worldwide* (Robert Hale, London, 1991); *Collins Encyclopedia of New and Rediscovered Animals* (HarperCollins, London, to be published October 1993).

GAMBO

THE BEAKED BEAST OF BUNGALOW BEACH

ABOUT THE AUTHOR

DR KARL SHUKER is a zoologist with a long-standing interest in the scientific study of mysterious and unexplained animals. He is the author of *Mystery Cats of the World* (1989) and *Extraordinary Animals Worldwide* (1991), both published by Robert Hale. Dr Shuker has also written our pull-out supplement on 'living fossils'.

ABOVE : The meg-amouth shark, the third largest known shark species, discovered off the Hawaiian island of Oahu in 1976.

During the night of 11 June 1983, the corpse of a strange marine creature was washed up on the West African coast below Bungalow Beach Hotel, Gambia. It was discovered about 8:30am the following morning by Owen Burnham, on holiday from Senegal with his father, brother and sister. Mr Burnham had grown up in Senegal, took a particular interest in the local fauna (both terrestrial and aquatic) and was quite familiar with the carcases of decomposing dolphins and sharks. He had no idea what the dead creature might be. Though he didn't have a camera, he made descriptive notes and took measurements. When he was living back in England in 1986, he described the creature in *BBC Wildlife* (#4, May 1986, p.220) and appealed for help in identifying the creature.

For the purposes of this article, we shall refer to the creature as Gambo [1]. It was about 15 feet long and five feet wide, with a smooth, scaleless skin, dark brown on the

"It was about 15 feet long and five feet wide, with a smooth, scaleless skin..."

top and white below, to midway down the tail; there was no actual median line, but the colour was distinctly separate. The five-foot-long pointed tail had no flukes. The carcase was foul-smelling, but not disintegrating; virtually intact, apart from the terminal portion of its right hind limb and most of its left hind limb, which had been torn off. The body was distended internally by gas, but still streamlined in shape and not notably flattened. It had a very short neck, and the front 18 inches of the 50-inch-long dolphin-like head was drawn out into long jaws containing 80 evenly distributed and uniform teeth, very sharp, conical like barracuda teeth, but whiter and thicker. There was no blow hole; the nostrils seemed to be at the tip of the jaws; and the rather small, brown eyes were clearly visible, though not protruding.

The long body had no dorsal fin or sign of having borne one; nor was there any sign of tail flukes. The hind- and forelimbs or flippers were the same size, 18 inches long, pad-

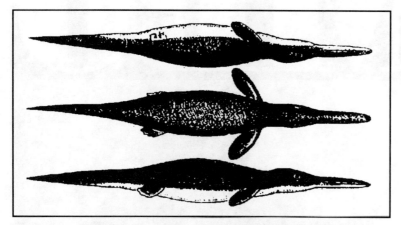

Three views of Gambo as created by a BBC Wildlife artist based on Owen Burnham's eyewitness drawings.

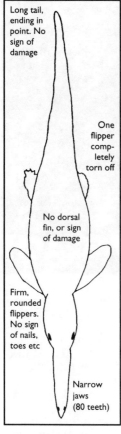

The Gambian sea-serpent as seen by Owen Burnham, June 1983.

Long tail, ending in point. No sign of damage

One flipper completely torn off

No dorsal fin, or sign of damage

Firm, rounded flippers. No sign of nails, toes etc

Narrow jaws (80 teeth)

COLOURATION: brown above, white below. No actual median line, but colours distinctly separate.

DIMENSIONS:
Length: 15-16ft.
Head & Body: 10ft.
Tail: 4.5-5ft.
Jaws: 1.5ft.
Flipper: 1.5ft.

The U-28 sea-serpent, 1915, after Richard Hennig

dle-shaped and solid, lacking toes or claws. Parts of the digestive tract, whitish in colour, and fatty tissue protruded from a tear in the abdomen.

When Burnham came upon the carcase, two local fishermen were busy hacking off its head with a machete, so that they could sell it to tourists. This took 20 minutes, as the vertebræ were very thick. The flesh was red and looked rather like beef. Burnham considered buying the head, but thought the difficulties of getting it out of the country too great. It is a pity he did not procure some smaller body part, such as vertebræ, flipper bones or a tissue sample.

Burnham was fluent in Mandinka, and asked the machete-wielding fishermen what they called the creature. 'Kunthum Belein' they replied – 'cutting jaws'. At every coastal village of Gambia and Senegal which he subsequently visited, notably Kap Skirring in Senegal where he once saw a dolphin's head for sale, Burnham asked the fishermen to draw the animal known to them by that name. Each time, the result was a dolphin. However, in the Mandinka language, the name (or a very similar one) of a common animal is also given to a rare or unknown one which resembles the familiar type. Thus the elusive, spotted serval cat translates as 'little leopard'. None of the fishermen who had drawn 'Kunthum Belein' for Burnham recognised Gambo from his description.

According to Bernard Heuvelmans in his monumental *In the Wake of the Sea-Serpents* (1968), 'The Great Sea Serpent' of marine tradition was an umbrella term for several distinct, but unknown, sea creatures, such as giant eels and turtles, modified seals, primitive serpentine whales called archæocetes (currently known only from fossils) and various 'extinct' reptiles.

In the last 60 years, marine biologists have become increasingly open to the idea that large marine creatures remain undiscovered. Several remarkable finds have contributed to this view; for instance, the Shepherd's Beaked Whale (1937); the Coelacanth, belonging to a fish group believed extinct in the Cretaceous, 64 million years ago (22 December 1938); the Japanese Beaked Whale (1958); the Conchito Porpoise from the Gulf of California (1958); the Megamouth Shark, the third largest known shark species, found off the Hawaiian island of Oahu (1976); and Prudes's Bay Killer Whale from the Antarctic (1983). One scientist has compared our attempts to sample the ocean fauna to an alien spaceship in earth orbit sampling life on the planet with a butterfly-net on the end of a long piece of string.

Most 'sea serpents' are observed only briefly, rarely offering more than a glimpse of head and neck, plus the occasional hump or flipper, and usually moving rapidly away from the observer. Stranded corpses are usually fragmentary or in advanced decomposition, which can lead to misidentifications; decomposed basking sharks, for instance, tend to look like plesiosaurs.

Complete corpses of large unknown marine creatures in reasonable condition are very rare. These include: two eel-like sharks caught alive off the eastern seaboard of America (late 1890s) [2]; a 45ft, snow-white monster with a trunk, observed fighting two whales and discovered dead days later on a beach at Margate, South Africa (1922) [3]; a smaller, trunked creature stranded on Glacier Island, Alaska (1930) [4]; and the four-limbed lizard-like beast washed ashore at Gourock, Scotland, in 1942, which was cremated and buried under what is now a football pitch [5]. Gambo belongs in this rare category.

With its fin-like limbs, Gambo is obviously not a fish. Neither is it an amphibian. The only known species of exclusively marine amphibians were from a fossil group called the trematosaurs, and they all had clawed feet. We can also forget the pinnipeds (seals and sea lions) which lost their tails before their limbs transformed into paddled flippers. Pinnipeds, like most mammals, living or extinct, have just over 40 teeth; the exceptions to this rule are marsupials, armadillos and certain whales. Furthermore, these teeth are of more than one type, unlike the 80 uniform teeth of the presumed carnivore Gambo.

The streamlined body, long jaws and

domed forehead are reminiscent of the cetaceans (whales, dolphins and porpoises); however, all known living species have either single or paired blow-holes sited dorsally on the head. Nostrils near the snout are characteristic of pinnipeds and terrestrial mammals. The archæocetes, such as *Basilosaurus*, better known as *Zeuglodon, did* possess nostrils near the end of the snout, but they only had 40 or so teeth. Conversely, certain extant cetaceans, like the elusive Shepherd's Beaked Whale (*Tasmacetus shepherdi*) do have 80 or so teeth, but no nostrils. *Tasmacetus* does resemble the Gambian creature in body colouration (brown above, white below), but the few specimens recorded all originate from New Zealand or South America.

Furthermore, no cetaceans have long, pointed tails without flukes. The clincher is Gambo's fully-formed hind limbs: in all living cetaceans, and even the archæocetes, the hind limbs and the entire pelvic girdle are vestigial, not even visible externally. This is also characteristic of the third principal group of marine mammals – the sirenians (manatees and sea cows). Besides, these herbivorous creatures all have broad tails with a pronounced horizontal fin, and jaws and teeth quite unlike Gambo's.

We can also exclude any living reptiles. Turtles possess paddled limbs like Gambo, but no teeth; most are enclosed within thick, horny shells. Living crocodilians are covered in tough scales and have fully-formed legs and clawed feet.

If Gambo isn't a variety of known living creature, perhaps it is a living fossil. The likely candidates are four reptilian groups: the plesiosaurs, mosasaurs, ichthyosaurs and thalattosuchians, all of which had supposedly died out by the end of the Cretaceous Era, about 64 million years ago.

The plesiosaurs comprise the long-necked elasmosaurs (Nessie has been interpreted as a surviving example) and the short-necked pliosaurs, which conform more nearly to some of Gambo's characteristics: short neck and long head, elongated jaws with uniform teeth, streamlined body, two sets of paddled limbs and a long, pointed tail. This morphological combination was also found in the mosasaurs and thalattosuchians, a classic example of convergent evolution. Pliosaurs were most probably smooth skinned, like whales, sealions and Leathery Turtles – and Gambo. They were also much the same size as Gambo, apart from giants like the 40ft *Kronosaurus*.

Unlike the pliosaurs, the mosasaurs do have living relatives: the monitor lizards, including the formidable Komodo Dragon. However, they had scales, a long dorsal fin and a tail fin. The ichthyosaurs, remarkably dolphin- or fish-like, had reduced hind flippers, a very prominent dorsal fin, vertical tail flukes and extremely large eyes. The thalattosuchians were ancient smooth-skinned crocodilians, exclusively marine and with paddled limbs; they also had eyes similar in size and location to those of Gambo, but their tails terminated in a fish-like fin.

It is worth noting in this context a sighting made on 30 July 1915 by the German U-Boat *U28*. This U-Boat had just sunk the steamer *Iberian*, which blew up at an estimated depth of 500 fathoms, shooting pieces of wreckage more than 60 feet in the air; among them was a "gigantic sea animal, writhing and struggling wildly." The U-Boat commander described it as about 60ft long, like a crocodile, with four limbs, powerful webbed feet and a long, tapering tail [6].

Weighing all the similarities and differences, it seems that Gambo most closely resembles either a pliosaur or a thalattosuchian. Against such fossil survivals, it has been pointed out that fossil evidence for any of these creatures in at least the last 64 million years is lacking. Fossils of large creatures, however, are extremely rare; besides, the Coelacanth was thought extinct for the same length of time until one was found alive in 1938. Another argument is that living mystery animals do not conform exactly to any known fossil. This overlooks possible evolution over the last 64 million years; after all, our ancestors in the Cretaceous probably looked like rats.

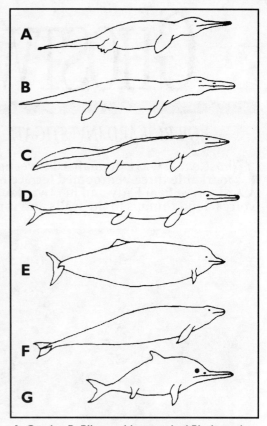

A: Gambo B: Pliosaur (short-necked Plesiosaur)
C: Mosasaur (giant marine lizard) D: Thalattosuchian (sea crocodile) E: Shepherd's Beaked Whale (Tasmacetus shepherdi) F: Archæocete (primitive whale) G: Ichthyosaur (fish-like reptile)

> "...Among them was a 'gigantic sea animal, writhing and struggling wildly'. The U-Boat commander described it as about 60ft long, like a crocodile, with four limbs, powerful webbed feet and a long, tapering tail."

NOTES

[1] This article is condensed from a two-part report that Dr Shuker wrote for *The Unknown* (Sept 1986, pp49-53 and Oct 1986, pp31-36).
[2] S.W.Hanna: 'Description of an eel-like creature taken in a net at New Harbor, Maine, in 1880.' (*Bulletin of the US Fish Commission* (1883) vol3, pp407-410.)
[3] *D.Mail*, 27 Dec 1924.
[4] 'Monster in Ice had Long Snout' (*New York Sun*, 28 Nov 1930.)
[5] Simon Welfare & John Fairley: *Arthur C.Clarke's Mysterious World* , (Collins 1980, pp81-82.)
[6] Freiherr von Forster: *Das schottische Seeungeheuer schon von U.28 gesichtet* (Deutsche Allgemeine Zeitung, Tübingen, 19 Dec 1933.)

GHOSTWATCH: Whatever

BOB RICKARD INVESTIGATES BBC TV'S RECENT MEDIA HOAX. ALTHOUGH INTENDED

Ghostwatch was a dramatised investigation of "the most haunted house in Britain". The unremarkable three-bedroomed terrace house "in Foxhill Drive, Northolt, Middlesex" was home to divorcee Pam Early and her two daughters. They had been tormented for several years by voices, loud thumps in the walls and pipes, objects moving inexplicably around the house.

The chief players - Michael Parkinson (centre) is one of Britain's longest serving chat-show hosts; although he occasionally branches out (eg. hosting *Give Us a Clue*), these efforts are not well remembered. Sarah Greene (left) is one of the presenters of the popular children's show *Going Live*. Mike Smith (right) - Greene's husband - is best known for fronting family shows, like *That's Show Business*. Another presenter with a massive following among the young was Craig Charles, star of the cult SF comedy *Red Dwarf*, who stayed in character as the cheeky, jovial, cynical

Solemnly, as he strolls across an all-purpose set, Michael Parkinson, personification of the no-nonsense Yorkshireman, intones: "The programme you are about to watch is a unique investigation of the supernatural. It contains material which some viewers may find disturbing." When it finished, 90 minutes later, the BBC phones were clogged with 20,000 callers wanting to know if it was 'real'. Perhaps as many again, turned away by busy lines, called police stations, newspapers and other TV companies.

Outside the house, the 'live broadcast' started up, with support vans, lights, generators, crew and crowds. Sarah Greene was with the girls inside the house; and Craig Charles was interviewing neighbours – each with their camera and sound teams. In the studio, Mike Smith was monitoring ranks of telethon-type phone operators.

These first scenes were important in establishing an atmosphere of realism. The studio chat-show, the phone-in, and the current affairs set-up, formed a compendium of familiar elements from many TV shows – for example, the functional chaos of C4's *The Big Breakfast* and the BBC's popular Saturday morning children's show *Going Live;* and the live reports of *Crimewatch* and *Watchdog.*

SCEPTIC SCIENTISTS

Michael Parkinson, as anchorman, talked to the chief psychical investigator of the case, smart, forty-something 'Dr Lyn Pascoe' (representing the Society for Psychical Research), and to 'Dr Sylvester' in New York (representing CSICOP, the organization of sceptical scientists). Of these characters, writer Stephen Volk told us: "I attempted to update the crumpled raincoat image of parapsychologists, usually a cross between Harry Price and Van Helsing"; and the 'sceptic' with whom she argues was depicted as an American because "we wanted

Possessed Parkinson?

POOF HALLOWE'EN DRAMA, MANY PEOPLE BELIEVED THAT THE EVENTS WERE REAL

to use as many TV devices as possible, and the satellite link-up was too good a trick to miss!"

Viewers were invited to phone in with their psychic experiences, on 081 811 8181 - a number familiar to millions as that used by *Going Live, Crimewatch* and other programmes. Maurice Grosse, who was supervising some lines on behalf of the SPR, later told us: "At first people wanted to tell of their experiences, but this quickly changed to an inundation of complaints [..] It was apparent that some callers were scared out of their wits [..] I got the impression this was very satisfactory. After all, that was the whole idea, wasn't it?"

A film insert, said to be taken by researchers monitoring the family, showed the two girls - Suzanne, the eldest, and Kimmy - screaming as they fled from a poltergeist tantrum. Someone phones in, saying they saw a phantom figure in the curtains of the girls' bedroom. We learn that a previous owner of the house was a child-molester, who killed himself in the cellar surrounded by the cats he tortured; and that the site has an ancient history of evil deeds. More phone-ins: watches stopping, mirrors jumping off walls and plates off tables in callers' houses.

After another film clip – showing researchers studying Suzanne who is talking as though possessed – we see more phenomena at the house. One of the girls is found banging on the heating pipes, but then the noises start up on their own. Suzanne goes into a trance; scratches appear on her face and she speaks strangely in a gruff voice. 'Dr Pascoe' suggests Suzanne is possessed by the suicide's spirit. Cries of tortured cats fill the house.

Sarah Greene's team trace screeching noises to the cellar, and her soundman faints when its door is opened. He is taken to hospital. At this point, Parkinson says he's had enough, that it's all rubbish! Suddenly the transmission from the house ceases; screens go blank; outside technicians mill about

helplessly. Poltergeist activity breaks out in the studio, and in the chaos, we glimpse Parkinson, shuffling about, talking in the gruff voice. He is obviously possessed. Fade to credits.

Writer Stephen Volk, an SPR member, said he wanted to draw attention to "the real emotional hell

> **"The very first thing Michael Parkinson says is 'Don't watch, this is disturbing.' Twenty minutes later it is repeated; and later on he actually says to a fictitious caller 'Switch off. Send your son to bed. It is very disturbing'."**

that families go through. In the drama, the audience is asked by 'Dr Pascoe' to care about such families and take such cases seriously." Volk added: "My own belief is that if haunted houses don't exist, haunted people do. These things happen, whether one attributes them to discarnate entities (I don't) or yet-to-be-understood psychological reasons. [..] Our story *demanded* a ghost. My idea was to elaborate on parapsychologist Hilary Evans' idea of the 'Need-based Experience', which he applies to UFOs and Virgin Mary sightings as well as apparitions. The ghost was what the hungry mass audience of TV wanted, and therefore created."

DELIBERATE HOAX?

Ghostwatch was promptly compared to Orson Wells' *War of the Worlds* broadcast of 1938, Richard Dimbleby's 1957 *Panorama* documentary on the spaghetti harvest, and (perhaps the closest parallel) Anglia TV's infamous *Alternative Three* - see **FT64** - though some of my correspondents thought it lacked the bravado of the first, the humour of the second, and the subtlety of the third.

On *Back Bite* – a BBC's viewer complaint forum - Sue Lawley put it to the producer Ruth Baumgarten and executive producer Richard Brooke, that their deliberate use of familiar TV presenters was intended to deceive. They denied this, stressing that the pro-

gramme was conceived, produced and billed as drama; that they wanted to create "a good ghost story", not a media hoax.

One viewer on *Back Bite*, who spoke for many, complained to the producers: "You toyed with our emotions, because we weren't actually sure whether it was fact or fiction, whether it was live or drama [..] *because* it was Michael Parkinson." Another agreed: "Michael Parkinson is a well-respected fatherly figure. Sarah Greene and Mike Smith are synonymous with children's TV. I thought it was going to be safe."

Much of the public reaction was about whether or not there was adequate warning about the nature of the programme. Ruth Baumgarten said that, apart from the pre-publicity, some "arrows" were built into the programme. "The very first thing Michael Parkinson says is 'Don't watch. This is disturbing.' Twenty minutes later it is repeated; and later on he actually says to a fictitious caller 'Switch off. Send your son to bed. It is very disturbing.'"

The viewers on *Back Bite* dismissed the published warnings as useless, because not everyone read the publications they were in. Others *had* vetted the programme for their children, but "still didn't know it was a drama". When a viewer asked if the real reason for the warnings was for dramatic effect, Ruth Baumgarten said, with some exasperation: "We can't win. What do we do? Never make a programme about anything disturbing?"

Having publicised the fact that well-known presenters were in it, the BBC should have realised that many children would be watching. Sue Lawley put it to the producers that a watershed between children's and adult viewing, in today's society, was non-existent and relying on one was impractical. Richard Brooke protested that it was not fair to accuse the BBC of hiding behind the policy. He said: "I'm sorry children watched it. It *was* unsuitable for children. The watershed begins at 9pm and this policy is published every week."

Stephen Volk, the writer of *Ghostwatch*, told us: "Hindsight is always a marvellous thing. Some people have said it was a great shame the programme was labelled as drama, as they would have preferred to discover it for themselves. In fact, I must point out that the BBC received many letters (many from teenagers and children) saying it was "brilliant", the best they'd seen on TV for a while. Many wanted a video or wanted it repeated." One reader has told us he has met people firmly convinced it all really happened anyway.

POLTERGEIST SEX PEST

Some of the comments from viewers, in *Back Bite* and elsewhere, show the extent of general ignorance about the findings of psychical research and poltergeists in particular. One teenager thought that the involvement of children in the story was "sick"; while others questioned the "taste" of portraying the polt as a child-molesting, cat-torturing deviant.

The polts usually encountered by researchers, Maurice Grosse assures us, "are more mischievous than evil or demonic." But *Ghostwatch* was not a documentary, and Stephen Volk was quite at liberty to dramatise his poltergeist as – in John Haddington's words – "an intensely evil pædophile mainly interested in pursuing prepubescent girls around their bedroom." The story merely extended the popular belief that terrible events somehow imprint themselves onto locations, which gifted people can 'pick up' and perhaps even 'amplify'.

In the current climate, any suggestive association between children, violence, sexuality, and the occult is politically sensitive - yet these elements have been observed in some cases of hauntings and poltergeists from the beginnings of proper psychical research. Our own mentor Charles Fort was possibly the first to observe the now commonly-accepted relationship of polt outbreaks to the psychological stresses of puberty. The Earlys were a typical modern family, and their nightmare is made universal by their ordinariness.

Rightly or wrongly, the public today expects clear signs that it is watching something really real or pretend real. Boundaries do get blurred between fiction and fact, and, depending upon your predisposition at the time, you will find such ambiguity entertaining or disturbing. Stephen Volk is correct in pointing to the venerable tradition of movies and TV drama which has used news and documentary techniques to frame a story; and he has every right to create a drama in this tradition. I suspect such fictions work best when the signals are clear, and I offer my analysis of why, in the case of *Ghostwatch*, they were not.

I was intrigued from the start, and once past the odour of rodents, I sat back to enjoy the ride. It was well done, spoiled (for me) only by Dr Pascoe's fake spontaneity and the OTT ending.

Like other viewers, if I noticed any 'warnings' at all, I thought they were part of the drama. Like many children, my own wanted to watch because of SG and CC – and like many others, my youngest became anxious without being able to say why and had to leave the room. However, I was in the fortunate position of being able to explain to the kids what (I thought) was going on, and (so far) there have been no nightmares.

I accept the production team's claim that they simply wanted to tell a rattling good ghost story, using, and even satirising, modern TV presentations. I enjoyed the joke of an overtly crass and materialistic medium (TV) coming up against its inability to cope with the truly unpredictable and unknown (the deviant-driven polt). I particularly appreciated the retribution visited on Parkinson. The idea of an ancient evil, energised by millions of curious viewers, bursting from the cellar like an unbottled genie to 'take over' the scoffers in the studio is a twist in the grand tradition of Gothic horror. Thank heavens they stopped there; imagine the results if they had dramatised the polt then leap-frogging from the studio into every viewer's household via their TV!

WARNINGS

In the days that followed, it was clear a lot of people had been upset. According to a BBC statement, the majority of callers wanted reassurance that the programme was not 'real', and when that was given, relief turned to anger. This shows clearly that despite the BBC's intentions and preparations, they seriously miscalculated both the nature of the 'warnings' and the consequence of that ineffectiveness. (People felt "duped" and "betrayed".)

GHOSTWATCH BLAMED FOR SUICIDE

After Michael Parkinson's scornful comments on gullibility, a leader in the Nottingham *Evening Post* accused him of self-congratulatory arrogance, and predicted that the programme must have deeply worried the psychologically vulnerable.

Sadly, three days later - on the morning of 5 November, 1992, just five days after the screening of *Ghostwatch* – they were proved correct by the suicide of 18-year-old Martin Denham, whose body was found hanging from a tree in Bestwood Lodge Park, in Nottingham.

The Denham family had no doubt that Martin - who had a mental age of 13 – had been seriously disturbed by the BBC's drama. His elder brother Carl told the *Evening Post*: "He was so timid, and the programme frightened him, but he wouldn't talk about it. Our mother sat up with him. She told him it was rubbish but he didn't believe her." Stepfather Percy Denham said that Martin watched "as if he were hypnotised."

That night Martin refused to go to bed without a torch, and, when he heard knocking in the central heating pipes - a phenomenon featured in the BBC drama - he became convinced there were ghosts in the house, tearing up the carpet in his room to locate the sound. A note, found in Martin's pocket reads: "Mother do not be upset. If there is ghosts I will now be one and I will always be with you as one. Love Martin."

Mr Denham described Martin as a "happy-go-lucky lad" who had attended a special unit for children with learning difficulties and then trained as a machinist. "We blame the BBC ", he said. After the case, Ms Aideen Hanley, a solicitor representing the BBC, stated that those concerned with the programme had expressed their sympathy to Mr and Mrs Denham.

Sources: Mostly Nottingham Evening Post, 7, 9, 10 Nov 1992. Coroner's verdict was in D.Telegraph, 23 Dec 1992.

The 'warnings' failed in their stated purpose because they were paradoxical; after all, why put warnings *in* a drama unless it is to heighten the dramatic effect? The Magritte-like surrealism of a drama which says 'I am not a drama' was sure to go over most viewers' head.

LESS EXPLICIT

There was a second, less explicit, clue that the programme was fiction; the polt's activities were a pastiche of details from cases, well-known to enthusiasts and researchers, but (probably) not to many viewers, who would have been disturbed by the sheer range and intensity of phenomena packed into a single 'case'. This variety made it simultaneously 'real' and 'unreal' for different audiences.

Those viewers who failed to recognise the 'warnings' and the artificial nature of the 'case' nevertheless expected to see a light documentary on a fascinating topic appropriate to Hallowe'en - this is what Parkinson, Greene, Smith and Charles meant to them. In this sense, I *do* think the public were misled; perhaps not deliberately, but that was the perceived effect.

While a BBC spokesman shrugged off responsibility saying "We billed it as drama, but people are entitled to their own opinions," Michael Parkinson antagonised people further by accusing those who had been fooled of "living under a stone for the previous two weeks. I have no concerns whatever about the show. You always get a certain percentage who believe everything on TV is real. If people were scared, we did our jobs well."

DELUSION

Parky said: "It shows what a capacity TV has for delusion." Stephen Volk explained: "I wanted to point up the blurring of fact and fiction in what we are shown on our TV screens every day. If the ambiguity of the style served to make people suspicious that television in general is not to be believed, then I'm delighted." Not many people could distinguish the message from the medium, with at least one disastrous consequence – see panel.

The presenters were *trusted* to be in control, and viewers became increasingly alarmed with each new event that showed they were not in control at all but – *mirabili dictu* – acting. Then,

THE ENFIELD POLTERGEIST

Scenes at the original haunted house in Enfield, Middlesex, in 1977, which inspired *Ghostwatch*. Top: Mother dodges a flying brick. Below: The children watch anxiously as phenomena occur. Asked about the parallels between fact and fiction, author of the study of the Enfield case, Guy Lyon Playfair, said: "I will not comment on that here except to urge viewers to wait for the reissue of my book - *This House is Haunted* (1980) - which will contain a longish epilogue describing some of the various spin-offs and rip-offs of the Enfield case, which was far more varied and dramatic than the BBC's fictional one. Art, in this case, has not yet caught up with real life."

just when they expected an explanatory wrap-scene, it faded to credits. The phone-calls were inevitable.

It is true that no amount of forewarning will prepare some people. How else can you explain the fact that, in 1988, on the 50th anniversary of Orson Welles' WOTW broadcast, a Portuguese radio station recreated it, causing widespread panic in the northern town of Braga? (AP 31 Oct 1988). But if the public are slow to learn, so too

are the media. In this I am reminded of a postmortem on the original WOTW panic in 1938, in the *New York Times* a few days later. It went: "Radio officials should have thought twice before mingling this news technique with fiction so terrifying. Horror for the sake of thrill has been legitimately exploited on air, but to disguise it as news with the deplorable results achieved underlines the need for careful self-searching in broadcasting."

Hoax!

WHAT THE EXPERTS SAID

Did Ghostwatch do the field of parapsychology more harm than good? We asked a number of prominent parapsychologists for their reactions.

GUY LYON PLAYFAIR – "Parts of *Ghostwatch* were certainly true to life, notably the TV crew climbing all over the family's home and directing their lives by remote control from Thought Control House. I found the acting and the direction pretty good. Will it do more good than harm? Possibly, if more real cases come to light and more people investigate them properly. Perhaps Darwin College will one day give its Perrott-Warwick fellowship to somebody who actually believes in psychical research and is prepared to do some. Did viewers really expect a serious probe into the poltergeist by a TV company on Hallowe'en? Whatever happened to the great British sense of humour?"

JOHN, LORD HADDINGTON, founder member of CCCS – "I happened on the programme shortly after it had started, and at first thought, as did many other viewers, that it was for real until some obviously scripted conversations ensued in situations that were supposed to be spontaneous interviews with alleged experts and members of the public. Clearly this programme was designed to shock [..] and would not have been much help to those viewers seeking a greater understanding of poltergeist activity. The two girls are to be commended for their acting; it scared the living daylights out of me."

MAURICE GROSSE, Chairman of the 'Spontaneous Phenomena Group', SPR – "Allowing for artistic licence, I thought it was well produced, but I do question whether it was right to portray a real case (thinly dis-

guised as a fake documentary) when the horror was so ridiculously overdone. It must have given the impression that poltergeists are evil and demonic. In my experience, which is exten-

sive, this is not so. They are more mischievous than evil. I would have preferred the BBC to have made a factual film of the Enfield poltergeist case. It would have been more interesting, more dramatic and more convincing. It certainly would have done a lot more for the credibility of psychical research. However, as we have to experience the paranormal 'Hollywood style', I suppose any sort of cheating is permissible, even if it does scare the pants off all and sundry, including small children.

ALAN GAULD, psychologist, University of Nottingham – "The money spent on 90 minutes of Hallowe'en nonsense would probably have funded some sensible research into poltergeists for several years."

SUSAN BLACKMORE, psychologist, University of Bristol – "My general feeling was that it treated the audience unfairly. It can be exciting to play on the edge of fantasy and reality, or stretch the accepted norms of television conventions, but this was neither true to its format nor fun. It was horrid to watch the distress of the girls - real or faked. The 'experts' (who were unconvincing as experts) could have given useful information - eg. refer-

ring to past cases, typical features of poltergeists, or methods of research, etc. (The Rosenheim case is referred to, but only briefly in the midst of an argument.) I found it over-long and occasionally disgusting; the totally gratuitous and revolting detail of the mutilated pregnant dog was the worst - just the sort of thing some stupid copycat might find amusing. The lack of adequate warnings was irresponsible."

ANTHONY D. CORNELL, Vice President of the SPR – "The most seriously misleading element of the programme was the depiction of poltergeists as uncontrollable, malevolent and evil entities that could produce mayhem on a scale I have never come across. Its most dangerous aspect was the portrayal of the widespread possession of anyone taking part by discarnate entities. Possession does occur in some cases, but not to the extent suggested by *Ghostwatch*. Similarly, one does encounter inexplicable malfunctions of equipment, but not to the ludicrous level at the end. Cases of haunting do involve considerable tension and emotional distress for members of the household, which an investigator has a duty to remove, rather than behave in a way that exacerbates the situation."

MANFRED CASSIRER – "Thumbs down. This kids' stuff, with people wearing silly t-shirts, and starring phoney SPR members, was in equal parts confused and confusing. It is likely to bring psychical research into contempt by its frivolity."

Ghostwatch was a Screen One Special, produced by Richard Brooke and Ruth Baumgarten of the BBC1 drama department; directed by Lesley Manning; written by Stephen Volk; broadcast at 9:25 pm on BBC1, 31 October 1992; and starred Michael Parkinson, Sarah Greene, Mike Smith, and Craig Charles.
Sources: Pre-publicity for *Ghostwatch* appeared throughout the week leading to 31 Oct 1992, including *Radio Times* and other listings. Reviews and comments used here: *S.Express, News of World, Mail on Sunday, 1 Nov; D.Telegraph, Guardian, D.Record, 2 Nov; D.Telegraph 4 Nov; Psychic News 14 Nov 1992. Plus letters, leaders etc in Nottingham Eve.Post, 2, 4, 6 & 10 Nov 1992.*

FT

ARCHIVE GEMS:
1. The Italian Martians

HILARY EVANS, CURATOR OF THE MARY EVANS PICTURE LIBRARY, LOOKS BACK AT A STRIKING IMAGE OF AN EARLY ALIEN ENCOUNTER

To read the American UFO literature, you would think the Americans invented the alien landing scenario; but the Italian case of Rosa Lotti, on 1 November 1954, anticipates all but a few of them, and offers an unsurpassed wealth of detail.

Since it was All Saints' Day, Rosa woke at 6:30 to go early to mass at Cennina church, carrying with her a bunch of flowers to offer the Madonna. She also carried her shoes and stockings so as not to soil them on the way. As she passed through a wood, she was surprised to see through the trees a strange object. Though she had no idea what it might be, she would probably have continued on her way if two little creatures, half the height of a normal man, but perfectly human-like in appearance, had not suddenly appeared.

They spoke to her in a language she could not understand, grabbed the flowers and stockings from her hands, deposited them in their 'rocket', and then produced a small tubular object which they pointed at her as if to photograph her. At this point Rosa began to feel uneasy, and started to move away. The creatures made no attempt to restrain or follow her. Looking back from a turn in the path, she saw them still standing by their 'craft'. That was the last she saw of them as she continued on her way.

A simple peasant, 40-year-old Rosa was a respectably married mother of four. Investigators found no reason to suspect a tendency to hysteria or hallucination. It was her parish priest who, when she told him of her experience, associated it with '*dischi volanti*' (flying saucers) and suggested that the creatures she had met were '*i Marziani*'.

This splendid colour painting by Walter Molino featured on the cover of the Italian weekly *La Domenica del Corriere* for 14 November 1954, just two weeks after Rosa Lotti's encounter with the 'men from Mars'.

Whatever the explanation for her experience, it remains one of the most appealing, as well as one of the most enigmatic of 'encounter' cases. "I hope that one day or another they manage to capture one of these beings," observed Rosa's husband in a 1977 interview, "then we would know that my wife was speaking the truth."

Hilary Evans is a UFO historian and co-proprietor of the Mary Evans Picture Library (59 Tranquil Vale, London SE3 0BS), which has a fine range of UFO-related pictures from which this illustration is taken. The case history is in *UFO in Italia* and the artwork is by Walter Molino. This item originally appeared in *The Skeptic* (PO Box 475, Manchester M60 2TH, UK), and is reprinted with their kind permission.

UNEARTHED:
1. SOMETHING NAZI

STEVE MOORE INVESTIGATES THE MYSTERIOUS FATE OF HITLER'S CORPSE...

According to the official version, Adolf Hitler and his mistress, Eva Braun, committed suicide on the 30th April 1945. Close aides then poured petrol over the corpses and set fire to them, and the charred bodies were believed to have been lost during heavy Soviet shelling of Berlin in the days that followed.

In a strange precursor to later events, a rumour circulated last spring (*NY Post, 17 Mar 1992*) that ABC Television's 'Nightline' programme was preparing a show based on Soviet Intelligence files concerning the last days of Hitler. It was claimed that, for the grand finale, the programme would show Hitler's head in a jar, preserved by the KGB. A spokeswoman for 'Nightline' denied that any such programme was being planned.

Perhaps this was the source of subsequent rumours turning up in July that Hitler's remains might still be preserved in Russia. According to Lev Bezymensky, a 72-year-old historian/journalist, the Soviet Army found the burned corpses in a shallow grave in the Chancellery grounds on 4 May 1945; they were almost immediately reburied in the same grave when stories flashed round Berlin that Hitler was still alive. They were later exhumed and reburied six (or nine) times, and autopsied once (or twice) – reports vary.

> "It was claimed that for the grand finale the programme would show Hitler's head in a jar, preserved by the KGB."

The bodies were apparently preserved, along with those of Joseph Goebbels and his family, by the counterintelligence unit of the Soviet 3rd Army, known as SMERSH (a Russian acronym for 'Death to Spies') and in 1946 they were finally buried in Magdeburg, in what was then East Germany. Finally, in 1970, the bodies of Hitler and Braun were dug up yet again and destroyed, except for their teeth and dental work, used in identifying bodies, which are said to remain in Russian military archives. Bezymensky says he got the information from the KGB, but only on condition that he said, in his 1968 book, that the bodies had been destroyed in the original fire. The Russian Security Ministry (successor to the KGB) refused to confirm or deny his claims.

If all this doesn't sound dubious enough, the story surfaced again in September, when Russian TV showed a few seconds' worth of grainy film-footage from KGB archives, purporting to show Hitler's corpse. Perhaps the best that could be said of this is that it showed a man who *looked like* Hitler, with a dark moustache and similar hairstyle, lying on his back and wearing a military

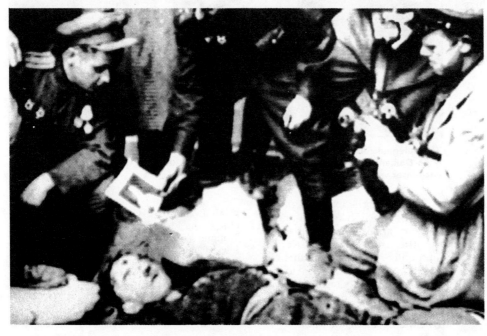

TOP: Victory, as Adolf Hitler celebrates becoming Chancellor of Germany on January 30th 1933.

LEFT: Still from the KGB film purporting to show Hitler's corpse.

uniform. At one point, Russian soldiers are seen gathering round the body, comparing it with a photograph. The significant detail, though, is that the body is not burnt. The next thing we know, Bezymensky is claiming that the bodies were not burnt when they were found (*Rocky Mountain News*, 17 Sept 1992). Apart from that, though, he seems to have been largely forgotten as two old adversaries from the 'Hitler's Diary' days took the field. Lord Dacre (Hugh Trevor-Roper) said he didn't dispute the idea that the Russians had taken the remains back to the USSR, but he still thought they were partially burned; though how much he wasn't sure. Right-wing historian David Irving thought there was a 'great possibility' that the Russians still had the unmarked preserved body, and speculated about

KGB disinformation making all reports unreliable.

Almost immediately, the film and photos came under attack and with near-suspicious swiftness the original cameraman was produced: Michail Poselsky, a member of SMERSH. He said that he had doubts about the corpse's identity at the time, when he saw that it was wearing darned socks. He added that the body was one of *two* Hitler doubles who'd been found dead in the ruins of the Chancellery and dragged out into the daylight because the cameramen weren't carrying lighting equipment. Apparently, officials at the Krasnogorsk archives were fully aware that the body in the film was that of a double, leading to further speculation about KGB disinformation.

Independent, 18 Sept; S.Express, 20 Sept 1992.

2. SHOOTING TSARS

... AND CLAIMS THAT THE ROMANOV BONES MAY HAVE BEEN DISCOVERED IN A FOREST NEAR SVERDLOVSK

Such is the bewildering British obsession with royalty that it even seems to extend to dead foreign monarchs. So much has been written on the Romanov saga in the last year that we can only summarise briefly here.

The story really got off the ground in July 1991, when it was announced that a grave containing nine skeletons had been found in the forest near Sverdlovsk. Few details were made available at the time, but the remains were said to be those of Tsar Nicholas II and his family, along with their servants.

In December, an eye-witness account of the executions at Ekaterinburg was released. This was written by the late Alexei Kabanov, one of the execution squad, and told how the family was woken at 2:00am on the night of 17 July 1918 and taken downstairs to a previously cleared room. Eleven people were present: the Tsar, his wife Alexandra, the crippled heir Alexei, the four daughters, the family doctor and three servants. The Tsar was killed with a single shot; the rest shot as they ran about. When the noise of the shooting began to disturb the neighbourhood, those who were still alive were finished off with bayonets and three of the family dogs were hanged to prevent them barking. It's perhaps not surprising that this account makes no mention of the alternative version, that the family was raped before execution.

By May 1992, Russian archæologists had examined the burial pit and further details emerged. It appears that the killers went to great lengths to hide their crime. The bodies were stripped and burned, using 150 gallons of petrol. Nine of the bodies were then thrown into a pit and had sulphuric acid poured over them. Finally, a lorry was driven back and forth over the pit to crush the remains. Findings in the burial pit, which had been covered with railway sleepers, seemed to confirm this. One of the skulls had bullet wounds; other bones were crushed or showed bayonet wounds; there was no clothing; and remains of two ceramic jars, thought to have contained the acid, were also found.

Curiously, these first reports mention that the body of the Tsar's

daughter, Anastasia, had been identified, as one of two skeletons found outside the pit. This detail rapidly disappears and there is no further mention of any other bodies being found apart from the nine in the pit. Indeed, not everyone was convinced. It was suggested that these bodies were not those of the royal family, but a family of rich merchants, also killed by the Bolsheviks.

June brought 'positive identifications' of the Tsar, Alexandra and the doctor, Sergei Botkin, using computer-modelling to compare the skulls with old photographs. It also brought the contradictory detail that 'bits of the Tsar's clothing' had been found at the site.

By July, Dr William Maples of the C.A. Pound Human Identification Laboratory in Florida had been brought in to help, and he added identifications of three of the Tsar's daughters, Olga, Maria and Tatyana. He also said that the remaining skeletons corresponded to a middle-aged woman and two middle-aged men, thought to be the servants. There were no remains that could be identified as Anastasia or Alexei. (*D.Express + Aberdeen Press & Journal, 29 July 1992.*) This throws interesting light on the long-held claim of the late 'Anna Anderson' that she was actually Anastasia, who'd been pulled clear of the execution by one of the guards; she's usually written off as an impostor, but who can say for sure?

Finally, samples of the bones were brought to Britain in September for DNA testing at the Government Forensic Laboratory at Aldermaston. Samples will be compared with known locks of hair from the family, preserved in Moscow, and various surviving members of the Romanovs, as well as several European royals, are said to have volunteered genetic material. There's also the possibility that some of Anna Anderson's hair will be tested. The tests are expected to take some months, so we await developments. In the meantime, the search is said to be continuing for the remains of Alexei and Anastasia, still thought, officially, to be buried somewhere in the Sverdlovsk forest.

S.Times, 13 Sept; D.Telegraph, 14+18 Sept 1992.

Tsar Nicholas II and the Tsarina Alexandria, dressed in mediæval robes

WATER BABIES

BOB RICKARD chronicles the thwarted attempts of a group of women who wished to give birth in the presence of dolphins

Back in August 1992, worldwide publicity was given to the imaginative plan of a London obstetrician to develop a new type of human capable of communicating with marine intelligences. Dr Gowri Motha, who runs a holistic obstetric clinic in East London, declared her intention to fly a group of pregnant women to the Israeli resort of Eilat so they could give birth in the presence of dolphins. "Dolphins communicate with one another by ultrasound and may be able to communicate with a fœtus," she said. Using the analogy of the familiar ultrasound scanner, her literature even talks of dolphins being "able to see the baby" inside the mother's body.

COMMUNING WITH NATURE

Dr Motha's vision sounded like an updated version of the hippy creed of communing with Nature, but she is serious and backs up her ideas with reference material. She told *FT* that she was inspired by hearing of 'wild' water-births practised in Russia, and was inspired by the reputed talents of dolphins in helping people suffering from autism and depression. The aim is "to make these children more in tune with nature and the environment, and able to communicate with other mammals who are as intelligent as we are." If funding is forthcoming, said Dr Motha, the babies would be periodically reintroduced to dolphins throughout their early lives and monitored to see if they manifest any "extra communication skills".

In early September, six women – in their last month of pregnancy – travelled to Israel and swam daily with the dolphin colony in Eilat Bay for four weeks, hoping to deliver their babies surrounded by the "gentle and peaceful animals", either in the sea or in a specially-constructed glass birthing pool. During this time, the Israeli health ministry stepped in, warning all the parties involved that births were "forbidden at unlicensed installations". According to an Israeli radio news bulletin, the ministry privately threatened to shut down the sanctuary and prosecute its managers if the births occurred as planned. Dr Chaim Boykes, one of Jerusalem's chief physicians, clearly annoyed,

told Uri Dan of the *New York Post*, that Dr Motha and her patients "can go and give birth among *English* dolphins if they wanted, but they were not welcome to turn the pristine lagoon into a maternity ward." She told *FT* that one advocate offered her free representation, advising her that there was no laws preventing waterbirths.

Despite considerable support from unexpected quarters, Dr Motha's pacifist principles insisted she back down from a fight with the stick-in-the-mud Old Guard health authorities. However, the women had come too far to be thwarted and arranged a compromise: they could give birth submerged, but it would have to be in Eilat's Yosef Tal Hospital. Dr Motha said that one woman's birth went according to plan out on a reef, in the special glass tub with filtered water; another occurred spontaneously in their hotel; and the rest took place in the hospital, all but one conventionally. The exception was a waterbirth – now in the record books as Israel's first – which was attended by the hospital obstetricians eager to learn Dr Motha's method.

INDIAN TRIP PLANNED

The entire trip – which was free to the mothers – has cost Dr Motha over £45,000; a burden made heavier when several sponsors retreated at the first objections from the Israeli authorities. "I am not discouraged. We learned many things from this project," she told *FT*. "Next time I will probably take mothers to India, where the water is warmer and cleaner, and there are wild dolphins in place of the domesticated ones at Eilat." Dr Motha would like to hear from anyone with a yacht big enough for a small party of heavily pregnant mums and a truckload of equipment.

FOOTNOTE:

Benjamin B'Hahn – whose father pioneered underwater births in Britain – fell into the River Avon and drowned in February 1992. An inquest in Plymouth recorded a verdict of accidental death. Five-year-old Benjamin was himself one of the first babies in Britain to be born underwater in a 'birthing tub'.
D.Telegraph, 15 April 1992.

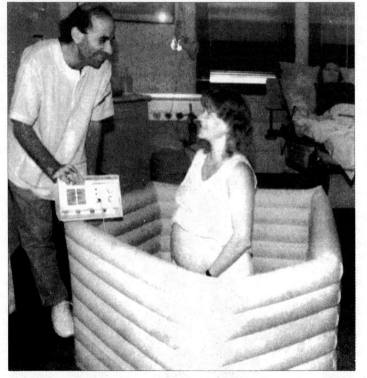

With no dolphins in sight, one of Dr Motha's expectant mothers demonstrates the plastic waterbirthing pool to an obstetrician in Yosef Tal Hospital, Eilat, Israel.

THE BATTLE TRIANGLE GHOST

Well-known ghost writer ANDREW GREEN looks at a rare multiple-witness case

The small town of Battle in Sussex will forever be haunted by the horrifying event of 14 October 1066 when King Harold slugged it out with William of Normandy on Senlac Hill. The community formed by the artisans and general traders who settled here during the building of the Abbey shortly after the Norman Conquest now numbers around 7,000, many of whom take considerable pride in the twinning with St Valery-sur-Somme, the town from which William departed to invade Britain. There are still only two main streets, with a pleasant clutter of mediæval, Georgian, Victorian and modern buildings, but most old residences are to be found in Mount Street, leading down from Caldbec Hill, where Harold amassed his footsore and weary troops before the fatal battle.

In the mid-1920s, Mount Street boasted a couple of churches, a courthouse, the 15th century King's Head, a couple of small shops and a number of houses for residents engaged in farming, gypsum mining in neighbouring Mountfield, and fishing in Hastings, some five miles to the south. One house, now known as the Bayeux Restaurant, was then home to the 23-strong Coade family, the head of which was a well-known and highly-respected butcher. Of his large family, 17 actually reached adolescence and all were blond.

GOLDEN-HAIRED CHILD

Some years after their departure, a farm bailiff moved in and used a small hatchway on the west-facing wall to pay out wages to the workers from the nearby farm. After a few years, an elderly couple took over the property, but by the 1970s they were too old to cope with the stairs and retired to Hastings. Their solicitor assured me that his clients, though in their eighties, were "acute and certainly had all their marbles". They told him that, on autumn evenings, they heard footsteps approach the west wall, stop there for a few moments and then continue into Mount Street. This point was where they had filled in a small hatchway, and they assumed that the sound was "the ghosts of the farm workers coming for their pay". There was also the sound of "someone young running along the upstairs landing and entering one of the empty bedrooms". They felt that the invisible phantom "exuded a feeling of great love and friendliness – nothing to be scared of at all."

Some little time later, Joyce Pain, an artist living in one of the cottages on the north side of the street, facing the restaurant, was quietly dozing in her front room with Muriel, a close friend, when she happened to glance towards the bay window.

"The phantom 'exuded a feeling of great love and friendliness ... nothing to be scared of at all'."

She saw the figure of a young golden-haired girl glide through and stand looking at her friend with "such love and affection that I just wanted to cuddle her but was afraid she would vanish if I approached. She really was so attractive, but I was completely unaware of how she was dressed. All I can recall is that she was about five years of age and had beautiful fair golden hair. She was so lovely." After a few minutes of gazing at her drowsy friend, the girl turned to smile at Joyce and then simply vanished.

The artist learnt from neighbours that the ghostly child had been seen repeatedly during the 1970s in a building only a few doors away, now called the Bayeux Café, opposite the unrelated restaurant of the same name. Once, the phantom was seen walking upstairs and, on another occasion, "standing near the grand piano, having actually touched the owner on the shoulder." The description of the child was identical to that seen by Joyce Pain.

PHANTOM FOOTSTEPS

Immediately opposite, in what might well have been the girl's original home, Sally McCabe was woken at three o'clock one morning in December 1989 by her five-year-old daughter Candy, asking for a glass of water. What astonished and intrigued Mrs McCabe was to see standing, immediately behind her daughter, the figure of another little girl, "fair haired and with such a charming, lovable smiling face that I forgot all about candy. It was only when my daughter repeated her request that I realised that the little stranger was not physical; but she didn't go away, even after blinking my eyes. There was nothing scary about her; she just had a great feeling of love and affection."

The case was filmed by TVS in August 1990 for their popular *Coast to Coast* programme, but for some inexplicable reason it was never transmitted. As far as I know, the young child has not been seen since 1989, but late in October 1992, Ginny Brown, wife of the licensee of the King's Head, only yards from the restaurant and opposite Joyce Pain's house, said that, whilst clearing up in the pub one night, she heard the sound of 'someone' running along the corridor at the top of the three-storeyed building. Thinking it might be her four-year-old daughter Harriet, she rushed upstairs only to find both her children, Harriet and her two-year-old son, fast asleep.

The running has since been repeated and has been heard by members of the staff. Is the unknown little girl now visiting another site and about to change the haunting of the Battle Triangle into an oblong?

FEAR AND LOATHING IN FRANCE

PAUL SIEVEKING looks at hysterical claims of child-murder in the Calais slums

In its most common application, mass hysteria refers to outbreaks of physical symptoms such as dizziness, fainting, nausea and vomiting, with no apparent physical cause, most frequently among workers with dull repetitive jobs (telephone switchboard operators and toll booth collectors come to mind), or among schoolchildren, sometimes (though not always) under stress of some kind. The stress can be political, as exemplified by outbreaks among Arab schoolgirls in Jordan's West Bank in March/April 1983 and among Albanian children in Serbia's Kosovo province in March 1990.

A more elusive variety of mass hysteria is manifested in collective delusions, such as the scare in Yorkshire in 1938-39, when a razor-wielding maniac was widely believed to be terrorising the back alleys of Halifax and neighbouring towns. After a massive police operation, the 'Slasher' was declared to be imaginary. Now, news of a similar episode comes to us from Calais.

The story begins on Friday, 25 September. Someone's child – nobody knows whose – told a parent that a man was taking photographs outside the Georges-Andrique school in the Beau-Marais, a bleak working-class area of Calais with an unemployment rate of over 50 per cent, where 24,000 people live in crumbling high rise blocks. In fact, a city surveyor was taking photographs as part of a study for the construction of a new square.

ENRAGED PARENTS

Headmaster Armand Pierrot was called to the door of the school, where 20 enraged parents told him there were children with their throats slit. One woman said there were two children in the field behind the school with their stomachs cut open. Pierrot pressed them to provide evidence, none was forthcoming and the parents dispersed. By the evening, accounts had begun to circulate that 13 children had been found with their throats slit in the cellar of one of the high-rises; in the gym of a local school called La Greuze it was said that a young girl had been mutilated. Signs could be seen in the neighbourhood saying: "Blond girls and boys, I will have you". The rumours were reinforced by the presence of

> "Racist violence is rare in Calais, where xenophobia is reserved for the hordes of English who pour across the Channel."

police – who in reality had arrived to stop a man threatening suicide from a sixth floor window.

A scapegoat for the imagined crimes was found in Christophe Beddeleem, 19, a former drug addict with a heavily pockmarked face, who had arrived from Paris to stay with his mother, Marie-Christine Tueux, three days earlier. Beddeleem was raised in an orphanage after his Tunisian father disappeared and his mother was jailed for theft. After a life of petty thefts and drugs in Paris, he was seeking a new start in a new town, reconciled to his mother.

Beddeleem was stopped at gunpoint by a group of men who accused him of taking lewd photographs of their children and being a rapist. They branded him 'bougnoule' (which roughly translates as 'dirty Arab'). He was also called 'Dracula', 'Frankenstein' and 'Freddy the long-nailed rapist'.

LEWD PHOTOGRAPHS

By Monday, 200 people gathered outside the Georges-Andrique school, some with megaphones, screaming that countless children had been burnt alive and vowing to lynch Beddeleem. The hapless 'bougnoule' was held for two days by the police. Asked to describe the man who allegedly had been taking pictures, some children said he was blond, others dark; some that he was fat, others thin; some that he had blue eyes, others that he was wearing sun glasses. No evidence of any kind was turned up by the police; no children had disappeared, no one was raped, no lewd photographs were found.

A month later, Mrs Tueux, surrounded by four of her eight children in her subsidised flat next to the school, was still besieged. Her door had twice been broken down. Beddeleem himself was in hiding. Professional 'explainers' were still puzzling over the case. Racist violence is rare in Calais, where xenophobia is reserved for the hordes of English who pour across the Channel. It was suggested that a concoction of boredom, frustration, fear, anger and ghoulish TV-fed fantasy had finally exploded. Sorbonne sociologist Olivier Duhamel saw the incident as symptomatic of a period of deep uncertainty in Europe.
Int. Herald Tribune, 31 Oct 1992.

DIARY OF A MAD PLANET
OCTOBER—NOVEMBER 1992

This diary aims to record, in two-month segments, the geophysical highlights of our planet: the tempests and tantrums, the oddities and extremities. Compiled by the editors and various correspondents.

DROUGHT 7 October
ZIMBABWE:

The dryspell continues. Hundreds of goats and chickens killed by starving baboons.

METEOR SHOWER 9 October
NEW YORK:

The Draconid meteor shower gave its usual bright display on this day: a lime-green fireball was seen by thousands along the US eastern seaboard. The 30-pound meteorite, one foot in diameter, which slammed into the boot (trunk) of a 1980 Chevy Malibu parked in the New York suburb of Peekskill at the same time, was probably a remnant of the fireball. It passed straight through and made a crater in the driveway. "We felt the rock and it was pretty hot", said owner Michelle Knapp, 18. "My car is totalled". [AP] 11 Oct 1992.

WILDLIFE 9 October
TASMANIA:

Only 15 out of 76 whales stranded off a west coast beach survived. Four were guided out to sea from shallow water off Strahan.

EARTHQUAKE 12 October
CAIRO:

(29.888N/ 31.223E) Depth: 25km. Magnitude: 5.9R. Strongest in living memory; 2 tremors only minutes apart, one lasting 20 seconds. At least 541 killed, 6,500 injured.

Damage blamed on shoddy buildings, which often fall down even without an earthquake; much of the death blamed on panic.

Aksam Sayed Ismail Hamouda, 37, was found alive by a dog after being buried for 81 hours in the rubble of a 14-storey building. He had survived by drinking his own urine; but his mother, wife and daughter died beside him. His only apparent injury was a twisted ankle.

The quake was felt over much of Egypt, from Alexandria to Aswan, and in Israel from Eilat to Jerusalem and Tel Aviv. Estimated damage: 300 million US dollars (see map below).

OZONE LAYER 13 October
ANTARCTICA:

Analysis of September 23rd data from US satellite Nimbus-7 showed Antarctic ozone hole had opened earlier and grown bigger than ever, 8.9 million square miles across, up 15% on 1991. It is now nearly the size of North America. Usually damage is between eight and 15 miles up, but balloon research shows that, due to polluting discharges from two volcanoes in 1991 (presumably Pinatubo and Hudson), almost 50% of ozone above and below this belt has also been destroyed.

The World Meteorological Organisation said ozone levels over Northern Europe, Russia and Canada last winter were 12% below seasonal average. *Nature* detailed further dire consequences of carbon dioxide buildup in the atmosphere: an Arctic version of the annual Antarctic ozone hole. Since northern populations greatly outnumber those in equivalent southern latitudes, health hazards are likely to be greater, even though there should still be greater protection in the Arctic.

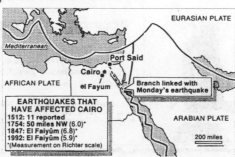

Special thanks to the Global Seismology Group of the British Geological Survey for the earthquake data.

EARTHQUAKE 18 October
COLOMBIA:

(7.123N/76.887W) Depth: 10km. Magnitude:6.6R. Second severe earthquake in two days; 11 killed, 10 of these by an explosion of a mud volcano at San Pedro de Uraba. 115 injured and 1,500 made homeless. Slight damage in Bogota, felt as far south as Cali as well as in eastern Panama and western Venezuela.

WILDLIFE 24 October
MEXICO:

During the previous three weeks, hundreds of birds from 16 different species, migrating from Canada and northern USA to winter feeding grounds in South America, plummeted to earth, dying on impact at Campeche on the Yucatan coast. More than 200 had fallen on a single ranch. They appeared to have died from head injuries when they hit the ground. The Pronatura environmental group ruled out such causes as contaminated air or feather deterioration. [Reuters] 24 Oct 1992.

RAINFALL 5 November
TUSCANY:

Following 40 days and 40 nights of rain, when various cities in the Tuscany region of Italy were brought to a complete standstill by serious flooding, rivers finally fell below danger level.

FLOODING 30 November
SOUTH WALES:

Flood alerts covering nearly a dozen rivers following four inches of rain, which was a fitting conclusion to the wettest November in Wales for 22 years. Railway lines blocked by flood water at Yeoford, Devon; in mid-Glamorgan; near Llanelli, Dyfed; 100 homes flooded in Tredegar, Gwent. Floods were accentuated by drought-hardened ground unable to absorb the rain.

WHO'S SPYING ON SWEDEN?

SVEN ROSÉN on the continuing mystery submarine intrusions in the Baltic

Unidentified submarine objects in the Baltic continue to worry the Swedish navy. In 1981, a Soviet Whiskey-class patrol submarine ran aground while snooping near the Swedish naval base at Karlskrona, and since the great 'USO flap' of 1983, the Swedish government has complained about submarines in its territorial waters. These USOs could not be caught in the navy's nets, nor damaged by depth charges; and in December 1987 the Swedes announced that henceforth

Swedish Commander-in-Chief Bengt Gustafsson: on 19th February 1992 he called a press conference and said the sub mystery was over.

spying submarines would be sunk without warning. These uncatchable USOs have been seen by anomalists as either a submarine branch of the UFO enigma or as a modern variation of the water monsters deeply rooted in Nordic folklore. *Fortean Times* has published numerous bulletins on this fascinating enigma [*FT42:7, 48:16, 49:63, 51:26, 60:64, 61:32.*]

Sweden expected the USOs to go away after the collapse of the Soviet Union in 1991. In a press conference on 19 February 1992, the Swedish Commander-in-Chief, Bengt Gustafsson, said he thought that the vexing saga was over and that an explanation would soon emerge. In Moscow, however, Commodore Emil Svensson conducted talks with the Russian authorities, who denied any knowledge of the USOs, while insisting that they had no reason to hide the mistakes of the old regime.

The summer of 1992, however, saw more USO intrusions than ever, and the armed forces couldn't conceal their bewilderment. It seemed that wide areas of the Stockholm 'skärgard' (archipelago) were under attack, particularly the naval bases of Muskö and Berga. Muskö is the headquarters of the East Coast Fleet, an atomic bomb-proof mountain fortress harbouring some of the elite

This ad, printed in *Moskovskaya Pravda*, was paid for by *Expressen Magazine*, (hoping for a scoop, one supposes) but it was the Commander-in-Chief who took the initiative.

vessels of the Swedish navy. Its primary task is to protect Stockholm and prevent invaders from reaching the coast of Norrland through the Åland Sea.

In May, the presence of at least two subs, including a 28-metre-long 'mini-mother sub', was fully established, according to the C-in-C, who added that the evidence for the intrusion was the most conclusive for a decade. In July and August, subs were reported from both the north and the south archipelagoes of Stockholm, particularly round the islands of Muskö, Möja and Bjärkskär. The weather was hot, however, and the 24,000 islands of the archipelago were swarming with holiday makers and sailing boats, preventing the navy from mounting an attack.

SMART TORPEDO

The third USO hunt began on 13 September in the waters off Oxelösund, when a 'smart' homing torpedo ('torpedo 442', made in Italy and worth three million kronor), was fired at a supposed sub near the Hävringe lighthouse. Though these torpedoes are described as 'foolproof', this one failed to explode and just disappeared. The navy was still looking for it in November.

On the morning of 16 September, a sub was believed to be in the waters north of the Gustav Dalén lighthouse; clear recordings were made of electric motors, and the typical sound of screw blades was recognised. A "carpet of depth charges" was dropped over the target, whereupon it was showered with electromagnetic anti-submarine shells. All signs of sub activity ceased after the charge, but there was no wreck, no oil spots, nothing but shoals of dead herring.

Another sub was depth-charged on 21

September, but again, nothing was found. On 23 September, two or three subs were believed to be in or near Oxelösund harbour, and the three navigable passages were blockaded to prevent an escape. As always, nothing was found, and on 26 September the hunt was called off. Swedish Premier Carl Bildt said that the September hunt involved "the greatest concentration of grave incidents that have occurred in Sweden in more than a decade" (ie since the Soviet sub ran aground in 1981).

Submarines are said to produce three types of sound: electric motor hum; noise of hydraulics (pipes, pumps etc); and the sound made by the screw-blades. This last is apparently quite distinctive for every individual sub, a sort of 'fingerprint', according to press officer Wyn Enqvist. This sonar evidence shows that the 1992 USOs are the same ones that have haunted the coast in previous years; some craft have been recorded at least 40 times. Said Björn Borg, head of the navy's information service: "We recognise each individual intruder. Their sounds are neatly registered in the navy's sound library." The navy esti-

The lore of secret submarines began early in Europe. This illustration appears in G. Le Faure's novel *La Guerre Sous L'Eau* (1892) in which a mini-submarine travels up the Rhine, surfacing only at night.

mates that the intruding 'fleet' comprises at least eight mini-mother-subs and 14 minisubs, some equipped with caterpillar tracks "to perform precision work on the sea bed."

In the 1980s, identification of the craft was more of a political than a scientific problem for the Swedes, as relations with their powerful Soviet neighbour had to be kept sweet. The situation today, however, is rather different; last summer, Premier Bildt didn't hesitate to blame Russia for the subs, although he stressed that he didn't hold the Russian *government* responsible. Until 1987, the Swedes blamed the Russian navy; then suspicion shifted to Soviet military intelligence, the GRU. Now, the supposed culprit is some covert intelligence organisation or 'gang' (*liga*), unknown to the Russian government.

RUSSIAN DIE-HARDS?

It might well be asked why this hypothetical outfit is mounting pointless spying missions. Gustafsson has suggested that it is a hardline communist group waiting for the old political order to be restored; meanwhile, it continues its old routines as before, rather like the Japanese soldiers who continued to fight World War II in the jungles of the Far East. The idea is certainly bizarre in the extreme: a diversionary brigade of 500-700 men with 22 submarines, diverse frogmen equipment, submarine mopeds and so forth, with bases unknown to any government in the region and bankrolled by god-knows who... One might prefer the equally outlandish conspiracy theory that the Swedish navy is fabricating evidence, perhaps to increase its state subsidies.

If a covert Russian organisation, working against the

Russian government, *is* behind the USOs, it is putting its very existence at stake in the Baltic, where the Swedish navy is under orders to sink any unidentified craft. It has been suggested that the intruders are placing mine-barriers in important channels of approach (to Muskö, for example) which will be activated in the event of war; or perhaps they are trying to retrieve something top secret. One would expect the subs to avoid trouble as much as possible, but they have frequently appeared with conning-towers, periscopes and masts in full view, and seemed quite unwilling to disappear until they were certain that they had been observed. The sub hunt last September started when USOs appeared *in the middle of the Swedish coast fleet*, on conscript-training manœuvres. This was no exception; USOs have often appeared during manœuvres. If they are spying, what could they possibly learn that they didn't already know?

ADVERTISING FOR SPIES

A Defence Staff informant suggested (*Expressen* 2 October) that there were no subs outside Oxelösund in September and that the sonic traces came from a series of small transmitters hidden in crevices on the sea bed, placed as a decoy while *real* submarine reconnaissance was going on elsewhere. If this were true, one could further speculate that such a system of transmitters could start up on its own through some technical mishap. This might explain why the smart torpedo didn't find a target and why there were so many sub reports in 1992 despite the fact that the USSR has been dismantled. However, the many visual sightings of subs negates this line of thought. On 23 September, a navy press officer confirmed that 'navy personnel' had seen USOs on at least two occasions in September, and said that a strangely torn fishing-net had been sent to a Linköping laboratory for analysis.

Gustafsson appealed on Swedish TV for any information, pointing out that exposing an organization that is working against its own government is not an act of treason. Subsequently, advertisements appeared in *Expressen* (24 September), the Russian army journal *Kraznaya Zvezda* (29 September) and the newspaper *Moskovskaya Pravda* (10 October), offering western cash to ex-Soviet sailors or spies with any information on the Baltic intrusions to ring Gustafsson on Stockholm 7887500 (fax 6646144). Advertising for spies seems like a last resort; but a couple of million pounds for the truth would be a bargain, considering the cost of each year's USO hunts.

Sources: Dagens Nyheter, 13 Oct; Expressen, 23 June, 15,17,18,22,24,25 Sept, 2,15 Oct; Skänska Dagbladet, 17,24 Sept, 15 Oct; Sydsvenska Dagbladet, 17,18,19,22,23,24,25,26,27 Sept, 2.15,17,24 Oct 1992.

SECRET COUNTRY

Mysterious places to visit in Great Britain compiled by Janet & Colin Bord

7: Dinas Bran, Llangollen, Clwyd

The ramparts of the Iron Age hillfort and the ruins of the mediæval castle crowning the hill can be clearly seen.

Standing high above the wooded Dee valley, this prominent hill may be an important site in Arthurian legend. Its name means Bran's Stronghold, Bran being a king of Britain and the hero of a *Mabinogion* tale. He was killed following an invasion of Ireland and his head was buried in the White Hill, believed to be Tower Hill in London. So long as the head remained buried, this island was protected against invasion; but King Arthur had the head exhumed, since he wished to protect the island through his strength alone. 'Bran' means raven, and the story of his buried head is thought to be connected with the belief that the presence of ravens at the Tower keeps the country safe from invasion. There might also be an echo of the ancient Celtic head-cult: severed heads were kept as talismans, and stone heads were carved to represent guardian deities.

Bran the Blessed's links with the mysterious hill in the Dee valley may seem tenuous, but they are nevertheless intriguing. Bran means rave nor crow, and so does Corbin, an old French word and the name given to the Castle of the Grail by Malory in the 15th century. Dinas Bran has been called Crow Castle in more recent centuries. The Fisher King of the Grail Castle was, in one version of the legend, called King Bron, and more than once it has been suggested that Dinas Bran was the hiding place of the mystical Holy Grail. The place is even mentioned in the romance *Perlesvaus*, or *The High History of the Holy Grail*. According to folklore, a golden harp is said to be hidden in the hill, but it can only be found by a boy who has a white dog with a silver eye: such dogs were said to be able to see the wind. The hill of Dinas Bran has also been known as a haunt of the Little People, and a young lad called Tudur who was watching sheep on the hillside was drawn into the fairy dance one summer's night. The scene was a hollow called Nant yr Ellyllon (goblins' brook), halfway up the hillside. First Tudur saw a tiny man with a fiddle; then the dancers arrived and the music began. Tudur was entranced by the scene, though he hesitated joining in for fear that the devil might be responsible and he would be spirited away. However, he couldn't resist, and as he danced he cried "Play away, old devil; brimstone and water, if you like!"

As soon as he spoke, the musician turned into the devil and the fairies became animals, and as they danced they looked like a wheel of fire. Tudur danced all night because he couldn't stop and his master, searching for the lost sheep and their shepherd, came upon him still spinning around in the hollow.

Today, the hill is crowned with the ruins of a mediæval castle, as well as the ramparts of an Iron Age hillfort, and from the top is a breathtaking view of the valley, the town of Llangollen and the surrounding countryside. It's a steep climb, but for those fit enough a path leads up from the north end of town, by the school.

Janet and Colin Bord are authors of Mysterious Britain, The Secret Country, Alien Animals, The Atlas of Magical Britain, and Modern Mysteries of Britain among many other books.

FT

On top of the hill, among the ruins of Castell Dinas Bran.

UFOLOGY:
Andy Roberts is a residential social-worker who edits *UFO Brigantia*, which looks at the underside and otherside of ufology. (Inquiries to: 44 Elland Rd, Brighouse, W.Yorks HD6 2QR.)

SCIENCE WATCH:
Dennis Stacy is a freelance science journalist living in San Antonio, Texas. He edits the monthly *Journal* of MUFON, the largest UFO research organisation in the USA.

FOLKLORE:
Paul Screeton is a feature writer and sub-editor on a newspaper in north-east England. Formerly editor of *The Ley Hunter*, he currently produces the controversial magazine *Folklore Frontiers*.

EARTH MYSTERIES:
David Sutton has written many horror short stories. He has edited the UK's award-winning genre magazine *Fantasy Tales* for 15 years and is also co-editor of Pan Books Horror series *Dark Voices*.

Ufology

Curiouser and Curiouser

Andy Roberts looks at a contentious new case of UFO abduction from the USA

The name Linda Napolitano, or 'Linda Cortile' as she is pseudonymously known, most likely means nothing to you; but you're going to hear of little else in ufology over the next two or three years. Her name will be better known than that of Betty and Barney Hill or J. Allen Hynek. The Napolitano case offers proof positive that aliens exist – or at least Budd Hopkins and his colleagues in abduction research think it does.

Napolitano is one of Hopkins' stable of abductees with whom he has been working for some time. He believes she has undergone UFO experiences and abductions since early childhood. In November 1989 she intimated to Hopkins that she might have had another abduction experience only hours previously, and so he placed her under hypnotic regression once more. Linda related how several small figures had taken her from her room through a *closed* window and up through a bluish-white beam of light into a large UFO hovering above her block of flats. Here she underwent the usual medical examination before being returned to her bedroom, where she found that her husband and children

were in a deep sleep from which it was hard to awaken them.

So far, so-so. Just another abduction case. But in February 1991, Budd received a letter purporting to come from two 'police officers' who described seeing an event (woman floats out of window into blue light and up into UFO) from the identical time and place as that of Napolitano's experience. Either this was a hoax, a coincidence of abductions (!) or that most rare occurrence, the third party witness to a Close Encounter of the Fourth Kind (a CE4).

In Autumn 1991 yet another witness to the event came forward and, unaware of what had gone before, gave further corroborative evidence. Weird? It gets better. The two 'police officers' then revealed themselves to be security agents guarding none other than Javier Perez de Cuellar, then Secretary General of the United Nations.

So now we have an abductee, two

security agents, another visual witness, a further witness who claims she experienced a car stop in the same location *and* de Cuellar, all of whom saw or were part of the same abduction event. Hopkins is certain none of them are connected (thus ruling out a hoax) and that all are telling the truth.

According to Hopkins, the whole abduction was specially staged so the important political figure could witness it "as a demonstration of alien intentions and power". He could be right: if the witnesses aren't lying and all came forward independent of each other, then something pretty damned strange took place.

Hopkins goes into the case in some detail in the September 1992 issue of *MUFON Journal*. I think this is going to be *the* case on which abductions as alien events stand or fall. If (and in my opinion when) it all falls down, the nonsense that aliens are abducting human beings can be laid to rest and we can sort out just what *is* behind these experiences.

There are serious problems with the Napolitano case, despite backing from several American UFO luminaries, such

> "According to Hopkins, the whole abduction was specially staged so the important political figure could witness it 'as a demonstration of alien intentions and power'."

as David Jacobs and Walt Andrus. It would appear that Hopkins has not actually met the two security agents; all his information comes via the postal service or through Napolitano herself. In addition, and most curiously, Napolitano claims to have been kidnapped by the two agents, sexually abused and almost murdered. Furthermore, one of the agents, by Hopkins' own admission, has a "clearly deteriorating mental state" and in his letters claims that Napolitano is part alien herself. Despite her claims of kidnapping and abuse, Napolitano has not gone to the police; Hopkins and the other ufologists have backed her inaction. It has been claimed that involving the police would be 'politically damaging' to ufology.

It looks as if once again American ufology will be torn apart by disputes over what constitutes proof. Hopkins has provided himself with the ultimate escape clause in the *MUFON Journal* article, which ends: "If rumours are true and there are officially sanctioned intelligence agents within the various UFO investigation networks, these people will also be mobilized to subvert the case from the inside, even before its full dimensions are made known to the public at large. The stakes are that high." Thus anyone who criticises the Napolitano case is likely to be dismissed as a government agent. I rest my case!

Hawking Hawking

Dennis Stacy casts a wary eye over the business of selling a scientist

Not since Einstein's glory days at Princeton has a scientist been so universally feted and lionised as Cambridge cosmologist Stephen Hawking. His *Brief History of Time* is one of the most popular non-fiction books of the last half of this century. *History* spent some 100 weeks on the bestseller list of the *NY Times* and sold approximately five million copies worldwide. (Some critics have carped that it's probably the most widely-bought and *un*read book of all time.)

Victim of a degenerative motor neurone affliction known as amyotrophic lateral sclerosis, Hawking is now confined to a special wheelchair and can only communicate with the outside world through a digitized speech synthesiser. As Lucasian Professor of Mathematics at Cambridge, he currently occupies Isaac Newton's old chair.

Hawking's *History* has been followed up by *Stephen Hawking's A Brief History of Time: A Reader's Companion* and a documentary film by the celebrated Errol Morris.

Certainly no one should begrudge Hawking – referred to by one wag as "the Mick Jagger of cosmology" – his astounding and unforeseen success. Still, a little perspective seems in order. After all, Hawking's current marketability stems more from his own personal physical plight than from theoretical work, which is basically as incomprehensible to the unwashed masses as Einstein's own theory of Relativity was once said to be.

Although the notion of scientist as rock star is a fruitful jumping-off point for examining the phenomenon of Hawking adulation, science itself is undergoing a public resurgence and Hawking is simply perceived as one of the foremost scientists of his (or any other) day. His physical plight also pulls at our heart-strings, not so much out of pity, but because Hawking's story is an ennobling one; that of the human spirit actually *thriving* in the face of

> "Hawking *is* HAL; the first human consciousness to wholly abandon his body and speak to us through a silicon chip."

all adversity. Hawking has not only absorbed everything God has hurled against him, but spat back by threatening to read the very mind of the Creator and unravel the most esoteric secrets of the universe. Hawking the atheist has got guts in other words; or soon hopes to have, in the form of a Grand Unified Theory of Everything – GUT for short.

However, another perception is at work here, that of Hawking as disembodied mind, divorced from all the restraints of a physical body, now freed to visit some cosmic chalk-board in the sky and then return to Earth, Prometheus-like, with his GUT equations intact, astral traveller and heavenly messenger rolled into one. Of course, some people think of God as a disembodied consciousness, too, but never mind.

Hawking also recently divorced Jane Wilde, his wife of almost 25 years and mother of their three children, to take up with his long-time nurse. This intimate drama was one of the few landmarks in his extraordinary career strictly verboten to filmmaker Morris. (The break was reportedly occasioned in part by Hawking's atheism versus his wife's religiosity). Ordinarily, I wouldn't care about the personal life and peccadilloes of a world-class scientist, either, except that in Hawking's case it's the only thing that renders him fully human.

It is this ambiguously human aspect of cosmology's leading light, I think, that drives the perception of Hawking as the first living embodiment of virtual reality. Hawking isn't so much a man connected to a computer as a computer connected to a man. Hawking *is* HAL; the first human consciousness wholly to abandon his body and speak to us through a silicon chip. For all practical purpose and intent, Hawking now only lives and works inside cyberspace. It seems to me that he's not so much the Mick Jagger of cosmology, then, as the made-over Michael Jackson of theoretical physics – composed of computer chips and integrated circuitry with a hard drive, monitor and CD-ROM attached – the INTEL of his age, cranking out newer and bigger hits in the face of a relentlessly ticking clock.

The *real* history of time is that it's all too brief, for Hawking and all of us.

FORUM is a column in which anyone with something to say about a particular field, theory or incident can share their thoughts with our readership. If you'd like to join in with an opinion on any area of Forteana, send it in to the editorial address. Ideal length: 500-1000 words. Please enclose a head and shoulders photo of yourself with all Forum submissions.

Dubious Transmissions

Paul Screeton listens to weird interruptions from unexpected voices

The congregation in an Oslo church were halfway through singing the hymn 'Nearer My God to Thee' when they heard a voice booming: "Get ready for take-off." The church's electronic organ had, by a technical freak, picked up an air control tower 13 miles away. As with many stories we read in newspapers, this one is doubtless apocryphal. As a collector of modern folklore, I have dubbed this motif the 'dubious transmission'.

Forteana deals with the anomalous, and the rare but feasible act of one piece of machinery being activated by another is not impossible. An oft-repeated tale concerns a woman whose teeth begin to play music. Electronics experts would deduce that a radio signal was being picked up by her gold and amalgam fillings, combined with saliva acid, creating a primitive crystal set. These could very well be true stories. I will shortly place this in context, but would like to draw attention to modern folklorists' methodology when confronted with such a claim.

One has only to look at a recent issue of *Dear Mr Thoms*, a modern folklore miscellany magazine, covering alien big cats, travelling garden gnomes and the kitten in the spin-dryer. Academic folklorists seem too ready to place all manner of themes common to Forteana – such as ice falls, 'Saharan' dust, entombed toads, rat kings, spontaneous human combustion – within the contemporary folklore canon. They seem reluctant to consider anomalies as true and repeating events of phenomenal reality; and they make no attempt to ascertain the veracity of unlikely events aired by the media. We can put this down to prejudice or intellectual laziness; perhaps any truth would be too uncomfortable to face.

The American guru of urban belief tales, Jan Harold Brunvand, has gone to some lengths to seek historical antecedents for today's popular legends. I would suggest that not only do all contemporary stories have examples going back centuries (prehistoric Jack and Jill went up the hill to fetch a pail of water – from a Neolithic dewpond), but that every 'new' motif which surfaces in the media, however bizarre or unlikely, will eventually be played out in reality.

To return to our 'dubious transmission' motif, the majority of tales cluster around three key elements of both life and lore. These are sex, religion and travel. All three are essential for our wellbeing and we might ask

> "A service at St Martin's Grimsby, Humberside, was interrupted: 'The Lord is my... Rubber Duck calling Balsa Bandit.'"

whether it is wise or necessary to attempt an analysis of which tales are 'true' and which 'apocryphal'.

Dipping into my files, I find religion and sex often feature together. For instance, fans of a TV hot-gospel show could not believe their eyes when a technical hitch gave them a torrid treat of topless beauties as viewers were preparing to join in the closing hymn, "Something Good is Going to Happen to You". In another version, evangelist Oral Roberts was replaced by Lolita, Rita, Amazon and other girls for several minutes, supposedly due to a satellite malfunction.

Churches keep cropping up in these stories. A couple were about to take their vows when from the organ speakers boomed a voice observing, "They're bloody well still in the bloody church". The couple complained to Tameside Consumer Forum, Greater Manchester, that the taxi driver's lookout had spoiled the ceremony and officials were consequently preparing a code of practice.

Then there was an interruption at St Martin's, Grimsby, Humberside: "The Lord is my... Rubber Duck calling Balsa Bandit." The voice belonged to a Citizen's Band enthusiast broadcasting in the area and the organ amplifiers acted as a receiver.

These two stories involve vehicles and the travel element extends to Brazilian Formula 1 Grand Prix ace Ayrton Senna. Racing along at 150mph, his newly-fitted helmet phone was meant to keep him in touch with his back-up team, but an instruction came over for fast food. "I'm already going as fast as I can", he responded upon hearing a request for the speedy delivery of six hamburgers, having intercepted a call from a Brands Hatch catering firm.

Messages from taxis, police and CB have been picked up from fruit machines at four different pubs according to my files; and I have clippings of such other receivers as radios, baby alarms, double-glazing, Jimi Hendrix's guitar at the Isle of Wight pop festival and a shop's electronic cash register which would burst out with Elvis Presley's 'Love Me Tender'. Then there are sexually explicit broadcasts heard at vulnerable locations such as ambulance stations and air traffic control points.

Another occasionally newsworthy event is the innocent video with an incongruous insertion, usually unadulterated pornography. Particularly Fortean in its irony was the evidently bona fide case of toothpaste giant Colgate Palmolive. Customers saved coupons from toothpaste tubes for a free two-hour cassette containing a 10-minute film encouraging children to clean their teeth. One of the 160,000 who received a copy realised it was a pornographic film and took the cassette to Lothian Regional Trading Standards office. She had received one of 50 copies of *Dracula Sucks* accidentally dispatched. The evil aristocrat was seen in a sex romp with the inmates of a lunatic asylum. Colgate apologised and blamed the London firm which copied the film onto the cassettes. Was this embarrassing episode an example of another motif – the 'employee's revenge'?

As they almost say, there's nowt so queer as folklore...

Spirits versus Energy

David Sutton questions some of our assumptions about straight lines in the landscape

The ghost story writer Robert Aickman described, in *The Real Road to the Church* (published in the collection *Cold Hand In Mine*, Gollancz 1975), the superstitious beliefs of the residents of an unnamed French island:

"All over the island, Mrs Du Quesne had said, all over the island when one knew, were these paths: *'le vrais chemins de l'eglise'*. It was the way one went to one's church - when one knew. Several other things were said that Rosa had not comprehended. There was another pause and then the nub of the matter was hinted at: by these paths one also went to one's grave... they had made those dead who were unquiet, almost visible and tangible in Mrs Du Quesne's homestead."

Aickman was supremely adept at strange, psychological stories that are often only loosely classifiable as 'ghost' or 'horror'. I speculate, but it seems unlikely that he was interested in leys, and may not even have been aware of the Fortean 'subculture'. He did, though, have a belief in paranormal phenomena and worked at Borley Rectory at one time. His interests outside the field of literature were opera, ballet, drama and film criticism. Robert Aickman died in 1981, leaving an œuvre of some 40 incomparable ghost stories and two novels.

The home of the aforementioned story's character was, of course, built next to one of these ghostly pathways... And so it may be that Aickman was aware of some obscure folkloristic belief, tucked away somewhere in the French countryside.

Paul Devereux is probably right to dismiss the idea that leys are 'energy' lines - Forum, *FT65:56*. Instead, he offers the intriguing notion of them being associated with 'death' tracks or roads. Hence the frisson created by Aickman's short story, published some 17 years ago.

Since the *kwei* (malign spirits) of Feng Shui travel in straight lines and therefore must be avoided, the theory that leys and similar alignments are to do with the fear of death, ghosts and the mystery surrounding man's mortality, takes on an extra significance.

While I was researching for my novel *Feng Shui*, I found that the superstitious Chinese were very careful to ensure the correct alignments for their tombs and buildings. However, the Chinese *do* describe their landscape lines as 'energy' lines, the *ch'i* (beneficial, cosmic breath) and *sha ch'i* (the breath of ill fortune). Perhaps 'energy' is a misnomer and the oriental leys are spiritual – or ghostly – influences *on* such pathways? The *Kwei*, if you like? This would fit in well with the Dutch and German ghost paths and the fairy roads of Celtic legend, which Paul Devereux mentions.

The practice of Feng Shui is, of course, very much alive. A few weeks ago, I was chatting to a waiter in a Chinese restaurant in Birmingham and was delighted to find out that he was a student of Feng Shui. He described the restaurant as being in a slightly unfortuitous position, as two straight roads fed onto the corner of the building. The city fathers, very much in favour of the continued development of a Chinatown district, do not employ a Feng Shui specialist! Anyway, our waiter was trying to figure out a way to deflect the bad *kwei* without completely re-designing the interior of the dining area, a prospect his employers would no doubt baulk at.

Perhaps the most interesting development in this field will be the synthesis of the more recent theories with the landscapes of Alfred Watkins, which all ley fans have held in such esteem since the heady 1960s and which have already metamorphosed since hippiedom into various concepts. Watkins might not have been amused at his ideas being interpreted as energy sources for UFOs, or their landing strips.

However, if ancient landscapes were crossed with a multitude of old straight tracks, surely not all of them could be associated with spirit paths – the 'real roads to the church'? Perhaps we need a broader perspective, to examine other belief systems, myths, archæology and so on, in order to extract the wheat from the chaff. I can think of no one better qualified than the ubiquitous Paul Devereux, who already appears to be leading the field in researching, sensibly, as an interdiciplinarian.

We should avoid the impression that 'spirit paths' are literally everywhere in neolithic and mediæval landscapes, in the manner of the old ley enthusiasts' opinion that any alignment of a barrow, a hill and a church indicated a ley - unless, of course, spirits/ghosts are and have been far more influential upon our subconscious than we have been prepared to accept heretofore.

> "Perhaps 'energy' is a misnomer and the oriental leys are spiritual – ghostly – influences *on* such pathways? This would fit in well with the Dutch and German ghost paths and the fairy roads of Celtic legend."

REVIEWS

AMERICAN DISCOVERY
by Gunnar Thompson.

Argonauts of the Misty Isles, 4739 University Way NE, Suite 1618, Seattle, WA 98105, USA. 1992, pb $17.95 (inc US postage; apply for overseas rate), pp400, illus, refs, bib, sources, credits, index.

Well, we can look back on Columbus Year and breathe a sigh of relief – but what will we remember of the history fest hooha, with its endless rehashes, beautiful photographs, brave re-enactments and pedantic documentation? Gunnar Thompson's *American Discovery* arrived at Fortean Towers rather late in the day, but it knocks all the other books of the 'who got there first' tribe into a cocked hat.

Thompson was born in Seattle of Norwegian and Native Indian stock, and grew up outside mainstream WASP traditions. He remembers that during an exam, at the age of 12, when asked "Who discovered America?", "I was the dumb Norwegian who wrote 'The Indians'." Later, he was confused and angered to find that it was more fashionable to offer the honour to Leif Erikson instead of Columbus. There and then, "I decided to become a detective of American history."

In the years that followed, Thompson gained degrees in anthropology and psychology, but because his enquiries often brought him into conflict with hide-bound academics, he hiked the byways of any subject that might illuminate the origins of human culture in North America - mythology, archæology, anthropology, history, linguistics and so on. His starting point was simple: if the Native Indians were here to greet the Western explorers, where did *they* come from? He believes that, from the time their ancestors crossed the great land bridge between Alaska and Siberia around 300,000 BC up to the coming of the Europeans in the 16th century, America was "the world's most cosmopolitan society" attracting traders, refugees, and wanderers of countless other cultures.

This, then, is the story of America from the point of view of the multi-ethnic society of Native Peoples - many we know about (the Phœnicians, Celts, Jews, Greeks, Irish, Romans, Hindus, Chinese, Japanese, Africans, Indo-Sumerians, Polynesians,

Scots, Egyptians, Arabs, etc - and many more that we don't. The picture Thompson paints is of a highly mobile world, not in the least daunted – technologically *or* psychologically – by long ocean voyages; as just one of many examples discussed, I was astonished to learn that there is evidence the Kwakiutl Indians from the coast of Northern Canada settled in Hawaii.

To call the book encyclopædic is to be mealy-mouthed; it is 20-years' worth of looting squillions of half-forgotten books in countless libraries, and myriads of objects, artifacts and remains from digs and museums beyond number, all stuffed into one

This Ming dynasty version of an ancient map used to plot voyages 5,000 years earlier, shows the Americas as a ring continent surrounding Asia.

handsomely hefty book. We are treated to perfectly concise presentations on tents, ship building, navigation, hunting, skinning and weaving, agriculture, pottery, flint knapping, writing, games, mining and metallurgy, head gear, and so on, as well as competent re-evaluations of all the enigmatic remains of people and their dwellings and achievements.

Thompson fires off in more directions than a blazing firework factory. There is much here about the plants – like chili peppers and the hibiscus – which reached Asia Minor via China; and the pineapple and maize which reached Europe via Atlantic traders; and many more plants and animals of American origin, found in Europe and Asia before the time of Columbus. He has a sure grasp of his material, and, important for an exposition of such diversity, writes

clearly. An excellent draughtsman, he has filled the book with maps, vignettes and stand-alone pages which compare people, symbols, artifacts or objects from both the Old World and the New. It is the well-thought-out work of a craftsman who *can* communicate his enthusiasm.

This is Thompson's third book. His *Spirit Sign* (1974) was about Mexican symbols of spiritual power; followed by *Nu Sun* (1989), a treatise on contacts between America and China around 500 BC, and the migration of the Yin-Yang symbol (that power-sign) to American peoples. Gunnar Thompson represents a vital new force in New World anthropology, and I think we'll hear a lot more from him. If you read only one book on pre-Columbian America, this is the one you need.

Bob Rickard

AYURVEDA:
LIFE, HEALTH AND LONGEVITY
by Robert E. Svoboda

Arkana (Penguin), London. 1992, pb £8.99, pp332, bib, index.

Ayurveda is the ancient Indian system of medicine derived from the Atharva-Veda, the youngest of the four Indian Vedas, composed sometime in the second millennium BC. Two of its main treatises, the Charaka and Sushruta Samhitas, on medicine and surgery, were compiled as long ago as 1000 BC - their ongoing traditions having certainly withstood the test of time.

Perhaps the greatest beauty of such an ancient and integral medical system is that, unlike most contemporary alternative and holistic forms of medicine, it needs no credentials to validate itself against the statistics and technology of modern medical science. Little is known of Ayurveda in the western world, and doubtless it will soon come under scrutiny; but perhaps from the perspective of the stable heights of its three-thousand-year-old trunk it may well be justified in viewing modern allopathic medicine as a proud sapling, whose growth is prodigious but is still young in learning the interdependence of roots and branches within the present environmental climate of stress, pollution and the search for real meaning.

Svoboda is the first and only westerner to become a fully qualified Ayurvedic physician, graduating in 1980 with flying colours. His writing is extremely lucid and comprehensible - in no way is this work a dry and guarded technical manual. The topics are covered with great insight and include chapters on history, anatomy, diet, diagnosis and treatment, rejuvenation and virilization, along with a detailed pharmacology of herbal, mineral and animal materia medica.

However, Ayurveda is not only the Indian art of medicine, but also the art of life, and an equal part of this book deals with the perennial philosophy of man's identity within the universe. The author's understanding of such topics as Kundalini and the Chakra system reveal the repetitive ignorance and paucity of the very many books on these subjects which line the shelves of New Age bookstores.

Svoboda was very fortunate in having been adopted by a wonderfully charismatic mentor, Vimalananda, a fearless and uncompromising practitioner of Hindu tantra, who taught him far more than may be glimpsed from this book. Inquisitive readers with a healthy disposition towards Indian Tantra are referred to his previous book, *Aghora - At the Left Hand of God* (published by Brotherhood of Life, Albuquerque, New Mexico).

Robert Beer

GENESIS REVISITED
IS MODERN SCIENCE CATCHING UP WITH ANCIENT KNOWLEDGE?
by Zecharia Sitchin.

Bear & Co, Santa Fe, New Mexico 87504, USA. 1991, hb £12.50, pp343, illus, index.

Most scientists accept the tectonic plate theory that land masses drift slowly across the surface of the globe and were once part of a vast supercontinent named Pangæa which split apart – but what was the origin of this single landmass surrounded by water?

According to Sitchin, the Biblical statement in *Genesis* that waters originally covered the face of the Earth and later 'gathered into' one side to reveal the dry land is based on physical facts, described by the Sumerians 6000 years ago; most of modern science being a rediscovery of ancient knowledge. This reads like science fiction, but Sitchin displays a most convincing and impressive knowledge of science and ancient history. The book is one of a series by the author, called 'The Earth Chronicles'.

Sitchin states that four billion years ago, a cosmic collision caused a massive upheaval of the solar system. A large planet, named Tiamat (Maiden of Life) by the Sumerians, completely covered by water, was struck by a cosmic intruder, which knocked off a large chunk. The chunk became the Moon and a collection of asteroids and comets. The remainder was this Earth, with its tilted axis and a big cavity which filled with water, leaving a large mass of mountainous dry land, the proto Pangæa.

The Sumerians named the invader from outer space Nibiru (Planet of the Crossing), and the encounter with the solar system – expressively called the 'Big Whack' theory – caused it to go into a very elliptical and retrograde solar orbit with a period of 3,600 years. There is much more in the book, including the catastrophic effects of the satellites of Tiamat and Nibiru. Some years ago astronomers suggested a similar idea – an intruder named Nemesis or Planet X, causing periodic disturbances – still a controversial subject.

An even more startling claim is that the

Sumerians described intelligent beings (Anunnaki) living on the Nibiru system, who, according to Sitchin, were capable of space travel 450,000 years ago. In astronomical terms, this is like yesterday, but astrophysicists do not apply the same criterion to the possibility of extra-terrestrial intelligence in the solar system, otherwise they would have realised years ago that there is evidence for an ancient civilisation on Mars, as described in *FT65*.

During the closest passage of the Nibiru planet and its satellites to the Sun, every 3,600 years, the Anunnaki take the opportunity to inspect the other planets and have left records, which explains why it appears that the ancients had as much knowledge about remote planets as we have. The date suggested by Sitchen for their most recent visit is 3760 BC, so they should have turned up in 160 BC and might again in 3440 AD. However, Sitchin does not comment on the fact that there seems to be no evidence for the passage of Nibiru in 160 BC. The book includes a chapter on the artifices on Mars, suggesting the Anunnaki had a space base there and that there were even signs of recent activity in connection with the Russian probes which visited the Martian satellite Phobos.

The Biblical story in *Genesis*, properly interpreted with regard to the timescale and with errors of translation corrected, seems to show remarkable knowledge of astronomy and biology.

Sitchin covers a very wide field; the only thing I found really disquieting and illogical is his claim that Anunnaki are almost immortal, because their year is equivalent to 3,600 Earth years. They must be deprived of effective sunlight for a very large part of their orbit, so I would like to have seen some speculation about how they may have evolved and developed in near darkness.

Eric Crew

BROTHER TWELVE
THE INCREDIBLE STORY OF CANADA'S FALSE PROPHET AND HIS DOOMED CULT OF GOLD, SEX AND BLACK MAGIC
by John Oliphant.

McClelland & Stewart, Toronto. 1992, hb £15.99, pp371, photos, index.

Brother Twelve is a fairy-tale about the endless gullibility of mankind, with lashings of weird craziness. An original guru of the New Age teaching, Edward Arthur Wilson was an early hippy cross between L. Ron Hubbard and Joe Stalin who started out as a merchant seaman and ended up a reclusive confidence trickster, faking his own death, in Hubbardesque fashion, following two fascinating courtroom battles with his own followers, in which both plaintiffs and defendants were quite obviously completely hatstand.

Oliphant's book is a well-researched in-depth study of a man who exemplified L. Ron's axiom that the only way to serious riches is to set up your own religion. Wilson established the Aquarian Foundation in the mid-1920s on a group of islands off the west coast of British Columbia, and waited for the insects to land on the fly-paper. Sure enough, off-balance and lonely people started to flock to it, attracted by a theology based on a lot of dodgy occult mumbo-jumbo and the occasional Egyptian deity. Wilson separated them from their money, which he kept in a secret stash under his floorboards, and put them to work building a new civilisation.

In addition to being a religious nutter, Bro 12 was of course also a political nutter. In 1927 he launched a campaign for the US presidency, although this foundered before the '28 election. He developed links with the Ku Klux Klan in his "Protestant Crusade", and ranted about Negroes, Jews, Communists and Catholics. However, in the end a platform couldn't be hacked out between the various unsavoury groups in the Crusade and the campaign disintegrated.

The Aquarian Foundation had branches across North America and some small-scale support in Europe, but it faced difficulties when Wilson began an affair with a woman he'd met on a train journey from Seattle, whom he installed on campus. The members divided over the ethics of the situation and the debate ended up in court with the collapse of the Foundation as a name.

Wilson continued his work, travelled around a bit, and eventually took up with an Elena Ceaucescu-like figure called Madame Zee. The pair ran the settlements as a sort of personal gulag, forcing those who misbehaved into isolation without food, and making hard labour the rule of the camp. Wilson took a 14-year-old boy, Dion Sepulveda, as his personal slave, and there were rumours of sexual abuse, which Sepulveda always denied. Eventually the inmates began to get restless and the end result was another court case. The followers had to be given lucky talismans to get them to give evidence, as they feared Wilson had cursed them. They won their case and were awarded all the money they'd had taken off them, with damages. Wilson, meanwhile, fled with Madame Zee and was not seen again by his ex-followers. He turned up briefly in England before going to Switzerland for medical treatment where his death certificate was signed. After that there were a couple of brief sightings of him, then nothing.

Oliphant's book is a compelling monument to human folly. He has clearly conducted an enormous amount of research, and there are many fascinating details about Wilson's life and times. It'll be right up there on my bookshelf next to the collected works of Morris Cerrulo.

Richard Furlong

DARK DOORWAY OF THE BEAST
by Gareth Hewitson-May.

New World Publishing, Unit 3c, Plumtree Industrial Estate, Harworth, Doncaster, S.Yorks DN11 8EW. 1992, hb £14.95 + 55p p&p, p260, illus, bib, index.

LIBER TzBA
by Aleister Crowley.

Iemanja Press, PO Box 196, London WC1A 2DY. 1992, pb £5.95 + 55p p&p, pp72.

CONDENSED CHAOS
by Phil Hine.

Chaos International, BM Sorcery, London WC1N 3XX. 1992, pb £3.50 inc p&p, pp36, illus, bib.

One of the most enjoyable features of the British occult scene is its thriving small press, ranging from hardbacks to pamphlets, and supported by some excellent magazines. Seriously-intentioned and often inspired, the published material covers a broad spectrum of which these three items give us an interesting cross-section.

Dark Doorway of the Beast is a well-produced hardback in which Hewitson-May attempts to provide an occult model of the origin of thought, based on the symbolic system of the Kabbalah. He proposes that thought-images originate beyond consciousness and that the mind operates a veto, only allowing a small amount of material through a narrow 'gateway' that can be arranged in a linear sequence of conscious thought. Some knowledge of the Kabbalah would assist the reader, as Hewitson-May traces thought from its origin in the 'Astral Light' and along the pathways of the 'Tree of Life'; but the book ranges widely through mythology, tantra, sigils and the occultism

R'yleh, featuring Cthulhu. A drawing by Letebre in *Dark Doorway*

of Aleister Crowley. One occasionally gets the impression that the author is perhaps too involved with his system and may be mistaking the map for the territory - but there's a great deal of interesting material here, if, at times, awkwardly written.

Whatever one thinks of Aleister Crowley may well have been coloured by what one first read about him; but there is little doubt that he was one of the major figures of occultism of this century. *Liber TzBA*, written in 1922 but never before published, at least allows him to speak in his own, very personal, words. This is a transcription– excellently annotated by Steve Wilson – of Crowley's magical diary for the period in which he was attempting to break an addiction to heroin (first medically prescribed for him as a treatment for bronchitis). It is a painful account of a failed struggle (not tidied-up for publication), allowing a view of Crowley the man, rather than the image. A valuable historical item, rather depressing but arousing considerable sympathy, highly recommended to anyone with an interest in Crowley, drug addiction or 20th century occultism.

By far the most fun of the three is Phil Hine's *Condensed Chaos*, a follow-up to his previous booklet *Chaos Servitors*. Here we have a brief look at the history, theory and practice of Chaos Magick. Easy to understand and occasionally hilarious, with a somewhat Discordian bent, it's a fine introduction for any beginner who wants to know what these guys are up to, but still containing enough of Hine's own theorising and experimentation to make it of interest to those already familiar with the subject. I thought it a splendid little book, even though my computer broke down completely as soon as I began writing this review. I guess that's Chaos for you.

As Forteans, we're supposed to be "connoisseurs of explanations", so here are three models of thought-processes which merit our attention as much as any other. They got me thinking, anyway.

Steve Moore

DEATH, DISSECTION AND THE DESTITUTE
by Ruth Richardson.

Pelican, London. 1989, pb £7.99, pp 426, index, bib, notes and refs, illus, appendices

In 1832, the Anatomy Act visited the fate of dissection, previously reserved for convicted murderers, on the poor who died unclaimed in the workhouse. How this came to pass, the political intrigues, social climate, scientific hypocrisy, public outcry and criminal activity which surrounded it is vividly and fascinatingly brought to life by Ruth Richardson.

We meet the Benthamites with their Malthusian 'survival of the fittest' approach to poverty, incompetent surgeons in whose hospital the sick were more likely to die than if they stayed at home, and necrophiliac anatomists who encouraged the trade in human corpses while preparing impregnable tombs for themselves. We travel with body-snatchers into the foul depths of early 19th century graveyards, overcrowded, noxious, rippling with neglect, disease and vermin, from which the snatchers prised the newly buried, but hours after their funerals, the sooner the better – they got more for fresh ones.

Then there's the infamous Burke and Hare, *not* bodysnatchers, but murderers who found they could profit from stifling itinerants and selling their bodies. Hare turned King's Evidence and was released while Burke was hanged and publicly dissected. The horror of their crimes started one of the 19th century's biggest social panics – 'Burkophobia' – where people feared suffocation with pitch plasters on dark streets (not the method Burke and Hare used, though), and spawned imitators like the London Burkers, Bishop and Williams.

Until the plentiful supply of paupers stifled their trade, Snatchers and Burkers stuffed corpses into impossibly small boxes, jammed them in barrels, dragged them up with hooks, imported them from Paris packed in salt and removed their teeth for dentures, while politicians and scientists ignored public outrage and covertly encouraged them until it suited them to act.

Richardson's masterful examination of the 1832 Act, its consequences and precedents, is combined with diversions into the origins of the 19th century's greatest fictional horrors, the vampire and Frankenstein's monster, the folklore of death and the sociology of popular vilification or 'rough music'. The author brings an unwavering light to bear into the dark crevices of early 19th century history wherein dwell many superstitions and popular fears which still thrive, leaving their indelible mark on our culture and public imagination.

Ian Simmons

THE WIDOW OF BORLEY
by Robert Wood.

For someone like myself who was almost weaned on the story of 'The most haunted house in England', and who has read just about everything published on the alleged hauntings at Borley Rectory, this new book on the saga was essential reading. In fact Wood's intention was not to study the phenomena in the case, but one of the main characters who lived at the rectory while the events were taking place - Marianne Foyster, the wife of the then incumbent rector.

There is a strong suspicion that she - in addition to others, including the 'investigator' Harry Price - was responsible for most of the phenomena that occurred during her residence there. But that is tame when set against all the other things she may have been guilty of in her eventful life: bigamist, pathological liar, psychopath, nymphomaniac, murderess – and she may still be alive, aged 93 – Wood presents evidence to support all these definitions of this extraordinary woman. The Rev. Foyster had some skeletons in his cupboard, too, if Wood's conclusions are valid. For students of human psychology, this book is a must; for students of the Borley phenomenon it is essential. *Duckworth, London. 1992, hb £14.99, pp168, illus, index, bib.* **Janet Bord**

BYE-GONES
by Richard Holland.

FT contributor Richard Holland has gathered together a varied and entertaining selection from the *Oswestry Advertizer's* eponymous weekly column which ran from 1871 to 1939. Absorbing tales of ghosts, witches, eccentrics, folk traditions, festivals, plus personal experiences of natural and supernatural phenomena, mainly connected with Wales and the Border Counties. Excellent value. *Published*

by Gwasg Carreg Gwalch, Capel Garmon, Llanrwst, Gwynedd, Wales, 1992, pb £3.50, illus.   **Paul Sieveking**

THE WRITE STUFF
by Barry L. Beyerstein and Dale F. Beyerstein.

Everything you ever wanted to know about graphology and the analysis of handwriting. The underlying idea – that handwriting is an indicator of personality traits – is tested in a collection of essays by proponents and critics. Also discussed is the role of graphology in crime detection and the courts, its use in brain research and employment interviews, and how it compares with phrenology and astrology as a 'character reading' system. The fact that this substantial and academic study comes from a well-known sceptics' press almost makes it a foregone conclusion that the overall verdict is that graphology is a 'pseudoscience' with very little to commend it. Even so, there were a few interesting gems in a lot of heavy going. *Prometheus Books, Buffalo, NY; and in the UK, 10 Crescent View, Loughton, Essex IG10 4PZ. 1992, hb £37.95, pb£15.95, pp515, refs, illus, indexes.*   **Bob Rickard**

THE ENCYCLOPEDIA OF GHOSTS AND SPIRITS
by Rosemary Ellen Guiley.

Following her earlier *Harper's Encyclopedia of Mystical and Psychic Experiences*, and *Encyclopedia of Witches and Witchcraft*, Rosemary Guiley has compiled a helpful and readable A-Z of paranormal activity. Important cases (eg. Bell Witch) and haunted places (eg. Borley Rectory) are covered in detail, full biographies of researchers and investigators are given, types of phenomena are explained (eg. seance, materialisation, apport, survival of death). A book equally useful for a straight-through read, dipping into, or as a reference tool. *Facts on File, Oxford & New York. 1992, hb £21.95, pp374, bibs, index, illus.*   **Janet Bord**

WEATHER WATCH
by Stephen Moss and Paul Simons.

This well-illustrated general introduction to modern meteorology accompanied the BBC series of the same name – featured in *FT65* – and covers the same territory in slightly more detail. Topics with a Forteans flavour are the sections on giant hail, falls of frogs and fishes, ball lightning, whirlwinds and tornadoes, and extreme weather conditions, but there is nothing too deep, too complicated or too jargon-ridden here, making it a splendid gift to an interested child or general reader. *BBC Books, London. 1992, pb £8.99, pp112, further reading, index.*   **Bob Rickard**

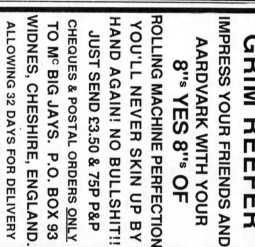

DEAR FT...

CAT'S CRADLE

■ I was interested in the Forum article on straight roads [FT65:56]. I am currently living in Kiribati (former Gilbert Islands), a collection of coral atolls straddling the Equator in the central Pacific. The people are mixed Polynesian/ Melanesian/ Micronesian. The Polynesian component of their culture is probably responsible for their belief in spirit paths. The island of Makin in the extreme north is supposed to be the road of the dead. The spirits travel along a promontory until they reach Naakaa's Point where they launch towards Paradise in the west.

Another belief connected with Naakaa, the god who judges the dead, is that he tries to capture spirits in his fishing net. One way of evading Naakaa and other perils is to perform the sequence of cat's cradle figures that metaphorically represent the creation of the world. This process was known as 'straightening the path' and was described by Professor H. Maude in his 1958 pamphlet *Gilbertese String Figures*, published by The Polynesian Society.

Most of the pre-Christian beliefs have been 'missionised' into superstitious dread and I have not seen anyone practising string figures, once a vital part of life here. Every Gilbertese had to know the six figures necessary safely to traverse the road to Paradise.

Adelaide Doble
Tarawa, Kiribati

VERY LOCAL WEATHER

■ On 21 October 1992, my sister and I were walking along London Road in Mitcham, Surrey. At about 7:00pm we stopped to look in a shop window at some Hallowe'en items. As we moved on, my sister said that it was raining quite heavily. I was in front of her and could see no rain, but I walked back and saw that it was indeed raining in one small spot near the shop. We both walked away and back again several times to check that we had seen things clearly. I told my sister that I had just bought a magazine called *Fortean Times* which had a mention of a similar localised rain in New York City [FT65:30 – see also FT60:64 – Eds.] I would be interested to know if anyone has an explanation.

Julia Harrington
Surbiton, Surrey

SHAMAN ROBIN

■ Paul Devereux [FT66:58] makes reference to a Koryak shaman whose spirit was said to leave his body along the path traced by an arrow released from his bow. Could this have a bearing on the legend of Robin Hood? As he died, he fired an arrow to indicate where his body should lie. Perhaps the saga of the Shaman of Nottingham Forest was misinterpreted by later narrators who couldn't conceive of spirits leaving the body except in death.

Tim Beswick
Saltburn

VALLEY FEVER

■ Your report *Pioneering Briton [FT66:11]* states that valley fever is found only in Arizona. This is not true. Valley fever is a fungus which may produce tuberculosis-like symptoms resulting in death if not properly diagnosed. TB therapy is not effective against the fungus. It exists as spores in much of the Southwest. There are outbreaks from Bakersfield to Sacramento when there are duststorms that lift the spores and they are inhaled.

Kirk McLoren
Billings, Montana

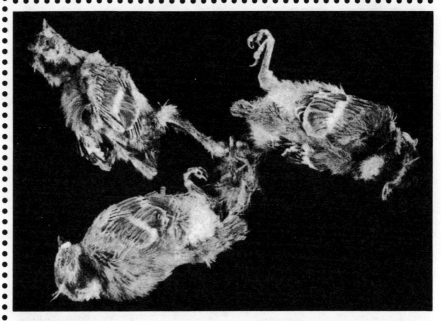

BIRD KING

■ After reading about the squirrel kings in *FT63:13*, I thought you might be interested in this account, from 1953, of a 'king' of young bluetits, from the German science journal *Natur und Volk* (83 (5), 1953, p169f). According to the journal's correspondent, Dr J. Steinbacher, the three young bluetits were about 15 days old and barely alive when found in a nesting-box with other young ones.

The heading to the notice translates as 'Death from entanglement of feet', implying that their legs were entangled directly with each other (as appears in the accompanying photograph) in the same way the tails of the squirrels were knotted. On this point the account is rather ambiguous, stating simply that their legs had become caught up in a clump of the nest lining material (ie. hair, plant fibres and feathers), from which they could not free themselves.

It was Steinbacher's opinion that the ill-fated fledglings could not beg for food as well as their nest-mates and so became weaker. The caption to the photo implied the tangled tableau was given to the Natur-Museum in Senckenberg after their death.

Lars Thomas, *Valby, Denmark*

COINCIDENCE OR PRECOGNITION?

■ This photograph shows the box of the game 'Fortress America' that came out in 1986. You will see that the aggressor is none other than Saddam Hussein, who at the time was considered to be an ally (of sorts) of the West. Did the game's maker, Milton Bradley Company, employ a clairvoyant?

Arthur Chrenkoff
Annerley, Australia

SURGICAL RUMOURS AND THUNDERBIRDS

■ The Turkish boy born 'circumcised' or 'leipoderm' *[FT65:10]* has a condition once claimed for Moses and a handful of other Jewish holy men (Felix Bryk: *Sex and Circumcision: A Study of Phallic Worship*, 1930). Horapollo also ascribed this trait to baboons (Lynn Thorndike: *History of Magic and Experimental Science*, vol 1, 1923.)

However, the boy's ability to speak at the age of 40 days makes him unique. It might put him under pressure to disclose his political allegiance; a canny politician could seek the endorsement of this Lamarckian wonder. Mass circumcision rallies in Turkey are used to attract voters. In 1991, the finest blade of Ozal's Motherland Party defected to Demirel's True Path Party. Kemal Ozkan, who claims to have snipped 1,650 boys in one day without a single mistake, decided his skills were being taken for granted (*Economist*, 5 Oct 1991.)

To the article on organ kidnappers *[FT65:50]*, I can add an early rumour from the Soviet Union. In 1982 the newspaper *Rigass Bals* (Voice of Riga) claimed that the bodies of three female students of the Latvian Medical Institute, all orphans, had been found floating in the Baltic with their livers missing. Despite an official coverup, a persistent novice detective discovered that the organs had been flown to Georgia, where they were used in unsuccessful attempts to save the life of a high-ranking official's son (see Ilya Gerol and Geoffrey

Molyneux: *The Manipulators: Inside the Soviet Media*, 1988.)

The state-controlled media in Serbia demonise their enemies by accusing them of (among other atrocities) cutting out Serbs' hearts and kidneys and selling them in Germany (AP report, 17 June 1992.) One German who would have been delighted to accept the kidneys was the organ broker Count Adelmann von Adelmannsfelden. He studied public bankruptcy notices in 1988 and would offer insolvent businesspeople the equivalent of £30,000 for one of their kidneys (*Victoria Times Colonist*, 22 Nov 1988.) The extraordinary letter he sent to them ("You donate a kidney for the preservation of Croesus, Croesus pays a sum for your preservation") was reprinted in *Harper's Magazine* in March 1989 under the headline 'Count Dracula Makes An Offer'.

Somatic entrepreneurs interested in harvesting bits and pieces of themselves can refer to a helpful book by Jim Hogshire, *Sell Yourself to Science*, "the first book that shows how to really tap your human potential", published in 1992 by Loompanics Unlimited of Port Townsend, Washington. Hogshire makes the novel suggestion that the trader could temporarily store 'extra' organs in his own body, "buying, say, a kidney from a cheap source and then reselling it later for a better price."

In the *Fortean Times* interview *[FT65:30]*, John Keel tells of his fruitless search for the photograph of a captured Thunderbird, stating: "In my mind I can see the entire photograph". In an earlier interview (*Strange*

Magazine #5, p39), he says confidently: "I could almost make a drawing of it. I can remember all the details." Yet his memory seems to be inconsistent. In FT, he describes the group of men in the photograph: "The caption said they were college professors, but they were all dressed like cowboys. They were seedy types, some wearing top hats." In *Strange* he says: "One guy had on a top hat and they referred to him in the caption as a college professor." Did some wear top hats, or just one, and how many professors did the caption refer to? Perhaps Mr Keel should indeed make a drawing as a mnemonic.

Brian Chapman
Victoria, British Columbia

SHARP PRACTICE

■ The article on kidney kidnapping *[FT65:50]* merits a codicil. About four and a half years ago, a young woman of Turkish extraction on a visit to Istanbul from the UK was advised that one of her kidneys was diseased and should be removed. Smelling a rat, I suggested that she obtain a second opinion on her return to London, which she did. Both of her kidneys were and still are healthy, and remain in their original location. The aspect of this anecdote that appeals to my warped sense of humour is that the surgeon concerned proposed charging her a substantial sum for the service he offered. Neat.

Professor Robert T. Green
London

RENT-A-READ

■ Rent-a-read *[FT66:9]* may be a straight hoax or a case of life imitating art, but either way the idea is a rip-off. Myles na Gopaleen (Flann O'Brian/Brian O'Nolan) invented the concept of book-handling for rich philistines in one of his columns for the *Irish Times* back in the 1940s ("Buchhandlung, Dog Ears – four a penny"). The service involved creasing pages, underlining key passages, marginal notes and the insertion of tram tickets as forgotten book marks. De luxe handing included thorough distressing of the volumes and forged messages of affection from some of the authors. He also suggested an automatic book-distressing machine, but rejected it on the grounds of artistic integrity.

David Longhorn
Sunderland

■ Later columns [by Miles na Gopaleen] extended the book-handling to include an Escort Service, composed of ventriloquists, who would allow you to appear stunningly well educated at public functions, as they carried out both sides of the conversation in a loud voice. Watch out for this one in Ulm!

Actually, I've often wondered if someone was offering the book service for real, ever since I bought a second hand book that included an old programme (in French) for a performance of an opera in Egypt in 1927. I still use it myself.

Nigel A. Callaghan
Peterborough, Cambs

NOT A KANGAROO

■ The photograph showing a carcass of a supposed kangaroo on the Isle of Wight *[FT65:18]* is not a marsupial. A 'post-orbital bar' – a bony structure around the eye not found in marsupials – is visible. I would suggest a foal as the most likely identification, one with its forelegs removed as well as a lot of other things.

H. Godthelp
Kensington, Sydney, Australia

GAS OR GOD?

■ To those living in Bristol, maybe the *Hueytown Hum [FT65:12]* is not all hooey. In my article 'Dr Hu?' published in *Prediction* some years back, I pointed out that the Bristol Hum, as the local media dubbed it, has haunted sufferers in the city for decades. The list of possible causes is very long.

Like the ancient Egyptians who called their god of the inaccessible *Hu*, many today use the sound *hu/hoo* (short for hu-man or god-man) as a daily mantra. Regular use of this so-called 'seed-sound of creation' lifts all levels of hu-man consciousness. It seems that whether we hear inner thunder, running water, bees buzzing or a single high-pitched sound, singing the Hu Song heals the hearer homeopathically, curing like with like. A sound cure, indeed.

Perhaps Hueytown is well named and its inhabitants are being called (Hu knows?) to higher frequencies of inner tonics – tone-ics. I write more fully about the phenomena of tinnitus and related issues of inexplicable inner sounds in my forthcoming book *Have Angels hairy Legs ...?*

Christopher Gilmore
Dursley, Gloucestershire

CHILDHOOD TERRORS

■ The four-year-old boy of a friend of mine recently underwent a tonsillectomy, but regained consciousness while still in the operating theatre. The experience seems to have affected his personality drastically. He used to be a happy-go-lucky, friendly child; now he will not go to bed – at all – and is terrified of the dark. If he dozes he will suddenly wake and run around the room crashing into furniture, saying ghosts are chasing him. This can continue for several minutes until he is reassured.

Many children regain consciousness, after operations, while still in the theatre, and although this is no fault of the theatre staff, it is obviously distressing for the child. Could this not provide an origin for the imagery used by UFO abductees and in 'ritual abuse' cases where there is no evidence of sexual abuse?

My theory is that a child waking in an operating theatre will be in an altered state of consciousness, in some

pain, and surrounded (unexpectedly?) by masked beings (emphasising the eyes?) wearing gloves, gowns, etc; apparel totally alien, yet somehow familiar. Even if the child has only been exposed to the odd 'spooky' tale on children's television, at a later date this experience could manifest as a half-real, half-imaginary incident incorporating similarly-dressed ghosts or bogeymen. Abductees frequently tell of undergoing a medical examination in an operating theatre type of environment, conducted by strangely dressed creatures; perhaps a garbled recollection of a childhood operation.

Peter Smith
Preston, Lancs

BR replies – According to Daniel Farson's biography of Bram Stoker, it was the recollection of a similar childhood experience that inspired the creation of Dracula. Childhood trauma – whether from operations, accidents, abductions, sexual and other abuse – obviously has a great influence upon the nature, structure and imagery of subsequent reverie, dream and fantasy. Discussions of these matters in specialist magazines deserve a wider reading, and we will explore ways of presenting them in future issues.

THE PIMLICO MYSTERY

■ I was fascinated to read Nigel Pennick on nineteenth century ether drinking *[FT66:65]*. This practice may well provide the solution to one of the century's most baffling murder cases, that which led to Adelaide Bartlett's trial for the murder of her husband by the administration of liquid chloroform in 1886.

The Pimlico Mystery, as the case became known, came about when Edwin Bartlett was found dead in bed with a stomach full of chloroform. He had lately suffered from inflammation of the stomach and was suffering from toothache at the time.

English medical opinion, led by the surgeon Sir James Paget, held that suicide by ingestion of liquid organic solvents was too painful to be possible. Nevertheless, since there was not a shred of evidence that his wife had administered the lethal dose, Adelaide Bartlett was acquitted by the jury.

Nigel Pennick's information that etheromaniacs could ingest a pint of solvent a day may well provide the solution to this mystery of criminology.

Nick Warren
Greenford, Middlesex

GIANT SNAKES

■ I have caught and measured gigantic snakes of every species and was first British breeder of the reticulated python. You published an item about a 35-foot anaconda which is said to have eaten a fisherman *[FT58:16]*. Using the information in the photograph – such as the size of the people and the width of the truck – the snake is no more than 21 feet with a head no more than seven inches long. This is by no means remarkable for an adult anaconda, though it is large.

The length of the ingested animal is no more than four feet; assuming that the snake is dead, the meal was eaten at least a day earlier, and the snake's stomach and the prey have expanded in the heat. The prey in this case was probably a capybara, the staple diet of large anacondas.

John Cheetham *Tonbridge, Kent.*

[Editors' note: According to a report in the Guardian (27 Mar 1992): "A 25-yard [sic] boa constrictor swallowed a 15-year-old child it found asleep in the Peruvian Amazon jungle. The body was found in the snake's belly after it was killed by local people."]

This photo of a python eating a pig was found by FT editor Bob Rickard in a photo shop in Klang, Malaysia, in 1992

noticeboard

EXCHANGE & MART

● **MkIV CARR-SCHMIDT DREAM MACHINE:** biofeedback-linked strobe shades. Illuminatory my dear Watson. S.A.E to Highland Psionics, Scoraig, Scotland, 1V23 2RE.

● **THE ENIGMA –** Articles on horror, politics, psychology, the occult and religion plus subjects enigmatic but not a puzzle. £1.50 UK, £2.00 overseas. Payment to: THE ENIGMA, 1 Austin Close, Irchester, Northants NN9 7AX.

● **WICCA-BRIEF –** newsletter for Wiccans and pagans in German. Inquiries to W-B: Georgstr. 4, 2000 Hamburg, Germany.

● **INVESTIGATING CONTACT** with non-human intelligences - "The Wild Places" is out now price £1.65 ($4) – Issue subscription £6 ($15) From New Ventures, 42 Victoria Rd, St Austell, Cornwall, PL25 4QD.

● **CATALYST – NEW AGE DIRECTORY** – limited edition. Extensive resource for New Age/Metaphysical / holistic / health / UFO / pschotronic / networking newsletters, publications. Unique products. Large 'personal' resource section. Book reviews. $6.95 ≠ $2.00 p&p ($5.00 overseas p&p) to Catalyst pc, POB 670022, Marietta, GA 30066, USA.

● **VISIONS OF BOWMEN AND ANGELS** - The full story of the Angels of Mons 1914. £2 ($4) From Kevin McClure, 42 Victoria Rd, St Austell, Cornwall, PL25 4QD.

● **CHINESE NEW YEAR** - Be prepared! Let us research and supply your Chinese horoscope. Send s.a.e for details to: Dragon Research, 32 The Fairway, Saltburn, Cleveland, TS12 1NQ.

● **MAKE THE PILGRIMAGE** to Middle Earth – Tarot, crystals, oils, lava lamps, jewellery, incense, cards, tarot readings by appointment. 102 Walton Street, Jericho, Oxford. Tel 0865 511522.

● **WANTED - DR HEARNE** type dream machine with instructions (Must have lucidity inducer) Contact 12 Green Row, Idle, Bradford, BD10 8SP.

● **NEW DIMENSIONS** –The monthly magazine of esoteric information. The best for occult articles, Qabalah, metaphysics, psychology, book and music reviews. Dynamic in origin. The best all-rounder. Magic at its best. £1.25 UD, £1.75 overseas. Dept MS, 1 Austin Close, Irchester, Northants NN9 7AX.

● **MILLENNIUM BOOKS** – 2nd hand books on UFOs, mysteries and all kinds of weird and wonderful things. For free lists write, fax or phone Millennium Books, 9 Chesham Road, Brighton, Sussex BN2 1NB. Fax/Phone 0273 671967.

● **UFO NEWSCLIPPING**

SERVICE – keeps you up with the real 'close encounters'. Many fascinating UFO reports from the world's press are reproduced facsimile, along with newswire items from the major agencies. UFONS is 20 foolscap pages monthly, with a Fortean section strong on cryptozoology. Foreign language reports are provided in translation. For information and sample pages, write today to: UFONS - Lucius Farrish, Route 1 - Box 220, Plumerville, AR 72127, USA.

● **FUNNY/SERIOUS SECOND HAND LIST** books, paperbacks, jigsaws, games, fortean, eccentric, occult, UFO's etc. Large s.a.e Offbeat, 53 Keepers Lane, Weaverham, Northwich,Cheshire CW8 3BN.

● **THE SKEPTIC** – takes an entertaining, rational and humourous look at pseudoscience and claims of the paranormal. Articles, reviews, columns, cartoons and much more. If you like FT you'll like The Skeptic. Sample issue £1.85; annual sub (6 issues) £12. The Skeptic, PO Box 475, Manchester M60 2TH.

● **COUNTER PRODUCTIONS** – Forteana and beyond! Send s.a.e for our extensive, descriptive catalogue of weird shit, false prophets, surrealist and anarchist titles. PO Box 556, London, SE5 ORL.

● **UFO AFRINEWS** – edited by Cynthia Hind. The only UFO magazine in Africa. #1-4 available at £2; #5 at £2.50. Write: Gemini, Box MP49, Mt Pleasant, Harare, Zimbabwe.

● **MARYAM** - Lived over 2,000 years ago but speaks now to groups and individuals worldwide. She seeks to warn and advise all. For basic info send s.a.e £1, for bookpack £5 to Vida Publications 17 Stapenhall Rd, Solihull, B90 4XX.

EVENTS

● **SOCIETY FOR PSYCHICAL RESEARCH** – Lectures. 18 March, 'Exploring dowsing' (Berwyn Eastwood); 22 April, 'Clairvoyance, how far can we see?' (Montague Keen); 20 May, 'Alien contact, the inner space dimension of the UFO mystery' (Jenny Randles). Venue: the Lecture Hall of Kensington Central Library, Campden Hill Road, London W8, at 6:30pm. Non-members £3, student cards £1. Further information from the SPR at 49 Marloes Rd, Kensington, London W8 6LA. Tel: 071 937 8984.

● **FOLKLORE SOCIETY EVENTS** – 'Talking folklore with Jeremy Bentham', informal evenings at the Jeremy Bentham pub in University St, London WC1, 6:30pm for 7: 17 Feb, 'Februaryish things'; 21 April, 'Contemporary legends'. Full details on this and other events from Steve Roud at the

Folklore Society, University College London, Gower St, London WC1E 6BT. Tel: 071 387 5894.

● **PAGAN VOICE** – monthly magazine of paganism and magick, holds talks at King William Ale House (upstairs), King St, central Bristol, 7:30pm - 22 Feb, 'Robin Hood and the Green Man' (John Matthews); 15 Mar, 'Sex, drugs and magick' (Dave Rankine). For full details phone 0272 531626, or write to 13 Barnstaple Walk, Knowle, Bristol BS4 1JQ.

● **THE HISTORY OF UFOLOGY** – slide lecture by Lionel Beer, BUFORA vp, 17 March, in Guildford. Details from Gordon Millington 0483 576914. For full BUFORA lecture list, send SAE to BUFORA, The Leys, Suite 1, 2c Leyton Rd, Harpenden, Herts AL5 2TL. (Tel: 0582 763218).

● **LONDON EARTH MYSTERIES CIRCLE** – Evening meetings in St Andrew's Seminar Room, Maria Assumpta Centre, 23 Kensington Square, London W8, at 7pm on the 2nd and 4th Tuesdays in each month. Members £1.00, non-members £2.00, unwaged £1.50. Lectures: 13 Oct (Reclaiming our Heritage), 27 Oct (Earth Mysteries and Magnetism), 10 Nov (social eve.), 24 Nov (UFOs & Psychic phenomena). Contact: Rob Stephenson, 18 Christchurch Ave, London NW6 7QN.

● **UFOS – FACT, FRAUD OR FANTASY?** – Independent UFO Network international conference. Speakers include: Bud Hopkins, Jenny Randles, Cynthia Hind, Paul Devereux, Hilary Evans, Dr Sue Blackmore and others. 14-15 August 1993 at Sheffield Polytechnic. For full details send SAE to: Stu Smith, 15 Rydal St, Burnley, Lancs BB10 1HS - or Phone: 0282 24837.

RESEARCH

● **WEIRD? YOUNG WRITER OF FICTION** seeks unusual people and lifestyles for inspiration. Really anything, surprise me. Bryan Kennerley, 21 Graham Drive, Rhyl, LL18 3RS.

● **CONTACT DESIRED** with genuine practitioners of black arts for willing student and research. Sincerity, confidentiality assured. Any distance. PO Box 321 Prestatyn Clywd, LL19 9YA.

● **CHINESE NEW YEAR** - Be prepared! Let us research and supply your Chinese horoscope. Send s.a.e for details to: Dragon Research, 32 The Fairway, Saltburn, Cleveland, TS12 1NQ.

● **ANCIENT DWARFS** – For my MSc dissertation I am researching the prevalence, diagnosis and social reaction to dwarfism (mainly achondroplasia), acromegaly and cleft palate. I am aware that in ancient Egypt, dwarfs were revered and linked to the god Bes. I am

particularly interested in discovering the European attitude, historically and prehistorically. I would appreciate any obscure but related information, or pointers on mystery little or large people of the Wildman/Bigfoot genre, artistic depictions, and societies dealing with dwarfism. Contact Philip Kiberd: Department of Archaeology, University of Sheffield, Sheffield S10 2TN.

● **UFO RESEARCH** – scientific establishments and individuals sought for voluntary assistance. Contact Philip Mantle, IUFON, 1 Woodhall Drive, Batley, W.Yorks WF17 7SW.

● **PET GHOSTS NEEDED** – I am researching a TV documentary on the 'Ghosts of Domestic Pets'. Have you had a direct experience of the ghost of a dying or dead pet, or know anyone who has? Do you have any theories about this? Any contacts, information or pointers on this unusual phenomenon gratefully received. Contact Dominic Santana: 48 Langdale Rd, Hove, Sussex BN3 4HP - or phone 0273 746928.

MISCELLANEOUS

● **DAVID BOWIE** – I have evidence proving that he's been influenced by aliens. The UFO community doesn't want to know. The media may not want to know, but sooner or later we will all know – like it or not. Send SAE for information/stickers to: DBINFO, 11 Wharton Street, London WC1X.

● **DRUIDS!** – Discover what they do and how Druidry answers our need for a spirituality that is connected to the land and our ancient heritage. For info send SAE to: ODOB (FT) 260 Kew Road, Richmond, Surrey TW9 3EG.

● **WELSH HOLIDAY COTTAGE** – Self-catering accomodation in historic North Wales town of Denbigh. For further details, contact Janet Bord, Melysfan, Llangwm, Corwen, Clwyd LL21 0RD. Tel: 049 082 472. Fax: 049 082 321.

● **GLASTONBURY COTTAGE** – Forget expensive hotels or B&Bs – charming 2 bed house to let in mystic Glastonbury town centre. Central-heating, fully furnished with necessary utensils, crockery etc, and unique view over Abbey grounds. Tel: 0234 211606 (answerphone) for leaflet.

● **FORTEAN PICTURES** – The Fortean Picture Library is a self-funding project for the rescue and preservation of valuable documentary material, photographs and drawings etc. If you have anything of this nature, please let FPL look after it. 50% of any revenue from the commercial use of the material (in books etc) could come back to you. FPL covers all expenses from its half. Contact Janet Bord, FPL, Melysfan, Llangwm,

If you have enjoyed this book you'll want to bring your interests up to date with the latest news, reviews and articles on current strange phenomena.

Subscribe to

For details of current subscription offers, write to us at
Fortean Times, FREEPOST
(SW6096) Bristol BS12 0BR

Or call 01454 202515
Or E-mail ft@johnbrown.co.uk